STUDENT ATLAS

First published 1996, reprinted 1997
Revised 1998, reprinted 1998, 1999(twice), 2000
New edition published 2001, reprinted 2001, 2002

© Collins-Longman Atlases 1996, 1998, 2001

The maps in this atlas are licensed to Collins-Longman Atlases
and are derived from databases © Bartholomew Ltd.

HarperCollins Publishers, Westerhill Road, Bishopbriggs, Glasgow G64 2QT

Pearson Education Ltd., Edinburgh Gate, Harlow, Essex CM20 2JE

Printed in Singapore

The contents of this atlas are believed correct at the time of
printing. Nevertheless the publisher can accept no responsibility
for errors or omissions, changes in the detail given or for any
expense or loss thereby caused.

PL11386

2 CONTENTS

SYMBOLS

Maps use special signs or symbols to represent location and to give information of interest.

Map symbols can be points, lines or areas and vary in size, shape and colour. This allows a great range of different symbols to be created. These have to be carefully selected to make maps easy to understand. Usually the same symbols are used to represent features on maps of the same type and scale within an atlas.

An important part of any map is the key which explains what the symbols represent. Each map in this atlas has its own key. Shown below are typical examples of the keys found on each reference map in the atlas. The first is found on all of the British Isles 1:1 200 000 series of maps. The second is found on the smaller scale maps of the rest of the world.

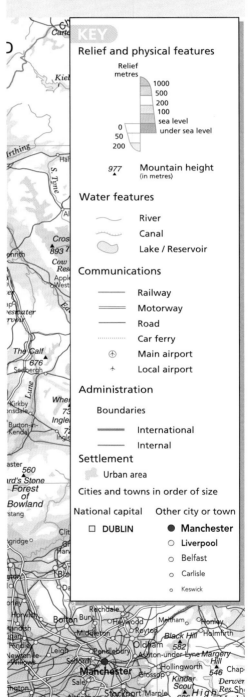

KEY

Relief and physical features

Relief
metres
1000
500
200
100
0 sea level
50 under sea level
200

977 ▲ Mountain height
(in metres)

Water features

~~~ River
~~~ Canal
◯ Lake / Reservoir

Communications

───── Railway
═════ Motorway
───── Road
········· Car ferry
⊕ Main airport
✈ Local airport

Administration

Boundaries

───── International
───── Internal

Settlement

▨ Urban area

Cities and towns in order of size

National capital | Other city or town
□ DUBLIN | ● Manchester
| ◯ Liverpool
| ◦ Belfast
| ◦ Carlisle
| ◦ Keswick

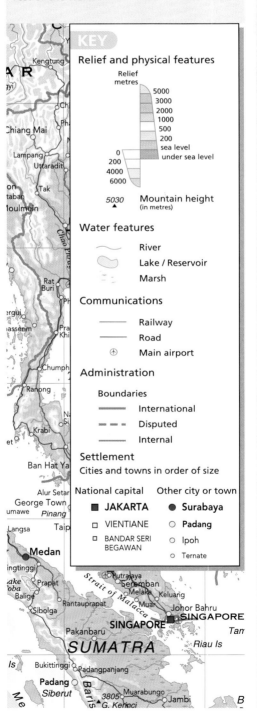

KEY

Relief and physical features

Relief
metres
5000
3000
2000
1000
500
200
sea level
under sea level
200
4000
6000

5030 ▲ Mountain height
(in metres)

Water features

~~~ River
◯ Lake / Reservoir
Marsh

Communications

───── Railway
───── Road
⊕ Main airport

Administration

Boundaries

───── International
– – – Disputed
───── Internal

Settlement

Cities and towns in order of size

National capital | Other city or town
■ JAKARTA | ● Surabaya
□ VIENTIANE | ◯ Padang
□ BANDAR SERI BEGAWAN | ◦ Ipoh
| ◦ Ternate

TYPE STYLES

Various type styles are used to show the difference between features on the maps in this atlas. Physical features are shown in italic and a distinction is made between land and water features.

Mountain Peaks are shown in small italics.

eg. *Ben Nevis   Mt Kenya   Fuji-san*

Large mountain ranges are shown in bold italic capitals.

eg. ***HIMALAYA   ALPS***
ROCKY MOUNTAINS

Rivers are also shown in small italics but in a different typeface from mountain peaks.

eg. *Thames   Euphrates   Rhine   Amazon*

Oceans are shown in large bold italic capitals.

eg. ***ATLANTIC OCEAN***
PACIFIC OCEAN
INDIAN OCEAN

When a feature covers a large area the type is letterspaced and sometimes curved to follow the shape of the feature.

eg. *S A H A R A*
B E A U F O R T   S E A

Settlements are shown in upright type. Country capitals are shown in capitals.

eg. LONDON
PARIS
TOKYO
MOSCOW

The size and weight of the type increases with the population of a settlement.

eg. Westbury
Chippenham
Bristol
Birmingham

Administrative names are shown in capitals.

eg. EAST SUSSEX
RONDONIA
KERALA
CALIFORNIA

Country names are shown in large bold capitals.

eg. **CHINA**
KENYA
MEXICO

An atlas map of the world shows the whole world on a flat surface of the page. yet in reality the earth is actually a sphere. This means that a system has to be used to turn the round surface of the earth into a flat map of the world, or part of the world. This cannot be done without some distortion - on a map some parts of the world have been stretched, other parts have been compressed.

A system for turning the globe into a flat map is called a **projection.**

There are many different projections, each of which distort different things to achieve a flat map. Correct area, correct shape, correct distances or correct directions can be achieved by a projection; but by achieving any one of these things the others have to

be distorted. When choosing the projection to use for a particular map it is important to decide which of these things is the most important to have correct.

The projections below illustrate the main types of projections, and include some of those used in this atlas.

Cylindrical projection

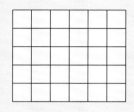

Cylindrical projections are constructed by projecting the surface of the globe on to a cylinder just touching the globe.

Conic projection

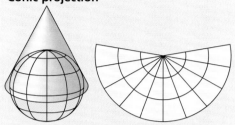

Conic projections are constructed by projecting part of the globe on to a cone which just touches a circle on the globe.

Azimuthal projection

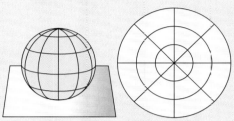

Azimuthal projections are constructed by projecting part of a globe on to a plane which touches the globe only at one point

Examples of projections

Mercator
Southeast Asia pp104-105

Mercator is a cylindrical projection. It is a useful projection for areas 15° N or S of the equator where distortion of shape is minimal. The projection is useful for navigation as directions can be plotted as straight lines.

Albers Equal Area Conic
Europe pp 34-35

Conic projections are best suited for areas between 30° and 60° N and S with longer east-west extent than north-south. Such an area would be Europe. Meridians are straight and equally spaced.

Lambert Azimuthal Equal Area
Australia p 110

Lambert's projection is uselful for areas which have similar east-west, north-south dimensions such as Australia.

Eckert IV
World pp 114-115

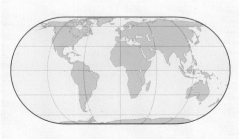

Eckert IV is an equal area projection. Equal area projections are useful for world thematic maps where it is important to show the correct relative sizes of continental areas. Ecker IV has a straight central meridian but all others are curved which help suggest the spherical nature of the earth.

Chamberlin Trimetric
Canada pp 62-63

Chamberlin trimetric is an equidistant projection. It shows correct distances from approximately three points. It is used for areas with a greater north-south than east-west extent, such as North America.

Polar stereographic
Antarctica p 112

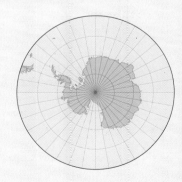

This projection shows no angular or shape distortion over small areas. All points on the map are in constant relative position and distance from the centre.

LATITUDE

Lines of latitude are imaginary lines which run in an east-west direction around the world. They are also called **parallels** of latitude because they run parallel to each other. Latitude is measured in **degrees** (°).

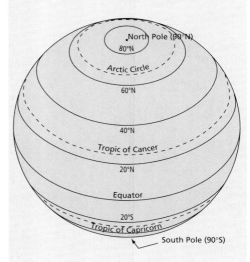

The most important line of latitude is the **Equator** (0°). The North Pole is 90° North (90°N) and the South Pole is 90° South (90°S). All other lines of latitude are given a number between 0° and 90°, either North (N) or South (S) of the Equator. Some other important lines of latitude are the Tropic of Cancer (23$\frac{1}{2}$°N), Tropic of Capricorn (23$\frac{1}{2}$°S), Arctic Circle (66$\frac{1}{2}$°N) and Antarctic Circle (66$\frac{1}{2}$°S).

The Equator can also be used as a line to divide the Earth into two halves. The northern half, north of the Equator, is the **Northern Hemisphere**. The southern half, south of the Equator, is the **Southern Hemisphere**.

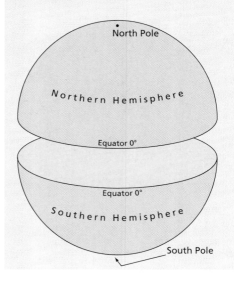

LONGITUDE

Lines of longitude are imaginary lines which run in a north-south direction, from the North Pole to the South Pole. These lines are also called **meridians** of longitude. They are also measured in **degrees** (°).

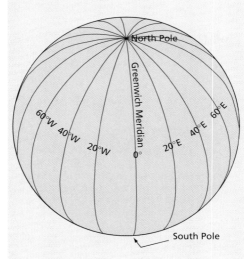

The most important line of longitude is the prime meridian (0°). This line runs through the Greenwich Observatory in London and is therefore known as the Greenwich Meridian. Exactly opposite the Greenwich Meridian on the other side of the world is the 180° line of longitude known as the International Date Line. All the other lines of longitude are given a number between 0° and 180°, either East (E) or West (W) of the Greenwich Meridian.

The Greenwich Meridian (0°) and the International Date Line (180°) can also be used to divide the world into two halves. The half to the west of the Greenwich Meridian is the Western Hemisphere. The half to the east of the Greenwich Meridian is the Eastern Hemisphere.

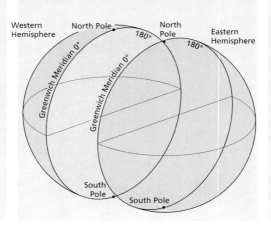

FINDING PLACES USING LATITUDE AND LONGITUDE

When lines of latitude and longitude are drawn on a map they form a grid pattern, very much like a pattern of squares.

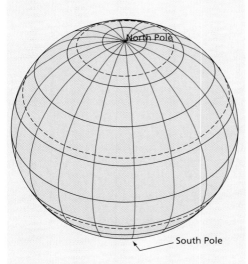

By stating the **latitude** and then the **longitude** of a place, it becomes much easier to find. On the map (below) Point A is very easy to find because it is exactly latitude 58° North of the Equator and longitude 4° West of the Greenwich Meridian (58°N,4°W).

To be even more accurate in locating a place, each degree of latitude and longitude can also be divided into smaller units called **minutes** ('). There are 60 minutes in each degree. On the map (below) Halkirk is one half (or 30/60ths) of the way past latitude 58°N, and one-half (or 30/60ths) of the way past longitude 3°W. Its latitude is therefore 58 degrees 30 minutes North and its longitude is 3 degrees 30 minutes West. This can be shortened to 58°30'N, 3°30'W.

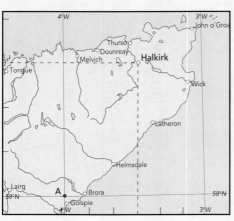

SCALE

To draw a map of any part of the world, the area must be reduced in size, or scaled down so that it will fit on to a page. The scale of a map tells us by how much the area has been reduced in size.

The scale of a map can also be used to work out distance and area. The scale of a map will show the relationship between distances on the map and distances on the ground.

Scale can be shown on a map in a number of ways:

(a) **in words**
e.g. 'one cm. to one km.' (one cm. on the map represents one km. on the ground). 'one cm. to one m.' (one cm. on the map represents one m. on the ground).

(b) **in numbers**
e.g. '1 : 100 000' or '1/100 000' (one cm. on the map represents 100 000 cm., or one km., on the ground).
'1 : 25 000' or '1/25 000' (one cm. on the map represents 25 000 cm, or 250 m., on the ground).
'1 : 100' or '1/100' (one cm. on the map represents 100 cm, or one m., on the ground).

(c) **as a line scale**
e.g.

MEASURING DISTANCE ON A MAP

When a map does not have distances printed on it, we can use the scale of the map to work out how far it is from one place to another. The easiest scale to use is a line scale. You must find out how far the places are apart on the map and then see what this distance represents on the line scale. To measure the straight line distance between two points:

a) Place a piece of paper between the two points on the map,
(b) Mark off the distance between the two points along the edge of the paper,
(c) Place the paper along the line scale,
(d) Read off the distance on the scale.

Step 1

Line up the paper and mark off the distance from A to B.

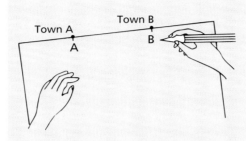

Step 2

Compare this distance with the line scale at the bottom of the map. The distance between A and B is 1.5 km on the line scale.

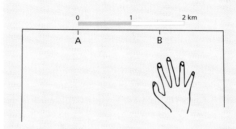

To measure the distance between two points where there are bends or curves:
(a) Place a sheet of paper on the map and mark off the start point on the edge of the paper,
(b) Now move the paper so that its edge follows the bends and curves on the map (Hint: Use the tip of your pencil to pin the edge of the paper to the curve as you pivot the paper around the curve),
(c) Mark off the end point on your sheet of paper,
(d) Place the paper along the line scale,
(e) Read off the distance on the scale.

Using a sheet of paper around a curve : Mark off the start point then twist the paper to follow the curve.

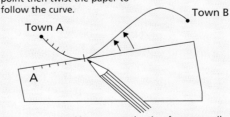

You can use the tip of your pencil to pin the paper to the curve. This stops the paper jumping off course.

MAP SCALE AND MAP INFORMATION

The scale of a map also determines how much information can be shown on it. As the area shown on a map becomes larger and larger, the amount of detail and the accuracy of the map becomes less and less.

The scale of this map is 1:5 000 000

The scale of this map is 1:10 000 000

The scale of this map is 1:20 000 000

UNITED KINGDOM

SCOTLAND
Edinburgh
ENGLAND
London
NORTHERN IRELAND
Belfast
REPUBLIC OF IRELAND
WALES
Cardiff

WEST CENTRAL SCOTLAND
1. WEST DUNBARTONSHIRE
2. EAST DUNBARTONSHIRE
3. EAST RENFREWSHIRE

Greenock
INVER-CLYDE
Dumbarton
Kirkintilloch
1.
2.
NORTH LANARKSHIRE
Motherwell
RENFREW-SHIRE
Paisley
GLASGOW CITY
Giffnock
3.

EAST CENTRAL SCOTLAND
Haddington
EAST LOTHIAN
Dalkeith
MIDLOTHIAN
CLACKMANNAN-SHIRE
Alloa
CITY OF EDINBURGH
WEST LOTHIAN
Bathgate
FALKIRK
Falkirk

SHETLAND
Lerwick

ORKNEY
Kirkwall

WESTERN ISLES
Stornoway

HIGHLAND
Inverness

MORAY
Elgin
Banff
Inverurie
ABERDEEN-SHIRE
ABERDEEN CITY
Stonehaven

SCOTLAND

PERTH AND KINROSS
ANGUS
Forfar
DUNDEE CITY
FIFE
Glenrothes
Perth

ARGYLL AND BUTE
Lochgilphead

STIRLING
Stirling

FALKIRK
Kirkintilloch
WEST EDINBURGH
CITY OF EDINBURGH
MID-LOTHIAN
EAST LOTHIAN
Haddington

SCOTTISH BORDERS
Newtown St-Boswells

NORTH AYRSHIRE
Dumbarton
RENFREW-SHIRE
GLASGOW CITY
Hamilton
SOUTH LANARK-SHIRE

Irvine
Kilmarnock
EAST AYRSHIRE

Ayr
SOUTH AYRSHIRE

DUMFRIES & GALLOWAY

NORTHUMBERLAND
Morpeth
Newcastle

Londonderry

SCOTLAND
1. WEST DUNBARTONSHIRE
2. EAST DUNBARTONSHIRE
3. EAST RENFREWSHIRE
4. INVERCLYDE
5. NORTH LANARKSHIRE
6. CLACKMANNANSHIRE

International boundary
National boundary
Administrative boundary
■ Capital city
○ Administrative centre

SCALE 1 : 3 000 000

0   25   50   75   100 km

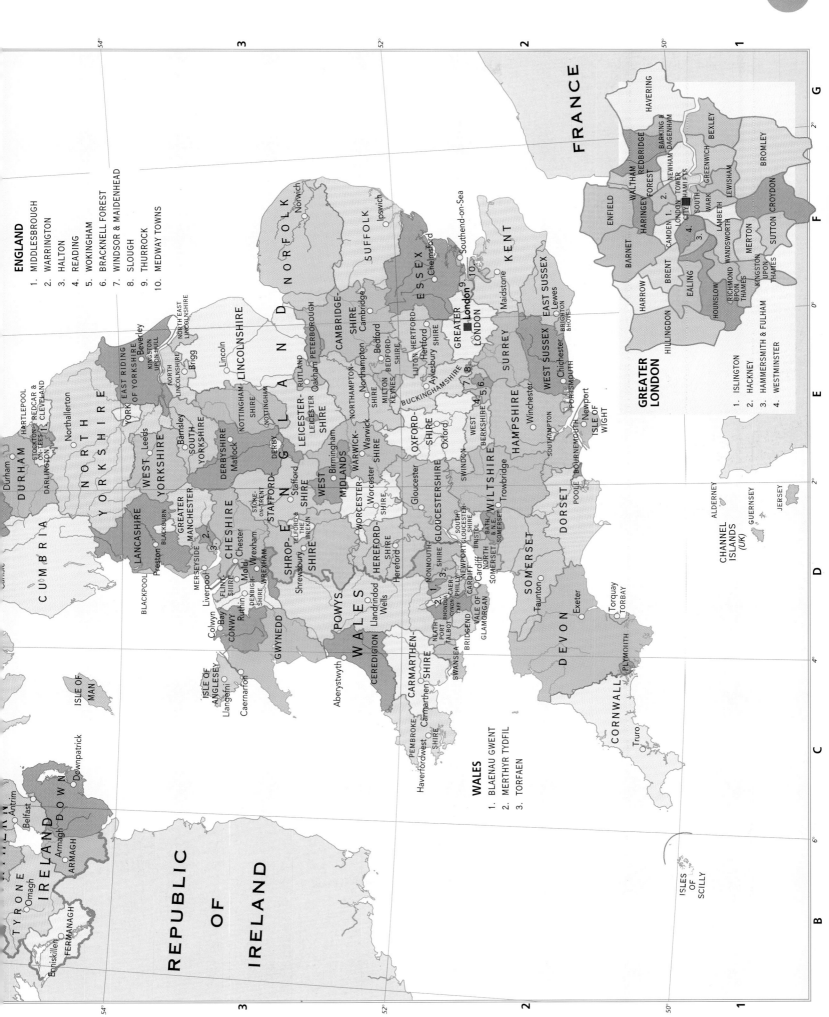

ENGLAND

1. MIDDLESBROUGH
2. WARRINGTON
3. HALTON
4. READING
5. WOKINGHAM
6. BRACKNELL FOREST
7. WINDSOR & MAIDENHEAD
8. SLOUGH
9. THURROCK
10. MEDWAY TOWNS

WALES

1. BLAENAU GWENT
2. MERTHYR TYDFIL
3. TORFAEN

GREATER LONDON

1. ISLINGTON
2. HACKNEY
3. HAMMERSMITH & FULHAM
4. WESTMINSTER

FRANCE

REPUBLIC OF IRELAND

Conic projection

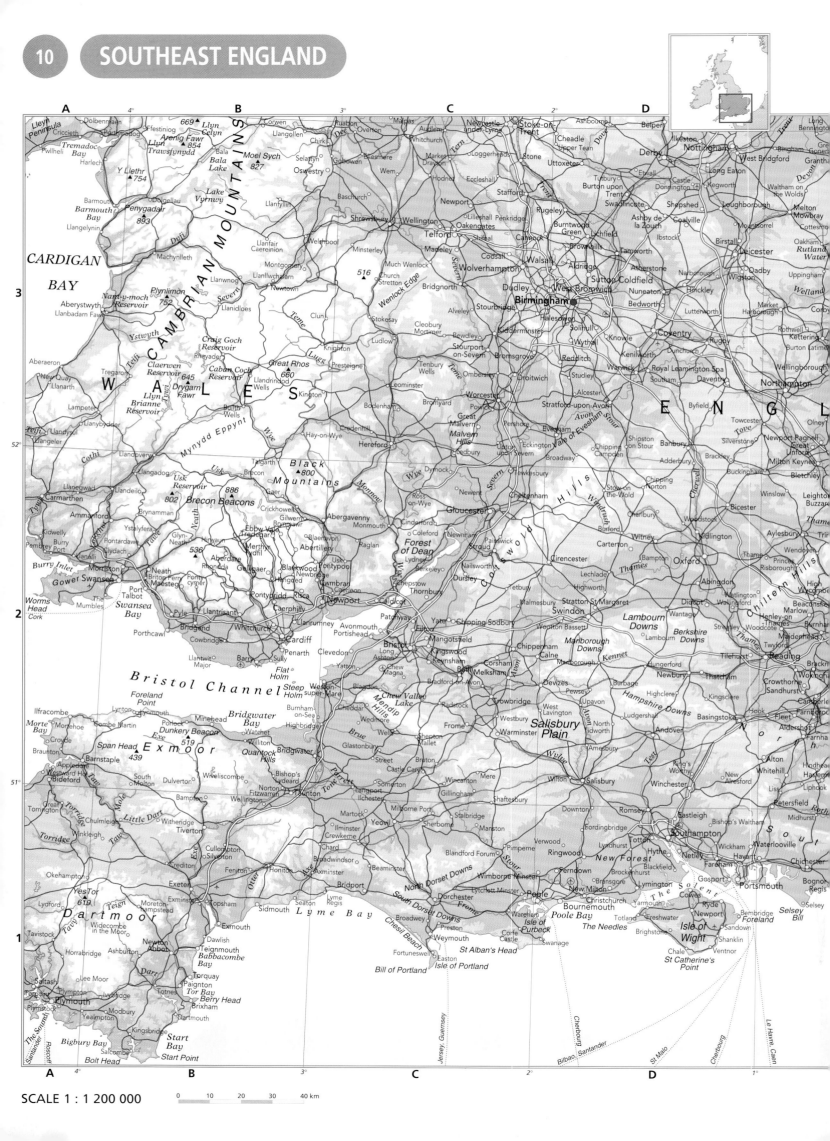

0   10   20   30   40 km

E 0° F 1° G 2° 53°

Holland Fen Sibsey Wrangle Old Leake
Sleaford Heckington Swineshead Boston
Gosberton Sutterton **The Marsh**
Holbeach Marsh **The Wash**
Spalding Holbeach Terrington Marsh Hunstanton Heacham Snettisham Wells-next-the-Sea Docking Sheringham Cromer
Bourne Market Deeping Crowland Wisbech Sutton Bridge King's Lynn South Wootton Dersingham Fakenham Holt Mundesley
Stamford Glinton Peterborough Whittlesey March Downham Market Narborough East Dereham Swaffham Watton Wymondham Bure North Walsham Aylsham Stalham Coltishall Caister-on-Sea
The Fens West Fen Nene **Bedford Levels** Wimblington Littleport Methwold Mundford **Breckland** Brandon Thetford Wensum Taverham Norwich Sprowston Acle **Bure** Great Yarmouth
Rockingham Forest Stilton Dundle Sawtry Ramsey Chatteris Soham Ely Isle of Ely Mildenhall Little Ouse Thetford Diss Scole Long Stratton Bungay Beccles Corton Lowestoft
Thrapston Warboys Sutton Burwell Newmarket Bury St Edmunds Stowmarket Needham Market Wickham Market Aldeburgh Southwold
Huntingdon Godmanchester St Ives Cambridge Stretham Cottenham **East Anglian Heights** Stanton Ixworth Dove Debenham Framlingham Saxmundham Leiston
Eaton Socon St Neots Great Shelford Sawston Melbourn Haverhill Lavenham Claydon Ipswich Hadleigh Woodbridge Orford Ness Hollesley Bay
Bedford Sandy Biggleswade Royston Saffron Walden Sudbury Stour Felixstowe Landguard Point Harwich The Naze
Kempston Ampthill Stotfold Baldock Newport Thaxted Halstead Coggeshall Colchester Wivenhoe Frinton-on-Sea
Luton Harpenden Letchworth Hitchin Stevenage Stansted Mountfitchet Braintree Great Dunmow Kelvedon Witham Tiptree Brightlingsea West Mersea Clacton-on-Sea
Hemel Hempstead St Albans Welwyn Garden City Hertford Hoddesdon Bishop's Stortford Harlow Chelmsford Maldon Tollesbury Blackwater
Chesham Watford Barnet Enfield Epping Chipping Ongar Great Baddow Ingatestone South Woodham Ferrers Southminster
Uxbridge Ealing **LONDON** Loughton Brentwood Billericay Wickford Rayleigh Rochford Burnham-on-Crouch Foulness Point
Wembley Hendon Ilford Romford Basildon Southend-on-Sea
Slough Hounslow Kingston-upon-Thames Bromley Grays Tilbury Gravesend Cliffe Canvey Island Thames Grain Sheerness Queenborough Herne Bay Margate North Foreland Broadstairs
Staines Wandsworth Greenwich Dartford Swanley Rochester Gillingham Chatham Isle of Sheppey Whitstable Ramsgate Pegwell Bay
Walton on Thames Weybridge Epsom Croydon New Addington Bromley Sittingbourne Faversham Sturry Canterbury East **Isle of Thanet** Sandwich
Woking Leatherhead Caterham Warlingham West Malling Maidstone Chilham Barham Aylesham Deal
Guildford Redhill Oxted Sevenoaks **North Downs** Wye Ashford Temple Ewell Whitfield Dover
Leith Hill Dorking Reigate Lingfield Tonbridge Pembury Headcorn Sellindge
Godalming Horley Southborough Royal Tunbridge Wells Kingsnorth Hamstreet Hythe Folkestone Channel Tunnel
Cranleigh Crawley Worth East Grinstead **The Weald** Bewl Water Hawkhurst Tenterden Romney Marsh Dymchurch
Billingshurst Horsham Crowborough Wadhurst Ticehurst Salehurst New Romney
Pulborough Lindfield Uckfield Heathfield Icklesham Rye Lydd Dungeness
Storrington Henfield Hurstpierpoint Maresfield Battle Rye Bay
Downs Arundel Steyning Hailsham Hollington Hastings
Littlehampton Worthing Hove Brighton Lewes Polegate Willingdon Bexhill
Newhaven Peacehaven Seaford Eastbourne **Beachy Head**

NORTH SEA

Norfolk Broads Brooke Loddon Oulton Kessingland Harleston Eye Stradbroke Halesworth Southwold

Leigh

ENGLISH CHANNEL

Greenwich (Prime) Meridian
Dieppe

Strait of Dover

Oostende
Nieuwpoort Veurne **BELGIUM** Diksmuide
Dunkerque **WEST-VLAANDEREN** Ieper
Gravelines HAINAUT
Calais Coulogne
Guines
Wimereux St-Omer Hazebrouck
Boulogne Desvres **NORD-**
FRANCE
PAS-DE-CALAIS Béthune
Bruay-en-Artois Lievin Carvin
Étaples Montreuil Artois Lens
Berck
Hesdin Arras

Conic projection

KEY

Relief and physical features

Relief metres
1000
500
200
100
0 sea level
50 under sea level
200

893 ▲ Mountain height (in metres)

Water features

~ River
~ Canal
Lake / Reservoir

Communications

Railway
Motorway
Road
Car ferry
⊕ Main airport
✈ Local airport

Administration

Boundaries
International
Internal

Settlement

Urban area

Cities and towns in order of size

National capital   Other city or town
■ LONDON   ● Birmingham
○ Reading
○ Oxford
○ Colchester
○ Wantage

H 3° I

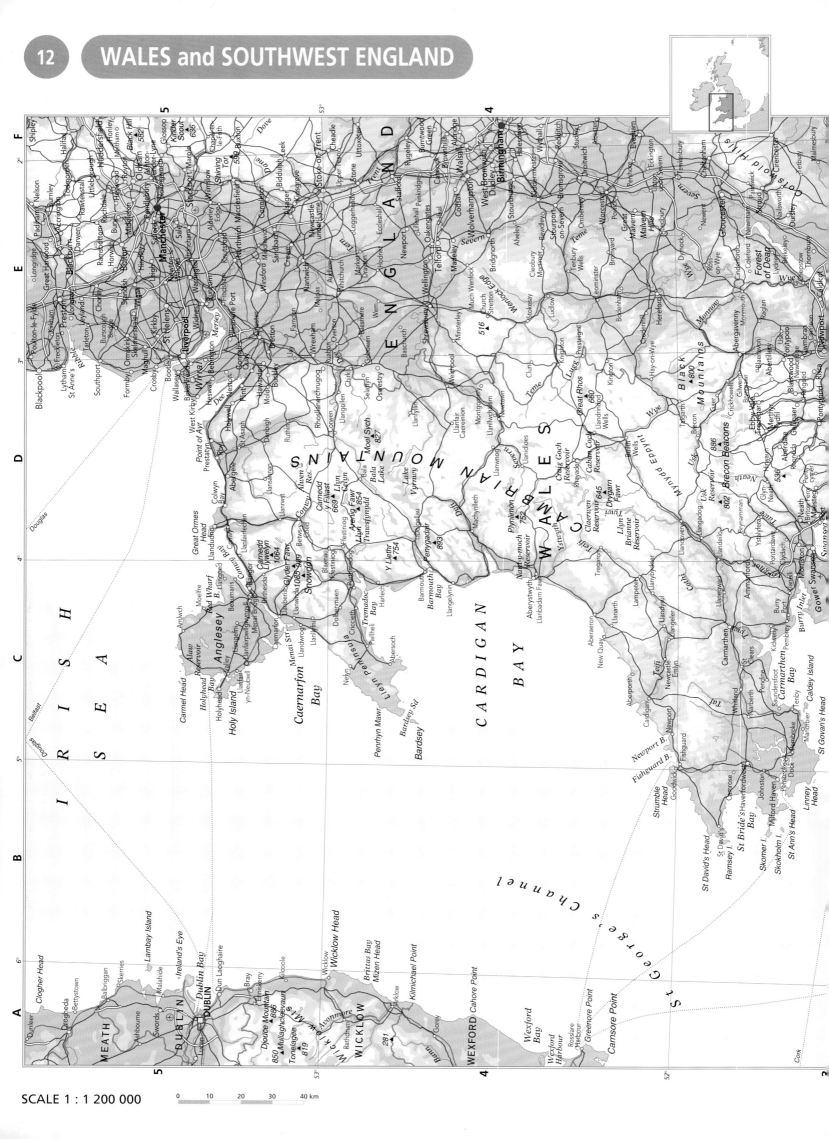

SCALE 1 : 1 200 000

0   10   20   30   40 km

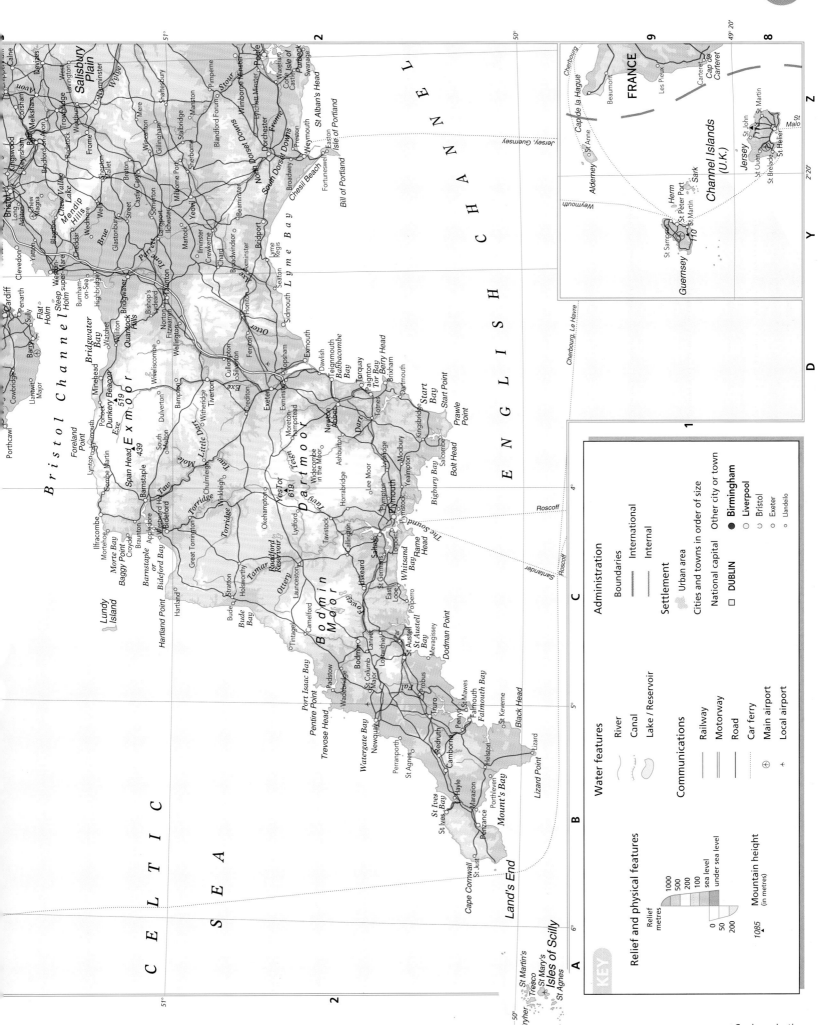

Conic projection

CELTIC SEA

Isles of Scilly

St Martin's
Tresco
Bryher
St Mary's
St Agnes

Land's End
Cape Cornwall
St Just
Penzance
Marazion
Newlyn
Mousehole
Porthleven
Mount's Bay
St Ives
St Ives Bay
Hayle
Camborne
Redruth
St Agnes
Perranporth
Newquay
Watergate Bay
Helston
Trevose Head
Lizard Point
Lizard
Black Head
St Keverne
Falmouth Bay
Falmouth
Penryn
Truro
St Mawes
Probus
Mevagissey
Dodman Point
St Austell Bay
St Austell
Lostwithiel
Lanreath
St Columb Major
Wadebridge
Bodmin
Padstow
Pentire Point
Port Isaac Bay
Tintagel
Camelford
Bodmin Moor
Polperro
Looe
East Looe
St Germans
Liskeard
Callington
Launceston
Holsworthy
Stratton
Bude
Bude Bay
Hartland
Hartland Point

Bristol Channel
Porthcawl
Cowbridge
Llantwit Major
Barry
Penarth
Sully
Cardiff
Clevedon
Bristol
Long Ashton
Keynsham
Kingswood
Corsham
Calne
Bath
Melksham
Bradford on Avon
Trowbridge
Westbury
Warminster
Salisbury Plain
West Lavington
Devizes
Avon
Radstock
Midsomer Norton
Frome
Shepton Mallet
Mere
Gillingham
Shaftesbury
Stalbridge
Sturminster Newton
Blandford Forum
Wimborne Minster
Poole
Wareham
Isle of Purbeck
Corfe Castle
Swanage
St Alban's Head

Mendip Hills
Cheddar
Wedmore
Wells
Glastonbury
Street
Somerton
Langport
Ilchester
Yeovil
Sherborne
Stalbridge
Wincanton
Castle Cary
Bruton
Chew Valley Lake
Chew Magna
Weston-super-Mare
Burnham-on-Sea
Highbridge
Bridgwater
Bridgwater Bay
Quantock Hills
Watchet
Minehead
Brue
Ilminster
Crewkerne
Chard
Axminster
Beaminster
Bridport
North Dorset Downs
Beaminster
Dorchester
Maiden Newton
South Dorset Downs
Weymouth
Easton
Isle of Portland
Bill of Portland
Chesil Beach
Abbotsbury
Bridport
Lyme Regis
Seaton
Sidmouth
Lyme Bay
Broadwindsor
Fortuneswell

Steep Holm
Flat Holm
Foreland Point
Lynton
Lynmouth
Combe Martin
Ilfracombe
Morthoe
Morte Bay
Baggy Point
Croyde
Braunton
Barnstaple or Bideford Bay
Westward Ho!
Appledore
Bideford
Barnstaple
Great Torrington
Exmoor
Dunkery Beacon 519
Span Head 439
South Molton
Chulmleigh
Crediton
Okehampton
Tiverton
Bampton
Dulverton
Wiveliscombe
Wellington
Taunton
Norton Fitzwarren
Bishop's Lydeard
Wellington
Cullompton
Silverton
Honiton
Exmouth
Budleigh Salterton
Topsham
Exeter
Exminster
Dawlish
Teignmouth
Babbacombe Bay
Torquay
Paignton
Tor Bay
Berry Head
Brixham
Dartmouth
Start Bay
Start Point
Prawle Point
Salcombe
Bolt Head
Kingsbridge
Modbury
Bigbury Bay
Yealmpton
Plympton
Plymouth
The Sound
Torpoint
Whitsand Bay
Rame Head
Saltash

Dartmoor
Yes Tor 619
Widecombe in the Moor
Moretonhampstead
Newton Abbot
Ashburton
Buckfastleigh
Totnes
Ivybridge
Lydford
Tavistock
Horrabridge
Lee Moor

Lundy Island

Roadford Reservoir

Winkleigh
Hatherleigh
Northam

Rivers/physical labels: Avon, Wylye, Stour, Frome, Parrett, Tone, Yeo, Isle, Brue, Axe, Otter, Exe, Little Dart, Taw, Mole, Torridge, Tamar, Otery, Fowey, Fal, Dart, Teign, Plym

ENGLISH CHANNEL

Roscoff (Santander)
Roscoff (Le Havre)
Cherbourg, Le Havre

Jersey, Guernsey
Weymouth

Cherbourg, Le Havre

Inset: Channel Islands (U.K.)

Cap de la Hague
Cherbourg
Cap de Carteret
Carteret
Les Pieux
Beaumont
FRANCE
St Anne
Alderney
St Martin
Guernsey
St Sampson
St Peter Port
Herm
Sark
St Martin
110
Jersey
St Ouen
St John
St Martin
St Helier
St Brelade
St Malo
St Malo
2° 20′
49° 20′

8 9

Z Y

KEY

Relief and physical features

Relief
metres
1000
500
200
100
sea level
under sea level
0
50
200

▲ 1085 **Mountain height**
(in metres)

Water features
River
Canal
Lake / Reservoir

Communications
Railway
Motorway
Road
⊕ Car ferry
⊕ Main airport
✈ Local airport

Administration

Boundaries
International
Internal

Settlement
Urban area

Cities and towns in order of size

National capital   Other city or town
□ DUBLIN   ● Birmingham
                    ○ Liverpool
                    ○ Bristol
                    ○ Exeter
                    ○ Llandeilo

Grid references: A B C D 1 2 4 5 6 50° 51°

A   B   C   D

Islay
Portnahaven
Port Askaig
Gigha
Port Ellen
Mull of Oa
Claonaig
Millport
Beith
Newton Mearns
East Kilbride
Hamilton
Wishaw
Carluke
Pentland Hills
Gala Water
Sound of Bute
Lochranza
Ardrossan
Saltcoats
Kilwinning
Dalry
Stewarton
Strathaven
Lanark
Peebles
Galashiels
Tweed
Melrose
Selkirk
Newto
Goat Fell 874
Arran
Brodick
Lamlash
Irvine
Kilmarnock
Galston
Muirkirk
Douglas
Rigside
Tinto 707
Biggar
Broad Law 840
Ettrick Forest
Teviot
Kintyre
Kilbrannan Sound
Troon
Prestwick
Ayr
Mauchline
Cumnock
Abington
Hart Fell 808
Ettrick Water
Hawick
Machrihanish
Campbeltown
Firth of Clyde
Culzean Bay
Dalrymple
Maybole
New Cumnock
Kirkconnel
Sanquhar
691
Moffat
Teviothead

4

Rathlin Island
Mull of Kintyre
Sanda Island
Ailsa Craig
Girvan
Dailly
Doon
Loch Doon
Dalmellington
Carsphairn
Moniaive
Thornhill
Nith
Langholm
Benbane Head
Fair Head
Bushmills
Ballycastle
Knocklayd 517
Armoy
Trostan 554
Garron Point
Cushendall
Stinchar
Ballantrae
843 Merrick
Corserine 813
Dalry
New Galloway
Lochmaben
Lockerbie
Ecclefechan
Esk
Esk
SCOTLAND
5

55°
Kilrea
Bann
Dunloy
Ballymoney
Ballymena
Broughshane
Antrim Hills
Carnlough
Glenarm
Larne
Milleur Point
Kirkcolm
Loch Ryan
Cairnryan
Newton Stewart
711
Castle Douglas
Dumfries
Annan
Gretna
Longtown
Brampton
Irthing
Carlisle
Thursby
Wigton
Aspatria
Maryport

North Channel
Stranraer
The Rinns of Galloway
Portpatrick
Glenluce
Wigtown
Kirkcudbright
Kirkbean
Criffell 569
Solway Firth
Abbey Head
Cockermouth
Skiddaw 931
Penrith

NORTHERN IRELAND
Lough Neagh
Antrim
Randalstown
Crumlin
Glengormley
Newtownabbey
Belfast Lough
Bangor
Donaghadee
Whitehead
Island Magee
Larne Lough
Carrickfergus
Ballyclare
Lisburn
Belfast
Dundonald
Newtownards
Comber
Kircubbin
Portavogie
Ards Peninsula
Luce Bay
Port William
Whithorn
Wigtown Bay
Burrow Head
Seaton
Workington
Great Clifton
Whitehaven
Distington
Keswick
Derwent Water
Bassenthwaite L.
Crummock Water
Helvellyn 949
Thirlmere
Ullswater
Pooley Bridge
Shap
Haweswater Reservoir
Lake District
Harter Fell 765
Kendal

3

Dunmurry
Lagan
Lurgan
Craigavon
Portadown
Tandragee
Banbridge
Dromore
Ballynahinch
Saintfield
Crossgar
Quoile
Strangford Lough
Downpatrick
Portaferry
Ballyquintin Point
Point of Ayre
Andreas
Ramsey Bay
Ramsey
Maughold Head
St Bees Head
Cleator Moor
St Bees
Egremont
Ennerdale Water
Scafell Pike
Gosforth
977
Ambleside
Coniston
Windermere
The
Newry
Bann
Rathfriland
Bessbrook
Newcastle
Slieve Donard 852
Dundrum Bay
St John's Point
Ardglass
Kirk Michael
Isle of Man
Snaefell 625
Peel
Laxey
Seascale
Wast Water
Black Combe 600
The Old Man of Coniston 803
Coniston Water
Levens
Kirkby Lonsdale
Sedb
Mourne Mts
Warrenpoint
Carlingford L. 588
Kilkeel
Annalong
Clay Head
Onchan
Douglas
Millom
Ulverston
Dalton-in-Furness
Barrow-in-Furness
Cartmel
Grange-over-Sands
Carnforth
Burton
Kenda
Port Erin
Castletown
Calf of Man
Isle of Walney
Hilpsford Point
Morecambe Bay
Morecambe
Heysham
Lancaster
56

54°
Dundalk
Ballagan Point
Dunany Point
Fane
Dundalk Bay
LOUTH
Dunleer
Clogher Head
Ward's S
Fore of Bowla
Fleetwood
Cleveleys
Thornton
Poulton-le-Fylde
Blackpool
Lancaster Canal
Ribble

MEATH
Drogheda
Bettystown
Balbriggan
Skerries
Ashbourne
Lambay Island
Malahide
Swords
I   R   I   S   H
S   E   A
Lytham
St Anne's
Freckleton
Kirkham
Preston
Longto
Tarleton
Leyland
Southport
Burscough Bridge
Chorley

2
Dublin
Ireland's Eye
Dublin Bay
DUBLIN
Dun Laoghaire
Bray
Carmel Head
Amlwch
Holyhead Bay
Alaw Reservoir
Moelfre
Great Ormes Head
West Kirby
Point of Ayr
Colwyn Bay
Southport
Formby
Ormskirk
Skelmersdale
Maghull
Crosby
Bootle
St Helens
Newton
Willo
Wigan
Standish
Horwi

Djouce Mountain 886
Enniskerry
Kilcoole
Holy Island
Holyhead
Valley
Llanfaethlu
Llangefni
Anglesey
Red Wharf Bay
Llangoed
Beaumaris
Menai Bridge
Bangor
Llandudno
Conwy
Conwy Bay
Llanfairfechan
Abergele
Colwyn Bay
Rhyl
Prestatyn
Holywell
St Asaph
Denbigh
Mold
Buckley
Wallasey
Birkenhead
Liverpool
Washington
Wirral
Bebington
Heswall
Neston
Connah's Quay
Ellesmere Port
Mersey
Runco
Flint
Widnes
Frodsham

WICKLOW
Tonelagee 819
Llanfairpwllgwyngyll
Carnarfon
Llanwnda
Bethesda
Carnedd Llywelyn 1064
Llanberis
Glyder Fawr 999
Betws-y-Coed
Conwy
Llansannan
Ruthin
WALES
Hawarden
Chester
Bretton
Farndon
Wrexham
Nanty
Malpas

1
53°
Wicklow Mts
Rathdrum
Wicklow
Wicklow Head
Caernarfon Bay
Menai Str
Llandwrog
Llanllyfni
Snowdon 1085
Carnedd y Filiast 669
Blaenau Ffestiniog
Alwen Res.
Corwen
Rhosllanerchrugog
Ruabon

A   6°   B   5°   C   4°   D   3°

SCALE 1 : 1 200 000

0   10   20   30   40 km

KEY

Relief and physical features

Relief
metres
1000
500
200
100
sea level
0
50
200
under sea level

▲ 977 Mountain height
(in metres)

Water features

〜 River

〜 Canal

◯ Lake / Reservoir

Communications

—— Railway

══ Motorway

—— Road

······ Car ferry

⊕ Main airport

✈ Local airport

Administration

Boundaries

══ International

—— Internal

Settlement

▨ Urban area

Cities and towns in order of size

National capital | Other city or town

☐ DUBLIN | ● Manchester
| ○ Liverpool
| ○ Belfast
| ○ Carlisle
| ○ Keswick

Conic projection

SCALE 1 : 1 200 000

0   10   20   30   40 km

F   3°   **G**   2°   **H**   1°

NORTH SEA

KEY

Relief and physical features

Relief metres

1000
500
200
100
sea level
0
50
200
under sea level

▲ 1214   Mountain height (in metres)

Water features

~~~ River

~~~ Canal

⬭ Lake / Reservoir

Communications

═══ Railway

═══ Motorway

─── Road

········· Car ferry

⊕ Main airport

✦ Local airport

Administration

Boundaries

═══ International

─── Internal

Settlement

▪ Urban area

Cities and towns in order of size

○ **Glasgow**

○ Londonderry

○ Lancaster

∘ Peebles

Conic projection

KEY

Relief and physical features

Relief
metres
1000
500
200
100
0 sea level
50
200 under sea level

1344 Mountain height
(in metres)

Water features

River
Canal
Lake / Reservoir

Communications

Railway
Road
Car ferry
⊕ Main airport
✈ Local airport

Settlement

Cities and towns in order of size

○ Aberdeen
○ Inverness
○ Kirkwall

SCALE 1 : 1 200 000

0   10   20   30   40 km

ATLANTIC

OCEAN

Outer Hebrides

Flannan Isles

St Kilda

Mealasta Island

Scarp

Pabbay
Berneray
Boreray

Sd of Monach

Monach Islands

Benbecula

Balivanich

Sd of Barra

Vatersay

Pabbay

Mingulay

Berneray

Barra
Castlebay

Sandray

Eriskay

South Uist

Lochboisdale

North Uist

Lochmaddy

Sound of Harris

Rodel

Loch Langavat

Harris

Loch Langavat

Tarbert

Tirga Mor
679

Clisham
799

E. L. Tarbert

Scalpay

West Loch Roag

Great Bernera

Callanish

LEWIS

Stornoway

Broad Bay

Eye Peninsula

Kebock Head

Butt of Lewis

Port of Ness

Muirneag
248

Tolsta Head

Little Minch

L. Dunvegan

Rubha Hunish

Uig

Loch Snizort

L. Bracadale

Skye

Portree

Soay

Cuillin Hills
993
Sgurr Alasdair

Blaven
928

Canna

Rum

Eigg

Muck

Coll

Coll

Point of Ardnamurchan

Loch Sunart

Eilean Shona

Sound of Arisaig

Shiant Islands

Rubha Reidh

Gruinard Bay

Gair Loch

Gairloch

Greenstone Point

The Minch

Summer Isles

Rubha Coigeach

Point of Stoer

Cape Wrath

Kyle of Durness

Loch Eriboll

Kinlochbervie
Loch Inchard
L. Laxford
Handa Island
Scourie

Foinaven
915

Loch More

Point of Stoer

Lochinver

Loch Assynt

Canisp
846

Ben More Assynt
998

Cul Mor
849

Loch Lurgainn

Loch Broom

Ullapool

An Teallach
1062

Fionn Loch

Beinn Dearg
1084

Loch Maree

Sgurr Mor
1110

WESTER ROSS

Loch Fannich

L. Torridon

Torridon

Shieldaig

Rona

Sound of Raasay

Raasay

Inner Sound

Scalpay

Kyle of Lochalsh

L. Eishort

Sd of Sleat

Ardvasar

L. Hourn
1020
Ladhar Bheinn

Mallaig

L. Nevis

Arisaig

Loch Morar

Cuillin Sound

Orrin

Loch Monar

Càrn Eighe
1183

A'Chralaig
1120

Loch Cluanie

L. Loyne

Garry

Glen Moriston

Glen Garry

Loch Quoich

Loch Arkaig

L. Lochy

Loch Shiel

Sgurr Dhomhnuill
888

Loch Linnhe

Fort William

Loch Leven

1344

Stob Choire Claurigh
1177

Ben Nevis

Loch Treig

Kinlochleven

Bidean nam Bian 1150

Glen Coe

E 4° F 3° G 2° X 2° Y 1° Z

Herma Ness

Lerwick
Noup Head Mull Head Unst
Papa North
Westray Ronaldsay Torshavn
N. Ronaldsay Firth
Westray The Point of Fetlar
North Sound Fethaland
Westray Firth Eday Sanday Yell Sound Yell

Sanday Ronas Hill
Sound 450
Brough Head Rousay Esha Ness Voe
Stronsay Toft
Egilsay St. Magnus Cut Skerries
Orkney Stronsay Bay Muckle
Loch of Firth Roe Whalsay
Islands Harray Shapinsay Auskerry Papa Melby
Loch of Wide Firth Stour
Stenness Kirkwall Foula Shetland
Stromness Mainland Skaill Islands Lerwick
Ward Hill Scapa Copinsay West Isle o'
479 Flow Burray Burra Noss
Hoy Flotta Burray Bressay
St Margaret's Hope Bergen (& Hanstholm)
South (summer only)
Pentland Walls Ronaldsay Mousa
Firth Burwick
Brough Ness Sumburgh
Dunnet Head Island of Pentland Skerries Sumburgh
Stroma John o'Groats Head
Strathy Thurso Dunnet Duncansby
Point B. Dunnet Bay Head
Thurso Dounreay Stromness
Melvich Halkirk Loch Sinclair's Fair Isle
Watten Bay
Tongue Dounreay Aberdeen
Ben Loyal Loch CAITHNESS Wick
764 Loyal Wick
L. Naver Ben Latheron
Klibreck
961
Helmsdale 60°

Helmsdale
Brora

Lairg
Golspie
Bonar Bridge Brora
Dornoch 8
Dornoch Firth Tarbat Ness
Tain
Balintore
Loch Glass Lossiemouth
Ben Wyvis Invergordon Nigg Burghead Portknockie Troup Head Fraserburgh
1046 Bay Cromarty Elgin Buckie Cullen Portsoy Macduff
Black Kinloss Banff Loch of Strathbeg
Isle Fortrose Forres Fochabers Knock Hill New Rattray Head
Conon Bridge Nairn Lossie 430 Aberchirder Pitsligo Crimond
Moray Isla Deveron N. Ugie
Beauly Firth Firth Rothes Keith Turriff Mintlaw Peterhead
Inverness Spey Huntly Boddam
Findhorn Dufftown Deveron Ythan Cruden Bay
Ness Nairn Strathspey STRATHBOGIE 2
Grantown Bogie Insch
-on-Spey Hills of Urie Oldmeldrum
Cromdale Inverurie
Kemnay Kintore
Aviemore Don Dyce
Geal Charn Westhill
821 Avon Aberdeen
Kingussie Cairn Gorm 1245 Dee Portlethen
Newtonmore Ben Macdui Cairngorm Mts Aboyne Banchory Newtonhill
1291 1309 Ballater 57°
Cairn Toul Braemar Dee Mount Keen Stonehaven
1008 1155 939 N. Esk
Carn nan Lochnagar Inverbervie
Beinn Dearg Gabhar Mayar Water of Saughs Laurencekirk
Forest of Atholl 1121 928 S. Esk 1
Ben Alder Glenshee Hillside
148 Backwater Brechin
Loch Reservoir
Garry Blair Atholl Isla Montrose
L. Rannoch Forfar
Schiehallion Loch Kirriemuir Lunan Bay
1083 Tummel

NORTH

SEA

E 4° F 3° G 2° H 1° I

Conic projection

KEY

Relief and physical features

Relief metres
1000
500
200
100
sea level
0
under sea level
200
4000

1041 ▲ Mountain height (in metres)

Water features
River
Canal
Lake / Reservoir
Marsh

Communications
Railway
Motorway
Road
✈ Main airport

Administration
Boundaries
International
Internal

Settlement
Cities and towns in order of size
National capital   Other city or town
□ DUBLIN   ○ Cork
                    ○ Killarney

SCALE 1 : 2 000 000

0   20   40   60   80 km

Conic projection

Map labels

SCOTLAND
Islay
785 ▲   Tarbert
Sound of Bute
Port Ellen   Gigha   Goat Fell 874 ▲   Arran
Mull of Oa
Campbeltown
Kilbrannan Sound
Mull of Kintyre
Sanda Island
Cairnryan
Stranraer

Inishtrahull
Malin Head
Glengad Head
Giant's Causeway
Rathlin Island
Fair Head
Garron Point
Tory I.
Bloody Foreland
Inishowen
Slieve Snaght 615 ▲
Buncrana
Portrush
Coleraine
Bushmills   Ballycastle
Ballymoney
Trostan 554 ▲
Carnlough
North Channel
Aran Island
L. Swilly
L. Foyle
Limavady
Ballymena
Island Magee
Larne
Gweebarra Bay
Derryveagh Mts
Errigal 752 ▲
Letterkenny
Londonderry
LONDONDERRY
ANTRIM
Antrim Hills
Ballyclare
Carrickfergus
Lifford
Strabane
Finn
Sperrin Mts 683 ▲
Maghera
Magherafelt
Antrim
Newtownabbey
DONEGAL
Blue Stack Mts 676 ▲
Derg
Foyle
Newtownstewart
Omagh
NORTHERN
TYRONE
Cookstown
Lough Neagh
Belfast L.
Belfast
Bangor
Newtownards
Killybegs
Donegal
IRELAND
Dungannon
Crumlin
Lisburn
Dundrum
Ards Pen.
Ballyshannon
Lower Lough Erne
Portadown
Lurgan
Lagan
Strangford Lough
Donegal Bay
Bundoran
Fintona
FERMANAGH
Enniskillen
ARMAGH
Armagh
Banbridge
DOWN
Portaferry
Erris Head
Downpatrick Head
Killala Bay
Sligo Bay
Manorhamilton
Lough Melvin
Monaghan
Lisnaskea
MONAGHAN
Clones
Newry
Warrenpoint
Mourne Mts 852 ▲
Slieve Donard
St John's Point
Newcastle
Downpatrick
Ardglass
Belmullet
The Mullet
Carrowmore Lake
Sligo
542 ▲ Knockalongy
LEITRIM
L. Gill
Upper Lough Erne
Castleblayney
Carrickmacross
Kingscourt
588 ▲
Carlingford L.
Kilkeel
Dundalk Bay
Blacksod Bay
772 ▲
Slieve Car
Nephin 806 ▲
Ballina
SLIGO
L. Allen
L. Key
CAVAN
Cavan
Bailieborough
Annalee
Fane
Dundalk
LOUTH
Dunany Point
Achill Island
Foxford
Charlestown
Boyle
Tubbercurry
Moy
L. Gara
Carrick-on-Shannon
L. Gowna
L. Sheelin
Kells
Drogheda
Clogher Head
Clare Island
Castlebar
MAYO
ROSCOMMON
L. Oughter
Longford
LONGFORD
Blackwater
Boyne
Balbriggan
Skerries
Clew Bay
Westport
Claremorris
Ballyhaunis
Lanesborough
MEATH
Navan
Lambay Island
Inishturk
Inishbofin
Partry Mts
L. Carra
Roscommon
Lough Ree
Athboy
Ashbourne
Swords
Ireland's Eye
IRISH
Lough Mask
Tuam
WESTMEATH
Mullingar
Trim
Slyne Head
Lough Corrib
GALWAY
Athlone
Inny
Kinnegad
Malahide
Liverpool
Connemara
Athenry
Ballinasloe
OF
Clara
Tullamore
Leixlip
Dublin
Iar Connaught
Galway
Oranmore
Brosna
OFFALY
KILDARE
DUBLIN
Dun Laoghaire
Holyhead
Galway Bay
Inishmore
Loughrea
Shannon
Banagher
Kilcormac
Newbridge
Naas
Bray
SEA
Aran Islands
Inishmaan
Inisheer
Gort
Portumna
Birr
Mountmellick
Kildare
Kilcullen
Pollaphuca Res.
Wicklow Mts
Hag's Head
Liscannor Bay
Ennistymon
Scalp 327 ▲
Lough Derg
Roscrea
LAOIS
Portlaoise
Athy
WICKLOW
Wicklow
Wicklow Head
391 ▲ Slievecallan
CLARE
Ennis
Newmarket-on-Fergus
Castleconnell
Nenagh
481 ▲
Templemore
Abbeyleix
337 ▲
Carlow
Tullow
281 ▲
Rathdrum
Mizen Head
Donegal Point
Kilkee
IRELAND
Castlecomer
Derry
Arklow
Kilmichael Point
Loop Head
Mouth of The Shannon
Kilrush
Limerick
TIPPERARY
Thurles
Kilkenny
CARLOW
Muine Bheag
Bunclody
Gorey
Ballybunnion
Rathkeale
Croom
Tipperary
Cashel
KILKENNY
Callan
Thomastown
Enniscorthy
Cahore Point
Kerry Head
Listowel
Newcastle West
Kilmallock
820 ▲ Galtee Mts
Nore
Suir
WEXFORD
Wexford Bay
Brandon Head
953 ▲
Tralee Bay
Abbeyfeale
Rathluirc
Mitchelstown
Clonmel
Slievenamon
Carrick-on-Suir
New Ross
Sybil Point
Brandon Mtn
Tralee
Mullaghareirk Mts
Castleisland
Galtee Mts
Tar
Comeragh Mts 728 ▲
Waterford
Rosslare Harbour
Great Blasket I.
Dingle
KERRY
Buttevant
Knockmealdown Mts
Seefin
WATERFORD
Tramore
Carnsore Point
Fishguard
L. Leane
Killarney
Mallow
Fermoy
Blackwater
Lismore
Dungarvan
Dunmore East
Hook Head
Saltee Islands
Bray Head
Carrantuohill 1041 ▲
Macgillycuddy's Reeks 774 ▲
840 ▲
Kenmare
Boggeragh Mts
Blarney
Midleton
Youghal
Knockadoon Head
WALES
St David's Head
Ramsey Island
Cahirciveen
Lee
CORK
Macroom
Cork
Cobh
Bolus Head
Knockboy 707 ▲
Caha Mts
Kenmare River
Bandon
Kinsale
Pembroke Dock
Dursey Head
Bantry
Clonakilty
Old Head of Kinsale
St George's Channel
Swansea
Mizen Head
Cape Clear
Clear Island
Galley Head
Seven Heads
Roscoff, Le Havre
Le Havre, Roscoff
Cherbourg, Roscoff
REPUBLIC OF IRELAND
GALWAY BAY

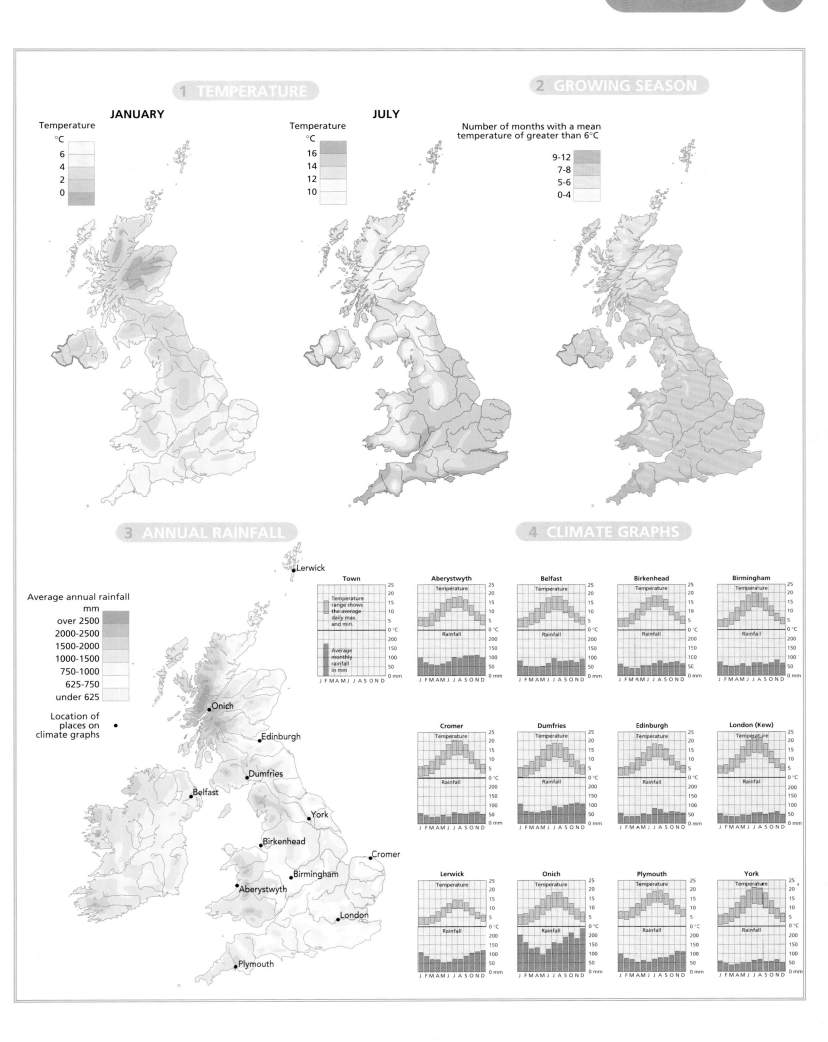

1 TEMPERATURE

JANUARY

Temperature
°C
6
4
2
0

JULY

Temperature
°C
16
14
12
10

2 GROWING SEASON

Number of months with a mean
temperature of greater than 6°C

9-12
7-8
5-6
0-4

3 ANNUAL RAINFALL

Average annual rainfall
mm
over 2500
2000-2500
1500-2000
1000-1500
750-1000
625-750
under 625

Location of
places on
climate graphs ●

Lerwick
Onich
Edinburgh
Dumfries
Belfast
York
Birkenhead
Cromer
Birmingham
Aberystwyth
London
Plymouth

4 CLIMATE GRAPHS

Town
Temperature range shows the average daily max. and min.
Average monthly rainfall in mm

Aberystwyth
Belfast
Birkenhead
Birmingham

Cromer
Dumfries
Edinburgh
London (Kew)

Lerwick
Onich
Plymouth
York

SCALE 1 : 4 000 000

0   50   100   150 km

Conic projection

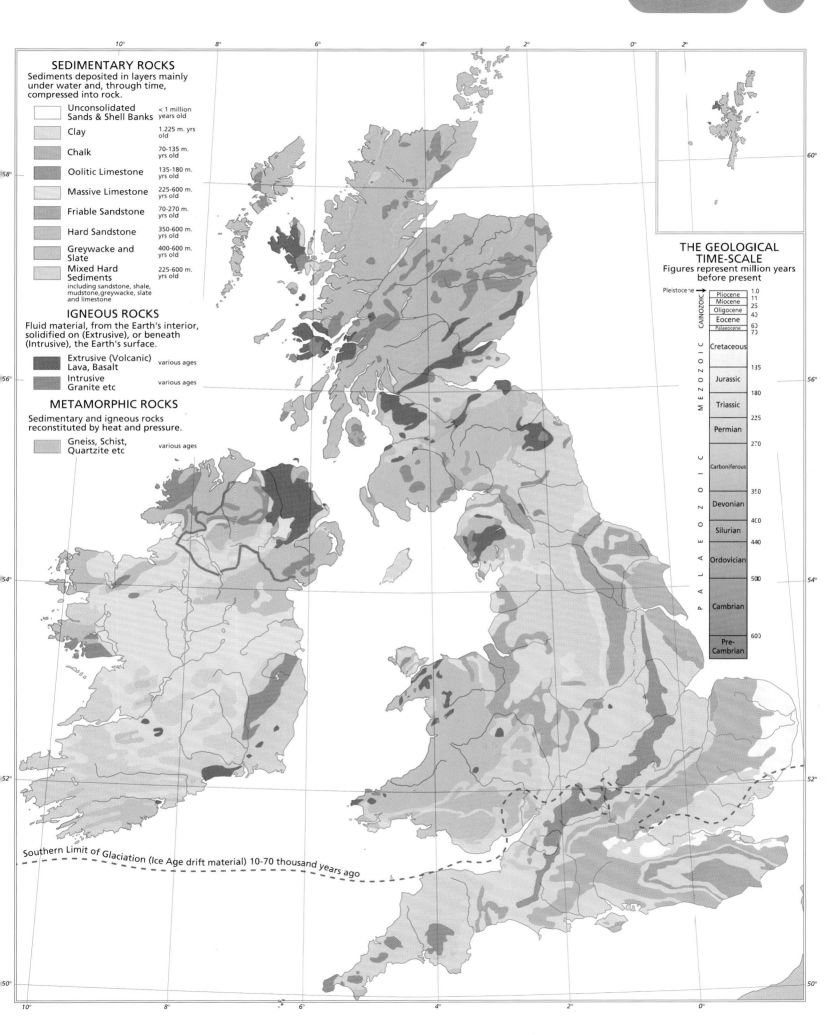

SEDIMENTARY ROCKS

Sediments deposited in layers mainly under water and, through time, compressed into rock.

	Unconsolidated Sands & Shell Banks	< 1 million years old
	Clay	1.225 m. yrs old
	Chalk	70-135 m. yrs old
	Oolitic Limestone	135-180 m. yrs old
	Massive Limestone	225-600 m. yrs old
	Friable Sandstone	70-270 m. yrs old
	Hard Sandstone	350-600 m. yrs old
	Greywacke and Slate	400-600 m. yrs old
	Mixed Hard Sediments	225-600 m. yrs old

including sandstone, shale, mudstone, greywacke, slate and limestone

IGNEOUS ROCKS

Fluid material, from the Earth's interior, solidified on (Extrusive), or beneath (Intrusive), the Earth's surface.

	Extrusive (Volcanic) Lava, Basalt	various ages
	Intrusive Granite etc	various ages

METAMORPHIC ROCKS

Sedimentary and igneous rocks reconstituted by heat and pressure.

	Gneiss, Schist, Quartzite etc	various ages

THE GEOLOGICAL TIME-SCALE

Figures represent million years before present

Pleistocene →			
CAINOZOIC		Pliocene	1.0
		Miocene	11
		Oligocene	25
		Eocene	40
		Palaeocene	60 / 70
MEZOZOIC		Cretaceous	
			135
		Jurassic	
			180
		Triassic	
			225
		Permian	
			270
PALAEOZOIC		Carboniferous	
			350
		Devonian	
			400
		Silurian	
			440
		Ordovician	
			500
		Cambrian	
			600
		Pre-Cambrian	

Southern Limit of Glaciation (Ice Age drift material) 10-70 thousand years ago

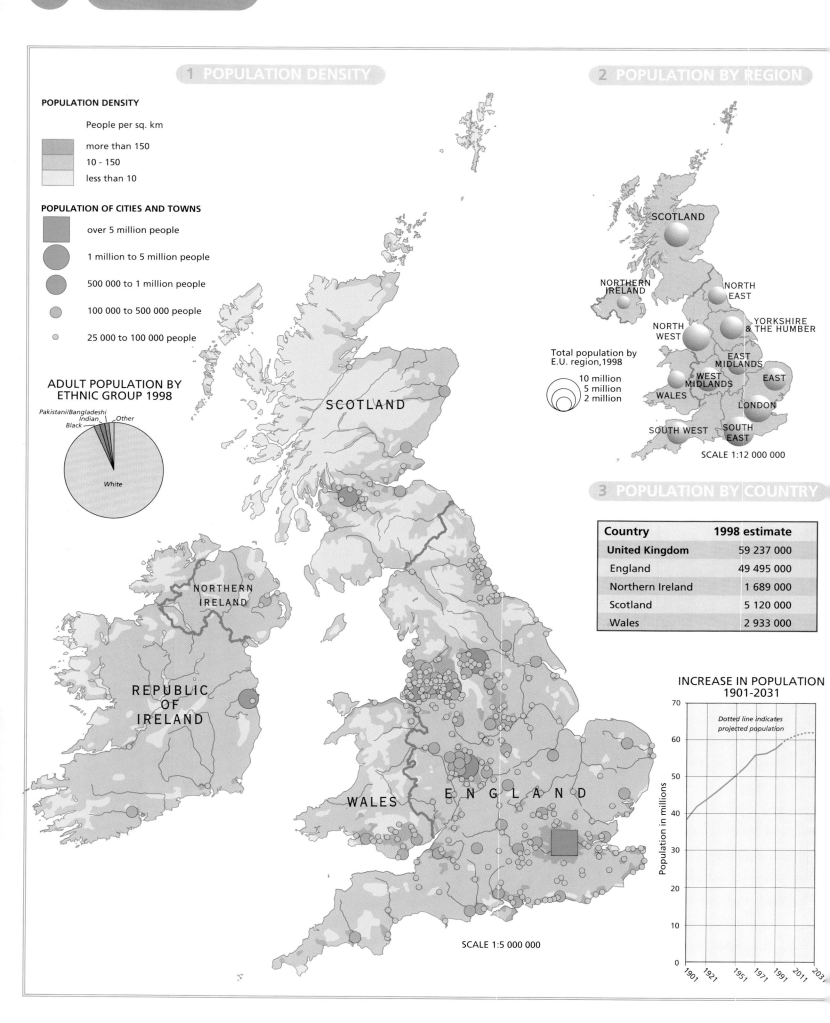

1 POPULATION DENSITY

POPULATION DENSITY

People per sq. km

more than 150

10 - 150

less than 10

POPULATION OF CITIES AND TOWNS

over 5 million people

1 million to 5 million people

500 000 to 1 million people

100 000 to 500 000 people

25 000 to 100 000 people

ADULT POPULATION BY ETHNIC GROUP 1998

Pakistani/Bangladeshi
Indian
Black
Other
White

SCOTLAND

NORTHERN IRELAND

REPUBLIC OF IRELAND

WALES

E N G L A N D

SCALE 1:5 000 000

2 POPULATION BY REGION

SCOTLAND

NORTHERN IRELAND

NORTH EAST

YORKSHIRE & THE HUMBER

NORTH WEST

EAST MIDLANDS

WEST MIDLANDS

EAST

WALES

LONDON

SOUTH WEST

SOUTH EAST

Total population by E.U. region, 1998

10 million
5 million
2 million

SCALE 1:12 000 000

3 POPULATION BY COUNTRY

Country	1998 estimate
United Kingdom	59 237 000
England	49 495 000
Northern Ireland	1 689 000
Scotland	5 120 000
Wales	2 933 000

INCREASE IN POPULATION 1901-2031

Dotted line indicates projected population

Population in millions

1901 1921 1951 1971 1991 2011 2031

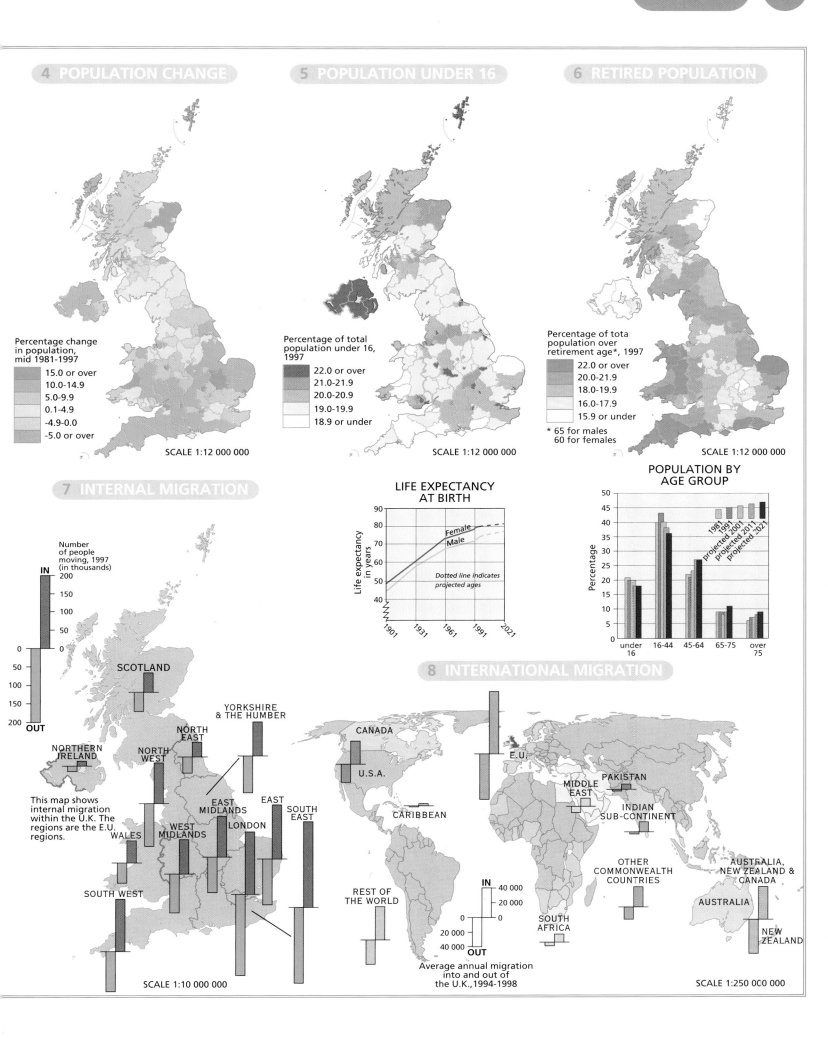

4 POPULATION CHANGE

Percentage change in population, mid 1981-1997
- 15.0 or over
- 10.0-14.9
- 5.0-9.9
- 0.1-4.9
- -4.9-0.0
- -5.0 or over

SCALE 1:12 000 000

5 POPULATION UNDER 16

Percentage of total population under 16, 1997
- 22.0 or over
- 21.0-21.9
- 20.0-20.9
- 19.0-19.9
- 18.9 or under

SCALE 1:12 000 000

6 RETIRED POPULATION

Percentage of total population over retirement age*, 1997
- 22.0 or over
- 20.0-21.9
- 18.0-19.9
- 16.0-17.9
- 15.9 or under

* 65 for males
60 for females

SCALE 1:12 000 000

7 INTERNAL MIGRATION

Number of people moving, 1997 (in thousands)

IN
200
150
100
50
0
0
50
100
150
200
OUT

SCOTLAND
NORTHERN IRELAND
NORTH WEST
NORTH EAST
YORKSHIRE & THE HUMBER
EAST MIDLANDS
EAST
WEST MIDLANDS
LONDON
SOUTH EAST
WALES
SOUTH WEST

This map shows internal migration within the U.K. The regions are the E.U. regions.

SCALE 1:10 000 000

LIFE EXPECTANCY AT BIRTH

Life expectancy in years
90
80
70
60
50
40

Female
Male

Dotted line indicates projected ages

1901 1931 1961 1991 2021

POPULATION BY AGE GROUP

Percentage
50
45
40
35
30
25
20
15
10
5
0

1981
1991
projected 2001
projected 2011
projected 2021

under 16 | 16-44 | 45-64 | 65-75 | over 75

8 INTERNATIONAL MIGRATION

CANADA
U.S.A.
CARIBBEAN
REST OF THE WORLD
E.U.
MIDDLE EAST
PAKISTAN
INDIAN SUB-CONTINENT
SOUTH AFRICA
OTHER COMMONWEALTH COUNTRIES
AUSTRALIA, NEW ZEALAND & CANADA
AUSTRALIA
NEW ZEALAND

IN
40 000
20 000
0
20 000
40 000
OUT

Average annual migration into and out of the U.K., 1994-1998

SCALE 1:250 000 000

1 EMPLOYMENT BY REGION

EMPLOYMENT STRUCTURE
- Agriculture
- Manufacturing
- Services

LABOUR FORCE, 1997 (thousands)
- 2000
- 1000
- 500

SCOTLAND

NORTHERN IRELAND

NORTH EAST

NORTH WEST

YORKSHIRE & THE HUMBER

EAST MIDLANDS

EAST

WEST MIDLANDS

WALES

LONDON

SOUTH WEST

SOUTH EAST

SCALE 1:10 000 000

2 EMPLOYMENT BY SECTOR

UNITED KINGDOM

1948   1994   1997

EMPLOYMENT STRUCTURE
- Agriculture
- Manufacturing
- Services

FRANCE

GERMANY

U.S.A

SPAIN

ITALY

JAPAN

BRAZIL

KENYA

BANGLADESH

SCALE 1:250 000 000

UNEMPLOYMENT RATES
(showing highest and lowest rates)

North East
United Kingdom
South East

Percentage: 12.5, 10.0, 7.5, 5.0, 2.5, 0
Years: 1994, 1995, 1996, 1997, 1998

UNEMPLOYMENT BY SELECTED COUNTRY

1976, 1981, 1986, 1993, 1998

Percentage: 25, 20, 15, 10, 5, 0

Spain   Germany   UK   Sweden   Japan

3 CHANGE IN EMPLOYMENT 1981-1997

AGRICULTURE

Percentage change in percentage of total workforce employed in agriculture, 1981-1997
- -49.9 or under
- -50.0 - -74.9
- -75.0 - -84.9
- -85.0 - -89.9
- -90.0 or over

SCALE 1:12 000 000

MANUFACTURING

Percentage change in percentage of total workforce employed in manufacturing, 1981-1997
- -25.9 or under
- -26.0 - -29.9
- -30.0 - -34.9
- -35.0 - -49.9
- -50.0 or over

SCALE 1:12 000 000

SERVICES

Percentage change in percentage of total workforce employed in services, 1981-1997
- 30.0 or over
- 25.0 - 29.9
- 20.0 - 24.9
- 15.0 - 19.9
- 14.9 or under

SCALE 1:12 000 000

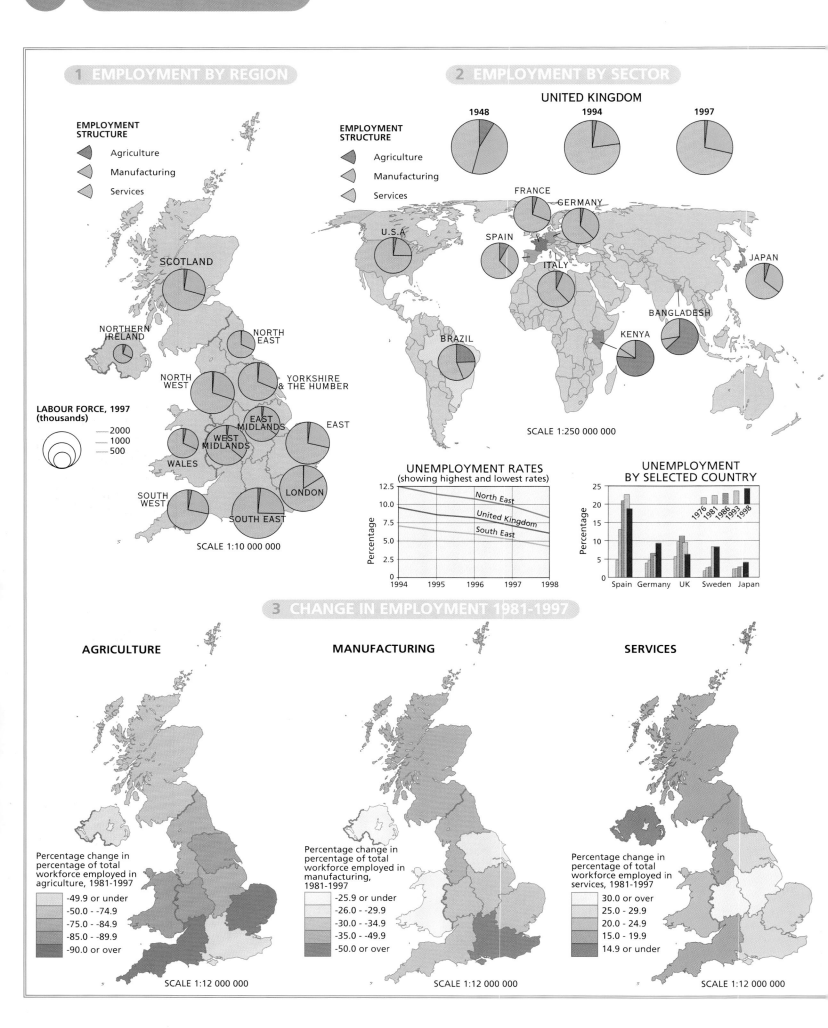

CHANGE IN AGRICULTURAL LAND USE 1961-1998

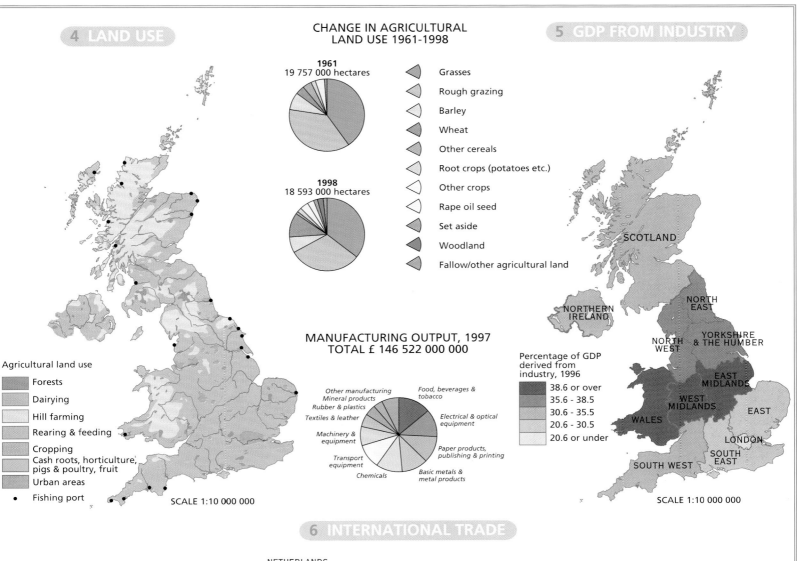

1961
19 757 000 hectares

- Grasses
- Rough grazing
- Barley
- Wheat
- Other cereals
- Root crops (potatoes etc.)
- Other crops
- Rape oil seed
- Set aside
- Woodland
- Fallow/other agricultural land

1998
18 593 000 hectares

MANUFACTURING OUTPUT, 1997
TOTAL £ 146 522 000 000

Other manufacturing
Mineral products
Rubber & plastics
Textiles & leather
Machinery & equipment
Transport equipment
Chemicals
Basic metals & metal products
Paper products, publishing & printing
Electrical & optical equipment
Food, beverages & tobacco

Agricultural land use
- Forests
- Dairying
- Hill farming
- Rearing & feeding
- Cropping
- Cash roots, horticulture, pigs & poultry, fruit
- Urban areas
- • Fishing port

SCALE 1:10 000 000

SCOTLAND

NORTHERN IRELAND

NORTH EAST

NORTH WEST

YORKSHIRE & THE HUMBER

EAST MIDLANDS

WEST MIDLANDS

WALES

EAST

LONDON

SOUTH EAST

SOUTH WEST

Percentage of GDP derived from industry, 1996
- 38.6 or over
- 35.6 - 38.5
- 30.6 - 35.5
- 20.6 - 30.5
- 20.6 or under

SCALE 1:10 000 000

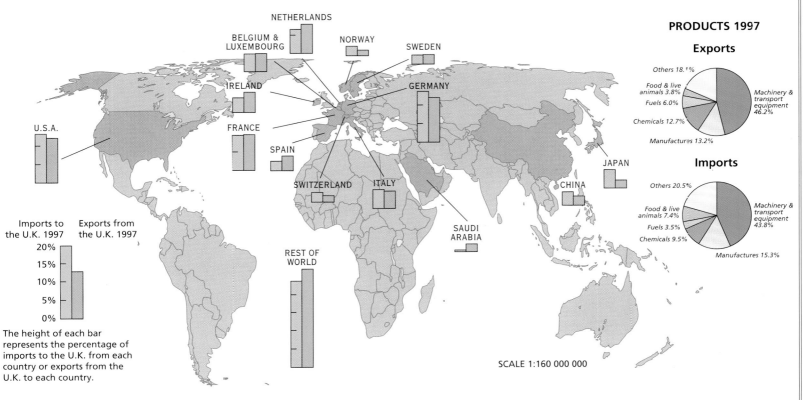

NETHERLANDS

BELGIUM & LUXEMBOURG

NORWAY

SWEDEN

IRELAND

GERMANY

U.S.A.

FRANCE

SPAIN

SWITZERLAND

ITALY

JAPAN

CHINA

SAUDI ARABIA

REST OF WORLD

Imports to the U.K. 1997   Exports from the U.K. 1997
- 20%
- 15%
- 10%
- 5%
- 0%

The height of each bar represents the percentage of imports to the U.K. from each country or exports from the U.K. to each country.

SCALE 1:160 000 000

PRODUCTS 1997

Exports

- Others 18.1%
- Food & live animals 3.8%
- Fuels 6.0%
- Chemicals 12.7%
- Manufactures 13.2%
- Machinery & transport equipment 46.2%

Imports

- Others 20.5%
- Food & live animals 7.4%
- Fuels 3.5%
- Chemicals 9.5%
- Manufactures 15.3%
- Machinery & transport equipment 43.8%

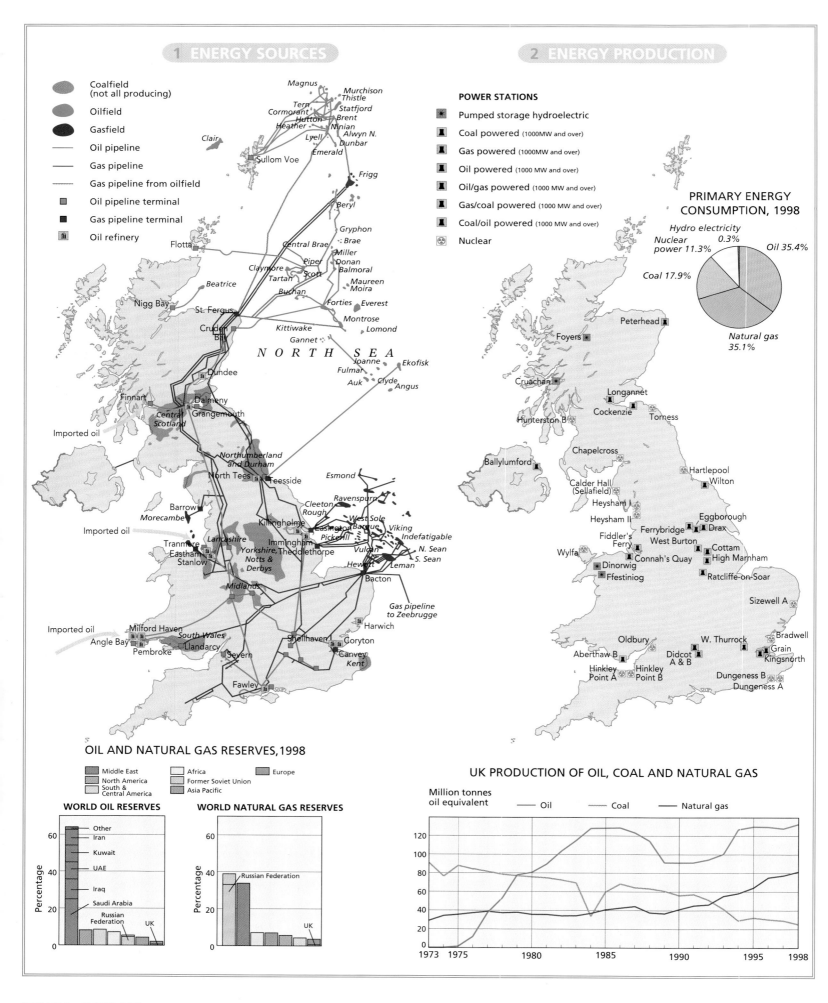

1 ENERGY SOURCES

- Coalfield (not all producing)
- Oilfield
- Gasfield
- Oil pipeline
- Gas pipeline
- Gas pipeline from oilfield
- Oil pipeline terminal
- Gas pipeline terminal
- Oil refinery

Magnus
Murchison
Thistle
Tern
Statfjord
Cormorant
Brent
Hutton
Ninian
Heather
Alwyn N.
Lyell
Dunbar
Clair
Emerald
Sullom Voe
Frigg
Beryl
Gryphon
Brae
Flotta
Central Brae
Miller
Donan
Claymore
Scott
Balmoral
Tartan
Maureen
Beatrice
Buchan
Moira
Nigg Bay
Forties
Everest
St. Fergus
Montrose
Cruden
Lomond
Bay
Kittiwake
Gannet
NORTH SEA
Dundee
Joanne
Ekofisk
Fulmar
Finnart
Auk
Clyde
Dalmeny
Angus
Central
Grangemouth
Scotland
Imported oil
Northumberland
and Durham
North Tees
Teesside
Esmond
Ravenspurn
Barrow
Cleeton
Morecambe
Rough
West Sole
Killingholme
Barque
Viking
Tranmere
Lancashire
Easington
Indefatigable
Eastham
Immingham
Pickerill
Yorkshire,
Theddlethorpe
Vulcan
N. Sean
Stanlow
Notts &
Hewett
S. Sean
Derbys
Leman
Midlands
Bacton
Gas pipeline
to Zeebrugge
Imported oil
Milford Haven
Harwich
Angle Bay
South Wales
Shellhaven
Coryton
Pembroke
Llandarcy
Canvey
Severn
Kent
Fawley

OIL AND NATURAL GAS RESERVES, 1998

- Middle East
- North America
- South & Central America
- Africa
- Former Soviet Union
- Asia Pacific
- Europe

WORLD OIL RESERVES

Percentage
60
40
20
0
Other
Iran
Kuwait
UAE
Iraq
Saudi Arabia
Russian Federation
UK

WORLD NATURAL GAS RESERVES

Percentage
60
40
20
0
Russian Federation
UK

2 ENERGY PRODUCTION

POWER STATIONS

- Pumped storage hydroelectric
- Coal powered (1000MW and over)
- Gas powered (1000MW and over)
- Oil powered (1000 MW and over)
- Oil/gas powered (1000 MW and over)
- Gas/coal powered (1000 MW and over)
- Coal/oil powered (1000 MW and over)
- Nuclear

PRIMARY ENERGY CONSUMPTION, 1998

- Hydro electricity 0.3%
- Nuclear power 11.3%
- Oil 35.4%
- Coal 17.9%
- Natural gas 35.1%

Peterhead
Foyers
Cruachan
Longannet
Cockenzie
Torness
Hunterston B
Chapelcross
Ballylumford
Hartlepool
Calder Hall
Wilton
(Sellafield)
Heysham I
Heysham II
Eggborough
Ferrybridge
Drax
Fiddler's
West Burton
Ferry
Cottam
Wylfa
Connah's Quay
High Marnham
Dinorwig
Ratcliffe-on-Soar
Ffestiniog
Sizewell A
Oldbury
W. Thurrock
Bradwell
Aberthaw B
Didcot
Grain
A & B
Kingsnorth
Hinkley
Hinkley
Dungeness B
Point A
Point B
Dungeness A

UK PRODUCTION OF OIL, COAL AND NATURAL GAS

Million tonnes oil equivalent

— Oil — Coal — Natural gas

120
100
80
60
40
20
1973 1975 1980 1985 1990 1995 1998

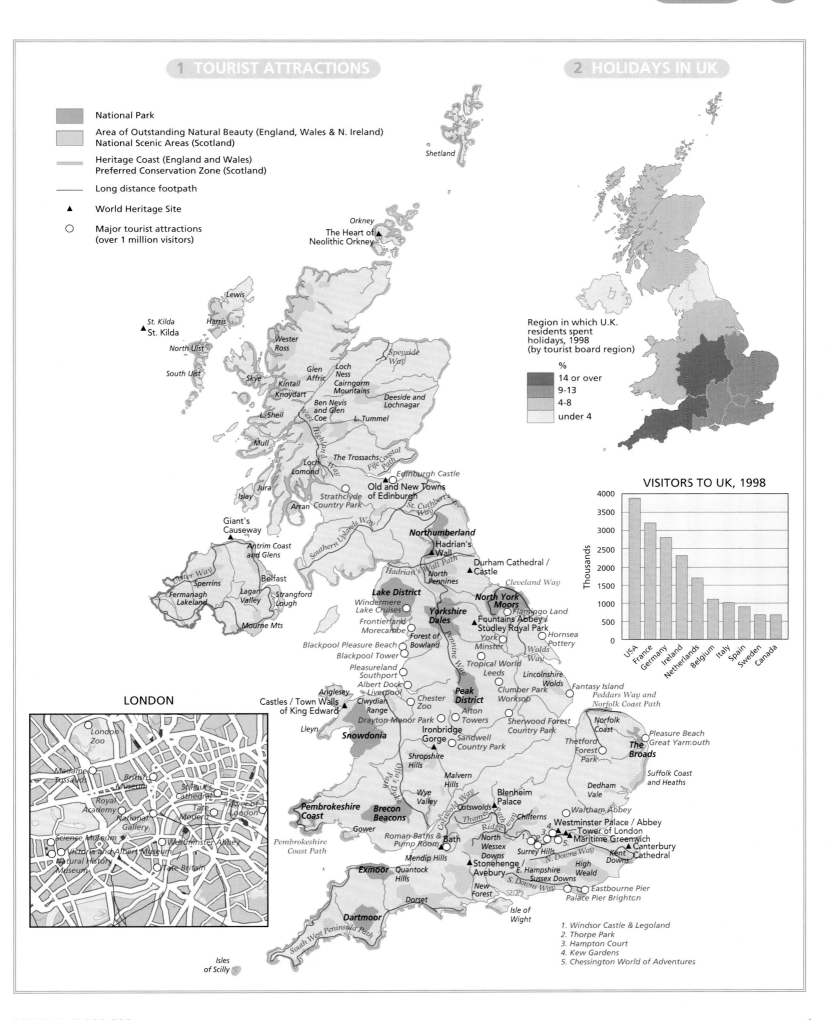

1 TOURIST ATTRACTIONS

Legend:
- National Park
- Area of Outstanding Natural Beauty (England, Wales & N. Ireland)
  National Scenic Areas (Scotland)
- Heritage Coast (England and Wales)
  Preferred Conservation Zone (Scotland)
- Long distance footpath
- ▲ World Heritage Site
- ○ Major tourist attractions (over 1 million visitors)

Shetland

Orkney
The Heart of ▲ Neolithic Orkney

Lewis
St. Kilda
▲ St. Kilda
Harris
North Uist
South Uist
Wester Ross
Speyside Way
Skye
Glen Affric
Loch Ness
Cairngorm Mountains
Kintail
Knoydart
Deeside and Lochnagar
Ben Nevis and Glen Coe
L. Sheil
L. Tummel
Mull
Loch Lomond
The Trossachs
Fife Coastal Path
Jura
Islay
Edinburgh Castle
○ Old and New Towns of Edinburgh
Strathclyde Country Park
St. Cuthbert's Way
Arran
West Highland Way
Giant's Causeway ▲
Antrim Coast and Glens
Southern Uplands Way
Northumberland
Belfast
Hadrian's ▲ Wall
Ulster Way
Sperrins
Lagan Valley
Strangford Lough
Hadrian's Wall Path
North Pennines
Durham Cathedral / Castle ▲
Cleveland Way
Fermanagh Lakeland
Mourne Mts
Lake District
North York Moors
Windermere Lake Cruises
Yorkshire Dales
○ Flamingo Land
Frontierland Morecambe
Forest of Bowland
Fountains Abbey / ▲ Studley Royal Park
York ○
Hornsea Pottery
Blackpool Pleasure Beach ○
Minster
Wolds Way
Blackpool Tower ○
Tropical World
Pleasureland Southport ○
Leeds
Lincolnshire Wolds
Fantasy Island
Albert Dock
Anglesey
Liverpool
Chester Zoo
Peak District
Clumber Park Worksop
Peddars Way and Norfolk Coast Path
Castles / Town Walls of King Edward ▲
Clwydian Range
Alton Towers
Sherwood Forest Country Park
Norfolk Coast
Lleyn
Drayton Manor Park
Snowdonia
Ironbridge Gorge ▲
Sandwell Country Park
Thetford Forest Park
Pleasure Beach Great Yarmouth
The Broads
Shropshire Hills
Suffolk Coast and Heaths
Olfa's Dyke Path
Malvern Hills
Dedham Vale
Wye Valley
Blenheim Palace ▲
Pembrokeshire Coast
Brecon Beacons
Cotswolds
Cotswold Way
Chilterns
Waltham Abbey
Gower
Thames Ridge
Westminster Palace / Abbey ▲
Roman Baths & Pump Room ▲ Bath
Tower of London ▲
Maritime Greenwich ▲
Pembrokeshire Coast Path
North Wessex Downs
Surrey Hills
Canterbury Cathedral
Mendip Hills
N. Downs Way
Kent Downs
Exmoor
Quantock Hills
▲ Stonehenge / Avebury
E. Hampshire
High Weald
Sussex Downs
New Forest
S. Downs Way
Eastbourne Pier
Palace Pier Brighton
Dorset
Isle of Wight
Dartmoor
South West Peninsula Path
Isles of Scilly

LONDON
- London Zoo
- Madame Tussauds
- British Museum
- Royal Academy
- St Paul's Cathedral
- National Gallery
- Tate Modern
- Tower of London
- Science Museum
- Westminster Abbey
- Victoria and Albert Museum
- Natural History Museum
- Tate Britain

2 HOLIDAYS IN UK

Region in which U.K. residents spent holidays, 1998 (by tourist board region)

%
- 14 or over
- 9-13
- 4-8
- under 4

VISITORS TO UK, 1998

Thousands (y-axis: 0, 500, 1000, 1500, 2000, 2500, 3000, 3500, 4000)

USA, France, Germany, Ireland, Netherlands, Belgium, Italy, Spain, Sweden, Canada

1. Windsor Castle & Legoland
2. Thorpe Park
3. Hampton Court
4. Kew Gardens
5. Chessington World of Adventures

SCALE 1 : 5 000 000

Conic projection

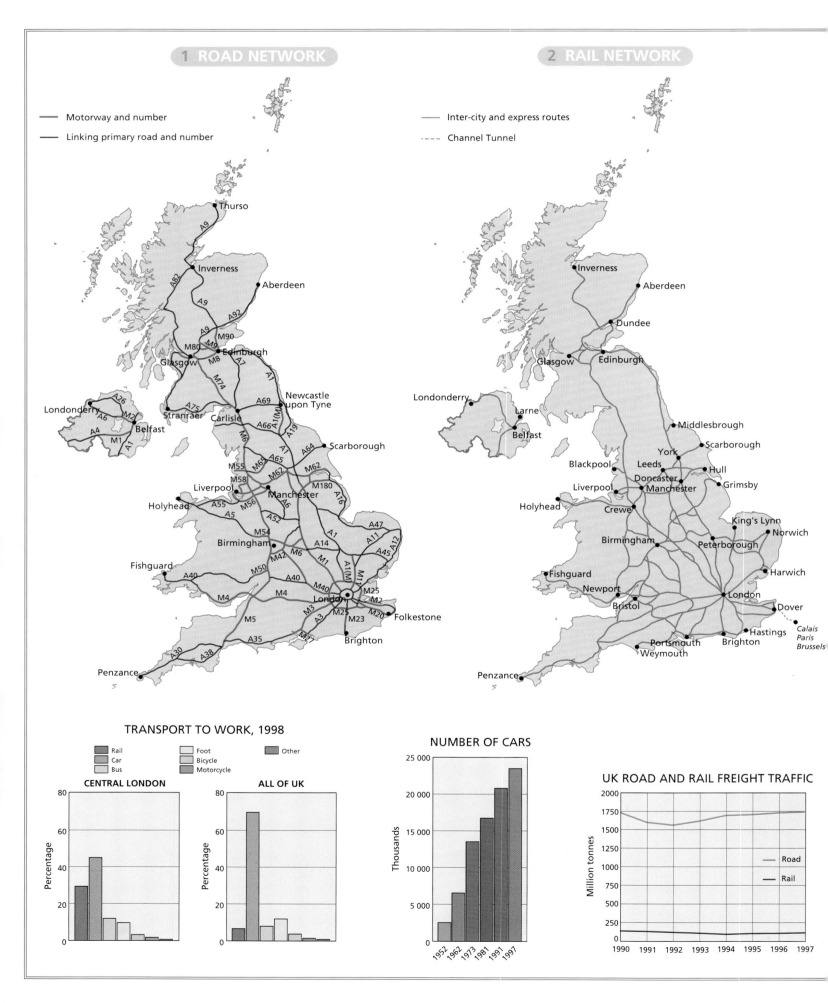

1 ROAD NETWORK

— Motorway and number
— Linking primary road and number

Thurso
A9
Inverness
Aberdeen
A9
A92
A9
M90
M80 M9
Edinburgh
Glasgow M8
A7
M74
Newcastle upon Tyne
A75
A69
Londonderry
A26
A6 M2
Stranraer Carlisle
A66 A1(M)
Belfast
A4
A19
M1 A1
Scarborough
A64
M6
A1
M55 M65 A65
M62
M58 M62
Liverpool M180
Manchester
A16
Holyhead A6
A55 M56
A5 A52
A47
M54
A1 A11
Birmingham A14
A45 A12
Fishguard M42 M6 M1 A1(M) M11
M50 A1
A40 M25
A40 M40 London M2
M4 M3 M25 M20
M4 M23
M5 A3 Folkestone
A35 M27 Brighton
A30 A38
Penzance

2 RAIL NETWORK

— Inter-city and express routes
---- Channel Tunnel

Inverness
Aberdeen
Dundee
Glasgow Edinburgh
Londonderry
Larne
Belfast
Middlesbrough
York Scarborough
Blackpool Leeds Hull
Doncaster
Liverpool Manchester Grimsby
Holyhead Crewe King's Lynn
Birmingham Norwich
Peterborough
Fishguard Harwich
Newport London
Bristol Dover
Hastings Calais Paris Brussels
Portsmouth Brighton
Weymouth
Penzance

TRANSPORT TO WORK, 1998

■ Rail
■ Car
□ Bus
□ Foot
■ Bicycle
■ Motorcycle
■ Other

CENTRAL LONDON

Percentage (0–80)

ALL OF UK

Percentage (0–80)

NUMBER OF CARS

Thousands (0–25 000)

1952 1962 1973 1981 1991 1997

UK ROAD AND RAIL FREIGHT TRAFFIC

Million tonnes (0–2000)

— Road
— Rail

1990 1991 1992 1993 1994 1995 1996 1997

SCALE 1 : 8 000 000

3 PORTS

4 AIRPORTS

PASSENGERS HANDLED PER YEAR (thousands)
- Over 10 000
- 5 000 - 10 000
- 2000 - 5 000
- 1 000 - 2 000
- Other airports

Ports handling more than 1 million tonnes of cargo
Ferry routes with destinations
Ferry terminal

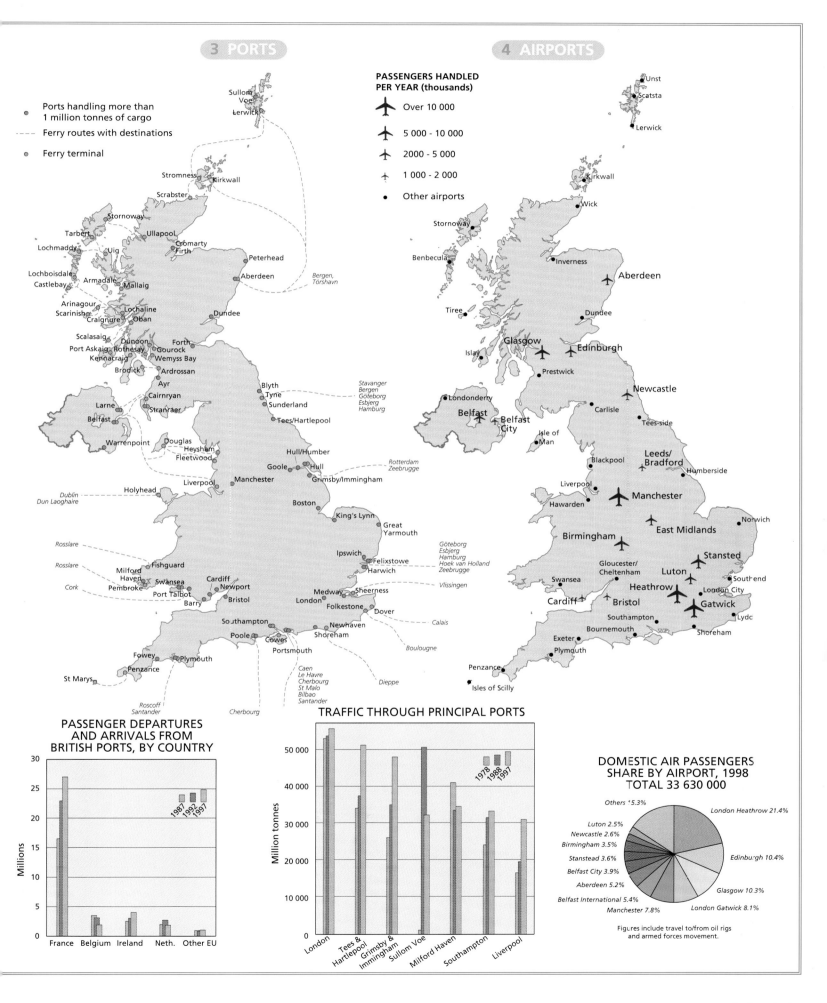

PASSENGER DEPARTURES AND ARRIVALS FROM BRITISH PORTS, BY COUNTRY

Millions — 1987, 1992, 1997

France, Belgium, Ireland, Neth., Other EU

TRAFFIC THROUGH PRINCIPAL PORTS

Million tonnes — 1978, 1988, 1997

London, Tees & Hartlepool, Grimsby & Immingham, Sullom Voe, Milford Haven, Southampton, Liverpool

DOMESTIC AIR PASSENGERS SHARE BY AIRPORT, 1998
TOTAL 33 630 000

- Others 15.3%
- Luton 2.5%
- Newcastle 2.6%
- Birmingham 3.5%
- Stansted 3.6%
- Belfast City 3.9%
- Aberdeen 5.2%
- Belfast International 5.4%
- Manchester 7.8%
- London Gatwick 8.1%
- Glasgow 10.3%
- Edinburgh 10.4%
- London Heathrow 21.4%

Figures include travel to/from oil rigs and armed forces movement.

Conic projection

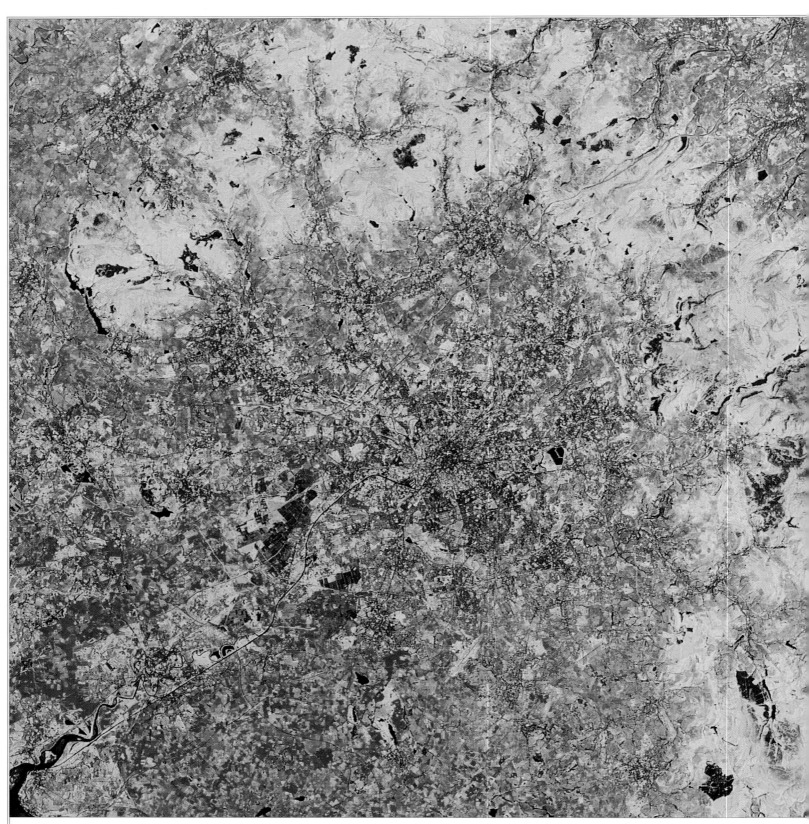

 Highland

The blue/green colour corresponds to grassland over 300 metres above sea level on the map opposite. In the higher areas of the Pennines the colour becomes greener as grassland changes to moorland, for example around Shining Tor.

 Lowland and arable land

The areas around Manchester appear as shades of orange and red. The cultivated areas near the river Mersey are redder.

 Built up area

These areas are dark blue on the satellite image. The largest area is the Manchester urban sprawl. In the top left of the image the built up areas of Blackburn and Accrington stand out from the surrounding farmland.

 Woodland

Some areas of woodland can be seen on the lower slopes of Shining Tor. There is also a small area near Alderley Edge.

 Reservoir

The small distinctive shape of these can be seen in the Pennines area. Examples are Watergrove Reservoir near Whitworth and Errwood Reservoir south of Whaley Bridge.

 Canal

The straight line of the Manchester Ship Canal can be seen running alongside the winding course of the river Mersey.

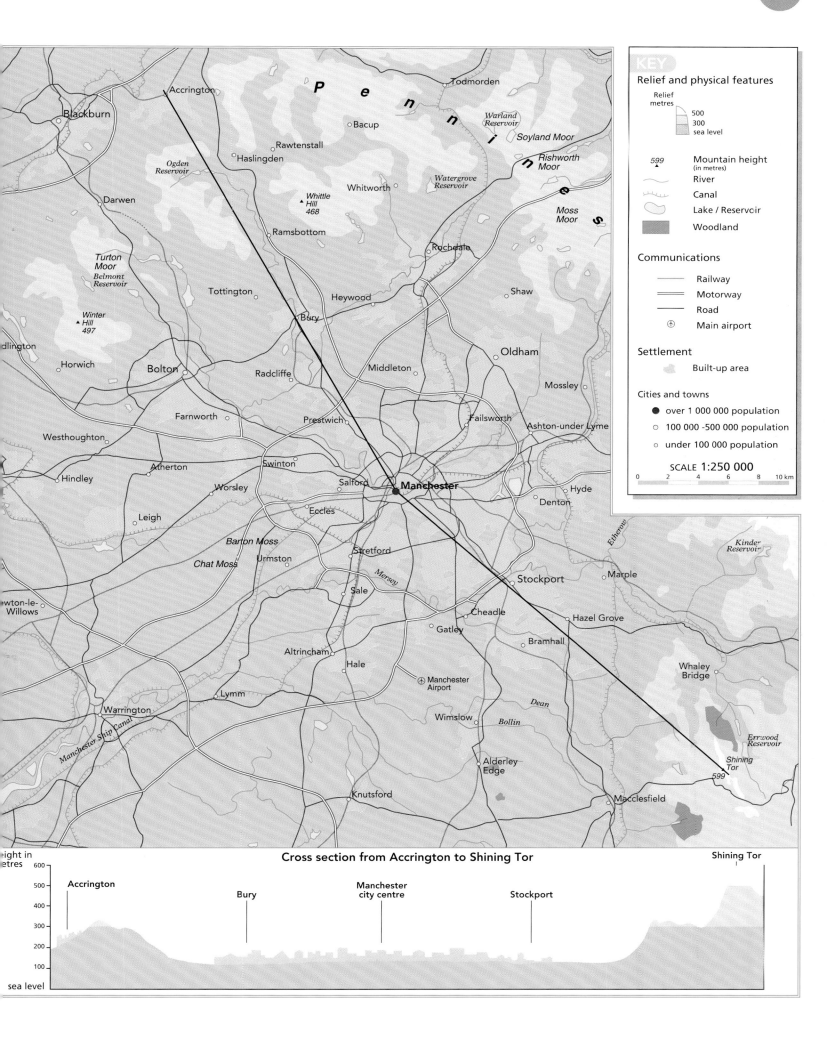

Relief and physical features

Relief
metres
500
300
sea level

599 ▲ Mountain height (in metres)

〜〜 River

〰 Canal

Lake / Reservoir

Woodland

Communications

Railway

Motorway

Road

⊕ Main airport

Settlement

Built-up area

Cities and towns

● over 1 000 000 population

○ 100 000 -500 000 population

○ under 100 000 population

SCALE **1:250 000**

0 2 4 6 8 10 km

Cross section from Accrington to Shining Tor

Height in metres

600
500
400
300
200
100
sea level

Accrington

Bury

Manchester city centre

Stockport

Shining Tor

Relief

Relief metres
5000
3000
2000
1000
500
200
0
sea level
200
4000
6000
under sea level

Ice cap

Arctic Circle

Jan Mayen

Faxaflói
Húnaflói
Vestmannaeyjar
Snaefell 1833
Vatnajökull
Fontur

Iceland

A T L A N T I C   O C E A N

Norwegian Sea

North Cape
Sørøya
Vesterålen
Lofoten
Vestfjorden

Lappland

Oz. Ima

Faeroes

Shetland

S c a n d i n a v i a

Lule
Ume
Kemi
Indals
Gulf of Bothnia

Inarijärvi

Lo
Lac

Orkney
Outer Hebrides

Mälaren
Vänern
Vättern
Åland
Gulf of Finland

Hiiumaa
Saaremaa

Lake Peipus

Ben Nevis 1344

British Isles

N o r t h

Skagerrak
Kattegat

Gotland
Öland
Gulf of Riga

B a l t i c   S e a

Malin Head
Donegal Bay

S e a

Sjaelland
Fyn
Bornholm

N O R T H   E U R O P E

Galway Bay
Shannon

Ireland
Irish Sea
The Pennines

Great Britain
Snowdon 1085

St George's Channel

Cape Clear

Frisian Islands

IJsselmeer

Weser
Elbe
Vistula
Warta

Pripet Marshes

Land's End
Isles of Scilly
Channel Islands

The Wash
Thames

Strait of Dover

English Channel

Maas
Rhine
Moselle
Ardennes
Taunus

Elbe
Ore Mts
Bohemian Forest
Oder
Sudeten Mts
Vistula

Bug

Brittany

Seine
Marne

Dniester

B a y   o f

Loire
Seine
Saône
Jura
Vosges
Rhine
Danube
Bodensee
Inn
Danube

Carpathian Mts

B i s c a y

Vienne
Mt Dore 1885
Allier
L. Geneva
Mont Blanc 4808
Matterhorn 4478
Gross Glockner 3798
Balaton
Tisza

Hungarian Plain

Mureş

Gulf of Gascony

Gironde
Massif Central
Rhône

A L P S

Po
Sava

Dinaric Alps

Transylvanian Alps

C. Finisterre

Danube
Morava

Cantabrian Mts
Douro

Pyrenees
Pico de Aneto 3404

Gulf of Lions
Côte d'Azur

Gulf of Genoa
Ligurian Sea

A p e n n i n e s

A d r i a t i c   S e a

Balkan Mts
Rhodope Mts

Duero
Ebro

Corsica

Mt Olympus 2911

Tagus

Sierra Morena
Guadalquivir

Gulf of Valencia

Balearic Is
Ibiza

Menorca
Mallorca

Strait of Bonifacio

Sardinia

Vesuvius 1281

G. of Taranto

Pindus Mts

A e g e a n

C. St. Vincent

Sierra Nevada

M E D I T E R R

Tyrrhenian Sea

Corfu
Evvoia

Sea Mar

I o n i a n

S e a

Strait of Gibraltar

Stromboli
Sicily

Mt Etna 3323
C. Passero

Zakynthos

Naxos

Dodeca

High Atlas
Toubkal 4167

Hauts Plateaux

Saharan Atlas

A N E A N

G. of Gabes

Crete

SCALE 1 : 16 000 000

0   200   400   600   800 km

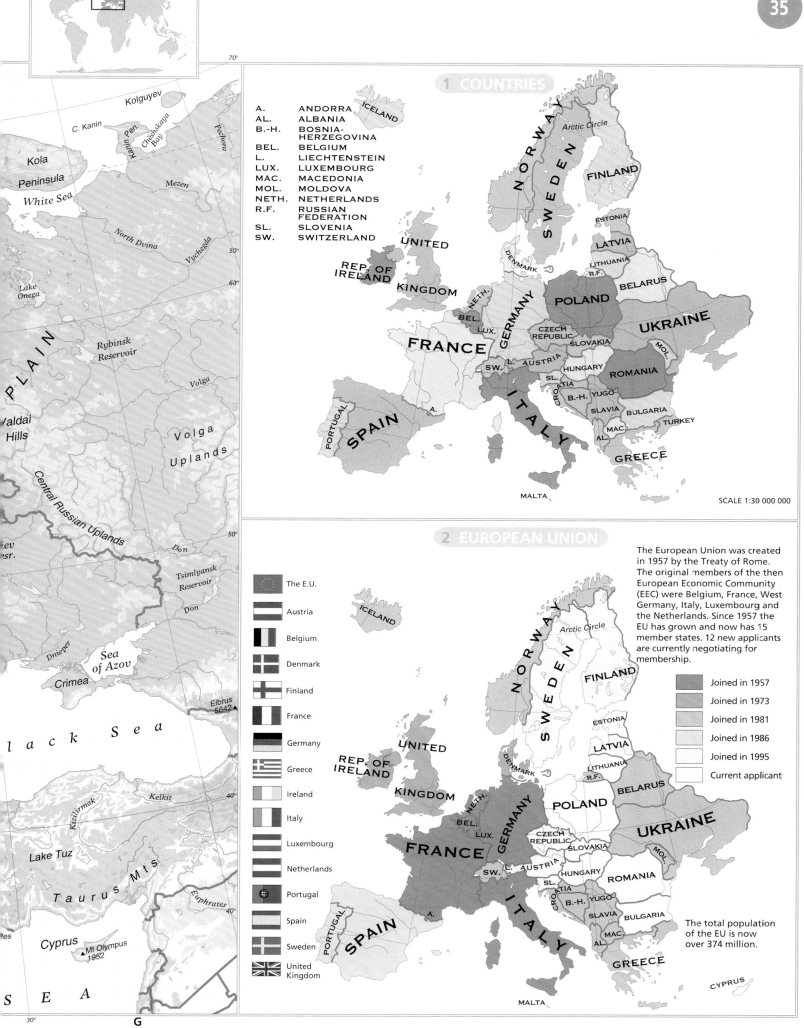

1 COUNTRIES

A.	ANDORRA
AL.	ALBANIA
B.-H.	BOSNIA-HERZEGOVINA
BEL.	BELGIUM
L.	LIECHTENSTEIN
LUX.	LUXEMBOURG
MAC.	MACEDONIA
MOL.	MOLDOVA
NETH.	NETHERLANDS
R.F.	RUSSIAN FEDERATION
SL.	SLOVENIA
SW.	SWITZERLAND

SCALE 1:30 000 000

2 EUROPEAN UNION

The European Union was created in 1957 by the Treaty of Rome. The original members of the then European Economic Community (EEC) were Belgium, France, West Germany, Italy, Luxembourg and the Netherlands. Since 1957 the EU has grown and now has 15 member states. 12 new applicants are currently negotiating for membership.

- Joined in 1957
- Joined in 1973
- Joined in 1981
- Joined in 1986
- Joined in 1995
- Current applicant

The total population of the EU is now over 374 million.

The E.U.
Austria
Belgium
Denmark
Finland
France
Germany
Greece
Ireland
Italy
Luxembourg
Netherlands
Portugal
Spain
Sweden
United Kingdom

Albers Equal Area Conic projection

Conic projection

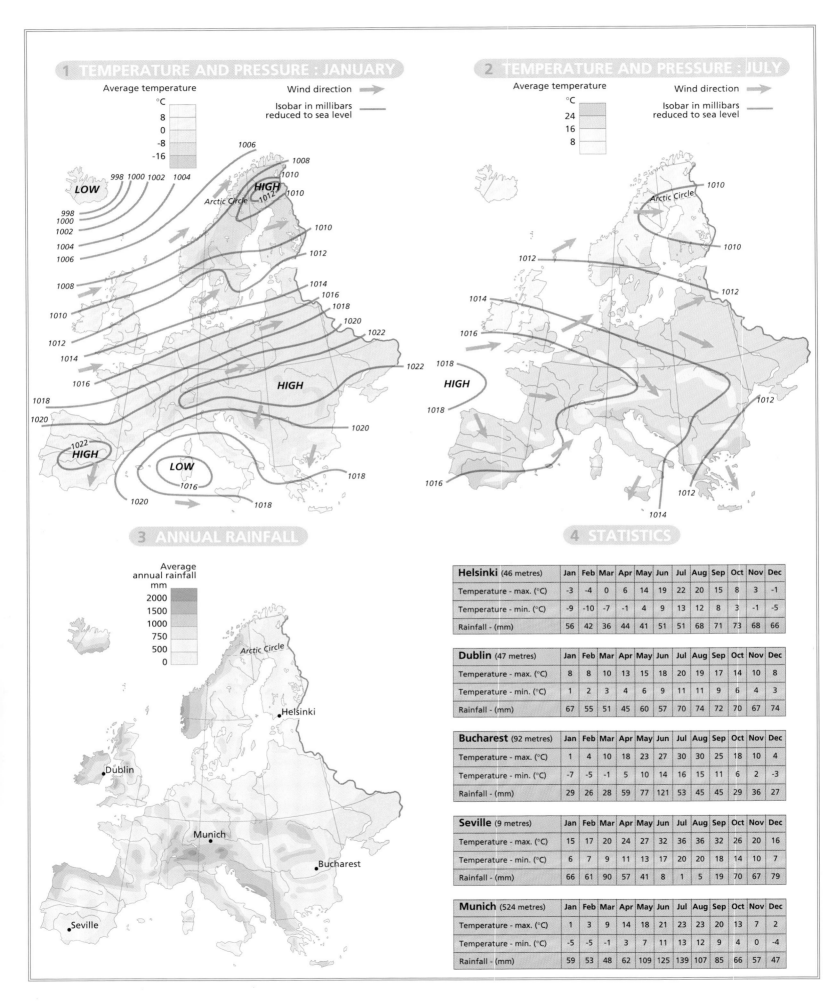

1 TEMPERATURE AND PRESSURE : JANUARY

Average temperature

°C
8
0
-8
-16

Wind direction →

Isobar in millibars
reduced to sea level

2 TEMPERATURE AND PRESSURE : JULY

Average temperature

°C
24
16
8

Wind direction →

Isobar in millibars
reduced to sea level

3 ANNUAL RAINFALL

Average
annual rainfall
mm
2000
1500
1000
750
500
0

4 STATISTICS

Helsinki (46 metres)	Jan	Feb	Mar	Apr	May	Jun	Jul	Aug	Sep	Oct	Nov	Dec
Temperature - max. (°C)	-3	-4	0	6	14	19	22	20	15	8	3	-1
Temperature - min. (°C)	-9	-10	-7	-1	4	9	13	12	8	3	-1	-5
Rainfall - (mm)	56	42	36	44	41	51	51	68	71	73	68	66

Dublin (47 metres)	Jan	Feb	Mar	Apr	May	Jun	Jul	Aug	Sep	Oct	Nov	Dec
Temperature - max. (°C)	8	8	10	13	15	18	20	19	17	14	10	8
Temperature - min. (°C)	1	2	3	4	6	9	11	11	9	6	4	3
Rainfall - (mm)	67	55	51	45	60	57	70	74	72	70	67	74

Bucharest (92 metres)	Jan	Feb	Mar	Apr	May	Jun	Jul	Aug	Sep	Oct	Nov	Dec
Temperature - max. (°C)	1	4	10	18	23	27	30	30	25	18	10	4
Temperature - min. (°C)	-7	-5	-1	5	10	14	16	15	11	6	2	-3
Rainfall - (mm)	29	26	28	59	77	121	53	45	45	29	36	27

Seville (9 metres)	Jan	Feb	Mar	Apr	May	Jun	Jul	Aug	Sep	Oct	Nov	Dec
Temperature - max. (°C)	15	17	20	24	27	32	36	36	32	26	20	16
Temperature - min. (°C)	6	7	9	11	13	17	20	20	18	14	10	7
Rainfall - (mm)	66	61	90	57	41	8	1	5	19	70	67	79

Munich (524 metres)	Jan	Feb	Mar	Apr	May	Jun	Jul	Aug	Sep	Oct	Nov	Dec
Temperature - max. (°C)	1	3	9	14	18	21	23	23	20	13	7	2
Temperature - min. (°C)	-5	-5	-1	3	7	11	13	12	9	4	0	-4
Rainfall - (mm)	59	53	48	62	109	125	139	107	85	66	57	47

SCALE 1 : 40 000 000

0   400   800   1200   1600 km

Conic projection

1 POPULATION DENSITY

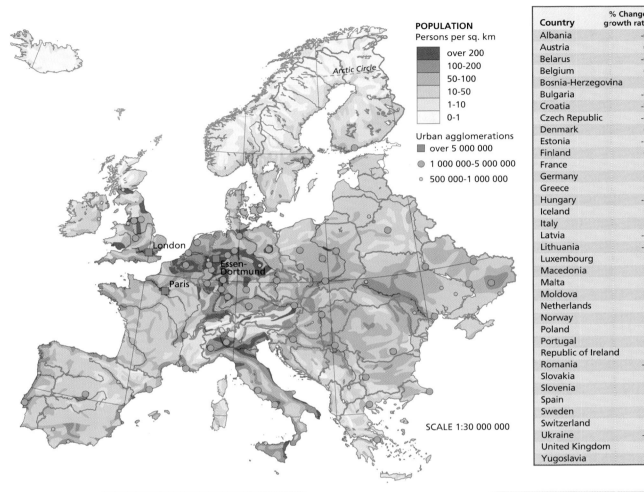

POPULATION
Persons per sq. km

	over 200
	100-200
	50-100
	10-50
	1-10
	0-1

Urban agglomerations

over 5 000 000

1 000 000-5 000 000

500 000-1 000 000

London
Essen-Dortmund
Paris

SCALE 1:30 000 000

2 POPULATION TABLE

Country	% Change in annual growth rate 1995-2000	Life expectancy (years) 1995-2000
Albania	-0.4	73
Austria	0.5	77
Belarus	-0.3	68
Belgium	0.1	77
Bosnia-Herzegovina	3.0	73
Bulgaria	-0.7	71
Croatia	-0.1	73
Czech Republic	-0.2	74
Denmark	0.3	76
Estonia	-1.2	69
Finland	0.3	77
France	0.4	78
Germany	0.1	77
Greece	0.3	78
Hungary	-0.4	71
Iceland	0.9	79
Italy	0.0	78
Latvia	-1.5	68
Lithuania	-0.3	70
Luxembourg	1.1	77
Macedonia	0.6	73
Malta	0.7	77
Moldova	0.0	68
Netherlands	0.4	78
Norway	0.5	78
Poland	0.1	73
Portugal	0.0	75
Republic of Ireland	0.7	76
Romania	-0.4	70
Slovakia	0.1	73
Slovenia	0.0	74
Spain	0.0	78
Sweden	0.2	79
Switzerland	0.7	79
Ukraine	-0.4	69
United Kingdom	0.2	77
Yugoslavia	0.1	73

3 POPULATION UNDER 16

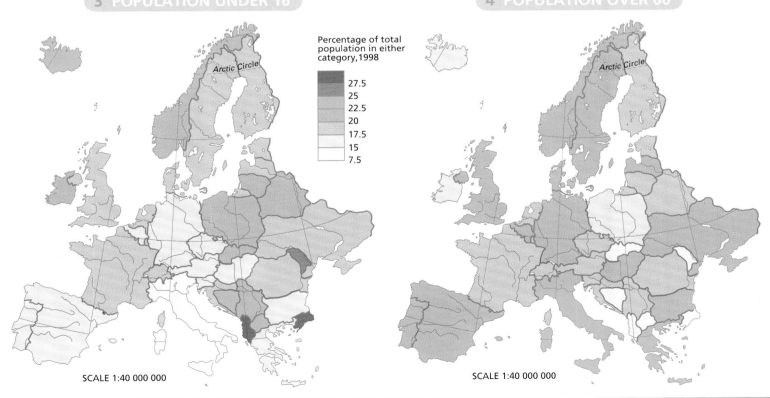

Percentage of total population in either category, 1998

	27.5
	25
	22.5
	20
	17.5
	15
	7.5

Arctic Circle

SCALE 1:40 000 000

4 POPULATION OVER 60

Arctic Circle

SCALE 1:40 000 000

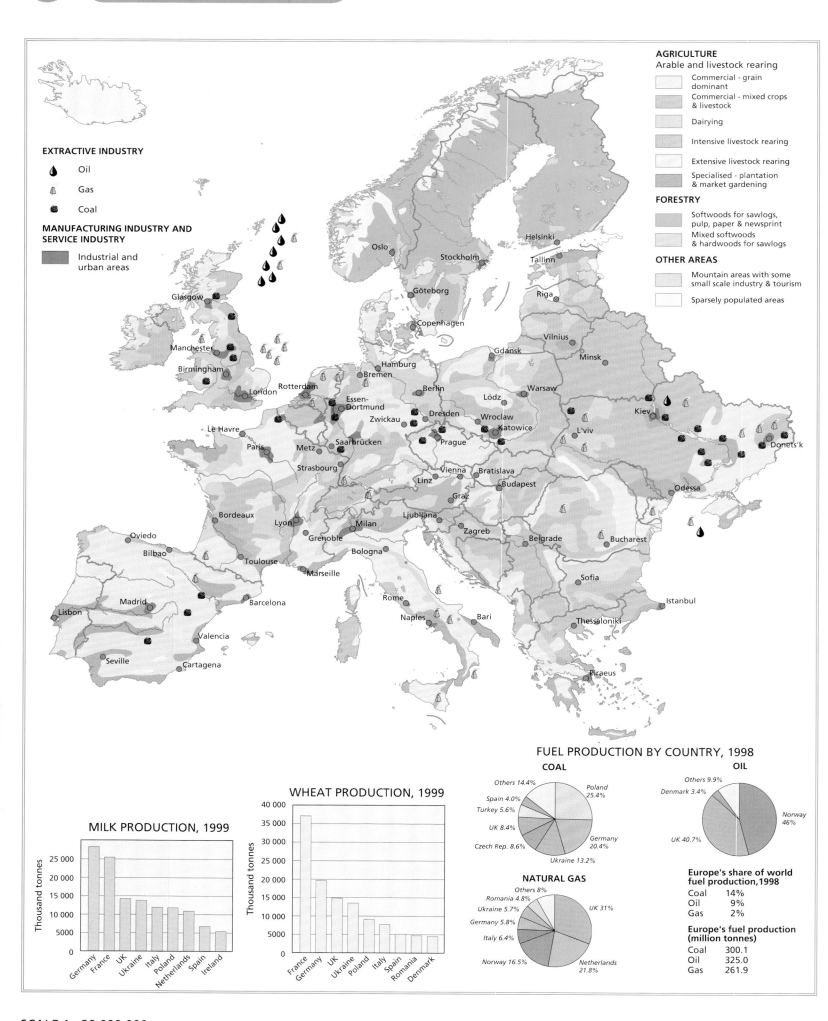

EXTRACTIVE INDUSTRY
- Oil
- Gas
- Coal

MANUFACTURING INDUSTRY AND SERVICE INDUSTRY
- Industrial and urban areas

AGRICULTURE
Arable and livestock rearing
- Commercial - grain dominant
- Commercial - mixed crops & livestock
- Dairying
- Intensive livestock rearing
- Extensive livestock rearing
- Specialised - plantation & market gardening

FORESTRY
- Softwoods for sawlogs, pulp, paper & newsprint
- Mixed softwoods & hardwoods for sawlogs

OTHER AREAS
- Mountain areas with some small scale industry & tourism
- Sparsely populated areas

MILK PRODUCTION, 1999

Thousand tonnes (y-axis: 0, 5000, 10 000, 15 000, 20 000, 25 000)

Countries: Germany, France, UK, Ukraine, Italy, Poland, Netherlands, Spain, Ireland

WHEAT PRODUCTION, 1999

Thousand tonnes (y-axis: 0, 5000, 10 000, 15 000, 20 000, 25 000, 30 000, 35 000, 40 000)

Countries: France, Germany, UK, Ukraine, Poland, Italy, Spain, Romania, Denmark

FUEL PRODUCTION BY COUNTRY, 1998

COAL
- Poland 25.4%
- Germany 20.4%
- Ukraine 13.2%
- Czech Rep. 8.6%
- UK 8.4%
- Turkey 5.6%
- Spain 4.0%
- Others 14.4%

OIL
- Norway 46%
- UK 40.7%
- Denmark 3.4%
- Others 9.9%

NATURAL GAS
- UK 31%
- Netherlands 21.8%
- Norway 16.5%
- Italy 6.4%
- Germany 5.8%
- Ukraine 5.7%
- Romania 4.8%
- Others 8%

Europe's share of world fuel production, 1998
- Coal 14%
- Oil 9%
- Gas 2%

Europe's fuel production (million tonnes)
- Coal 300.1
- Oil 325.0
- Gas 261.9

SCALE 1 : 20 000 000

Albers equal area conic projection

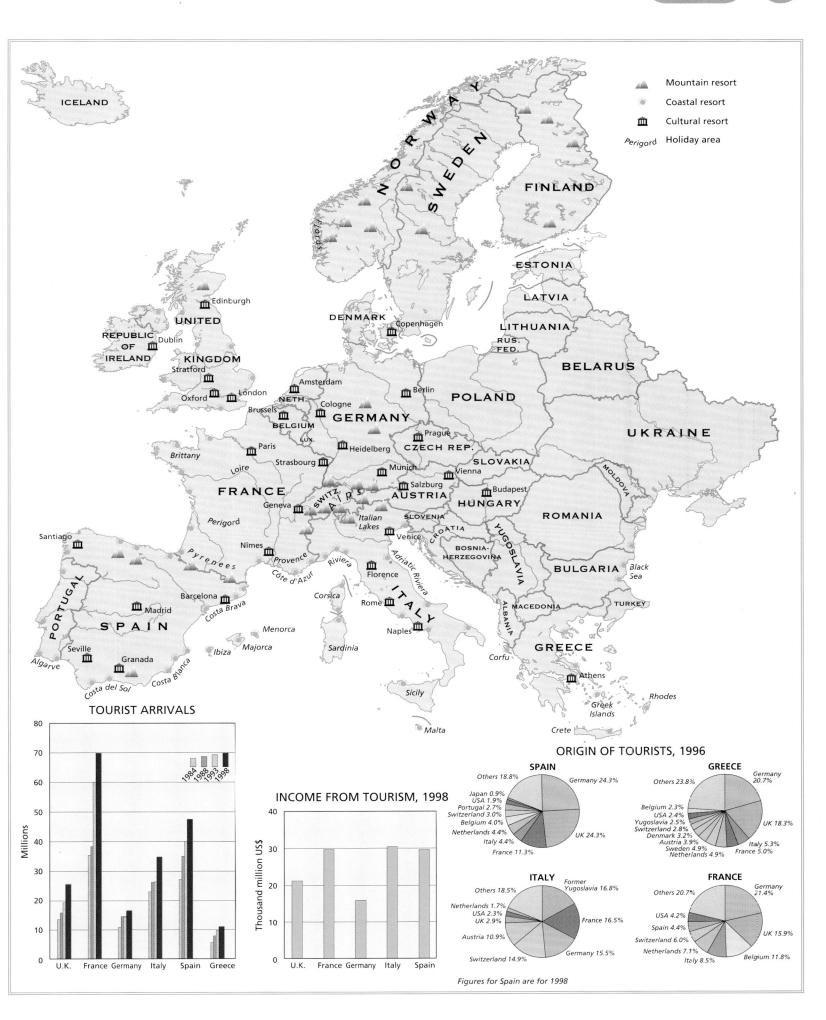

Mountain resort
Coastal resort
Cultural resort
Perigord Holiday area

ICELAND

NORWAY
SWEDEN
FINLAND
Fjords

ESTONIA
LATVIA
LITHUANIA
RUS. FED.
BELARUS

DENMARK
Copenhagen

UNITED
Edinburgh
REPUBLIC
OF
IRELAND
Dublin
KINGDOM
Stratford
Oxford
London
Brittany

Amsterdam
NETH.
Berlin
POLAND
Cologne
Brussels
BELGIUM
GERMANY
Lux.
Paris
Heidelberg
Prague
CZECH REP.
Strasbourg
UKRAINE

Loire
Munich
Vienna
SLOVAKIA
FRANCE
Geneva
SWITZ.
Alps
Salzburg
AUSTRIA
HUNGARY
MOLDOVA
Perigord
Italian
Lakes
SLOVENIA
Venice
CROATIA
ROMANIA
Santiago
Nîmes
Provence
Adriatic Riviera
BOSNIA-
HERZEGOVINA
YUGOSLAVIA
BULGARIA
Black
Sea
Pyrenees
Riviera
Florence
Côte d'Azur
Corsica
ITALY
PORTUGAL
Barcelona
Rome
ALBANIA
MACEDONIA
TURKEY
Costa Brava
Madrid
SPAIN
Menorca
Naples
GREECE
Seville
Ibiza
Majorca
Granada
Sardinia
Corfu
Algarve
Costa del Sol
Costa Blanca
Athens
Sicily
Rhodes
*Greek
Islands*
Malta
Crete

TOURIST ARRIVALS

1984
1988
1993
1998

Millions

80
70
60
50
40
30
20
10
0

U.K. France Germany Italy Spain Greece

INCOME FROM TOURISM, 1998

Thousand million US$

40
30
20
10
0

U.K. France Germany Italy Spain

Figures for Spain are for 1998

ORIGIN OF TOURISTS, 1996

SPAIN
Others 18.8%
Germany 24.3%
Japan 0.9%
USA 1.9%
Portugal 2.7%
Switzerland 3.0%
Belgium 4.0%
Netherlands 4.4%
Italy 4.4%
France 11.3%
UK 24.3%

GREECE
Others 23.8%
Germany 20.7%
Belgium 2.3%
USA 2.4%
Yugoslavia 2.5%
Switzerland 2.8%
Denmark 3.2%
Austria 3.9%
Sweden 4.9%
Netherlands 4.9%
UK 18.3%
Italy 5.3%
France 5.0%

ITALY
Others 18.5%
Former
Yugoslavia 16.8%
Netherlands 1.7%
USA 2.3%
UK 2.9%
France 16.5%
Austria 10.9%
Switzerland 14.9%
Germany 15.5%

FRANCE
Others 20.7%
Germany 21.4%
USA 4.2%
Spain 4.4%
Switzerland 6.0%
UK 15.9%
Netherlands 7.1%
Italy 8.5%
Belgium 11.8%

SCALE 1 : 20 000 000

Albers equal area conic projection

Built-up area
The main built up areas, which can be identified on the satellite image, are Rotterdam, Dordrecht and Antwerpen.

Farmland
These areas appear as a greenish yellow pattern in the top right of the satellite image.

Woodland
Patchy areas of darkbrown/red lying north of Antwerpen are areas of woodland.

Canal
The pattern of dark thin lines is the canal system which cuts across islands and peninsulas to link the cities of Rotterdam and Antwerpen.

Dunes
Dunes appear as white linear features along most of the coast. Extensive areas of dunes are also found in the Schelde estuary.

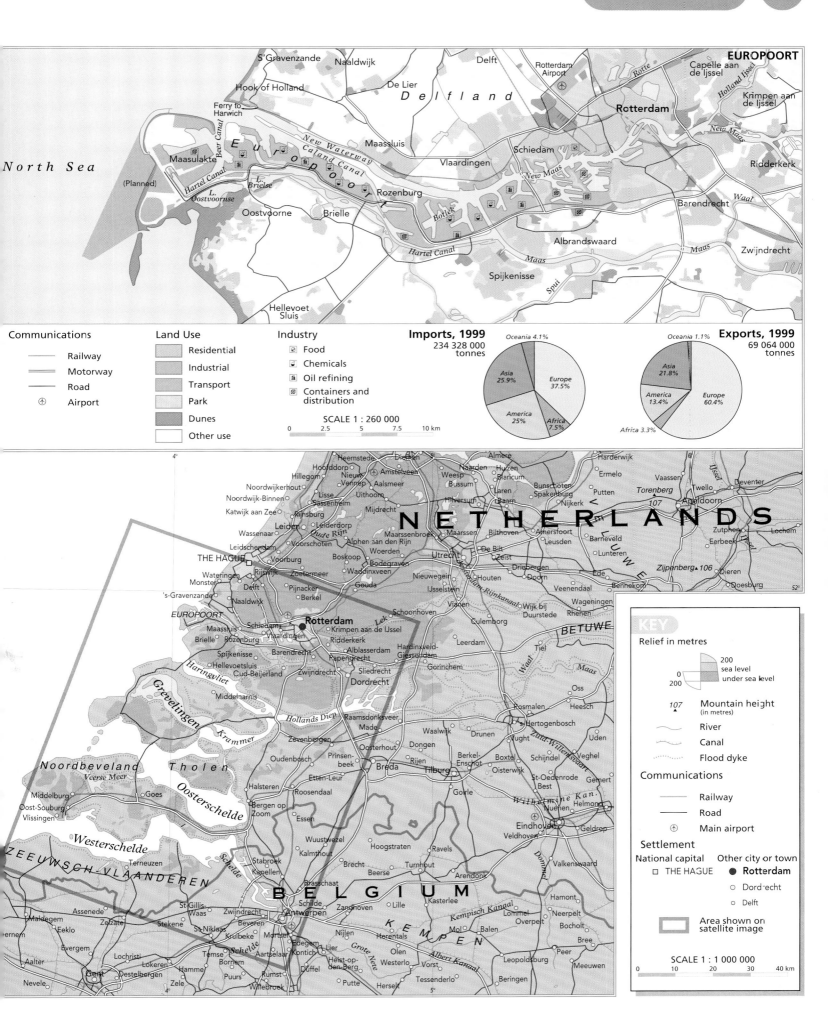

Lambert Azimuthal Equal Area projection

KEY

Relief and physical features

Relief metres
5000
3000
2000
1000
500
200
0 sea level
under sea level
200
4000
6000

818 ▲ Mountain height (in metres)

Permanent ice

Water features

River
Canal
Lake / Reservoir
Marsh

Communications

Railway
Motorway
Road
⊕ Main airport

Administration

Boundaries
International
Internal

Settlement
Cities and towns in order of size

National capital   Other city or town
■ AMSTERDAM   ● Rotterdam
□ THE HAGUE   ○ Dortmund
□ BONN   ○ Maastricht
□ LUXEMBOURG ○ Oostende

SCALE 1 : 2 000 000

0   20   40   60   80 km

Conic projection

SCALE 1 : 7 500 000

0   100   200   300 km

Conic projection

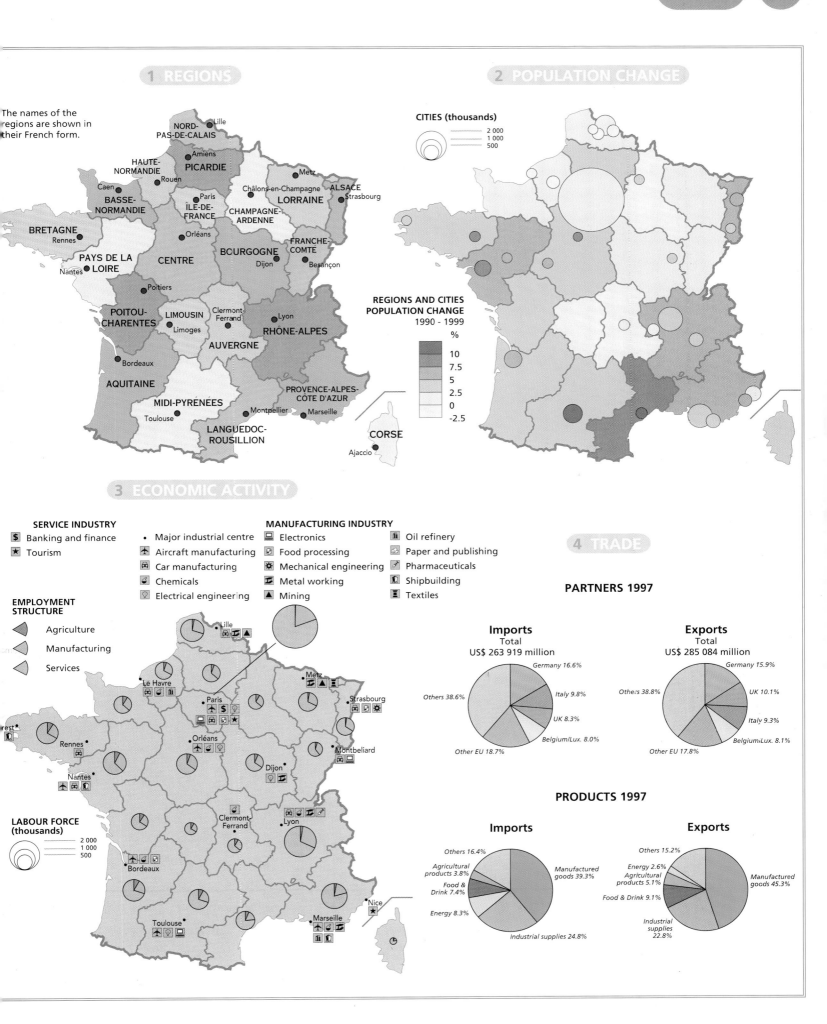

1 REGIONS

The names of the regions are shown in their French form.

NORD-PAS-DE-CALAIS
Lille
Amiens
PICARDIE
HAUTE-NORMANDIE
Metz
Caen
Rouen
Châlons-en-Champagne
ALSACE
LORRAINE
Strasbourg
BASSE-NORMANDIE
Paris
ÎLE-DE-FRANCE
CHAMPAGNE-ARDENNE
BRETAGNE
Rennes
Orléans
FRANCHE-COMTÉ
PAYS DE LA LOIRE
CENTRE
BOURGOGNE
Nantes
Dijon
Besançon
Poitiers
POITOU-CHARENTES
LIMOUSIN
Clermont-Ferrand
Lyon
Limoges
RHÔNE-ALPES
Bordeaux
AUVERGNE
AQUITAINE
MIDI-PYRÉNÉES
Montpellier
PROVENCE-ALPES-CÔTE D'AZUR
Marseille
Toulouse
LANGUEDOC-ROUSILLION
CORSE
Ajaccio

2 POPULATION CHANGE

CITIES (thousands)
2 000
1 000
500

REGIONS AND CITIES POPULATION CHANGE
1990 - 1999
%
10
7.5
5
2.5
0
-2.5

3 ECONOMIC ACTIVITY

SERVICE INDUSTRY
$ Banking and finance
★ Tourism

• Major industrial centre
✈ Aircraft manufacturing
🚗 Car manufacturing
Chemicals
Electrical engineering

MANUFACTURING INDUSTRY
Electronics
Food processing
✳ Mechanical engineering
Metal working
▲ Mining

Oil refinery
Paper and publishing
Pharmaceuticals
Shipbuilding
Textiles

EMPLOYMENT STRUCTURE
Agriculture
Manufacturing
Services

Lille
Le Havre
Metz
Strasbourg
Brest
Rennes
Paris
Orléans
Montbeliard
Nantes
Dijon
Clermont-Ferrand
Lyon
Bordeaux
Toulouse
Marseille
Nice

LABOUR FORCE (thousands)
2 000
1 000
500

4 TRADE

PARTNERS 1997

Imports
Total
US$ 263 919 million

Germany 16.6%
Italy 9.8%
UK 8.3%
Belgium/Lux. 8.0%
Other EU 18.7%
Others 38.6%

Exports
Total
US$ 285 084 million

Germany 15.9%
UK 10.1%
Italy 9.3%
Belgium/Lux. 8.1%
Other EU 17.8%
Others 38.8%

PRODUCTS 1997

Imports

Others 16.4%
Agricultural products 3.8%
Food & Drink 7.4%
Energy 8.3%
Industrial supplies 24.8%
Manufactured goods 39.3%

Exports

Others 15.2%
Energy 2.6%
Agricultural products 5.1%
Food & Drink 9.1%
Industrial supplies 22.8%
Manufactured goods 45.3%

SCALE 1 : 10 000 000

0   100   200   300 km

KEY

Relief and physical features

Relief
metres
5000
3000
2000
1000
500
200
sea level
0
200
under sea level
4000
6000

3482 ▲ Mountain height (in metres)

Water features

~~~ River
~~~ Intermittent river
~~~ Canal
Lake / Reservoir
Marsh

Communications

Railway
Motorway
Road
⊕ Main airport

Administration

Boundaries
International

Settlement

Cities and towns in order of size

National capital
■ MADRID
□ ANDORRA LA VELLA

Other city or town
● Barcelona
○ Málaga
○ Pamplona
○ Benidorm

SCALE 1 : 5 000 000

0   50   100   150   200 km

Lambert Conformal Conic projection

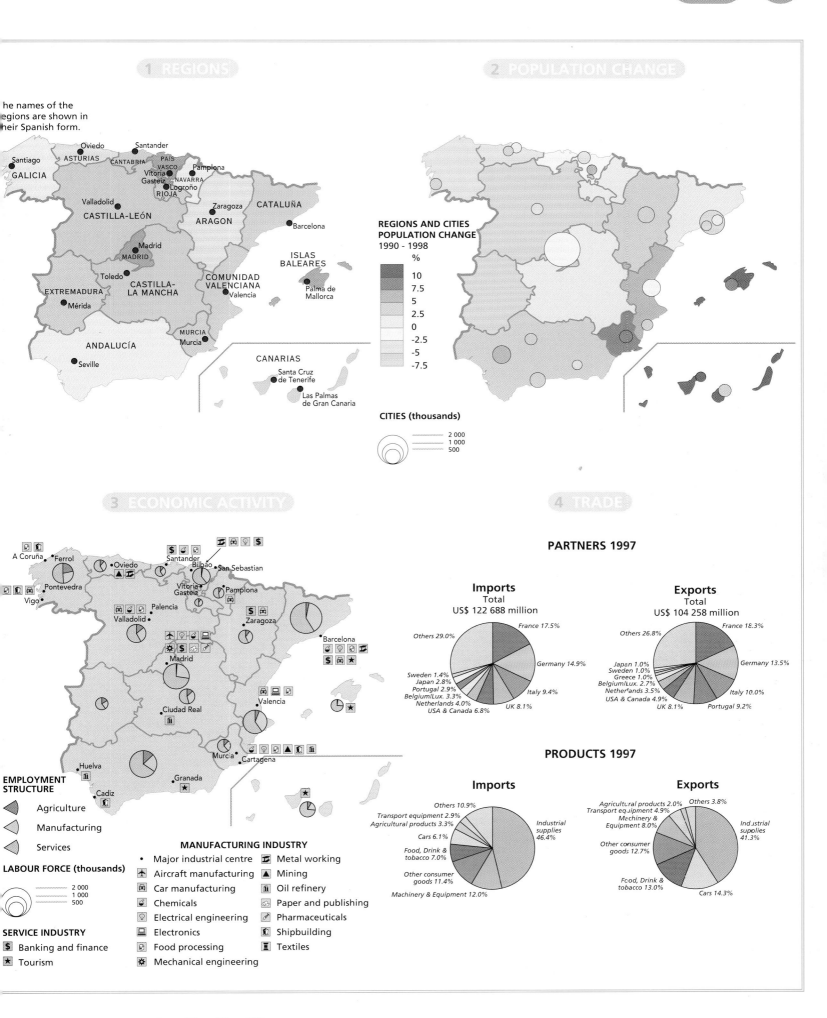

1 REGIONS

The names of the regions are shown in their Spanish form.

GALICIA · Santiago · Oviedo · Santander
ASTURIAS · CANTABRIA · PAÍS VASCO
Vitoria Gasteiz · NAVARRA · Pamplona
Logroño · RIOJA
Valladolid · CASTILLA-LEÓN
ARAGON · Zaragoza · CATALUÑA · Barcelona
Madrid · MADRID
ISLAS BALEARES
Toledo · CASTILLA-LA MANCHA · COMUNIDAD VALENCIANA · Valencia
Palma de Mallorca
EXTREMADURA · Mérida
MURCIA · Murcia
ANDALUCÍA · Seville
CANARIAS
Santa Cruz de Tenerife
Las Palmas de Gran Canaria

2 POPULATION CHANGE

REGIONS AND CITIES POPULATION CHANGE
1990 - 1998
%
10
7.5
5
2.5
0
-2.5
-5
-7.5

CITIES (thousands)
2 000
1 000
500

3 ECONOMIC ACTIVITY

A Coruña · Ferrol · Oviedo · Santander · Bilbao · San Sebastian
Pontevedra · Vitoria Gasteiz · Pamplona
Vigo · Palencia · Valladolid · Zaragoza · Barcelona
Madrid · Valencia
Ciudad Real
Huelva · Murcia · Cartagena
Cadiz · Granada

EMPLOYMENT STRUCTURE
Agriculture
Manufacturing
Services

LABOUR FORCE (thousands)
2 000
1 000
500

SERVICE INDUSTRY
$ Banking and finance
★ Tourism

MANUFACTURING INDUSTRY
• Major industrial centre
✈ Aircraft manufacturing
🚗 Car manufacturing
Chemicals
Electrical engineering
Electronics
Food processing
Mechanical engineering
Metal working
▲ Mining
Oil refinery
Paper and publishing
Pharmaceuticals
Shipbuilding
Textiles

4 TRADE

PARTNERS 1997

Imports
Total
US$ 122 688 million

France 17.5%
Germany 14.9%
Italy 9.4%
UK 8.1%
USA & Canada 6.8%
Netherlands 4.0%
Belgium/Lux. 3.3%
Portugal 2.9%
Japan 2.8%
Sweden 1.4%
Others 29.0%

Exports
Total
US$ 104 258 million

France 18.3%
Germany 13.5%
Italy 10.0%
Portugal 9.2%
UK 8.1%
USA & Canada 4.9%
Netherlands 3.5%
Belgium/Lux. 2.7%
Greece 1.0%
Sweden 1.0%
Japan 1.0%
Others 26.8%

PRODUCTS 1997

Imports
Industrial supplies 46.4%
Machinery & Equipment 12.0%
Other consumer goods 11.4%
Food, Drink & tobacco 7.0%
Cars 6.1%
Agricultural products 3.3%
Transport equipment 2.9%
Others 10.9%

Exports
Industrial supplies 41.3%
Cars 14.3%
Food, Drink & tobacco 13.0%
Other consumer goods 12.7%
Machinery & Equipment 8.0%
Transport equipment 4.9%
Agricultural products 2.0%
Others 3.8%

SCALE 1 : 12 000 000

0   100   200   300 km

A 4° B 6° C 8° D 10° E 12° F 14° G H

Map labels

NORTH SEA

Baltic Sea

Kiel Bay *Heligoland Bay* *North Frisian Is* *East Frisian Islands* *West Frisian Islands* *Waddenzee*

Flensburg, Schleswig, Husum, Kiel, Kiel Canal, Neumünster, Itzehoe, Cuxhaven, Lübeck Bay, Rostock, Wismar, Schwerin, Greifswald, Stralsund, Sassnitz, *Rügen*, *Fehmarn*, *Lolland*, *Falster*, Nyköbing, Naksköv

Słupsk, Koszalin, Kołobrzeg, Świnoujście, Szczecinek, Piła, Stargard, Szczecin, Schwedt, Eberswalde, Neustrelitz, *L. Müritz*, Neubrandenburg

Wilhelmshaven, Bremerhaven, Emden, Leer, Oldenburg, Bremen, Hamburg, Lüneburg, Uelzen, Wittenberge, *Elbe*, Rathenow, Brandenburg, *Havell*, BERLIN, Potsdam, Frankfurt, Eisenhüttenstadt

Groningen, Leeuwarden, Den Helder, Texel, Zaandam, Haarlem, AMSTERDAM, Leiden, THE HAGUE, Delft, Rotterdam, Dordrecht, Breda, Tilburg, Utrecht, Hilversum, Apeldoorn, Arnhem, Nijmegen, Enschede, *IJsselmeer*, *Lek*, *Rhine*, *Mark*

NETHERLANDS

Lingen, Osnabrück, Münster, Hannover, Celle, *Aller*, Wolfsburg, Braunschweig, Salzgitter, Hildesheim, Bielefeld, Paderborn, Göttingen, Kassel, Magdeburg, Dessau, Halle, Leipzig

POLAND, Poznań, Gorzów Wielkopolski, Kostrzyn, Grodzisk Wielkopolski, Zielona Góra, Leszno, Głogów, Żary, Forst, Cottbus, *Spree*, *Oder*, *Bóbr*, *Warta*, Note

Zeebrugge, Oostende, Brugge, Antwerpen, Gent, Mechelen, BRUSSELS, Anderlecht, Roubaix, Lille, Tournai, Mons, Charleroi, Namur, Dinant, *Sambre*, *Meuse*

BELGIUM, Maastricht, Aachen, Liège, Eindhoven, Mönchengladbach, Krefeld, Duisburg, Essen, Gelsenkirchen, Dortmund, Hamm, Bochum, Wuppertal, Düsseldorf, Leverkusen, Bergisch Gladbach, Cologne, Bonn, Siegen, Marburg, *Lippe*, *Ruhr*

GERMANY

Eifel, Neuwied, Koblenz, Wetzlar, Giessen, Fulda, Meiningen, *Taunus*, Wiesbaden, Mainz, Frankfurt am Main, Offenbach am Main, Darmstadt, Worms, Ludwigshafen, Mannheim, Heidelberg, Speyer, *Hunsrück*, *Mosel*, Trier, LUXEMBOURG, LUXEMBOURG, Arlon, Bastogne, Thionville, Saarbrücken, Kaiserslautern, *Ardennes*

Erfurt, Jena, Gotha, *Thüringian Forest*, Suhl, Coburg, Schweinfurt, Würzburg, Bamberg, Bayreuth, Nordhausen, Mühlhausen, Eisleben, Hoyerswerda, Meissen, Dresden, Freiberg, Chemnitz, Zwickau, Gera, Altenburg, Plauen, Hof, *Ore Mts*, *Saale*

Görlitz, Legnica, Wrocław, Jelenia Góra, *Sudeten Mountain*, Wałbrzych, Kłodzko, 1015, Liberec, Děčín, Teplice, Most, Ústí, Karlovy Vary, Cheb, 940, *Bohemian Forest*, PRAGUE, Kladno, Plzeň, Písek, CZECH REPUBLIC, Tábor, České Budějovice

Würzburg, Ansbach, Fürth, Nürnberg, Erlangen, Regensburg, Straubing, Ingolstadt, Landshut, Passau, *Isar*, *Danube*, *Lech*, *Inn*

Heilbronn, Karlsruhe, Pforzheim, Baden-Baden, Stuttgart, Reutlingen, Tübingen, Aalen, Ulm, Augsburg, Biberach, Memmingen, Kempten, Munich, Rosenheim, *Swabian Alps*, *Black Forest*, *Neckar*, Offenburg, Freiburg im Breisgau, Tuttlingen, Friedrichshafen, *Bodensee*, Konstanz, Schaffhausen, Winterthur, St Gallen, Dornbirn, Garmisch-Partenkirchen, Zugspitze 2962, 2287

FRANCE, Nancy, Lunéville, Strasbourg, Metz, Verdun, St-Dié, Épinal, Colmar, Mulhouse, Montbéliard, Besançon, Vesoul, Lure, *Vosges*, *Meuse*, *Moselle*, *Saône*, *Rhine*

SWITZERLAND, Basel, Zürich, *Jura*, LIECH., Innsbruck, AUSTRIA, Salzburg, Judenburg, *ALPS*, 2277, Kapfenberg, Leoben, Wiener Neustadt, Aspang-Markt, VIENNA, St Pölten, Steyr, Linz, Gmünd, *Enns*, *Danube*, Hollabrunn, Znojmo, Brno, *Chiemsee*

SLOVENIA, LJUBLJANA, Klagenfurt, Villach, *Drau*, Maribor, Varaždin, Kranj, Celje, Udine, ZAGREB, Gorizia, Trieste, 1796, Rijeka, CROATIA, *Istra*, *Sava*, *Kupa*, Karlovac, Sisak, Bihać, Gospić, *Pag*, *Cres*, *Krk*, Pula

KEY

Relief and physical features

Relief metres
5000
3000
2000
1000
500
200
0 — sea level
200 — under sea level
4000
6000

▲ 1142 Mountain height (in metres)

Permanent ice

Water features

~ River
~ Intermittent river
~ Canal
Lake / Reservoir
Marsh

Communications

Railway
Motorway
Road
⊕ Main airport

Administration

Boundaries
— International

Settlement

Cities and towns in order of size

National capital | Other city or town
■ BERLIN | ● Munich
□ ZAGREB | ○ Dortmund
□ LJUBLJANA | ○ Ulm
□ LUXEMBOURG | ○ Tuttlingen

SCALE 1 : 4 500 000

0 50 100 150 200 km

Lambert Conformal Conic projection

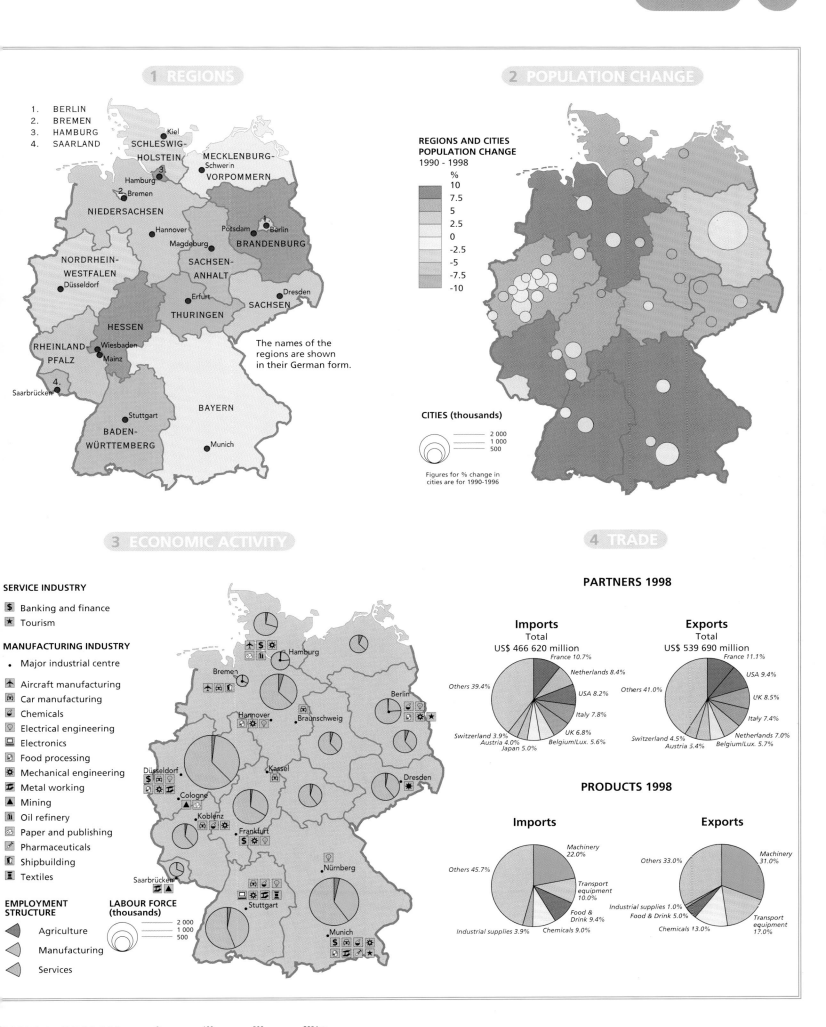

1 REGIONS

1. BERLIN
2. BREMEN
3. HAMBURG
4. SAARLAND

Kiel
SCHLESWIG-HOLSTEIN
Hamburg 3.
2. Bremen
MECKLENBURG-VORPOMMERN
Schwerin
NIEDERSACHSEN
Hannover
Magdeburg
Potsdam 1. Berlin
BRANDENBURG
NORDRHEIN-WESTFALEN
Düsseldorf
SACHSEN-ANHALT
Erfurt
Dresden
THURINGEN
SACHSEN
HESSEN
Wiesbaden
RHEINLAND-PFALZ
Mainz
4.
Saarbrücken
Stuttgart
BADEN-WÜRTTEMBERG
BAYERN
Munich

The names of the regions are shown in their German form.

2 POPULATION CHANGE

REGIONS AND CITIES POPULATION CHANGE
1990 - 1998
%
10
7.5
5
2.5
0
-2.5
-5
-7.5
-10

CITIES (thousands)
2 000
1 000
500

Figures for % change in cities are for 1990-1996

3 ECONOMIC ACTIVITY

SERVICE INDUSTRY
$ Banking and finance
★ Tourism

MANUFACTURING INDUSTRY
• Major industrial centre
✈ Aircraft manufacturing
🚗 Car manufacturing
Chemicals
Electrical engineering
💻 Electronics
Food processing
✺ Mechanical engineering
Metal working
▲ Mining
Oil refinery
Paper and publishing
Pharmaceuticals
Shipbuilding
Textiles

EMPLOYMENT STRUCTURE
Agriculture
Manufacturing
Services

LABOUR FORCE (thousands)
2 000
1 000
500

Hamburg
Bremen
Hannover
Braunschweig
Berlin
Düsseldorf
Cologne
Kassel
Dresden
Koblenz
Frankfurt
Saarbrücken
Nürnberg
Stuttgart
Munich

4 TRADE

PARTNERS 1998

Imports
Total
US$ 466 620 million
France 10.7%
Netherlands 8.4%
Others 39.4%
USA 8.2%
Italy 7.8%
Switzerland 3.9%
Austria 4.0%
Japan 5.0%
UK 6.8%
Belgium/Lux. 5.6%

Exports
Total
US$ 539 690 million
France 11.1%
USA 9.4%
UK 8.5%
Others 41.0%
Italy 7.4%
Netherlands 7.0%
Switzerland 4.5%
Austria 5.4%
Belgium/Lux. 5.7%

PRODUCTS 1998

Imports
Machinery 22.0%
Others 45.7%
Transport equipment 10.0%
Food & Drink 9.4%
Industrial supplies 3.9%
Chemicals 9.0%

Exports
Machinery 31.0%
Others 33.0%
Industrial supplies 1.0%
Food & Drink 5.0%
Chemicals 13.0%
Transport equipment 17.0%

SCALE 1 : 7 500 000

0   100   200   300 km

AUSTRIA
HUNGARY
SWITZERLAND
FRANCE
SLOVENIA
CROATIA
BOSNIA-HERZEGOVINA
LIECH.

Administration

Boundaries
——— International

Settlement
Cities and towns in order of size

National capital	Other city or town
■ ROME	● Milan
□ SARAJEVO	○ Genoa
□ SAN MARINO	○ Venice
	○ Ragusa

Sea and water labels

Gulf of Genoa
Ligurian Sea
Tyrrhenian Sea
Adriatic Sea
Ionian Sea
Gulf of Venice
Gulf of Taranto
Gulf of Gaeta
Gulf of Salerno
Gulf of Asinara
Gulf of Orosei
Gulf of Oristano
Gulf of Valinco

Islands

Corsica (France)
Sardinia (Italy)
Sicily
Elba
Capraia
Pianosa
Montecristo
San Pietro
Pantelleria (Italy)
Lipari Islands
Stromboli
Ustica
Pontine Is
Capri
Ischia
Linosa
Gozo
MALTA
Dugi Otok
Brac
Hvar
Korcula
Mljet
Cres
Pag
Krk

Selected cities

Geneva, Bern, Turin, Milan, Genoa, Monaco, Nice, Marseille, Aosta, Novara, Pavia, Como, Bergamo, Brescia, Verona, Padua, Venice, Trento, Bolzano, Trieste, Udine, LJUBLJANA, Rijeka, ZAGREB, Parma, Modena, Bologna, Ferrara, Ravenna, Rimini, Forlì, Florence, Pisa, Livorno, Siena, Arezzo, Perugia, SAN MARINO, Ancona, Pesaro, Jesi, Terni, Viterbo, Civitavecchia, ROME, Tivoli, Frosinone, Latina, Gaeta, Naples, Salerno, Avellino, Caserta, Foggia, Bari, Brindisi, Taranto, Lecce, Potenza, Matera, Cosenza, Catanzaro, Reggio di Calabria, Messina, Palermo, Catania, Siracusa, Agrigento, Marsala, Trapani, Cagliari, Sassari, Oristano, Nuoro, Alghero, VALLETTA

Mountains

Mt Blanc 4808, Mt Rosa 4634, Matterhorn 4478, Gran Paradiso 4061, Mt Viso 3841, Mt Pelat 3051, Mt Cinto 2710, Mt Vettore 2476, Mt Corno 2912, Mt Terminillo, Mt Velino 2487, Mt Greco 2283, Mt Pollino 2248, Mt Etna 3323, Gr. Glockner 3798, Gran Paradiso

KEY

Relief and physical features

Relief metres
5000
3000
2000
1000
500
200
0 sea level
under sea level
200
4000
6000

▲ 4634 Mountain height (in metres)

Permanent ice

Water features

River
Canal
Lake / Reservoir

Communications

Railway
Motorway
Road
⊕ Main airport

SCALE 1 : 5 000 000

0   50   100   150   200 km

Lambert Conformal Conic projection

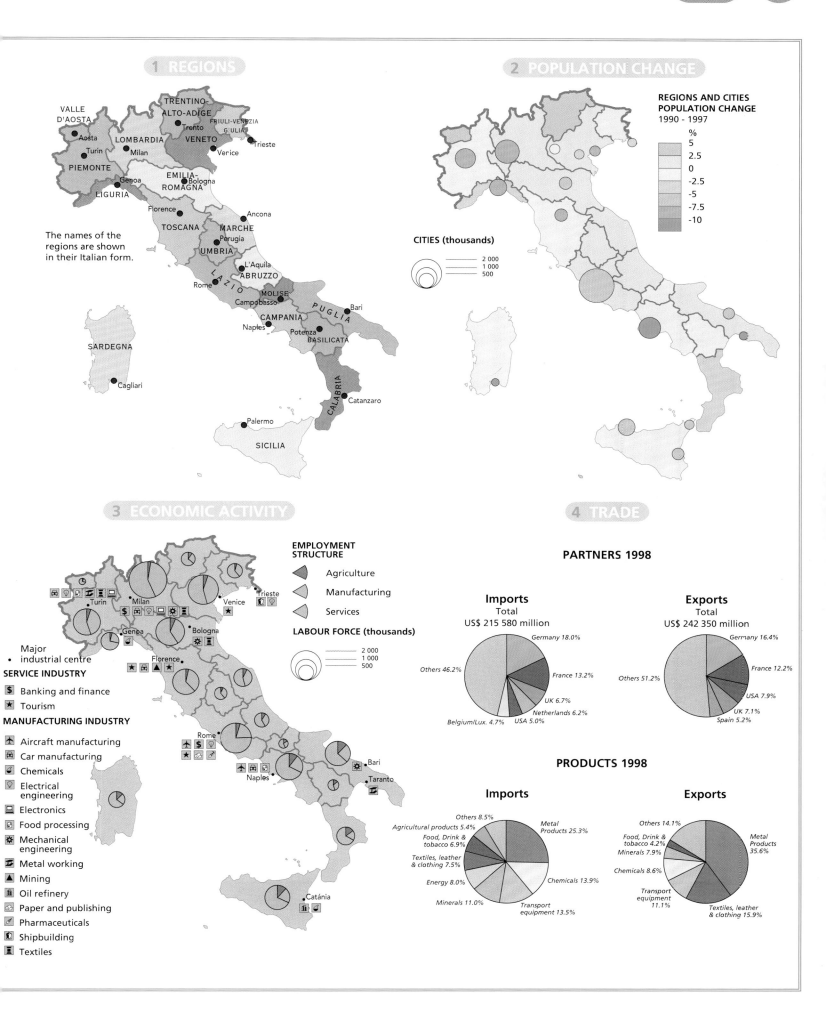

1 REGIONS

VALLE D'AOSTA
Aosta
Turin
PIEMONTE
LOMBARDIA
Milan
TRENTINO-ALTO-ADIGE
Trento
VENETO
Venice
FRIULI-VENEZIA GIULIA
Trieste
Genoa
LIGURIA
EMILIA-ROMAGNA
Bologna
Florence
TOSCANA
MARCHE
Ancona
Perugia
UMBRIA
L'Aquila
ABRUZZO
LAZIO
Rome
MOLISE
Campobasso
CAMPANIA
Naples
Potenza
BASILICATA
PUGLIA
Bari
CALABRIA
Catanzaro
SARDEGNA
Cagliari
Palermo
SICILIA

The names of the regions are shown in their Italian form.

2 POPULATION CHANGE

REGIONS AND CITIES POPULATION CHANGE
1990 - 1997
%
5
2.5
0
-2.5
-5
-7.5
-10

CITIES (thousands)
2 000
1 000
500

3 ECONOMIC ACTIVITY

Trieste
Turin
Milan
Venice
Genoa
Bologna
Florence
Rome
Naples
Bari
Taranto
Catánia

EMPLOYMENT STRUCTURE
Agriculture
Manufacturing
Services

LABOUR FORCE (thousands)
2 000
1 000
500

• Major industrial centre

SERVICE INDUSTRY
$ Banking and finance
★ Tourism

MANUFACTURING INDUSTRY
Aircraft manufacturing
Car manufacturing
Chemicals
Electrical engineering
Electronics
Food processing
Mechanical engineering
Metal working
▲ Mining
Oil refinery
Paper and publishing
Pharmaceuticals
Shipbuilding
Textiles

4 TRADE

PARTNERS 1998

Imports
Total
US$ 215 580 million

Germany 18.0%
France 13.2%
UK 6.7%
Netherlands 6.2%
USA 5.0%
Belgium/Lux. 4.7%
Others 46.2%

Exports
Total
US$ 242 350 million

Germany 16.4%
France 12.2%
USA 7.9%
UK 7.1%
Spain 5.2%
Others 51.2%

PRODUCTS 1998

Imports

Others 8.5%
Agricultural products 5.4%
Food, Drink & tobacco 6.9%
Textiles, leather & clothing 7.5%
Energy 8.0%
Minerals 11.0%
Transport equipment 13.5%
Chemicals 13.9%
Metal Products 25.3%

Exports

Others 14.1%
Food, Drink & tobacco 4.2%
Minerals 7.9%
Chemicals 8.6%
Transport equipment 11.1%
Textiles, leather & clothing 15.9%
Metal Products 35.6%

SCALE 1 : 10 500 000

0   100   200   300 km

Conic projection

KEY

Relief and physical features

Relief metres

5000
3000
2000
1000
500
200
sea level
0
200
4000
6000
under sea level

3798 ▲ Mountain height (in metres)

Permanent ice

Water features

~ River
═ Canal
Lake / Reservoir
Marsh

Communications

Railway
Motorway
Road
⊕ Main airport

Administration

Boundaries

International
Internal

Settlement

Cities and towns in order of size

National capital	Other city or town
■ WARSAW	● Kharkiv
□ CHIŞINĂU	○ Kraków
□ BRATISLAVA	○ Brno
□ VADUZ	○ Chelm

SCALE 1 : 5 000 000

0   50   100   150   200 km

Baltic Sea

Gulf of Gdańsk

SWEDEN

Helsingør, Helsingborg, Kristianstad, Hässleholm, Karlshamn, Karlskrona

COPENHAGEN

Hundested, Hillerød, Holbæk, Lund, Malmö, Ystad, Trelleborg, Køge

DENMARK

Kalundborg, Store Bælt, Sjælland, Svendborg, Næstved, Møn, Vordingborg, Nakskov, Lolland, Falster, Nykøbing, Fehmarn

Ronne, Bornholm, Neksø

Lübeck Bay, Stralsund, Rügen, Sassnitz, Greifswald, Rostock, Świnoujście, Kołobrzeg, Koszalin, Słupsk, Lębork, Gdynia, Gdańsk, Elblag

Klaipėda, Šilutė, Courland Lagoon, Neman, Sovetsk, Baltiysk, Kaliningrad, Chernyakhovsk, Marijampė, Turbarkas, Mažeikiai, Plungė, Šiauliai

RUSSIAN FED. **LITH**

Pregel, Bartoszyce, Suwałki, Elk, Pisz, Szczytno, Białystok, Łomża

GERMANY

Schwerin, Neubrandenburg, L. Müritz, Neustrelitz, Wittenberge, Rathenow, Elbe, Brandenburg, Havel, **BERLIN**, Potsdam, Magdeburg, Dessau, Eisenhüttenstadt, Eisleben, Halle, Leipzig, Jena, Gera, Altenburg, Zwickau, Chemnitz, Freiberg, Plauen, Hof, Ore Mts, Meissen, Dresden, Görlitz

Szczecin, Stargard Szczeciński, Piła, Gorzów Wielkopolski, Zielona Góra, Żary, Forst, Cottbus, Spree, Bóbr, Głogów, Oder, Hoyerswerda, Jelenia Góra, Liberec, Teplice

POLAND

Kościerzyna, Chojnice, Szczecinek, Bydgoszcz, Inowrocław, Toruń, Grudziądz, Włocławek, Płock, Konin, Gniezno, **Poznań**, Grodzisk Wielkopolski, Leszno, Rawicz, Wschowa, Kalisz, Ostrzeszów, Wieluń

Olsztyn, Masurian Lakes, Nidzica, Omulew, Malbork, Ostrów Mazowiecka, Pułtusk, Wkra, Vistula, Siedlce, **WARSAW**, Łowicz, Pruszków, **Łódź**, Tomaszów Mazowiecki, Piotrków Trybunalski, Radomsko, Radom, Skarżysko-Kamienna, Kielce, Lublin, Ostrów Podl.

Legnica, **Wrocław**, Wałbrzych, ▲1015, Sudeten Mts, Opole, Częstochowa, Silesian Plateau, Dąbrowa Górnicza, Bytom, Gliwice, Sosnowiec, Katowice, Rybnik, Ostrava, Olomouc, **Kraków**, Tarnów, Bielsko-Biała, Babia Góra 1725, Nowy Sącz, Krosno, Przemyśl, Rzeszów

CZECH REPUBLIC

Karlovy Vary, Cheb 940, Kladno, **PRAGUE**, Hradec Králové, Pardubice, Plzeň, Vltava, Tábor, Písek, Svitavy, Jihlava, Brno, Znojmo, Zlín, Břeclav, Olomouc

Bohemian Forest, Regensburg, Straubing, Passau, České Budějovice, Gmünd

SLOVAKIA

Žilina, Martin, Prievidza, Banská Bystrica, Zvolen, Lučenec, Poprad, 2043, Tatra 1346, Košice, Trebišov, Uzhhorod, Mukachev, Ozd

AUSTRIA

Swabian Alps, Tuttlingen, Biberach, Danube, Augsburg, Landshut, **Munich**, Memmingen, Kempten, Chiemsee, Rosenheim, Salzburg, Linz, Steyr, Enns, St Pölten, Hollabrunn, **VIENNA**, **BRATISLAVA**, Leoben, Kapfenberg, Wiener Neustadt, Aspang-Markt, Judenburg, Gr. Glockner 3798, Lienz

Inn, Garmisch-Partenkirchen, Zugspitze 2962, Innsbruck, Brenner Pass, Isar, Lech

SWITZERLAND **LIECH**

St Gallen, Konstanz, Friedrichshafen, Dornbirn, **VADUZ**, Chur, Scuol, St Moritz, Bozen, Merano

ITALY

ALPS, Como, Bergamo, Monza, Brescia, L. di Garda, Verona, Vicenza, Padua, Trento, Bolzano, Dolomites, Adda, Adige, Piave, Treviso, Udine, Gorizia, Trieste, Istra, Piacenza, Cremona, Mantua, Po, Parma, Reggio, Modena, Bologna, Reno, Gulf of Venice, Venice

HUNGARY

Szombathely, Győr, Nové Zámky, Nitra, Vác, Gyöngyös, Nyíregyháza, Miskolc, **BUDAPEST**, Várpalota, Székesfehérvár, Cegléd, Debrecen, Karcag, Kecskemét, Balaton, Nagykanizsa, Kaposvár, Szekszárd, Baja, Pécs, Szeged, Békéscsaba, 680

SLOVENIA

LJUBLJANA, Kranj, Celje, Maribor, Villach, Klagenfurt, Drau, 2140, Graz, 1796, Varaždin, Metlika, Kupa

CROATIA

ZAGREB, Karlovac, Ogulin, Rijeka, Krk, Cres, Pula

BOSNIA-HERZEGOVINA

Bosanska Dubica, Bihać, Una, Sava, Drava, Tisa, Sombor

YUGOSLAVIA

VOJVODINA, Novi Sad, Subotica, Kikinda, Zrenjanin, Vinkovci, Ruma, Vršac

Oradea, Arad, Lipova, Timișoara, Lugoj, Deva, Reșița, Varful Bihor 1849, Mureș, Beiuș, Zalău, Satu Mare, Cărei, Tisza

Conic projection

A 14° B 16° C 18° D 20° E 22° F 24° G

KEY

Relief and physical features

Relief
metres
5000
3000
2000
1000
500
200
sea level
0
200
4000
6000
under sea level

3971 ▲ Mountain height
(in metres)

Water features

River
Intermittent river
Canal
Lake / Reservoir
Intermittent lake
Marsh

Communications

Railway
Motorway
Road
⊕ Main airport

Administration

Boundaries
International
Internal
Ceasefire line

Settlement

Cities and towns in order of size

National capital   Other city or town
■ ATHENS   ● İstanbul
□ SKOPJE   ○ Konya
□ NICOSIA   ○ Split
                   ○ Dubrovnik

SCALE 1 : 5 000 000

0   50   100   150   200 km

CROATIA

ZAGREB
Metlika
Rijeka
Krk
Cres
Pula
Istra
Karlovac
Kupa
Sisak
Sava
1796 ▲
Gospić
1758
Dugi Otok
Zadar
Knin
Šibenik
Split
Brač
Hvar
Vis
Korčula
Mljet
Dubrovnik

Bosanska
Dubica
Bihać
Banja Luka
Una
Vrbas
Doboj
Bosna
Tuzla
Zenica
Travnik
SARAJEVO
Mostar
Metković
Neretva
BOSNIA-
HERZEGOVINA
Dinaric Alps
Dalmatia

Drava
Varaždin
16°
46°
46°

Subotica
Sombor
Kikinda
Novi Sad
Ruma
VOJVODINA
Zrenjanin
Vinkovci
Vršac
Šabac
Loznica
BELGRADE
Požarevac
Valjevo
YUGOSLAVIA
SERBIA
Kragujevac
Titovo Užice
Kraljevo
Kruševac
Pljevlja
2522 Tara
Novi Pazar
Ibar
MONTE
NEGRO
Nikšić
Podgorica
Kotor
Bar
2656 Peć
Daravica
Kosovska
Mitrovica
Đakovica
KOSOVO
Priština
Vranje
Prizren
L. Shkodër
Shkodër
2650
Kumanovo
SKOPJE
Kočani
Veles
MACEDONIA
Peshkopi
Debar
Prilep
Strumica
Gevgelija
TIRANË
ALBANIA
Elbasan
Lake
Ohrid
Ohrid
L. Prespa
Bitola
Korçë
Berat
Seman
Vlorë

Arad
Timișoara
Reșița
Timiș
Lugoj
Deva
Lipova
Brad
Alba Iulia
Sibiu
Mureș
Vârful
Moldoveanu ▲ 2544
Transylvanian Alps
ROMANIA
Petroșani
Mt Mindra
2519
Târgu Jiu
Drobeta-
Turnu
Severin
Orșova
Drăgășani
Râmnica Vâlcea
Jiu
Craiova
Slatina
Caracal
Olt
Turnu
Măgurele
Lom
Vidin
Zaječar
Negotin
Vrdnik
Vrața
Botevgrad
SOFIA
Pernik
Blagoevgrad
Kyustendil
Struma
Pazardzhik
Plovdiv
Rhodope Mts
Smolyan
Mesta
Petrich
Serres
Drama
Kavala
Kilkis
Edessa
Vardar
Thessaloniki
Kalamaria

Sfântu
Gheorghe
Brașov
Focșani
Buzău
Ploiești
Ialomița
BUCHAREST
Oltenița
Călărași
Silistra
Slobozia
Danube
Zimnicea
Ruse
Pleven
Osăm
Lovech
Veliko
Târnovo
Iskăr
Balkan Mts
BULGARIA
Stara
Zagora
Kazanlăk
Tundzha
Sliven
Karnobat
Burg
Maritsa
Dimitrovgrad
Khaskovo
Kürdzhali
Kırklareli
Edirne
Loleburga
Ergene
Keşan
Komotini
Xanthi
Nestos
Alexandroupoli
Thasos
Samothraki
Gökçeada
G. of
Saros
Gallipoli
Biga
Çanakkale
Ezine
Edremit
Ayvalık
Dardanelles
Tekir
Onești
Târgu
Secuiesc
Ted

ADRIATIC SEA
ITALY
Termoli
San Severo
Campobasso
Brindisi
Lecce
Gallipoli
Otranto
C. Sta Maria
di Leuca
Strait of Otranto

Durrës
Seman
Pindus Mountains
Smolikas
2637
Sarandë
Corfu
Corfu
Ioannina
Igoumenitsa
Preveza
Arta
Lefkada
Kefallonia
Mesolongion
G. of Patras
Patras
Pyrgos
Zakynthos
Kyparissia
IONIAN
SEA
Ionian Islands

Florina
Kastoria
Kozani
Aliakmonas
Trikala
Pineios
Larisa
Karditsa
Farsala
GREECE
Mt Olympus
2911
Ossa
1978
Volos
Northern Sporades
Lamia
Oiti
2152
Ramossos
2457
Chalkida
Evvoia
Kyllini
2376
Corinth
G. of Corinth
Megara
Piraeus
ATHENS
Marathonas C.
Kafireas
Tripoli
Nafplio
Aigina
Kea
Kythnos
Sparti
Kalamata
G. of
Messina
G. of
Lakonia
C. Matapan
Kythira
C. Maléa
Antikythira
C. Spátha
Chania
Rethymno
Crete
Idi
2456
Iraklion
Sitela

Mt Athos
2033
C. Platí
Limnos
Agios
Efstratios
Aegean Sea
Skyros
Psara
Lesvos
Mytilini
Chios
Chios
Samos
Sökö
İzmir
Mani
Karakaya
G. of İzmir
Cyclades
Andros
Tinos
Ikaria
Naxos
Paros
Milos
Amorgos
Ios
Thira
Sea of Crete
Karpathos
Kasos

MEDITERRANEAN

D 20° E 22° F 24° G 26° H

6
5
4
3
2
1

Conic projection

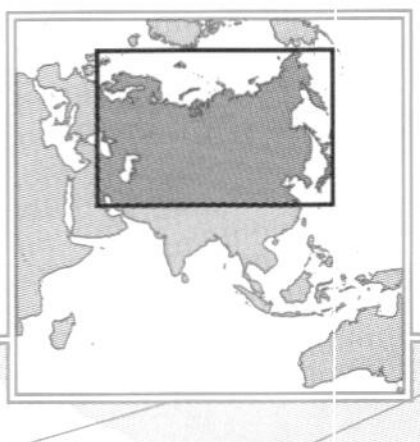

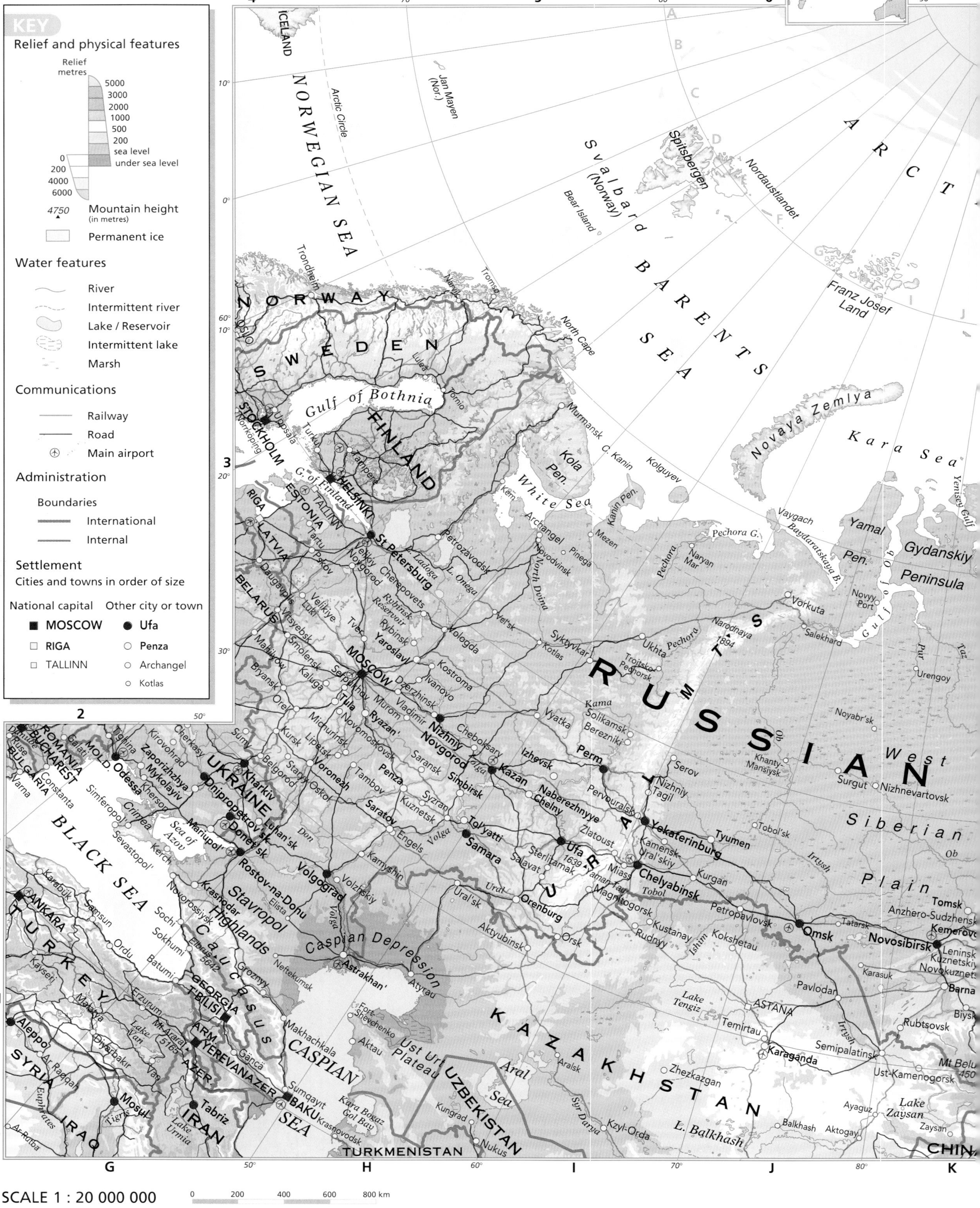

KEY
Relief and physical features
Relief metres
5000
3000
2000
1000
500
200
sea level
under sea level
0
200
4000
6000
4750 Mountain height (in metres)
Permanent ice
Water features
River
Intermittent river
Lake / Reservoir
Intermittent lake
Marsh
Communications
Railway
Road
Main airport
Administration
Boundaries
International
Internal
Settlement
Cities and towns in order of size
National capital
Other city or town
MOSCOW
Ufa
RIGA
Penza
TALLINN
Archangel
Kotlas
ICELAND
NORWEGIAN SEA
Arctic Circle
Jan Mayen (Nor.)
Svalbard (Norway)
Spitsbergen
Nordaustlandet
Bear Island
BARENTS SEA
ARCTIC
Franz Josef Land
Novaya Zemlya
Kara Sea
NORWAY
SWEDEN
FINLAND
Gulf of Bothnia
STOCKHOLM
HELSINKI
TALLINN
RIGA
ESTONIA
LATVIA
BELARUS
G. of Finland
Murmansk
Kola Pen.
White Sea
C. Kanin
Kolguyev
Kanin Pen.
Archangel
Pechora G.
Vaygach
Yamal Pen.
Gydanskiy Peninsula
Novyy Port
Gulf of Ob
Vorkuta
Salekhard
St Petersburg
L. Ladoga
L. Onega
Petrozavodsk
Rybinsk Reservoir
Yaroslavl
MOSCOW
Vologda
Kostroma
Ivanovo
Syktyvkar
Kotlas
Ukhta
Narodnaya 1894
Urengoy
Noyabr'sk
RUSSIAN
Nizhniy Novgorod
Kazan
Perm
Izhevsk
Vyatka
Solikamsk
Berezniki
Surgut
Nizhnevartovsk
West Siberian Plain
Yekaterinburg
Tyumen
Chelyabinsk
Ufa
Samara
Tol'yatti
Saratov
Penza
Volgograd
Orenburg
Magnitogorsk
Kurgan
Omsk
Novosibirsk
Kemerovo
Petropavlovsk
Kustanay
Kokshetau
Pavlodar
ASTANA
Karaganda
Semipalatinsk
Ust-Kamenogorsk
Barnaul
Rubtsovsk
KAZAKHSTAN
Aral Sea
L. Balkhash
Lake Zaysan
UZBEKISTAN
TURKMENISTAN
Kzyl-Orda
Zhezkazgan
Caspian Depression
Astrakhan'
Atyrau
CASPIAN SEA
Makhachkala
BAKU
TBILISI
YEREVAN
GEORGIA
ARM.
AZER.
Caucasus
Elbrus 5642
Mt Ararat 5165
Stavropol Highlands
Rostov-na-Donu
Krasnodar
Sochi
BLACK SEA
Sea of Azov
Crimea
UKRAINE
Kharkiv
Donets'k
Odessa
Dnipropetrovs'k
MOLD.
ROMANIA
BUCHAREST
BULGARIA
TURKEY
ANKARA
SYRIA
Aleppo
IRAQ
Mosul
IRAN
Tabriz
CHINA
SCALE 1 : 20 000 000
0 200 400 600 800 km

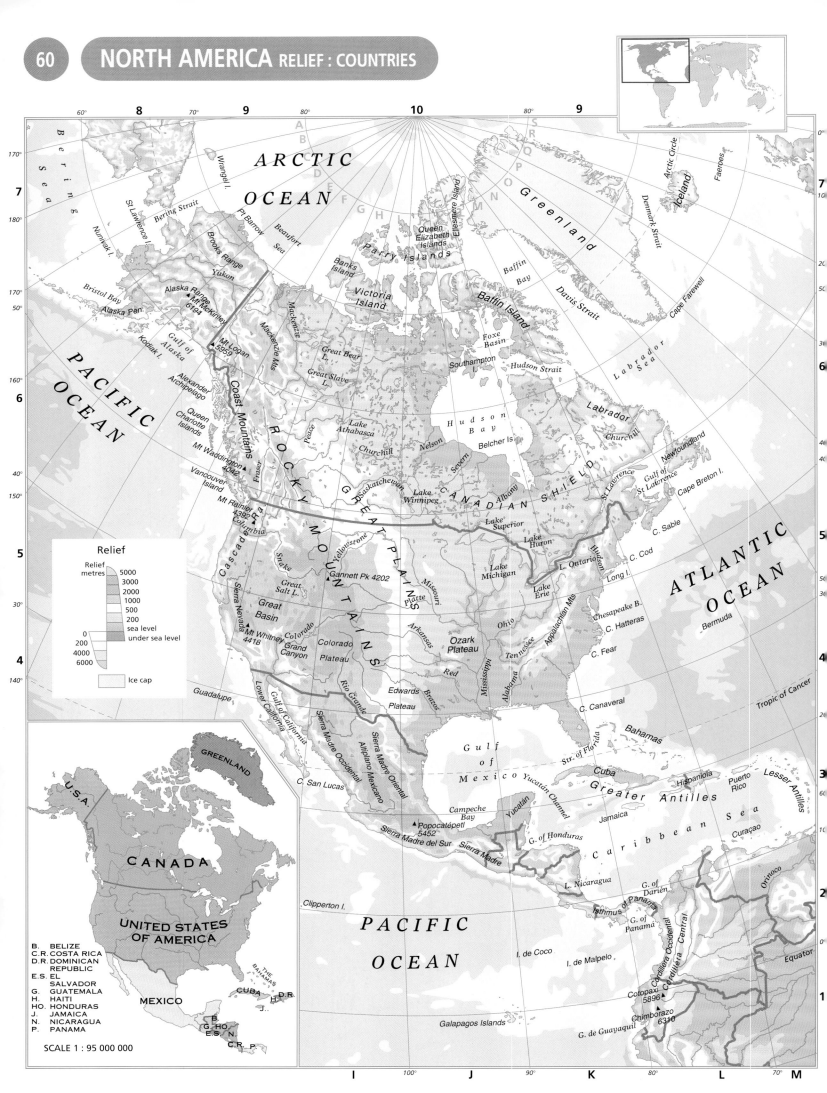

ARCTIC OCEAN

PACIFIC OCEAN

ATLANTIC OCEAN

PACIFIC OCEAN

Greenland

Bering Sea

Wrangel I.

Nunivak I.

St Lawrence I.

Bering Strait

Pt Barrow

Beaufort Sea

Brooks Range

Yukon

Alaska Range ▲ Mt McKinley 6194

Alaska Pan.

Kodiak I.

Gulf of Alaska

Alexander Archipelago

Queen Charlotte Islands

Mt Waddington 4042 ▲

Vancouver Island

Coast Mountains

Mt Logan 5959 ▲

Mackenzie Mts

Mackenzie

Great Bear L.

Great Slave L.

Victoria Island

Banks Island

Parry Islands

Queen Elizabeth Islands

Ellesmere Island

Baffin Bay

Baffin Island

Davis Strait

Cape Farewell

Denmark Strait

Iceland

Faeroes

Arctic Circle

Foxe Basin

Southampton I.

Hudson Strait

Hudson Bay

Labrador Sea

Labrador

Churchill

Belcher Is

Nelson

Severn

Albany

CANADIAN SHIELD

Peace

Fraser

Lake Athabasca

Churchill

Saskatchewan

Lake Winnipeg

Lake Superior

Newfoundland

Gulf of St Lawrence

Cape Breton I.

St Lawrence

C. Sable

ROCKY MOUNTAINS

GREAT PLAINS

Columbia

Mt Rainier 4392 ▲

Cascades

Snake

Yellowstone

Gannett Pk 4202 ▲

Great Salt L.

Sierra Nevada

Mt Whitney 4418 ▲

Great Basin

Colorado

Colorado Plateau

Grand Canyon

Missouri

Platte

Lake Michigan

Lake Huron

Lake Erie

L. Ontario

Long I.

C. Cod

Hudson

Chesapeake B.

Bermuda

Ohio

Arkansas

Red

Ozark Plateau

Tennessee

Appalachian Mts

C. Hatteras

C. Fear

Mississippi

Alabama

Edwards Plateau

Bravos

Rio Grande

Guadalupe

Lower California

Gulf of California

Sierra Madre Occidental

C. San Lucas

Altiplano Mexicano

Sierra Madre Oriental

▲ Popocatépetl 5452

Sierra Madre del Sur

Sierra Madre

Campeche Bay

Yucatán

Yucatán Channel

C. Canaveral

Tropic of Cancer

Bahamas

Str. of Florida

Gulf of Mexico

Cuba

Hispaniola

Jamaica

Puerto Rico

Lesser Antilles

Greater Antilles

Curaçao

Caribbean Sea

G. of Honduras

L. Nicaragua

G. of Darién

Isthmus of Panama

G. of Panama

Clipperton I.

I. de Coco

I. de Malpelo

Galapagos Islands

G. de Guayaquil

Orinoco

Cordillera Occidental

Cordillera Central

Cotopaxi 5896 ▲

Chimborazo 6310

Equator

Relief

Relief metres
- 5000
- 3000
- 2000
- 1000
- 500
- 200
- sea level
- under sea level
- 0
- 200
- 4000
- 6000

Ice cap

GREENLAND

U.S.A.

CANADA

UNITED STATES OF AMERICA

MEXICO

THE BAHAMAS

CUBA

D.R.

J.

B.
G. HO.
E.S. N.
C.R. P.

B. BELIZE
C.R. COSTA RICA
D.R. DOMINICAN REPUBLIC
E.S. EL SALVADOR
G. GUATEMALA
H. HAITI
HO. HONDURAS
J. JAMAICA
N. NICARAGUA
P. PANAMA

SCALE 1 : 95 000 000

SCALE 1 : 40 000 000

Chamberlin Trimetric projection

1 TEMPERATURE AND PRESSURE : JANUARY

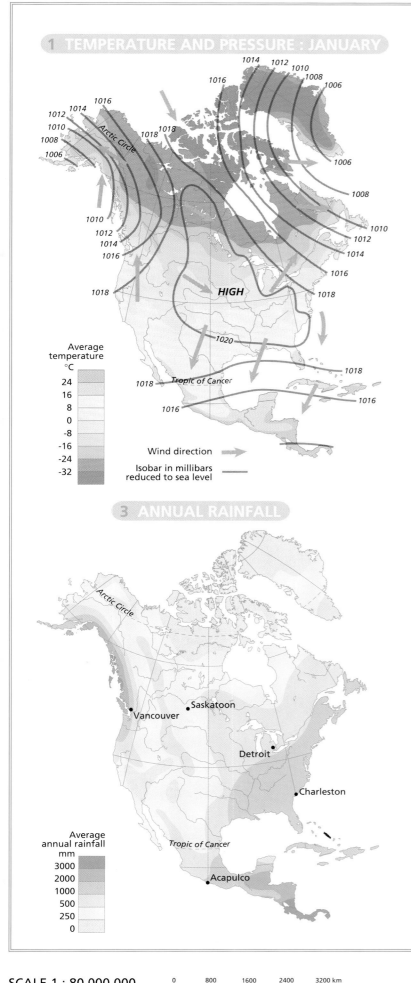

Average temperature °C

| 24 |
| 16 |
| 8 |
| 0 |
| -8 |
| -16 |
| -24 |
| -32 |

Wind direction →

Isobar in millibars reduced to sea level ——

2 TEMPERATURE AND PRESSURE : JULY

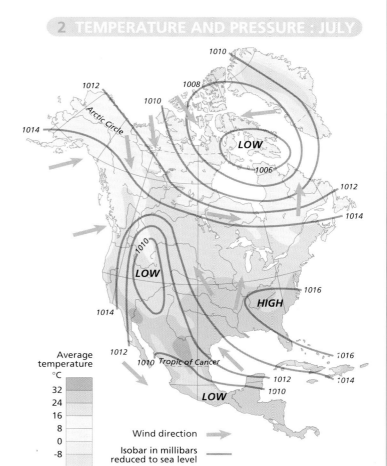

Average temperature °C

| 32 |
| 24 |
| 16 |
| 8 |
| 0 |
| -8 |

Wind direction →

Isobar in millibars reduced to sea level ——

3 ANNUAL RAINFALL

Average annual rainfall mm

| 3000 |
| 2000 |
| 1000 |
| 500 |
| 250 |
| 0 |

4 STATISTICS

Saskatoon (515 metres)	Jan	Feb	Mar	Apr	May	Jun	Jul	Aug	Sep	Oct	Nov	Dec
Temperature - max. (°C)	-13	-11	-3	9	18	22	25	24	17	11	-1	-9
Temperature - min. (°C)	-24	-22	-14	-3	3	9	11	9	3	-3	-11	-19
Rainfall - (mm)	23	13	18	18	36	66	61	48	38	23	13	15

Vancouver (14 metres)	Jan	Feb	Mar	Apr	May	Jun	Jul	Aug	Sep	Oct	Nov	Dec
Temperature - max. (°C)	5	7	10	14	18	21	23	23	18	14	9	6
Temperature - min. (°C)	0	1	3	4	8	11	12	12	9	7	4	2
Rainfall - (mm)	218	147	127	84	71	64	31	43	91	147	211	224

Charleston (3 metres)	Jan	Feb	Mar	Apr	May	Jun	Jul	Aug	Sep	Oct	Nov	Dec
Temperature - max. (°C)	14	15	19	23	27	30	31	31	28	24	19	15
Temperature - min. (°C)	6	7	10	14	19	23	24	24	22	16	11	7
Rainfall - (mm)	74	84	86	71	81	119	185	168	130	81	58	71

Acapulco (3 metres)	Jan	Feb	Mar	Apr	May	Jun	Jul	Aug	Sep	Oct	Nov	Dec
Temperature - max. (°C)	31	31	31	32	32	33	32	33	32	32	32	31
Temperature - min. (°C)	22	22	22	23	25	25	25	25	24	24	23	22
Rainfall - (mm)	6	1	0	1	36	281	256	252	349	159	28	8

Detroit (189 metres)	Jan	Feb	Mar	Apr	May	Jun	Jul	Aug	Sep	Oct	Nov	Dec
Temperature - max. (°C)	-1	0	6	13	19	25	28	27	23	16	8	2
Temperature - min. (°C)	-7	-8	-3	3	9	14	17	17	13	7	1	-4
Rainfall - (mm)	53	53	64	64	84	91	84	69	71	61	61	58

KEY

Relief and physical features

Relief
metres
5000
3000
2000
1000
500
200
sea level
under sea level
200
4000
6000

6194 ▲ Mountain height
(in metres)

Permanent ice

Water features

~~~ River
Lake / Reservoir
Intermittent lake
Marsh

Communications

Railway
Road
✈ Main airport

Administration

Boundaries
International
Internal

Settlement

Cities and towns in order of size

National capital | Other city or town
■ **OTTAWA** | ● **Montréal**
□ REYKJAVÍK | ○ **Winnipeg**
| ○ Québec
| ○ Churchill

SCALE 1 : 17 000 000

0   200   400   600   800 km

I 90° J 80° K 70° L 60° M 80° 50° N 40° O 5 30° P 20° 70° Q 4 10°

GREENLAND
(Denmark)

ICELAND

Arctic Circle

Akureyri
Siglufjördhur
Seydhisfjördhur
1763 Hofsjökull
Faxaflói Akranes Höfn
Keflavík REYKJAVÍK

Denmark Strait

Kong Christian IX Land Gunnbjörn Fjeld 3700

Ísafjördhur

10°

60°

20°

Axel
Heiberg
Island

Amund
Ringnes I.

Ellesmere Island

Cape
Parry

Qaanaaq
(Thule)

Cape York Melville
Bay

Upernavik

Kong Frederick VI Kyst

Tasiilaq

30°

Jones Sound
Devon Island

nwallis I.

Resolute
Bay

Somerset
Island

Lancaster Sound

Bylot
Island

Arctic Bay

Borden
Peninsula

Pond Inlet
(Mittimatalik)

Clyde River

Saqqaq

Disko
I.

Oqaatsut

Qasigiannguit

Davis Strait

Sisimiut

Maniitsoq

NUUK
(Godthåb)

C. Dyer

Davis Strait

Labrador

Sea

ATLANTIC

OCEAN

3

Somerset
Island

Gulf of Boothia

Boothia
Peninsula

Baffin Island

Home Bay

Penny
Icecap

Pangnirtung

Paamiut

Iittoqqortoormiit

Nanortalik Cape Farewell

30°

Taloyoak

Melville

Hall
Beach

Prince
Charles I.

Nettilling
Lake

Cumberland Sound

Amadjuak
Lake

V U T

Foxe
Basin

Foxe
Peninsula

Iqaluit

Frobisher Bay

Resolution
Island

Repulse
Bay

Southampton
Island

Coral
Harbour

Fisher Str.

Coats I.

Foxe Channel

Hudson Strait

Akpatok I. C. Chidley

N

40°

A D A

Baker Lake
Qamanittuaq

Baker
Lake

nkin Inlet

Mansel I.

Salluit Kangiqsujuaq

Ottawa Is

Puvurnituq

Ungava
Bay

Kangiqsualujjuaq

Nain

Cape Harrison

Hopedale

50°

40°

Cape Churchill

Churchill

Hudson

Bay

Inukjuak

Feuilles

Kuujjuaq

George

Baleine

Smallwood
Reservoir

Schefferville

Churchill

Happy Valley
Goose Bay

Port Hope
Simpson

St Anthony

N E W F O U N D L A N D

O B A

Nelson

Fort Severn

Belcher
Islands

Cape
Henrietta Maria

Lac à
l'Eau Claire

Rés. de
La Grande 2

Caniapiscau

Réservoir
Caniapiscau

Rés. de
La Grande 4

Labrador
City

Wabush

Strait of Belle Isle

Grand
Falls

Corner
Brook

Gander

Bonavista

St John's

2

Winisk

Big Trout Lake

Sandy Lake

James

Bay

Ekwan

Fort
George
(Chisasibi)

Akimiski
Island

Eastmain

Fort
Albany

Rés. de
La Grande 3

Q U É B E C

Eastmain

Fort Rupert
(Waskaganish)

Gagnon

Havre-St-Pierre

Sept-Îles

Île d'Anticosti

Newfoundland

Channel-Port
aux Basques

St Pierre
& Miquelon
(Fr.)

Cabot Strait

Red Lake

Lac
St Joseph

Sioux
Lookout

O N T A R I O

Albany

Missinaibi

Moosonee

L. Mistassini

Mistissini
(Baie-du-Poste)

Chibougamau

L. Evans

Réservoir
Gouin

Baie Comeau

St Lawrence

Gaspé Gaspé
Pen.

Gulf of
St Lawrence

St Pierre
& Miquelon

Lake of
the Woods

rt Frances

Lake
Nipigon

Longlac

Kapuskasing

Groundhog

Timmins

Amos

Roberval

Chicoutimi

Jonquière

Rivière-du-Loup

Rimouski

Edmundston

Bathurst

PRINCE EDWARD
ISLAND

Charlottetown

Sydney
Glace Bay

Cape Breton
Island

NNESOTA

ridji

Duluth

Lake Superior

Nipigon

Chapleau

Kirkland Lake

Val d'Or

Hurricana

Québec

NEW
BRUNSWICK

Moncton

Fredericton

St John

NOVA SCOTIA

Truro

Halifax

Sable I.

1

Ashland

MI

Marquette

Sault Ste
Marie

Sudbury

North Bay

Ottawa

Montréal

Trois Rivières

Sherbrooke

MAINE

Bangor

Bay of Fundy

Cape Sable

Minneapolis-
St Paul

Green Bay

WISCONSIN

Albert Lea

Escanaba

MICHIGAN

Cadillac

Bay
City

Flint

Georgian B.

Owen
Sound

Oshawa

Peterborough

OTTAWA

North Bay

VER. 1917

Mt Washington

N.H.

MASS.

Augusta

Portland

Yarmouth

Cape Sable

50°

40°

Milwaukee

Rockford

IOWA

Cedar
Rapids

Chicago

Grand
Rapids

Detroit

Toledo

Cleveland

PENNSYLVANIA

Williamsport

Lake Huron

L. Ontario

Toronto

London

Rochester

Syracuse

Albany

Hartford

Worcester

Boston

Lowell

Manchester

CONN. R.I.

New Haven

Long Island

New York

Providence

Cape Cod

L. Erie

Erie

Buffalo

Binghamton

Scranton

N.J.

C A

Chamberlin Trimetric projection

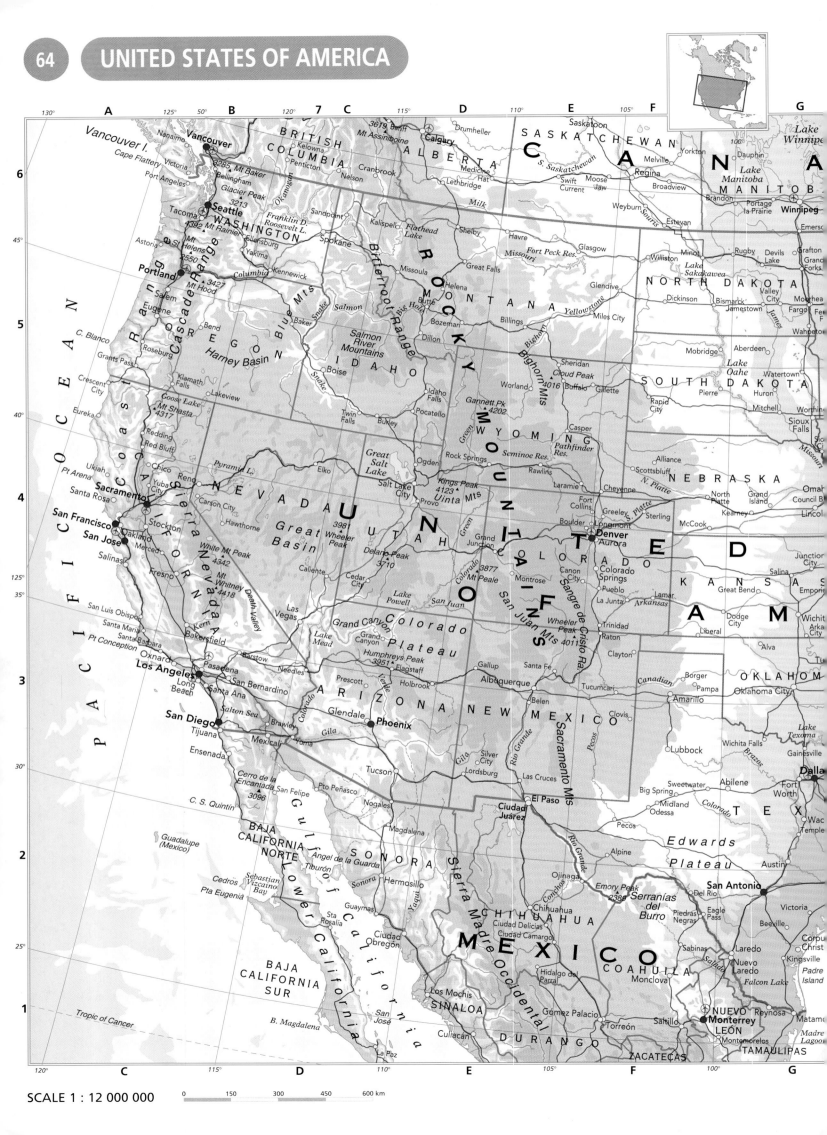

KEY

Relief and physical features

Relief metres

5000
3000
2000
1000
500
200
sea level
0
200
4000
6000
under sea level

4418 ▲ Mountain height (in metres)

Water features

River

Intermittent river

Lake / Reservoir

Intermittent lake

Marsh

Communications

Railway

Road

⊕ Main airport

Administration

Boundaries

International

Internal

Settlement

Cities and towns in order of size

National capital | Other city or town
■ WASHINGTON D.C. | ● New York
□ NASSAU | ○ Norfolk
| ○ Savannah
| ○ Elko

Lambert Conformal Conic projection

1 POPULATION DENSITY

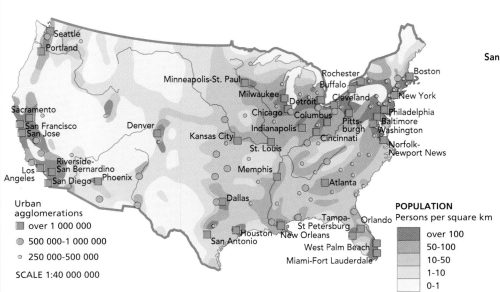

Urban agglomerations
- ■ over 1 000 000
- ● 500 000-1 000 000
- ○ 250 000-500 000

SCALE 1:40 000 000

POPULATION
Persons per square km
- over 100
- 50-100
- 10-50
- 1-10
- 0-1

4 STATE COMPARISONS

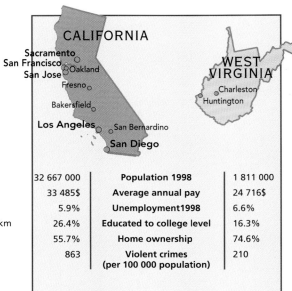

CALIFORNIA

WEST VIRGINIA

CALIFORNIA		WEST VIRGINIA
32 667 000	Population 1998	1 811 000
33 485$	Average annual pay	24 716$
5.9%	Unemployment 1998	6.6%
26.4%	Educated to college level	16.3%
55.7%	Home ownership	74.6%
863	Violent crimes (per 100 000 population)	210

2 MAIN URBAN AGGLOMERATIONS

Urban agglomeration	1980	1998	% change
New York	15 600 000	16 626 000	6.6
Los Angeles	9 500 000	13 129 000	38.2
Chicago	6 780 000	6 945 000	2.4
Philadelphia	4 116 000	4 398 000	6.9
San Francisco	3 201 000	4 051 000	26.6
Washington	2 777 000	3 927 000	41.4
Dallas	2 468 000	3 912 000	58.5
Detroit	3 806 000	3 785 000	-0.6
Houston	2 424 000	3 365 000	38.8
San Diego	1 718 000	2 983 000	73.6
Boston	2 681 000	2 915 000	8.7

5 POPULATION GROWTH

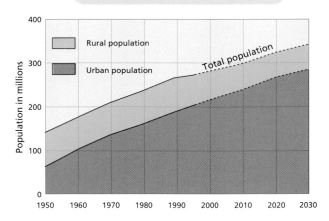

Rural population
Urban population
Total population

Population in millions

3 POPULATION CHANGE

SCALE 1:40 000 000

POPULATION CHANGE
1985 - 1998
%
- over 50
- 31-50
- 16-30
- 0-15
- -1 - -10

CO.	CONNECTICUT	PENN.	PENNSYLVANIA
DEL.	DELAWARE	R.I.	RHODE ISLAND
MASS.	MASSACHUSETTS	S.C.	SOUTH CAROLINA
N.H.	NEW HAMPSHIRE	V.	VERMONT
N.J.	NEW JERSEY	W.V.	WEST VIRGINIA

6 IMMIGRATION

IMMIGRATION INTO U.S.A
BY COUNTRY 1997
Total 798 400

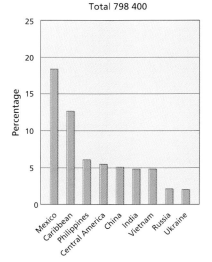

Percentage

7 ECONOMIC ACTIVITY

- Major industrial centre

SERVICE INDUSTRY

- $ Banking and finance
- ★ Tourism

MANUFACTURING INDUSTRY

- Aircraft manufacturing
- Car manufacturing
- Chemicals
- Electrical engineering
- Food processing
- Mechanical engineering
- Metal working
- Oil refinery
- Paper and publishing
- Shipbuilding
- Textiles

SCALE 1:40 000 000

Seattle
San Francisco/Oakland
Los Angeles
Minneapolis/St. Paul
Milwaukee
Chicago
Kansas City
St. Louis
Dallas
Houston
New Orleans
Detroit
Cleveland
Indianapolis
Birmingham
Atlanta
Miami
Buffalo
Pittsburgh
Washington
Boston
New York
Philadelphia
Baltimore

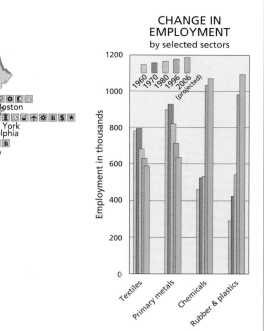

CHANGE IN EMPLOYMENT
by selected sectors

Employment in thousands

1960 1970 1980 1996 2006 (projected)

Textiles — Primary metals — Chemicals — Rubber & plastics

8 TRADE

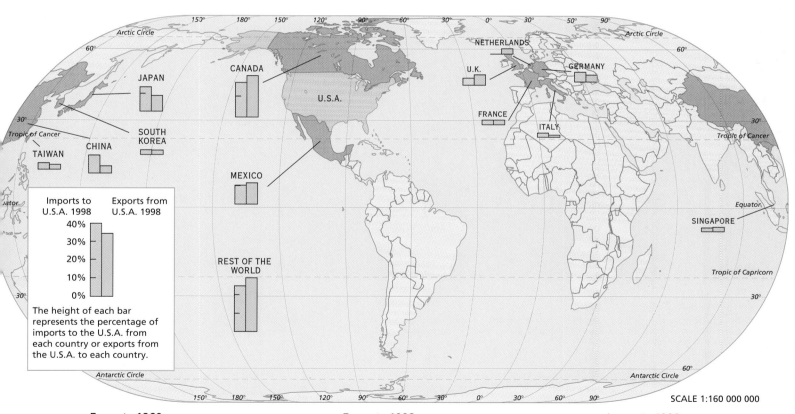

JAPAN
TAIWAN
CHINA
SOUTH KOREA
CANADA
U.S.A.
MEXICO
REST OF THE WORLD
NETHERLANDS
U.K.
FRANCE
GERMANY
ITALY
SINGAPORE

Arctic Circle
Tropic of Cancer
Equator
Tropic of Capricorn
Antarctic Circle

Imports to U.S.A. 1998   Exports from U.S.A. 1998

40%
30%
20%
10%
0%

The height of each bar represents the percentage of imports to the U.S.A. from each country or exports from the U.S.A. to each country.

SCALE 1:160 000 000

Exports 1960
Total: US$ 20 717 million

Others 9.4%
Textiles 10.8%
Chemicals 11.7%
Food 12.9%
Metals & manufactures 13.1%
Machinery & vehicles 42.1%

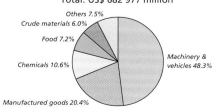

Exports 1998
Total: US$ 682 977 million

Others 7.5%
Crude materials 6.0%
Food 7.2%
Chemicals 10.6%
Manufactured goods 20.4%
Machinery & vehicles 48.3%

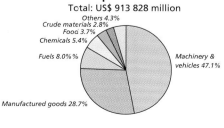

Imports 1998
Total: US$ 913 828 million

Others 4.3%
Crude materials 2.8%
Food 3.7%
Chemicals 5.4%
Fuels 8.0%
Manufactured goods 28.7%
Machinery & vehicles 47.1%

Built-up area

The built up area shown as blue/green on the satellite image surrounds San Francisco Bay and extends south to San Jose. Three bridges link the main built up areas across San Francisco Bay.

Woodland

Areas of dense woodland cover much of the Santa Cruz Mountains to the west of the San Andreas Fault Zone. Other areas of woodland are found on the ridges to the east of San Francisco Bay.

Marsh / Salt Marsh

Areas of dark green on the satellite image represent marshland in the Coyote Creek area and salt marshes between the San Mateo and Dumbarton Bridges.

Reservoir / lake

Lakes and reservoirs stand out from the surrounding land. Good examples are the Upper San Leandro Reservoir east of Piedmont and the San Andreas Lake which lies along the fault line.

Airport

A grey blue colour shows San Francisco International Airport as a flat rectangular strip of land jutting out into the bay.

SAN FRANCISCO FAULT LINES

— Fault line
— Major road
— Railway
▢ Built-up area
⊕ Airport

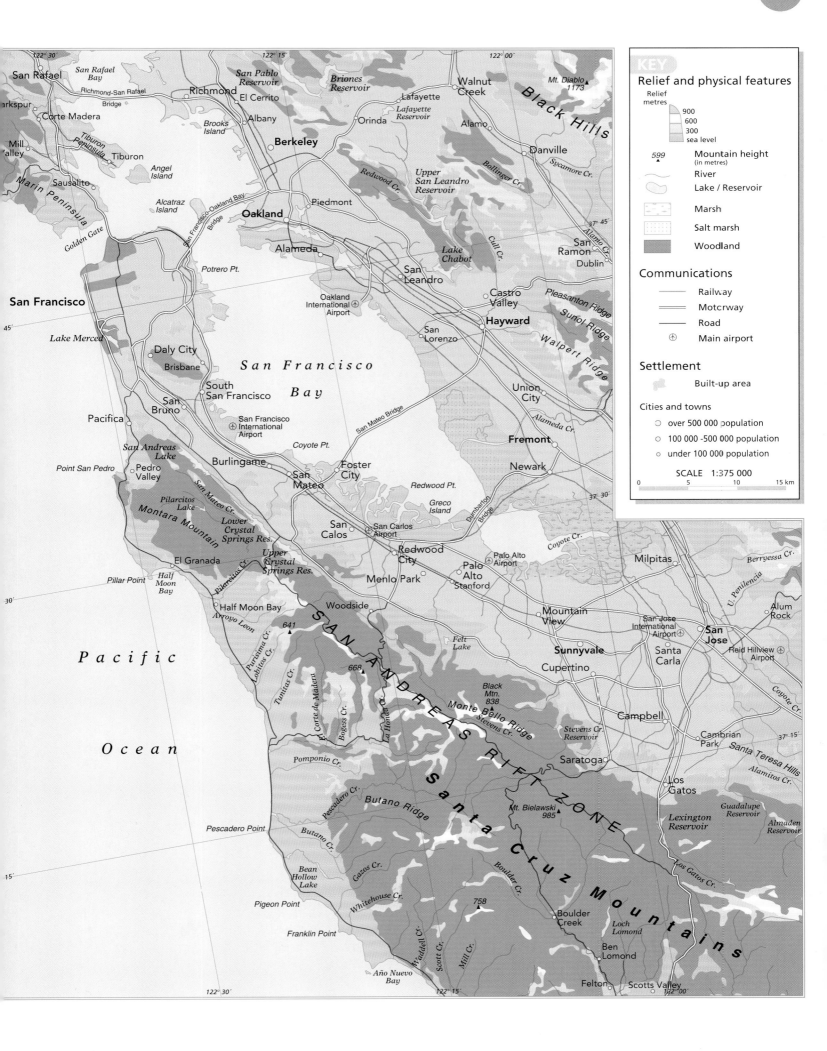

KEY

Relief and physical features

Relief
metres

900
600
300
sea level

599 ▲ Mountain height (in metres)

River

Lake / Reservoir

Marsh

Salt marsh

Woodland

Communications

Railway

Motcrway

Road

⊕ Main airport

Settlement

Built-up area

Cities and towns

◯ over 500 000 population

○ 100 000 -500 000 population

○ under 100 000 population

SCALE 1:375 000

0   5   10   15 km

San Rafael
San Rafael Bay
arkspur
Corte Madera
Mill Valley
Tiburon Peninsula
Tiburon
Sausalito
Marin Peninsula
Golden Gate
San Francisco
Lake Merced
Daly City
Brisbane
San Bruno
Pacifica
Point San Pedro
San Andreas Lake
Pedro Valley
Pilarcitos Lake
Montara Mountain
El Granada
Half Moon Bay
Pillar Point
Half Moon Bay
Arroyo Leon
Lower Crystal Springs Res.
Upper Crystal Springs Res.

Richmond-San Rafael Bridge
Richmond
El Cerrito
Albany
Brooks Island
Berkeley
Angel Island
Alcatraz Island
San Francisco-Oakland Bay Bridge
Oakland
Alameda
Potrero Pt.
San Francisco Bay
South San Francisco
San Francisco International Airport
Burlingame
San Mateo
Coyote Pt.
Foster City
Redwood Pt.
Greco Island
San Calos
San Carlos Airport
Redwood City
Menlo Park

San Pablo Reservoir
Briones Reservoir
Lafayette
Lafayette Reservoir
Orinda
Piedmont
Redwood Cr.
Upper San Leandro Reservoir
Lake Chabot
San Leandro
Oakland International Airport
San Lorenzo
San Mateo Bridge
Walnut Creek
Alamo
Danville
Sycamore Cr.
Bollinger Cr.
Cull Cr.
Castro Valley
Hayward
Union City
Alameda Cr.
Fremont
Newark
Dumbarton Bridge
Palo Alto Airport
Palo Alto
Stanford

Black Hills
Mt. Diablo 1173 ▲
San Ramon
Dublin
Pleasanton Ridge
Sunol Ridge
Walpert Ridge
Coyote Cr.
Milpitas
Berryessa Cr.
U. Penitencia
Alum Rock

Pacific Ocean

641 ▲
668 ▲
Purisima Cr.
Lobitos Cr.
Tunitas Cr.
El Corte de Madera
Bogess Cr.
La Honda
Woodside
Felt Lake
Mountain View
Sunnyvale
Cupertino
San Jose International Airport
San Jose
Santa Carla
Reid Hillview Airport
Campbell
Cambrian Park
Santa Teresa Hills
Alamitos Cr.

SAN ANDREAS RIFT ZONE
Black Mtn. 838
Monte Bello Ridge
Stevens Cr.
Stevens Cr. Reservoir
Saratoga
Los Gatos
Lexington Reservoir
Guadalupe Reservoir
Almaden Reservoir

Pomponio Cr.
Pescadero Cr.
Butano Ridge
Mt. Bielawski 985 ▲
Santa Cruz Mountains
Pescadero Point
Butano Cr.
Bean Hollow Lake
Gazos Cr.
Whitehouse Cr.
Pigeon Point
758 ▲
Boulder Cr.
Los Gatos Cr.
Boulder Creek
Loch Lomond
Ben Lomond
Franklin Point
Waddell Cr.
Scott Cr.
Mill Cr.
Año Nuevo Bay
Felton
Scotts Valley

122° 30'
122° 15'
122° 00'
45'
45'
37° 45'
30'
37° 30'
15'
37° 15'
122° 30'
122° 15'
122° 00'

UNITED STATES OF AMERICA

OKLAHOMA

TENNESS

TEXAS

MISSISSIPPI

ALABAM

LOUISIANA

ARKANSAS

ARIZONA

NEW MEXICO

CALIFORNIA

San Diego
Tijuana
Ensenada
Cerro. de la Encantada ▲3096
San Felipe
Mexicali
Glendale
Phoenix
Tucson
Nogales
Lordsburg
Las Cruces
El Paso
Ciudad Juárez

BAJA CALIFORNIA NORTE

BAJA CALIFORNIA SUR

Gulf of California (Lower California)

Angel de la Guarda
Sta Rosalía
Sebastián Vizcaíno B.
Sa Vizcaína
B. Magdalena
La Paz
C. San Lucas
I. Marías

Tropic of Cancer

PACIFIC OCEAN

I. San Benedicto
I. Socorro
Revillagigedo Is (Mexico)

MEXICO

Mexican States numbered on map
1. AGUASCALIENTES
2. DISTRITO FEDERAL
3. TLAXCALA

GULF OF MEXICO

Campeche Bay

YUCATÁN

QUINTANA ROO

CAMPECHE

BELIZE

BELMOPAN

Gulf of Honduras

GUATEMALA

GUATEMALA CITY

HON

TEGUCIGAL

SAN SALVADOR
EL SALVADOR

MANAGU

KEY

Relief and physical features

Relief metres
5000
3000
2000
1000
500
200
sea level
under sea level
0
200
4000
6000

5775 ▲ Mountain height (in metres)

Water features

~~~ River
~~~ Intermittent river
⬯ Lake / Reservoir
⬯ Intermittent lake
⬯ Marsh

Communications

— Railway
— Road
⊕ Main airport

Administration

Boundaries
——— International
——— Internal

Settlement

Cities and towns in order of size

National capital
■ **HAVANA**
□ BELMOPAN
□ CASTRIES

Other city or town
● **Puebla**
○ El Paso
○ Acapulco
○ Guanajuato

SCALE 1 : 13 000 000

0   200   400   600   800 km

Lambert Azimuthal Equal Area projection

Yucatan Channel
Bahamas
Cuba
Greater Antilles
Yucatán
Hispaniola
Puerto Rico
Jamaica
Leeward Is
Sierra Madre
G. of Honduras
CARIBBEAN SEA
Lesser Antilles
Windward Is

ATLANTIC
OCEAN

L. Nicaragua
Gallinas Pt.
Curaçao
Trinidad

G. of Darien
L. Maracaibo
Llanos
Orinoco

I. de Coco
Cordillera Occidental
Cordillera Central
Meta
2810 Mt Roraima
Guiana Highlands
Essequibo

I. de Malpelo
Caquetá

Amazon Delta
Equator

Cotopaxi 5896
6310 Chimborazo
Japurá
Amazon
Negro
Amazon
Fernando de Noronha

G. of Guayaquil
Marañón
Juruá
Purús
Madeira
Tapajós
Xingu
Tocantins
Parnaíba
C. de São Roque

Pta Negra
Selvas

Galapagos Islands

6768 Huascarán

A N D E S

Planalto do Mato Grosso
Araguaia
Brazilian

PACIFIC

L. Titicaca
Altiplano
L. Poopó
Highlands
São Francisco

OCEAN

Atacama Desert
Gran Chaco
Paraguay
Paraná
2797 Agulhas Negras
Trindade Martin Vaz Is
Tropic of Capricorn

6908 Ojos del Salado
Paraná
Uruguay

6960 Aconcagua

ATLANTIC
OCEAN

Pampas
Paraná
Rio de la Plata

Golfo San Matías

Isla de Chiloé
Patagonia

Bahía Grande
Str. of Magellan
Falkland Islands

Tierra del Fuego
Cape Horn
South Georgia

South Sandwich Is

Inset map (lower left):

VENEZUELA
COLOMBIA
GUYANA
SURINAME
FR. GUIANA
ECUADOR
Equator
PERU
BRAZIL
BOLIVIA
PARAGUAY
Tropic of Capricorn
CHILE
ARGENTINA
URUGUAY

SCALE 1 : 80 000 000

Relief legend:

Relief
Relief metres
5000
3000
2000
1000
500
200
0 sea level
200 under sea level
3000
5000

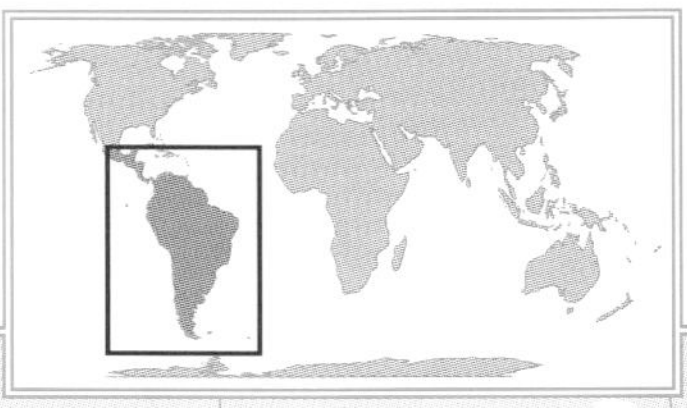

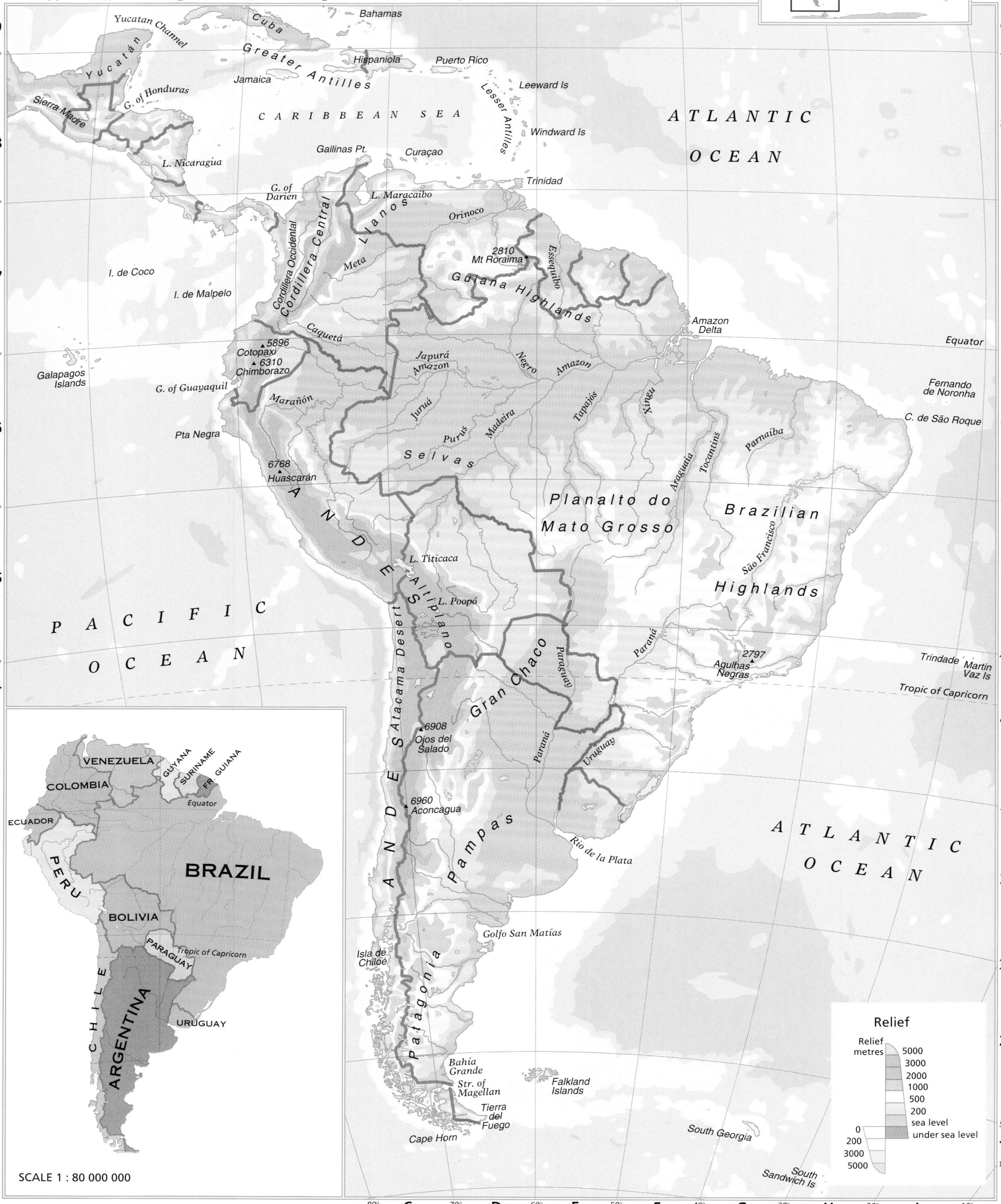

SCALE 1 : 35 000 000

Lambert Azimuthal Equal Area projection

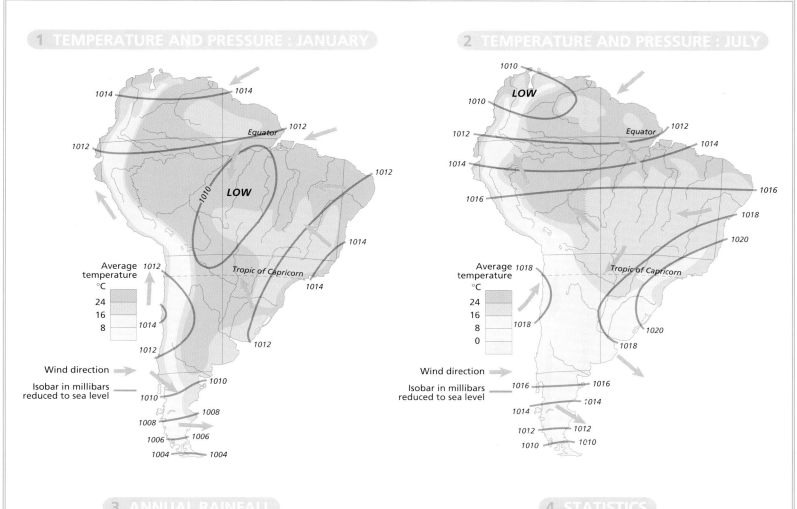

1 TEMPERATURE AND PRESSURE : JANUARY

1014
1014
1012
Equator
1012
1012
1010
LOW
1012
1014
Average temperature °C
24
16
8
1014
Tropic of Capricorn
1014
1012
1012
Wind direction
Isobar in millibars reduced to sea level
1010
1010
1008
1008
1006
1006
1004
1004

2 TEMPERATURE AND PRESSURE : JULY

1010
1010
LOW
1012
Equator
1012
1014
1014
1016
1016
1018
1020
Average temperature °C
24
16
8
0
1018
Tropic of Capricorn
1018
1020
1018
Wind direction
Isobar in millibars reduced to sea level
1016
1016
1014
1014
1012
1012
1010
1010

3 ANNUAL RAINFALL

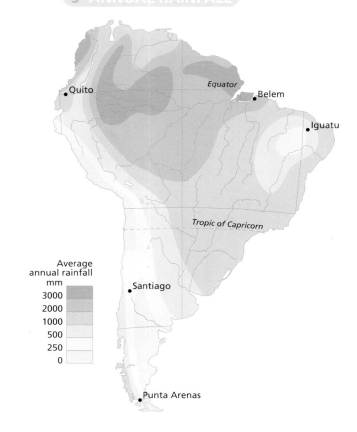

Quito
Equator
Belem
Iguatu
Tropic of Capricorn
Average annual rainfall mm
3000
2000
1000
500
250
0
Santiago
Punta Arenas

4 STATISTICS

Quito (2879 metres)	Jan	Feb	Mar	Apr	May	Jun	Jul	Aug	Sep	Oct	Nov	Dec
Temperature - max. (°C)	22	22	22	21	21	22	22	23	23	22	22	22
Temperature - min. (°C)	8	8	8	8	8	7	7	7	7	8	7	8
Rainfall - (mm)	99	112	142	175	137	43	20	31	69	112	97	79

Belem (13 metres)	Jan	Feb	Mar	Apr	May	Jun	Jul	Aug	Sep	Oct	Nov	Dec
Temperature - max. (°C)	31	30	31	31	31	31	31	31	32	32	32	32
Temperature - min. (°C)	22	22	23	23	23	22	22	22	22	22	22	22
Rainfall - (mm)	318	358	358	320	259	170	150	112	89	84	66	155

Iguatu (209 metres)	Jan	Feb	Mar	Apr	May	Jun	Jul	Aug	Sep	Oct	Nov	Dec
Temperature - max. (°C)	34	33	32	31	31	31	32	32	35	36	36	36
Temperature - min. (°C)	23	23	23	23	22	22	21	22	22	23	23	23
Rainfall - (mm)	89	173	185	160	61	61	36	5	18	18	10	33

Santiago (520 metres)	Jan	Feb	Mar	Apr	May	Jun	Jul	Aug	Sep	Oct	Nov	Dec
Temperature - max. (°C)	29	29	27	23	18	14	15	17	19	22	26	28
Temperature - min. (°C)	12	11	9	7	5	3	3	4	6	7	9	11
Rainfall - (mm)	3	3	5	13	64	84	76	56	31	15	8	5

Punta Arenas (8 metres)	Jan	Feb	Mar	Apr	May	Jun	Jul	Aug	Sep	Oct	Nov	Dec
Temperature - max. (°C)	14	14	12	10	7	5	4	6	8	11	12	14
Temperature - min. (°C)	7	7	5	4	2	1	-1	1	2	3	4	6
Rainfall - (mm)	38	23	33	36	33	41	28	31	23	28	18	36

SCALE 1 : 70 000 000

0   1000   2000   3000 km

Lambert Azimuthal Equal Area projection

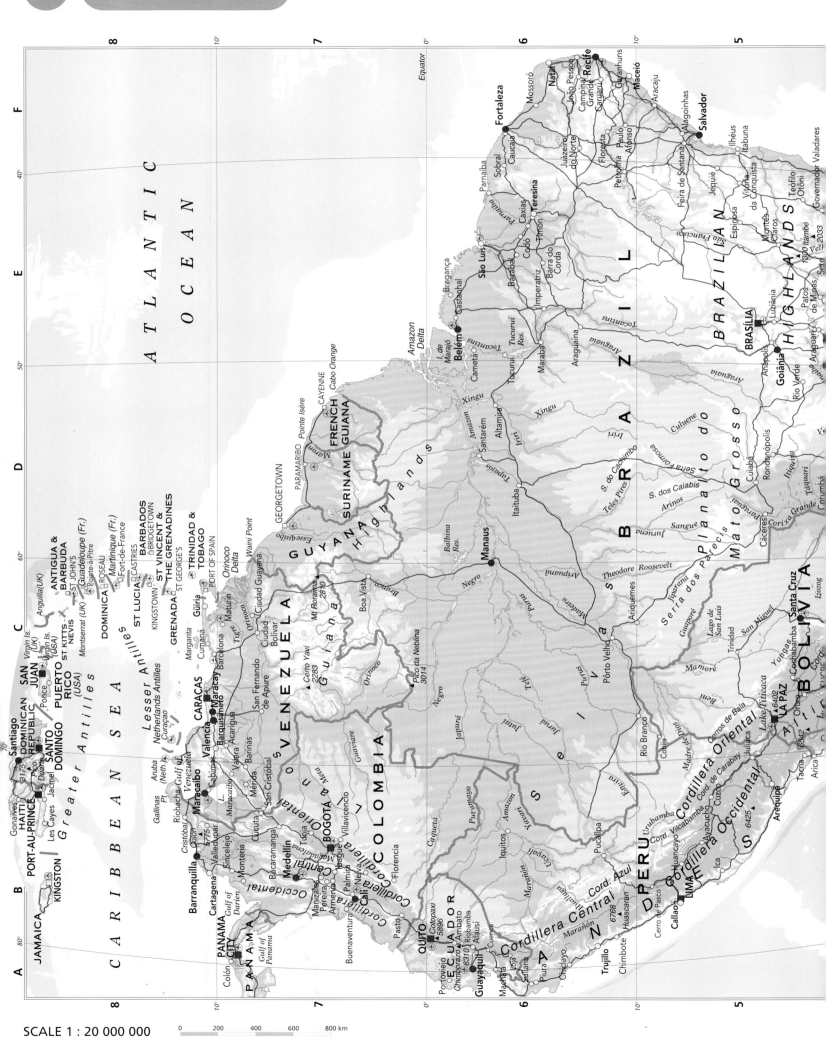

SCALE 1 : 20 000 000

0   200   400   600   800 km

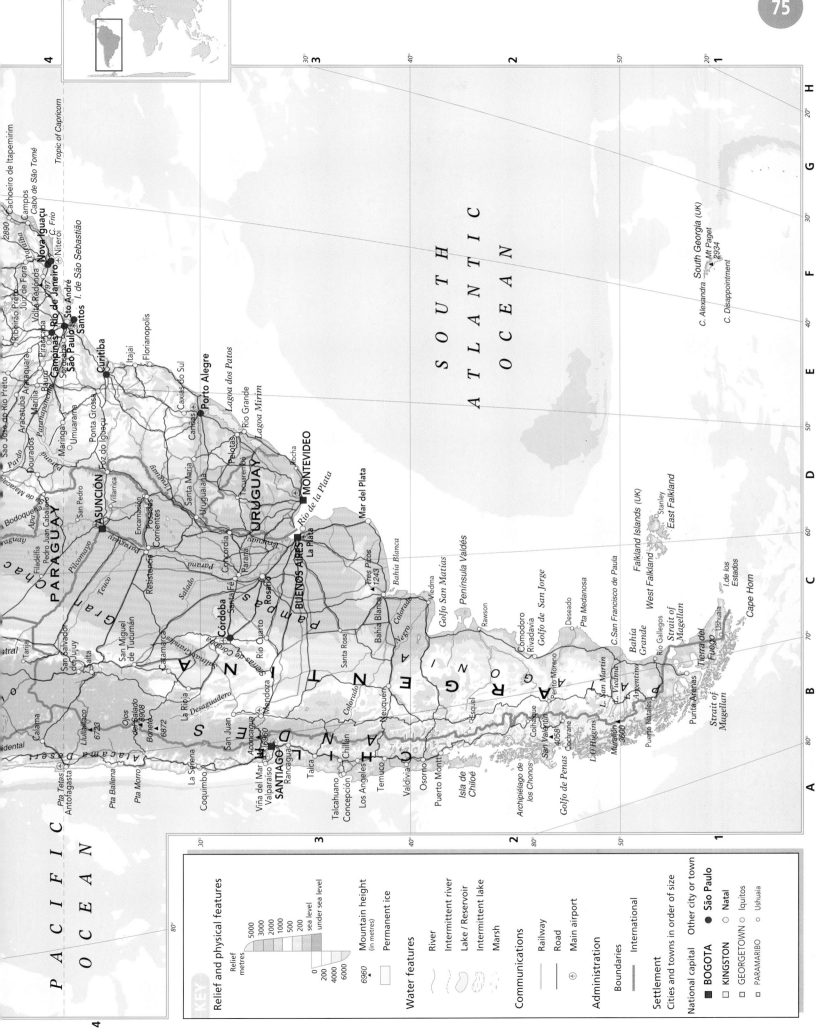

Sinusoidal projection

KEY

Relief and physical features

Relief
metres
5000
3000
2000
1000
500
200
sea level
under sea level
0
200
4000
6000

6960 ▲ **Mountain height**
(in metres)

Permanent ice

Water features

River

Intermittent river

Lake / Reservoir

Intermittent lake

Marsh

Communications

Railway

Road

⊕ Main airport

Administration

Boundaries

International

Settlement

Cities and towns in order of size

National capital   Other city or town

■ **BOGOTA**   ● **São Paulo**

□ **KINGSTON**   ○ Natal

□ GEORGETOWN   ○ Iquitos

□ PARAMARIBO   ○ Ushuaia

PACIFIC OCEAN

SOUTH ATLANTIC OCEAN

Tropic of Capricorn

ARGENTINA

CHILE

PARAGUAY

URUGUAY

ASUNCIÓN

MONTEVIDEO

BUENOS AIRES

SANTIAGO

Córdoba

Rosario

Santa Fé

Mar del Plata

La Plata

São Paulo

Rio de Janeiro

Curitiba

Porto Alegre

Campinas

Santos

Sto André

Niterói

Nova Iguaçu

Volta Redonda

Ribeirão Preto

Juiz de Fora

Cabo de São Tomé

C. Frio

I. de São Sebastião

Florianópolis

Itajaí

Ponta Grossa

Foz do Iguaçu

Caxias do Sul

Canoas

Pelotas

Rio Grande

Lagoa dos Patos

Lagoa Mirim

Rocha

Rio de la Plata

Tres Picos 1243

Bahía Blanca

Bahia Blanca

Colorado

Negro

Neuquén

Santa Rosa

Río Cuarto

Mendoza

San Juan

La Rioja

Desaguadero

Catamarca

San Miguel de Tucumán

Salta

San Salvador de Jujuy

Sierras de Córdoba

Aconcagua 6960

Ojos del Salado 6908

Bonete 6872

Llullaillaco 6723

Calama

Antofagasta

Pta Tetas

Pta Ballena

Pta Morro

Coquimbo

La Serena

Viña del Mar

Valparaíso

Rancagua

Talca

Chillán

Concepción

Talcahuano

Los Angeles

Temuco

Valdivia

Osorno

Puerto Montt

Isla de Chiloé

Golfo de Penas

Archipiélago de los Chonos

Coihaique

San Valentín 4058

Cochrane

Puerto Natales

Muralón 3600

L. O'Higgins

L. San Martín

L. Viedma

L. Argentina

Esquel

Cesque

Rawson

Comodoro Rivadavia

Golfo de San Jorge

Deseado

Pta Medanosa

C. San Francisco de Paula

Bahía Grande

Río Gallegos

Punta Arenas

Strait of Magellan

Tierra del Fuego

Ushuaia

I. de los Estados

Cape Horn

Falkland Islands (UK)

West Falkland

East Falkland

Stanley

South Georgia (UK)

Mt Paget 2934

C. Alexandra

C. Disappointment

Golfo San Matías

Península Valdés

Viedma

Perito Moreno

Florianópolis

Santa Maria

Uruguaiana

Villarrica

Encarnación

Posadas

Corrientes

Resistencia

Concordia

Paraná

Paraguay

Pilcomayo

Teuco

Salado

San Pedro

Pedro Juan Caballero

Filadélfia

Bodoquena

Paraguay

Apa

Ñeembucú

GRAN CHACO

Paraná

Uruguay

Ibicuí

Ivinheima

Paranapanema

Pardo

Dourados

Maringá

Umuarama

Bauru

Marília

Araçatuba

Araraquara

São José do Rio Preto

Piracicaba

Sorocaba

Campos

Cachoeiro de Itapemirim

2890

797

Paraíba

Paranapanema

Los Andes

Chiquimula

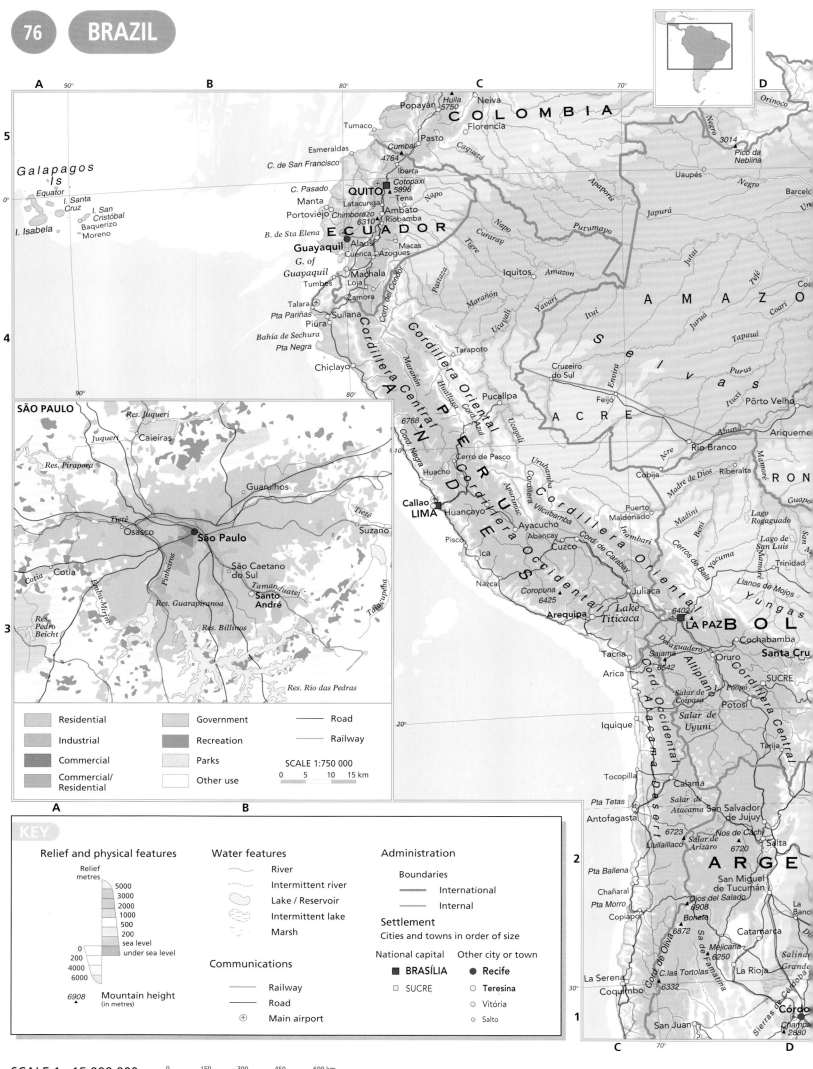

SÃO PAULO

Residential	Government	—— Road
Industrial	Recreation	—— Railway
Commercial	Parks	
Commercial/Residential	Other use	

SCALE 1:750 000

0   5   10   15 km

KEY

Relief and physical features

Relief metres
5000
3000
2000
1000
500
200
sea level
under sea level
0
200
4000
6000

▲ 6908   Mountain height (in metres)

Water features

River
Intermittent river
Lake / Reservoir
Intermittent lake
Marsh

Communications

—— Railway
—— Road
⊕ Main airport

Administration

Boundaries
International
Internal

Settlement
Cities and towns in order of size

National capital
■ BRASÍLIA
□ SUCRE

Other city or town
● Recife
◉ Teresina
○ Vitória
○ Salto

SCALE 1 : 15 000 000

0   150   300   450   600 km

Lambert Azimuthal Equal Area projection

1 POPULATION DENSITY

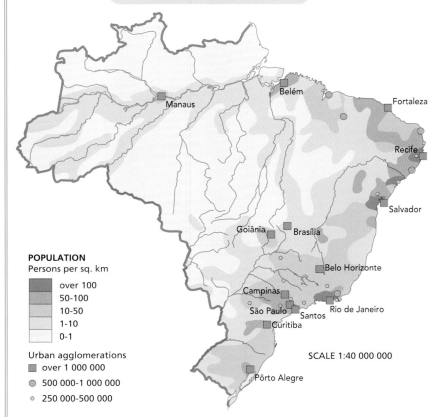

POPULATION
Persons per sq. km

- over 100
- 50-100
- 10-50
- 1-10
- 0-1

Urban agglomerations
- over 1 000 000
- 500 000-1 000 000
- 250 000-500 000

SCALE 1:40 000 000

3 MAIN URBAN AGGLOMERATIONS

Urban agglomeration	1980	1995	% change
São Paulo	12 497 000	16 417 000	31.4
Rio de Janeiro	8 741 000	9 888 000	13.1
Belo Horizonte	2 588 000	3 899 000	50.7
Pôrto Alegre	2 273 000	3 349 000	47.3
Recife	2 337 000	3 168 000	35.6
Salvador	1 754 000	2 819 000	60.7
Fortaleza	1 569 000	2 660 000	69.5
Curitiba	1 427 000	2 270 000	59.1
Brasília	1 162 000	1 778 000	53.0
Belém	992 000	1 574 000	58.7

4 POPULATION GROWTH

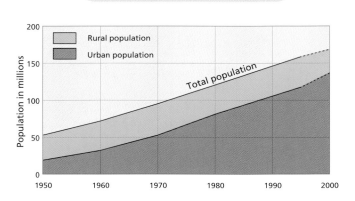

Rural population
Urban population

Total population

Population in millions

1950   1960   1970   1980   1990   2000

2 POPULATION CHANGE

POPULATION CHANGE
1980 - 1995

%
- over 200
- 100-200
- 50-100
- 30-50
- 20-30
- 0-20

SCALE 1:40 000 000

5 MIGRATION

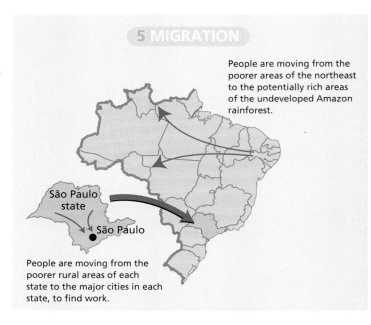

People are moving from the poorer areas of the northeast to the potentially rich areas of the undeveloped Amazon rainforest.

São Paulo state

São Paulo

People are moving from the poorer rural areas of each state to the major cities in each state, to find work.

6 REGIONAL COMPARISONS

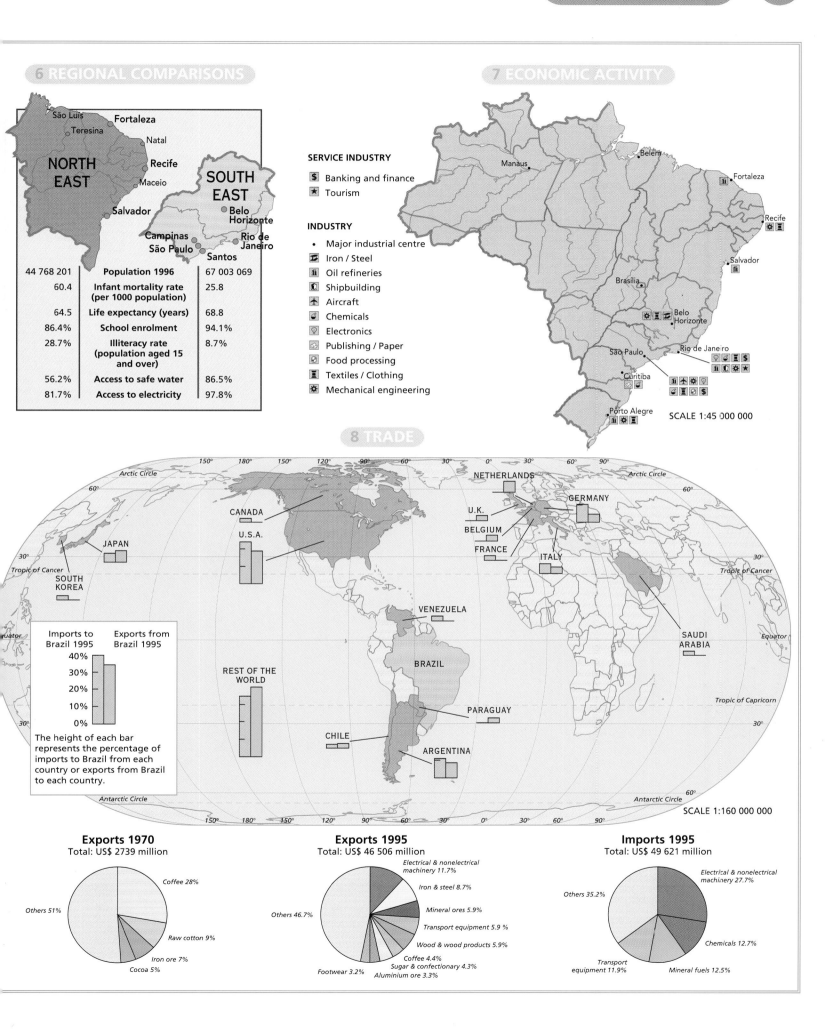

NORTH EAST

São Luís
Teresina
Fortaleza
Natal
Recife
Maceio
Salvador

SOUTH EAST

Belo Horizonte
Campinas
São Paulo
Rio de Janeiro
Santos

NORTH EAST		SOUTH EAST
44 768 201	**Population 1996**	67 003 069
60.4	**Infant mortality rate (per 1000 population)**	25.8
64.5	**Life expectancy (years)**	68.8
86.4%	**School enrolment**	94.1%
28.7%	**Illiteracy rate (population aged 15 and over)**	8.7%
56.2%	**Access to safe water**	86.5%
81.7%	**Access to electricity**	97.8%

7 ECONOMIC ACTIVITY

SERVICE INDUSTRY

- $ Banking and finance
- ★ Tourism

INDUSTRY

- • Major industrial centre
- Iron / Steel
- Oil refineries
- Shipbuilding
- ✈ Aircraft
- Chemicals
- Electronics
- Publishing / Paper
- Food processing
- Textiles / Clothing
- ✳ Mechanical engineering

Manaus
Belém
Fortaleza
Recife
Salvador
Brasilia
Belo Horizonte
São Paulo
Rio de Janeiro
Curitiba
Porto Alegre

SCALE 1:45 000 000

8 TRADE

Arctic Circle
NETHERLANDS
GERMANY
U.K.
BELGIUM
FRANCE
ITALY
CANADA
U.S.A.
JAPAN
SOUTH KOREA
Tropic of Cancer
VENEZUELA
SAUDI ARABIA
REST OF THE WORLD
BRAZIL
PARAGUAY
CHILE
ARGENTINA
Equator
Tropic of Capricorn
Antarctic Circle

Imports to Brazil 1995 **Exports from Brazil 1995**

40%
30%
20%
10%
0%

The height of each bar represents the percentage of imports to Brazil from each country or exports from Brazil to each country.

SCALE 1:160 000 000

Exports 1970
Total: US$ 2739 million

- Coffee 28%
- Others 51%
- Raw cotton 9%
- Iron ore 7%
- Cocoa 5%

Exports 1995
Total: US$ 46 506 million

- Electrical & nonelectrical machinery 11.7%
- Iron & steel 8.7%
- Mineral ores 5.9%
- Transport equipment 5.9 %
- Wood & wood products 5.9%
- Coffee 4.4%
- Sugar & confectionary 4.3%
- Aluminium ore 3.3%
- Footwear 3.2%
- Others 46.7%

Imports 1995
Total: US$ 49 621 million

- Electrical & nonelectrical machinery 27.7%
- Chemicals 12.7%
- Mineral fuels 12.5%
- Transport equipment 11.9%
- Others 35.2%

Forest
Dense forest covers much of this area and the courses of the many tributaries of the river Guaporé can be followed cutting through the forest areas.

Marshy Savanna
An area of marshy savanna lies between the forest and the river Guaporé. Similar areas can also be seen south of the river around Laguna Bella Vista.

Deforested Areas
Large rectangular areas of pale blue on the satellite image are areas of deforestation, probably from commercial logging. In the bottom right of the image the pale blue line patterns are systematic deforestation due to the practice of slash and burn farming.

Highland
The highland of the Serra dos Parecis can be seen at the top right of the image.

Lakes
Several small dark blue/black outlines of lakes can be seen along the course of the river Guaporé. Laguna Bella Vista stands out clearly as a much larger feature.

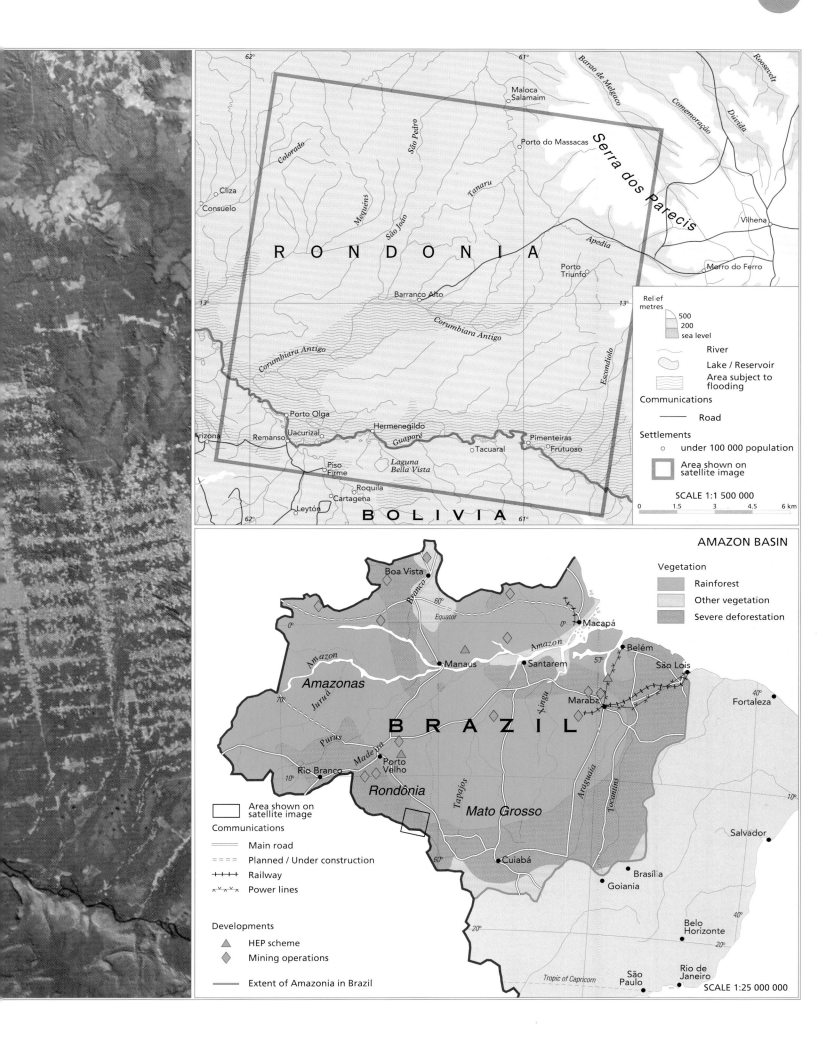

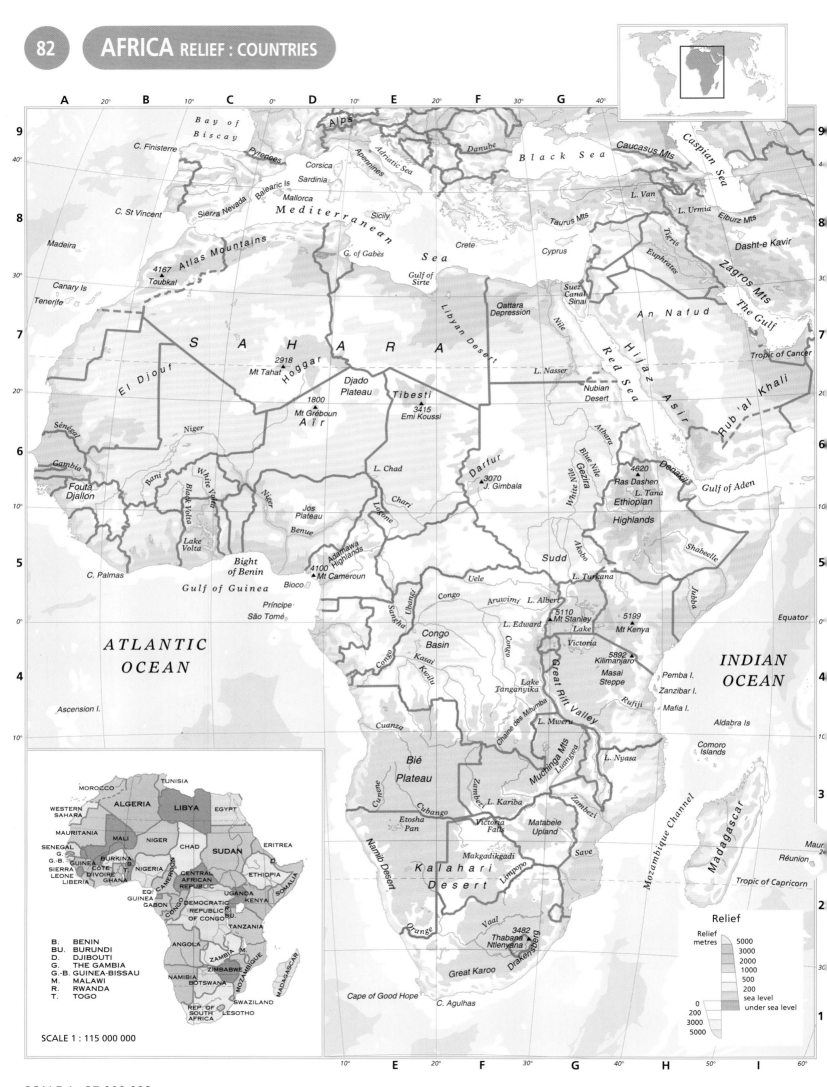

A B C D E F G

20° 10° 0° 10° 20° 30° 40°

9 *Bay of Biscay* Alps *Black Sea* Caucasus Mts *Caspian Sea* 9

C. Finisterre Pyrenees Danube

40° Corsica *Adriatic Sea* L. Van

C. St Vincent Sierra Nevada Balearic Is *Mediterranean* Sicily Taurus Mts L. Urmia Elburz Mts 8

Madeira Mallorca Sardinia Crete Cyprus Tigris Euphrates Dasht-e Kavir Zagros Mts

30° *Atlas Mountains* G. of Gabès *Sea* Qattara Depression Suez Canal An Nafud The Gulf

4167 ▲ Toubkal

Canary Is *Libyan Desert* Sinai Hijaz Asir Rub' al Khali

Tenerife 7 S A H A R A Nile L. Nasser *Red Sea* Tropic of Cancer 7

20° El Djouf 2918 ▲ Mt Tahat Hoggar Djado Plateau Tibesti Nubian Desert 20°

Niger 1800 ▲ Mt Gréboun Aïr 3415 ▲ Emi Koussi

Sénégal 6 Bani *White Volta* Niger L. Chad Darfur Athara Blue Nile Gezira 4620 ▲ Ras Dashen Denakil Gulf of Aden 6

Gambia Chari ▲3070 J. Gimbala White Nile L. Tana Ethiopian

10° Fouta Djallon *Black Volta* Logone Jos Plateau Benue Highlands

C. Palmas Lake Volta Adamawa Highlands Sudd Akobo Shabeelle

5 *Bight of Benin* 4100 ▲ Mt Cameroun Uele L. Turkana Jubba 5

Gulf of Guinea Bioco Congo Aruwimi L. Albert 5110 ▲ Mt Stanley 5199 ▲ Mt Kenya

Príncipe Sangha Ubangi L. Edward Lake

São Tomé Congo Basin Victoria 5892 ▲ Kilimanjaro Pemba I. *INDIAN OCEAN*

0° *ATLANTIC OCEAN* Kasai Congo Masai Steppe Zanzibar I. Equator 0°

4 Kwilu Lake Tanganyika Great Rift Valley Rufiji Mafia I. 4

Ascension I. Cuanza Chaine des Mitumba L. Mweru Aldabra Is

10° Comoro Islands

Cunene Bié Plateau Muchinga Mts Luangwa L. Nyasa

3 Cubango Zambezi L. Kariba Zambezi *Mozambique Channel* Madagascar Maur. 3

Etosha Pan Victoria Falls Matabele Upland Save Réunion

Namib Desert Makgadikgadi Tropic of Capricorn

2 *Kalahari Desert* Limpopo **Relief** 2

Orange Vaal Thabana ▲ 3482 Ntlenyana Drakensberg

Great Karoo

Cape of Good Hope C. Agulhas

10° E F G H I 50° 60°

SCALE 1 : 37 000 000

Lambert Azimuthal Equal Area projection

Inset map:

MOROCCO TUNISIA

WESTERN SAHARA ALGERIA LIBYA EGYPT

MAURITANIA MALI NIGER CHAD SUDAN ERITREA

SENEGAL BURKINA NIGERIA CENTRAL AFRICAN REPUBLIC ETHIOPIA

G. GUINEA CÔTE D'IVOIRE CAMEROON UGANDA SOMALIA

G.-B. SIERRA LEONE GHANA EQ. GUINEA DEMOCRATIC REPUBLIC OF CONGO KENYA

LIBERIA GABON CONGO R. BU. TANZANIA

ANGOLA ZAMBIA M.

NAMIBIA ZIMBABWE MOZAMBIQUE MADAGASCAR

BOTSWANA

SWAZILAND

REP. OF SOUTH AFRICA LESOTHO

B. BENIN
BU. BURUNDI
D. DJIBOUTI
G. THE GAMBIA
G.-B. GUINEA-BISSAU
M. MALAWI
R. RWANDA
T. TOGO

SCALE 1 : 115 000 000

Relief

Relief metres	
	5000
	3000
	2000
	1000
	500
	200
0	sea level
	under sea level

200
3000
5000

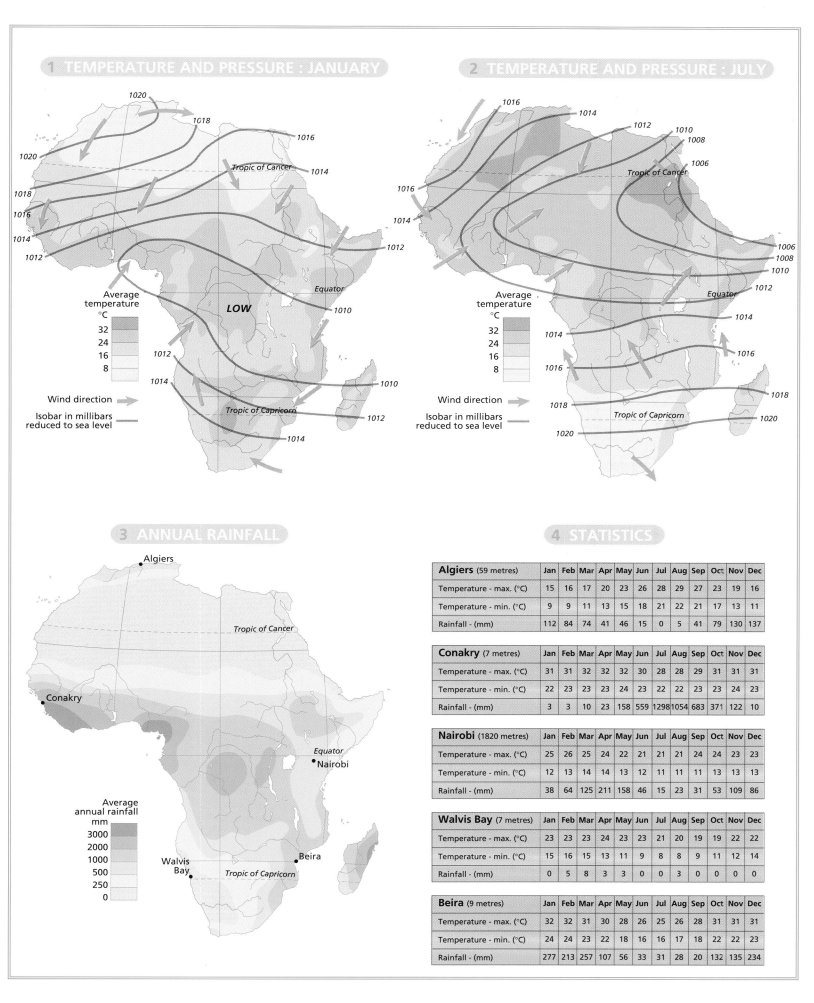

1 TEMPERATURE AND PRESSURE : JANUARY

1020
1018
1016
1020
Tropic of Cancer
1014
1018
1016
1014
1012
1012
Equator
1010
LOW
1012
1010
1014
Tropic of Capricorn
1012
1014

Average temperature °C
32
24
16
8

Wind direction

Isobar in millibars reduced to sea level

2 TEMPERATURE AND PRESSURE : JULY

1016
1014
1012
1010
1008
Tropic of Cancer
1006
1016
1014
1006
1008
1010
Equator
1012
1014
1014
1016
1016
1018
Tropic of Capricorn
1020
1018
1020

Average temperature °C
32
24
16
8

Wind direction

Isobar in millibars reduced to sea level

3 ANNUAL RAINFALL

Algiers

Tropic of Cancer

Conakry

Equator
Nairobi

Average annual rainfall mm
3000
2000
1000
500
250
0

Walvis Bay
Beira
Tropic of Capricorn

4 STATISTICS

Algiers (59 metres)	Jan	Feb	Mar	Apr	May	Jun	Jul	Aug	Sep	Oct	Nov	Dec
Temperature - max. (°C)	15	16	17	20	23	26	28	29	27	23	19	16
Temperature - min. (°C)	9	9	11	13	15	18	21	22	21	17	13	11
Rainfall - (mm)	112	84	74	41	46	15	0	5	41	79	130	137

Conakry (7 metres)	Jan	Feb	Mar	Apr	May	Jun	Jul	Aug	Sep	Oct	Nov	Dec
Temperature - max. (°C)	31	31	32	32	32	30	28	28	29	31	31	31
Temperature - min. (°C)	22	23	23	23	24	23	22	22	23	23	24	23
Rainfall - (mm)	3	3	10	23	158	559	1298	1054	683	371	122	10

Nairobi (1820 metres)	Jan	Feb	Mar	Apr	May	Jun	Jul	Aug	Sep	Oct	Nov	Dec
Temperature - max. (°C)	25	26	25	24	22	21	21	21	24	24	23	23
Temperature - min. (°C)	12	13	14	14	13	12	11	11	11	13	13	13
Rainfall - (mm)	38	64	125	211	158	46	15	23	31	53	109	86

Walvis Bay (7 metres)	Jan	Feb	Mar	Apr	May	Jun	Jul	Aug	Sep	Oct	Nov	Dec
Temperature - max. (°C)	23	23	23	24	23	23	21	20	19	19	22	22
Temperature - min. (°C)	15	16	15	13	11	9	8	8	9	11	12	14
Rainfall - (mm)	0	5	8	3	3	0	0	3	0	0	0	0

Beira (9 metres)	Jan	Feb	Mar	Apr	May	Jun	Jul	Aug	Sep	Oct	Nov	Dec
Temperature - max. (°C)	32	32	31	30	28	26	25	26	28	31	31	31
Temperature - min. (°C)	24	24	23	22	18	16	16	17	18	22	22	23
Rainfall - (mm)	277	213	257	107	56	33	31	28	20	132	135	234

SCALE 1 : 77 000 000

0   1000   2000   3000 km

Lambert Azimuthal Equal Area projection

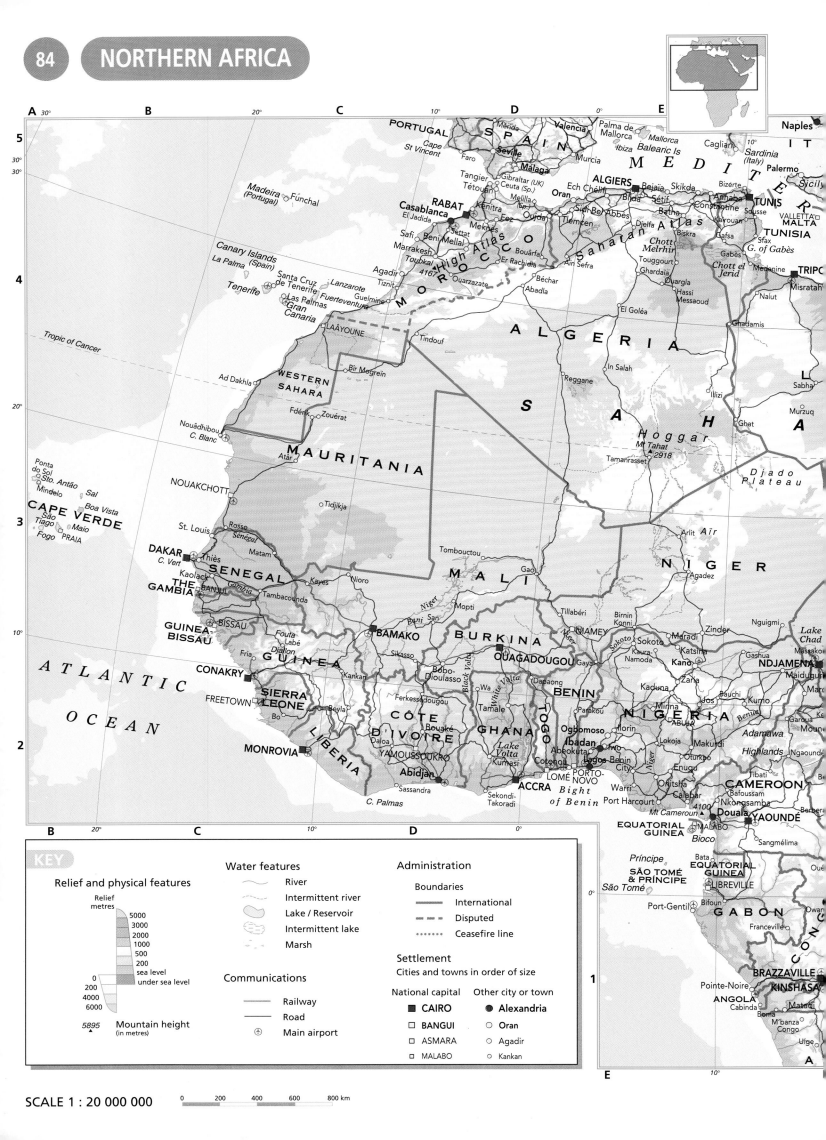

A 30° B 20° C 10° D 0° E

PORTUGAL — Cape St Vincent — Faro — Seville — Málaga — Murcia — Valencia — Palma de Mallorca — Ibiza — Balearic Is — Mallorca — Cagliari — Sardinia (Italy) — Palermo — **Naples** — **IT** — **MEDITER** — Sicily

SPAIN — Mérida

Madeira (Portugal) — Funchal

Tangier — Tétouan — Gibraltar (UK) — Ceuta (Sp.) — Melilla — **ALGIERS** — Bejaïa — Skikda — Bizerte — Annaba — **TUNIS** — VALLETTA — **MALTA** — **TUNISIA**

Canary Islands (Spain) — La Palma — Santa Cruz de Tenerife — Lanzarote — Fuerteventura — Las Palmas — Gran Canaria — Tenerife

RABAT — **Casablanca** — El Jadida — Kénitra — Settat — Meknes — Fez — Oujda — Tlemcen — Sidi Bel Abbès — Oran — Ech Chélif — Blida — Sétif — Batna — Constantine — Sousse — Kairouan — Sfax — G. of Gabès — Gabès — Medenine

Safi — Beni Mellal — Marrakesh — Toubkal — **M O R O C C O** — Bouârfa — Er Rachidia — Béchar — Abadla — El Goléa — Djelfa — Ghardaïa — Touggourt — Ouargla — Hassi Messaoud — Ghadamis — Nalut — **TRIPC** — Misratah — Sahra

Agadir — Tiznit — 4167 — Ouarzazate — Aïn Sefra — High Atlas — Saharan Atlas — Chott Melrhir — Chott el Jerid — Biskra — Gafsa

Tropic of Cancer

Ad Dakhla — **WESTERN SAHARA** — LAÂYOUNE — Tindouf — Bir Megreïn — **A L G E R I A** — Reggane — In Salah — Illizi — Ghadamis — Sabha — **L** — Murzuq — Ghat

Nouâdhibou — C. Blanc — Fdérik — Zouérat — **S A H A R A** — Hoggar — Mt Tahat 2918 — Tamanrasset — Djado Plateau

CAPE VERDE — Ponta do Sol — Sto. Antão — Sal — Mindelo — Boa Vista — São Tiago — Maio — **PRAIA** — Fogo

Atâr — **M A U R I T A N I A** — NOUAKCHOTT — Tidjikja — Tombouctou — Arlit — Aïr — Agadez — **N I G E R** — Nguigmi — Lake Chad

St. Louis — Rosso — Sénégal — Matam — Nioro — Gao — **M A L I** — Tillabéri — Birnin Konni — Zinder — Maradi — Katsina — Gashua — Maiduguri

DAKAR — C. Vert — Thiès — Kaolack — **SENEGAL** — Kayes — Niger — Mopti — Niamey — **NIAMEY** — Sokoto — Kano — Zinder — **NDJAMENA**

THE GAMBIA — BANJUL — Gambia — Tambacounda — Kaolack — San — Bani — **BURKINA** — **OUAGADOUGOU** — Gaya — Kaura Namoda — Sokoto — Kano — Maradi

GUINEA-BISSAU — BISSAU — Labé — Fouta Djallon — Fria — **GUINEA** — Sikasso — Bobo-Dioulasso — **NIGERIA** — **ABUJA** — Kaduna — Zaria — Jos — Bauchi — Kumo — Garoua

CONAKRY — Kankan — Ferkessédougou — Wa — Black Volta — White Volta — **BENIN** — Parakou — Minna — Ilorin — Lokoja — Makurdi — Adamawa Highlands — Ngaounde

FREETOWN — **SIERRA LEONE** — Bo — Beyla — Tamale — **GHANA** — Dapaong — **TOGO** — Ogbomoso — Oyo — Enugu — Onitsha — Calabar — Tibati — **CAMEROON**

A T L A N T I C   O C E A N — **LIBERIA** — **MONROVIA** — Daloa — **CÔTE D'IVOIRE** — Bouaké — **YAMOUSSOUKRO** — Lake Volta — Kumasi — Abeokuta — Ibadan — Lagos — Benin City — Warri — Port Harcourt — Mt Cameroon 4100 — **Douala** — **YAOUNDÉ** — Bafoussam — Nkongsamba — Berber

Sassandra — C. Palmas — Sekondi-Takoradi — **ACCRA** — Cotonou — **PORTO-NOVO** — LOMÉ — Bight of Benin — **EQUATORIAL GUINEA** — MALABO — Bioco — Sangmélima

Príncipe — **SÃO TOMÉ & PRÍNCIPE** — São Tomé — Bata — **EQUATORIAL GUINEA** — **LIBREVILLE** — **G A B O N** — Oué

Port-Gentil — Bifoun — Franceville — Owan

ANGOLA — **BRAZZAVILLE** — **KINSHASA** — Pointe-Noire — Cabinda — Boma — M'banza Congo — Matadi — Uíge

KEY

Relief and physical features

Relief metres	
5000	
3000	
2000	
1000	
500	
200	
0	sea level
	under sea level
200	
4000	
6000	

5895 ▲ Mountain height (in metres)

Water features

~~~ River
---- Intermittent river
Lake / Reservoir
Intermittent lake
Marsh

Communications

Railway
Road
⊕ Main airport

Administration

Boundaries

—— International
– – – Disputed
········· Ceasefire line

Settlement

Cities and towns in order of size

National capital

■ **CAIRO**
□ BANGUI
□ ASMARA
□ MALABO

Other city or town

● **Alexandria**
○ Oran
○ Agadir
○ Kankan

SCALE 1 : 20 000 000

0   200   400   600   800 km

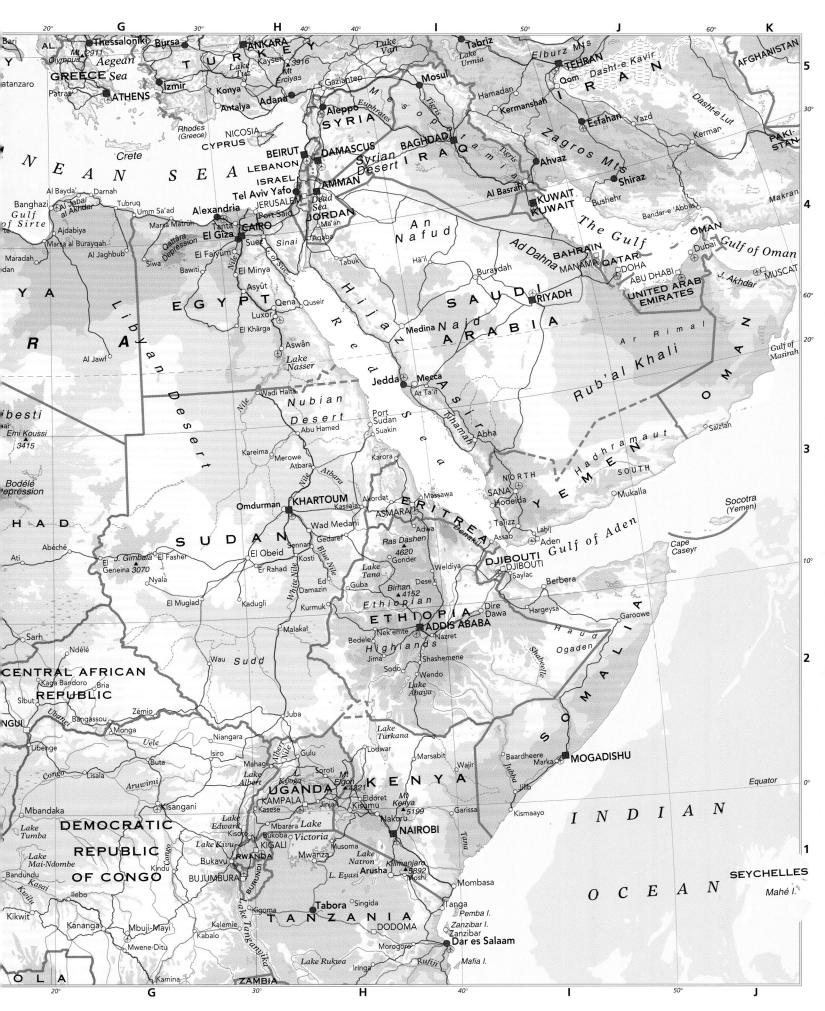

Millers Stereographic projection

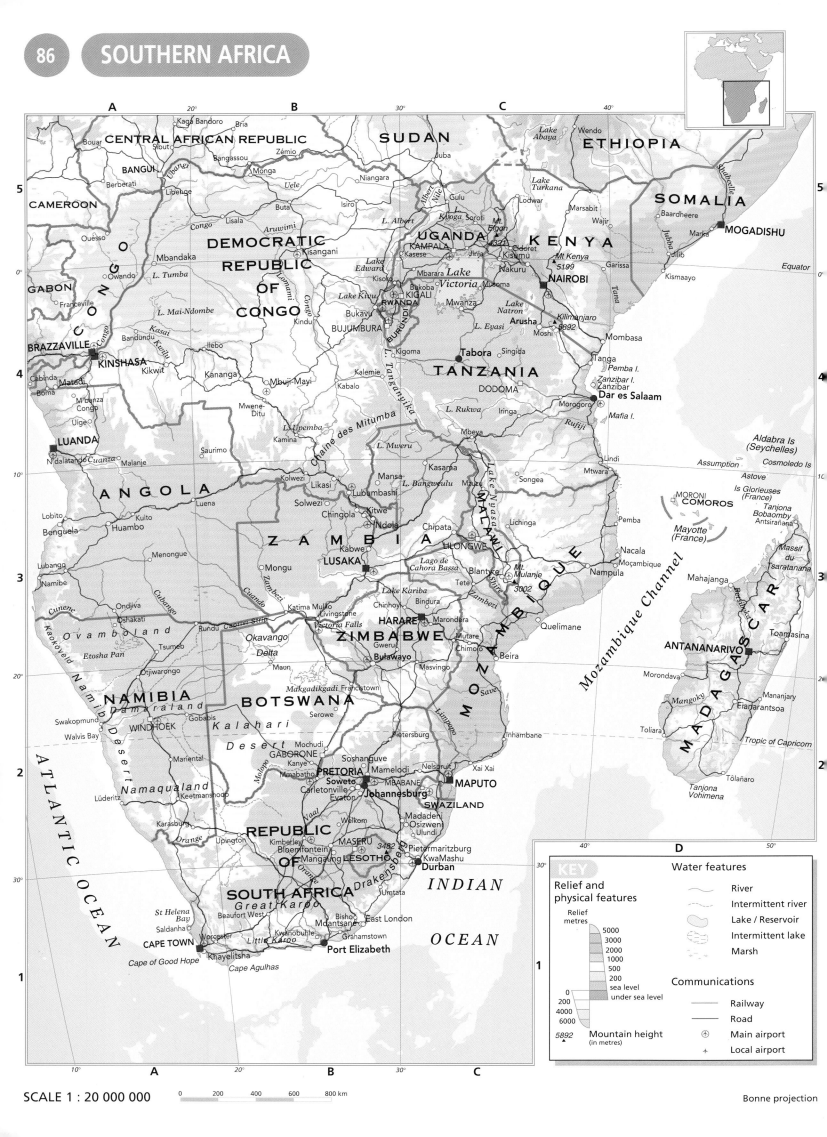

SCALE 1 : 20 000 000

0   200   400   600   800 km

Bonne projection

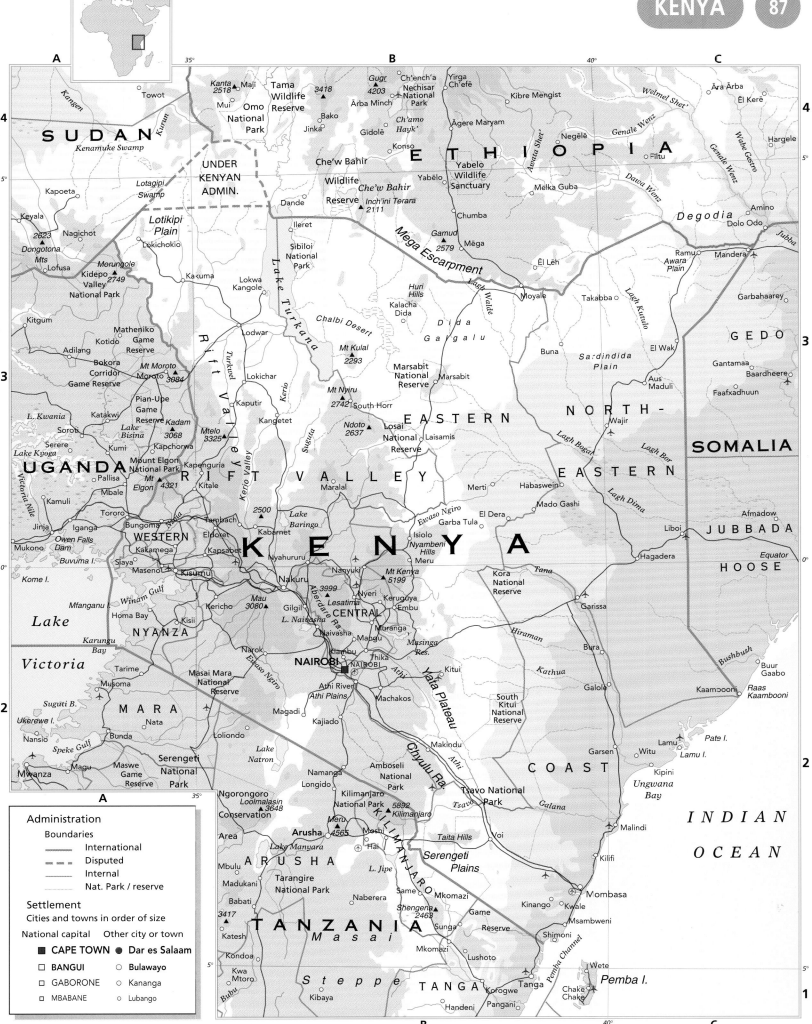

A

SUDAN

Towot
Kangen
Kurun
Kenamuke Swamp
Kapoeta
Keyala
2623
Dongotona
Mts
Lofusa
Nagichot
Lotagipi
Swamp
Lokichokio
Kitgum
Morungole
Kidepo
Valley
2749
National Park
Matheniko
Game
Reserve
Adilang
Kotido
Bokora
Corridor
Game Reserve
Mt Moroto
Moroto
3084
Pian-Upe
Game
Reserve
L. Kwania
Katakwi
Kadam
3068
Soroti
Serere
Lake
Bisina
Kapchorwa
Kumi
Mtelo
3325
Lake Kyoga
Mount Elgon
National Park

UGANDA
Pallisa
Mbale
Mt
Elgon 4321
Kitale
Kamuli
Tororo
Kapenguria
Victoria Nile
Jinja
Iganga
Bungoma
Tambach
Owen Falls
Dam
Kakamega
Eldoret
Kabarnet
2500
Buvuma I.
Mukono
WESTERN
Kapsabet
Siaya
Maseno
Nyahururu
Kome I.
Kisumu
Nakuru
Mfangano I.
Winam Gulf
Kericho
Mau
3080
Gilgil
Homa Bay
Kisii
L. Naivasha
Lake Victoria
NYANZA
Naivasha
Karungu
Bay
Narok
Tarime
Musoma
Masai Mara
National
Reserve
Magadi
Suguti B.
Ukerewe I.
Nansio
MARA
Nata
Loliondo
Speke Gulf
Bunda
Lake
Natron
Mwanza
Magu
Maswe
Game
Reserve
Serengeti
National
Park
Ngorongoro
Loolmalasin
3648
Conservation
Area
Mbulu
ARUSHA
Lake Manyara
Arusha
Madukani
Tarangire
National Park
Babati
3417
Katesh
TANZANIA
Kondoa
Masai
Kwa
Mtoro
Bubu
Steppe

35°

B

Kanta
2518
Maji
Mui
Omo
National
Park
Tama
Wildlife
Reserve
3418
Bako
Jinka
Gugr
4203
Ch'ench'a
Nechisar
National
Park
Arba Minch
Gidole
Che'w Bahir
Wildlife
Reserve
Dande
Inch'ini Terara
2111
Che'w Bahir
Ileret
Sibiloi
National
Park
Lake Turkana
Lokwa
Kangole
Lodwar
Turkwel
Lokichar
Kerio
Kaputir
Mt Nyiru
2742 South Horr
Kangetet
Suguta
Ndoto
2637
Losai
National
Reserve
RIFT VALLEY
Maralal
Kerio Valley
Kabarnet
Lake
Baringo
KENYA
Nanyuki
Mt Kenya
5199
Nyeri
3999
Aberdare Ra.
Lesatima
Keruguya
Embu
CENTRAL
Muranga
Mangu
Musinga
Res.
Thika
Kiambu
NAIROBI
NAIROBI
Athi
Athi River
Athi Plains
Machakos
Magadi
Kajiado
Yata Plateau
Kitui
Makindu
Namanga
Longido
Amboseli
National
Park
Kilimanjaro
National Park
5892
Chyulu Ra.
Meru
4565
Moshi
Hai
KILIMANJARO
Tsavo
Tsavo National
Park
Taita Hills
Same
Mkomazi
Voi
Serengeti
Plains
L. Jipe
Shengena
2463
Game
Reserve
Naberera
Sunga
Mkomazi
Lushoto
TANGA
Kibaya
Handeni
Korogwe
Pangani

B

ETHIOPIA

Yirga
Ch'efe
Kibre Mengist
Welmel Shet'
Ara Arba
El Kere
Hargele
Agere Maryam
Konso
Yabelo
Yabelo
Wildlife
Sanctuary
Chumba
Mega Escarpment
Gamud
2579
Mega
El Leh
Awata Shet'
Negele
Melka Guba
Genale Wenz
Wabe Gestro
Genale Wenz
Amino
Dolo Odo
Jubba
Degodia
Moyale
Ramu
Awara
Plain
Mandera
Lagh Walde
Takabba
Lagh Kutulo
Garbahaarey
Huri
Hills
Kalacha
Dida
Dida
Galgalu
Buna
El Wak
GEDO
Gantamaa
Baardheere
Aus
Maduli
Faafxadhuun
EASTERN
Marsabit
National
Reserve
Marsabit
Laisamis
Sardindida
Plain
NORTH-
EASTERN
SOMALIA
Wajir
Merti
Habaswein
Lagh Bogal
Lagh Bor
Afmadow
Ewaso Ngiro
El Dera
Garba Tula
Mado Gashi
Lagh Dima
Liboi
JUBBADA
Isiolo
Nyambeni
Hills
Meru
Hagadera
HOOSE
Kora
National
Reserve
Tana
Garissa
Hiraman
Bura
Bushbush
Buur
Gaabo
Kathua
Galole
Kaamooni
Raas
Kaambooni
South
Kitui
National Reserve
Equator
Lamu
Pate I.
Lamu I.
Garsen
Witu
Kipini
Ungwana
Bay
Galana
Malindi
INDIAN
OCEAN
Kilifi
Kinango
Kwale
Mombasa
Msambweni
Shimoni
Pemba Channel
Wete
Pemba I.
Chake
Chake

40°

C

Kibre Mengist

ETHIOPIA

Welmel Shet'

Ara Arba

El Kere

Hargele

Genale Wenz

Wabe Gestro

Amino

Dolo Odo

Jubba

Degodia

Mandera

Garbahaarey

GEDO

Gantamaa

Baardheere

Faafxadhuun

SOMALIA

Afmadow

JUBBADA

HOOSE

Buur
Gaabo

Raas
Kaambooni

SCALE 1 : 5 000 000

0   50   100   150   200 km

Oblated Stereographic projection

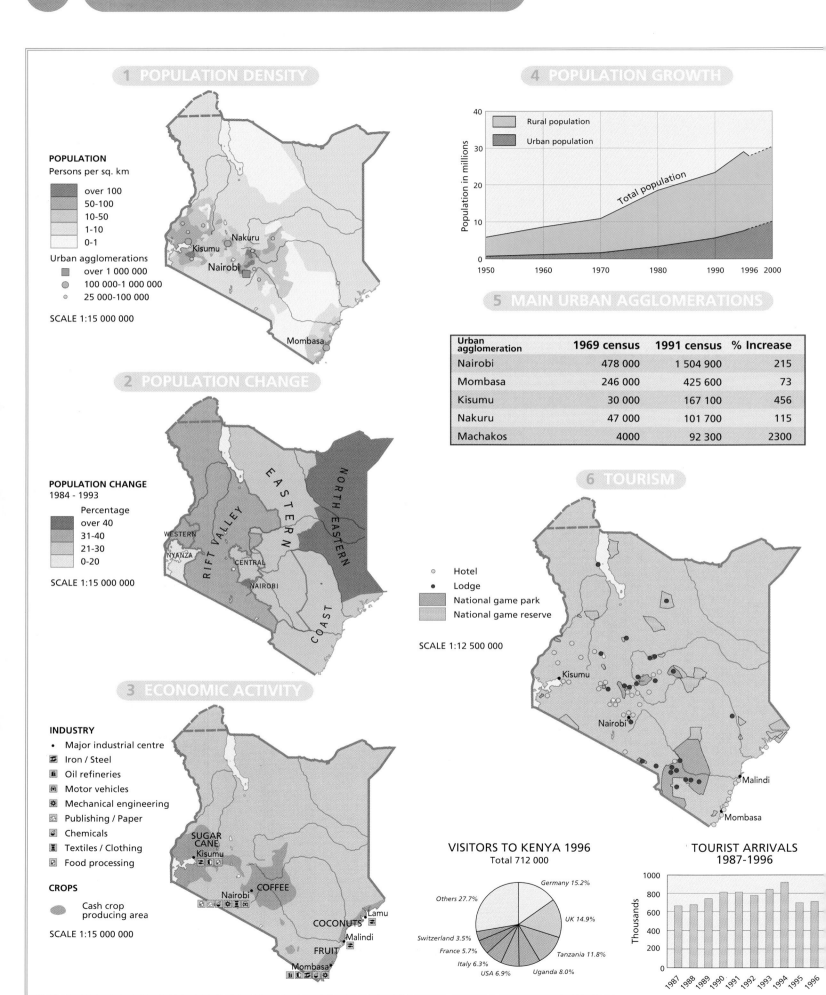

1 POPULATION DENSITY

POPULATION
Persons per sq. km

- over 100
- 50-100
- 10-50
- 1-10
- 0-1

Urban agglomerations
- over 1 000 000
- 100 000-1 000 000
- 25 000-100 000

SCALE 1:15 000 000

Nakuru
Kisumu
Nairobi
Mombasa

2 POPULATION CHANGE

POPULATION CHANGE
1984 - 1993

Percentage
- over 40
- 31-40
- 21-30
- 0-20

SCALE 1:15 000 000

WESTERN
NYANZA
RIFT VALLEY
CENTRAL
NAIROBI
EASTERN
NORTH EASTERN
COAST

3 ECONOMIC ACTIVITY

INDUSTRY
- Major industrial centre
- Iron / Steel
- Oil refineries
- Motor vehicles
- Mechanical engineering
- Publishing / Paper
- Chemicals
- Textiles / Clothing
- Food processing

CROPS
- Cash crop producing area

SCALE 1:15 000 000

SUGAR CANE
Kisumu
COFFEE
Nairobi
COCONUTS
Lamu
Malindi
FRUIT
Mombasa

4 POPULATION GROWTH

Legend:
- Rural population
- Urban population

Total population

Population in millions

1950 1960 1970 1980 1990 1996 2000

5 MAIN URBAN AGGLOMERATIONS

Urban agglomeration	1969 census	1991 census	% Increase
Nairobi	478 000	1 504 900	215
Mombasa	246 000	425 600	73
Kisumu	30 000	167 100	456
Nakuru	47 000	101 700	115
Machakos	4000	92 300	2300

6 TOURISM

- Hotel
- Lodge
- National game park
- National game reserve

SCALE 1:12 500 000

Kisumu
Nairobi
Malindi
Mombasa

VISITORS TO KENYA 1996
Total 712 000

Germany 15.2%
UK 14.9%
Tanzania 11.8%
Uganda 8.0%
USA 6.9%
Italy 6.3%
France 5.7%
Switzerland 3.5%
Others 27.7%

TOURIST ARRIVALS
1987-1996

Thousands

1987 1988 1989 1990 1991 1992 1993 1994 1995 1996

7 NAIROBI

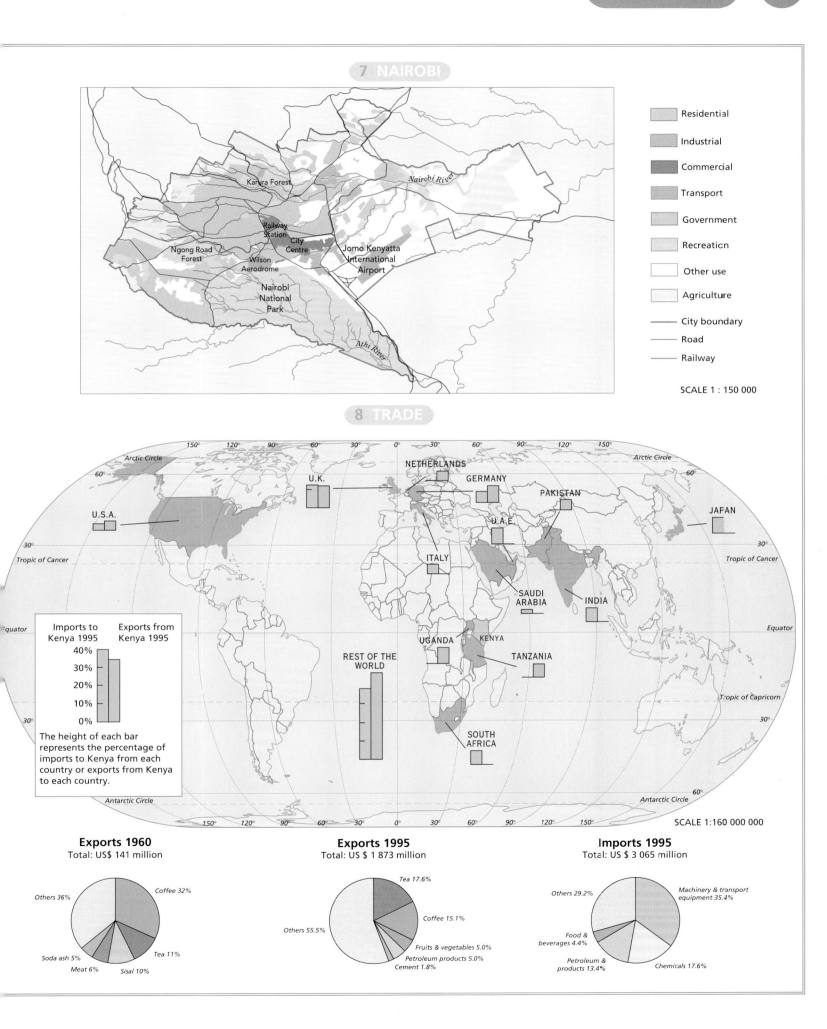

Residential
Industrial
Commercial
Transport
Government
Recreation
Other use
Agriculture
City boundary
Road
Railway

SCALE 1 : 150 000

Karura Forest
Nairobi River
Railway Station
City Centre
Ngong Road Forest
Wilson Aerodrome
Jomo Kenyatta International Airport
Nairobi National Park
Athi River

8 TRADE

Arctic Circle
Tropic of Cancer
Equator
Tropic of Capricorn
Antarctic Circle

NETHERLANDS
U.K.
GERMANY
PAKISTAN
JAPAN
U.S.A.
U.A.E.
ITALY
SAUDI ARABIA
INDIA
UGANDA
KENYA
TANZANIA
REST OF THE WORLD
SOUTH AFRICA

Imports to Kenya 1995   Exports from Kenya 1995

40%
30%
20%
10%
0%

The height of each bar represents the percentage of imports to Kenya from each country or exports from Kenya to each country.

SCALE 1:160 000 000

Exports 1960
Total: US$ 141 million

Coffee 32%
Others 36%
Soda ash 5%
Meat 6%
Sisal 10%
Tea 11%

Exports 1995
Total: US $ 1 873 million

Tea 17.6%
Coffee 15.1%
Others 55.5%
Fruits & vegetables 5.0%
Petroleum products 5.0%
Cement 1.8%

Imports 1995
Total: US $ 3 065 million

Machinery & transport equipment 35.4%
Others 29.2%
Food & beverages 4.4%
Petroleum & products 13.4%
Chemicals 17.6%

SCALE 1 : 40 000 000

0   400   800   1200   1600 km

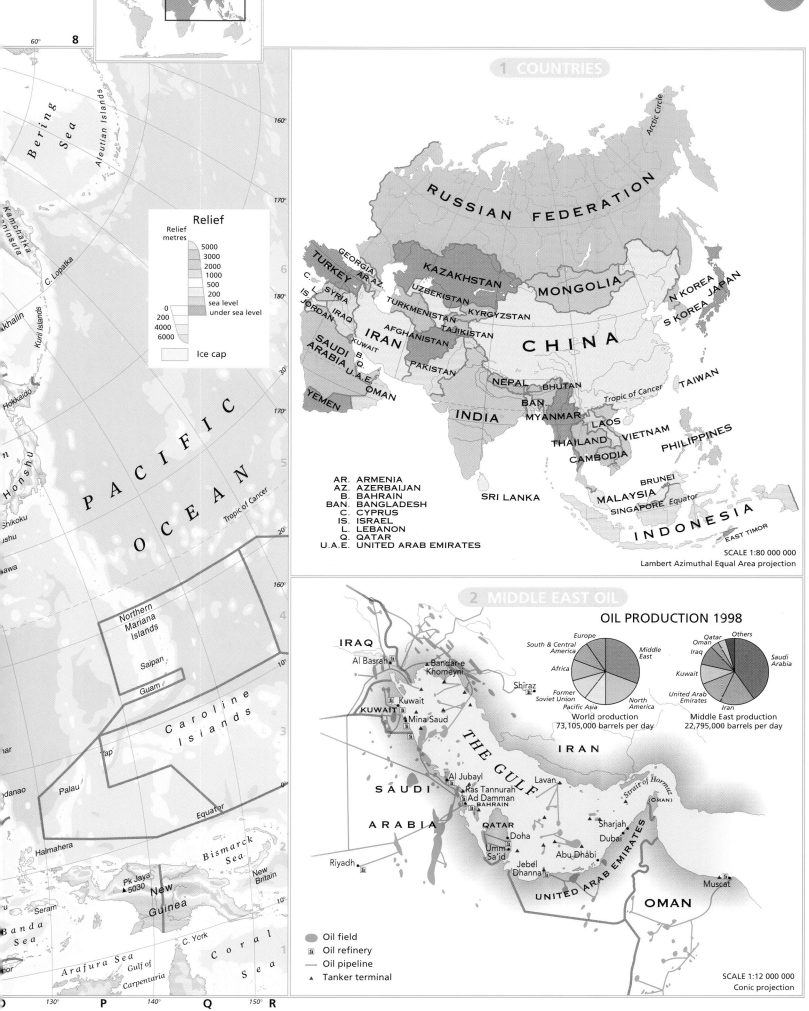

8

60°

Bering Sea

Aleutian Islands

Kamchatka Peninsula

C. Lopatka

160°

170°

Sakhalin

Kuril Islands

180°

Hokkaido

Honshu

Shikoku

170°

ushu

awa

n

Relief

Relief
metres

5000
3000
2000
1000
500
200
0
sea level
200
under sea level
4000
6000

Ice cap

P A C I F I C

O C E A N

Tropic of Cancer

160°

20°

Northern
Mariana
Islands

Saipan

Guam

C a r o l i n e
I s l a n d s

10°

ar

Yap

Palau

danao

Equator

0°

Halmahera

Bismarck
Sea

New
Britain

Pk Jaya
5030

New
Guinea

10°

Seram

*Banda
Sea*

C. York

Coral

Sea

Gulf of
Carpentaria

Arafura Sea

or

O   130°   P   140°   Q   150°   R

Lambert Azimuthal Equal Area projection

1 COUNTRIES

R U S S I A N   F E D E R A T I O N

Arctic Circle

TURKEY GEORGIA
C. L SYRIA AR. AZ.
IS. IRAQ
JORDAN
SAUDI KUWAIT
ARABIA U.A.E. OMAN B. Q.
YEMEN

KAZAKHSTAN

UZBEKISTAN

TURKMENISTAN KYRGYZSTAN

IRAN AFGHANISTAN TAJIKISTAN

PAKISTAN

MONGOLIA

C H I N A

N KOREA JAPAN
S KOREA

NEPAL BHUTAN *Tropic of Cancer* TAIWAN

BAN.
INDIA MYANMAR
LAOS
THAILAND VIETNAM PHILIPPINES
CAMBODIA

SRI LANKA

BRUNEI

MALAYSIA
SINGAPORE *Equator*

I N D O N E S I A
EAST TIMOR

AR.   ARMENIA
AZ.   AZERBAIJAN
B.   BAHRAIN
BAN.   BANGLADESH
C.   CYPRUS
IS.   ISRAEL
L.   LEBANON
Q.   QATAR
U.A.E.   UNITED ARAB EMIRATES

SCALE 1:80 000 000
Lambert Azimuthal Equal Area projection

2 MIDDLE EAST OIL

OIL PRODUCTION 1998

IRAQ

Al Basrah
Bandar-e
Khomeyni
Shīrāz

KUWAIT Kuwait

Mina Saud

T H E   G U L F

IRAN

Al Jubayl
SAUDI Ras Tannurah
Ad Damman
ARABIA BAHRAIN

Lavan

Strait of Hormuz
(OMAN)

QATAR Doha
Umm
Sa'id
Riyadh
Jebel
Dhanna

Sharjah
Dubai
Abu Dhabi

U N I T E D   A R A B   E M I R A T E S

Muscat

O M A N

Europe
South & Central
America
Africa
Former
Soviet Union
Pacific Asia
Middle
East
North
America

World production
73,105,000 barrels per day

Qatar
Oman Others
Iraq
Kuwait Saudi
Arabia
United Arab
Emirates Iran

Middle East production
22,795,000 barrels per day

Oil field
Oil refinery
Oil pipeline
Tanker terminal

SCALE 1:12 000 000
Conic projection

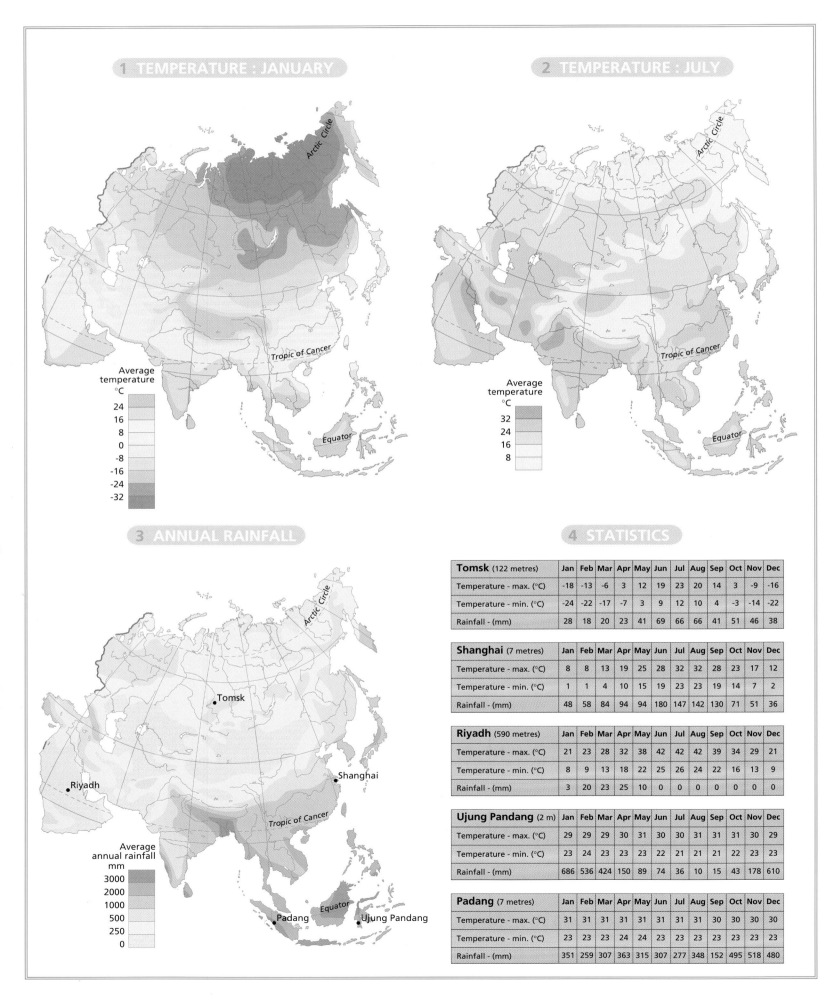

1 TEMPERATURE : JANUARY

Average
temperature
°C

24
16
8
0
-8
-16
-24
-32

Tropic of Cancer

Equator

2 TEMPERATURE : JULY

Average
temperature
°C

32
24
16
8

Tropic of Cancer

Equator

3 ANNUAL RAINFALL

Average
annual rainfall
mm

3000
2000
1000
500
250
0

Tomsk

Riyadh

Shanghai

Tropic of Cancer

Padang   Ujung Pandang

Equator

4 STATISTICS

Tomsk (122 metres)	Jan	Feb	Mar	Apr	May	Jun	Jul	Aug	Sep	Oct	Nov	Dec
Temperature - max. (°C)	-18	-13	-6	3	12	19	23	20	14	3	-9	-16
Temperature - min. (°C)	-24	-22	-17	-7	3	9	12	10	4	-3	-14	-22
Rainfall - (mm)	28	18	20	23	41	69	66	66	41	51	46	38

Shanghai (7 metres)	Jan	Feb	Mar	Apr	May	Jun	Jul	Aug	Sep	Oct	Nov	Dec
Temperature - max. (°C)	8	8	13	19	25	28	32	32	28	23	17	12
Temperature - min. (°C)	1	1	4	10	15	19	23	23	19	14	7	2
Rainfall - (mm)	48	58	84	94	94	180	147	142	130	71	51	36

Riyadh (590 metres)	Jan	Feb	Mar	Apr	May	Jun	Jul	Aug	Sep	Oct	Nov	Dec
Temperature - max. (°C)	21	23	28	32	38	42	42	42	39	34	29	21
Temperature - min. (°C)	8	9	13	18	22	25	26	24	22	16	13	9
Rainfall - (mm)	3	20	23	25	10	0	0	0	0	0	0	0

Ujung Pandang (2 m)	Jan	Feb	Mar	Apr	May	Jun	Jul	Aug	Sep	Oct	Nov	Dec
Temperature - max. (°C)	29	29	29	30	31	30	30	31	31	31	30	29
Temperature - min. (°C)	23	24	23	23	23	22	21	21	21	22	23	23
Rainfall - (mm)	686	536	424	150	89	74	36	10	15	43	178	610

Padang (7 metres)	Jan	Feb	Mar	Apr	May	Jun	Jul	Aug	Sep	Oct	Nov	Dec
Temperature - max. (°C)	31	31	31	31	31	31	31	31	30	30	30	30
Temperature - min. (°C)	23	23	23	24	24	23	23	23	23	23	23	23
Rainfall - (mm)	351	259	307	363	315	307	277	348	152	495	518	480

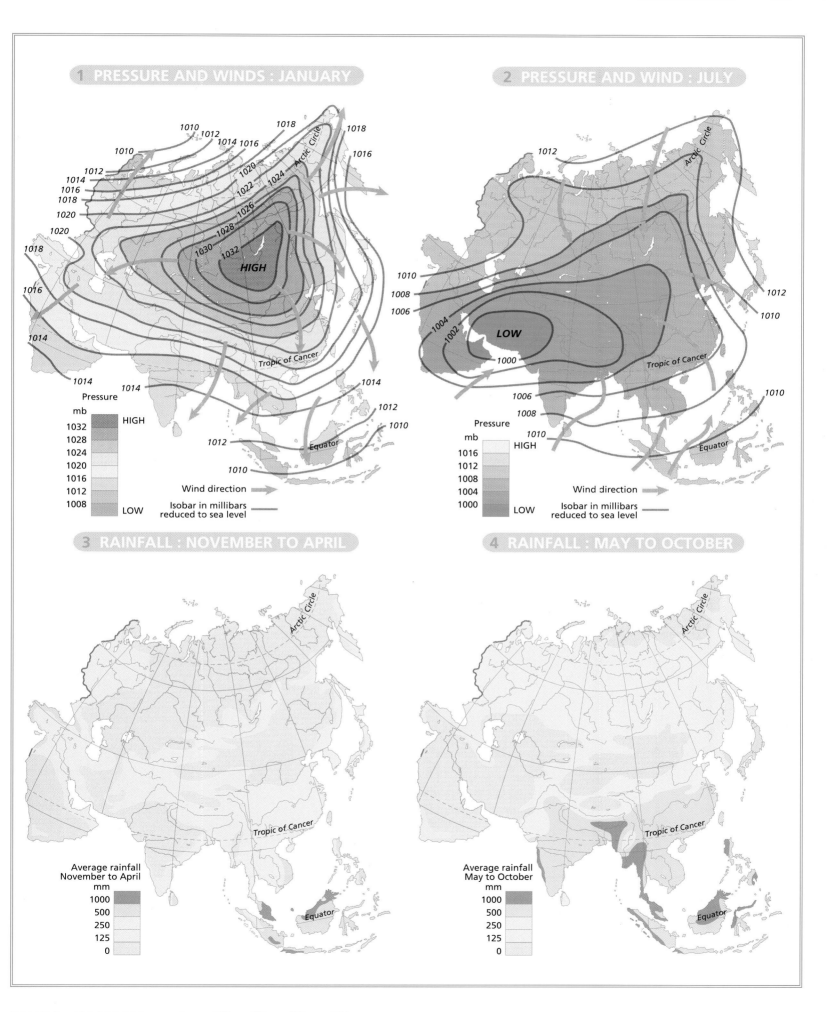

1 PRESSURE AND WINDS : JANUARY

1010 1012 1014 1016 1018 1018
1010 1016
1012
1014 1020
1016 1022
1018 1024 Arctic Circle
1020 1026
1020 1028
1018 1030 1028
1016 1032
1014 HIGH

1018
1016
1014 1014

1014 1014 1014
Tropic of Cancer

1012

Pressure
mb
1032 HIGH
1028
1024
1020
1016
1012
1010
1008 LOW

1012 1012
1010

Equator

1010

Wind direction →
Isobar in millibars
reduced to sea level ——

2 PRESSURE AND WIND : JULY

1012 Arctic Circle

1010
1008
1006
1004
1002 LOW 1012
1000 1010
Tropic of Cancer

1006
1008 1010
1010

Pressure
mb
1016 HIGH
1012
1008
1004
1000 LOW

Equator

Wind direction →
Isobar in millibars
reduced to sea level ——

3 RAINFALL : NOVEMBER TO APRIL

Arctic Circle

Tropic of Cancer

**Average rainfall
November to April**
mm
1000
500
250
125
0

Equator

4 RAINFALL : MAY TO OCTOBER

Arctic Circle

Tropic of Cancer

**Average rainfall
May to October**
mm
1000
500
250
125
0

Equator

SCALE 1 : 100 000 000

0 1000 2000 3000 4000 km

Lambert Azimuthal Equal Area projection

5165
Mt Ararat
AZ

Grid columns: A 20° B 25° C 30° D 35° E F

Ionian Sea

Zakynthos
Patras
Corinth
Kyparissia
Tripoli
Kalamata
Sparti
C. Matapan

Chalkida
ATHENS
Piraeus
Andros
Samos
Tinos
Ikaria
Paros
Naxos
Milos
Ios
Thira
Kythira
Chania
Iraklion
Karpathos

Aegean Sea
Sea of Crete
Crete
Dodecanese
Rhodes
Rodos

Manisa
Izmir
Aydin
Söke
Yatağan
Denizli
Fethiye
Gulf of Antalya
Antalya
Karamad

Akhisar
Uşak
Eğridir
Dinar
Burdur
Eğirdir L.
Beyşehir L.
Konya
Karaman

Afyon
Lake Tuz
Akşehir
Ereğli
Niğde

TURKEY
Sivas
3916
Mt Erciyas
Kayseri
Kahraman Maraş
Gaziantep
Adana
Tarsus
Mersin
İskenderun
Taurus Mountains

Elazig
Malatya
Şanliurfa
Diyarbakır
Mardin
Siirt
Van
Tatvan
Lake Van
L. Urmi
Urmi
Zakho
Haydara
Khvo

MEDITERRANEAN SEA

NICOSIA
Keryneia
Famagusta
CYPRUS
Limassol
Latakia
Tripoli

Aleppo
Ar Raqqah
Euphrates
Dayr az Zawr
Âl Bu Kamal
Âna
Mosul
Kirkuk
Tikrit
Samarra'
Ba'quban
Ar Ramadi
BAGHDAD
Karbala'
Al Hillah
An Najaf
Ad Diwaniya

SYRIA
Hamâh
Homs
Palmyra
IRA

BEIRUT
Sidon
Tyre
Haifa
Nazareth
Tel Aviv-Yafo
Holon
Gaza
GAZA
DAMASCUS
Zahlé
LEBANON
L. Tiberias
Dar'a
Irbid
Mafraq
Zarqa'
AMMAN
JERUSALEM
WEST BANK
Hebron
Dead Sea
Karak
Beersheba
Negev
JORDAN
Ma'an

Syrian Al Widyan Desert
Ar Rutba
Badanah
As Sama
Sakakah
Al Jauf
Rafea'

Banghazi
Al Marj
Al Bayda'
Darnah
Al Jabal al Akhdar
Gulf of Sirte
As Sidrah
Ajdabiya
Al 'Uqaylah
Marsa al Burayqah
Maradah
As Sarir
Jalu
Calanscio Sand Sea
Al Jaghbub

Tubruq
Umm Sa'ad
Marsa Matruh
Siwa
Qattâra Depression
Libyan Plateau

Alexandria
Damanhûr
Tanta
Dumyât
Port Said
Zagazig
El Mansûra
Isma'iliya
Suez Canal

El Giza
CAIRO
El Faiyûm
Beni Suef
El Minya
Bawiti
Bahariya Oasis
Farafra Oasis
Suez
Gulf of Suez
Sinai
El Ein
Katherina
2637
G. of Aqaba
Aqaba
Al Mudawwara

An Nafud
Tabuk
Tayma'
Hâ'il
Buraydah
Unayza

LIBYA
Western Desert
EGYPT
Al Jaghbub

Great Sand Sea
Mut
Dakhla Oasis
Asyût
Sohâg
Nile
Qena
Luxor
El Khârga
The Great Oasis
Idfu
Aswân
Eastern Desert
Hurghada
Bûr Safâga
Quseir
Marsa Alam

SAHARA
SUDAN
Al Khufrah
Al 'Uwaynat
Gilf Kebir Plateau
Rebiana Sand Sea

Libyan Desert
Erdi
Dépression du Mourdi
CHAD
Massif Ennedi

Lake Nuba
Abu Simbel
Lake Nasser
Wadi Halfa
Nile
Nubian Desert
Kerma
Dungunab
Muhammad Qol

Yanbu 'al Bahr
Medina
Rabigh
RED SEA
Jedda
Mecca
At Tâ'if
Turabah
As Suq

Hijaz
NAJD
SAU
AR

Port Sudan
Suakin
Sinkat
Al Qunfidhah
Abha
Najran
Sabya
Jizan
Abu 'Arish

Jebel Abyad Plateau
Abu Hamed
Kareima
Shereiq
Merowe
Ed Debba
Berber
Musmar
Atbara
Ed Damer
Haiya
Karora

Baiyuda Desert
Nile
Derudeb
Hagar Nish Plateau
Massawa
Dahlak Archipelago

SUDAN
Omdurman
KHARTOUM
Athara
Kassala
Khashm el Girba
Teseney
Akordat
ASMARA
Keren
Hodeida
SANA
NOR

El Geneina
Kebkabiya
Abyad
El Fasher
Umm Keddada
Marra Plateau
J. Gimbala
3070
Bara
En Nahud
El Obeid
Er Rahad
Umm Ruwaba
Ed Dueim
Kosti
Singa
Sennar
Wad Medani
Gedaref
Gallabat
Gonder
Lake Tana

Aglwat Hills
ERITREA
Adi Ugri
Adi Quala
Aksum
Adwa
Ādī Ārk'ay
Simēn Mts
4620
Ras Dashen
Mek'elē
Ādīgrat
Koluli
Zabid
Ibb
Ta'izz
Dhamar
Denaki
Bab al Mandab
Assab
Ade

Nyala
Ed Da'ein
Abu Matariq
Birao

SAHARA
ETHIOPIA
White Nile
Blue Nile
Nuba Mts

0   100   200   300   400 km

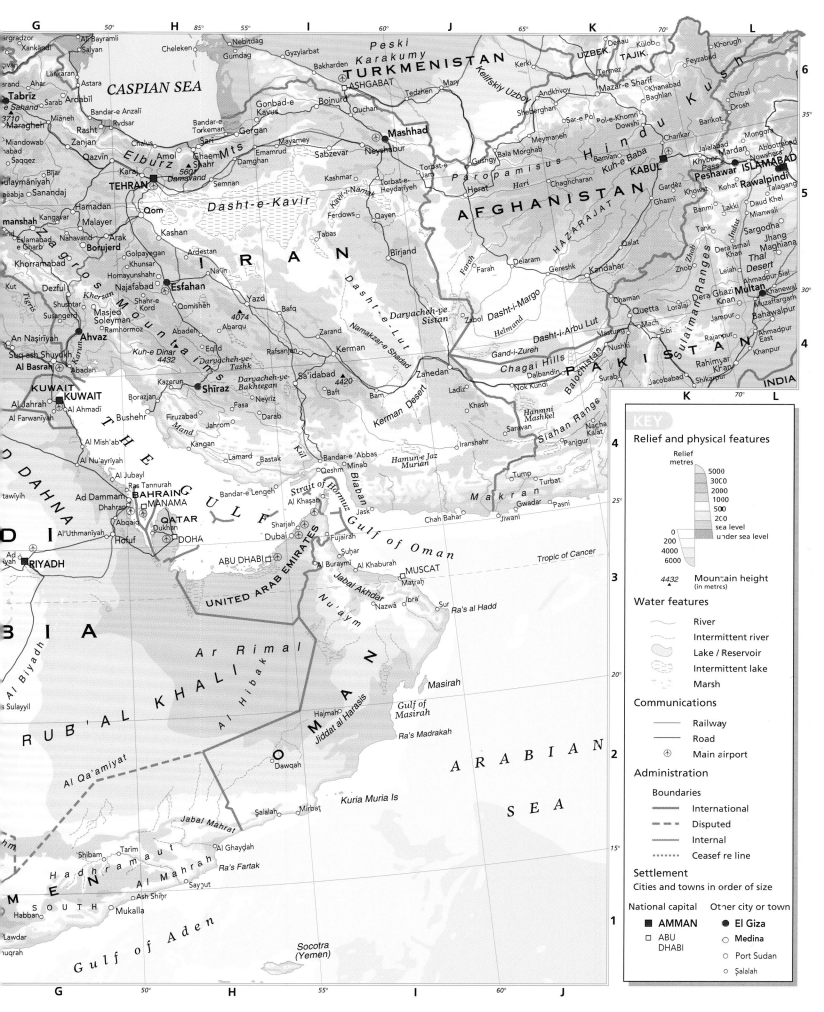

Albers Conic Equal Area projection

KEY

Relief and physical features

Relief
metres

5000
3000
2000
1000
500
200
sea level
0
200
under sea level
4000
6000

▲ 4432   Mountain height
         (in metres)

Water features

~~~~ River

~~~~ Intermittent river

Lake / Reservoir

Intermittent lake

Marsh

Communications

Railway

Road

⊕ Main airport

Administration

Boundaries

International

Disputed

Internal

Ceasefire line

Settlement

Cities and towns in order of size

National capital   Other city or town

■ AMMAN   ● El Giza

□ ABU   ○ Medina
  DHABI

                         ○ Port Sudan

                         ○ Şalalah

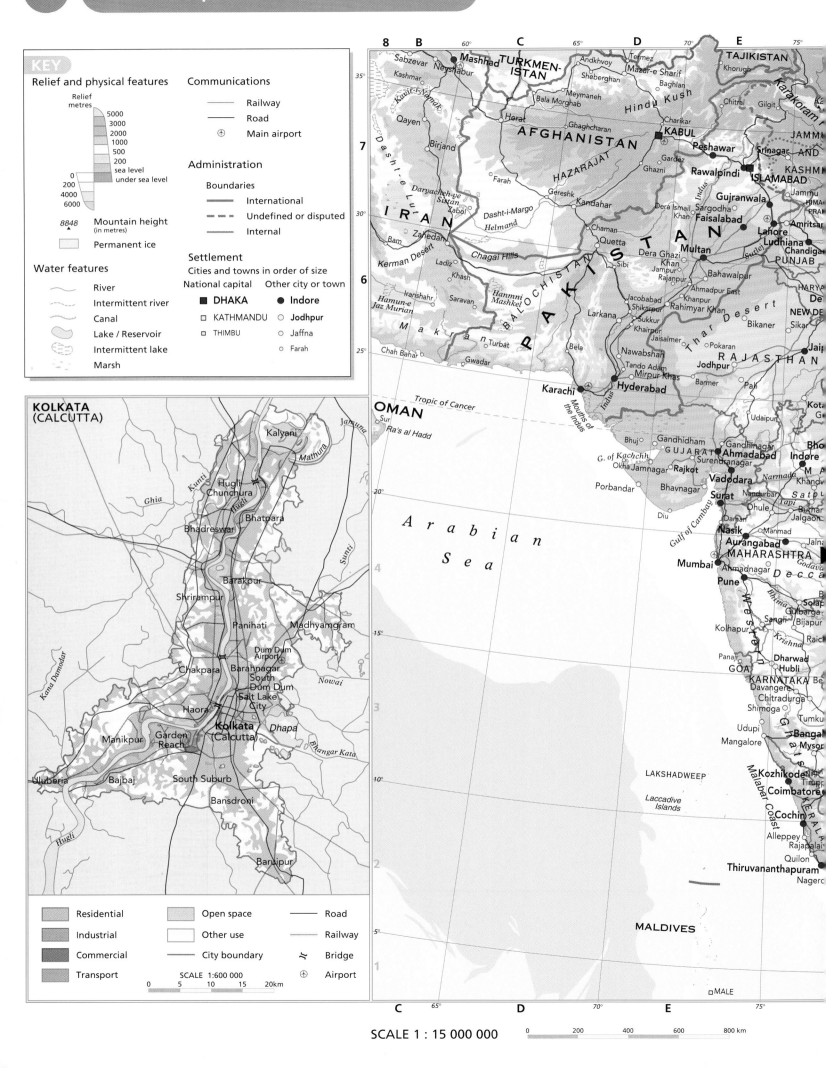

KEY

Relief and physical features

Relief metres
5000
3000
2000
1000
500
200
sea level
0
200
4000
6000
under sea level

8848 ▲ Mountain height (in metres)

☐ Permanent ice

Water features

~~~ River
- - - Intermittent river
Canal
Lake / Reservoir
Intermittent lake
Marsh

Communications

Railway
Road
⊕ Main airport

Administration

Boundaries

International
— — — Undefined or disputed
Internal

Settlement

Cities and towns in order of size

National capital   Other city or town

■ DHAKA   ● Indore

☐ KATHMANDU   ○ Jodhpur

☐ THIMBU   ○ Jaffna

                      ○ Farah

KOLKATA (CALCUTTA)

Kalyani
Jamuna
Mathura
Kunti
Hugli Chunchura
Ghia
Hugli
Bhatpara
Bhadreswar
Barakpur
Shrirampur
Panihati
Madhyamgram
Suntti
Nowai
Dum Dum Airport
Chakpara
Barahnagar
South Dum Dum
Salt Lake City
Kana Damodar
Haora
Kolkata (Calcutta)
Dhapa
Manikpur
Garden Reach
Bhangar Kata
Uluberia
Bajbaj
South Suburb
Bansdroni
Hugli
Baruipur

Residential
Industrial
Commercial
Transport

Open space
Other use
City boundary
SCALE 1:600 000
0   5   10   15   20km

Road
Railway
⤩ Bridge
⊕ Airport

TURKMEN-ISTAN
Sabzevar
Neyshabur
● Mashhad
Kashmar
Kavir-i-Namak
Andkhvoy
Termez
Sheberghan
Mazar-e Sharif
Baghlan
Khorugh
TAJIKISTAN
Meymaneh
Bala Morghab
Hindu Kush
Chitral
Gilgit
Karakoram
Qayen
Herat
Charikar
Ghaghcharan
■ KABUL
Srinagar
JAMM
Birjand
AFGHANISTAN
Peshawar
AND
Dasht-e Lut
HAZARAJAT
Gardez
Rawalpindi
KASHM
Farah
Ghazni
ISLAMABAD
Jammu
Daryacheh-ye Sistan
Gereshk
Kandahar
Dera Ismail Khan
Sargodha
Gujranwala
HIMA
Zabol
Dasht-i-Margo
Chaman
Quetta
Faisalabad
PRA
IRAN
Helmand
Multan
Lahore
Amritsar
Bam
Zahedan
Dera Ghazi Khan
Ludhiana
Kerman Desert
Chagai Hills
Sibi
Jampur
Bahawalpur
Chandigarh
Ladiz
Khash
Rajanpur
Ahmadpur East
Bikaner
PUNJAB
Iranshahr
Hamun-e Jaz Murian
Hanmni Mashkel
Larkana
Jacobabad
Shikarpur
Khanpur
Rahimyar Khan
HARYA
Saravan
Sukkur
De
Thar Desert
Khairpur
Jaisalmer
NEW DE
Makran
Turbat
Bela
Nawabshah
Pokaran
RAJASTHAN
Sikar
Chah Bahar
Gwadar
Tando Adam
Mirpur Khas
Barmer
Jaip
Karachi
Hyderabad
Jodhpur
Pali
Tropic of Cancer
Mouths of the Indus
Indus
Udaipur
Kota
OMAN
Bhuj
Gandhidham
Gandhinagar
Sur
Ra's al Hadd
GUJARAT
Ahmadabad
Bho
Okha
Jamnagar
Surendranagar
Indore
Porbandar
Rajkot
Vadodara
Narmada
Khand
Bhavnagar
Diu
Surat
Satp
Daman
Nandurbar
Dhule
Jalgaon
Arabian Sea
Nasik
Manmad
Jalna
Aurangabad
MAHARASHTRA
Mumbai
Ahmadnagar
Decca
Pune
Godava
Bhima
Solap
Gulbarga
Kolhapur
Bijapur
Sangli
Krishna
Raic
Panaji
Dharwad
GOA
Hubli
KARNATAKA
Be
Davangere
Chitradurga
Shimoga
Tumku
Udupi
Banga
Mangalore
Mysor
LAKSHADWEEP
Kozhikode
Tirupp
Laccadive Islands
Coimbatore
Cochin
KERALA
Alleppey
Rajapalai
Quilon
Thiruvananthapuram
Nagerc
MALDIVES
☐ MALE

SCALE 1 : 15 000 000
0   200   400   600   800 km

Conic projection

1 POPULATION DENSITY

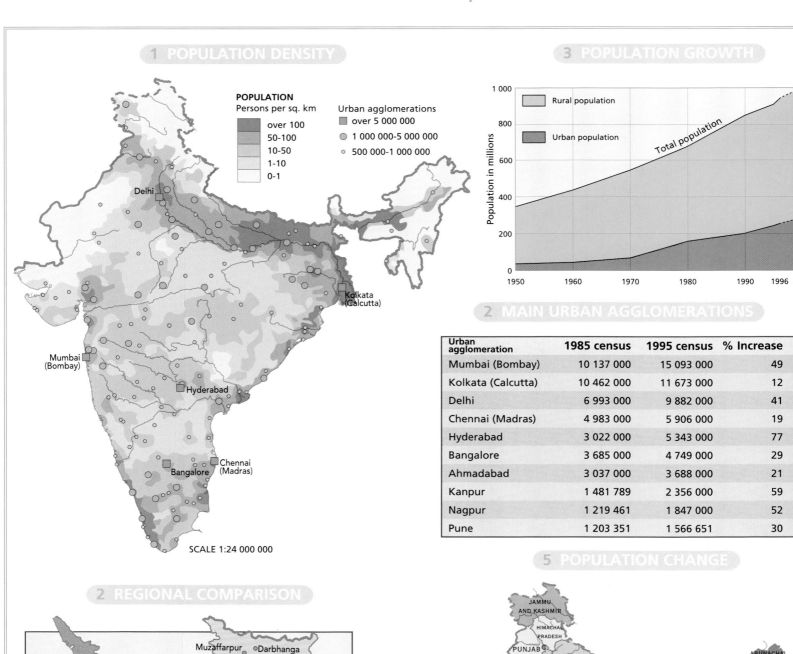

POPULATION
Persons per sq. km
- over 100
- 50-100
- 10-50
- 1-10
- 0-1

Urban agglomerations
- over 5 000 000
- 1 000 000-5 000 000
- 500 000-1 000 000

Delhi
Kolkata (Calcutta)
Mumbai (Bombay)
Hyderabad
Bangalore
Chennai (Madras)

SCALE 1:24 000 000

3 POPULATION GROWTH

Rural population
Urban population
Total population

Population in millions

1950 1960 1970 1980 1990 1996 20

2 MAIN URBAN AGGLOMERATIONS

Urban agglomeration	1985 census	1995 census	% Increase
Mumbai (Bombay)	10 137 000	15 093 000	49
Kolkata (Calcutta)	10 462 000	11 673 000	12
Delhi	6 993 000	9 882 000	41
Chennai (Madras)	4 983 000	5 906 000	19
Hyderabad	3 022 000	5 343 000	77
Bangalore	3 685 000	4 749 000	29
Ahmadabad	3 037 000	3 688 000	21
Kanpur	1 481 789	2 356 000	59
Nagpur	1 219 461	1 847 000	52
Pune	1 203 351	1 566 651	30

2 REGIONAL COMPARISON

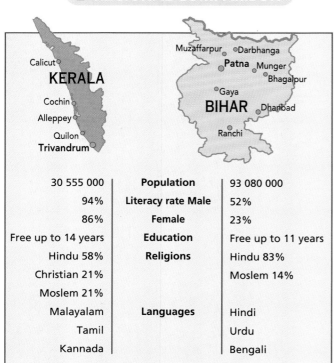

Calicut
KERALA
Cochin
Alleppey
Quilon
Trivandrum

Muzaffarpur · Darbhanga
Patna · Munger
· Bhagalpur
· Gaya
BIHAR · Dhanbad
Ranchi

30 555 000	**Population**	93 080 000
94%	**Literacy rate Male**	52%
86%	**Female**	23%
Free up to 14 years	**Education**	Free up to 11 years
Hindu 58%	**Religions**	Hindu 83%
Christian 21%		Moslem 14%
Moslem 21%		
Malayalam	**Languages**	Hindi
Tamil		Urdu
Kannada		Bengali

5 POPULATION CHANGE

JAMMU AND KASHMIR
HIMACHAL PRADESH
PUNJAB
HARYANA
D.
RAJASTHAN
UTTAR PRADESH
BIHAR
GUJARAT
MADHYA PRADESH
WEST BENGAL
MAHARASHTRA
ORISSA
ANDHRA PRADESH
GOA
KARNATAKA
KERALA
TAMIL NADU
ARUNACHAL PRADESH
S.
ASSAM
MEGHALAYA
MA.
N.
T.
MI.

C. CHANDIGARGH
D. DELHI
MA. MANIPUR
MI. MIZORAM
N. NAGALAND
S. SIKKIM
T. TRIPURA

POPULATION CHANGE
1981 - 1994

Percentage
- over 50
- 41-50
- 31-40
- 0-30

SCALE 1:30 000 000

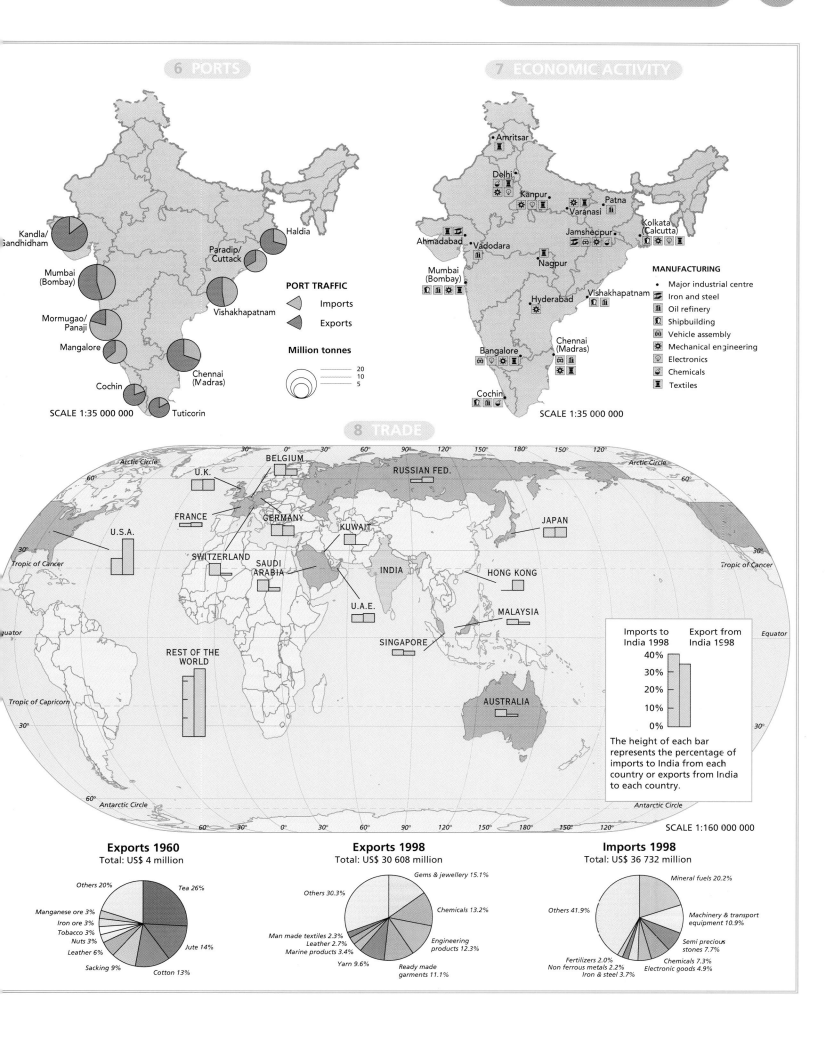

6 PORTS

Kandla/
Gandhidham

Haldia

Paradip/
Cuttack

Mumbai
(Bombay)

Vishakhapatnam

Mormugao/
Panaji

Mangalore

Chennai
(Madras)

Cochin

Tuticorin

PORT TRAFFIC

Imports

Exports

Million tonnes

20
10
5

SCALE 1:35 000 000

7 ECONOMIC ACTIVITY

Amritsar

Delhi

Kanpur

Patna

Varanasi

Jamshedpur

Kolkata
(Calcutta)

Ahmadabad

Vadodara

Nagpur

Mumbai
(Bombay)

Hyderabad

Vishakhapatnam

Bangalore

Chennai
(Madras)

Cochin

MANUFACTURING

• Major industrial centre

Iron and steel

Oil refinery

Shipbuilding

Vehicle assembly

Mechanical engineering

Electronics

Chemicals

Textiles

SCALE 1:35 000 000

8 TRADE

Arctic Circle

BELGIUM

RUSSIAN FED.

Arctic Circle

U.K.

FRANCE

GERMANY

KUWAIT

JAPAN

U.S.A.

SWITZERLAND

SAUDI
ARABIA

INDIA

HONG KONG

Tropic of Cancer

Tropic of Cancer

U.A.E.

MALAYSIA

SINGAPORE

REST OF THE
WORLD

AUSTRALIA

Tropic of Capricorn

Antarctic Circle

Antarctic Circle

Imports to India 1998	Export from India 1998
40%	
30%	
20%	
10%	
0%	

The height of each bar represents the percentage of imports to India from each country or exports from India to each country.

SCALE 1:160 000 000

Exports 1960
Total: US$ 4 million

Others 20%
Tea 26%
Manganese ore 3%
Iron ore 3%
Tobacco 3%
Nuts 3%
Leather 6%
Jute 14%
Sacking 9%
Cotton 13%

Exports 1998
Total: US$ 30 608 million

Gems & jewellery 15.1%
Others 30.3%
Chemicals 13.2%
Man made textiles 2.3%
Leather 2.7%
Marine products 3.4%
Engineering products 12.3%
Yarn 9.6%
Ready made garments 11.1%

Imports 1998
Total: US$ 36 732 million

Mineral fuels 20.2%
Others 41.9%
Machinery & transport equipment 10.9%
Semi precious stones 7.7%
Fertilizers 2.0%
Non ferrous metals 2.2%
Iron & steel 3.7%
Chemicals 7.3%
Electronic goods 4.9%

1 POPULATION DENSITY

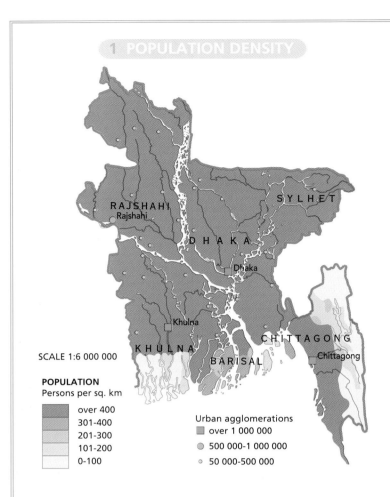

SCALE 1:6 000 000

POPULATION
Persons per sq. km

over 400
301-400
201-300
101-200
0-100

Urban agglomerations
over 1 000 000
500 000-1 000 000
50 000-500 000

Forest

Dense forests known as the Sundarbans are found along the southwest co of Bangladesh. The same green on the right of the image is wooded forest found on the highlands along the border with Myanmar.

Silt laden water

The red/browm area on the satellite image is the silt laden water at the mouth of the Ganges. Silt carried down by the rivers Ganges and Brahmaputra is deposited at the delta which is steadily growing out into the Bay of Bengal.

Cultivated land

When silt is deposited on the deltaic plains extremely fertile ground is left. This is most suitable for the growing of rice, especially floating varieties which are adapted to cope with seasonal flooding.

Rivers

Bangladesh has two major rivers, the Ganges and the Brahmaputra or Jamuna, whose many tributaries criss cross the country.

Reservoir
In addition to its many small natural lakes, Bangladesh has a large reservoir, the Karnafuli Reservoir, in the hills near Chittagong.

2 MAIN URBAN AGGLOMERATIONS

Urban agglomeration	1991 census	1998 estimate	% Increase
Dhaka	6 105 160	10 979 000	80
Chittagong	2 040 663	2 906 000	42
Khulna	877 388	1 229 000	40

3 ECONOMIC ACTIVITY

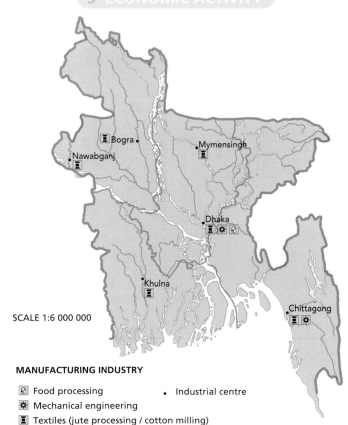

SCALE 1:6 000 000

MANUFACTURING INDUSTRY

- Food processing
- Mechanical engineering
- Textiles (jute processing / cotton milling)
- Industrial centre

4 TRADE

PARTNERS 1997

Imports
Total: US$ 7100 million

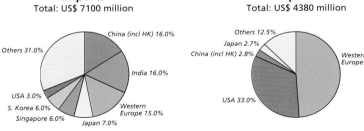

China (incl HK) 16.0%
Others 31.0%
India 16.0%
USA 3.0%
S. Korea 6.0%
Singapore 6.0%
Japan 7.0%
Western Europe 15.0%

Exports
Total: US$ 4380 million

Others 12.5%
Japan 2.7%
China (incl HK) 2.8%
Western Europe 45
USA 33.0%

PRODUCTS 1997

Imports

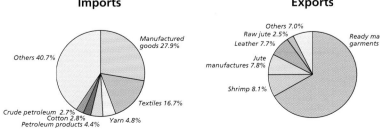

Manufactured goods 27.9%
Others 40.7%
Crude petroleum 2.7%
Cotton 2.8%
Petroleum products 4.4%
Yarn 4.8%
Textiles 16.7%

Exports

Others 7.0%
Raw jute 2.5%
Leather 7.7%
Jute manufactures 7.8%
Shrimp 8.1%
Ready made garments 66

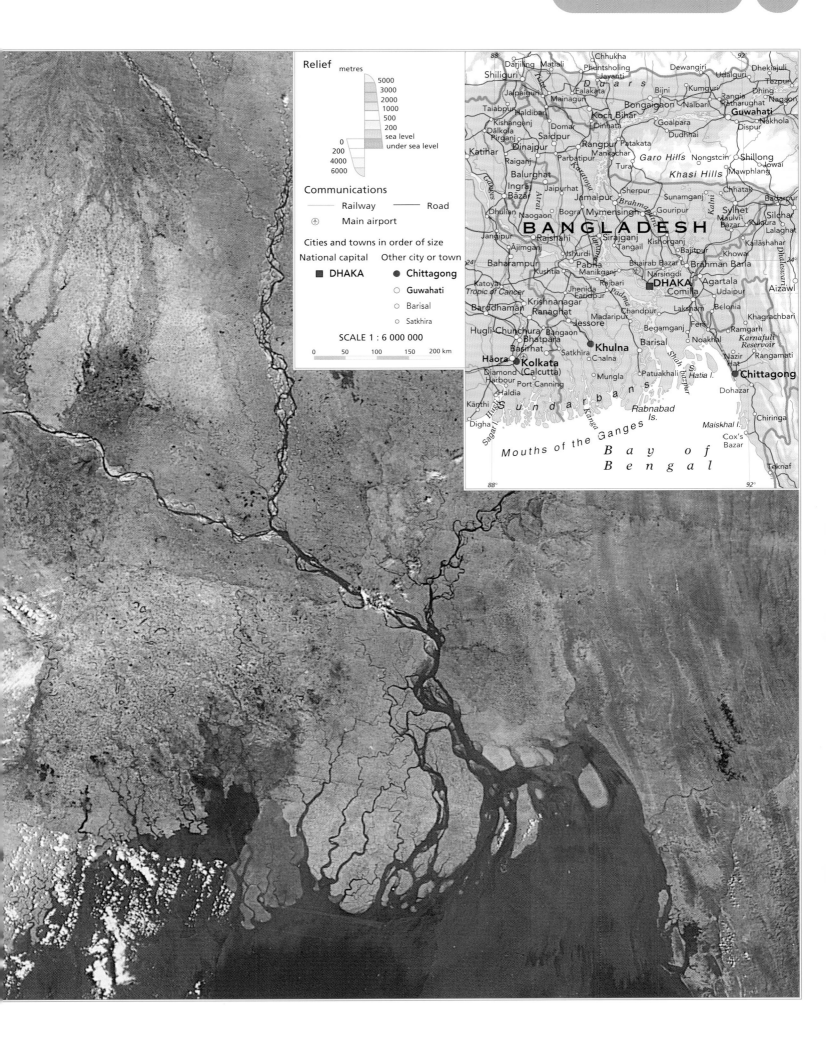

Relief
metres

5000	
3000	
2000	
1000	
500	
200	
0	sea level
200	under sea level
4000	
6000	

Communications

—— Railway   —— Road

⊕   Main airport

Cities and towns in order of size

National capital   Other city or town

■ **DHAKA**   ● **Chittagong**

○ **Guwahati**

○ Barisal

○ Satkhira

SCALE 1 : 6 000 000

0   50   100   150   200 km

Chhukha
Darjiling   Matiali   Phuntsholing   Dewangiri   Udalguri   Dhekiajuli
Shiliguri   Jayanti
Jalpaiguri   Mainaguri   D u a r s   Bijni   Kumguri   Rangia   Patharughat   Dhing
Taiabpur   Haldibar   Bongaigaon   Nalbari   Nagaon
Kishanganj   Domar   Dinhata   Koch Bihar   Goalpara   Dudhnai   Dispur   **Guwahati**   Nakhola
Dalkola   Pirganj   Patakata
Katihar   Dinajpur   Saidpur   Rangpur   Mankachar   Garo Hills   Nongstcin   Shillong
Raiganj   Parbatipur   Tura   Khasi Hills   Jowai   Mawphlang
Balurghat   Ingraj   Jaipurhat   Sherpur   Sunamganj   Gouripur   Kalni   Chhatak   Badarpur
Bāzār   Jamalpur   Brahma   Sylhet   Silchar
Dhulian   Naogaon   Bogra   Mymensingh   Gouripur   Maulvi   Lalaghat
BANGLADESH   Bāzār   Kulaura
Jangipur   Rajshahi   Sirajganj   Kishorganj   Kailāshahar
Ājimganj   Ishurdi   Tangail   Bajitpur   Khowai
Baharampur   Pabna   Bhairab Bazar   Brahman Barla   Aizawl
Tropic of Cancer   Manikganj   Narsingdi
Katoya   Kushtia   Rejbari   **DHAKA**   Agartala
Krishnanagar   Jhenida   Padma   Comilla   Udaipur
Barddhaman   Faridpur   Laksham   Belonia
Ranaghat   Madaripur   Chandpur   Khagrachbari
Hugli-Chunchura   Bangaon   Jessore   Begamganj   Feni   Ramgarh
Bhatpara   Satkhira   Karnafuli   Rangamati
Basirhat   **Khulna**   Barisal   Noakhal   Reservoir
Hãora   **Kolkata**   Chalna   Nazir   Dohazar
Diamond   (Calcutta)   Mungla   Patuakhali   S.   Hat   **Chittagong**
Harbour   Port Canning   Hatia I.
Haldia   S u n d a r b a n s   Rabnabad   Chiringa
Kānthi   Is.   Maiskhal I.   Cox's
Digha   Sagar I.   Kanega   Bazar
Mouths of the Ganges   B a y   o f   Teknaf
B e n g a l

SCALE 1 : 15 000 000

0   200   400   600   800 km

Conic projection

Grid references: A 95° · B 100° · C · D 105° · E 110° · F 115° · 120°

INDIA

CHINA

GUANGDONG

Nanning · Yulin

GUANGXI ZHUANGZU ZIZHIQU · CHINA · Kowloon · Macau · HONG KONG · Gaoxio · TAIWAN

Shwebo · Monywa

Mandalay · Myingyan

Mt Pakokku · Victoria · 3053

MYANMAR · Meiktila · Taung-gyi · Kengtung

Magwe · Pyinmana · Chiang Rai · Yunjinghong · Lao Cai · Cao Bang · Pingxiang · Qinzhou · Beihai · Zhanjiang

Sittwe · Phongsali · Thai Nguyen · HANOI · Hai Phong · Nam Dinh · Thai Binh · Haikou · Qionghai

Sandoway · Pye · Louang Namtha · Chiang Mai · Phayao · Nan · Xiangkhoang · Thanh Hoa · Gulf of Tongking · HAINAN · Dongfang

Henzada · Shwegyn · Pegu · Lampang · Phrae · Louangphrabang · VIENTIANE · Vinh · Ha Tinh · Leizhou Pen. · Xuwen

Bassein · Thaton · Martaban · Moulmein · Uttaradit · Udon Thani · Savannakhét · Dong Hoi · Quang Tri · Huê

Bay of Bengal · Arakan Yoma · Irrawaddy · Salween · Mekong

YANGON · Gulf of Martaban · Phitsanulok · Khon Kaen · Da Nang

Tavoy · Nakhon Sawan · THAILAND · Ubon Ratchathani · Pakxé · Quang Ngai · Paracel Is

Mouths of the Irrawaddy · Sara Buri · Nakhon Ratchasima · Surin · Qui Nhon · SOUTH

Preparis I. · Ayutthaya · Nonthaburi · Sisophon · CHINA · San Fernando · Bagulo · Dagupan · Cabanatua · Mt Pinatubo 1600 · Olongapo · Quez · MANILA

Mergui · Rat Buri · BANGKOK · Chon Buri · Phet Buri · Batdâmbâng · Tônlé Sap · CAMBODIA · Buôn Mê Thuôt · Nha Trang · Cam Ranh · SEA · Mindoro

Andaman Islands (India) · Tenasserim · Chanthaburi · Pouthisat · Kâmpóng Cham · Da Lat · Phan Thiet · Calamian Group

Port Blair · Khiri Khan · Prachuap · PHNOM PENH · Tây Ninh · Mindoro

Little Andaman · Chumphon · Sihanoukville · Kâmpôt · My Tho · Hô Chi Minh City

Andaman · Ranong · Gulf of Thailand · Long Xuyên · Rach Gia · Vung Tau

Ten Degree Channel · Sea · Nakhon Si Thammarat · Bac Liêu · Cân Tho · Mouths of the Mekong · Con Son · Spratly Is · Palawan · Puerto Princesa

Car Nicobar · Krabi · Phatthalung · Mui Ca Mau

Nicobar Islands (India) · Phuket · Songkhla · Brooke's Point · Sul Se

Ban Hat Yai · Yala · Balabac Strait · Jol

Great Nicobar · Alur Setar · Kota Bharu · MALAYSIA · Kota Kinabalu · G. Kinabalu 4094 · SABAH · Sandakan · Lahad Datu

Banda Aceh · George Town · Butterworth · Kuala Terengganu · BRUNEI · Miri · Seria · Tawau · Tawita

Lhokseumawe · Pinang · Taiping · Ipoh · Dungun · BANDAR SERI BEGAWAN · Igan

Langsa · MALAYA · PENINSULAR · Kuantan · Natuna Besar · Anambas Is · SARAWAK · Bintulu · Tanjungredeb

G. Leuser 3145 · Medan · Tebingtinggi · KUALA LUMPUR · Putrajaya · Seremban · Melaka · MALAYSIA · Natuna Is · Sibu · Iran Ra. 2988 · Tarakan

Simeuluë · Prapat · Baligé · Rantauprapat · Keluang · Muar · Johor Bahru · SINGAPORE · Kuching · Debak · Ce

Lake Toba · Sibolga · SINGAPORE · Tambelan Is · Sambas · Singkawang · BORNEO

Nias · Pakanbaru · Riau Is · Kuala Lumpur · Simanggang · Kalimantan

Batu Is · Bukittinggi · SUMATRA · Karimata Strait · Pontianak · Sangulirang · Makassar Strait

INDIAN · Padang · Padangpanjang · Bangka · Sukadana · Schwaner Mts · Samarinda · Tom Gu

Siberut · Muarabungo · Pangkalpinang · Ketapang · Kendawangan · Palangkaraya · Amuntai · Balikpapan · Palu · Poso

Sipura · Jambi · Mentok · Tanjungpandan · Sampit · Pangkalanbuun · Sulawe

Barisan Range · 3805 · G. Kerinci · Sungaipenuh · Belitung · Banjarmasin · Mamuju · 3074 · Bt Gandadiwata

OCEAN · Utara I. · Lubuklinggau · Palembang · Toboali · Tg Puting · Majene · Makale

Mentawai Is · Selatan I. · Prabumulih · Lahat · Tg Selatan · Parepare · Watampone

Dempo 3159 · Bengkulu · Martapura · Java Sea · Laut · Ujung Pandang · 287

Enggano · Kotabumi · Bontosunggu · Buluku · Salayar

Tanjungkarang Telukbetung · Bawean · INDONE · Kangean Is

Sunda Str. · JAKARTA · Cirebon · Pekalongan · Tuban · Madura · Bali Sea · Flore

Serang · Bogor · Bandung · Semarang · Surabaya · Probolinggo · Singaraja · Lombok · 3726 · Raba · Ruteng

Sukabumi · 3428 · Slamet · Surakarta · Malang · Singaraja · Bali

Tasikmalaya · Cilacap · Yogyakarta · 3676 · Jember · Denpasar · Mataram · Sumbawa

JAVA · Waingapu · Sumba

Christmas I. (Aust.)

SCALE 1 : 15 000 000 · 0 · 200 · 400 · 600 · 800 km

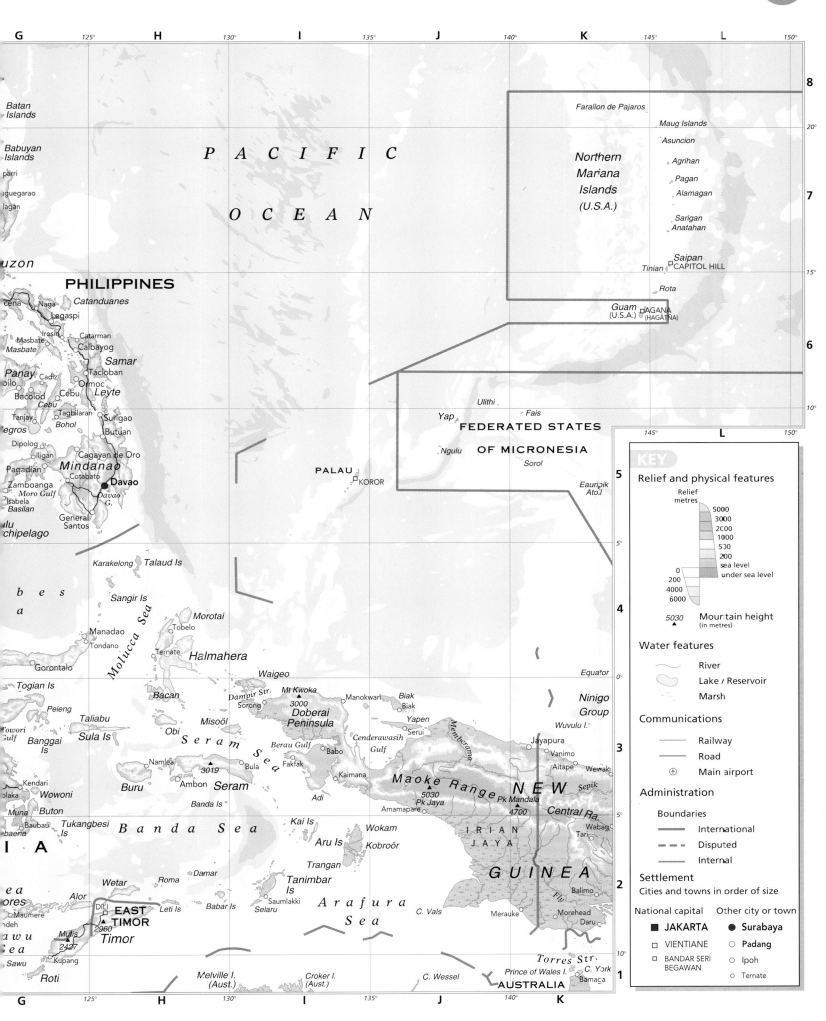

Mercator projection

A 130° B 135° C 140° D E

5

Fangzheng
Shangzhi
Linkou
Jixi
Hulin
Dongfanghong
Muling
Wanda Shan
Iman
Amgu

La Pérouse Strait
Sea of Okhotsk
Iturup

Wakkanai

4

Zhangguangcai Ling
Mudan
CHINA
Pipa Dingzi ▲1397
RUSSIAN FEDERATION
Sikhote-Alin Range
Lake Khanka
Ussuri
Spassk Dal'niy
Ussuriysk
Vladivostok
Rudnaya Pristan'
Hokkaido
Monbetsu
Abashiri
Kitami
Asahikawa ▲2290
Asahi-dake
Hidaka-sanmyaku
Kunashir
Shikotan-to

Dunhua
Wangqing
Kanji
Tumen
Hunchun
Muling
Suchan
Nakhodka
Otaru
Iwanai
Bibai
Yubari
Sapporo
Obihiro
Kushiro

Helong ▲1677
Zengfeng Shan
Tumen
Unggi
Najin
Yakumo
Mori
Muroran
Tomakomai
Samani

Kambo Ho ▲2541
Chongjin
Hakodate
Tsugaru-kaikyo

Kimchaek
NORTH KOREA
Mutsu
Goshogawara
Aomori
Towada
Hachinohe

40°

Sea of Japan
Hirosaki
Noshiro
Odate
Morioka
Miyako

Akita
Hanamaki
Kamaishi

Sakata
Ichinoseki
Kesennuma

Kangnung
Nogwak-san ▲1321
SOUTH KOREA
Ullung-do
Tok-to (Take-shima)
Sadoga-shima
Ryotsu
Yamagata
Tendo
Ishinomaki
Sendai

3

Ulchin
Suzu
Nanao
Toyama-wan
Kashiwazaki
Niigata
Agano
Nagaoka
Fukushima
Aizu-wakamatsu
Koriyama
Iwaki

Changgi Gap
P'ohang
Oki-shoto
Takaoka
Kanazawa
Toyama
Joetsu
Nagano
Utsunomiya
Hitachi
Honshu

Ulsan
Matsue
Komatsu
Yariga-take ▲3180
Matsumoto
Ueda
Maebashi
Oyama
Mito

Pusan
Tsushima
Tottori
Yonago
Fukui
Okaya
Kofu
Urawa
Sakura
Tsuchiura
Choshi

35°

Korea Strait
Higashi-suido
Masuda
Chugoku-sanchi
Maizuru
Tsuruga
Ogaki
Gifu
Ichinomiya
Nagoya
Toyota
Tenryu
Fuji-san ▲3776
TOKYO
Yokohama
Funabashi
Chiba
Kawasaki
Yokosuka

Iki-shima
Shimonoseki
Okayama
Kobe
Osaka
Suzuka
Tsu
Numazu
Shizuoka

Hiroshima
Sakai
Matsusaka
Hamamatsu

Kita-Kyushu
Seto-naikai
Takamatsu
Ise
Izu-shoto

Sasebo
Fukuoka
Kurume
Matsuyama ▲1981
Shikoku-sanchi ▲1955
Tokushima
Wakayama

Arao
Oita ▲1788
Yawatahama
Kochi
Shingu

Nagasaki
Kumamoto ▲1759
Uwajima ▲1229
Shikoku

2

▲1739
Nobeoka
Hachijo-jima

▲1700
Miyazaki
Kyushu

Kagoshima
Osumi-kaikyo

Yaku-shima
Tanega-shima

PACIFIC OCEAN

1

Tokara-retto

KEY

Relief and physical features

Relief metres
5000
3000
2000
1000
500
200
sea level
0
200 under sea level
4000
6000

3776 ▲ Mountain height (in metres)

Water features

River

Lake / Reservoir

Communications

Railway

Road

⊕ Main airport

Administration

Boundaries

International

Settlement

Cities and towns in order of size

National capital
■ TOKYO

Other city or town
● Osaka
○ Sendai
○ Niigata
○ Wakkanai

SCALE 1 : 7 500 000

0 100 200 300 400 km

Albers Equal Area Conic projection

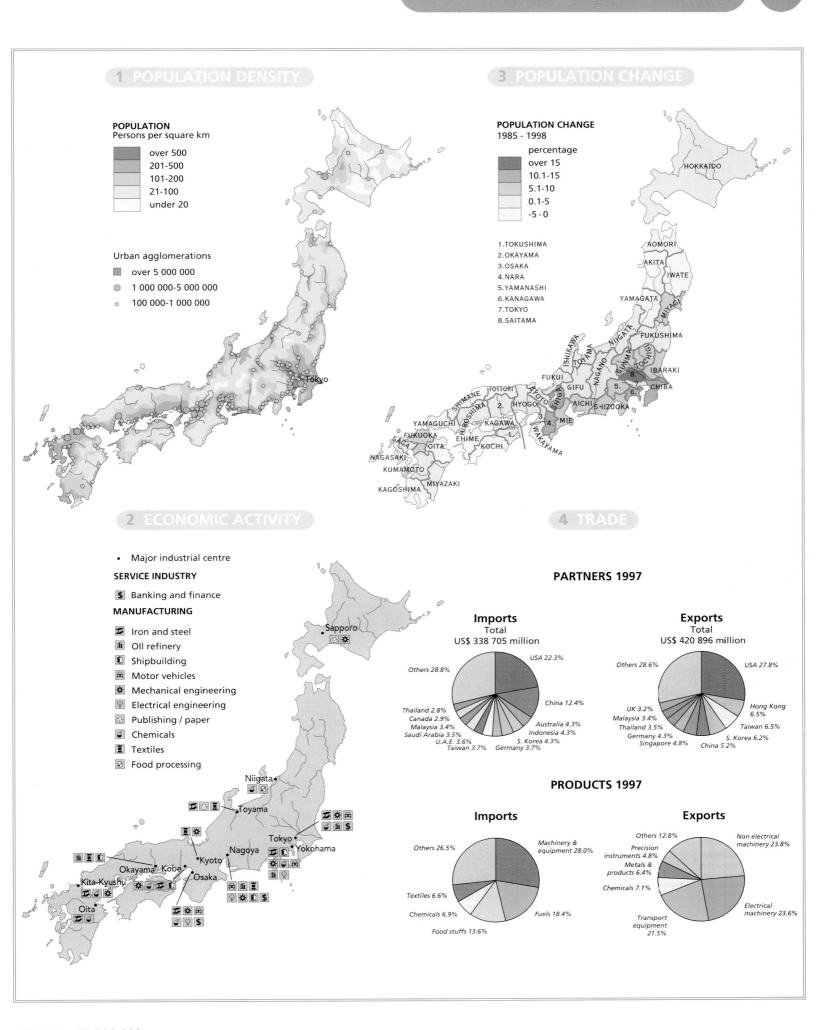

1 POPULATION DENSITY

POPULATION
Persons per square km

- over 500
- 201-500
- 101-200
- 21-100
- under 20

Urban agglomerations

- over 5 000 000
- 1 000 000-5 000 000
- 100 000-1 000 000

Tokyo

3 POPULATION CHANGE

POPULATION CHANGE
1985 - 1998

percentage
- over 15
- 10.1-15
- 5.1-10
- 0.1-5
- -5 - 0

1. TOKUSHIMA
2. OKAYAMA
3. OSAKA
4. NARA
5. YAMANASHI
6. KANAGAWA
7. TOKYO
8. SAITAMA

HOKKAIDO

AOMORI
AKITA
IWATE
YAMAGATA
MIYAGI
FUKUSHIMA
NIIGATA
ISHIKAWA
TOYAMA
NAGANO
GUNMA
TOCHIGI
IBARAKI
FUKUI
GIFU
SHIGA
AICHI
SHIZUOKA
CHIBA
TOTTORI
KYOTO
HYOGO
MIE
SHIMANE
OKAYAMA
HIROSHIMA
KAGAWA
WAKAYAMA
YAMAGUCHI
EHIME
KOCHI
FUKUOKA
SAGA
OITA
NAGASAKI
KUMAMOTO
MIYAZAKI
KAGOSHIMA

2 ECONOMIC ACTIVITY

- • Major industrial centre

SERVICE INDUSTRY
$ Banking and finance

MANUFACTURING
- Iron and steel
- Oil refinery
- Shipbuilding
- Motor vehicles
- Mechanical engineering
- Electrical engineering
- Publishing / paper
- Chemicals
- Textiles
- Food processing

Sapporo
Niigata
Toyama
Tokyo
Yokohama
Nagoya
Kyoto
Okayama Kobe
Osaka
Kita-Kyushu
Oita

4 TRADE

PARTNERS 1997

Imports
Total
US$ 338 705 million

Others 28.8%
USA 22.3%
China 12.4%
Australia 4.3%
Indonesia 4.3%
S. Korea 4.3%
Germany 3.7%
Taiwan 3.7%
U.A.E. 3.6%
Saudi Arabia 3.5%
Malaysia 3.4%
Canada 2.9%
Thailand 2.8%

Exports
Total
US$ 420 896 million

Others 28.6%
USA 27.8%
Hong Kong 6.5%
Taiwan 6.5%
S. Korea 6.2%
China 5 2%
Singapore 4.8%
Germany 4.3%
Thailand 3.5%
Malaysia 3.4%
UK 3.2%

PRODUCTS 1997

Imports

Others 26.5%
Machinery & equipment 28.0%
Fuels 18.4%
Food stuffs 13.6%
Chemicals 6.9%
Textiles 6.6%

Exports

Others 12.8%
Non electrical machinery 23.8%
Electrical machinery 23.6%
Transport equipment 21.5%
Chemicals 7.1%
Metals & products 6.4%
Precision instruments 4.8%

SCALE 1 : 15 000 000

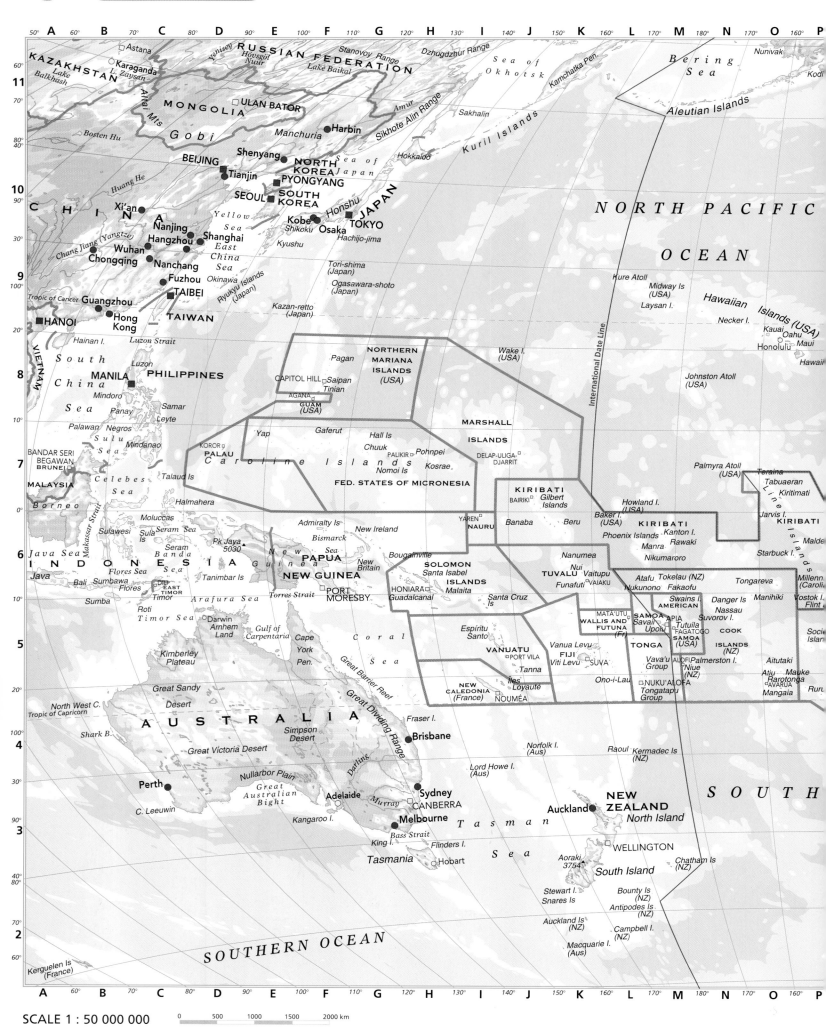

SCALE 1 : 50 000 000

0   500   1000   1500   2000 km

KEY

Relief and physical features

Relief metres
5000
3000
2000
1000
500
200
sea level
under sea level
0
200
3000
5000

6960 ▲ Mountain height (in metres)

Administration

Boundaries
International

Settlement
Cities and towns in order of size

National capital
■ MEXICO CITY
□ ULAN BATOR
□ CANBERRA
□ SUVA
▫ VAIAKU

Other city or town
● Seattle
○ Adelaide
○ Honolulu

▲ Mt Logan 5959

Caribou Mts
Peace
Lake Athabasca
Nelson

HUDSON BAY
Belcher Is

Gulf of Alaska

CANADA

Queen Charlotte Islands

Coast Mountains
ROCKY

Vancouver
Vancouver Island
Seattle

Columbia
Cascade Range
Coast Range
Sierra Nevada

Lake Winnipeg
L. Nipigon
Lake Superior

UNITED STATES OF AMERICA

Yellowstone
Missouri
M ts

San Francisco
Mt Whitney ▲ 4418

Denver
Arkansas
Kansas City

Colorado
Los Angeles
San Diego

Gulf of California
Lower California

Rio Grande

Guadalupe (Mexico)

Revillagigedo Is. (Mexico)

Gulf of Mexico
Str. of Florida

Miami/Fort Lauderdale
NASSAU
HAVANA
THE BAHAMAS

Tropic of Cancer

MEXICO

Guadalajara
MEXICO CITY
Popocatepetl 5452

Yucatán Channel
Yucatán

CUBA

Greater Antilles
JAMAICA
Kingston

DOMINICAN REP.
HAITI
SANTO DOMINGO
PORT-AU-PRINCE
PUERTO RICO (USA)

BELIZE
BELMOPAN

GUATEMALA
GUATEMALA CITY
HONDURAS
TEGUCIGALPA
SAN SALVADOR
NICARAGUA
MANAGUA
EL SALVADOR

Caribbean Sea
Lesser Antilles

Clipperton I. (France)

COSTA RICA
SAN JOSÉ
PANAMA CITY
PANAMA

CARACAS

VENEZUELA

I. del Coco (Costa Rica)

Medellín

Llanos
Orinoco
GUYANA
SURINAME
FRENCH GUIANA

BOGOTÁ

I. de Malpelo (Colombia)

COLOMBIA

Galapagos Islands (Ecuador)

QUITO
ECUADOR
Chimborazo 6310

Equator

Negro
Amazon

B R A Z I L

Marañón
Selvas

Nuku Hiva
Marquesas Islands
Hiva Oa

Huascaran ▲ 6768

Madeira
Araguaia

Tuamotu Islands
giroa
Îles du Désappointement

LIMA
A
PERU
N
D

hiti
PEETE
FRENCH
POLYNESIA

Groupe Actéon

LA PAZ
L. Titicaca
BOLIVIA
SUCRE

BRASÍLIA

uai
Mururoa
Raivavae
Gambier Is

Henderson I. (UK)
Ducie I. (UK)
Pitcairn I. (UK)

S
E
Atacama Desert
Gran Chaco
Paraguay

(Fr)
Rapa
Marotiri

I. Sala y Gómez (Chile)
Easter I. (Chile)

San Félix (Chile)
San Ambrosio (Chile)

PARAGUAY
ASUNCIÓN

Tropic of Capricorn

Ojos del Salado 6908
Paraná

PACIFIC OCEAN

Juan Fernandez Is (Chile)

Aconcagua 6960
A
N
D
E
S

Pampas
URUGUAY
MONTEVIDEO
BUENOS AIRES

SANTIAGO
C
H
ARGENTINA

I. de Chiloé

Golfo San Matías

Patagonia
Golfo de San Jorge

ATLANTIC OCEAN

Tierra del Fuego
Str. of Magellan

Falkland Islands (UK)

South Georgia (UK)

Cape Horn

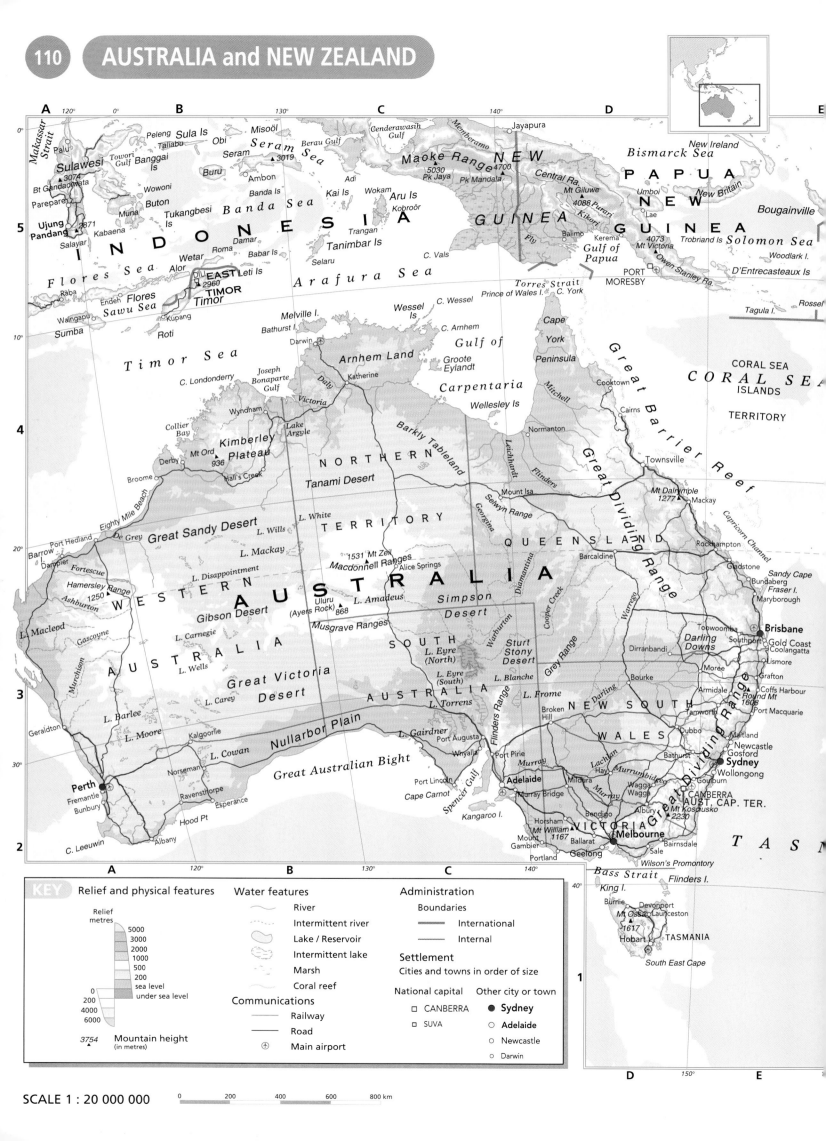

KEY

Relief and physical features

Relief metres
5000
3000
2000
1000
500
200
sea level
0
200 under sea level
4000
6000

3754 ▲ Mountain height (in metres)

Water features

River
Intermittent river
Lake / Reservoir
Intermittent lake
Marsh
Coral reef

Communications

Railway
Road
⊕ Main airport

Administration

Boundaries
International
Internal

Settlement
Cities and towns in order of size

National capital
□ CANBERRA
□ SUVA

Other city or town
● Sydney
○ Adelaide
○ Newcastle
○ Darwin

SCALE 1 : 20 000 000
0   200   400   600   800 km

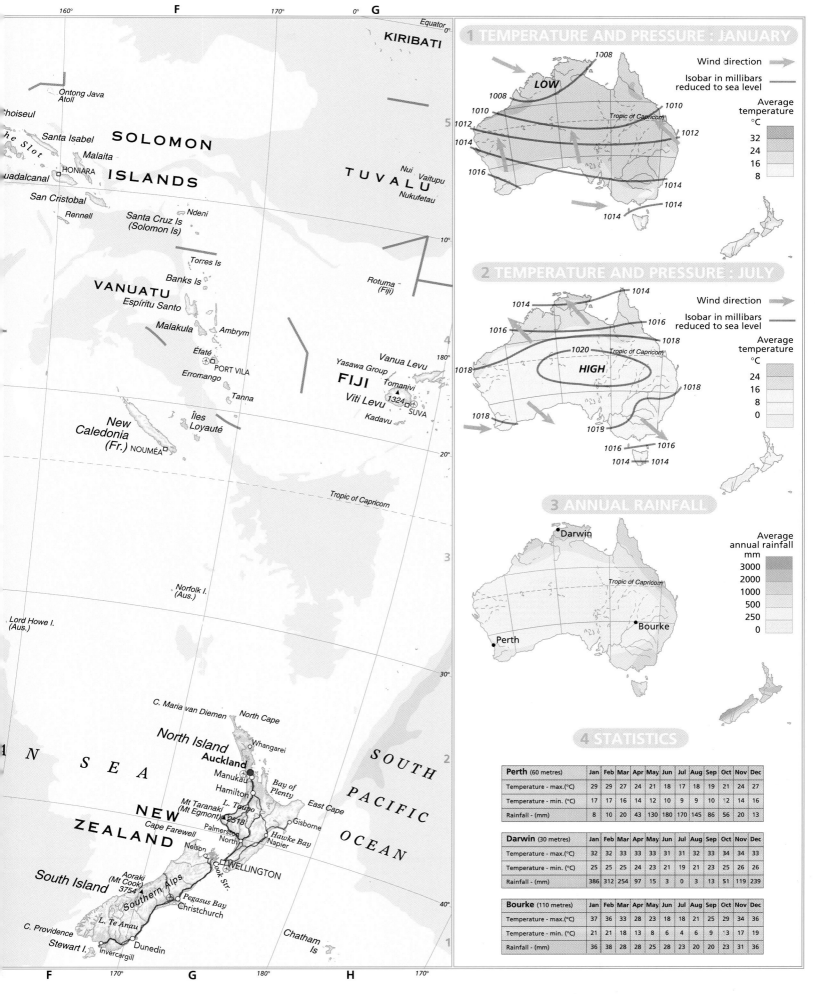

1 TEMPERATURE AND PRESSURE : JANUARY

Wind direction
Isobar in millibars reduced to sea level

Average temperature °C
32
24
16
8

2 TEMPERATURE AND PRESSURE : JULY

Wind direction
Isobar in millibars reduced to sea level

Average temperature °C
24
16
8
0

3 ANNUAL RAINFALL

Average annual rainfall mm
3000
2000
1000
500
250
0

4 STATISTICS

Perth (60 metres)	Jan	Feb	Mar	Apr	May	Jun	Jul	Aug	Sep	Oct	Nov	Dec
Temperature - max.(°C)	29	29	27	24	21	18	17	18	19	21	24	27
Temperature - min. (°C)	17	17	16	14	12	10	9	9	10	12	14	16
Rainfall - (mm)	8	10	20	43	130	180	170	145	86	56	20	13

Darwin (30 metres)	Jan	Feb	Mar	Apr	May	Jun	Jul	Aug	Sep	Oct	Nov	Dec
Temperature - max.(°C)	32	32	33	33	33	31	31	32	33	34	34	33
Temperature - min. (°C)	25	25	25	24	23	21	19	21	23	25	26	26
Rainfall - (mm)	386	312	254	97	15	3	0	3	13	51	119	239

Bourke (110 metres)	Jan	Feb	Mar	Apr	May	Jun	Jul	Aug	Sep	Oct	Nov	Dec
Temperature - max.(°C)	37	36	33	28	23	18	18	21	25	29	34	36
Temperature - min. (°C)	21	21	18	13	8	6	4	6	9	13	17	19
Rainfall - (mm)	36	38	28	28	25	28	23	20	20	23	31	36

Lambert Azimuthal Equal Area projection

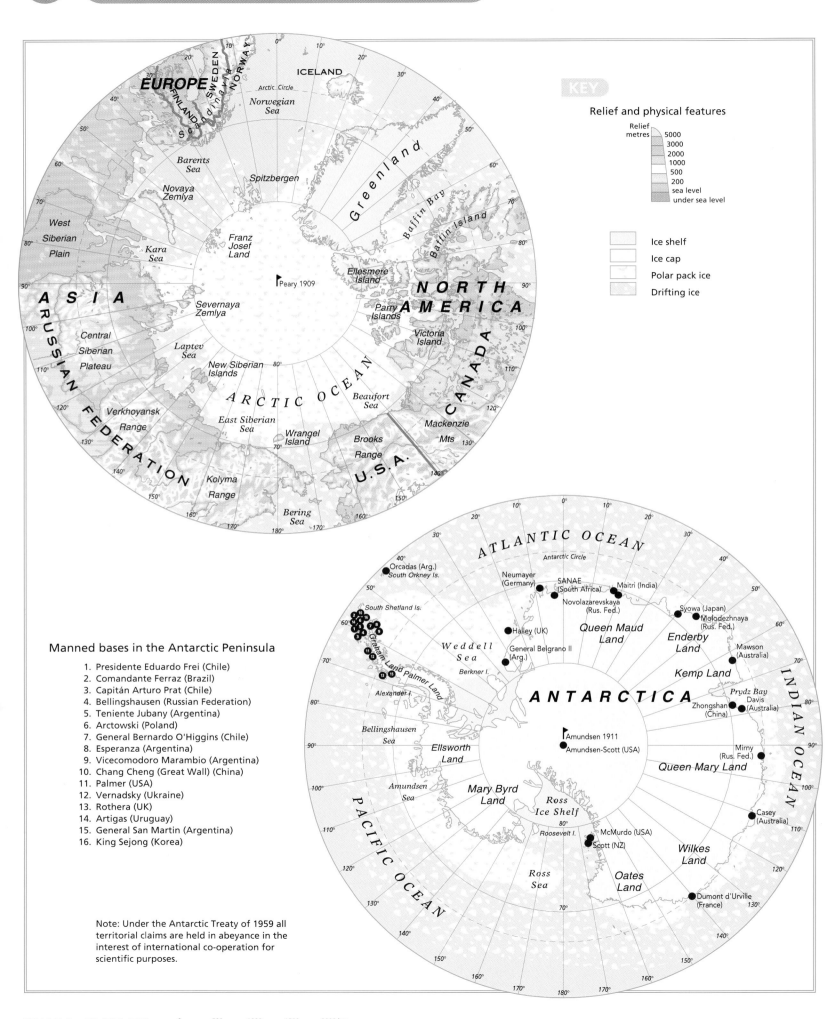

KEY

Relief and physical features

Relief metres	
	5000
	3000
	2000
	1000
	500
	200
	sea level
	under sea level

Ice shelf

Ice cap

Polar pack ice

Drifting ice

Arctic Ocean map labels:

EUROPE
ICELAND
SWEDEN
FINLAND
NORWAY
Arctic Circle
Norwegian Sea
Barents Sea
Spitzbergen
Novaya Zemlya
West Siberian Plain
Kara Sea
Franz Josef Land
Greenland
Baffin Bay
Baffin Island
Ellesmere Island
Peary 1909
NORTH AMERICA
ASIA
RUSSIAN FEDERATION
Severnaya Zemlya
Parry Islands
Victoria Island
CANADA
Central Siberian Plateau
Laptev Sea
New Siberian Islands
ARCTIC OCEAN
Beaufort Sea
Verkhoyansk Range
East Siberian Sea
Wrangel Island
Brooks Range
Mackenzie Mts
U.S.A.
Kolyma Range
Bering Sea

Manned bases in the Antarctic Peninsula

1. Presidente Eduardo Frei (Chile)
2. Comandante Ferraz (Brazil)
3. Capitán Arturo Prat (Chile)
4. Bellingshausen (Russian Federation)
5. Teniente Jubany (Argentina)
6. Arctowski (Poland)
7. General Bernardo O'Higgins (Chile)
8. Esperanza (Argentina)
9. Vicecomodoro Marambio (Argentina)
10. Chang Cheng (Great Wall) (China)
11. Palmer (USA)
12. Vernadsky (Ukraine)
13. Rothera (UK)
14. Artigas (Uruguay)
15. General San Martin (Argentina)
16. King Sejong (Korea)

Note: Under the Antarctic Treaty of 1959 all territorial claims are held in abeyance in the interest of international co-operation for scientific purposes.

Antarctica map labels:

ATLANTIC OCEAN
Antarctic Circle
Orcadas (Arg.)
South Orkney Is.
Neumayer (Germany)
SANAE (South Africa)
Maitri (India)
Novolazarevskaya (Rus. Fed.)
Syowa (Japan)
Molodezhnaya (Rus. Fed.)
South Shetland Is.
Halley (UK)
Queen Maud Land
Enderby Land
Mawson (Australia)
Graham Land
Palmer Land
Weddell Sea
General Belgrano II (Arg.)
Berkner I.
Kemp Land
Alexander I.
ANTARCTICA
Prydz Bay
Davis (Australia)
Zhongshan (China)
Bellingshausen Sea
Ellsworth Land
Amundsen 1911
Amundsen-Scott (USA)
Mirny (Rus. Fed.)
Queen Mary Land
INDIAN OCEAN
Amundsen Sea
Mary Byrd Land
Ross Ice Shelf
Casey (Australia)
PACIFIC OCEAN
Roosevelt I.
McMurdo (USA)
Scott (NZ)
Wilkes Land
Ross Sea
Oates Land
Dumont d'Urville (France)

SCALE 1 : 50 000 000

0   500   1000   1500   2000 km

Polar Stereographic projection

1 TIME ZONES

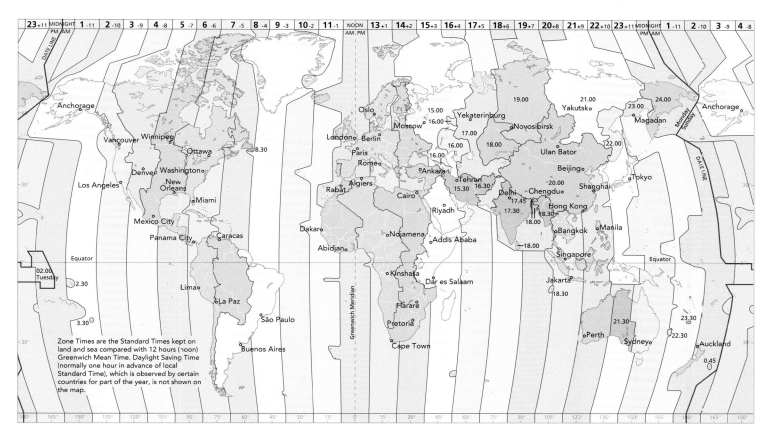

| 23 +11 | MIDNIGHT | 1 -11 | 2 -10 | 3 -9 | 4 -8 | 5 -7 | 6 -6 | 7 -5 | 8 -4 | 9 -3 | 10 -2 | 11 -1 | NOON | 13 +1 | 14 +2 | 15 +3 | 16 +4 | 17 +5 | 18 +6 | 19 +7 | 20 +8 | 21 +9 | 22 +10 | 23 +11 | MIDNIGHT | 1 -11 | 2 -10 | 3 -9 | 4 -8 |
| | PM AM | | | | | | | | | | | | AM PM | | | | | | | | | | | | PM AM | | | | |

Anchorage · Vancouver · Winnipeg · Ottawa · Denver · Washington · Los Angeles · New Orleans · Miami · Mexico City · Panama City · Caracas · Lima · La Paz · São Paulo · Buenos Aires

Oslo · London · Berlin · Paris · Moscow · Rome · Algiers · Rabat · Cairo · Riyadh · Dakar · Abidjan · Ndjamena · Addis Ababa · Kinshasa · Dar es Salaam · Harare · Pretoria · Cape Town

Yekaterinburg · Novosibirsk · Ulan Bator · Ankara · Tehran · Delhi · Chengdu · Beijing · Shanghai · Hong Kong · Bangkok · Manila · Singapore · Jakarta · Tokyo · Yakutsk · Magadan · Perth · Sydney · Auckland

15.00 · 16.00 · 17.00 · 16.00 · 18.00 · 19.00 · 21.00 · 24.00 · 23.00 · 22.00 · 20.00 · 17.45 · 17.30 · 18.00 · 18.30 · 18.00 · 15.30 · 16.30 · 18.30 · 21.30 · 22.30 · 23.30 · 0.45 · 8.30 · 02.00 Tuesday · 2.30 · 3.30

DATE LINE · Monday Sunday · DATE LINE · Equator · Greenwich Meridian

Zone Times are the Standard Times kept on land and sea compared with 12 hours (noon) Greenwich Mean Time. Daylight Saving Time (normally one hour in advance of local Standard Time), which is observed by certain countries for part of the year, is not shown on the map.

180° · 165° · 150° · 135° · 120° · 105° · 90° · 75° · 60° · 45° · 30° · 15° · 0° · 15° · 30° · 45° · 60° · 75° · 90° · 105° · 120° · 135° · 150° · 165° · 180° · 165° · 150°

2 INTERNATIONAL ORGANIZATIONS

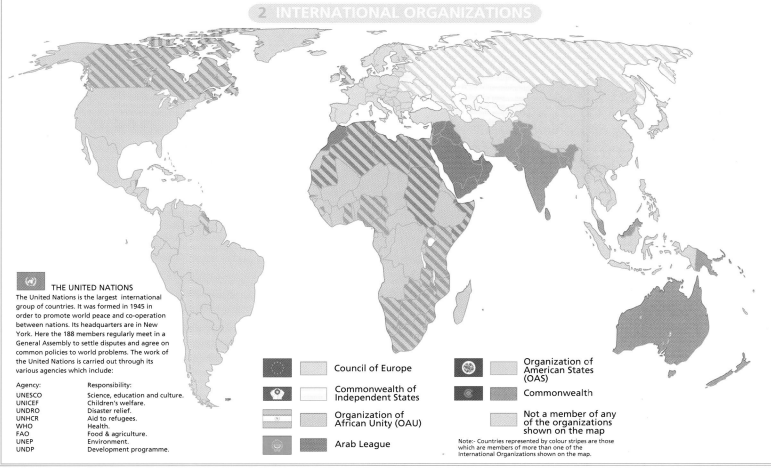

THE UNITED NATIONS

The United Nations is the largest international group of countries. It was formed in 1945 in order to promote world peace and co-operation between nations. Its headquarters are in New York. Here the 188 members regularly meet in a General Assembly to settle disputes and agree on common policies to world problems. The work of the United Nations is carried out through its various agencies which include:

Agency:	Responsibility:
UNESCO	Science, education and culture.
UNICEF	Children's welfare.
UNDRO	Disaster relief.
UNHCR	Aid to refugees.
WHO	Health.
FAO	Food & agriculture.
UNEP	Environment.
UNDP	Development programme.

Council of Europe

Commonwealth of Independent States

Organization of African Unity (OAU)

Arab League

Organization of American States (OAS)

Commonwealth

Not a member of any of the organizations shown on the map

Note:- Countries represented by colour stripes are those which are members of more than one of the International Organizations shown on the map.

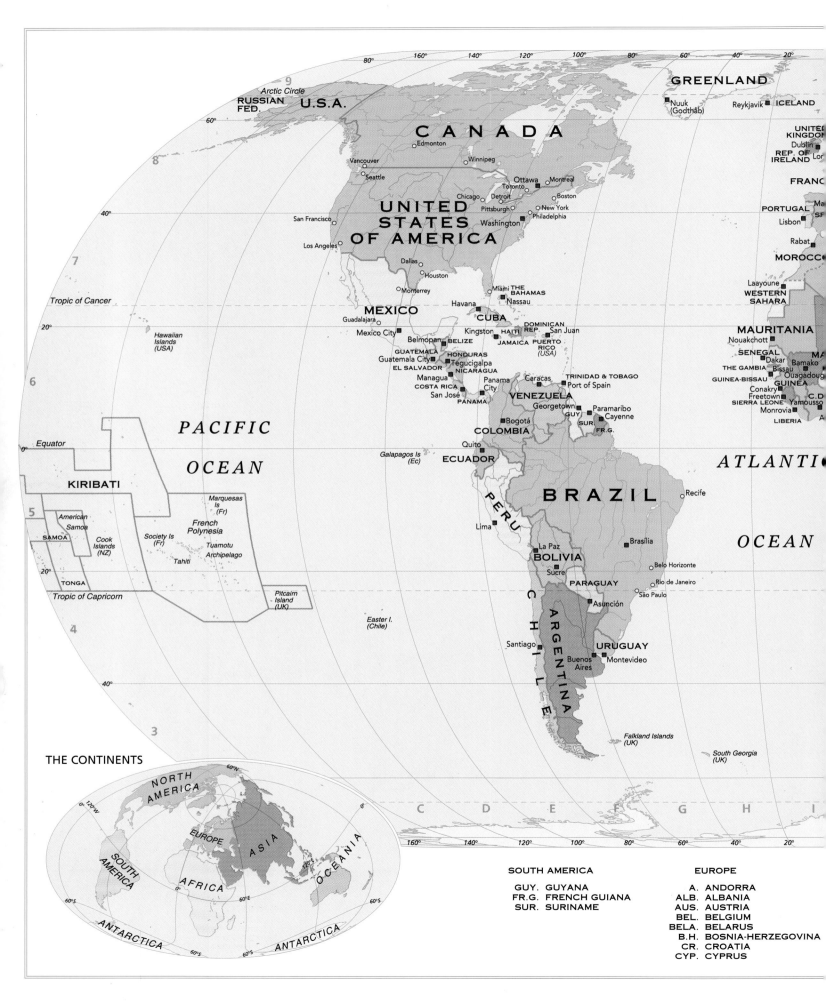

THE CONTINENTS

SOUTH AMERICA		EUROPE	
GUY.	GUYANA	A.	ANDORRA
FR.G.	FRENCH GUIANA	ALB.	ALBANIA
SUR.	SURINAME	AUS.	AUSTRIA
		BEL.	BELGIUM
		BELA.	BELARUS
		B.H.	BOSNIA-HERZEGOVINA
		CR.	CROATIA
		CYP.	CYPRUS

SCALE 1 : 77 500 000

0   800   1600   2400   3200 km

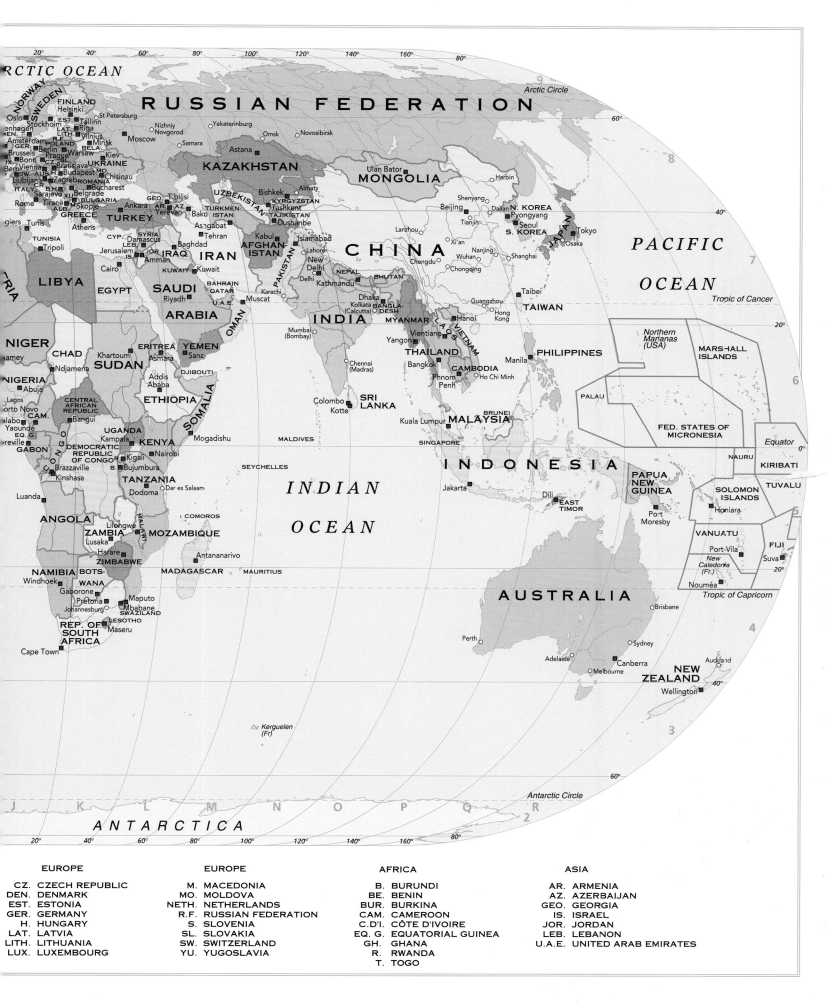

Arctic Circle
Tropic of Cancer
Equator
Tropic of Capricorn
Antarctic Circle

ARCTIC OCEAN

PACIFIC
OCEAN

INDIAN

OCEAN

RUSSIAN FEDERATION

NORWAY
SWEDEN
FINLAND
Oslo
Helsinki
St Petersburg
Stockholm
EST. Tallinn
enhagen
LAT. Riga
Amsterdam LITH. Vilnius
EN. Minsk
GER. BELA.
Brussels POLAND Moscow
Bonn Berlin Warsaw Kiev
Bern Vienna Prague UKRAINE
SW. AUS H. Bratislava MO. Chisinau
ITALY Budapest ROMANIA
Ljubljana CR. Zagreb Bucharest
Rome Sarajevo B.H. Belgrade
Tiranë YU. BULGARIA
giers Tunis ALB. MSkopje
GREECE TURKEY
Athens
CYP.
TUNISIA
Tripoli
SYRIA LEB.
Damascus
Jerusalem JOR. IRAQ
IS. Amman Baghdad
Cairo KUWAIT Kuwait

Nizhniy
Novgorod
Yekaterinburg
Omsk
Novosibirsk
Samara

Astana

KAZAKHSTAN

UZBEKISTAN
Bishkek
Almaty
KYRGYZSTAN
GEO. T'bilisi Tashkent
AZ. Yerevan Baku TAJIKISTAN
Ankara TURKMEN- Dushanbe
ISTAN
Ashgabat
Tehran Kabul
AFGHAN-
ISTAN
IRAN Islamabad
New Lahore
Delhi

MONGOLIA
Ulan Bator
Harbin
Shenyang
Beijing Dalian N. KOREA
Tianjin Pyongyang
Seoul
Lanzhou S. KOREA
Xi'an
Chengdu Nanjing Shanghai
Chongqing Wuhan

Tokyo
Osaka

LIBYA

EGYPT

SAUDI
ARABIA
Riyadh
BAHRAIN
QATAR
U.A.E.
Muscat

OMAN
PAKISTAN
Karachi
Delhi
NEPAL
Kathmandu
BHUTAN
Dhaka
Kolkata BANGLA-
(Calcutta) DESH

CHINA

Guangzhou
Hong
Kong

Taibei

TAIWAN

Taipei

NIGER
CHAD
ERITREA YEMEN
Khartoum Asmara Sana
SUDAN DJIBOUTI
NIGERIA Addis
Abuja Ababa
CENTRAL ETHIOPIA
AFRICAN SOMALIA
REPUBLIC
Bangui

Mumbai
(Bombay)

INDIA

Chennai
(Madras)

Colombo SRI
Kotte LANKA

MYANMAR
Yangon
THAILAND
Bangkok
Vientiane
LAOS
VIETNAM
Hanoi

CAMBODIA
Phnom
Penh
Ho Chi Minh

Manila
PHILIPPINES

Northern
Marianas
(USA)

MARSHALL
ISLANDS

PALAU

FED. STATES OF
MICRONESIA

NAURU

KIRIBATI

NIGER
amey
Lagos
rto Novo CAM.
labo EQ. G.
Yaounde
reville GABON
DEMOCRATIC
REPUBLIC
OF CONGO
Kinshasa

UGANDA
Kampala KENYA
Kigali Nairobi
B. Bujumbura
TANZANIA
Dodoma
Dar es Salaam

Mogadishu

MALDIVES

SEYCHELLES

SINGAPORE

Kuala Lumpur
MALAYSIA

BRUNEI

INDONESIA

PAPUA
NEW
GUINEA
Port
Moresby

SOLOMON
ISLANDS
Honiara

TUVALU

Luanda
ANGOLA
ZAMBIA
Lusaka
Lilongwe
MOZAMBIQUE
Harare
ZIMBABWE
NAMIBIA BOTS-
Windhoek WANA
Gaborone
Johannesburg Pretoria Maputo
Mbabane
SWAZILAND
REP. OF LESOTHO
SOUTH Maseru
AFRICA
Cape Town

COMOROS

INDIAN

OCEAN

Antananarivo
MADAGASCAR MAURITIUS

Jakarta

Dili
EAST
TIMOR

AUSTRALIA

Perth

Adelaide
Melbourne

Sydney
Canberra

NEW
ZEALAND
Wellington

Brisbane

VANUATU
Port-Vila
New
Caledonia
(Fr.)
Nouméa

FIJI
Suva

Auckland

Kerguelen
(Fr)

ANTARCTICA

Eckert IV projection

EUROPE	EUROPE	AFRICA	ASIA
CZ. CZECH REPUBLIC	M. MACEDONIA	B. BURUNDI	AR. ARMENIA
DEN. DENMARK	MO. MOLDOVA	BE. BENIN	AZ. AZERBAIJAN
EST. ESTONIA	NETH. NETHERLANDS	BUR. BURKINA	GEO. GEORGIA
GER. GERMANY	R.F. RUSSIAN FEDERATION	CAM. CAMEROON	IS. ISRAEL
H. HUNGARY	S. SLOVENIA	C.D'I. CÔTE D'IVOIRE	JOR. JORDAN
LAT. LATVIA	SL. SLOVAKIA	EQ. G. EQUATORIAL GUINEA	LEB. LEBANON
LITH. LITHUANIA	SW. SWITZERLAND	GH. GHANA	U.A.E. UNITED ARAB EMIRATES
LUX. LUXEMBOURG	YU. YUGOSLAVIA	R. RWANDA	
		T. TOGO	

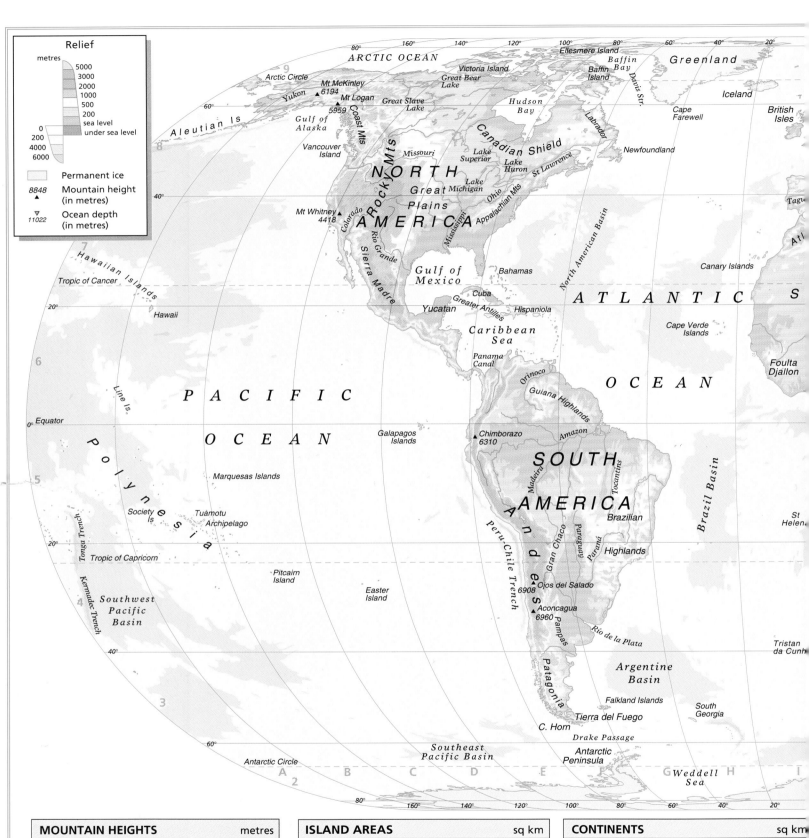

Relief

metres
- 5000
- 3000
- 2000
- 1000
- 500
- 200

0 sea level

under sea level
- 200
- 4000
- 6000

Permanent ice

8848 ▲ Mountain height (in metres)

11022 ▽ Ocean depth (in metres)

MOUNTAIN HEIGHTS	metres
Mt Everest (Nepal/China)	8848
K2 (Jammu & Kashmir/China)	8611
Kangchenjunga (Nepal/India)	8586
Dhaulagiri (Nepal)	8167
Annapurna (Nepal)	8091
Aconcagua (Argentina)	6960
Ojos del Salado (Arg./Chile)	6908
Chimborazo (Ecuador)	6310
Mt McKinley (USA)	6194
Mt Logan (Canada)	5959

ISLAND AREAS	sq km
Greenland	2 175 600
New Guinea	808 510
Borneo	745 561
Madagascar	587 040
Sumatra	473 606
Baffin Island	507 451
Honshu	227 414
Great Britain	218 476
Victoria Island	217 291
Ellesmere Island	196 236

CONTINENTS	sq km
Asia	45 036 492
Africa	30 343 578
North America	24 680 331
South America	17 815 420
Antarctica	12 093 000
Europe	9 908 599
Oceania	8 923 000

SCALE 1 : 80 000 000

0   800   1600   2400   3200 km

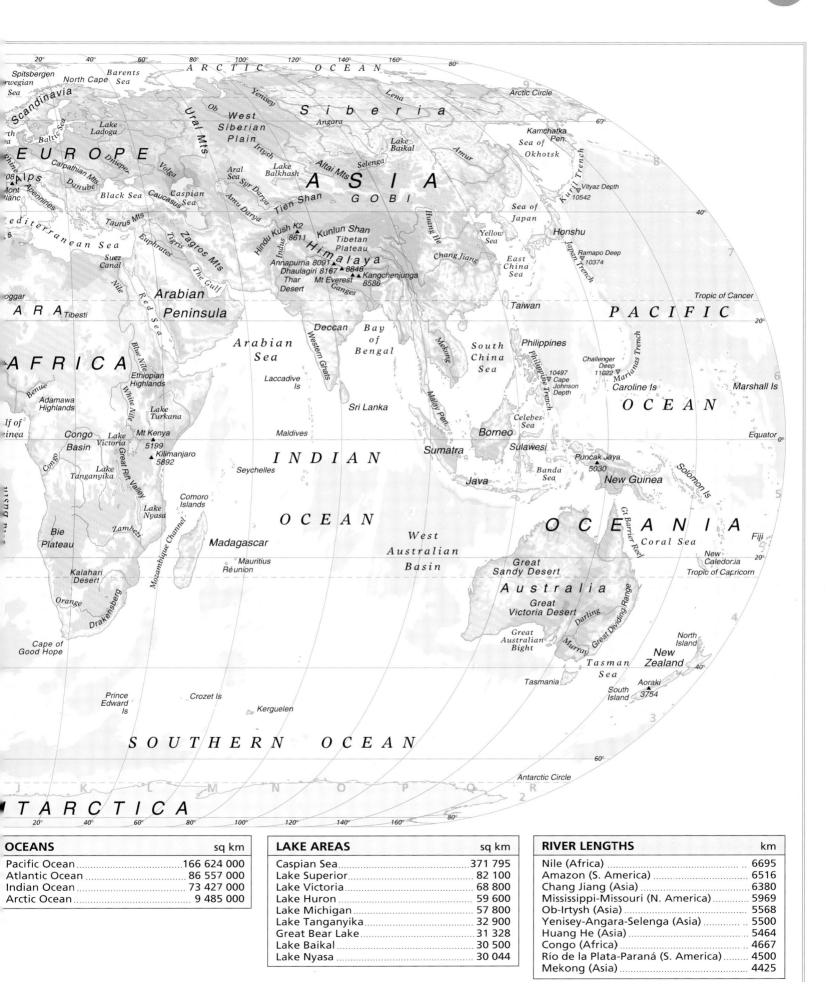

OCEANS	sq km
Pacific Ocean	166 624 000
Atlantic Ocean	86 557 000
Indian Ocean	73 427 000
Arctic Ocean	9 485 000

LAKE AREAS	sq km
Caspian Sea	371 795
Lake Superior	82 100
Lake Victoria	68 800
Lake Huron	59 600
Lake Michigan	57 800
Lake Tanganyika	32 900
Great Bear Lake	31 328
Lake Baikal	30 500
Lake Nyasa	30 044

RIVER LENGTHS	km
Nile (Africa)	6695
Amazon (S. America)	6516
Chang Jiang (Asia)	6380
Mississippi-Missouri (N. America)	5969
Ob-Irtysh (Asia)	5568
Yenisey-Angara-Selenga (Asia)	5500
Huang He (Asia)	5464
Congo (Africa)	4667
Río de la Plata-Paraná (S. America)	4500
Mekong (Asia)	4425

CLIMATIC GRAPHS

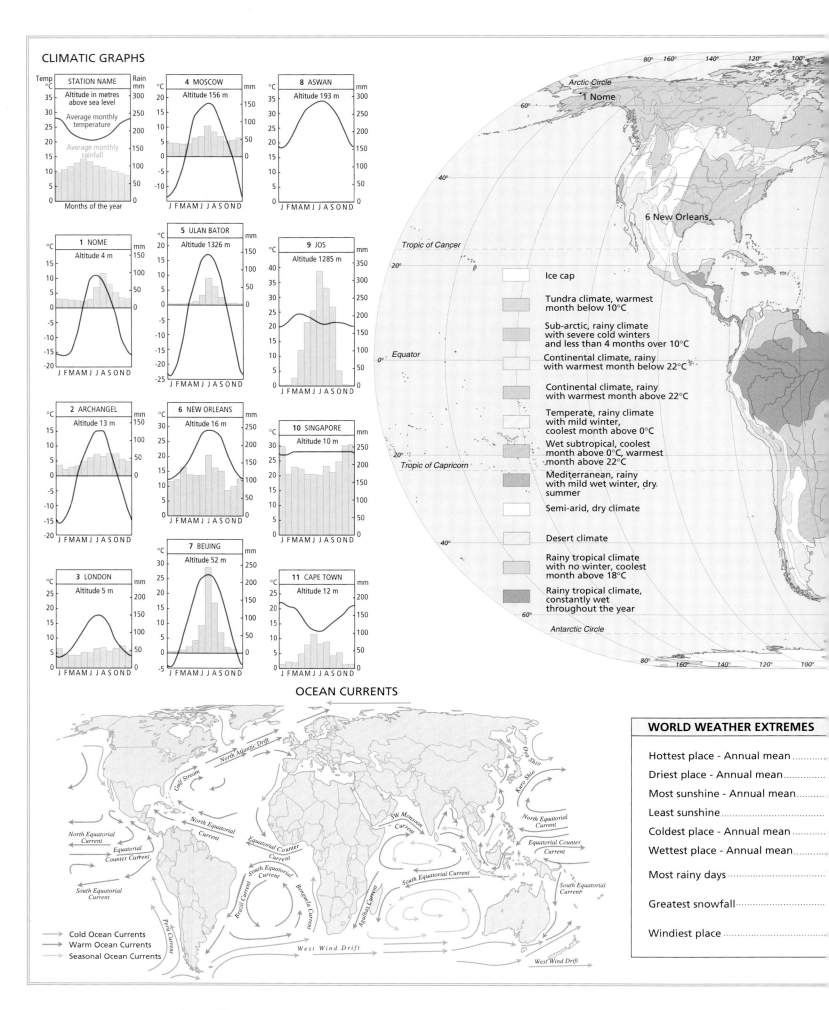

STATION NAME		
Temp °C		Rain mm
Altitude in metres above sea level		
Average monthly temperature		
Average monthly rainfall		
Months of the year		

4 MOSCOW — Altitude 156 m

8 ASWAN — Altitude 193 m

1 NOME — Altitude 4 m

5 ULAN BATOR — Altitude 1326 m

9 JOS — Altitude 1285 m

2 ARCHANGEL — Altitude 13 m

6 NEW ORLEANS — Altitude 16 m

10 SINGAPORE — Altitude 10 m

3 LONDON — Altitude 5 m

7 BEIJING — Altitude 52 m

11 CAPE TOWN — Altitude 12 m

Ice cap

Tundra climate, warmest month below 10°C

Sub-arctic, rainy climate with severe cold winters and less than 4 months over 10°C

Continental climate, rainy with warmest month below 22°C

Continental climate, rainy with warmest month above 22°C

Temperate, rainy climate with mild winter, coolest month above 0°C

Wet subtropical, coolest month above 0°C, warmest month above 22°C

Mediterranean, rainy with mild wet winter, dry summer

Semi-arid, dry climate

Desert climate

Rainy tropical climate with no winter, coolest month above 18°C

Rainy tropical climate, constantly wet throughout the year

Arctic Circle

1 Nome

6 New Orleans

Tropic of Cancer

Equator

Tropic of Capricorn

Antarctic Circle

OCEAN CURRENTS

North Atlantic Drift

Gulf Stream

Oya Shio

Kuro Shio

North Equatorial Current

North Equatorial Current

Equatorial Counter Current

SW Monsoon Current

North Equatorial Current

Equatorial Counter Current

Equatorial Counter Current

South Equatorial Current

South Equatorial Current

South Equatorial Current

South Equatorial Current

Brazil Current

Benguela Current

Agulhas Current

Peru Current

West Wind Drift

West Wind Drift

→ Cold Ocean Currents
→ Warm Ocean Currents
→ Seasonal Ocean Currents

WORLD WEATHER EXTREMES	
Hottest place - Annual mean	
Driest place - Annual mean	
Most sunshine - Annual mean	
Least sunshine	
Coldest place - Annual mean	
Wettest place - Annual mean	
Most rainy days	
Greatest snowfall	
Windiest place	

SCALE 1 : 100 000 000

0   1000   2000   3000   4000 km

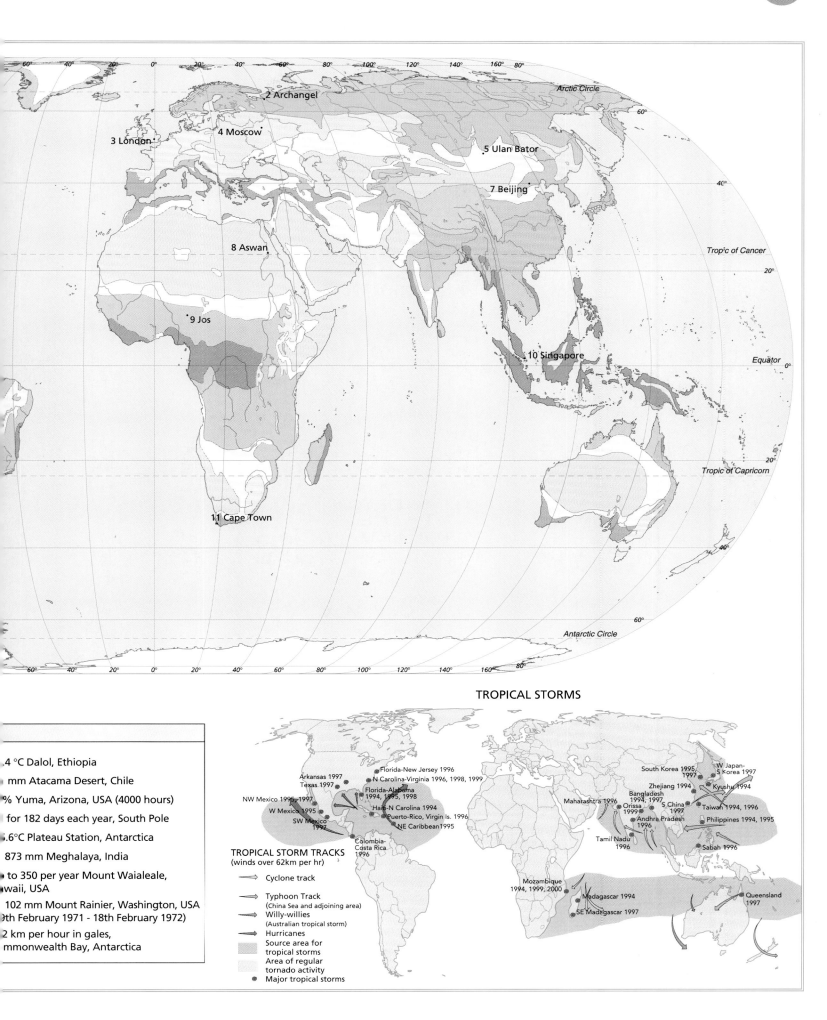

60° 40° 20° 0° 20° 40° 60° 80° 100° 120° 140° 160° 80°

Arctic Circle

2 Archangel

4 Moscow

3 London

5 Ulan Bator

7 Beijing

40°

Tropic of Cancer

8 Aswan

20°

9 Jos

10 Singapore

Equator 0°

Tropic of Capricorn 20°

11 Cape Town

40°

60°

Antarctic Circle

60° 40° 20° 0° 20° 40° 60° 80° 100° 120° 140° 160° 80°

TROPICAL STORMS

4 °C Dalol, Ethiopia

mm Atacama Desert, Chile

% Yuma, Arizona, USA (4000 hours)

for 182 days each year, South Pole

.6°C Plateau Station, Antarctica

873 mm Meghalaya, India

to 350 per year Mount Waialeale, waii, USA

102 mm Mount Rainier, Washington, USA th February 1971 - 18th February 1972)

2 km per hour in gales, mmonwealth Bay, Antarctica

Arkansas 1997
Texas 1997
Florida-New Jersey 1996
N Carolina-Virginia 1996, 1998, 1999
NW Mexico 1995-1997
Florida-Alabama 1994, 1995, 1998
W Mexico 1995
Haiti-N Carolina 1994
SW Mexico 1997
Puerto-Rico, Virgin Is. 1996
NE Caribbean 1995
Colombia-Costa Rica 1996

South Korea 1995, 1997
W Japan-S Korea 1997
Zhejiang 1994
Kyushu 1994
Bangladesh 1994, 1997
S China 1997
Taiwan 1994, 1996
Maharashtra 1996
Orissa 1999
Andhra Pradesh 1996
Philippines 1994, 1995
Tamil Nadu 1996
Sabah 1996
Mozambique 1994, 1999, 2000
Madagascar 1994
Queensland 1997
SE Madagascar 1997

TROPICAL STORM TRACKS
(winds over 62km per hr)

→ Cyclone track

→ Typhoon Track
(China Sea and adjoining area)

→ Willy-willies
(Australian tropical storm)

→ Hurricanes

Source area for tropical storms

Area of regular tornado activity

● Major tropical storms

Eckert IV projection

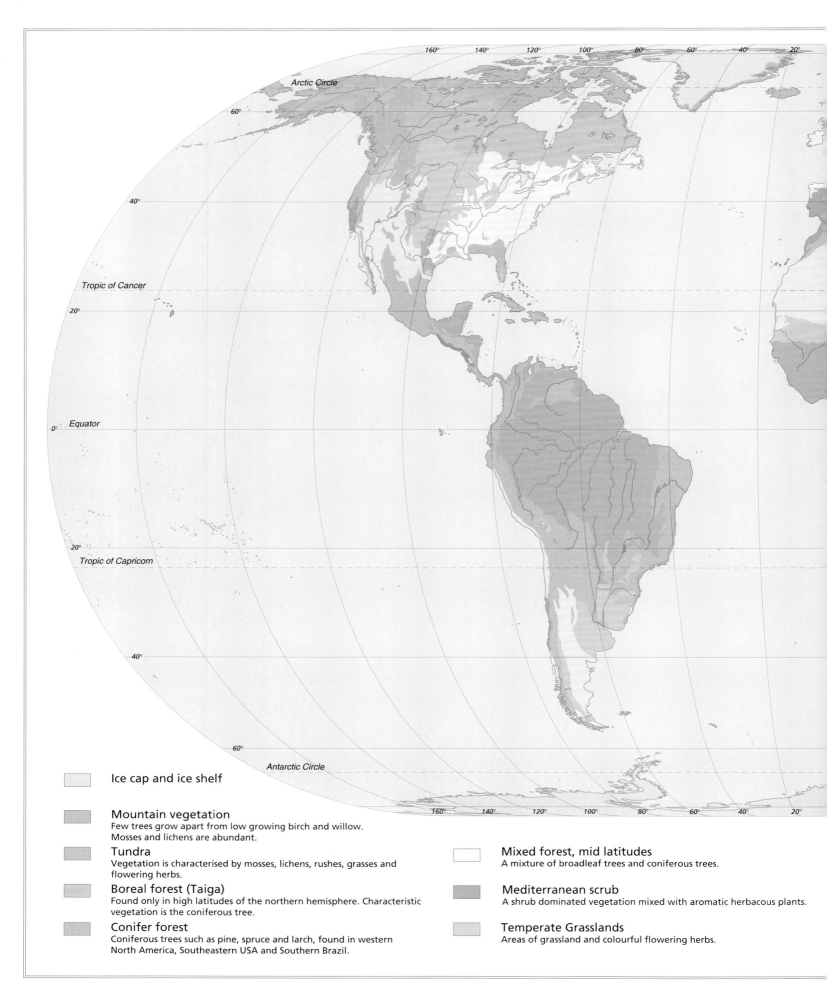

Ice cap and ice shelf

Mountain vegetation
Few trees grow apart from low growing birch and willow.
Mosses and lichens are abundant.

Tundra
Vegetation is characterised by mosses, lichens, rushes, grasses and
flowering herbs.

Boreal forest (Taiga)
Found only in high latitudes of the northern hemisphere. Characteristic
vegetation is the coniferous tree.

Conifer forest
Coniferous trees such as pine, spruce and larch, found in western
North America, Southeastern USA and Southern Brazil.

Mixed forest, mid latitudes
A mixture of broadleaf trees and coniferous trees.

Mediterranean scrub
A shrub dominated vegetation mixed with aromatic herbacous plants.

Temperate Grasslands
Areas of grassland and colourful flowering herbs.

SCALE 1 : 80 000 000   0   800   1600   2400   3200 km

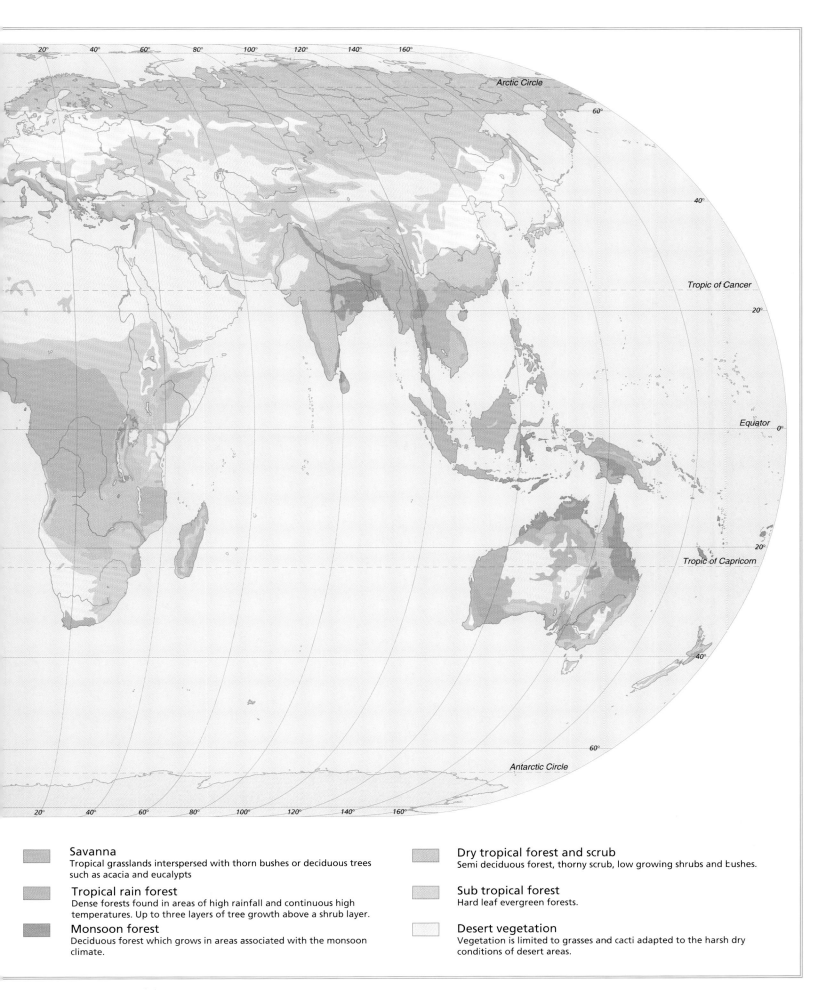

Savanna
Tropical grasslands interspersed with thorn bushes or deciduous trees such as acacia and eucalypts

Tropical rain forest
Dense forests found in areas of high rainfall and continuous high temperatures. Up to three layers of tree growth above a shrub layer.

Monsoon forest
Deciduous forest which grows in areas associated with the monsoon climate.

Dry tropical forest and scrub
Semi deciduous forest, thorny scrub, low growing shrubs and bushes.

Sub tropical forest
Hard leaf evergreen forests.

Desert vegetation
Vegetation is limited to grasses and cacti adapted to the harsh dry conditions of desert areas.

Eckert IV projection

CONTINENTAL DRIFT

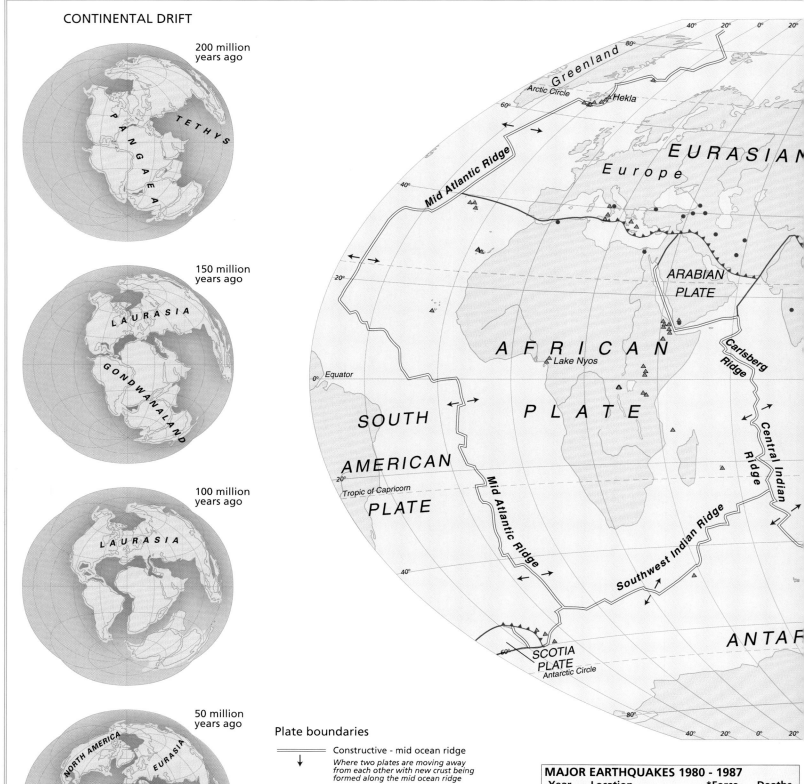

200 million years ago

PANGAEA · TETHYS

150 million years ago

LAURASIA · GONDWANALAND

100 million years ago

LAURASIA

50 million years ago

NORTH AMERICA · EURASIA · SOUTH AMERICA · AFRICA · ANTARCTICA · AUSTRALIA

Greenland · Arctic Circle · Hekla

Mid Atlantic Ridge

EURASIAN

Europe

ARABIAN PLATE

A F R I C A N   P L A T E

Lake Nyos

Carlsberg Ridge

Central Indian Ridge

SOUTH AMERICAN PLATE

Equator

Tropic of Capricorn

Mid Atlantic Ridge

Southwest Indian Ridge

SCOTIA PLATE
Antarctic Circle

ANTAR...

Plate boundaries

═══ ↓	**Constructive - mid ocean ridge** *Where two plates are moving away from each other with new crust being formed along the mid ocean ridge*
▲▲▲▲	**Destructive** *Where two plates are colliding and a subduction zone is created*
────	**Conservative** *Where two plates slide past one another without either being destroyed*

Earthquakes and volcanoes

- ●   Major earthquakes
- ▲   Major volcanoes

MAJOR EARTHQUAKES 1980 - 1987			
Year	**Location**	***Force**	**Deaths**
1980	El Asnam, Algeria	7.7	3500
1980	Southern Italy	6.9	3000
1981	Kerman, Iran	7.3	2500
1982	El Salvador	7.4	16
1982	Dhamar, Yemen	6.0	3000
1983	Eastern Turkey	7.1	1500
1985	Santiago, Chile	7.8	177
1985	Xinjiang Uygur, China	7.4	63
1985	Michoacán, Mexico	8.1	20 000
1986	El Salvador	7.5	1000
1987	Ecuador	7.0	2000

SCALE 1 : 100 000 000

0   1000   2000   3000   4000 km

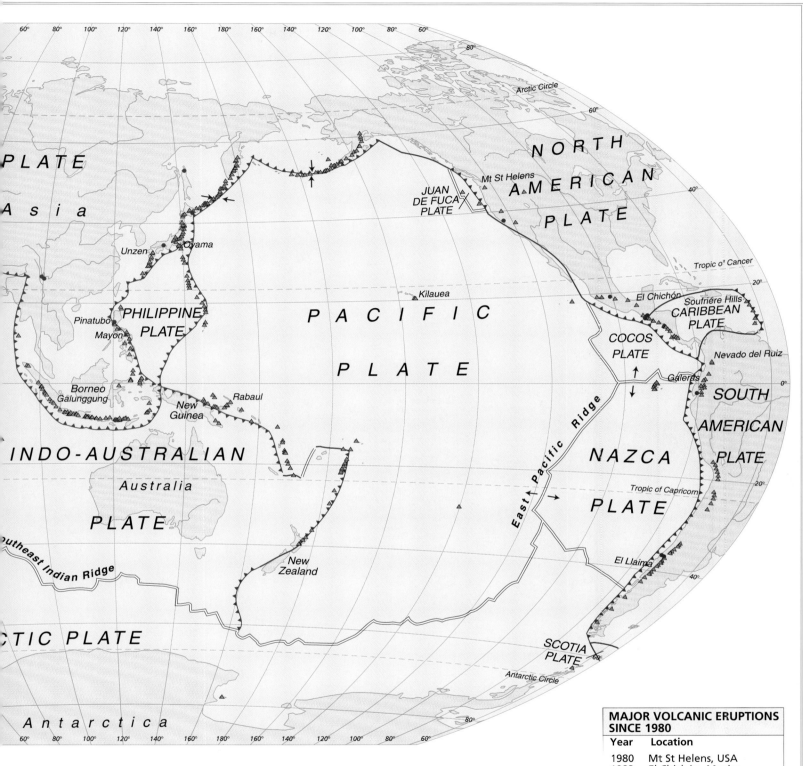

MAJOR EARTHQUAKES 1988 - 1992

Year	Location	*Force	Deaths
1988	Yunnan, China	7.6	1000
1988	Spitak, Armenia	6.9	25 000
1988	Nepal / India	6.9	1000
1989	San Francisco Bay, USA	7.1	67
1990	Manjil, Iran	7.7	50 000
1990	Luzon, Philippines	7.7	1600
1991	Georgia	7.1	114
1991	Uttar Pradesh, India	6.1	1600
1992	Flores, Indonesia	7.5	2500
1992	Erzincan, Turkey	6.8	500
1992	Cairo, Egypt	5.9	550

MAJOR EARTHQUAKES 1993 - 1999

Year	Location	*Force	Deaths
1993	Northern Japan	7.8	185
1993	Maharashtra, India	6.4	9700
1994	Kuril Islands, Japan	8.3	10
1995	Kobe, Japan	7.2	5200
1995	Sakhalin, Russian Fed	7.6	2500
1996	Yunnan, China	7.0	251
1997	Quae'n, Iran	7.1	2400
1999	Izmit, Turkey	7.4	15 657

* Earthquake force measured on the Richter scale

MAJOR VOLCANIC ERUPTIONS SINCE 1980

Year	Location
1980	Mt St Helens, USA
1982	El Chichón, Mexico
1982	Galunggung, Indonesia
1983	Kilauea, Hawaii
1983	Oyama, Japan
1985	Nevado del Ruiz, Colombia
1986	Lake Nyos, Cameroon
1991	Hekla, Iceland
1991	Pinatubo, Philippines
1991	Unzen, Japan
1993	Mayon, Philippines
1993	Galeras, Colombia
1994	El Llaima, Chile
1994	Rabaul, PNG
1997	Soufriére Hills, Montserrat

POPULATION DISTRIBUTION

Persons per sq km

- over 100
- 40-100
- 10-40
- 2-10
- 0-2

POPULATION STRUCTURE

USA 1999

MEXICO 1999

Male | Female

95+	75+	70-74
65-69		60-64
55-59		50-54
45-49		40-44
35-39		30-34
25-29		20-24
15-19		10-14
5-9		0-4

10 8 6 4 2 0 2 4 6 8 10%

Each full square represents 1% of the total population

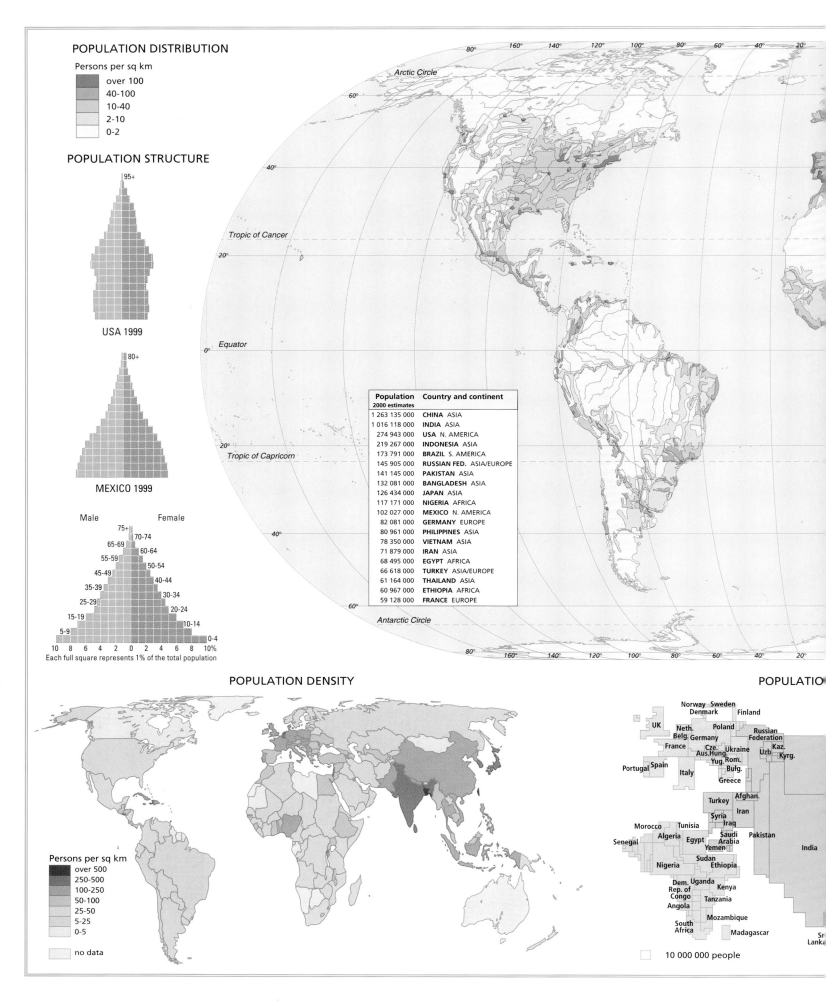

Population 2000 estimates	Country and continent
1 263 135 000	**CHINA** ASIA
1 016 118 000	**INDIA** ASIA
274 943 000	**USA** N. AMERICA
219 267 000	**INDONESIA** ASIA
173 791 000	**BRAZIL** S. AMERICA
145 905 000	**RUSSIAN FED.** ASIA/EUROPE
141 145 000	**PAKISTAN** ASIA
132 081 000	**BANGLADESH** ASIA
126 434 000	**JAPAN** ASIA
117 171 000	**NIGERIA** AFRICA
102 027 000	**MEXICO** N. AMERICA
82 081 000	**GERMANY** EUROPE
80 961 000	**PHILIPPINES** ASIA
78 350 000	**VIETNAM** ASIA
71 879 000	**IRAN** ASIA
68 495 000	**EGYPT** AFRICA
66 618 000	**TURKEY** ASIA/EUROPE
61 164 000	**THAILAND** ASIA
60 967 000	**ETHIOPIA** AFRICA
59 128 000	**FRANCE** EUROPE

POPULATION DENSITY

Persons per sq km

- over 500
- 250-500
- 100-250
- 50-100
- 25-50
- 5-25
- 0-5
- no data

POPULATIO

10 000 000 people

SCALE 1 : 100 000 000

0   1000   2000   3000   4000 km

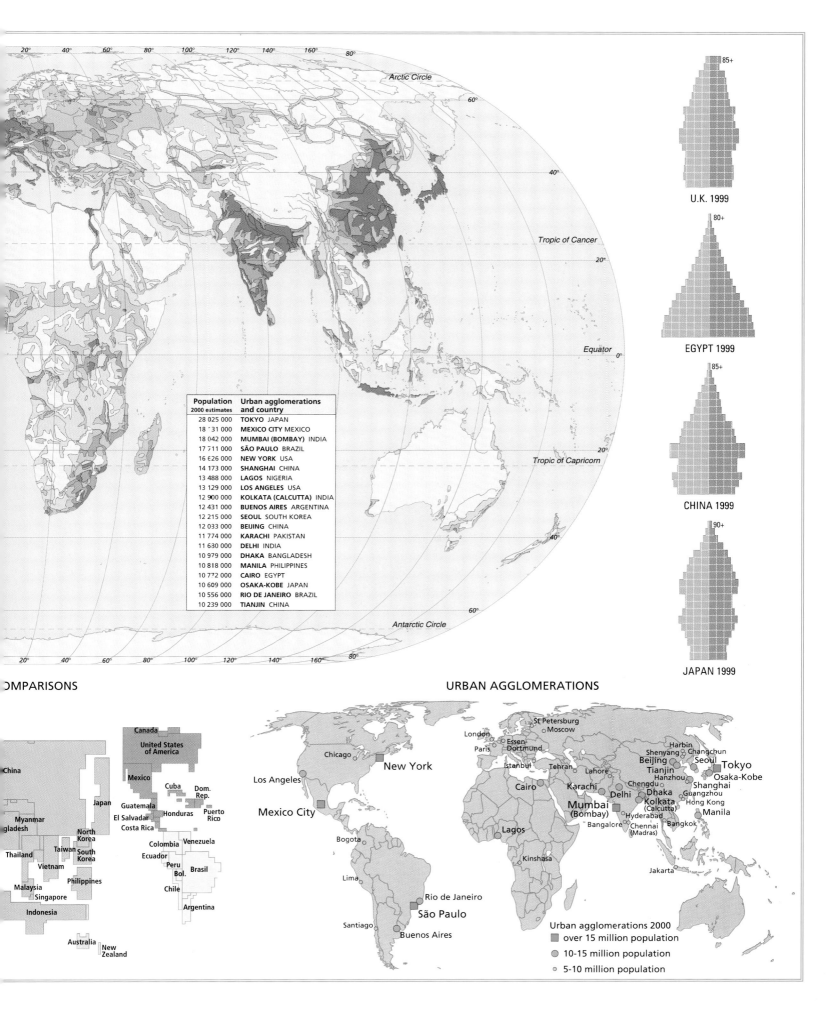

Population 2000 estimates	Urban agglomerations and country
28 025 000	**TOKYO** JAPAN
18 ´31 000	**MEXICO CITY** MEXICO
18 042 000	**MUMBAI (BOMBAY)** INDIA
17 711 000	**SÃO PAULO** BRAZIL
16 €26 000	**NEW YORK** USA
14 173 000	**SHANGHAI** CHINA
13 488 000	**LAGOS** NIGERIA
13 129 000	**LOS ANGELES** USA
12 900 000	**KOLKATA (CALCUTTA)** INDIA
12 431 000	**BUENOS AIRES** ARGENTINA
12 215 000	**SEOUL** SOUTH KOREA
12 033 000	**BEIJING** CHINA
11 774 000	**KARACHI** PAKISTAN
11 630 000	**DELHI** INDIA
10 979 000	**DHAKA** BANGLADESH
10 818 000	**MANILA** PHILIPPINES
10 772 000	**CAIRO** EGYPT
10 609 000	**OSAKA-KOBE** JAPAN
10 556 000	**RIO DE JANEIRO** BRAZIL
10 239 000	**TIANJIN** CHINA

U.K. 1999

EGYPT 1999

CHINA 1999

JAPAN 1999

OMPARISONS

URBAN AGGLOMERATIONS

Urban agglomerations 2000
■ over 15 million population
● 10-15 million population
○ 5-10 million population

Eckert IV projection

1 BIRTH RATES

BIRTH RATE
Birth rate is the number of
births per thousand of the
population in one year.
World average 23.
Statistics are for 1997.

Births per
1000 population

- 45 - 52
- 40 - 44.9
- 35 - 39.9
- 23 - 34.9
- 20 - 22.9
- 15 - 19.9
- 8 - 14.9

no data

FERTILITY RATE
(average births per
childbearing woman)

0 1 2 3 4 5 6

Europe
North America
Oceania
Asia
Latin America
Africa

BIRTH RATES
HIGHEST AND LOWEST

Rate
60
50
40
30
20
10
0

Niger
Angola, Malawi, Uganda,
Dem. Rep. of Congo, Mali
Belarus, Bulgaria, Czech Rep.,
Estonia, Italy, Russian Fed.,
Slovenia,
Latvia

2 DEATH RATES

DEATH RATE
Death rate is the number of
deaths per thousand of the
population in one year.
World average 9.
Statistics are for 1997.

Deaths per
1000 population

- 21 - 26
- 17 - 20.9
- 13 - 16.9
- 9 - 12.9
- 6 - 8.9
- 4 - 5.9
- 2 - 3.9

no data

DEATH RATE
(by continent)

0 2 4 6 8 10 12 14

Latin America
Oceania
North America
Asia
Europe
Africa

DEATH RATES
HIGHEST AND LOWEST

Rate
30
25
20
15
10
5
0

Sierra Leone
Malawi
Rwanda
Costa Rica, Jordan,
Saudi Arabia, Singapore
Bahrain, Oman, UAE, Brunei
Kuwait, Qatar

SCALE 1 : 140 000 000

Eckert IV projection

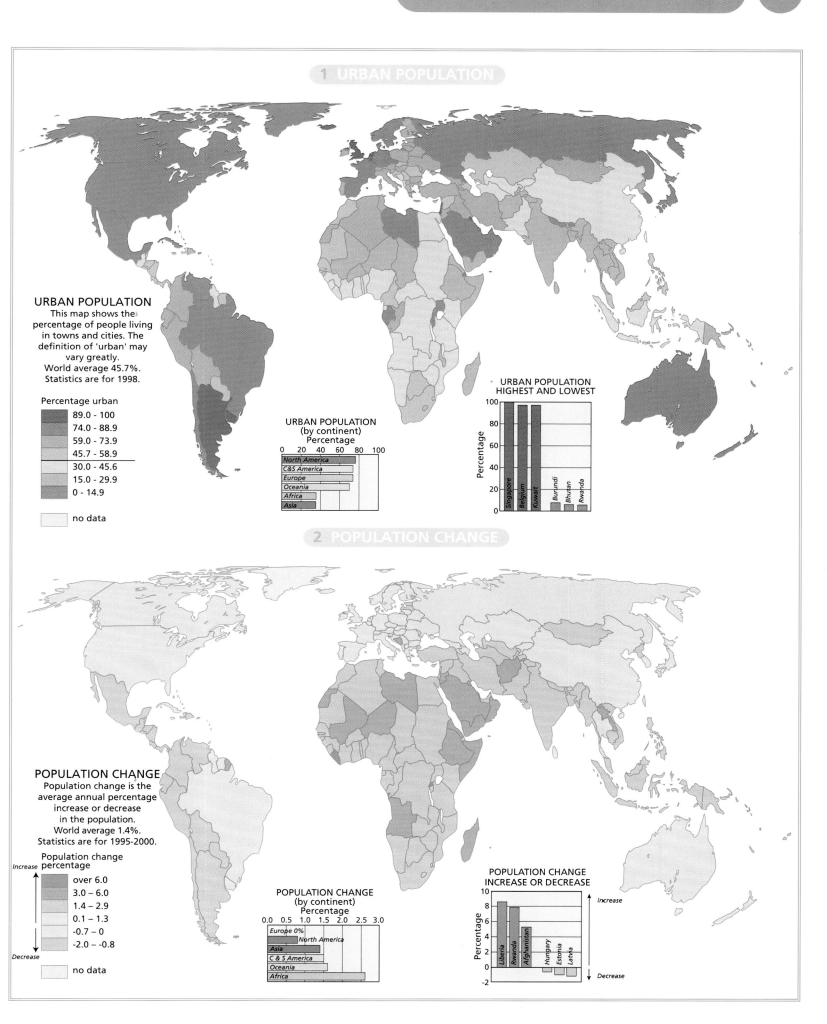

1 URBAN POPULATION

URBAN POPULATION

This map shows the percentage of people living in towns and cities. The definition of 'urban' may vary greatly.
World average 45.7%.
Statistics are for 1998.

Percentage urban

- 89.0 – 100
- 74.0 – 88.9
- 59.0 – 73.9
- 45.7 – 58.9
- 30.0 – 45.6
- 15.0 – 29.9
- 0 – 14.9

no data

URBAN POPULATION
(by continent)
Percentage

0   20   40   60   80   100

- North America
- C&S America
- Europe
- Oceania
- Africa
- Asia

URBAN POPULATION
HIGHEST AND LOWEST

Percentage

Singapore, Belgium, Kuwait, Burundi, Bhutan, Rwanda

2 POPULATION CHANGE

POPULATION CHANGE

Population change is the average annual percentage increase or decrease in the population.
World average 1.4%.
Statistics are for 1995-2000.

Population change percentage

Increase

- over 6.0
- 3.0 – 6.0
- 1.4 – 2.9
- 0.1 – 1.3
- -0.7 – 0
- -2.0 – -0.8

Decrease

no data

POPULATION CHANGE
(by continent)
Percentage

0.0   0.5   1.0   1.5   2.0   2.5   3.0

- Europe 0%
- North America
- Asia
- C & S America
- Oceania
- Africa

POPULATION CHANGE
INCREASE OR DECREASE

Percentage

Increase

Liberia, Rwanda, Afghanistan, Hungary, Estonia, Latvia

Decrease

SCALE 1 : 140 000 000

Eckert IV projection

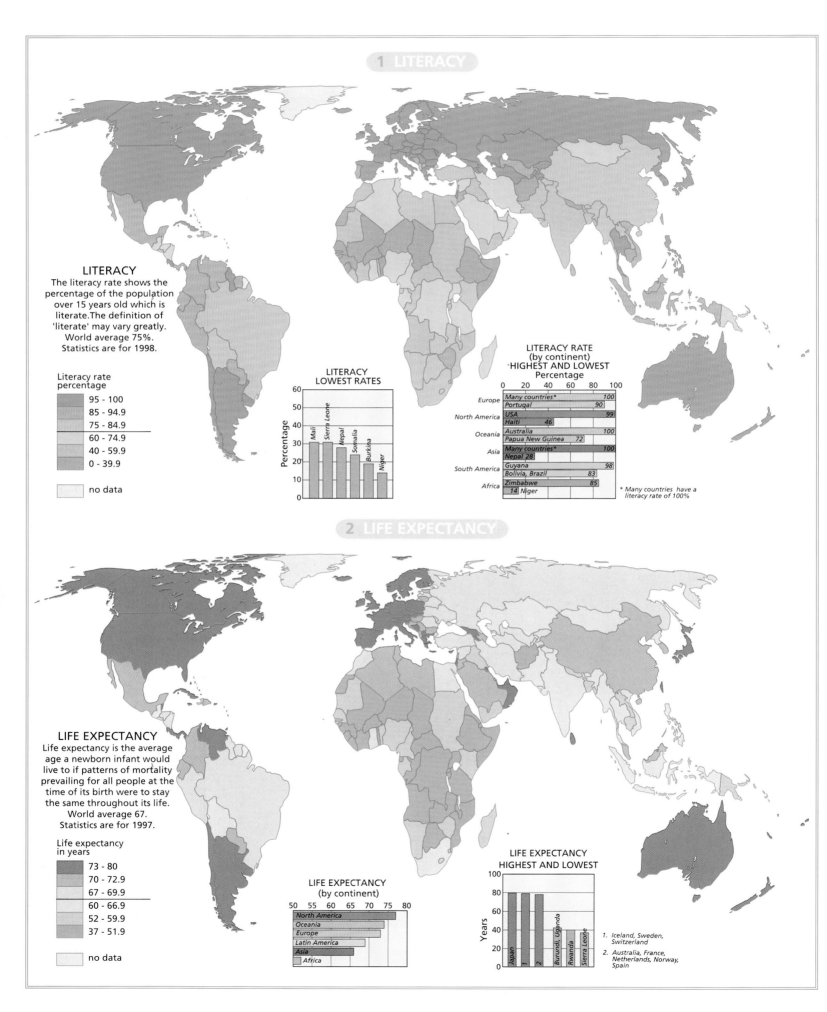

1 LITERACY

LITERACY
The literacy rate shows the percentage of the population over 15 years old which is literate. The definition of 'literate' may vary greatly. World average 75%. Statistics are for 1998.

Literacy rate percentage

- 95 - 100
- 85 - 94.9
- 75 - 84.9
- 60 - 74.9
- 40 - 59.9
- 0 - 39.9

no data

LITERACY LOWEST RATES
(Percentage)
Mali, Sierra Leone, Nepal, Somalia, Burkina, Niger

LITERACY RATE
(by continent)
HIGHEST AND LOWEST
Percentage

Continent	Country	Percentage
Europe	Many countries*	100
	Portugal	90
North America	USA	99
	Haiti	46
Oceania	Australia	100
	Papua New Guinea	72
Asia	Many countries*	100
	Nepal	28
South America	Guyana	98
	Bolivia, Brazil	83
Africa	Zimbabwe	85
	Niger	14

* Many countries have a literacy rate of 100%

2 LIFE EXPECTANCY

LIFE EXPECTANCY
Life expectancy is the average age a newborn infant would live to if patterns of mortality prevailing for all people at the time of its birth were to stay the same throughout its life. World average 67. Statistics are for 1997.

Life expectancy in years

- 73 - 80
- 70 - 72.9
- 67 - 69.9
- 60 - 66.9
- 52 - 59.9
- 37 - 51.9

no data

LIFE EXPECTANCY
(by continent)
North America, Oceania, Europe, Latin America, Asia, Africa

LIFE EXPECTANCY
HIGHEST AND LOWEST
(Years)
Japan, 1, 2, Burundi, Uganda, Rwanda, Sierra Leone

1. Iceland, Sweden, Switzerland
2. Australia, France, Netherlands, Norway, Spain

SCALE 1 : 140 000 000

Eckert IV projection

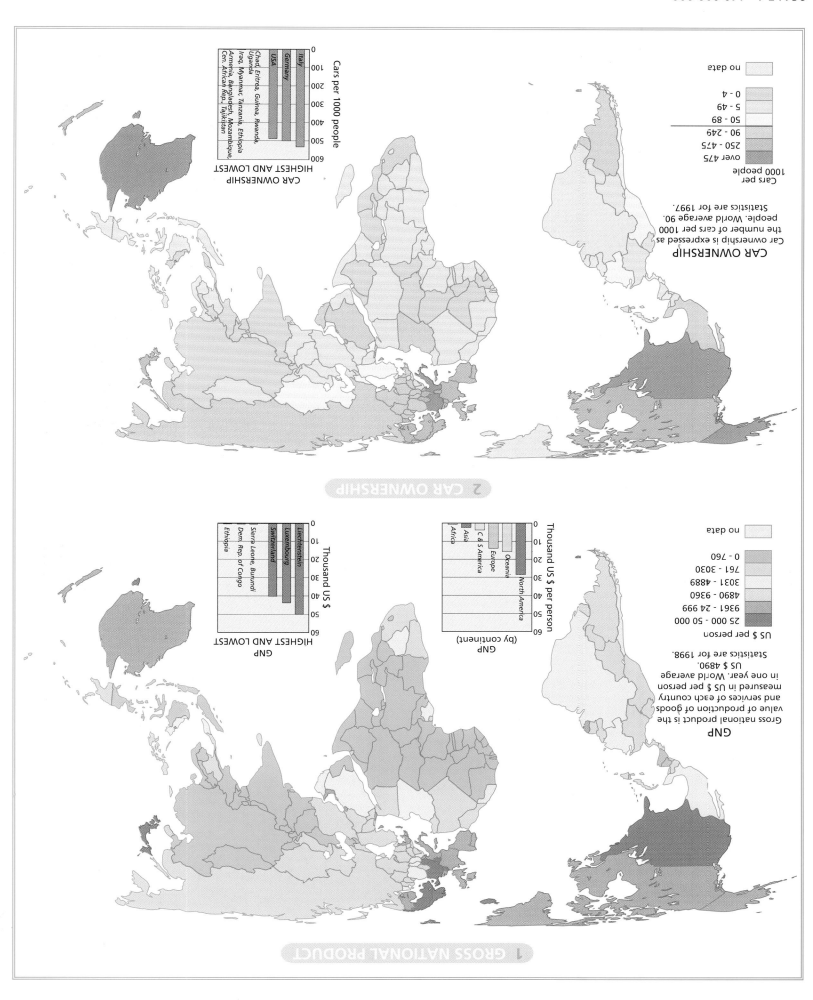

2 CAR OWNERSHIP

CAR OWNERSHIP

Car ownership is expressed as the number of cars per 1000 people. World average 90. Statistics are for 1997.

Cars per 1000 people

- over 475
- 250 - 475
- 90 - 249
- 50 - 89
- 5 - 49
- 0 - 4
- no data

CAR OWNERSHIP HIGHEST AND LOWEST

Cars per 1000 people

- Italy
- Germany
- USA
- Chad, Eritrea, Guinea, Rwanda, Uganda
- Iraq, Myanmar, Tanzania, Ethiopia
- Armenia, Bangladesh, Mozambique, Cen. African Rep., Tajikistan

(0, 100, 200, 300, 400, 500, 600)

1 GROSS NATIONAL PRODUCT

GNP

Gross national product is the value of production of goods and services of each country measured in US $ per person in one year. World average US $ 4890. Statistics are for 1998.

US $ per person

- 25 000 - 50 000
- 9361 - 24 999
- 4890 - 9360
- 3031 - 4889
- 761 - 3030
- 0 - 760
- no data

GNP (by continent)

Thousand US $ per person

- North America
- Europe
- Oceania
- C & S America
- Asia
- Africa

(0, 10, 20, 30, 40, 50, 60)

GNP HIGHEST AND LOWEST

Thousand US $

- Liechtenstein
- Luxembourg
- Switzerland
- Sierra Leone, Burundi
- Dem. Rep. of Congo
- Ethiopia

(0, 10, 20, 30, 40, 50)

SCALE 1 : 100 000 000

0 1000 2000 3000 4000 km

ATMOSPHERIC POLLUTION
(Carbon Dioxide emissions, 1997)

Tonnes per capita

- over 10.00
- 5.00-9.99
- 1.00-4.99
- 0.50-0.99
- 0.00-0.49
- no data

CO₂ EMISSIONS, 1997
Thousand million tonnes

USA
China
Russian Federation
Japan
Germany
India
UK
Canada
Italy
S. Korea
Ukraine
France
Poland
Mexico
S. Africa
Australia
Brazil
Iran
Saudi Arabia
Indonesia

0 0.5 1 1.5 2 2.5 3 3.5 4 4.5 5 5.5

CO₂ EMISSIONS FROM FOSSIL FUEL CONSUMPTION 1955-1997
Thousand million tonnes

5 10 15 20 25

1955 60 65 70 75 80 85 90 95

DEGREE OF HUMAN DISTURBANCE TO NATURAL LAND COVER (%)

- Low disturbance
- Medium disturbance
- High disturbance

South America
U.S.S.R. (former)
Oceania
North and Central America
Africa
Asia
Europe

0 20 40 60 80 100

THREATS TO THE ENVIRONMENT

- *Forest
- Severe marine pollution
- Partial marine pollution
- River pollution
- Forest areas under threat
- * Forest above global average of deforestation
- ☢ Current nuclear test site
- ☢ Former nuclear test site
- ● Major city with air pollution problem due to industry and vehicle exhaust
- ▼ Offshore oil production

*Includes Tropical rain forest, Monsoon forest and Dry tropical scrub. See World Natural Vegetation pp120-121.

Arctic Circle

New York

Lisbon

Nevada

Los Angeles

Mexico City

Johnston I.

Tropic of Cancer

Equator

Kiritimati (Christmas I.)

Mururoa Atoll

Tropic of Capricorn

São Paulo

Buenos Aires

Antarctic Circle

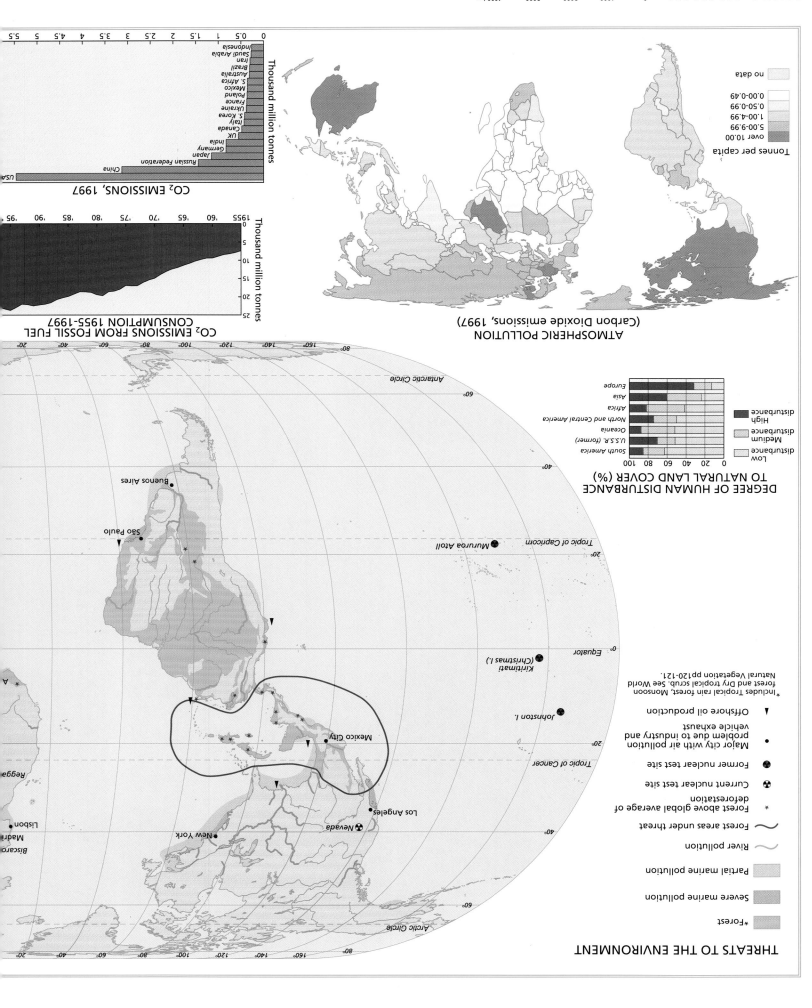

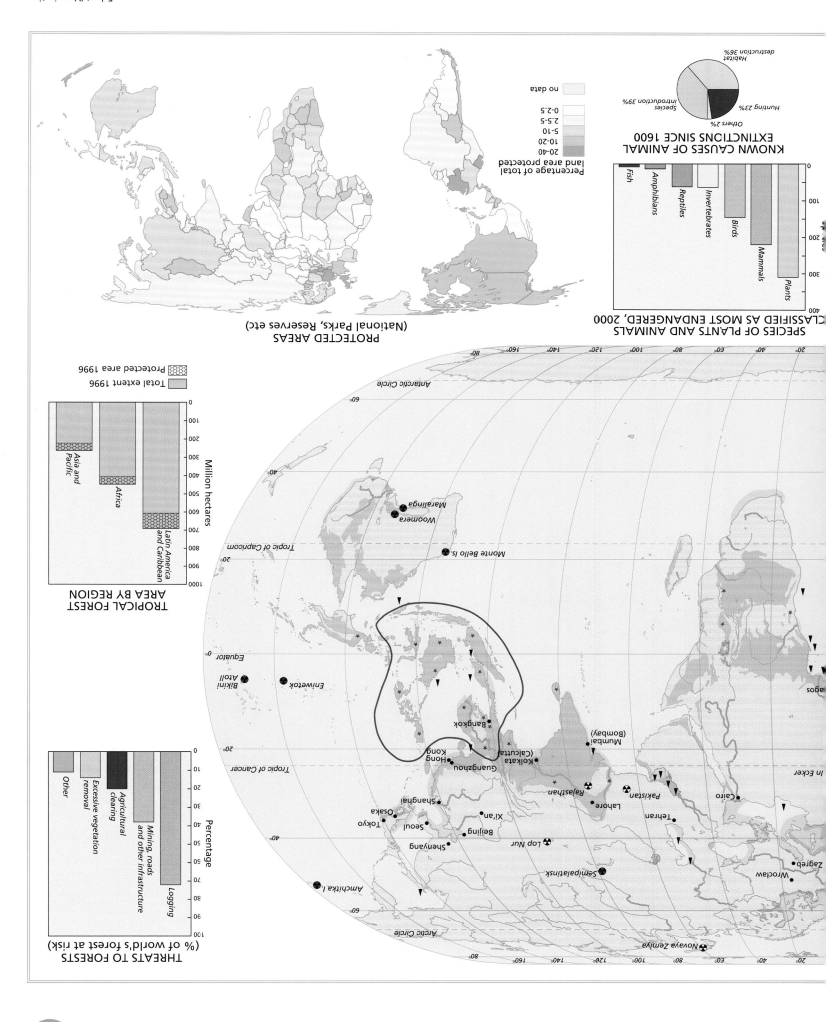

PROTECTED AREAS
(National Parks, Reserves etc)

Percentage of total land area protected
- 20–40
- 10–20
- 5–10
- 2.5–5
- 0–2.5
- no data

KNOWN CAUSES OF ANIMAL EXTINCTIONS SINCE 1600
- Species introduction 39%
- Habitat destruction 36%
- Hunting 23%
- Others 2%

SPECIES OF PLANTS AND ANIMALS CLASSIFIED AS MOST ENDANGERED, 2000
Fish, Amphibians, Reptiles, Invertebrates, Birds, Mammals, Plants

TROPICAL FOREST AREA BY REGION
- Total extent 1996
- Protected area 1996

Asia and Pacific, Africa, Latin America and Caribbean — Million hectares

THREATS TO FORESTS
(% of world's forest at risk)
- Logging
- Mining, roads and other infrastructure
- Agricultural clearing
- Excessive vegetation removal
- Other

Percentage

SCALE 1 : 140 000 000

Eckert IV projection

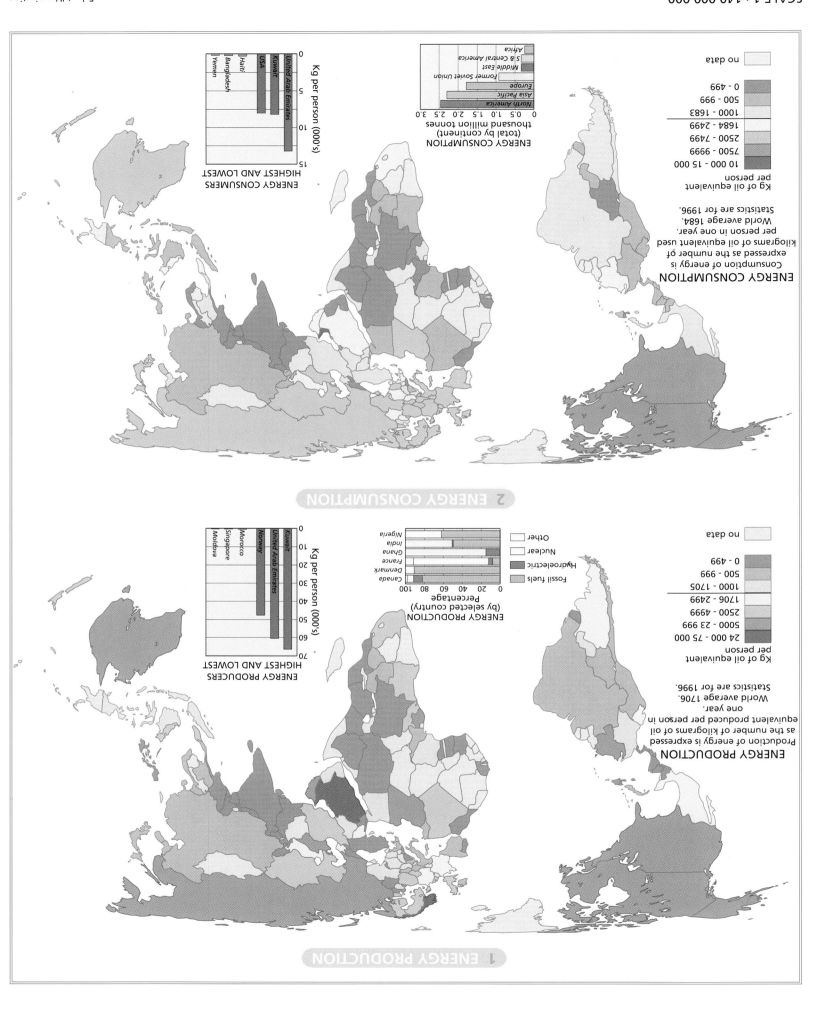

1 ENERGY PRODUCTION

ENERGY PRODUCTION

Production of energy is expressed
as the number of kilograms of oil
equivalent produced per person in
one year.
World average 1706.
Statistics are for 1996.

**Kg of oil equivalent
per person**

- 24 000 - 75 000
- 5000 - 23 999
- 2500 - 4999
- 1706 - 2499
- 1000 - 1705
- 500 - 999
- 0 - 499
- no data

**ENERGY PRODUCTION
(by selected country)**

Percentage

	0	20	40	60	80	100
Canada						
Denmark						
France						
Ghana						
India						
Nigeria						

- Fossil fuels
- Hydroelectric
- Nuclear
- Other

**ENERGY PRODUCERS
HIGHEST AND LOWEST**

Kg per person (000's)

0 10 20 30 40 50 60 70

- Kuwait
- United Arab Emirates
- Norway
- Moldova
- Singapore
- Morocco

2 ENERGY CONSUMPTION

ENERGY CONSUMPTION

Consumption of energy is
expressed as the number of
kilograms of oil equivalent used
per person in one year.
World average 1684.
Statistics are for 1996.

**Kg of oil equivalent
per person**

- 10 000 - 15 000
- 7500 - 9999
- 2500 - 7499
- 1684 - 2499
- 1000 - 1683
- 500 - 999
- 0 - 499
- no data

**ENERGY CONSUMPTION
(total by continent)**

thousand million tonnes

	0	0.5	1.0	1.5	2.0	2.5	3.0
North America							
Asia Pacific							
Europe							
Former Soviet Union							
Middle East							
S & Central America							
Africa							

**ENERGY CONSUMERS
HIGHEST AND LOWEST**

Kg per person (000's)

0 5 10 15

- United Arab Emirates
- Kuwait
- USA
- Haiti
- Bangladesh
- Yemen

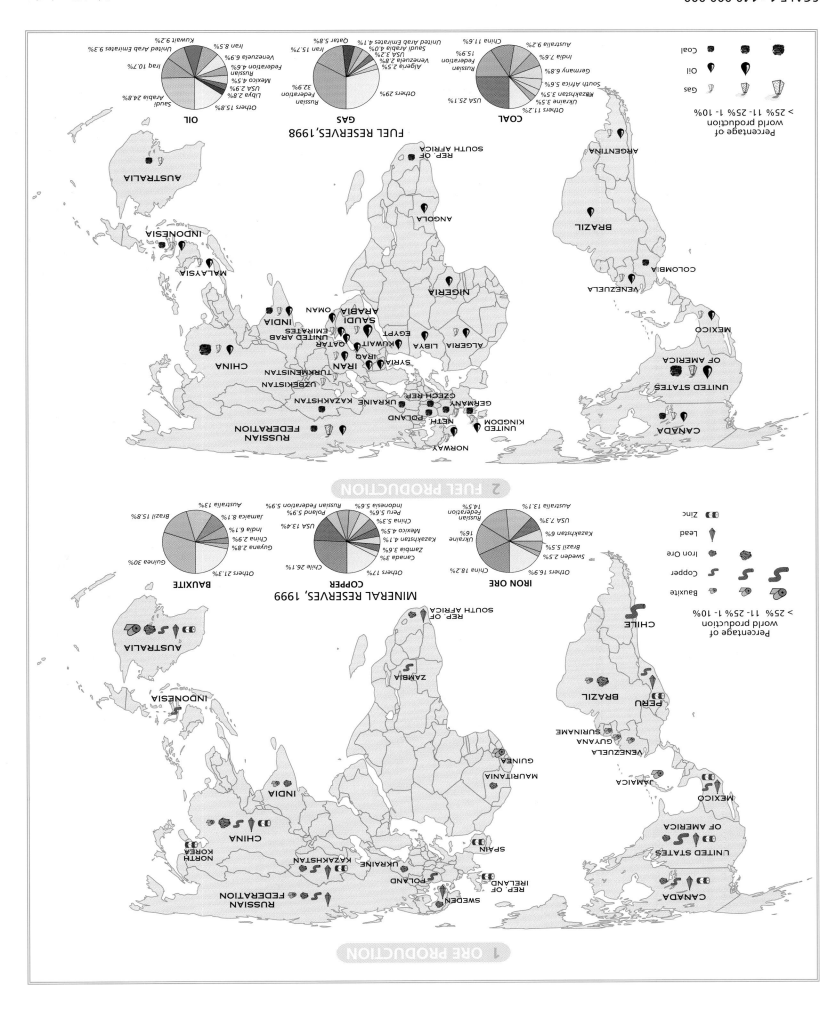

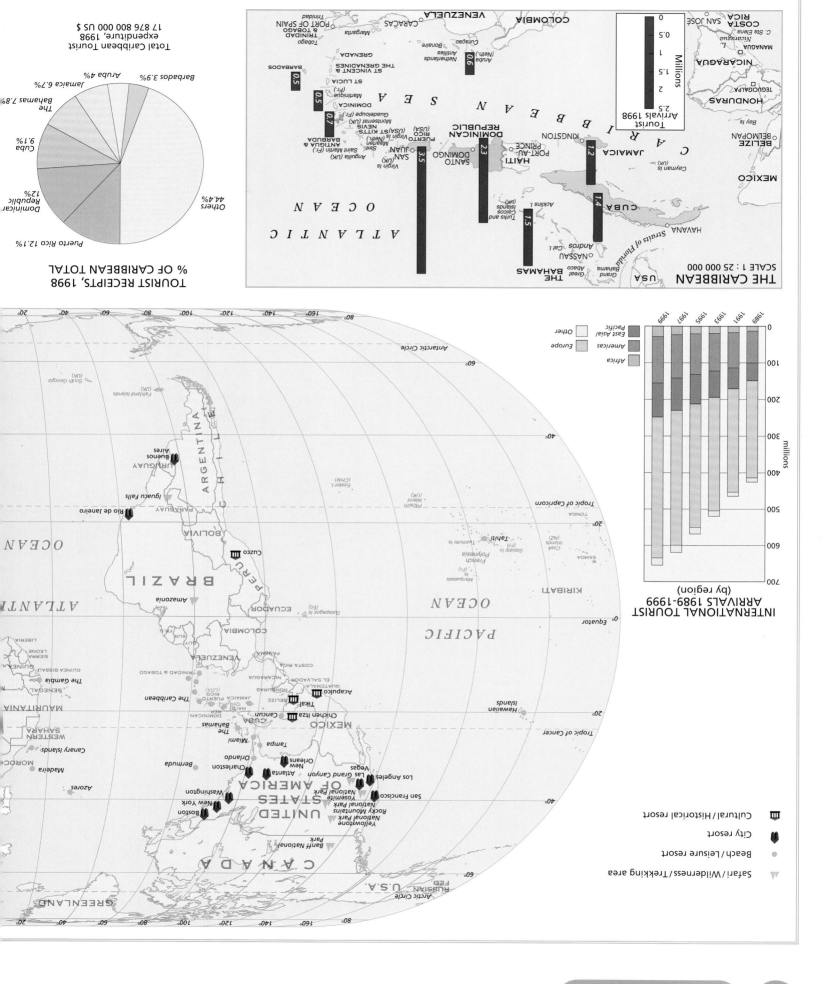

THE CARIBBEAN
SCALE 1 : 25 000 000

Tourist Arrivals 1998

Millions
2.5
2
1.5
1
0.5
0

TOURIST RECEIPTS, 1998
% OF CARIBBEAN TOTAL

Total Caribbean Tourist expenditure, 1998
17 876 800 000 US $

Others 44.4%
Dominican Republic 12%
Puerto Rico 12.1%
Cuba 9.1%
The Bahamas 7.8%
Jamaica 6.7%
Aruba 4%
Barbados 3.9%

INTERNATIONAL TOURIST ARRIVALS 1989-1999
(by region)

Africa
Americas
Europe
East Asia/ Pacific
Other

1989 1991 1993 1995 1997 1999
millions
0 100 200 300 400 500 600 700

Safari/ Wilderness/ Trekking area
Beach/ Leisure resort
City resort
Cultural/ Historical resort

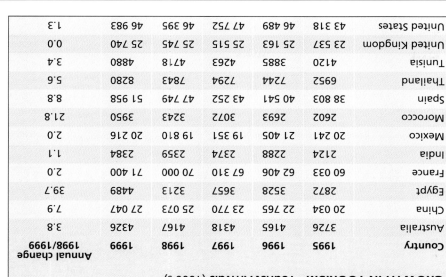

GROWTH IN TOURISM - Tourist Arrivals (1000's)

Country	1995	1996	1997	1998	1999	Annual change 1998/1999
Australia	3726	4165	4318	4167	4326	3.8
China	20 034	22 765	23 770	25 073	27 047	7.9
Egypt	2872	3528	3657	3213	4489	39.7
France	60 033	62 406	67 310	70 000	71 400	2.0
India	2124	2288	2374	2359	2384	1.1
Mexico	20 241	21 405	19 351	19 810	20 216	2.0
Morocco	2602	2693	3072	3243	3950	21.8
Spain	38 803	40 541	43 252	47 749	51 958	8.8
Thailand	6952	7244	7294	7843	8280	5.6
Tunisia	4120	3885	4263	4718	4880	3.4
United Kingdom	23 537	25 163	25 515	25 745	25 740	0.0
United States	43 318	46 489	47 752	46 395	46 983	1.3

FLORIDA
SCALE 1 : 12 000 000

National Park

Main expressway

★ Tourist attraction

TOURIST ARRIVALS, 1999
World total: 656 933 000 tourists

TOURIST RECEIPTS, 1999
World total: 441 255 000 US $

Europe
Africa
Middle East
Americas
South Asia
East Asia/ Pacific

TOP 10 TOURISM DESTINATIONS, 1999

Tourist arrivals (millions)

France
Spain
United States
Italy
China
UK
Mexico
Canada
Poland
Austria

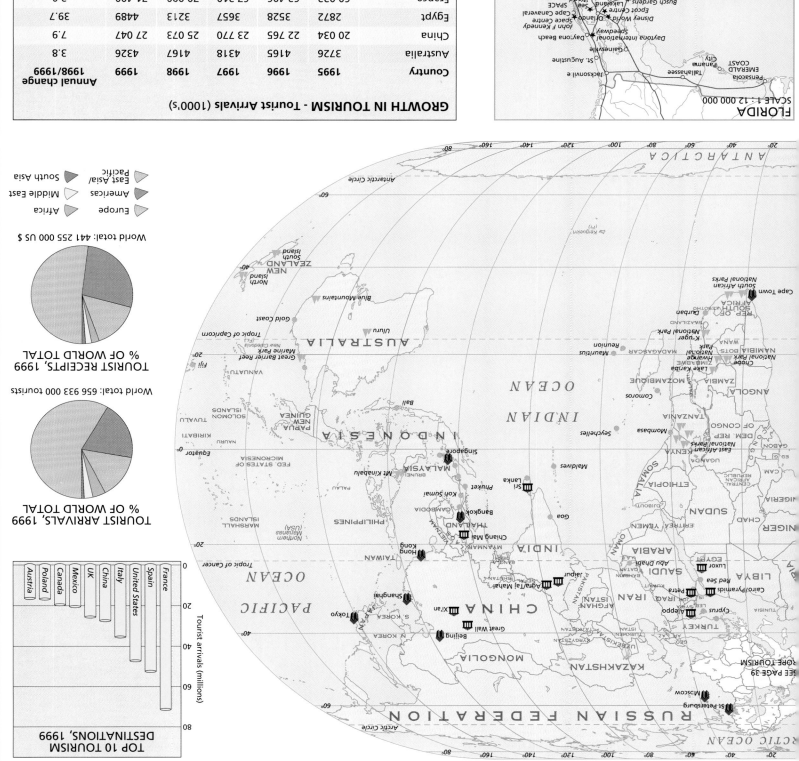

Eckert IV projection

KEY INFORMATION

POPULATION

FLAG	COUNTRY	CAPITAL CITY	TOTAL 1998	DENSITY persons per sq km 1998	BIRTH RATE per 1000 population 1997	DEATH RATE per 1000 population 1997	LIFE EXPEC-TANCY in years 1997	POP. CHANGE average % per annum 1995 - 2000	URBAN POP. % 1998
	Afghanistan	Kabul	21 354 000	32.7	43	18	46	5.3	20
	Albania	Tiranë	3 119 000	108.5	19	7	72	0.6	40
	Algeria	Algiers	30 081 000	12.6	27	5	70	2.3	59
	Angola	Luanda	12 092 000	9.7	48	19	46	3.3	33
	Argentina	Buenos Aires	36 123 000	13.1	20	8	73	1.3	89
	Armenia	Yerevan	3 536 000	118.7	12	9	74	0.2	69
	Australia	Canberra	18 520 000	2.4	14	7	78	1.1	85
	Austria	Vienna	8 140 000	97.1	10	10	77	0.6	65
	Azerbaijan	Baku	7 669 000	88.6	18	6	71	0.8	57
	Bahamas, The	Nassau	296 000	21.2	22	6	73	1.6	87
	Bahrain	Manama	595 000	861.1	22	3	69	2.1	91
	Bangladesh	Dhaka	124 774 000	866.5	28	10	58	1.6	23
	Barbados	Bridgetown	268 000	623.3	14	9	75	0.3	48
	Belarus	Minsk	10 315 000	49.7	9	13	68	-0.1	71
	Belgium	Brussels	10 141 000	332.3	11	10	77	0.3	97
	Belize	Belmopan	230 000	10.0	30	4	72	2.5	46
	Benin	Porto Novo	5 781 000	51.3	43	13	53	2.8	41
	Bhutan	Thimbu	2 004 000	43.0	40	9	66	2.8	6
	Bolivia	La Paz/Sucre	7 957 000	7.2	33	9	61	2.3	61
	Bosnia-Herzegovina	Sarajevo	3 675 000	71.9	13	7	73	3.9	42
	Botswana	Gaborone	1 570 000	2.7	34	15	47	2.2	49
	Brazil	Brasilia	165 851 000	19.5	21	7	67	1.2	80
	Brunei	Bandar Seri Begawan	315 000	54.6	25	3	71	2.1	70
	Bulgaria	Sofia	8 336 000	75.1	9	14	71	-0.5	69
	Burkina	Ouagadougou	11 305 000	41.2	45	19	44	2.8	17
	Burundi	Bujumbura	6 457 000	232.0	43	20	42	2.8	8
	Cambodia	Phnom Penh	10 716 000	59.2	34	12	54	2.2	15
	Cameroon	Yaoundé	14 305 000	30.1	39	11	57	2.7	47
	Canada	Ottawa	30 563 000	3.1	12	7	79	0.9	77
	Cape Verde	Praia	408 000	101.2	36	8	68	2.5	56
	Central African Republic	Bangui	3 485 000	5.6	37	19	45	2.1	40
	Chad	Ndjamena	7 270 000	5.7	45	17	49	2.8	23
	Chile	Santiago	14 824 000	19.6	20	6	75	1.4	85
	China	Beijing	1 262 817 000	132.0	17	8	70	0.9	31
	Colombia	Bogotá	40 803 000	35.7	25	6	70	1.7	73
	Comoros	Moroni	658 000	353.4	38	10	59	3.1	31
	Congo	Brazzaville	2 785 000	8.1	44	16	48	2.8	61
	Congo, Dem. Rep. of	Kinshasa	49 139 000	21.0	47	15	51	2.6	30
	Costa Rica	San José	3 841 000	75.2	23	4	77	2.1	47
	Côte d'Ivoire	Yamoussoukro	14 292 000	44.3	37	16	47	2.0	45
	Croatia	Zagreb	4 481 000	79.3	10	13	72	-0.1	57
	Cuba	Havana	11 116 000	100.3	14	7	76	0.4	75
	Cyprus	Nicosia	771 000	83.3	14	8	77	1.3	55
	Czech Republic	Prague	10 282 000	130.4	9	11	74	-0.1	75
	Denmark	Copenhagen	5 270 000	122.3	13	11	75	0.2	85

AREA sq km	CULTIV-ATED AREA '000s sq km 1997	FOREST '000s sq km 1997	ADULT LITERACY % 1998	*SCHOOL ENROL-MENT Secondary, gross % 1997	DOCTORS PER 100 000 PERSONS 1990-1998	FOOD INTAKE calories per capita per day 1997	ENERGY CONSU-MPTION million tonnes of oil equivalent 1997	TRADE BALANCE millions US $ 1996	GNP PER CAPITA US $ 1998	COUNTRY	TIME ZONES + OR - GMT
652 225	81	-	35.0	22	-	1747	-	-300	-	Afghanistan	+4¹/₂
28 748	7	10	83.7	35	141	2961	1.0	-960	810	Albania	+1
2 381 741	80	19	61.5	63	83	2853	26.5	2200	1550	Algeria	+1
1 246 700	35	222	42.0	12	-	1903	6.8	1500	340	Angola	+1
2 766 889	272	339	97.0	77	268	3093	61.7	-2220	8970	Argentina	-3
29 800	6	3	98.0	98	312	2371	1.8	-540	480	Armenia	+4
7 682 300	531	409	100.0	153	250	3224	101.6	-12 850	20 300	Australia	+8 to +10¹/₂
83 855	15	39	100.0	102	327	3536	27.8	-5810	26 850	Austria	+1
86 600	19	10	99.0	77	390	2236	12.0	-400	490	Azerbaijan	+4
13 939	-	-	95.0	86	141	2499	-	-230	-	Bahamas, The	-5
691	-	-	86.0	94	11	-	-	340	7660	Bahrain	+3
143 998	82	10	40.1	19	18	2086	24.3	-3410	350	Bangladesh	+6
430	-	-	97.0	98	113	3176	-	-760	7890	Barbados	-4
207 600	63	74	99.5	93	379	3226	25.1	-530	2200	Belarus	+2
30 520	8	7	99.0	147	365	3619	57.1	14 760	25 380	Belgium	+1
22 965	1	-	80.0	50	47	2907	-	-180	2610	Belize	-6
112 620	16	46	38.3	17	7	2487	2.1	-250	380	Benin	+1
46 620	2	-	42.0	-	20	-	-	0	390	Bhutan	+6
1 098 581	21	483	84.5	40	51	2174	4.3	-650	1000	Bolivia	-4
51 130	7	27	86.0	-	-	2266	1.8	-	-	Bosnia-Herzegovina	+1
581 370	3	139	75.6	68	20	2183	-	70	3600	Botswana	+2
8 511 965	653	5511	84.0	50	134	2974	172.0	-3760	4570	Brazil	-2 to -5
5 765	-	-	91.0	77	-	2857	-	90	24 000	Brunei	+8
110 994	45	32	98.5	77	333	2686	20.6	-1400	1230	Bulgaria	+2
274 200	34	43	22.4	9	<5**	2121	-	-430	240	Burkina	GMT
27 835	11	3	45.8	8	6	1685	-	-90	140	Burundi	+2
181 000	38	98	37.6	28	58	2048	-	-360	280	Cambodia	+7
475 442	72	196	73.5	26	7	2111	5.8	190	610	Cameroon	+1
9 970 610	457	2446	97.0	108	221	3119	238.0	18 190	20 020	Canada	-3¹/₂ to 8
4 033	-	0	73.0	10	29	3015	-	-230	1060	Cape Verde	-1
622 436	20	299	44.2	10	6	2016	-	-120	300	Central African Republic	+1
1 284 000	33	110	39.9	10	2	2032	-	10	230	Chad	+1
756 945	23	79	95.5	75	108	2796	23.0	510	4810	Chile	-4
9 562 000	1354	1333	83.3	71	115	2897	1113.1	29 210	750	China	+8
1 141 748	44	530	91.0	72	105	2597	30.5	910	2600	Colombia	-5
1 862	1	-	58.0	24	10	1858	-	-40	370	Comoros	+3
342 000	2	195	78.3	52	27	2144	1.2	1130	690	Congo	+1
2 345 410	79	-	71.0	30	10	1755	14.5	280	110	Congo, Dem. Rep. of	+1 to +2
51 100	5	12	95.0	50	126	2649	-	250	2780	Costa Rica	-6
322 463	74	55	44.7	24	10	2610	5.6	1150	700	Côte d'Ivoire	GMT
56 538	14	18	98.0	84	201	2445	7.7	-3500	4520	Croatia	+1
110 860	45	18	96.0	77	518	2480	14.3	-2360	-	Cuba	-5
9 251	1	-	97.0	-	231	3429	-	-2700	-	Cyprus	+2
78 864	33	26	100.0	103	293	3244	40.6	-2020	5040	Czech Republic	+1
43 075	24	4	100.0	123	283	3407	21.1	4520	33 260	Denmark	+1

*Total enrolment in secondary level of education, regardless of age, is expressed as a percentage of the official secondary school-age population.
**Estimate.

KEY INFORMATION

POPULATION

FLAG	COUNTRY	CAPITAL CITY	TOTAL 1998	DENSITY persons per sq km 1998	BIRTH RATE per 1000 population 1997	DEATH RATE per 1000 population 1997	LIFE EXPEC-TANCY in years 1997	POP. CHANGE average % per annum 1995 - 2000	URBAN POP. % 1998
	Djibouti	Djibouti	623 000	26.9	39	16	48	2.7	82
	Dominica	Roseau	71 000	94.7	19	8	78	0.1	70
	Dominican Republic	Santo Domingo	8 232 000	169.9	26	5	71	1.7	64
	Ecuador	Quito	12 175 000	44.8	25	6	70	2.0	63
	Egypt	Cairo	65 978 000	66.0	25	7	66	1.9	45
	El Salvador	San Salvador	6 032 000	286.7	28	6	69	2.2	46
	Equatorial Guinea	Malabo	431 000	15.4	44	18	48	2.5	43
	Eritrea	Asmara	3 577 000	30.5	41	12	51	3.7	18
	Estonia	Tallinn	1 429 000	31.6	9	13	70	-1.0	69
	Ethiopia	Addis Ababa	59 649 000	52.6	46	20	43	3.2	17
	Fiji	Suva	796 000	43.4	24	6	63	1.6	41
	Finland	Helsinki	5 154 000	15.2	12	10	77	0.3	66
	France	Paris	58 683 000	107.9	12	9	78	0.3	75
	Gabon	Libreville	1 167 000	4.4	37	16	52	2.8	79
	Gambia, The	Banjul	1 229 000	108.8	43	13	53	2.3	31
	Georgia	T'bilisi	5 059 000	72.6	10	7	73	-0.1	60
	Germany	Berlin	82 133 000	229.5	10	10	77	0.3	87
	Ghana	Accra	19 162 000	80.3	36	9	60	2.8	37
	Greece	Athens	10 600 000	80.3	10	10	78	0.3	60
	Guatemala	Guatemala City	10 801 000	99.2	34	7	64	2.8	39
	Guinea	Conakry	7 337 000	29.8	41	17	46	1.4	31
	Guinea-Bissau	Bissau	1 161 000	32.1	42	21	44	2.0	23
	Guyana	Georgetown	850 000	4.0	24	7	66	1.0	36
	Haiti	Port-au-Prince	7 952 000	286.6	32	13	54	1.9	34
	Honduras	Tegucigalpa	6 147 000	54.8	34	5	69	2.8	51
	Hungary	Budapest	10 116 000	108.7	10	14	71	-0.6	64
	Iceland	Reykjavík	276 000	2.7	15	7	79	1.0	92
	India	New Delhi	982 223 000	298.8	27	9	63	1.6	28
	Indonesia	Jakarta	206 338 000	107.5	24	8	65	1.5	39
	Iran	Tehran	65 758 000	39.9	22	6	69	2.2	61
	Iraq	Baghdad	21 800 000	49.7	33	10	58	2.8	71
	Ireland, Republic of	Dublin	3 681 000	52.4	14	9	76	0.2	59
	Israel	Jerusalem	5 984 000	288.1	21	6	77	1.9	91
	Italy	Rome	57 369 000	190.4	9	10	78	0.0	67
	Jamaica	Kingston	2 538 000	230.9	24	6	75	0.9	55
	Japan	Tokyo	126 281 000	334.3	10	7	80	0.2	79
	Jordan	Amman	6 304 000	70.7	31	4	71	3.3	73
	Kazakhstan	Astana	16 319 000	6.0	14	10	65	0.1	56
	Kenya	Nairobi	29 008 000	49.8	37	13	52	2.2	31
	Kuwait	Kuwait	1 811 000	101.6	22	2	76	3.0	97
	Kyrgyzstan	Bishkek	4 643 000	23.4	22	7	67	0.4	34
	Laos	Vientiane	5 163 000	21.8	38	14	53	3.1	22
	Latvia	Riga	2 424 000	38.1	8	13	69	-1.1	69
	Lebanon	Beirut	3 191 000	305.3	22	6	70	1.8	89
	Lesotho	Maseru	2 062 000	67.9	35	12	56	2.5	26

LAND			EDUCATION AND HEALTH				DEVELOPMENT				
AREA sq km	CULTIV-ATED AREA '000s sq km 1997	FOREST '000s sq km 1997	ADULT LITERACY % 1998	*SCHOOL ENROL-MENT Secondary, gross % 1997	DOCTORS PER 100 000 PERSONS 1990-1998	FOOD INTAKE calories per capita per day 1997	ENERGY CONSU-MPTION million tonnes of oil equivalent 1997	TRADE BALANCE millions US $ 1996	GNP PER CAPITA US $ 1998	COUNTRY	TIME ZONES + OR - GMT
23 200	-	-	46.0	14	20	2084	-	-300	-	Djibouti	+3
750	-	-	90.0	-	46	3059	-	-80	3010	Dominica	-4
48 442	15	16	83.0	50	77	2288	5.5	-4270	1770	Dominican Republic	-4
272 045	30	111	90.5	10	111	2679	8.5	1350	1530	Ecuador	-5
1 000 250	33	0	53.7	75	202	3287	39.6	-12 720	1290	Egypt	+2
21 041	8	1	77.9	33	91	2562	4.1	-2080	1850	El Salvador	-6
28 051	2	-	81.0	-	21	-	-	-20	1500	Equatorial Guinea	+1
117 400	4	3	51.9	21	2	1622	-	-	200	Eritrea	+3
45 200	11	136	98.0	103	312	2849	5.6	-1180	3390	Estonia	+2
1 133 880	105	-	36.0	12	4	1858	17.1	-890	100	Ethiopia	+3
18 330	3	-	92.0	70	38	2865	-	-300	2110	Fiji	+12
338 145	21	200	100.0	117	269	3100	33.1	10 100	24 110	Finland	+2
543 965	195	150	99.0	111	280	3518	247.5	9600	24 940	France	+1
267 667	5	179	63.3	-	19	2556	1.6	1190	3950	Gabon	+1
11 295	2	1	34.5	25	2	2350	-	-220	340	Gambia, The	GMT
69 700	11	30	99.0	73	436	2614	2.3	-360	930	Georgia	+4
357 868	121	107	100.0	102	319	3382	347.3	67 890	25 850	Germany	+1
238 537	46	90	68.9	31	4	2611	6.9	-140	390	Ghana	GMT
131 957	39	65	96.5	98	387	3649	25.6	19 090	11 650	Greece	+2
108 890	19	38	67.6	25	90	2339	5.6	-1850	1640	Guatemala	-6
245 857	15	64	36.0	12	15	2232	-	-290	540	Guinea	GMT
36 125	4	23	36.7	11	18	2430	-	-50	160	Guinea-Bissau	GMT
214 969	5	-	98.0	76	33	2530	-	-90	770	Guyana	-4
27 750	9	0	48.0	23	16	1869	1.8	-730	410	Haiti	-5
112 088	20	41	73.0	32	22	2403	3.2	-1650	730	Honduras	-6
93 030	50	17	99.0	103	337	3313	25.3	-3000	4510	Hungary	+1
102 820	-	-	100.0	104	-	3117	-	-510	28 010	Iceland	GMT
3 287 263	1699	650	53.3	49	48	2496	461.0	-8030	430	India	+5 1/2
1 919 445	310	1098	85.5	52	12	2886	138.8	24 570	680	Indonesia	+7 to +9
1 648 000	194	15	74.5	74	90	2836	108.3	2550	1770	Iran	+3 1/2
438 317	55	1	53.3	41	51	2619	27.1	2900	-	Iraq	+3
70 282	13	6	99.0	117	167	3565	12.5	24 050	18 340	Ireland, Republic of	GMT
20 770	4	1	96.0	88	459	3278	17.6	-7880	15 940	Israel	+2
301 245	109	65	98.5	91	550	3507	163.3	14 790	20 250	Italy	+1
10 991	3	2	86.0	71	57	2553	4.0	-1670	1680	Jamaica	-5
377 727	43	251	100.0	106	177	2932	514.9	108 740	32 380	Japan	+9
89 206	4	0	88.7	-	158	3014	4.8	-1970	1520	Jordan	+2
2 717 300	301	105	100.0	85	360	3085	38.4	1680	1310	Kazakhstan	+4 to +6
582 646	45	13	80.5	24	15	1977	14.1	-1170	330	Kenya	+3
17 818	-	0	80.6	65	178	3096	16.2	4500	-	Kuwait	+3
198 500	14	7	97.0	80	310	2447	2.8	-120	350	Kyrgyzstan	+5
236 800	9	-	45.8	29	20	2108	-	-180	330	Laos	+7
63 700	18	29	100.0	84	303	2864	4.5	-1180	2430	Latvia	+2
10 452	3	1	84.9	82	191	3277	5.2	-5490	3560	Lebanon	+2
30 355	3	0	82.2	29	5	2244	-	-710	570	Lesotho	+2

*Total enrolment in secondary level of education, regardless of age, is expressed as a percentage of the official secondary school-age population.
**Estimate.

KEY INFORMATION

POPULATION

FLAG	COUNTRY	CAPITAL CITY	TOTAL 1998	DENSITY persons per sq km 1998	BIRTH RATE per 1000 population 1997	DEATH RATE per 1000 population 1997	LIFE EXPEC- TANCY in years 1997	POP. CHANGE average % per annum 1995 - 2000	URBAN POP. % 1998
	Liberia	Monrovia	2 666 000	23.9	42	12	59	8.6	46
	Libya	Tripoli	5 339 000	3.0	29	5	70	3.3	87
	Lithuania	Vilnius	3 694 000	56.7	10	12	71	-0.3	68
	Luxembourg	Luxembourg	422 000	163.2	13	9	77	1.1	90
	Macedonia	Skopje	1 999 000	77.7	16	8	72	0.7	61
	Madagascar	Antananarivo	15 057 000	25.6	42	11	57	3.1	28
	Malawi	Lilongwe	10 346 000	87.3	48	23	43	2.5	22
	Malaysia	Kuala Lumpur	21 410 000	64.3	26	5	72	2.0	56
	Maldives	Male	271 000	909.4	26	5	69	3.4	27
	Mali	Bamako	10 694 000	8.6	47	16	50	3.0	29
	Malta	Valletta	384 000	1215.2	13	8	78	0.6	90
	Mauritania	Nouakchott	2 529 000	2.5	41	14	53	2.5	55
	Mauritius	Port Louis	1 141 000	559.3	17	7	71	1.1	41
	Mexico	Mexico City	95 831 000	48.6	25	5	72	1.6	74
	Micronesia, Fed. States of	Pohnpei	114 000	162.6	33	8	66	2.8	28
	Moldova	Chişinău	4 378 000	129.9	11	10	67	0.1	46
	Mongolia	Ulan Bator	2 579 000	1.6	23	7	66	2.1	62
	Morocco	Rabat	27 377 000	61.3	26	7	67	1.8	55
	Mozambique	Maputo	18 880 000	23.6	41	20	45	2.5	38
	Myanmar	Yangon	44 497 000	65.8	27	10	60	1.8	27
	Namibia	Windhoek	1 660 000	2.0	36	12	56	2.4	30
	Nepal	Kathmandu	22 847 000	155.2	34	11	57	2.5	11
	Netherlands	Amsterdam/The Hague	15 678 000	377.5	12	9	78	0.5	89
	New Zealand	Wellington	3 796 000	14.0	15	7	77	1.1	86
	Nicaragua	Managua	4 807 000	37.0	32	5	68	2.6	55
	Niger	Niamey	10 078 000	8.0	52	18	47	3.3	20
	Nigeria	Abuja	106 409 000	115.2	40	12	54	2.8	42
	North Korea	Pyonyang	23 348 000	193.7	21	9	63	1.6	60
	Norway	Oslo	4 419 000	13.6	14	10	78	0.4	75
	Oman	Muscat	2 382 000	7.7	30	3	73	4.2	81
	Pakistan	Islamabad	148 166 000	184.3	36	8	62	2.7	36
	Panama	Panama City	2 767 000	35.9	23	5	74	1.6	56
	Papua New Guinea	Port Moresby	4 600 000	9.9	32	10	58	2.2	17
	Paraguay	Asunción	5 222 000	12.8	31	5	70	2.6	55
	Peru	Lima	24 797 000	19.3	27	6	69	1.7	72
	Philippines	Manila	72 944 000	243.1	29	6	68	2.0	57
	Poland	Warsaw	38 718 000	123.8	11	10	73	0.1	65
	Portugal	Lisbon	9 869 000	111.0	11	11	75	-0.1	61
	Qatar	Doha	579 000	50.6	19	2	72	1.8	92
	Romania	Bucharest	22 474 000	94.6	10	13	69	-0.2	56
	Russian Federation	Moscow	147 434 000	8.6	9	14	67	-0.3	77
	Rwanda	Kigali	6 604 000	250.7	46	22	40	7.9	6
	Samoa	Apia	174 000	61.5	29	5	65	1.1	21
	São Tomé and Príncipe	São Tomé	141 000	146.0	43	9	64	2.0	44
	Saudi Arabia	Riyadh	20 181 000	9.2	35	4	71	3.4	85

LAND

EDUCATION AND HEALTH

DEVELOPMENT

AREA sq km	CULTIV- ATED AREA '000s sq km 1997	FOREST '000s sq km 1997	ADULT LITERACY % 1998	*SCHOOL ENROL- MENT Secondary, gross % 1997	DOCTORS PER 100 000 PERSONS 1990-1998	FOOD INTAKE calories per capita per day 1997	ENERGY CONSU- MPTION million tonnes of oil equivalent 1997	TRADE BALANCE millions US $ 1996	GNP PER CAPITA JS $ 1998	COUNTRY	TIME ZONES + OR - GMT
111 369	3	-	51.0	14	-	2044	-	100	-	Liberia	GMT
1 759 540	21	4	78.0	100	137	3289	15.1	3660	-	Libya	+2
65 200	30	20	99.0	86	399	3261	8.8	-1790	2440	Lithuania	+1
2 586	-	-	99.0	-	213	3619	-	14 760	45 570	Luxembourg	+1
25 713	7	10	89.0	58	219	2664	-	-	1290	Macedonia	+1
587 041	31	151	65.0	13	24	2022	-	-510	260	Madagascar	+3
118 484	17	33	58.3	17	2	2043	-	-120	200	Malawi	+2
332 965	76	155	86.6	62	43	2977	48.5	19 030	3600	Malaysia	+8
298	-	-	96.0	63	19	2485	-	-340	1230	Maldives	+5
1 240 140	47	116	38.4	11	4	2030	-	-190	250	Mali	GMT
316	-	-	91.0	86	250	3398	-	-860	9440	Malta	+1
1 030 700	5	6	41.4	16	11	2622	-	130	410	Mauritania	GMT
2 040	1	0	83.5	65	85	2917	-	-570	3700	Mauritius	+4
1 972 545	273	554	91.0	63	107	3097	141.5	-11 530	3970	Mexico	-6 to -8
701	-	-	81.0	-	46	-	-	-	1800	Micronesia	+10 to +11
33 700	22	4	98.5	79	356	2567	4.4	-90	410	Moldova	+2
1 565 000	13	94	61.5	56	268	1917	-	-100	400	Mongolia	+8
446 550	96	38	47.0	39	34	3078	9.3	-3350	1250	Morocco	GMT
799 380	32	169	42.0	7	<5**	1832	7.7	-1210	210	Mozambique	+2
676 577	102	272	84.0	35	28	2862	13.0	-1600	-	Myanmar	+6½
824 292	8	124	81.0	61	23	2183	-	-150	1940	Namibia	+1
147 181	30	48	39.7	37	5	2366	7.2	-780	210	Nepal	+5¾
41 526	9	3	100.0	140	260	3284	74.9	15 130	24 760	Netherlands	+1
270 534	33	79	100.0	120	210	3395	16.7	-1910	14 700	New Zealand	+12 to 12¾
130 000	27	56	67.5	47	82	2186	2.6	-1330	390	Nicaragua	-6
1 267 000	50	26	14.4	7	3	2097	-	-80	190	Niger	+1
923 768	307	138	60.9	34	21	2735	88.7	930	300	Nigeria	+1
120 538	20	62	95.0	-	-	1837	-	-320	-	North Korea	+9
323 878	9	81	100.0	119	250	3357	24.2	11 100	34 330	Norway	+1
309 500	-	0	68.2	66	120	-	6.8	2310	-	Oman	+4
803 940	216	17	44.0	30	52	2476	56.8	-1770	480	Pakistan	+5
77 082	7	28	91.1	69	119	2430	2.3	-2620	3080	Panama	-5
462 840	7	369	63.2	14	18	2224	-	680	890	Papua New Guinea	+10
406 752	23	115	92.5	44	67	2566	4.2	-1570	1760	Paraguay	-4
1 285 216	42	676	89.0	70	73	2302	15.1	-1950	2460	Peru	-5
300 000	95	68	97.5	79	11	2366	38.3	2320	1050	Philippines	+8
312 683	144	87	99.0	97	230	3366	105.2	-18 100	3900	Poland	+1
88 940	29	29	91.4	116	291	3667	20.4	-14 110	10 690	Portugal	GMT
11 437	-	-	80.0	78	143	-	-	1500	-	Qatar	+3
237 500	99	62	98.0	78	176	3253	44.1	-1740	1390	Romania	+2
17 075 400	1280	7635	99.0	86	380	2904	592.0	33 200	2300	Russian Federation	+2 to +12
26 338	12	3	63.9	13	<5**	2056	-	-230	230	Rwanda	+2
2 831	1	-	98.0	62	38	2828	-	-80	1020	Samoa	-11
964	-	-	-	-	32	2138	-	-20	280	São Tomé and Príncipe	GMT
2 200 000	38	2	66.5	61	166	2783	98.4	20 550	-	Saudi Arabia	+3

*Total enrolment in secondary level of education, regardless of age, is expressed as a percentage of the official secondary school-age population.
**Estimate.

KEY INFORMATION

POPULATION

FLAG	COUNTRY	CAPITAL CITY	TOTAL 1998	DENSITY persons per sq km 1998	BIRTH RATE per 1000 population 1997	DEATH RATE per 1000 population 1997	LIFE EXPEC-TANCY in years 1997	POP. CHANGE average % per annum 1995 - 2000	URBAN POP. % 1998
	Senegal	Dakar	9 003 000	45.8	40	13	52	2.7	46
	Seychelles	Victoria	76 000	167.0	19	8	70	1.0	35
	Sierra Leone	Freetown	4 568 000	63.7	46	26	37	3.0	34
	Singapore	Singapore	3 476 000	5439.7	13	4	76	1.5	100
	Slovakia	Bratislava	5 377 000	109.7	11	10	73	0.1	57
	Slovenia	Ljubljana	1 993 000	98.4	9	10	75	-0.1	50
	Solomon Islands	Honiara	417 000	14.7	37	4	70	3.2	18
	Somalia	Mogadishu	9 237 000	14.5	47	19	46	3.9	26
	South Africa, Republic of	Pretoria/Cape Town	39 357 000	32.3	25	8	65	2.2	53
	South Korea	Seoul	46 109 000	464.5	15	6	72	0.9	80
	Spain	Madrid	39 628 000	78.5	9	10	78	0.1	77
	Sri Lanka	Colombo	18 455 000	281.3	19	6	73	1.0	23
	St Lucia	Castries	150 000	244.0	22	7	70	1.3	38
	St Vincent and the Grenadines	Kingstown	112 000	288.0	21	7	73	0.9	50
	Sudan	Khartoum	28 292 000	11.3	33	12	55	2.2	34
	Suriname	Paramaribo	414 000	2.5	24	6	70	1.2	50
	Swaziland	Mbabane	952 000	54.8	42	10	39	2.8	32
	Sweden	Stockholm	8 875 000	19.7	10	11	79	0.3	83
	Switzerland	Bern	7 299 000	176.8	11	9	79	0.7	68
	Syria	Damascus	15 333 000	82.8	29	5	69	2.5	54
	Taiwan	Taibei	21 908 135	605.5	12	6	75	-	-
	Tajikistan	Dushanbe	6 015 000	42.0	23	6	68	1.9	28
	Tanzania	Dodoma	32 102 000	34.0	41	16	48	2.3	31
	Thailand	Bangkok	60 300 000	117.5	17	7	69	0.8	21
	Togo	Lomé	4 397 000	77.4	41	16	49	2.7	32
	Tonga	Nuku'alofa	98 000	131.0	24	7	72	0.4	42
	Trinidad and Tobago	Port of Spain	1 283 000	250.1	16	7	73	0.8	73
	Tunisia	Tunis	9 335 000	56.9	23	7	70	1.8	64
	Turkey	Ankara	64 479 000	82.7	22	7	69	1.6	73
	Turkmenistan	Ashgabat	4 309 000	8.8	24	7	66	1.9	45
	Tuvalu	Funafuti	11 000	440.0	24	9	-	-	48
	Uganda	Kampala	20 554 000	85.3	48	20	42	2.6	14
	Ukraine	Kiev	50 861 000	84.2	9	15	67	-0.4	68
	United Arab Emirates	Abu Dhabi	2 377 453	28.4	18	3	75	2.0	85
	United Kingdom	London	58 649 000	240.3	12	11	77	0.1	89
	United States of America	Washington	274 028 000	27.9	15	8	76	0.8	77
	Uruguay	Montevideo	3 289 000	18.7	18	10	74	0.6	91
	Uzbekistan	Tashkent	23 574 000	52.7	27	6	69	1.9	38
	Vanuatu	Port Vila	182 000	14.9	35	7	65	2.5	19
	Venezuela	Caracas	23 242 000	25.5	25	5	73	2.0	86
	Vietnam	Hanoi	77 562 000	235.3	21	7	68	1.8	20
	Yemen	Sana	16 887 000	32.0	40	13	54	3.7	24
	Yugoslavia	Belgrade	10 635 000	104.1	13	11	72	0.5	52
	Zambia	Lusaka	8 781 000	11.7	42	19	43	2.5	39
	Zimbabwe	Harare	11 377 000	29.1	31	12	52	2.1	34

AREA sq km	CULTIV-ATED AREA '000s sq km 1997	FOREST '000s sq km 1997	ADULT LITERACY % 1998	*SCHOOL ENROL-MENT Secondary, gross % 1997	DOCTORS PER 100 000 PERSONS 1990-1998	FOOD INTAKE calories per capita per day 1997	ENERGY CONSU-MPTION million tonnes of oil equivalent 1997	TRADE BALANCE millions US $ 1996	GNP PER CAPITA US $ 1998	COUNTRY	TIME ZONES + OR - GMT
LAND			**EDUCATION AND HEALTH**				**DEVELOPMENT**				
196 720	23	74	35.5	16	7	2418	2.8	-420	530	Senegal	GMT
455	-	-	84.0	-	104	2487	-	-330	6450	Seychelles	+4
71 740	5	13	31.5	17	10	2035	-	-90	140	Sierra Leone	GMT
639	-	0	92.0	73	147	-	26.9	3630	30 060	Singapore	+8
49 035	16	20	100.0	94	325	2984	17.2	-1000	3700	Slovakia	+1
20 251	3	11	99.0	93	219	3101	6.4	-1320	9760	Slovenia	+1
28 370	1	-	62.0	18	-	2122	-	-30	750	Solomon Islands	+11
637 657	11	-	24.0	5	4	1566	-	0	-	Somalia	+3
1 219 080	163	85	84.5	84	59	2990	107.2	-120	2880	South Africa, Republic of	+2
99 274	19	76	97.5	102	127	3155	176.4	-24 510	7970	South Korea	+9
504 782	192	84	97.0	132	400	3310	107.3	-35 530	14 080	Spain	+1
65 610	19	18	91.0	75	23	2302	7.2	-1290	810	Sri Lanka	+6
616	-	-	-	-	35	2734	-	-290	3410	St Lucia	-4
389	-	-	-	-	46	2472	-	-140	2420	St Vincent & the Grenadines	-4
2 505 813	169	416	55.5	20	10	2395	11.5	-1110	290	Sudan	+2
163 820	-	-	93.0	-	40	2665	-	-160	1660	Suriname	-3
17 364	2	-	78.0	52	-	2483	-	-290	1400	Swaziland	+2
449 964	28	244	100.0	139	299	3194	51.9	16 360	25 620	Sweden	+1
41 293	4	11	100.0	-	301	3223	26.2	450	40 080	Switzerland	+1
185 180	55	2	72.7	42	109	3352	14.6	-740	1020	Syria	+2
36 179	-	-	94.0	-	-	-	72.7	10 610	-	Taiwan	+8
143 100	9	4	99.0	76	210	2001	3.4	60	350	Tajikistan	+5
945 087	40	325	73.4	5	4	1995	14.3	-770	210	Tanzania	+3
513 115	204	116	95.0	57	24	2360	80.0	7870	2200	Thailand	+7
56 785	24	12	54.9	27	6	2469	-	-400	330	Togo	GMT
748	-	-	99.0	-	-	-	-	-70	1690	Tonga	+13
5 130	1	2	93.5	72	90	2661	8.2	-750	4430	Trinidad and Tobago	-4
164 150	49	6	68.6	66	67	3283	6.8	-2590	2050	Tunisia	+1
779 452	292	89	81.4	63	103	3525	71.3	-13 050	3160	Turkey	+2
488 100	17	38	98.0	111	353	2306	12.2	520	640	Turkmenistan	+5
25	-	-	99.0	-	89	-	-	-10	-	Tuvalu	+12
241 038	68	61	65.0	12	4	2085	-	-910	320	Uganda	+3
603 700	341	92	99.5	93	429	2795	150.1	-60	850	Ukraine	+2
83 600	1	1	74.3	80	168	3390	30.9	630	18 220	United Arab Emirates	+4
244 082	64	24	100.0	133	164	3276	228.0	-52 300	21 400	United Kingdom	GMT
9 809 386	1790	2125	99.0	97	245	3699	2162.2	-364 850	29 340	United States	-5 to -10
176 215	13	8	96.0	85	309	2816	2.9	-560	6180	Uruguay	-3
447 400	49	91	88.0	93	335	2433	42.6	-250	870	Uzbekistan	+5
12 190	1	-	64.0	21	-	2700	-	-60	1270	Vanuatu	+11
912 050	35	440	92.0	40	194	2321	57.5	3660	3500	Venezuela	-4
329 565	72	91	93.0	41	40	2484	39.3	-80	330	Vietnam	+7
527 968	16	0	45.0	34	26	2051	3.4	-120	300	Yemen	+3
102 173	41	18	98.0	64	200	3031	-	-	-	Yugoslavia	+1
752 614	53	314	76.4	29	10	1970	6.0	40	330	Zambia	+2
390 759	32	87	87.5	48	14	2145	10.0	660	610	Zimbabwe	+2

*Total enrolment in secondary level of education, regardless of age, is expressed as a percentage of the official secondary school-age population.
**Estimate.

How to use the Index

All the names on the maps in this atlas, except some of those on the special topic maps, are included in the index.

The names are arranged in **alphabetical order**. Where the name has more than one word the separate words are considered as one to decide the position of the name in the index:

Thetford
Thetford Mines
The Trossachs
The Wash
The Weald
Thiers

Where there is more than one place with the same name, the country name is used to decide the order:

London Canada
London England

If both places are in the same country, the county or state name is also used:

Avon *r.* Bristol England
Avon *r.* Dorset England

Each entry in the index starts with the name of the place or feature, followed by the name of the country or region in which it is located. This is followed by the number of the most appropriate page on which the name appears, usually the largest scale map. Next comes the alphanumeric reference followed by the latitude and longitude.

Names of physical features such as rivers, capes, mountains etc are followed by a description. The descriptions are usually shortened to one or two letters, these abbreviations are keyed below. Town names are followed by a description only when the name may be confused with that of a physical feature:

Big Spring *town*

To help to distinguish the different parts of each entry, different styles of type are used:

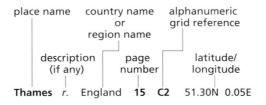

place name   country name or region name   alphanumeric grid reference

description (if any)   page number   latitude/ longitude

Thames *r.* England **15** **C2** 51.30N 0.05E

To use the **alphanumeric grid reference** to find a feature on the map, first find the correct page and then look at the black letters printed outside the blue frame along the top and bottom of the map and the black numbers printed outside the blue frame at the sides of the map. When you have found the correct letter and number follow the grid boxes up and along until you find the correct grid box in which the feature appears. You must then search the grid box until you find the name of the feature.

The **latitude and longitude reference** gives a more exact description of the position of the feature.

Page 6 of the atlas describes lines of latitude and lines of longitude, and explains how they are numbered and divided into degrees and minutes. Each name in the index has a different latitude and longitude reference, so the feature can be located accurately. The lines of latitude and lines of longitude shown on each map are numbered in degrees. These numbers are printed in black along the top, bottom and sides of the map frame.

The drawing above shows part of the map on page 20 and the lines of latitude and lines of longitude.

The index entry for Wexford is given as follows

Wexford Rep. of Ire. **20 E2** 52.20N 6.28W

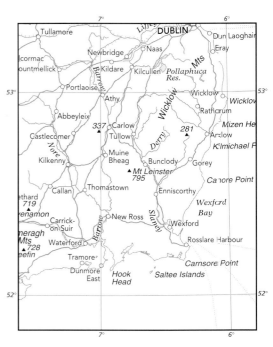

To locate Wexford, first find latitude 52N and estimate 20 minutes north from 52 degrees to find 52.20N, then find longitude 6W and estimate 28 minutes west from 6 degrees to find 6.28W. The symbol for the town of Wexford is where latitude 52.20N and longitude 6.28W meet.

On maps at a smaller scale than the map of Ireland, it is not possible to show every line of latitude and longitude. Only every 5 or 10 degrees of latitude and longitude may be shown. On these maps you must estimate the degrees and minutes to find the exact location of a feature.

Abbreviations

A. and B.	Argyll and Bute
Afghan.	Afghanistan
Ala.	Alabama
b., **B.**	bay, Bay
Bangla.	Bangladesh
Bosnia.	Bosnia-Herzegovina
B.V.Is.	British Virgin Islands
c., **C.**	cape, Cape
Cambs.	Cambridgeshire
C.A.R.	Central African Republic
Carib. Sea	Caribbean Sea
Colo.	Colorado
Czech Rep.	Czech Republic
d.	internal division eg. county, state
D. and G.	Dumfries and Galloway
Del.	Delaware
Derbys.	Derbyshire
des.	desert
Dom. Rep.	Dominican Republic
Equat. Guinea	Equatorial Guinea
E. Sussex	East Sussex
E. Yorks.	East Riding of Yorkshire
est.	estuary
f.	physical feature eg. valley, plain, geographic district
Fla.	Florida
g., **G.**	Gulf
Ga.	Georgia
Glos.	Gloucestershire
Hants.	Hampshire
Herts.	Hertfordshire
High.	Highland

i., **I.** , *is.*, **Is.**	island, Island, islands, Islands
Ill.	Illinois
I.o.M.	Isle of Man
I.o.W.	Isle of Wight
l., **L.**	lake, Lake
La.	Louisiana
Lancs.	Lancashire
Leics.	Leicestershire
Liech.	Liechtenstein
Lincs.	Lincolnshire
Lux.	Luxembourg
Man.	Manitoba
Med. Sea	Mediterranean Sea
Miss.	Mississippi
Mt.	Mount
mtn., **Mtn.**	mountain, Mountain
mts., **Mts.**	mountains, Mountains
N. Ayr.	North Ayrshire
N.C.	North Carolina
N. Cal.	New Caledonia
Neth.	Netherlands
Neth. Ant.	Netherlands Antilles
Nev.	Nevada
Nfld.	Newfoundland
N. Korea	North Korea
N. Mex.	New Mexico
Northum.	Northumberland
Notts.	Nottinghamshire
N.Y.	New York
Oc.	Ocean
Oreg.	Oregon
Oxon.	Oxfordshire
P. and K.	Perth and Kinross

Pem.	Pembrokeshire
pen., **Pen.**	peninsula, Peninsula
Phil.	Philadelphia
P.N.G.	Papua New Guinea
Pt.	Point
r., **R.**	river, River
Rep.of Ire.	Republic of Ireland
Resr.	Reservoir
R.S.A.	Republic of South Africa
Russian Fed.	Russian Federation
Sd.	Sound
S.C.	South Carolina
Shrops.	Shropshire
S. Korea	South Korea
Staffs.	Staffordshire
str., **Str.**	strait, Strait
Switz.	Switzerland
Tex.	Texas
U.A.E.	United Arab Emirates
U.K.	United Kingdom
U.S.A.	United States of America
U.S. V.Is.	United States Virgin Islands
Va.	Virginia
Warwicks.	Warwickshire
W. Isles	Western Isles
W. Sahara	Western Sahara
W. Sussex	West Sussex
W. Va.	West Virginia
Wilts.	Wiltshire
Wyo.	Wyoming
Yugo.	Yugoslavia

A

Aachen Germany 48 C4 50.46N 6.06E
Aalen Germany 48 E3 48.50N 10.05E
Aalst Belgium 42 D2 50.57N 4.03E
Abadan Iran 95 G5 30.21N 48.15E
Abadeh Iran 95 H5 31.10N 52.40E
Abadla Algeria 84 D5 31.01N 2.45W
Abakan Russian Fed. 59 L3 53.43N 91.25E
Abancay Peru 76 C3 13.35S 72.55W
Abarqu Iran 95 H5 31.09N 53.18E
Abashiri Japan 106 D4 44.02N 144.17E
Abaya, L. Ethiopia 85 H2 6.20N 38.00E
Abaza Russian Fed. 102 G8 52.44N 90.12E
Abbeville France 44 D7 50.06N 1.51E
Abbeyfeale Rep. of Ire. 20 B2 52.24N 9.18W
Abbey Head Scotland 17 F2 54.45N 3.58W
Abbeyleix Rep. of Ire. 20 D2 52.55N 7.20W
Abbottabad Pakistan 95 L5 34.12N 73.15E
Abéché Chad 85 G3 13.49N 20.49E
Åbenrå Denmark 43 B1 55.03N 9.26E
Abeokuta Nigeria 84 E2 7.10N 3.26E
Aberaeron Wales 12 C4 52.15N 4.16W
Aberchirder Scotland 19 G2 57.33N 2.38W
Aberdare Wales 12 D3 51.43N 3.27W
Aberdare Range mts. Kenya 87 B2 0.20S 36.07E
Aberdeen Scotland 19 G2 57.08N 2.07W
Aberdeen U.S.A. 64 G6 45.28N 98.30W
Aberdeen City d. Scotland 8 D5 57.08N 2.07W
Aberdeenshire d. Scotland 8 D5 57.22N 2.35W
Aberfeldy Scotland 17 F4 56.38N 3.52W
Aberford England 15 F2 53.51N 1.20W
Aberfoyle Scotland 16 E4 56.11N 4.23W
Abergavenny Wales 12 D3 51.49N 3.01W
Abergele Wales 12 D5 53.17N 3.34W
Aberporth Wales 12 C4 52.08N 4.33W
Abersoch Wales 12 C4 52.50N 4.31W
Abertillery Wales 12 D3 51.44N 3.09W
Aberystwyth Wales 12 C4 52.25N 4.06W
Abha Saudi Arabia 94 F2 18.13N 42.30E
Abidjan Côte d'Ivoire 84 D2 5.19N 4.01W
Abilene U.S.A. 64 G3 32.27N 99.45W
Abingdon England 10 D2 51.40N 1.17W
Abington Scotland 17 F3 55.29N 3.42W
Abitibi, L. Canada 65 K6 48.42N 79.45W
Aboyne Scotland 19 G2 57.05N 2.49W
Abqaiq Saudi Arabia 95 G4 25.55N 49.40E
Abu' Arīsh Saudi Arabia 94 F2 16.58N 42.50E
Abu Dhabi U.A.E. 95 H3 24.27N 54.23E
Abu Hamed Sudan 85 H3 19.32N 33.20E
Abuja Nigeria 84 E2 9.12N 7.11E
Abu Matariq Sudan 94 C1 10.58N 26.17E
Abunã r. Brazil 76 D4 9.41S 65.20W
Abu Simbel Egypt 94 D3 22.18N 31.40E
Abyad Sudan 94 C1 13.46N 26.28E
Acapulco Mexico 70 E4 16.51N 99.56W
Acarigua Venezuela 71 K2 9.35N 69.12W
Accra Ghana 84 D2 5.33N 0.15W
Accrington England 15 E2 53.46N 2.22W
Acheloös r. Greece 56 E3 38.20N 21.04E
Achill I. Rep. of Ire. 20 A3 53.57N 10.00W
Achinsk Russian Fed. 59 L3 56.10N 90.10E
A'Chralaig mtn. Scotland 18 D2 57.11N 5.09W
Acklins I. The Bahamas 71 J5 22.30N 74.10W
Acle England 11 G3 52.38N 1.33E
Aconcagua mtn. Argentina 75 B3 32.37S 70.00W
A Coruña Spain 46 A5 43.22N 8.24W
Acre r. Brazil 76 D4 8.45S 67.23W
Acre d. Brazil 76 C4 8.50S 71.30W
Actéon, Groupe is. French Polynesia 109 Q4 22.00S 136.00W
Adaja r. Spain 46 C4 41.32N 4.52W
Adamawa Highlands Nigeria/Cameroon 84 F2 7.05N 12.00E
Adana Turkey 57 L2 37.00N 35.19E
Adapazari Turkey 57 J4 40.45N 30.23E
Adda r. Italy 50 C6 45.08N 9.55E
Ad Dahna des. Saudi Arabia 95 G2 26.00N 47.00E
Ad Dakhla W. Sahara 84 C4 23.43N 15.57W
Ad Dammam Saudi Arabia 95 H4 26.23N 50.08E
Adderbury England 10 D3 52.01N 1.19W
Ad Dir'iyah Saudi Arabia 95 G4 24.45N 46.32E
Addis Ababa Ethiopia 85 H2 9.03N 38.42E
Ad Dīwanīyah Iraq 94 F5 31.59N 44.57E
Adelaide Australia 110 C2 34.56S 138.36E
Aden Yemen 94 F1 12.50N 45.00E
Aden, G. of Indian Oc. 85 I3 13.00N 50.00E
Adi i. Indonesia 105 I3 4.10S 133.10E
Ādī Ārk'ay Ethiopia 94 E1 13.35N 37.57E
Adige r. Italy 50 E6 45.10N 12.20E
Ādīgrat Ethiopia 94 E1 14.18N 39.31E
Adilang Uganda 87 A3 2.44N 33.28E
Adi Ugri Eritrea 94 E1 14.55N 38.53E
Adıyaman Turkey 57 N2 37.46N 38.15E
Admiralty Is. P.N.G. 108 J6 2.30S 147.20E
Adour r. France 44 C3 43.28N 1.35W
Adriatic Sea Med. Sea 50 F5 42.30N 16.00E
Adwa Ethiopia 85 H3 14.12N 38.56E
Aegean Sea Med. Sea 56 G3 39.00N 25.00E
Afghanistan Asia 95 K5 33.00N 65.30E
Afmadow Somalia 87 C3 0.27N 42.05E
Africa 82
Afyon Turkey 57 J3 38.46N 30.32E
Agadez Niger 84 E3 17.00N 7.56E
Agadir Morocco 84 D5 30.26N 9.36W
Agana Guam 105 K6 13.28N 144.45E
Agano r. Japan 106 C3 37.58N 139.02E
Agartala India 97 I5 23.49N 91.15E
Agde France 44 E3 43.19N 3.28E
Agen France 44 D4 44.12N 0.38E
Āgere Maryam Ethiopia 87 B4 5.40N 38.11E
Aghla Mtn. Rep. of Ire. 16 A2 54.50N 8.10W
Agios Efstratios i. Greece 56 G3 39.30N 25.00E
Agirwat Hills Sudan 94 E2 16.00N 35.10E
Agra India 97 F6 27.09N 78.00E
Ağrı Turkey 94 F6 39.44N 43.04E
Agrigento Italy 50 E2 37.19N 13.36E
Agrihan i. N. Mariana Is. 105 L7 18.44N 145.39E
Aguascalientes Mexico 70 D5 21.51N 102.18W
Aguascalientes d. Mexico 70 D4 22.00N 102.18W
Aguilar de Campóo Spain 46 C5 42.55N 4.15W
Aguilas Spain 46 E2 37.25N 1.35W
Agulhas, C. R.S.A. 86 B1 34.50S 20.00E
Agulhas Negras mtn. Brazil 72 F4 22.20S 44.43W
Ahar Iran 95 G6 38.25N 47.07E
Ahaus Germany 42 G4 52.04N 7.01E
Ahmadabad India 96 E5 23.03N 72.40E
Ahmadnagar India 96 E4 19.08N 74.48E
Ahmadpur East Pakistan 95 L4 29.09N 71.16E
Ahmadpur Sial Pakistan 95 L5 30.41N 71.46E
Ahvaz Iran 95 G5 31.17N 48.44E
Aigina i. Greece 56 F2 37.43N 23.30E
Ailsa Craig i. Scotland 16 D3 55.15N 5.07W
Aïn Beïda Algeria 52 E4 35.50N 7.27E
Aïn Sefra Algeria 84 D5 32.45N 0.35W
Aïr mts. Niger 84 E3 18.30N 8.30E
Airdrie Canada 62 G3 51.20N 114.00W
Airdrie Scotland 17 F3 55.52N 3.59W
Aisne r. France 44 E6 49.27N 2.51E
Aitape P.N.G. 105 K3 3.10S 142.17E
Aitutaki i. Cook Is. 108 P5 18.52S 159.46W
Aix-en-Provence France 44 F3 43.31N 5.27E
Aizu-wakamatsu Japan 106 C3 37.30N 139.58E
Ajaccio France 44 H2 41.55N 8.43E
Ajdabiya Libya 85 G5 30.48N 20.15E
Akhdar, Al Jabal al mts. Libya 85 G5 32.10N 22.00E
Akhdar, Jabal mts. Oman 95 I3 23.10N 57.25E
Akhisar Turkey 57 H3 38.54N 27.49E
Akimiski I. Canada 63 J3 53.00N 81.20W
Akita Japan 106 D3 39.44N 140.05E
Akkajaure l. Sweden 43 D4 67.40N 17.30E
Akobo r. Sudan/Ethiopia 82 G5 8.30N 33.15E
Akordat Eritrea 85 H3 15.35N 37.55E
Akpatok I. Canada 63 L4 60.30N 68.30W
Akranes Iceland 43 X2 64.19N 22.05W
Akron U.S.A. 65 J5 41.04N 81.31W
Aksaray Turkey 94 D5 38.22N 34.02E
Akşehir Turkey 57 J3 38.22N 31.24E
Aksu China 102 E6 42.10N 80.00E
Āksum Ethiopia 94 E1 14.08N 38.48E
Aktau Kazakhstan 58 H2 43.37N 51.11E
Aktogay Kazakhstan 102 D7 46.59N 79.42E
Aktyubinsk Kazakhstan 58 H3 50.16N 57.13E
Akureyri Iceland 43 Y2 65.41N 18.04W
Alabama r. U.S.A. 65 I3 31.05N 87.55W
Alabama d. U.S.A. 65 I3 33.00N 87.00W
Alagoas d. Brazil 77 G4 9.30S 37.00W
Alagoinhas Brazil 77 G3 12.09S 38.21W
Al Ahmadi Kuwait 95 G4 29.05N 48.04E
Alakol', L. Kazakhstan 102 E7 46.00N 81.40E
Alakurtti Russian Fed. 43 G4 67.00N 30.23E
Alamagan i. N. Mariana Is. 105 L7 17.35N 145.50E
Åland is. Finland 43 E3 60.20N 20.00E
Alanya Turkey 57 J2 36.32N 32.02E
Al Artawīyah Saudi Arabia 95 G4 26.31N 45.21E
Alaska d. U.S.A. 62 C4 65.00N 153.00W
Alaska, G. of U.S.A. 62 D3 58.45N 145.00W
Alaska Pen. U.S.A. 62 C3 56.00N 160.00W
Alaska Range mts. U.S.A. 62 C4 62.10N 152.00W
Alausí Ecuador 76 C4 2.00S 78.50W
Alavus Finland 43 E3 62.35N 23.37E
Alaw Resr. Wales 12 C5 53.20N 4.25W
Albacete Spain 46 E3 39.00N 1.52W
Alba Iulia Romania 56 F7 46.04N 23.33E
Albania Europe 56 E4 41.00N 20.00E
Albany Australia 110 A2 34.57S 117.54E
Albany Ga. U.S.A. 65 J3 31.37N 84.10W
Albany N.Y. U.S.A. 65 L5 42.40N 73.49W
Albany r. Canada 63 J3 52.10N 82.00W
Al Basrah Iraq 95 G5 30.33N 47.50E
Al Bayda' Libya 85 G5 32.50N 21.50E
Albenga Italy 50 C6 44.03N 8.13E
Alberche r. Spain 46 C4 40.00N 4.45W
Albert France 42 B1 50.00N 2.40E
Albert, L. Africa 86 C5 1.45N 31.00E
Alberta d. Canada 62 G3 55.00N 115.00W
Albert Lea U.S.A. 65 H5 43.39N 93.22W
Albert Nile r. Uganda 85 H2 3.30N 32.00E
Albi France 44 E3 43.56N 2.08E
Al Biyadah f. Saudi Arabia 95 G3 22.00N 47.00E
Alboran, Isla de i. Spain 46 D1 35.55N 3.10W
Ålborg Denmark 43 B2 57.03N 9.56E
Āl Bu Kamal Syria 94 F5 34.27N 40.55E
Albuquerque U.S.A. 64 E4 35.05N 106.38W
Al Buraymi U.A.E. 95 I3 24.15N 55.45E
Albury Australia 110 D2 36.03S 146.53E
Alcalá de Henares Spain 46 D4 40.28N 3.22W
Alcalá la Real Spain 46 D2 37.28N 3.55W
Alcañiz Spain 46 E4 41.03N 0.09W
Alcázar de San Juan Spain 46 D3 39.24N 3.12W
Alcester England 10 D3 52.13N 1.52W
Alcoy Spain 46 E3 38.42N 0.29W
Alcúdia Spain 46 G3 39.51N 3.09E
Aldabra Is. Indian Oc. 86 D4 9.00S 47.00E
Aldan Russian Fed. 59 O3 58.44N 125.22E
Aldan r. Russian Fed. 59 P4 63.30N 130.00E
Aldbrough England 15 G2 53.50N 0.07W
Aldeburgh England 11 G3 52.09N 1.35E
Alderley Edge England 15 E2 53.18N 2.15W
Alderney i. Channel Is. 13 Z9 49.42N 2.11W
Aldershot England 10 E2 51.15N 0.47W
Aldingham England 14 D3 54.08N 3.08W
Aldridge England 10 D3 52.36N 1.55W
Aleksandrovsk-Sakhalinskiy Russian Fed. 59 Q3 50.55N 142.12E
Aleksin Russian Fed. 55 O6 54.31N 37.07E
Alençon France 44 D6 48.25N 0.05E
Aleppo Syria 94 E6 36.14N 37.10E
Alès France 44 F4 44.08N 4.05E
Alessandria Italy 50 C6 44.54N 8.37E
Ålesund Norway 43 A3 62.28N 6.11E
Aleutian Is. U.S.A. 108 N12 52.00N 176.00W
Aleutian Range mts. U.S.A. 62 C3 58.00N 156.00W
Alexander Archipelago is. U.S.A. 62 E3 56.30N 134.30W
Alexander I. Antarctica 112 72.00S 70.00W
Alexandra, C. South Georgia 75 F1 54.05S 37.58W
Alexandria Egypt 94 C5 31.13N 29.55E
Alexandria Scotland 16 E3 55.59N 4.35W
Alexandria La. U.S.A. 65 H3 31.19N 92.29W
Alexandria Va. U.S.A. 65 K4 38.48N 77.03W
Alexandroupoli Greece 56 G4 40.50N 25.53E
Aleysk Russian Fed. 102 E8 52.32N 82.17E
Al Farwanīyah Kuwait 95 G4 29.04N 47.50E
Alford England 15 H2 53.17N 0.11E
Alfreton England 15 F2 53.06N 1.22W
Algarve f. Portugal 46 A2 37.20N 8.00W
Algeciras Spain 46 C2 36.08N 5.27W
Algeria Africa 84 E4 28.00N 2.00E
Al Ghaydah Yemen 95 H2 16.12N 52.16E
Alghero Italy 50 C4 40.33N 8.20E
Algiers Algeria 84 E5 36.50N 3.00E
Al Hamad des. Asia 94 E5 31.45N 39.00E
Al Hamadah al Hamra' f. Libya 52 F2 29.00N 12.00E
Al Ḥasakah Syria 94 F6 36.29N 40.45E
Al Hibak f. Saudi Arabia 95 H3 21.00N 53.30E
Al Hillah Iraq 94 F5 32.28N 44.29E
Al Hoceima Morocco 46 D1 35.15N 3.55W
Aliakmonas r. Greece 56 F4 40.30N 22.38E
Ali Bayramli Azerbaijan 95 G6 39.56N 48.55E
Alicante Spain 46 E3 38.21N 0.29W
Alice Springs town Australia 110 C3 23.42S 133.52E
Alingsås Sweden 43 C2 57.55N 12.30E
Al Jaghbub Libya 85 E4 29.42N 24.38E
Al Jaharah Kuwait 95 G4 29.20N 47.41E
Al Jauf Saudi Arabia 94 E4 29.49N 39.52E
Al Jawf Libya 85 G4 24.09N 23.19E
Al Jawsh Libya 52 F3 32.00N 11.40E
Al Jubayl Saudi Arabia 95 G4 26.59N 49.40E
Al Khaburah Oman 95 I3 23.58N 57.10E
Al Khaṣab Oman 95 I4 26.14N 56.15E
Al Khums Libya 53 F3 32.39N 14.15E
Alkmaar Neth. 42 D4 52.37N 4.44E
Al Kut Iraq 95 G5 32.30N 45.51E
Allahabad India 97 G6 25.57N 81.50E
Allegheny Mts. U.S.A. 65 K5 38.00N 81.00W
Allendale Town England 15 E3 54.54N 2.15W
Allen, Lough Rep. of Ire. 20 C4 54.07N 8.04W
Allentown U.S.A. 65 K5 40.37N 75.30W
Alleppey India 96 F2 9.30N 76.22E
Aller r. Germany 48 D5 52.57N 9.11E
Alliance U.S.A. 64 F5 42.08N 103.00W
Allier r. France 44 E5 46.58N 3.04E
Al Lith Saudi Arabia 94 F3 20.09N 40.16E
Alloa Scotland 17 F4 56.07N 3.49W
Al Mahrah f. Yemen 95 H2 15.30N 51.00E
Almansa Spain 46 E3 38.52N 1.06W
Almanzor mtn. Spain 46 C4 40.20N 5.22W
Al Marj Libya 53 H3 32.30N 20.50E
Almaty Kazakhstan 102 D6 43.19N 76.55E
Almeirim Brazil 77 E4 1.30S 52.35W
Almelo Neth. 42 F4 52.21N 6.40E
Almería Spain 46 D2 36.50N 2.26W
Almina, Punta c. Morocco 46 C1 35.54N 5.17W
Al Mish'ab Saudi Arabia 95 G4 28.00N 48.43E
Almodôvar Portugal 46 A2 37.31N 8.03W
Almond r. Scotland 17 F4 56.25N 3.28W
Al Mudawwara Jordan 94 E5 29.20N 36.00E
Al Mukha Yemen 94 F1 13.19N 43.15E
Almuñécar Spain 46 D2 36.44N 3.41W
Al Nu'ayriyah Saudi Arabia 95 G4 27.27N 48.17E
Alnwick England 15 F4 55.25N 1.41W
Alofi Niue 108 N5 19.03S 169.54W
Alor i. Indonesia 105 G2 8.20S 124.30E
Alpes Maritimes mts. France 44 G4 44.07N 7.08E
Alpine U.S.A. 64 F3 30.22N 103.40W
Alps mts. Europe 34 E2 46.00N 7.30E
Al Qa'amiyat f. Saudi Arabia 95 G2 18.30N 49.00E
Al Qaddahiyah Libya 53 G3 31.24N 15.12E
Al Qāmishlī Syria 94 F6 37.05N 41.11E
Al Qunfidhah Saudi Arabia 94 F2 19.08N 41.15E
Alsager England 15 E2 53.07N 2.20W
Alston England 15 E3 54.48N 2.26W
Alta r. Norway 43 E5 70.00N 23.15E
Altai Mts. Mongolia 102 G7 46.30N 93.30E
Altamira Brazil 77 E4 3.12S 52.12W
Altamura Italy 50 G4 40.50N 16.32E
Altay China 102 F7 47.48N 88.07E
Altay Mongolia 102 H7 46.20N 97.00E
Altenburg Germany 48 F4 50.59N 12.27E
Altiplano f. Bolivia 76 D3 18.00S 67.30W
Altiplano Mexicano mts. N. America 60 I4 24.00N 105.00W
Alton England 10 E2 51.08N 0.59W
Altoona U.S.A. 65 K5 40.32N 78.23W
Altrincham England 15 E2 53.25N 2.21W
Altun Shan mts. China 102 F5 38.10N 87.50E
Al'Uqaylah Libya 53 G3 30.15N 19.12E
Alur Setar Malaysia 104 C5 6.06N 100.23E
Al'Uthmanīyah Saudi Arabia 95 G4 25.16N 49.24E
Al'Uwaynat Libya 94 B3 21.53N 24.51E
Alva U.S.A. 64 G4 36.48N 98.40W
Älvdalen Sweden 43 C3 61.14N 14.05E
Alveley England 10 C3 52.28N 2.20W
Älvsbyn Sweden 43 E4 65.41N 21.00E
Al Wajh Saudi Arabia 94 E4 26.16N 36.28E
Alwen Resr. Wales 12 D5 53.05N 3.35W
Al Widyan f. Iraq/Saudi Arabia 94 F5 31.00N 42.00E
Alyth Scotland 17 F4 56.38N 3.14W
Alytus Lithuania 55 I6 54.24N 24.03E
Amadeus, L. Australia 110 C3 24.50S 130.45E
Amadjuak L. Canada 63 K4 65.00N 71.00W
Amadora Portugal 46 A3 38.45N 9.13W
Åmål Sweden 43 C2 59.04N 12.41E
Amamapare Indonesia 105 J3 4.56S 136.43E
Amapá d. Brazil 77 E5 2.00N 52.00W
Amarillo U.S.A. 64 F4 35.14N 101.50W
Amasya Turkey 57 L4 40.37N 35.50E
Amazon r. Brazil 77 E4 2.00S 50.00W
Amazonas d. Brazil 76 D4 4.50S 64.00W
Amazon Delta f. Brazil 77 F5 0.00 50.00W
Ambarchik Russian Fed. 59 S4 69.39N 162.27E
Ambato Ecuador 76 C4 1.18S 78.36W
Ambergate England 15 F2 53.03N 1.29W
Ambergris Cay i. Belize 70 G4 18.00N 87.58W
Amble England 15 F4 55.20N 1.34W
Ambleside England 14 E3 54.26N 2.58W
Ambon Indonesia 105 H3 3.50S 128.10E
Amboseli Nat. Park Kenya 87 B2 2.40S 37.10E
Ambrym i. Vanuatu 111 F4 16.15S 168.10E
Ameland i. Neth. 42 E5 53.28N 5.48E
American Samoa is. Pacific Oc. 108 O5 14.20S 170.00W
Amersfoort Neth. 42 E4 52.10N 5.23E
Amersham England 11 E2 51.40N 0.38W
Amesbury England 10 D2 51.10N 1.46W
Amgu Russian Fed. 106 C5 45.48N 137.36E
Amgun r. Russian Fed. 59 P3 53.10N 139.47E
Amiens France 44 E6 49.54N 2.18E
Amino Ethiopia 87 C3 4.25N 41.52E
Amlwch Wales 12 C5 53.24N 4.21W
Amman Jordan 94 E5 31.57N 35.56E
Ammanford Wales 12 C3 51.48N 4.00W
Amol Iran 95 H6 36.26N 52.24E
Amorgos i. Greece 56 G2 36.49N 25.54E
Amos Canada 63 K2 48.35N 78.05W
Ampthill England 11 E3 52.03N 0.30W
Amravati India 97 F5 20.58N 77.50E
Amritsar India 96 E7 31.35N 74.56E
Amstelveen Neth. 42 D4 52.18N 4.51E
Amsterdam Neth. 42 D4 52.22N 4.54E
Amu Darya r. Asia 90 H7 43.50N 59.00E
Amund Ringnes I. Canada 63 I5 78.00N 96.00W
Amundsen G. Canada 62 F5 70.30N 122.00W
Amundsen Sea Antarctica 112 70.00S 110.00W
Amuntai Indonesia 104 F3 2.24S 115.14E
Amur r. Russian Fed. 59 P3 53.17N 140.00E
Anabar r. Russian Fed. 59 N5 72.40N 113.30E
Anadyr Russian Fed. 59 T4 64.40N 177.32E
Anadyr r. Russian Fed. 59 T4 65.00N 176.00E
Anadyr, G. of Russian Fed. 59 U4 64.30N 177.50W
'Ānah Iraq 94 F5 34.29N 41.57E
Anambas Is. Indonesia 104 D4 3.00N 106.10E
Anamur Turkey 57 K2 36.06N 32.49E
Anápolis Brazil 77 F3 16.19S 48.58W
Anatahan i. N. Mariana Is. 105 L7 16.22N 145.38E
Anatolia f. Turkey 57 J3 38.30N 32.00E
Anchorage U.S.A. 62 D4 61.10N 150.00W
Ancona Italy 50 E5 43.37N 13.33E
Åndalsnes Norway 43 A3 62.33N 7.43E
Andaman Is. India 97 I3 12.00N 93.00E
Andaman Sea Indian Oc. 97 J3 11.00N 96.00E
Anderlecht Belgium 42 D2 50.51N 4.18E
Anderson U.S.A. 62 D4 64.25N 149.10W
Anderson r. Canada 62 F4 69.45N 129.00W
Andes mts. S. America 74 B5 15.00S 74.00W
Andfjorden est. Norway 43 D5 69.10N 16.20E
Andhra Pradesh d. India 97 F4 17.00N 79.00E
Andkhvoy Afghan. 95 K6 36.56N 65.05E
Andorra Europe 46 F5 42.30N 1.32E
Andorra La Vella Andorra 46 F5 42.30N 1.31E
Andover England 10 D2 51.13N 1.29W
Andøya i. Norway 43 C5 69.00N 15.30E
Andreas I.o.M. 14 C3 54.22N 4.26W
Andreas, C. Cyprus 57 L1 35.40N 34.35E
Andros i. Greece 56 G2 37.50N 24.50E
Andros i. The Bahamas 71 I5 24.30N 78.00W
Andújar Spain 46 C3 38.02N 4.03W
Anegada i. B.V.Is. 71 L4 18.46N 64.24W
Aneto, Pico de mtn. Spain 46 F5 42.40N 0.19E
Angara r. Russian Fed. 59 L3 58.00N 93.00E
Angarsk Russian Fed. 103 I8 52.31N 103.55E
Ånge Sweden 43 C3 62.31N 15.40E
Angel de la Guarda i. Mexico 70 B6 29.10N 113.20W
Ängelholm Sweden 43 C2 56.15N 12.50E
Angers France 44 C5 47.29N 0.32W
Angola Africa 86 A3 12.00S 18.00E
Angola Basin f. Atlantic Oc. 117 J5
Angoulême France 44 D4 45.40N 0.10E
Angren Uzbekistan 102 C6 41.01N 70.10E
Anguilla i. Leeward Is. 71 L4 18.14N 63.05W
Angus d. Scotland 8 D5 56.45N 3.00W
Anhui d. China 103 L4 31.30N 116.45E
Ankara Turkey 57 K3 39.55N 32.50E
Anlaby England 15 G2 53.45N 0.27W
Annaba Algeria 84 E5 36.55N 7.47E
An Nafud des. Saudi Arabia 94 F4 28.40N 41.30E
An Najaf Iraq 94 F5 31.59N 44.19E
Annalee r. Rep. of Ire. 20 D4 54.08N 7.25W
Annalong N. Ireland 16 D2 54.06N 5.55W
Annan Scotland 17 F2 54.59N 3.16W
Annan r. Scotland 17 F3 54.58N 3.16W
Annapurna mtn. Nepal 97 G6 28.34N 83.50E
Ann Arbor U.S.A. 65 J5 42.18N 83.45W
An Nāṣirīyah Iraq 95 G5 31.04N 46.16E
An Nawfaliyah Libya 53 G3 30.47N 17.50E
Annecy France 44 G4 45.54N 6.07E
Ansbach Germany 48 E3 49.18N 10.36E
Anshan China 103 M6 41.05N 122.58E
Anshun China 103 J3 26.15N 105.51E
Anstruther Scotland 17 G4 56.14N 2.42W
Antakya Turkey 57 M2 36.12N 36.10E
Antalya Turkey 57 J2 36.53N 30.42E
Antalya, G. of Turkey 57 J2 36.38N 31.00E
Antananarivo Madagascar 86 D3 18.52S 47.30E
Antarctica 112
Antarctic Pen. f. Antarctica 116 F2 65.00S 64.00W
An Teallach mtn. Scotland 18 D2 57.48N 5.16W
Antequera Spain 46 C2 37.01N 4.34W
Antibes France 44 G3 43.35N 7.07E
Anticosti, Île d' Canada 63 L2 49.20N 63.00W
Antigua i. Leeward Is. 71 L4 17.09N 61.49W
Antigua and Barbuda Leeward Is. 71 L4 17.30N 61.49W
Antikythira i. Greece 56 F1 35.52N 23.18E
Antipodes Is. Pacific Oc. 108 M2 49.42S 178.50E
Antofagasta Chile 76 C2 23.40S 70.23W
Antrim N. Ireland 16 C2 54.43N 6.14W
Antrim d. N. Ireland 20 E4 54.45N 6.15W
Antrim Hills N. Ireland 16 C2 55.00N 6.10W
Antsirañana Madagascar 86 D3 12.19S 49.17E
Antwerpen Belgium 42 D3 51.13N 4.25E
Antwerpen d. Belgium 42 D3 51.16N 4.45E
Anxi China 102 H6 40.32N 95.57E
Anyang China 103 K5 36.04N 114.20E
Anzhero-Sudzhensk Russian Fed. 58 K3 56.10N 86.10E
Aomori Japan 106 D4 40.50N 140.43E
Aoraki mtn. New Zealand 111 G1 43.36S 170.09E
Aosta Italy 50 B6 45.43N 7.19E
Apa r. Brazil/Paraguay 77 E2 22.08S 57.55W
Apalachee B. U.S.A. 65 J2 29.30N 84.00W
Apaporis r. Colombia 76 D4 1.40S 69.20W
Aparri Phil. 105 G7 18.22N 121.40E
Apatity Russian Fed. 43 H4 67.32N 33.21E
Apeldoorn Neth. 42 E4 52.13N 5.57E
Apennines mts. Italy 50 D6 44.00N 11.00E
Apia Samoa 108 N5 13.50S 171.44E
Aporé r. Brazil 77 E3 19.30S 50.55W
Appalachian Mts. U.S.A. 65 K4 39.30N 78.00W
Appleby-in-Westmorland England 15 E3 54.35N 2.29W
Appledore England 13 C3 51.03N 4.12W
Appleton U.S.A. 65 I5 44.16N 88.25W
Apucarana Brazil 77 E2 23.34S 51.28W
Apurimac r. Peru 76 C3 10.43S 73.55W
Aqaba Jordan 94 E4 29.32N 35.00E
Aqaba, G. of Asia 94 D4 28.45N 34.45E
Āra Ārba Ethiopia 87 C4 5.50N 41.30E
Arabian Pen. Saudi Arabia 90 G5 24.00N 45.00E
Arabian Sea Asia 96 C4 19.00N 65.00E
Aracaju Brazil 77 G3 10.54S 37.07W

B

Batdâmbâng Cambodia 104 C6 13.06N 103.13E
Bath England 10 C2 51.22N 2.22W
Bath and North East Somerset d. England 9 D2 51.20N 2.30W
Bathgate Scotland 17 F3 55.55N 3.38W
Bathurst Australia 110 D2 33.27S 149.35E
Bathurst Canada 63 L2 47.37N 65.40W
Bathurst I. Australia 110 C4 11.45S 130.15E
Bathurst I. Canada 63 H5 76.00N 100.00W
Bathurst Inlet town Canada 62 H4 66.48N 108.00W
Batley England 15 F2 53.43N 1.38W
Batna Algeria 84 E5 35.34N 6.11E
Baton Rouge U.S.A. 65 H3 30.30N 91.10W
Batticaloa Sri Lanka 97 G2 7.43N 81.42E
Battle England 11 F1 50.55N 0.30E
Batu Is. Indonesia 104 B3 0.30S 98.20E
Batumi Georgia 58 G2 41.37N 41.36E
Baubau Indonesia 105 G2 5.30S 122.37E
Bauchi Nigeria 84 E3 10.16N 9.50E
Bauru Brazil 77 F2 22.19S 49.07W
Bawean i. Indonesia 104 E2 5.50S 112.35E
Bawiti Egypt 94 C4 28.21N 28.51E
Bayamo Cuba 71 I5 20.23N 76.39W
Bayanhongor Mongolia 103 I7 46.42N 100.09E
Bayburt Turkey 57 O4 40.15N 40.16E
Bay City U.S.A. 65 J5 43.35N 83.52W
Baydaratskaya B. Russian Fed. 58 I4 70.00N 66.00E
Bay Is. Honduras 70 G4 16.10N 86.30W
Bayonne France 44 C3 43.30N 1.28W
Bayreuth Germany 48 E3 49.56N 11.35E
Bayy al Kabir, Wadi r. Libya 53 G3 31.20N 16.00E
Baza Spain 46 D2 37.30N 2.45W
Beachy Head England 11 F1 50.43N 0.15E
Beaconsfield England 10 E2 51.37N 0.39W
Beaminster England 10 C1 50.48N 2.44W
Bear I. Norway 58 D5 74.30N 19.00E
Beata, C. Dom. Rep. 71 J4 17.41N 71.24W
Beata I. Dom. Rep. 71 J4 17.38N 71.29W
Beaufort Sea N. America 62 D5 72.00N 141.00W
Beaufort West R.S.A. 86 B1 32.20S 22.34E
Beauly Scotland 19 E2 57.29N 4.28W
Beauly Firth est. Scotland 19 E2 57.29N 4.20W
Beaumaris Wales 12 C5 53.16N 4.07W
Beaumont U.S.A. 65 H3 30.04N 94.06W
Beaune France 44 F5 47.02N 4.50E
Beauvais France 44 E6 49.26N 2.05E
Beaver r. Canada 62 H3 55.30N 108.00W
Beaver Creek town Canada 62 D4 62.20N 140.45W
Bebington England 14 E2 53.23N 2.58W
Beccles England 11 G3 52.27N 1.33E
Béchar Algeria 84 D5 31.35N 2.17W
Beckingham England 15 G2 53.23N 0.50W
Bedale England 15 F3 54.18N 1.35W
Bedele Ethiopia 85 H2 8.29N 36.19E
Bedford England 11 E3 52.08N 0.29W
Bedford Levels f. England 11 F3 52.30N 0.06W
Bedfordshire d. England 9 E3 52.04N 0.28W
Bedlington England 15 F4 55.08N 1.34W
Bedworth England 10 D3 52.28N 1.29W
Beersheba Israel 94 D5 31.15N 34.47E
Beeville U.S.A. 64 G2 28.25N 97.47W
Bei'an China 103 N7 48.17N 126.33E
Beihai China 103 J2 21.29N 109.10E
Beijing China 103 L5 39.55N 116.25E
Beinn an Oir mtn. Scotland 16 C3 55.55N 6.00W
Beinn Dearg mtn. High. Scotland 18 E2 57.49N 4.55W
Beinn Dearg mtn. P. and K. Scotland 19 F1 56.52N 3.54W
Beinn Heasgarnich mtn. Scotland 16 E4 56.31N 4.34W
Beira Mozambique 86 C3 19.49S 34.52E
Beirut Lebanon 94 E5 33.52N 35.30E
Beith Scotland 16 E3 55.45N 4.37W
Beiuş Romania 54 H2 46.40N 22.21E
Beja Portugal 46 B3 38.01N 7.52W
Bejaïa Algeria 84 E5 36.45N 5.05E
Béjar Spain 46 C4 40.24N 5.45W
Békéscsaba Hungary 54 G2 46.41N 21.06E
Bela Pakistan 96 D6 26.12N 66.20E
Belarus Europe 55 J5 53.00N 28.00E
Belcher Is. Canada 63 K3 56.00N 79.00W
Belém Brazil 77 F4 1.27S 48.29W
Belen U.S.A. 64 E3 34.39N 106.48W
Belfast N. Ireland 16 D2 54.36N 5.57W
Belfast Lough N. Ireland 16 D2 54.41N 5.49W
Belford England 15 F4 55.36N 1.48W
Belgium Europe 42 D2 51.00N 4.30E
Belgorod Russian Fed. 55 O4 50.38N 36.36E
Belgrade Yugo. 56 E6 44.49N 20.28E
Belikh r. Syria 57 N1 35.58N 39.05E
Belitung i. Indonesia 104 D3 3.00S 108.00E
Belize Belize 70 G4 17.29N 88.20W
Belize C. America 70 G4 17.00N 88.30W
Bellac France 44 D5 46.07N 1.04E
Bellary India 96 F4 15.11N 76.54E
Belle-Île France 44 B5 47.20N 3.10W
Belle Isle, Str. of Canada 63 M3 50.45N 58.00W
Bellingham England 15 E4 55.09N 2.15W
Bellingham U.S.A. 64 B6 48.45N 122.29W
Bellingshausen Sea Antarctica 112 70.00S 88.00W
Bellinzona Switz. 44 H5 46.11N 9.02E
Bello Colombia 71 I2 6.20N 75.41W
Belmopan Belize 70 G4 17.25N 88.46W
Belmullet Rep. of Ire. 20 A4 54.13N 10.00W
Belo Horizonte Brazil 77 F3 19.45S 43.53W
Belorechensk Russian Fed. 57 N6 44.46N 39.54E
Belper England 15 F2 53.02N 1.29W
Belukha, Mt. Russian Fed. 58 K2 49.46N 86.40E
Belyy Russian Fed. 55 M6 55.49N 32.58E
Bembridge England 10 D1 50.41N 1.04W
Bemidji U.S.A. 65 H6 47.29N 94.52W
Ben Alder mtn. Scotland 19 E1 56.49N 4.28W
Benavente Spain 46 C5 42.00N 5.40W
Benbane Head N. Ireland 16 C3 55.15N 6.29W
Benbecula i. Scotland 18 B2 57.26N 7.18W
Ben Cruachan mtn. Scotland 16 D4 56.26N 5.18W
Bend U.S.A. 64 B5 44.04N 121.20W
Bendigo Australia 110 D2 36.48S 144.21E
Bengal, B. of Indian Oc. 97 H4 17.00N 89.00E
Bengbu China 103 L4 32.56N 117.27E
Bengkulu Indonesia 104 C3 3.46S 102.16E
Benguela Angola 86 A3 12.34S 13.24E
Ben Hope mtn. Scotland 19 E3 58.24N 4.36W
Beni r. Bolivia 76 D3 10.30S 66.00W
Benidorm Spain 46 E3 38.33N 0.09W
Beni Mellal Morocco 84 D5 32.21N 6.21W
Benin Africa 84 E3 9.00N 2.30E
Benin, Bight of Africa 84 E2 5.30N 3.00E
Benin City Nigeria 84 E2 6.19N 5.41E
Beni-Saf Algeria 52 C4 35.19N 1.23W
Beni Suef Egypt 94 D4 29.05N 31.05E
Ben Klibreck mtn. Scotland 19 E3 58.15N 4.22W
Ben Lawers mtn. Scotland 16 E4 56.33N 4.14W
Ben Lomond mtn. Scotland 16 E4 56.12N 4.38W
Ben Loyal mtn. Scotland 19 E3 58.24N 4.26W
Ben Lui mtn. Scotland 16 E4 56.23N 4.49W
Ben Macdhui mtn. Scotland 19 F2 57.04N 3.40W
Ben More mtn. A. and B. Scotland 16 C4 56.26N 6.02W
Ben More mtn. Stirling Scotland 16 E4 56.23N 4.31W
Ben More Assynt mtn. Scotland 18 E3 58.07N 4.52W
Ben Nevis mtn. Scotland 18 D1 56.48N 5.00W
Bentley England 15 F2 53.31N 1.09W
Benue r. Nigeria 84 E2 7.52N 6.45E
Ben Vorlich mtn. Scotland 16 E4 56.21N 4.13W
Ben Wyvis mtn. Scotland 19 E2 57.40N 4.35W
Benxi China 103 M6 41.21N 123.45E
Berat Albania 56 D4 40.42N 19.59E
Berau G. Indonesia 105 I3 2.20S 133.00E
Berber Sudan 94 D2 18.01N 33.59E
Berbera Somalia 85 I3 10.28N 45.02E
Berberati C.A.R. 86 A5 4.19N 15.51E
Berdyans'k Ukraine 55 O2 46.45N 36.47E
Berdychiv Ukraine 55 K3 49.54N 28.39E
Berens River town Canada 62 I3 52.22N 97.00W
Berezivka Ukraine 55 L2 47.12N 30.56E
Berezniki Russian Fed. 58 H3 59.26N 56.49E
Bergamo Italy 50 C6 45.42N 9.40E
Bergen Norway 43 A3 60.23N 5.20E
Bergerac France 44 D4 44.50N 0.29E
Bergisch Gladbach Germany 48 C4 50.59N 7.10E
Bering Sea N. America/Asia 60 A7 60.00N 170.00E
Bering Str. Russian Fed./U.S.A. 59 U4 65.00N 170.00W
Berkel r. Neth. 42 F4 52.10N 6.12E
Berkeley England 10 C2 51.42N 2.27W
Berkner I. Antarctica 112 79.30S 50.00W
Berkshire Downs hills England 10 D2 51.30N 1.15W
Berlin Germany 48 F5 52.32N 13.25E
Bermejo r. Argentina 77 E2 26.47S 58.30W
Bermuda i. Atlantic Oc. 71 L7 32.18N 65.00W
Bern Switz. 44 G5 46.57N 7.26E
Berneray i. W.Isles Scotland 18 B1 56.47N 7.38W
Berneray i. W.Isles Scotland 18 B2 57.43N 7.11W
Bernina Pass Switz. 50 D7 46.25N 10.02E
Berry Head England 13 D2 50.24N 3.28W
Beru i. Kiribati 108 M6 1.15S 176.00E
Berwick-upon-Tweed England 17 G3 55.46N 2.00W
Besançon France 44 G5 47.14N 6.02E
Bessbrook N. Ireland 16 C2 54.12N 6.25W
Betanzos Spain 46 A5 43.17N 8.13W
Bethel U.S.A. 62 B4 60.48N 161.46W
Bethesda Wales 12 C5 53.11N 4.03W
Béthune France 42 B2 50.32N 2.38E
Betsiboka r. Madagascar 86 D3 16.03S 46.36E
Betws-y-Coed Wales 12 D5 53.05N 3.48W
Beult r. England 11 F2 51.13N 0.26E
Beverley England 15 G2 53.52N 0.26W
Bewdley England 10 C3 52.23N 2.19W
Bewl Water l. England 11 F2 51.02N 0.22E
Bexhill England 11 F1 50.51N 0.29E
Beykoz Turkey 57 I4 41.09N 29.06E
Beyla Guinea 84 D2 8.42N 8.39W
Beypazarı Turkey 57 J4 40.10N 31.56E
Beyşehir L. Turkey 57 J2 37.47N 31.30E
Béziers France 44 E3 43.21N 3.13E
Bhagalpur India 97 H6 25.14N 86.59E
Bhamo Myanmar 97 J5 24.15N 97.15E
Bhavnagar India 96 E5 21.46N 72.14E
Bhima r. India 96 F4 16.30N 77.10E
Bhopal India 97 F5 23.17N 77.28E
Bhubaneshwar India 97 H5 20.15N 85.50E
Bhuj India 96 D5 23.12N 69.54E
Bhutan Asia 97 I6 27.25N 90.00E
Biaban f. Iran 95 I4 26.00N 57.40E
Biak Indonesia 105 J3 1.10S 136.05E
Biak i. Indonesia 105 J3 0.55S 136.00E
Biała Podlaska Poland 54 H5 52.02N 23.06E
Białystok Poland 54 H5 53.09N 23.10E
Biarritz France 44 C3 43.29N 1.33W
Bibai Japan 106 D4 43.21N 141.53E
Biberach Germany 48 D3 48.06N 9.48E
Bicester England 10 D2 51.53N 1.09W
Bidar India 96 F4 17.54N 77.33E
Biddulph England 15 E2 53.08N 2.11W
Bidean nam Bian mtn. Scotland 16 D4 56.39N 5.02W
Bideford England 13 C3 51.01N 4.13W
Bideford B. England 13 C3 51.04N 4.20W
Biel Switz. 44 G5 47.09N 7.16E
Bielefeld Germany 48 D5 52.02N 8.32E
Biella Italy 50 C6 45.34N 8.03E
Bielsko-Biała Poland 54 F3 49.49N 19.02E
Bié Plateau f. Angola 82 E3 13.00S 16.00E
Bifoun Gabon 84 E1 0.20S 10.25E
Biga Turkey 56 H4 40.13N 27.14E
Bigbury B. England 13 D2 50.15N 3.56W
Biggar Scotland 17 F3 55.38N 3.31W
Biggleswade England 11 E3 52.06N 0.16W
Big Hole r. U.S.A. 64 D6 45.52N 111.30W
Bighorn r. U.S.A. 64 E6 46.05N 107.20W
Bighorn Mts. U.S.A. 64 E5 44.00N 107.30W
Big Spring town U.S.A. 64 F3 32.15N 101.30W
Big Trout Lake town Canada 63 J3 53.45N 90.00W
Bihać Bosnia. 56 B6 44.49N 15.53E
Bihar d. India 97 H5 24.15N 86.00E
Bijapur India 96 F4 16.52N 75.47E
Bijar Iran 95 G6 35.52N 47.39E
Bikaner India 96 E6 28.01N 73.22E
Bilaspur India 97 G5 22.03N 82.12E
Bila Tserkva Ukraine 55 C3 49.49N 30.10E
Bilbao Spain 46 D5 43.15N 2.56W
Bilecik Turkey 57 I4 40.10N 29.59E
Bilhorod-Dnistrovs'kyy Ukraine 55 L1 46.10N 30.19E
Billericay England 11 F2 51.38N 0.25E
Billingham England 15 F3 54.36N 1.18W
Billinghay England 15 G2 53.05N 0.18W
Billings U.S.A. 64 E6 45.47N 108.30W
Billingshurst England 11 E2 51.02N 0.28W
Bill of Portland c. England 10 C1 50.31N 2.27W
Biloxi U.S.A. 65 I3 30.30N 88.53W
Bilston Scotland 17 F3 55.53N 3.09W
Bilton England 15 G2 53.46N 0.13W
Bimini Is. The Bahamas 71 I6 25.44N 79.15W
Bindura Zimbabwe 86 C3 17.18S 31.20E
Bingham England 10 E3 52.57N 0.57W
Binghamton U.S.A. 65 K5 42.06N 75.55W
Bingley England 15 F2 53.51N 1.50W
Bintulu Malaysia 104 E4 3.12N 113.01E
Bioco i. Equat. Guinea 84 E2 3.25N 8.45E
Birao C.A.R. 94 B1 10.17N 22.47E
Birecik Turkey 57 N2 37.03N 37.59E
Birhan mtn. Ethiopia 85 H3 11.00N 37.50E
Bīrjand Iran 95 I5 32.54N 59.10E
Birkenhead England 14 D2 53.24N 3.01W
Birmingham England 10 D3 52.30N 1.55W
Birmingham U.S.A. 65 I3 33.30N 86.55W
Bîr Mogreïn Mauritania 84 C4 25.10N 11.35W
Birnin Konni Niger 84 E3 13.49N 5.19E
Birobidzhan Russian Fed. 103 O7 48.49N 132.54E
Birr Rep. of Ire. 20 D3 53.06N 7.56W
Birstall England 10 D3 52.42N 1.06W
Biržai Lithuania 55 I7 56.10N 24.48E
Biscay, B. of France 44 B4 45.30N 3.00W
Bishkek Kyrgyzstan 102 C6 42.53N 74.46E
Bisho R.S.A. 86 B1 32.50S 27.30E
Bishop Auckland England 15 F3 54.40N 1.40W
Bishop's Lydeard England 13 D3 51.04N 3.12W
Bishop's Stortford England 11 F2 51.53N 0.09E
Bishop's Waltham England 10 D1 50.57N 1.13W
Bisina, L. Uganda 87 A3 1.40N 34.00E
Biskra Algeria 84 E5 34.48N 5.40E
Bismarck U.S.A. 64 F6 46.50N 100.48W
Bismarck Sea Pacific Oc. 110 D5 4.00S 146.30E
Bissau Guinea Bissau 84 C3 11.52N 15.39W
Bistriţa Romania 55 I2 47.08N 24.30E
Bistriţa r. Romania 55 J2 46.30N 26.54E
Bitburg Germany 42 F1 49.58N 6.31E
Bitola Macedonia 56 E4 41.02N 21.21E
Bitterroot Range U.S.A. 64 D6 47.06N 115.00W
Biwa-ko l. Japan 106 C3 35.20N 136.10E
Biysk Russian Fed. 58 K3 52.35N 85.16E
Bizerte Tunisia 84 E5 37.17N 9.51E
Black r. U.S.A. 65 H4 35.30N 91.20W
Blackburn England 15 E2 53.44N 2.30W
Blackburn d. England 9 D3 53.44N 2.30W
Black Combe mtn. England 14 D3 54.15N 3.20W
Blackfield England 10 D1 50.49N 1.22W
Black Forest f. Germany 48 D3 48.00N 8.00E
Black Head England 13 B2 49.59N 5.05W
Black Hill England 15 F2 53.30N 1.53W
Black Isle f. Scotland 19 E2 57.35N 4.15W
Black Mts. Wales 12 D3 51.52N 3.09W
Blackpool England 14 D2 53.48N 3.03W
Blackpool d. England 9 D3 53.48N 3.03W
Black Sea Europe 57 L5 43.00N 35.00E
Blacksod B. Rep. of Ire. 20 A4 54.04N 10.00W
Black Volta r. Ghana 84 D2 8.14N 2.11W
Blackwater r. England 11 F2 51.43N 0.42E
Blackwater r. N. Ireland 16 C2 54.31N 6.35W
Blackwater r. Meath Rep. of Ire. 20 E3 53.39N 6.42W
Blackwater r. Waterford Rep. of Ire. 20 D1 51.58N 7.52W
Blackwood Wales 12 D3 51.38N 3.13W
Blaenau Ffestiniog Wales 12 D5 53.00N 3.57W
Blaenau Gwent d. Wales 9 D2 51.45N 3.10W
Blaenavon Wales 12 D3 51.46N 3.05W
Blagdon England 10 C2 51.20N 2.43W
Blagoevgrad Bulgaria 56 F5 42.02N 23.04E
Blagoveshchensk Russian Fed. 59 O3 50.19N 127.30E
Blair Atholl Scotland 19 F1 56.48N 3.50W
Blairgowrie Scotland 17 F4 56.36N 3.21W
Blanca, Bahía b. Argentina 75 C3 39.15S 61.00W
Blanche, L. Australia 110 C3 29.15S 139.40E
Blanc, Mont mtn. Europe 44 G4 45.50N 6.52E
Blanco, C. U.S.A. 64 B5 42.50N 124.29W
Blandford Forum England 10 C1 50.52N 2.10W
Blanquilla i. Venezuela 71 L3 11.53N 64.38W
Blantyre Malawi 86 C3 15.46S 35.00E
Blarney Rep. of Ire. 20 C1 51.56N 8.34W
Blaven mtn. Scotland 18 C2 57.13N 6.05W
Bletchley England 10 E2 51.59N 0.45W
Blida Algeria 84 E5 36.30N 2.50E
Bloemfontein R.S.A. 86 B2 29.07S 26.14E
Blois France 44 D5 47.36N 1.20E
Bloody Foreland c. Rep. of Ire. 20 C5 55.09N 8.17W
Bloomington U.S.A. 65 I5 40.29N 89.00W
Bluefield U.S.A. 65 J4 37.14N 81.17W
Blue Mts. U.S.A. 64 C6 45.00N 118.00W
Blue Nile r. Sudan 85 H3 15.45N 32.25E
Blue Stack Mts. Rep. of Ire. 20 C4 54.44N 8.09W
Blumenau Brazil 77 F2 26.55S 49.07W
Blyth Northum. England 15 F4 55.07N 1.29W
Blyth Notts. England 15 F2 53.21N 1.03W
Bo Sierra Leone 84 C2 7.58N 11.45W
Boa Vista Brazil 77 D5 2.51N 60.43W
Boa Vista i. Cape Verde 84 B3 16.00N 22.55W
Bobo-Dioulasso Burkina 84 D3 11.11N 4.18W
Bóbr r. Poland 54 D4 52.04N 15.04E
Bocholt Germany 48 C4 51.49N 6.37E
Boda C.A.R. 85 F2 4.19N 17.26E
Boddam Scotland 19 H2 57.28N 1.48W
Bodélé Depression f. Chad 85 F3 16.50N 17.10E
Boden Sweden 43 E4 65.50N 21.44E
Bodenham England 10 C3 52.09N 2.41W
Bodensee l. Europe 48 D2 47.40N 9.30E
Bodmin England 13 C2 50.28N 4.44W
Bodmin Moor England 13 C2 50.35N 4.35W
Bodø Norway 43 C4 67.18N 14.26E
Bodoquena, Serra da mts. Brazil 75 D4 21.00S 57.00W
Boggeragh Mts. Rep. of Ire. 20 C2 52.04N 8.50W
Bogie r. Scotland 19 G2 57.30N 2.47W
Bognor Regis England 10 E1 50.47N 0.40W
Bogor Indonesia 104 D2 6.34S 106.45E
Bogotá Colombia 74 B7 4.38N 74.05W
Bo Hai g. China 103 L5 41.17N 118.56E
Bohain-en-Vermandois France 42 C1 49.59N 3.28E
Bohemian Forest mts. Germany/Czech Rep. 54 C3 49.20N 13.10E
Bohol i. Phil. 105 G5 9.45N 124.10E
Bohu China 102 F6 41.48N 86.10E
Boise U.S.A. 64 C5 43.38N 116.12W
Bojnurd Iran 95 I6 37.28N 57.20E
Bokora Corridor Game Res. Uganda 87 A3 2.30N 34.05E
Bolhrad Ukraine 55 K1 45.42N 28.40E
Bolivia S. America 76 D3 17.00S 65.00W
Bollnäs Sweden 43 D3 61.20N 16.25E
Bolmen l. Sweden 43 C2 57.00N 13.45E
Bologna Italy 50 D6 44.30N 11.20E
Bolsena, L. Italy 50 D5 42.36N 11.55E
Bolshevik i. Russian Fed. 59 M5 78.30N 102.00E
Bolshoi Lyakhovskiy i. Russian Fed. 59 Q5 73.30N 142.00E
Bolsover England 15 F2 53.14N 1.18W
Bolt Head c. England 13 D2 50.13N 3.48W
Bolton England 15 E2 53.35N 2.26W
Bolu Turkey 57 J4 40.45N 31.38E
Bolus Head Rep. of Ire. 20 A1 51.48N 10.21W
Bolzano Italy 50 D7 46.30N 11.20E
Boma Dem. Rep. of Congo 84 F1 5.50S 13.03E
Bombay see Mumbai India 96
Bømlo i. Norway 43 A2 59.37N 5.13E
Bonaire i. Neth. Ant. 71 K3 12.15N 68.27W
Bonar Bridge Scotland 19 E2 57.53N 4.22W
Bonavista Canada 63 M2 48.38N 53.08W
Bon, C. Tunisia 52 F4 37.05N 11.03E
Bone, G. of Indonesia 104 G3 4.00S 120.50E
Bo'ness Scotland 17 F4 56.01N 3.36W
Bonete mtn. Argentina 76 D2 27.55S 68.41W
Bonifacio France 44 H2 41.23N 9.10E
Bonifacio, Str. of Med. Sea 50 C4 41.18N 9.10E
Bonn Germany 48 C4 50.44N 7.06E
Bonnyrigg Scotland 17 F3 55.52N 3.07W
Bontosunggu Indonesia 104 F2 5.42S 119.44E
Boothia, G. of Canada 63 J4 70.00N 90.00W
Boothia Pen. Canada 63 I5 70.30N 95.00W
Bootle England 14 D2 53.28N 3.01W
Borås Sweden 43 C2 57.44N 12.55E
Borazjan Iran 95 H4 29.14N 51.12E
Bordeaux France 44 C4 44.50N 0.34W
Borden I. Canada 62 G5 78.30N 111.00W
Borden Pen. Canada 63 J5 73.00N 83.00W
Bordj Messaouda Algeria 52 E3 30.10N 9.19E
Boreray i. Scotland 18 B2 57.43N 7.17W
Borgarnes Iceland 43 X2 64.33N 21.53W
Borger U.S.A. 64 F4 35.39N 101.24W
Borken Germany 42 F3 51.50N 6.52E
Borkum i. Germany 42 F5 53.35N 6.45E
Borlänge Sweden 43 C3 60.29N 15.25E
Borneo i. Asia 104 E4 1.00N 114.00E
Bornholm i. Denmark 43 C1 55.02N 15.00E
Borodyanka Ukraine 55 K4 50.38N 25.59E
Boroughbridge England 15 F3 54.06N 1.23W
Borujerd Iran 95 G5 33.54N 48.47E
Boryslav Ukraine 54 H3 49.18N 23.28E
Boryspil' Ukraine 55 L4 50.21N 30.59E
Borzna Ukraine 55 M4 51.15N 32.25E
Borzya Russian Fed. 103 L8 50.24N 116.35E
Bosanska Dubica Croatia 56 C6 45.11N 16.50E
Bose China 103 J2 23.58N 106.32E
Bosna r. Bosnia./Croatia 56 D6 45.04N 18.27E
Bosnia-Herzegovina Europe 56 C6 44.00N 18.00E
Bosporus str. Turkey 57 I4 41.07N 29.04E
Bosten Hu l. China 102 F6 42.00N 87.00E
Boston England 15 G1 52.59N 0.02W
Boston U.S.A. 65 L5 42.15N 71.05W
Boston Spa England 15 F2 53.54N 1.21W
Botevgrad Bulgaria 56 F5 42.55N 23.57E
Bothnia, G. of Europe 43 D3 63.30N 20.30E
Botoşani Romania 55 J2 47.44N 26.41E
Botswana Africa 86 B2 22.00S 24.00E
Bottesford England 15 G2 53.32N 0.37W
Bouaké Côte d'Ivoire 84 D2 7.42N 5.00W
Bouar C.A.R. 86 A5 5.58N 15.35E
Bouârfa Morocco 84 D5 32.30N 1.59W
Bougainville i. P.N.G. 110 E5 6.00S 155.00E
Bouillon Belgium 42 E1 49.48N 5.03E
Boulder U.S.A. 64 E5 40.02N 105.16W
Boulogne France 44 D7 50.43N 1.37E
Boulogne-Billancourt France 44 E6 48.50N 2.15E
Bounty Is. Pacific Oc. 108 M2 48.00S 178.30E
Bourg-en-Bresse France 44 F5 46.12N 5.13E
Bourges France 44 E5 47.05N 2.23E
Bourke Australia 110 D2 30.09S 145.59E
Bourne England 11 E3 52.46N 0.23W
Bournemouth England 10 D1 50.43N 1.53W
Bournemouth d. England 9 E2 50.43N 1.53W
Bou Saâda Algeria 52 D4 35.12N 4.11E
Bowes England 15 E3 54.31N 2.01W
Boxtel Neth. 42 E3 51.36N 5.20E
Boyarka Ukraine 55 L4 50.20N 30.26E
Boyle Rep. of Ire. 20 C3 53.58N 8.20W
Boyne r. Rep. of Ire. 20 E3 53.43N 6.18W
Bozeman U.S.A. 64 D6 45.40N 111.00W
Bozüyük Turkey 57 J3 39.55N 30.03E
Braan r. Scotland 17 F4 56.34N 3.36W
Brabant Wallon d. Belgium 42 D2 50.47N 4.30E
Brac i. Croatia 56 C5 43.20N 16.38E
Bracadale, Loch Scotland 18 C2 57.20N 6.32W
Bräcke Sweden 43 C3 62.44N 15.30E
Brackley England 10 D3 52.02N 1.09W
Bracknell England 10 E2 51.26N 0.46W
Bracknell Forest d. England 9 E2 51.26N 0.46W
Brad Romania 56 F7 46.06N 22.48E
Bradano r. Italy 50 G4 40.23N 16.52E
Bradford England 15 F2 53.47N 1.45W
Bradford-on-Avon England 10 C2 51.20N 2.15W
Braemar Scotland 19 F2 57.00N 3.27W
Braga Portugal 46 A4 41.32N 8.26W
Bragança Brazil 77 F4 1.03S 46.46W
Bragança Portugal 46 B4 41.47N 6.46W
Brahmapur India 97 G4 19.21N 84.51E
Brahmaputra r. Asia 97 H5 23.50N 89.45E
Brăila Romania 55 J1 45.18N 27.58E
Braintree England 11 F2 51.53N 0.32E
Brämön i. Sweden 43 D3 62.15N 17.40E
Brampton England 14 E3 54.56N 2.43W
Branco r. Brazil 77 D4 1.30S 62.00W
Brandenburg Germany 48 F5 52.25N 12.34E
Brandesburton England 15 G2 53.55N 0.18W
Brandon Canada 62 I2 49.50N 99.57W
Brandon England 11 F3 52.27N 0.37E
Brandon Head Rep. of Ire. 20 A2 52.17N 10.11W
Brandon Mtn. Rep. of Ire. 20 A2 52.14N 10.15W
Bransgore England 10 D1 50.47N 1.45W
Brasília Brazil 77 F3 15.54S 47.50W
Braşov Romania 56 G6 45.40N 25.35E
Bratislava Slovakia 54 E3 48.10N 17.10E
Bratsk Russian Fed. 59 M3 56.20N 101.15E
Bratsk Resr. Russian Fed. 90 M8 54.40N 103.00E
Braunschweig Germany 48 E5 52.15N 10.30E
Braunton England 13 C3 51.06N 4.09W
Brawley U.S.A. 64 C3 33.10N 115.30W
Bray Rep. of Ire. 20 E3 53.12N 6.07W
Bray Head Rep. of Ire. 20 A1 51.52N 10.28W

Brazil S. America 77 E3 10.00S 52.00W
Brazil Basin f. Atlantic Oc. 116 H5
Brazilian Highlands Brazil 77 F3 17.00S 48.00W
Brazos r. U.S.A. 64 G2 28.55N 95.20W
Brazzaville Congo 86 F1 4.14S 15.14E
Brechin Scotland 19 G1 56.44N 2.40W
Breckland f. England 11 F3 52.28N 0.40E
Břeclav Czech Rep. 54 E3 48.46N 16.53E
Brecon Wales 12 D3 51.57N 3.23W
Brecon Beacons mts. Wales 12 D3 51.53N 3.27W
Breda Neth. 42 D3 51.35N 4.46E
Bredhafjördhur est. Iceland 43 X2 65.15N 23.00W
Breidhdalsvik Iceland 43 Z2 64.48N 14.00W
Bremen Germany 48 D5 53.05N 8.48E
Bremerhaven Germany 48 D5 53.33N 8.35E
Brenner Pass Italy/Austria 50 D7 47.00N 11.30E
Brentwood England 11 F2 51.38N 0.18E
Brescia Italy 50 D6 45.33N 10.12E
Bressay i. Scotland 19 Y9 60.08N 1.05W
Bressuire France 44 C5 46.50N 0.28W
Brest Belarus 55 H5 52.08N 23.40E
Brest France 44 A6 48.23N 4.30W
Brest-Nantes Canal France 44 B5 47.52N 2.20W
Bretton Wales 12 E5 53.10N 3.00W
Bria C.A.R. 85 G2 6.32N 21.59E
Briançon France 44 G4 44.53N 6.39E
Bride r. Rep. of Ire. 20 D2 52.06N 7.50W
Bridgend Wales 13 D3 51.30N 3.35W
Bridgend d. Wales 9 D2 51.33N 3.35W
Bridgeport U.S.A. 65 L5 41.12N 73.12W
Bridgetown Barbados 71 M3 13.06N 59.37W
Bridgnorth England 10 C3 52.33N 2.25W
Bridgwater England 13 D3 51.08N 3.00W
Bridgwater B. England 13 D3 51.15N 3.10W
Bridlington England 15 G3 54.06N 0.11W
Bridlington B. England 15 G3 54.03N 0.10W
Bridport England 10 C1 50.43N 2.45W
Brig Switz. 44 G5 46.19N 8.00E
Brigg England 15 G2 53.33N 0.30W
Brighstone England 10 D1 50.38N 1.24W
Brightlingsea England 11 G2 51.49N 1.01E
Brighton England 11 E1 50.50N 0.09W
Brighton and Hove d. England 9 E2 50.50N 0.09W
Brindisi Italy 50 G4 40.38N 17.57E
Brisbane Australia 110 E3 27.30S 153.00E
Bristol England 10 C2 51.26N 2.35W
Bristol d. England 9 D2 51.26N 2.35W
Bristol B. U.S.A. 62 C3 58.00N 158.50W
Bristol Channel England/Wales 13 D3 51.17N 3.20W
British Columbia d. Canada 62 F3 55.00N 125.00W
British Isles Europe 34 C3 54.00N 5.00W
Briton Ferry town Wales 12 D3 51.37N 3.50W
Brittany f. France 44 B6 48.00N 3.00W
Brive-la-Gaillarde France 44 D4 45.09N 1.32E
Brixham England 13 D2 50.24N 3.31W
Brno Czech Rep. 54 E3 49.11N 16.39E
Broad B. Scotland 18 C3 58.15N 6.15W
Broad Law mtn. Scotland 17 F3 55.30N 3.21W
Broadstairs England 11 G2 51.22N 1.27E
Broadview Canada 64 F7 50.20N 102.30W
Broadway England 10 D3 52.02N 1.50W
Broadwey England 10 C1 50.39N 2.29W
Broadwindsor England 10 C1 50.49N 2.48W
Brockenhurst England 10 D1 50.49N 1.34W
Brock I. Canada 62 G5 78.00N 114.30W
Brodeur Pen. Canada 63 J5 73.00N 88.00W
Brodick Scotland 16 D3 55.34N 5.09W
Broken Hill town Australia 110 D2 31.57S 141.30E
Bromley England 11 F2 51.24N 0.02E
Bromsgrove England 10 C3 52.20N 2.03W
Bromyard England 10 C3 52.12N 2.30W
Brønderslev Denmark 43 B2 57.16N 9.58E
Brønnøysund Norway 43 C4 65.38N 12.15E
Brooke England 11 G3 52.32N 1.25E
Brooke's Point town Phil. 104 F5 8.50N 117.52E
Brooks Range mts. U.S.A. 62 C4 68.50N 152.00W
Broome Australia 110 B4 17.58S 122.15E
Broom, Loch Scotland 18 D2 57.55N 5.15W
Brora Scotland 19 F3 58.01N 3.52W
Brora r. Scotland 19 F3 57.59N 3.51W
Brosna r. Rep. of Ire. 20 D3 53.12N 7.59W
Brotton England 15 G3 54.34N 0.55W
Brough Cumbria England 15 E3 54.32N 2.19W
Brough E.Yorks. England 15 G2 53.42N 0.34W
Brough Head Scotland 19 F4 59.09N 3.19W
Brough Ness c. Scotland 19 G3 58.44N 2.57W
Broughshane N. Ireland 16 C2 54.54N 6.12W
Brownhills England 10 D3 52.38N 1.57W
Broxburn Scotland 17 F3 55.57N 3.29W
Bruay-en-Artois France 42 B2 50.29N 2.36E
Brue r. England 13 E3 51.13N 3.00W
Brugge Belgium 42 C3 51.13N 3.14E
Brunei Asia 104 E4 4.56N 114.58E
Brunflo Sweden 43 C3 63.04N 14.50E
Brunswick U.S.A. 65 J3 31.09N 81.21W
Brussels Belgium 42 D2 50.50N 4.23E
Bruton England 13 E3 51.06N 2.28W
Bryansk Russian Fed. 55 N5 53.15N 34.09E
Bryher i. England 13 A1 49.57N 6.21W
Brynamman Wales 12 D3 51.49N 3.52W
Brynmawr Wales 12 D3 51.48N 3.10W
Buca Turkey 56 H3 38.22N 27.10E
Bucaramanga Colombia 71 J2 7.08N 73.01W
Bucharest Romania 56 H6 44.25N 26.06E
Buckhaven Scotland 17 F4 56.11N 3.03W
Buckie Scotland 19 G2 57.40N 2.58W
Buckingham England 10 E2 52.00N 0.59W
Buckinghamshire d. England 9 E2 51.50N 0.48W
Buckley Wales 12 D5 53.11N 3.04W
Budapest Hungary 54 F2 47.30N 19.03E
Buddon Ness c. Scotland 17 G4 56.29N 2.42W
Bude England 13 C2 50.49N 4.33W
Bude B. England 13 C2 50.45N 4.40W
Buenaventura Colombia 74 B7 3.54N 77.02W
Buenos Aires Argentina 75 D3 34.40S 58.30W
Buffalo N.Y. U.S.A. 65 K5 42.52N 78.55W
Buffalo Wyo. U.S.A. 64 E5 44.21N 106.40W
Bug r. Poland 54 G5 52.29N 21.11E
Bug r. Ukraine 55 L2 46.55N 31.59E
Buhayrat al Asad l. Syria 57 N2 36.10N 38.20E
Builth Wells Wales 12 D4 52.09N 3.24W
Buir Nur l. Mongolia 103 L7 47.50N 117.40E
Bujumbura Burundi 86 B4 3.22S 29.21E
Bukavu Dem. Rep. of Congo 86 B4 2.30S 28.49E
Bukittinggi Indonesia 104 C3 0.18S 100.20E
Bukoba Tanzania 86 C4 1.20S 31.49E
Bula Indonesia 105 I3 3.07S 130.27E
Bulawayo Zimbabwe 86 B2 20.10S 28.43E
Bulgan Mongolia 103 I7 48.34N 103.12E
Bulgaria Europe 56 G5 42.30N 25.00E
Bulukumba Indonesia 104 G2 5.35S 120.13E
Bulun Russian Fed. 59 O5 70.50N 127.20E
Buna Kenya 87 B3 2.49N 39.27E
Bunbury Australia 110 A2 33.20S 115.34E
Bunclody Rep. of Ire. 20 E2 52.39N 6.39W
Buncrana Rep. of Ire. 20 D5 55.08N 7.28W
Bunda Tanzania 87 A2 2.00S 33.57E
Bundaberg Australia 110 E3 24.50S 152.21E
Bundoran Rep. of Ire. 20 C4 54.28N 8.20W
Bungay England 11 G3 52.27N 1.26E
Bungoma Kenya 87 A3 0.33N 34.33E
Buôn Mê Thuôt Vietnam 104 D6 12.41N 108.02E
Bura Kenya 87 B2 1.09S 39.55E
Buraydah Saudi Arabia 94 F4 26.18N 43.58E
Burbage England 10 D2 51.22N 1.40W
Burdur Turkey 57 J2 37.44N 30.17E
Bure r. England 11 G3 52.36N 1.44E
Burford England 10 D2 51.48N 1.38W
Burgas Bulgaria 56 H5 42.30N 27.29E
Burgess Hill town England 11 E1 50.57N 0.07W
Burghead Scotland 19 F2 57.42N 3.30W
Burgh le Marsh England 15 H2 53.10N 0.15E
Burgos Spain 46 D5 42.21N 3.41W
Burhanpur India 96 F5 21.18N 76.08E
Burkina Africa 84 D3 12.15N 1.30W
Burley U.S.A. 64 D5 42.32N 113.48W
Burlington U.S.A. 65 L5 44.25N 73.14W
Burnham England 10 E2 51.35N 0.39W
Burnham-on-Crouch England 11 F2 51.37N 0.50E
Burnham-on-Sea England 13 D3 51.15N 3.00W
Burnie Australia 110 D1 41.03S 145.55E
Burniston England 15 G3 54.19N 0.27W
Burnley England 15 E2 53.47N 2.15W
Burns Lake town Canada 62 F3 54.14N 125.45W
Burntisland Scotland 17 F4 56.03N 3.15W
Burntwood Green England 10 D3 52.42N 1.54W
Burray i. Scotland 19 G3 58.51N 2.54W
Burrow Head Scotland 16 E2 54.41N 4.24W
Burry Inlet Wales 12 C3 51.40N 4.11W
Burry Port Wales 12 C3 51.41N 4.17W
Bursa Turkey 57 I4 40.11N 29.04E
Bûr Safâga Egypt 94 D4 26.45N 33.55E
Burscough Bridge England 14 E2 53.37N 2.51W
Burton-in-Kendal England 14 E3 54.12N 2.43W
Burton Latimer England 10 E3 52.23N 0.41W
Burton upon Trent England 10 D3 52.48N 1.39W
Buru i. Indonesia 105 H3 3.30S 126.30E
Burundi Africa 86 B4 3.30S 30.00E
Burwash Landing Canada 62 E4 61.21N 139.01W
Burwell England 11 F3 52.17N 0.20E
Burwick Scotland 19 G3 58.44N 2.57W
Bury England 15 E2 53.36N 2.19W
Bury St. Edmunds England 11 F3 52.15N 0.42E
Bush r. N. Ireland 16 C3 55.13N 6.33W
Bushbush r. Somalia 87 C2 1.08S 41.52E
Bushehr Iran 95 H4 28.57N 50.52E
Bushmills N. Ireland 16 C3 55.12N 6.32W
Buta Dem. Rep. of Congo 86 B5 2.49N 24.50E
Bute i. Scotland 16 D3 55.51N 5.07W
Bute, Sd. of Scotland 16 D3 55.44N 5.10W
Buton i. Indonesia 105 G2 5.00S 122.50E
Butte U.S.A. 64 D6 46.00N 112.31W
Butterworth Malaysia 104 C5 5.24N 100.22E
Buttevant Rep. of Ire. 20 C2 52.13N 8.40W
Butt of Lewis c. Scotland 18 C3 58.31N 6.15W
Butuan Phil. 105 H5 8.56N 125.31E
Buur Gaabo Somalia 87 C2 1.10S 41.50E
Buvuma I. Uganda 87 A3 0.12N 33.17E
Buxton England 15 F2 53.16N 1.54W
Buzău Romania 56 H6 45.10N 26.49E
Byarezina r. Belarus 55 L5 52.30N 30.20E
Bydgoszcz Poland 54 E5 53.16N 18.00E
Byfield England 10 D3 52.10N 1.15W
Bylot I. Canada 63 K5 73.00N 78.30W
Byrranga Mts. Russian Fed. 59 M5 74.50N 101.00E
Bytom Poland 54 F4 50.22N 18.54E

C

Caacupé Paraguay 77 E2 25.23S 57.05W
Cabanatuan Phil. 104 G7 15.30N 120.58E
Caban Coch Resr. Wales 12 D4 52.17N 3.34W
Cabimas Venezuela 71 J3 10.26N 71.27W
Cabinda Angola 84 F1 5.34S 12.12E
Cabonga, Resr. Canada 65 K6 47.20N 76.35W
Cabot Str. Canada 63 M2 47.00N 59.00W
Cabrera, Sierra mts. Spain 46 B5 42.10N 6.30W
Cabriel r. Spain 46 E3 39.13N 1.07W
Cáceres Brazil 77 E3 16.05S 57.40W
Cáceres Spain 46 B3 39.29N 6.23W
Cachimbo, Serra do mts. Brazil 77 E4 8.30S 55.00W
Cachoeiro de Itapemirim Brazil 77 F2 20.51S 41.07W
Cadera, C. Venezuela 71 K3 10.40N 66.05W
Cadillac U.S.A. 65 I5 44.15N 85.23W
Cadiz Phil. 105 G6 10.57N 123.18E
Cádiz Spain 46 B2 36.32N 6.18W
Cádiz, G. of Spain 46 B2 37.00N 7.10W
Caen France 44 C6 49.11N 0.22W
Caerleon Wales 12 E3 51.36N 2.57W
Caernarfon Wales 12 C5 53.08N 4.17W
Caernarfon B. Wales 12 C5 53.05N 4.25W
Caerphilly Wales 12 D3 51.34N 3.13W
Caerphilly d. Wales 9 D2 51.34N 3.13W
Cagayan de Oro Phil. 105 G5 8.29N 124.40E
Cagliari Italy 50 C3 39.14N 9.07E
Cagliari, G. of Med. Sea 50 C3 39.07N 9.15E
Caha Mts. Rep. of Ire. 20 B1 51.44N 9.45W
Cahirciveen Rep. of Ire. 20 A1 51.51N 10.14W
Cahora Bassa, Lago de l. Mozambique 86 C3 15.33S 32.42E
Cahore Pt. Rep. of Ire. 20 E2 52.33N 6.11W
Cahors France 44 D4 44.28N 0.26E
Cahul Moldova 55 K1 45.58N 28.10E
Caiabis, Serra dos mts. Brazil 77 E3 12.00S 56.30W
Caiapó, Serra do mts. Brazil 77 E3 17.10S 52.00W
Caicos Is. Turks & Caicos Is. 71 J5 21.30N 72.00W
Cairn Gorm mtn. Scotland 19 F2 57.06N 3.39W
Cairngorm Mts. Scotland 19 F2 57.04N 3.30W
Cairnryan Scotland 16 D2 54.58N 5.02W
Cairns Australia 110 D4 16.51S 145.43E
Cairn Toul mtn. Scotland 19 F2 57.04N 3.44W
Cairo Egypt 94 D4 30.03N 31.15E
Caister-on-Sea England 11 G3 52.38N 1.43E
Caistor England 15 G2 53.29N 0.20W
Caithness f. Scotland 19 F3 58.25N 3.25W
Calabar Nigeria 84 E2 4.56N 8.22E
Calais France 44 D7 50.57N 1.50E
Calama Chile 76 D2 22.30S 68.55W
Calamian Group is. Phil. 104 G6 12.00N 120.05E
Calamocha Spain 46 E4 40.54N 1.18W
Calanscio Sand Sea f. Libya 53 H2 27.00N 23.00E
Calapan Phil. 104 G6 13.23N 121.10E
Călărași Romania 56 H6 44.11N 27.21E
Calatayud Spain 46 E4 41.21N 1.39W
Calbayog Phil. 105 G6 12.04N 124.58E
Calcanhar, Punta do c. Brazil 77 G4 5.06S 35.30W
Calcutta see Kolkata India 97
Caldas da Rainha Portugal 46 A3 39.24N 9.08W
Caldey Island Wales 12 C3 51.38N 4.43W
Caldicot Wales 12 E3 51.36N 2.45W
Calf of Man i. I.o.M. 14 C3 54.03N 4.49W
Calgary Canada 62 G3 51.05N 114.05W
Cali Colombia 74 B7 3.24N 76.30W
Caliente U.S.A. 64 D4 37.36N 114.31W
California d. U.S.A. 64 B4 37.00N 120.00W
California, G. of Mexico 70 B6 28.30N 112.30W
Callan Rep. of Ire. 20 D2 52.33N 7.23W
Callander Scotland 16 E4 56.15N 4.13W
Callanish Scotland 18 C3 58.12N 6.45W
Callao Peru 76 C3 12.05S 77.08W
Callington England 13 C2 50.30N 4.19W
Calne England 10 D2 51.26N 2.00W
Caltanissetta Italy 50 F2 37.30N 14.05E
Calvi France 44 H3 42.34N 8.44E
Cam r. England 11 F3 52.34N 0.21E
Camaçari Brazil 77 G3 12.44S 38.16W
Camagüey Cuba 71 I5 21.25N 77.55W
Camagüey, Archipelago de Cuba 71 I5 22.30N 78.00W
Cambay, G. of India 96 E5 20.30N 72.00E
Camberley England 10 E2 51.21N 0.45W
Cambodia Asia 104 C6 12.00N 105.00E
Camborne England 13 B2 50.12N 5.19W
Cambrai France 42 C2 50.10N 3.14E
Cambrian Mts. Wales 12 D4 52.33N 3.33W
Cambridge England 11 F3 52.13N 0.08E
Cambridge Bay town Canada 62 H4 69.09N 105.00W
Cambridgeshire d. England 9 E3 52.15N 0.05W
Camelford England 13 C2 50.37N 4.41W
Cameroon Africa 84 F2 6.00N 12.30E
Cameroun, Mt. Cameroon 84 E2 4.20N 9.05E
Cametá Brazil 77 F4 2.12S 49.30W
Campbell I. Pacific Oc. 108 L1 52.30S 169.02E
Campbell River town Canada 62 F3 50.00N 125.18W
Campbellton Canada 65 M6 48.00N 66.40W
Campbeltown Scotland 16 D3 55.25N 5.36W
Campeche Mexico 70 F4 19.50N 90.30W
Campeche d. Mexico 70 F4 19.00N 90.00W
Campeche B. Mexico 70 F4 19.30N 94.00W
Campina Grande Brazil 77 G4 7.15S 35.53W
Campinas Brazil 77 F2 22.54S 47.06W
Campobasso Italy 50 F4 41.34N 14.39E
Campo Grande Brazil 77 E2 20.24S 54.35W
Campos Brazil 77 F2 21.46S 41.21W
Cam Ranh Vietnam 104 D6 11.54N 109.14E
Camrose Wales 12 B3 51.50N 5.01W
Canada N. America 62 H3 60.00N 105.00W
Canadian r. U.S.A. 64 G4 35.20N 95.40W
Canadian Shield f. N. America 60 K7 50.00N 80.00W
Çanakkale Turkey 56 H4 40.09N 26.26E
Canal du Midi France 44 D3 43.18N 2.00E
Canary Is. Atlantic Oc. 46 X2 29.00N 15.00W
Canaveral, C. U.S.A. 65 J2 28.28N 80.28W
Canberra Australia 110 D2 35.18S 149.08E
Cancún Mexico 70 G5 21.26N 86.51W
Caniapiscau r. Canada 63 L3 57.40N 69.30W
Caniapiscau, Résr. Canada 63 K3 55.05N 72.40W
Canindé r. Brazil 77 F4 6.14S 42.51W
Canisp mtn. Scotland 18 D3 58.07N 5.03W
Çankaya Turkey 57 K3 39.52N 32.52E
Çankırı Turkey 57 K4 40.35N 33.37E
Canna i. Scotland 18 C2 57.03N 6.30W
Cannes France 44 G3 43.33N 7.00E
Cannock England 10 C3 52.42N 2.02W
Canõas Brazil 77 E2 29.55S 51.10W
Canon City U.S.A. 64 E4 38.27N 105.14W
Cantabrian Mts. Spain 46 B5 43.00N 6.00W
Canterbury England 11 G2 51.17N 1.05E
Cân Tho Vietnam 104 D6 10.03N 105.46E
Canvey Island town England 11 F2 51.32N 0.35E
Cao Bang Vietnam 104 D8 22.40N 106.16E
Capbreton France 44 C3 43.38N 1.15W
Cape Breton I. Canada 63 L2 46.00N 61.00W
Capel St. Mary England 11 G2 51.59N 1.02E
Cape Town R.S.A. 86 A1 33.56S 18.28E
Cape Verde Atlantic Oc. 84 B3 16.00N 24.00W
Cape York Pen. Australia 110 D4 12.40S 142.20E
Cap Haïtien town Haiti 71 J4 19.47N 72.17W
Capim r. Brazil 77 F4 1.40S 47.47W
Capitol Hill N. Mariana Is. 105 L7 15.12N 145.45E
Capraia i. Italy 50 C5 43.03N 9.50E
Caprera i. Italy 50 C4 41.48N 9.27E
Capri i. Italy 50 F4 40.33N 14.13E
Capricorn Channel str. Australia 110 E3 23.00S 152.00E
Caprivi Strip f. Namibia 86 B3 17.50S 23.10E
Caquetá r. Colombia 76 C4 1.20S 70.50W
Carabay, Cordillera de mts. Peru 76 C3 13.50S 71.00W
Caracal Romania 56 G6 44.08N 24.18E
Caracas Venezuela 71 K3 10.35N 66.56W
Carajás, Serra dos mts. Brazil 77 E4 5.00S 51.00W
Caratasca Lagoon Honduras 71 H4 15.10N 84.00W
Caratinga Brazil 77 F3 19.50S 42.06W
Caravaca de la Cruz Spain 46 E3 38.06N 1.51W
Carbonara, C. Italy 50 C3 39.06N 9.32E
Carcassonne France 44 E3 43.13N 2.21E
Cardiff Wales 13 D3 51.28N 3.11W
Cardiff d. Wales 9 D2 51.30N 3.12W
Cardigan Wales 12 C4 52.06N 4.41W
Cardigan B. Wales 12 C4 52.30N 4.30W
Carei Romania 54 H2 47.42N 22.28E
Carey, L. Australia 110 B3 29.05S 122.15E
Cariacica Brazil 77 F2 20.15S 40.23W
Caribbean Sea C. America 71 I4 15.00N 75.00W
Caribou Mts. Canada 62 G3 58.30N 115.00W
Cark Mtn. Rep. of Ire. 16 B2 54.53N 7.53W
Carletonville R.S.A. 86 B2 26.21S 27.23E
Carlingford Lough Rep. of Ire./N. Ireland 16 C2 54.03N 6.09W
Carlisle England 14 E3 54.54N 2.55W
Carlow Rep. of Ire. 20 E2 52.50N 6.54W
Carlow d. Rep. of Ire. 20 E2 52.43N 6.50W
Carluke Scotland 17 E3 55.44N 3.51W
Carmacks Canada 62 E4 62.04N 136.21W
Carmarthen Wales 12 C3 51.52N 4.20W
Carmarthen B. Wales 12 C3 51.40N 4.30W
Carmarthenshire d. Wales 9 C2 52.00N 4.17W
Carmel Head Wales 12 C5 53.24N 4.35W
Carndonagh Rep. of Ire. 16 B3 55.15N 7.15W
Carnedd Llywelyn mtn. Wales 12 D5 53.10N 3.58W
Carnedd y Filiast mtn. Wales 12 D4 52.56N 3.40W
Carnegie, L. Australia 110 B3 26.15S 123.00E
Carn Eighe mtn. Scotland 18 D2 57.17N 5.07W
Carnforth England 14 E3 54.08N 2.47W
Carnic Alps mts. Italy/Austria 50 E7 46.40N 12.48E
Car Nicobar i. India 104 A5 9.06N 92.57E
Carnlough N. Ireland 16 D2 54.58N 6.00W
Carn nan Gabhar mtn. Scotland 19 F1 56.49N 3.44W
Carnot C.A.R. 84 F2 4.59N 15.56E
Carnot, C. Australia 110 C2 34.57S 135.38E
Carnoustie Scotland 17 G4 56.30N 2.44W
Carnsore Pt. Rep. of Ire. 20 E2 52.10N 6.21W
Caroline I. see Millennium I. Kiribati 109
Caroline Is. Pacific Oc. 108 J7 5.00N 150.00E
Carpathian Mts. Europe 34 F2 48.45N 23.45E
Carpentaria, G. of Australia 110 C4 14.00S 140.00E
Carpentras France 44 F4 44.03N 5.03E
Carra, Lough Rep. of Ire. 20 B3 53.40N 9.15W
Carrara Italy 50 D6 44.04N 10.06E
Carrauntoohil mtn. Rep. of Ire. 20 B2 52.00N 9.45W
Carrickfergus N. Ireland 16 D2 54.43N 5.49W
Carrickmacross Rep. of Ire. 20 E3 53.59N 6.44W
Carrick-on-Shannon Rep. of Ire. 20 C3 53.57N 8.06W
Carrick-on-Suir Rep. of Ire. 20 D2 52.21N 7.26W
Carron r. Falkirk Scotland 17 F4 56.01N 3.44W
Carron r. High. Scotland 19 E2 57.53N 4.22W
Carrowmore Lake Rep. of Ire. 20 B4 54.11N 9.48W
Carson City U.S.A. 64 C4 39.10N 119.46W
Carsphairn Scotland 16 E3 55.13N 4.15W
Cartagena Colombia 71 I3 10.24N 75.33W
Cartagena Spain 46 E2 37.36N 0.59W
Carter Bar pass Scotland/England 17 G3 55.21N 2.27W
Carterton England 10 D2 51.46N 1.35W
Cartmel England 14 E3 54.12N 2.57W
Caruarú Brazil 77 G4 8.15S 35.55W
Carvin France 42 B2 50.30N 2.58E
Casablanca Morocco 84 D5 33.39N 7.35W
Cascade Range mts. U.S.A. 64 B5 44.00N 121.30W
Cascavel Brazil 77 E2 24.59S 53.29W
Caserta Italy 50 F4 41.06N 14.21E
Caseyr, C. Somalia 85 J3 12.00N 51.30E
Cashel Rep. of Ire. 20 D2 52.31N 7.54W
Casper U.S.A. 64 E5 42.50N 106.20W
Caspian Depression f. Russian Fed./Kazakhstan 58 G2 47.00N 48.00E
Caspian Sea Asia 90 H7 42.00N 51.00E
Cassiar Mts. Canada 62 F3 60.00N 131.00W
Cassley r. Scotland 18 E3 57.58N 4.35W
Castanhal Brazil 77 F4 1.16S 47.51W
Castelló de la Plana Spain 46 E3 39.59N 0.03W
Castlebar Rep. of Ire. 20 B3 53.52N 9.19W
Castleblayney Rep. of Ire. 20 E4 54.08N 6.46W
Castle Cary England 13 E3 51.06N 2.31W
Castlecomer Rep. of Ire. 20 D2 52.48N 7.12W
Castleconnell Rep. of Ire. 20 C2 52.43N 8.30W
Castlederg N. Ireland 16 B2 54.43N 7.37W
Castle Donnington England 10 D3 52.51N 1.19W
Castle Douglas Scotland 17 F2 54.56N 3.56W
Castleford England 15 F2 53.43N 1.21W
Castleisland town Rep. of Ire. 20 B2 52.14N 9.29W
Castletown I.o.M. 14 C3 54.04N 4.38W
Castres France 44 E3 43.36N 2.14E
Castries St. Lucia 71 L3 14.01N 60.59W
Catamarca Argentina 76 D2 28.28S 65.46W
Catanduanes i. Phil. 105 G6 13.45N 124.20E
Catania Italy 50 F2 37.31N 15.05E
Catanzaro Italy 50 G3 38.55N 16.35E
Catarman Phil. 105 G6 12.28N 124.50E
Caterham England 11 E2 51.17N 0.04W
Cat I. The Bahamas 71 I5 24.30N 75.30W
Catoche, C. Mexico 70 G5 21.38N 87.08W
Catterick England 15 F3 54.23N 1.38W
Cauca r. Colombia 71 J2 8.57N 74.30W
Caucaia Brazil 77 G4 3.45S 38.45W
Caucasus mts. Europe 58 G2 43.00N 44.00E
Caudry France 42 C2 50.07N 3.25E
Cavan Rep. of Ire. 20 D3 53.59N 7.22W
Cavan d. Rep. of Ire. 20 D3 54.00N 7.15W
Cawston England 11 G3 52.46N 1.10E
Caxias Brazil 77 F4 4.53S 43.20W
Caxias do Sul Brazil 77 E2 29.14S 51.10W
Cayenne French Guiana 74 D7 4.55N 52.18W
Cayman Brac i. Cayman Is. 71 I4 19.44N 79.48W
Cayman Is. C. America 71 H4 19.00N 81.00W
Cayos Miskito is. Nicaragua 71 H3 14.30N 82.40W
Ceará d. Brazil 77 G4 4.50S 39.00W
Cebu Phil. 105 G6 10.17N 123.56E
Cebu i. Phil. 105 G6 10.15N 123.45E
Cedar r. U.S.A. 65 H5 41.15N 91.20W
Cedar City U.S.A. 64 D4 37.40N 113.04W
Cedar Rapids town U.S.A. 65 H5 41.59N 91.31W
Cedros i. Mexico 64 C2 28.15N 115.15W
Cefalù Italy 50 F3 38.01N 14.03E
Cegléd Hungary 54 F2 47.10N 19.48E
Celaya Mexico 70 D5 20.32N 100.48W
Celebes Sea Indonesia 105 G4 3.00N 122.00E
Celje Slovenia 54 D2 46.15N 15.16E
Celle Germany 48 E5 52.37N 10.05E
Cenderawasih G. Indonesia 105 J3 2.30S 135.20E
Central d. Kenya 87 B2 1.00S 37.00E
Central African Republic Africa 85 F2 6.30N 20.00E
Central, Cordillera mts. Bolivia 76 D3 20.00S 65.00W
Central, Cordillera mts. Colombia 74 B7 5.00N 75.20W
Central, Cordillera mts. Peru 76 C4 7.00S 79.00W
Central Range mts. P.N.G. 105 K3 5.00S 142.00E
Central Russian Uplands f. Russian Fed. 55 O5 53.00N 37.00E
Central Siberian Plateau f. Russian Fed. 59 M4 66.00N 108.00E
Ceredigion d. Wales 9 C3 52.15N 4.00W
Cernavodă Romania 57 I6 44.20N 28.02E

Cerralvo i. Mexico 70 C5 24.17N 109.52W
Cerro de Pasco Peru 76 C3 10.43S 76.15W
Cervo Spain 46 B5 43.40N 7.25W
České Budějovice Czech Rep. 54 D3 49.00N 14.30E
Ceuta Spain 46 C1 35.53N 5.19W
Cévennes mts. France 44 E4 44.25N 3.30E
Ceyhan r. Turkey 57 L2 36.54N 34.58E
Chad Africa 85 F3 13.00N 19.00E
Chad, L. Africa 84 F3 13.30N 14.00E
Chadan Russian Fed. 102 G8 51.20N 91.39E
Chagai Hills Pakistan 95 J4 29.10N 63.35E
Chaghcharan Afghan. 95 K5 34.32N 65.15E
Chagos Archipelago is. Indian Oc. 90 J2 7.00S 72.00E
Chah Bahar Iran 95 J4 25.17N 60.41E
Chake Chake Tanzania 87 B1 5.13S 39.46E
Chalbi Desert Kenya 87 B3 3.00N 37.20E
Chale England 10 D1 50.36N 1.19W
Chalkida Greece 56 F3 38.27N 23.36E
Challenger Deep Pacific Oc. 91 Q4 11.19N 142.15E
Châlons-en-Champagne France 44 F6 48.58N 4.22E
Chalon-sur-Saône France 44 F5 46.47N 4.51E
Chalus Iran 95 H6 36.40N 51.25E
Chaman Pakistan 96 D7 30.55N 66.27E
Chambéry France 44 F4 45.34N 5.55E
Ch'amo Hayk' l. Ethiopia 87 B4 5.49N 37.35E
Chamonix France 44 G4 45.55N 6.52E
Champaqui mtn. Argentina 76 D1 31.59S 64.59W
Champlain, L. U.S.A. 65 L5 44.45N 73.20W
Chañaral Chile 76 C2 26.21S 70.37W
Chandalar r. U.S.A. 62 D4 66.40N 146.00W
Chandeleur Is. U.S.A. 65 I2 29.50N 88.50W
Chandigarh India 96 F7 30.44N 76.54E
Chandrapur India 97 F4 19.58N 79.21E
Changchun China 103 N6 43.50N 125.20E
Changde China 103 K3 29.03N 111.35E
Changgi Gap b. S. Korea 106 A3 36.00N 129.30E
Chang Jiang r. China 103 M4 31.40N 121.15E
Changsha China 103 K3 28.10N 113.00E
Changzhi China 103 K5 36.09N 113.12E
Changzhou China 103 L4 31.45N 119.57E
Chania Greece 56 G1 35.30N 24.02E
Channel Is. U.K. 13 Z9 49.28N 2.13W
Channel-Port aux Basques town Canada 63 M2 47.35N 59.10W
Chanthaburi Thailand 104 C6 12.38N 102.12E
Chantilly France 42 B1 49.12N 2.28E
Chao Phraya r. Thailand 104 C6 13.35N 100.37E
Chapada de Maracás f. Brazil 77 F3 13.20S 40.00W
Chapada Diamantina f. Brazil 77 F3 13.30S 42.30W
Chapala, Lago de l. Mexico 70 D5 20.00N 103.00W
Chapecó Brazil 77 E2 27.14S 52.41W
Chapel-en-le-Frith England 15 F2 53.19N 1.54W
Chapeltown England 15 F2 53.28N 1.27W
Chapleau Canada 63 J2 47.50N 83.24W
Chaplynka Ukraine 55 M2 46.23N 33.32E
Chard England 13 E2 50.52N 2.59W
Chari r. Chad 82 E6 13.00N 14.30E
Charīkar Afghan. 95 K6 35.02N 69.13E
Charlbury England 10 D2 51.53N 1.29W
Charleroi Belgium 42 D2 50.25N 4.27E
Charleston S.C. U.S.A. 65 K3 32.48N 79.58W
Charleston W.Va. U.S.A. 65 J4 38.23N 81.20W
Charlestown Rep. of Ire. 20 C3 53.57N 8.50W
Charleville-Mézières France 44 F6 49.46N 4.43E
Charlotte U.S.A. 65 J4 35.05N 80.50W
Charlottesville U.S.A. 65 K4 38.02N 78.29W
Charlottetown Canada 63 L2 46.14N 63.09W
Chartres France 44 D6 48.27N 1.30E
Châteaubriant France 44 C5 47.43N 1.22W
Châteaudun France 44 D6 48.04N 1.20E
Châteauroux France 44 D5 46.49N 1.41E
Château-Thierry France 44 E6 49.03N 3.24E
Châtellerault France 44 D5 46.49N 0.33E
Chatham England 11 F2 51.23N 0.32E
Chatham Is. Pacific Oc. 111 H1 44.00S 176.35W
Chattahoochee r. U.S.A. 65 J2 30.52N 84.57W
Chattanooga U.S.A. 65 I4 35.01N 85.18W
Chatteris England 11 F3 52.27N 0.03E
Chaumont France 44 F6 48.07N 5.08E
Chauny France 42 C1 49.37N 3.13E
Cheadle England 10 D3 52.59N 1.59W
Cheb Czech Rep. 54 C4 50.04N 12.20E
Cheboksary Russian Fed. 58 G3 56.08N 47.12E
Cheboygan U.S.A. 65 J6 45.40N 84.28W
Cheddar England 13 E3 51.16N 2.47W
Cheju do i. S. Korea 103 N4 33.20N 126.30E
Chekhov Russian Fed. 55 O6 55.21N 37.31E
Cheleken Turkmenistan 95 H6 39.26N 53.11E
Chełm Poland 55 H4 51.10N 23.28E
Chelmer r. England 11 F2 51.43N 0.42E
Chelmsford England 11 F2 51.44N 0.28E
Cheltenham England 10 C2 51.53N 2.07W
Chelyabinsk Russian Fed. 58 I3 55.10N 61.25E
Chelyuskin, C. Russian Fed. 59 M5 77.20N 106.00E
Chemnitz Germany 48 F4 50.50N 12.55E
Ch'ench'a Ethiopia 87 B4 6.18N 37.37E
Chengde China 103 L6 40.48N 118.06E
Chengdu China 103 I4 30.37N 104.06E
Chennai India 97 G3 13.05N 80.18E
Chenzhou China 103 K3 25.45N 113.00E
Chepstow Wales 12 E3 51.38N 2.40W
Cher r. France 44 D5 47.21N 0.29E
Cherbourg France 44 C6 49.38N 1.37W
Cherepovets Russian Fed. 58 F3 59.05N 37.55E
Cherkasy Ukraine 55 M3 49.27N 32.04E
Chernihiv Ukraine 55 L4 51.30N 31.18E
Chernivtsi Ukraine 55 I3 48.19N 25.52E
Chernyakhovsk Russian Fed. 54 G6 54.36N 21.48E
Cherskogo Range mts. Russian Fed. 59 Q4 65.50N 143.00E
Chervonohrad Ukraine 55 I4 50.25N 24.10E
Cherwell r. England 10 D2 51.45N 1.15W
Chesapeake B. U.S.A. 65 K4 38.00N 76.00W
Chesham England 11 E2 51.43N 0.38W
Cheshire d. England 9 D3 53.14N 2.30W
Chëshskaya Bay Russian Fed. 35 H4 67.20N 46.30E
Cheshunt England 11 E2 51.43N 0.02W
Chesil Beach f. England 10 C1 50.37N 2.33W
Chester England 14 E2 53.12N 2.53W
Chesterfield England 15 F2 53.14N 1.26W
Chester-le-Street England 15 F3 54.53N 1.34W
Cheviot Hills U.K. 17 G3 55.22N 2.24W
Che'w Bahir f. Ethiopia 87 B3 4.40N 36.50E
Che'w Bahir Wildlife Res. Ethiopia 87 B4 5.00N 36.50E
Chew Magna England 10 C2 51.21N 2.37W
Chew Valley L. England 10 C2 51.20N 2.37W
Cheyenne U.S.A. 64 F5 41.08N 104.50W
Chiang Mai Thailand 104 B7 18.48N 98.59E
Chiang Rai Thailand 104 B7 19.56N 99.51E
Chiapas d. Mexico 70 F4 16.30N 93.00W
Chiba Japan 106 D3 35.38N 140.07E
Chibougamau Canada 63 K2 49.56N 74.24W
Chicago U.S.A. 65 I5 41.50N 87.45W
Chichester England 10 E1 50.50N 0.47W
Chiclayo Peru 76 C4 6.47S 79.47W
Chico U.S.A. 64 B4 39.46N 121.50W
Chicoutimi Canada 63 K2 48.26N 71.06W
Chidley, C. Canada 63 L4 60.30N 65.00W
Chiemsee l. Germany 48 F2 47.55N 12.30E
Chieti Italy 50 F5 42.22N 14.12E
Chihli, G. of China 103 L5 38.30N 119.30E
Chihuahua Mexico 70 C6 28.40N 106.06W
Chihuahua d. Mexico 70 C6 28.40N 105.00W
Chile S. America 75 B3 33.00S 71.00W
Chilham England 11 F2 51.15N 0.57E
Chillán Chile 75 B3 36.37S 72.10W
Chiloé, Isla de Chile 75 B2 43.00S 73.00W
Chilpancingo Mexico 70 E4 17.33N 99.30W
Chiltern Hills England 10 E2 51.40N 0.53W
Chimborazo mtn. Ecuador 76 C4 1.10S 78.50W
Chimbote Peru 74 B6 8.58S 78.34W
Chimoio Mozambique 86 C3 19.04S 33.29E
China Asia 103 H4 33.00N 103.00E
Chindwin r. Myanmar 97 J5 21.30N 95.12E
Chingola Zambia 86 B3 12.31S 27.53E
Chinhoyi Zimbabwe 86 C3 17.22S 30.10E
Chios Greece 56 H3 38.22N 26.08E
Chios i. Greece 56 G3 38.23N 26.04E
Chipata Zambia 86 C3 13.37S 32.40E
Chippenham England 10 C2 51.27N 2.07W
Chipping Campden England 10 D3 52.03N 1.46W
Chipping Norton England 10 D2 51.56N 1.32W
Chipping Ongar England 11 F2 51.43N 0.15E
Chipping Sodbury England 10 C2 51.31N 2.23W
Chiriquí, G. of Panama 71 H2 8.00N 82.20W
Chirk Wales 12 D4 52.56N 3.03W
Chirnside Scotland 17 G3 55.48N 2.12W
Chirripó mtn. Costa Rica 71 H2 9.31N 83.30W
Chisasibi see Fort George Canada 63
Chişinau Moldova 55 K2 47.00N 28.50E
Chita Russian Fed. 59 N3 52.03N 113.35E
Chitradurga India 96 F3 14.16N 76.23E
Chitral Pakistan 96 E8 35.52N 71.58E
Chittagong Bangla. 97 I5 22.20N 91.48E
Chittoor India 97 F3 13.13N 79.06E
Choiseul i. Solomon Is. 111 E5 7.00S 157.00E
Chojnice Poland 54 E5 53.42N 17.32E
Cholet France 44 C5 47.04N 0.53W
Chon Buri Thailand 104 C6 13.24N 100.59E
Chongjin N. Korea 103 N6 41.55N 129.50E
Chongqing China 103 J3 29.31N 106.35E
Chonju S. Korea 103 N5 35.50N 127.05E
Chorley England 14 E2 53.39N 2.39W
Chornobyl' Ukraine 55 L4 51.17N 30.15E
Chortkiv Ukraine 55 I3 49.01N 25.42E
Choshi Japan 106 D3 34.53N 140.51E
Chott ech Chergui f. Algeria 52 D3 34.00N 0.30E
Chott ech Hodna f. Algeria 52 D4 35.40N 5.00E
Chott el Jerid f. Tunisia 84 E5 33.30N 8.30E
Chott Melrhir f. Algeria 84 E5 34.15N 7.00E
Choybalsan Mongolia 103 K7 48.02N 114.32E
Christchurch England 10 D1 50.44N 1.47W
Christchurch New Zealand 111 G1 43.32S 172.37E
Christmas I. Indian Oc. 104 D1 10.30S 105.40E
Chuckchi Pen. Russian Fed. 59 U4 66.00N 174.30W
Chudovo Russian Fed. 54 G2 59.10N 31.41E
Chugoku-sanchi mts. Japan 106 B3 35.30N 133.00E
Chuhuyiv Ukraine 55 O3 49.51N 36.44E
Chukchi Sea Arctic Oc. 59 U4 69.30N 172.00W
Chulmleigh England 13 D2 50.55N 3.52W
Chumba Ethiopia 87 B3 4.30N 38.15E
Chumphon Thailand 104 B6 10.35N 99.14E
Chunchon S. Korea 103 N5 37.53N 127.45E
Chur Switz. 44 H5 46.52N 9.32E
Churchill Canada 63 I3 58.45N 94.00W
Churchill r. Man. Canada 63 I3 58.20N 94.15W
Churchill r. Nfld. Canada 63 L3 53.20N 60.00W
Churchill, C. Canada 63 I3 58.50N 93.00W
Church Stretton England 10 C3 52.32N 2.49W
Chuuk i. Fed. States of Micronesia 108 K7 7.23N 151.46E
Chuxiong China 103 I3 25.03N 101.33E
Chyulu Range mts. Kenya 87 B2 2.40S 37.53E
Ciego de Avila Cuba 71 I5 21.51N 78.47W
Cienfuegos Cuba 71 H5 22.10N 80.27W
Cigüela r. Spain 46 D3 39.08N 3.44W
Cihanbeyli Turkey 57 K3 38.40N 32.55E
Cijara L. Spain 46 C3 39.20N 4.50W
Cilacap Indonesia 104 D2 7.44S 109.00E
Cinca r. Spain 46 F4 41.22N 0.20E
Cincinnati U.S.A. 65 J4 39.10N 84.30W
Cinderford England 10 C2 51.49N 2.30W
Ciney Belgium 42 E2 50.17N 5.06E
Cinto, Monte mtn. France 44 H3 42.23N 8.57E
Cirebon Indonesia 104 D2 6.46S 108.33E
Cirencester England 10 D2 51.43N 1.59W
City of Edinburgh d. Scotland 8 D4 55.57N 3.13W
Ciudad Bolívar Venezuela 71 L2 8.06N 63.36W
Ciudad Camargo Mexico 70 C6 27.41N 105.10W
Ciudad Delicias Mexico 70 C6 28.10N 105.30W
Ciudad de Valles Mexico 70 E5 22.00N 99.00W
Ciudad Guayana Venezuela 71 L2 8.22N 62.40W
Ciudad Ixtepec Mexico 70 E4 16.32N 95.10W
Ciudad Juárez Mexico 70 C7 31.42N 106.29W
Ciudad Madero Mexico 70 E5 22.19N 97.50W
Ciudad Obregón Mexico 70 C6 27.28N 109.55W
Ciudad Real Spain 46 D3 38.59N 3.55W
Ciudad-Rodrigo Spain 46 B4 40.36N 6.33W
Ciudad Victoria Mexico 70 E5 23.43N 99.10W
Ciutadella de Menorca Spain 46 G4 40.00N 3.50E
Civitavecchia Italy 50 D5 42.06N 11.48E
Clackmannanshire d. Scotland 8 D5 56.10N 3.45W
Clacton-on-Sea England 11 G2 51.47N 1.10E
Claerwen Resr. Wales 12 D4 52.17N 3.40W
Claonaig Scotland 16 D3 55.43N 5.24W
Clara Rep. of Ire. 20 D3 53.21N 7.37W
Clare r. Rep. of Ire. 20 B3 53.20N 9.03W
Clare d. Rep. of Ire. 20 C2 52.52N 8.55W
Clare I. Rep. of Ire. 20 A3 53.50N 10.00W
Claremorris Rep. of Ire. 20 C3 53.44N 9.00W
Clarksville U.S.A. 65 I4 36.31N 87.21W
Claro r. Brazil 77 E3 19.05S 50.40W
Clay Cross England 15 F2 53.11N 1.26W
Claydon England 11 G3 52.06N 1.07E
Clay Head I.o.M. 14 C3 54.12N 4.23W
Clayton U.S.A. 64 F4 36.27N 103.12W
Clear, C. Rep. of Ire. 20 B1 51.25N 9.31W
Clear I. Rep. of Ire. 20 B1 51.26N 9.30W
Cleator Moor town England 14 D3 54.30N 3.32W
Cleethorpes England 15 G2 53.33N 0.02W
Cleobury Mortimer England 10 C3 52.23N 2.28W
Clermont France 42 B1 49.23N 2.24E
Clermont-Ferrand France 44 E4 45.47N 3.05E
Clevedon England 10 C2 51.26N 2.52W
Cleveland U.S.A. 65 J5 41.30N 81.41W
Cleveland Hills England 15 F3 54.25N 1.10W
Cleveleys England 14 D2 53.52N 3.01W
Clew B. Rep. of Ire. 20 B3 53.50N 9.47W
Cliffe England 11 F2 51.28N 0.30E
Clipperton I. Pacific Oc. 109 U8 10.17N 109.13W
Clitheroe England 15 E2 53.52N 2.23W
Clogher Head Rep. of Ire. 20 E3 53.48N 6.13W
Clonakilty Rep. of Ire. 20 C1 51.37N 8.55W
Clones Rep. of Ire. 20 D4 54.11N 7.15W
Clonmel Rep. of Ire. 20 D2 52.21N 7.44W
Cloud Peak mtn. U.S.A. 64 E5 44.23N 107.11W
Clovis U.S.A. 64 F3 34.14N 103.13W
Cluanie, Loch Scotland 18 D2 57.08N 5.05W
Cluj-Napoca Romania 55 H2 46.47N 23.37E
Clun England 10 B3 52.26N 3.02W
Clydach Wales 12 D3 51.42N 3.53W
Clyde r. Scotland 16 E3 55.58N 4.53W
Clydebank Scotland 16 E3 55.53N 4.23W
Clyde River town Canada 63 L5 70.30N 68.30W
Coahuila d. Mexico 70 D6 27.00N 103.00W
Coalville England 10 D3 52.43N 1.21W
Coari Brazil 76 D4 4.08S 63.07W
Coari r. Brazil 76 D4 4.08S 63.07W
Coast d. Kenya 87 B2 3.00S 40.00E
Coast Mts. Canada 62 F3 55.30N 128.00W
Coast Range mts. U.S.A. 64 B5 40.00N 123.00W
Coatbridge Scotland 17 E3 55.52N 4.02W
Coats I. Canada 63 J4 62.30N 83.00W
Coatzacoalcos Mexico 70 F4 18.10N 94.25W
Cobh Rep. of Ire. 20 C1 51.50N 8.18W
Cobija Bolivia 76 D3 11.01S 68.45W
Coburg Germany 48 E4 50.15N 10.58E
Cochabamba Bolivia 76 D3 17.26S 66.10W
Cochin India 96 F2 9.56N 76.15E
Cochrane Canada 65 J6 49.00N 81.00W
Cochrane Chile 75 B2 47.20S 72.30W
Cockburnspath Scotland 17 G3 55.56N 2.22W
Cockburn Town Turks & Caicos Is. 71 J5 21.30N 71.30W
Cockermouth England 14 D3 54.40N 3.22W
Coco r. Honduras 71 H3 14.58N 83.15W
Coco, Isla del i. Pacific Oc. 60 K2 5.32N 87.04W
Cod, C. U.S.A. 65 L5 42.08N 70.10W
Coddington England 15 G2 53.04N 0.45W
Codó Brazil 77 F4 4.28S 43.51W
Códoba, Sierras de mts. Argentina 76 D1 30.30S 64.40W
Codsall England 10 C3 52.37N 2.11W
Coffs Harbour Australia 110 E2 30.19S 153.05E
Coggeshall England 11 F2 51.53N 0.41E
Coiba, I. Panama 71 H2 7.23N 81.45W
Coihaique Chile 75 B2 45.35S 72.08W
Coimbatore India 96 F3 11.00N 76.57E
Coimbra Portugal 46 A4 40.12N 8.25W
Colatina Brazil 77 F3 19.35S 40.37W
Colchester England 11 F2 51.54N 0.55E
Cold Bay town U.S.A. 62 B3 55.10N 162.47W
Coldstream Scotland 17 G3 55.39N 2.15W
Coleford England 10 C2 51.46N 2.38W
Coleraine N. Ireland 16 C3 55.08N 6.41W
Colima Mexico 70 D4 19.14N 103.41W
Colima mtn. Mexico 70 D4 19.32N 103.36W
Colima d. Mexico 70 D4 19.05N 104.00W
Coll i. Scotland 16 C4 56.38N 6.34W
Collier B. Australia 110 B4 16.10S 124.15E
Colmar France 44 G6 48.05N 7.21E
Colne England 15 E2 53.51N 2.11W
Colne r. England 11 F2 51.50N 0.59E
Cologne Germany 48 C4 50.56N 6.57E
Colombia S. America 74 B7 5.00N 75.00W
Colombo Sri Lanka 97 F2 6.55N 79.52E
Colón Panama 71 I2 9.21N 79.54W
Colonsay i. Scotland 16 C4 56.04N 6.13W
Colorado r. Argentina 75 C3 39.50S 62.02W
Colorado r. Tex. U.S.A. 64 G2 28.30N 96.00W
Colorado r. U.S.A./Mexico 64 D3 31.45N 114.40W
Colorado d. U.S.A. 64 E4 39.00N 106.00W
Colorado Plateau f. U.S.A. 64 D4 36.00N 111.00W
Colorado Springs town U.S.A. 64 F4 38.50N 104.40W
Coltishall England 11 G3 52.44N 1.22E
Columbia U.S.A. 65 J3 34.00N 81.00W
Columbia r. U.S.A. 64 B6 46.10N 123.30W
Columbia, Mt. Canada 62 G3 52.09N 117.25W
Columbus Ga. U.S.A. 65 J3 32.28N 84.59W
Columbus Ohio U.S.A. 65 J4 39.59N 83.03W
Colville r. U.S.A. 62 C5 70.06N 151.30W
Colwyn Bay town Wales 12 D5 53.18N 3.43W
Combe Martin England 13 C3 51.12N 4.02W
Comber N. Ireland 16 D2 54.33N 5.45W
Comeragh Mts. Rep. of Ire. 20 D2 52.15N 7.35W
Como Italy 50 C6 45.48N 9.04E
Como, L. Italy 50 C7 46.05N 9.17E
Comodoro Rivadavia Argentina 75 C2 45.50S 67.30W
Comorin, C. India 90 J3 8.04N 77.35E
Comoros Africa 86 D3 12.15S 44.00E
Compiègne France 42 B1 49.25N 2.50E
Comrie Scotland 17 F4 56.23N 4.00W
Conakry Guinea 84 C2 9.30N 13.43W
Concarneau France 44 B5 47.53N 3.55W
Concepción Chile 75 B3 36.50S 73.03W
Conception, Pt. U.S.A. 64 B3 34.27N 120.26W
Conchos r. Chihuahua Mexico 70 D6 29.34N 104.30W
Conchos r. Tamaulipas Mexico 70 E6 25.00N 97.30W
Concord U.S.A. 65 L5 43.13N 71.34W
Concordia Argentina 77 E1 31.25S 58.00W
Condor, Cordillera del mts. Ecuador/Peru 76 C4 4.00S 78.30W
Congleton England 15 E2 53.10N 2.12W
Congo Africa 84 F1 1.00S 16.00E
Congo r. Africa 84 F1 6.00S 12.30E
Congo Basin f. Africa 82 E4 1.00S 20.00E
Congo, Dem. Rep. of Africa 85 G1 1.00S 21.00E
Coningsby England 15 G2 53.07N 0.09W
Coniston England 14 D3 54.22N 3.06W
Coniston Water l. England 14 D3 54.20N 3.05W
Connah's Quay town Wales 12 D5 53.13N 3.03W
Connecticut d. U.S.A. 65 L5 41.30N 73.00W
Connemara f. Rep. of Ire. 20 B3 53.30N 9.50W
Conn, Lough Rep. of Ire. 20 B4 54.01N 9.15W
Conon Bridge Scotland 19 E2 57.33N 4.26W
Consett England 15 F3 54.52N 1.50W
Con Son is. Vietnam 104 D5 8.30N 106.30E
Constanța Romania 57 I6 44.10N 28.31E
Constantine Algeria 84 E5 36.22N 6.38E
Conwy Wales 12 D5 53.17N 3.50W
Conwy r. Wales 12 D5 53.17N 3.49W
Conwy d. Wales 9 D3 53.10N 3.45W
Conwy B. Wales 12 D5 53.19N 3.55W
Cook Is. Pacific Oc. 108 O5 15.00S 160.00W
Cook, Mt. see Aoraki New Zealand 111
Cookstown N. Ireland 16 C2 54.39N 6.46W
Cook Str. New Zealand 111 G1 41.15S 174.30E
Cooktown Australia 110 D4 15.29S 145.15E
Coolangatta Australia 110 E3 28.10S 153.26E
Cooper Creek r. Australia 110 C3 28.33S 137.46E
Copenhagen Denmark 43 C1 55.43N 12.34E
Copiapo Chile 76 C2 27.20S 70.23W
Copinsay i. Scotland 19 G3 58.54N 2.41W
Coppermine see Kugluktuk Canada 62
Coquimbo Chile 76 C1 30.00S 71.25W
Coral Harbour town Canada 63 J4 64.10N 83.15W
Coral Sea Pacific Oc. 110 E4 13.00S 150.00E
Coral Sea Islands Territory Austa. 110 E4 15.00S 153.00E
Corbie France 42 B1 49.55N 2.31E
Corbridge England 15 E3 54.58N 2.01W
Corby England 10 E3 52.29N 0.41W
Córdoba Argentina 76 D1 31.25S 64.11W
Córdoba Mexico 70 E4 18.55N 96.55W
Córdoba Spain 46 C2 37.53N 4.46W
Corfe Castle town England 10 C1 50.38N 2.04W
Corfu Greece 56 D3 39.37N 19.50E
Corfu i. Greece 56 D3 39.35N 19.50E
Corigliano Calabro Italy 50 G3 39.36N 16.31E
Corinth Greece 56 F2 37.56N 22.55E
Corinth, G. of Greece 56 F3 38.15N 22.30E
Corixa Grande r. Brazil/Bolivia 77 E3 17.30S 57.55W
Cork Rep. of Ire. 20 C1 51.54N 8.28W
Cork d. Rep. of Ire. 20 C1 52.00N 8.40W
Çorlu Turkey 57 H4 41.11N 27.48E
Corner Brook town Canada 63 M2 48.58N 57.58W
Corno, Monte mtn. Italy 50 E5 42.29N 13.33E
Cornwall d. England 9 C2 50.26N 4.40W
Cornwall, C. England 13 B2 50.07N 5.44W
Cornwallis I. Canada 63 I5 75.00N 95.00W
Coro Venezuela 71 K3 11.27N 69.41W
Coronada B. Costa Rica 71 H2 9.00N 83.50W
Coronation G. Canada 62 G4 68.00N 112.00W
Coronel Oviedo Paraguay 77 E2 25.24S 56.30W
Coropuna mtn. Peru 76 C3 15.31S 72.45W
Corpus Christi U.S.A. 64 G2 27.47N 97.26W
Corralejo Canary Is. 46 Z2 28.43N 13.53W
Corrib, Lough Rep. of Ire. 20 B3 53.26N 9.14W
Corrientes Argentina 77 E2 27.30S 58.48W
Corrientes r. Argentina 77 E2 29.55S 59.32W
Corrientes, C. Mexico 70 C5 20.25N 105.42W
Corse, Cap c. France 44 H3 43.00N 9.21E
Corserine mtn. Scotland 16 E3 55.09N 4.22W
Corsham England 10 C2 51.25N 2.11W
Corsica i. France 44 H3 42.00N 9.10E
Corte France 44 H3 42.18N 9.08E
Cortegana Spain 46 B2 37.55N 6.49W
Corton England 11 G3 52.32N 1.44E
Çorum Turkey 57 L4 40.31N 34.57E
Corumbá Brazil 77 E3 19.00S 57.25W
Corwen Wales 12 D4 52.59N 3.23W
Cosenza Italy 50 G3 39.17N 16.14E
Cosmoledo Is. Indian Oc. 86 D4 9.30S 49.00E
Cosne France 44 E5 47.25N 2.55E
Costa Blanca f. Spain 46 F3 38.30N 0.05E
Costa Brava f. Spain 46 G4 41.30N 3.00E
Costa del Sol f. Spain 46 C2 36.30N 4.00W
Costa Rica C. America 71 H3 10.00N 84.00W
Cotabato Phil. 105 G5 7.14N 124.15E
Côte d'Azur f. France 44 G3 43.20N 6.45E
Côte d'Ivoire Africa 84 D2 7.00N 5.30W
Cothi r. Wales 12 C3 51.51N 4.10W
Cotonou Benin 84 E2 6.24N 2.31E
Cotopaxi mtn. Ecuador 76 C4 0.40S 78.30W
Cotswold Hills England 10 C2 51.50N 2.00W
Cottbus Germany 48 G4 51.43N 14.21E
Cottenham England 11 F3 52.18N 0.08E
Cottesmore England 10 E3 52.43N 0.39W
Coulogne France 42 A2 50.55N 1.54E
Council Bluffs U.S.A. 64 G5 41.14N 95.54W
Coupar Angus Scotland 17 F4 56.33N 3.17W
Courland Lagoon Russian Fed. 54 G6 55.00N 21.00E
Coutances France 44 C6 49.03N 1.29W
Coventry England 10 D3 52.25N 1.31W
Covilhã Portugal 46 B4 40.17N 7.30W
Cowan, L. Australia 110 B2 32.00S 122.00E
Cowbridge Wales 13 D3 51.28N 3.28W
Cowdenbeath Scotland 17 F4 56.07N 3.21W
Cowes England 10 D1 50.45N 1.18W
Cowfold England 11 E1 50.59N 0.17W
Cow Green Resr. England 15 E3 54.40N 2.19W
Cox's Bazar Bangla. 97 I5 21.25N 91.59E
Cozumel I. Mexico 70 G5 20.30N 87.00W
Craigavon N. Ireland 16 C2 54.28N 6.25W
Craig Goch Resr. Wales 12 D4 52.20N 3.35W
Craignure Scotland 16 D4 56.28N 5.42W
Crail Scotland 17 G4 56.16N 2.38W
Craiova Romania 56 F6 44.18N 23.46E
Cramlington England 15 F4 55.06N 1.33W
Cranbrook Canada 62 G2 49.29N 115.48W
Cranleigh England 11 E2 51.08N 0.29W
Crawley England 11 E2 51.07N 0.10W
Creag Meagaidh mtn. Scotland 19 E1 56.57N 4.38W
Credenhill England 10 C3 52.06N 2.49W
Crediton England 13 D2 50.47N 3.39W
Cree L. Canada 62 H3 57.20N 108.30W
Creil France 42 B1 49.16N 2.29E
Cremona Italy 50 D6 45.08N 10.03E
Crepy-en-Valois France 42 B1 49.14N 2.54E
Cres i. Croatia 56 B6 44.50N 14.20E
Crescent City U.S.A. 64 B5 41.46N 124.13W
Creston U.S.A. 65 H5 41.04N 94.20W
Creswell England 15 F2 53.16N 1.12W

Crete *i.* Greece 56 G1 35.15N 25.00E
Crete, Sea of Med. Sea 56 G1 36.00N 25.00E
Creuse *r.* France 44 D5 47.00N 0.35E
Crewe England 15 E2 53.06N 2.28W
Crewkerne England 13 E2 50.53N 2.48W
Crianlarich Scotland 16 E4 56.23N 4.37W
Criccieth Wales 12 C4 52.55N 4.15W
Criciúma Brazil 77 F2 28.40S 49.23W
Crickhowell Wales 12 D3 51.52N 3.08W
Crieff Scotland 17 F4 56.23N 3.52W
Criffell *mtn.* Scotland 17 F2 54.57N 3.38W
Crimea *pen.* Ukraine 55 N1 45.30N 34.00E
Crimond Scotland 19 H2 57.36N 1.55W
Cristóbal Colón *mtn.* Colombia 71 J3 10.53N 73.48W
Croatia Europe 56 C6 45.30N 17.00E
Cromarty Scotland 19 E2 57.40N 4.01W
Cromarty Firth *est.* Scotland 19 E2 57.41N 4.10W
Cromdale, Hills of Scotland 19 F2 57.18N 3.30W
Cromer England 11 G3 52.56N 1.18E
Cronamuck Mtn. Rep. of Ire. 16 B2 54.54N 7.52W
Crook England 15 F3 54.43N 1.45W
Crooked I. The Bahamas 71 J5 22.45N 74.00W
Crooked Island Passage The Bahamas 71 J5 22.45N 74.40W
Croom Rep. of Ire. 20 C2 52.30N 8.42W
Crosby England 14 D2 53.30N 3.02W
Cross Fell *mtn.* England 15 E3 54.43N 2.28W
Crossgar N. Ireland 16 D2 54.24N 5.45W
Crossmaglen N. Ireland 16 C2 54.05N 6.37W
Crotone Italy 50 G3 39.05N 17.06E
Crouch *r.* England 11 F2 51.37N 0.45E
Crowborough England 11 F2 51.03N 0.09E
Crowland England 11 E3 52.41N 0.10W
Crowle England 15 G2 53.36N 0.49W
Crowthorne England 10 E2 51.23N 0.49W
Croyde England 13 C3 51.07N 4.13W
Croydon England 11 E2 51.23N 0.06W
Crozet Is. Indian Oc. 117 L2 47.00S 52.00E
Cruden Bay *town* Scotland 19 H2 57.24N 1.51W
Crumlin N. Ireland 16 C2 54.38N 6.13W
Crummock Water *l.* England 14 D3 54.33N 3.19W
Cruz, Cabo *c.* Cuba 71 I4 19.52N 77.44W
Cruzeiro do Sul Brazil 76 C4 7.40S 72.39W
Cuando *r.* Africa 86 B3 18.30S 23.30E
Cuanza *r.* Angola 86 A4 9.22S 13.09E
Cuba C. America 71 I5 22.00N 79.00W
Cubango *r.* Botswana 86 B3 18.30S 22.04E
Cuckfield England 11 E2 51.00N 0.08W
Cúcuta Colombia 71 J2 7.55N 72.31W
Cuddalore India 97 F3 11.43N 79.46E
Cuddapah India 97 F3 14.30N 78.30E
Cuenca Ecuador 76 C4 2.54S 79.00W
Cuenca Spain 46 D4 40.04N 2.07W
Cuenca, Serrania de *mts.* Spain 46 E4 40.25N 2.00W
Cuernavaca Mexico 70 E4 18.57N 99.15W
Cuiabá Brazil 77 E3 15.32S 56.05W
Cuiabá *r.* Brazil 77 E3 18.00S 57.25W
Cuilcagh *mtn.* Rep. of Ire. 16 B2 54.12N 7.50W
Cuillin Hills Scotland 18 C2 57.12N 6.13W
Culiacán Mexico 70 C5 24.50N 107.23W
Cullen Scotland 19 G2 57.42N 2.50W
Cullera Spain 46 E3 39.10N 0.15W
Cullin Sound Scotland 18 C2 57.05N 6.20W
Cullompton England 13 D2 50.52N 3.23W
Cullybackey N. Ireland 16 C2 54.53N 6.21W
Cul Mor *mtn.* Scotland 18 D3 58.04N 5.10W
Culuene *r.* Brazil 77 E3 12.56S 52.51W
Culzean B. Scotland 16 E3 55.21N 4.50W
Cumaná Venezuela 71 L3 10.29N 64.12W
Cumbal *mtn.* Colombia 76 C5 0.59N 77.53W
Cumberland Sd. Canada 63 L4 65.00N 65.30W
Cumbernauld Scotland 17 F3 55.57N 4.00W
Cumbria *d.* England 9 D4 54.40N 3.00W
Cumnock Scotland 16 E3 55.27N 4.15W
Cunene *r.* Angola 86 A3 17.15S 11.50E
Cuneo Italy 50 B6 44.22N 7.32E
Cupar Scotland 17 F4 56.19N 3.01W
Cupica, G. of Colombia 71 I2 6.35N 77.25W
Curaçao *i.* Neth. Ant. 71 K3 12.15N 69.00W
Curaray *r.* Peru 76 C4 2.20S 74.05W
Curitiba Brazil 77 F2 25.24S 49.16W
Curuá *r.* Brazil 77 E4 5.23S 54.22W
Cushendall N. Ireland 16 C3 55.05N 6.04W
Cuttack India 97 H5 20.26N 85.56E
Cuxhaven Germany 48 D5 53.52N 8.42E
Cuzco Peru 76 C3 13.32S 72.10W
Cwmbran Wales 12 D3 51.39N 3.01W
Cyclades *is.* Greece 56 G2 37.00N 25.00E
Cyprus Asia 57 K1 35.00N 33.00E
Cyrenaica *f.* Libya 53 H2 28.00N 22.10E
Czech Republic Europe 54 D3 49.30N 15.00
Częstochowa Poland 54 F4 50.49N 19.07E

D

Dabrowa Gornicza Poland 54 F4 50.22N 19.20E
Dagupan Phil. 104 G7 16.02N 120.21E
Da Hinggan Ling *mts.* China 103 M7 50.00N 122.10E
Dahlak Archipelago *is.* Eritrea 94 F2 15.45N 40.30E
Dailly Scotland 16 E3 55.18N 4.43W
Dakar Senegal 84 C3 14.38N 17.27W
Dakhla Oasis Egypt 94 C4 25.30N 29.00E
Dakol'ka *r.* Belarus 55 K5 52.10N 29.00E
Dakovica Yugo. 56 E5 42.22N 20.26E
Dalaman Turkey 57 I2 36.47N 28.47E
Da Lat Vietnam 104 D6 11.56N 108.25E
Dalbandin Pakistan 95 J4 28.53N 64.25E
Dalbeattie Scotland 17 F2 54.55N 3.49W
Dali China 103 I3 25.42N 100.11E
Dalian China 103 M5 38.53N 121.37E
Dalkeith Scotland 17 F3 55.54N 3.04W
Dallas U.S.A. 64 G3 32.47N 96.48W
Dalmally Scotland 16 E4 56.25N 4.58W
Dalmatia *f.* Croatia 56 C5 43.30N 17.00E
Dalmellington Scotland 16 E3 55.19N 4.24W
Daloa Côte d'Ivoire 84 D2 6.56N 6.28W
Dalry D. and G. Scotland 16 E3 55.07N 4.10W
Dalry N.Ayr. Scotland 16 E3 55.43N 4.43W
Dalrymple Scotland 16 E3 55.24N 4.35W
Dalrymple, Mt. Australia 110 D3 21.02S 148.38E
Dalton-in-Furness England 14 D3 54.10N 3.11W
Daly *r.* Australia 110 C4 13.20S 130.19E
Daman India 96 E5 20.25N 72.58E
Damanhûr Egypt 94 D5 31.03N 30.28E
Damar *i.* Indonesia 105 H2 7.10S 128.30E
Damaraland *f.* Namibia 86 A2 22.20S 16.00E
Damascus Syria 94 E5 33.30N 36.19E
Damavand *mtn.* Iran 95 H6 35.47N 52.04E
Damghan Iran 95 H6 36.09N 54.22E
Dampier Australia 110 A3 20.40S 116.42E
Dampir Str. Pacific Oc. 105 I3 0.30S 130.50E
Da Nang Vietnam 104 D7 16.04N 108.14E
Dande Ethiopia 87 B3 4.53N 36.20E
Dandong China 103 M6 40.06N 124.25E
Dane *r.* England 15 E2 53.16N 2.30W
Danger Is. Cook Is. 108 O5 10.53S 165.49W
Dankov Russian Fed. 55 P5 53.15N 39.08E
Danube *r.* Europe 35 F2 45.26N 29.38E
Danube, Mouths of the *f.* Romania 55 K1 45.05N 29.45E
Danville U.S.A. 65 K4 36.34N 79.25W
Dapaong Togo 84 E3 10.58N 0.07E
Da Qaidam China 102 H5 37.44N 95.08E
Daqing China 103 N7 46.40N 125.00E
Dar'â Syria 94 E5 32.37N 36.06E
Darab Iran 95 H4 28.45N 54.34E
Darabani Romania 55 J3 48.11N 26.35E
Daravica *mtn.* Yugo. 56 E5 42.32N 20.08E
Darbhanga India 97 H6 26.10N 85.54E
Dardanelles *str.* Turkey 56 H4 40.15N 26.30E
Dar es Salaam Tanzania 86 C4 6.51S 39.18E
Darhan Mongolia 103 J7 49.34N 106.23E
Darién, G. of Colombia 71 I2 9.20N 77.00W
Darjiling India 97 H6 27.02N 88.20E
Darling *r.* Australia 110 D2 34.05S 141.57E
Darling Downs *f.* Australia 110 D3 28.00S 149.45E
Darlington England 15 F3 54.33N 1.33W
Darlington *d.* England 9 E4 54.33N 1.33W
Darmstadt Germany 48 D3 49.52N 8.30E
Darnah Libya 85 G5 32.45N 22.39E
Dart *r.* England 13 D2 50.24N 3.41W
Dartford England 11 F2 51.27N 0.14E
Dartmoor *hills* England 13 D2 50.33N 3.55W
Dartmouth England 13 D2 50.21N 3.35W
Darton England 15 F2 53.36N 1.32W
Daru P.N.G. 105 K2 9.05S 143.10E
Darwen England 15 E2 53.42N 2.29W
Darwin Australia 110 C4 12.23S 130.44E
Daryacheh-ye-Bakhtegan *l.* Iran 95 H4 29.20N 54.05E
Daryacheh-ye Sistan *f.* Iran 95 J5 31.00N 61.15E
Daryacheh-ye-Tashk *l.* Iran 95 H5 30.05N 54.00E
Dasht-e-Kavir *des.* Iran 95 H5 34.40N 55.00E
Dasht-e-Lut *des.* Iran 95 I5 31.30N 58.00E
Dasht-i-Arbu Lut *des.* Afghan. 95 J5 30.00N 65.00E
Dasht-i-Margo *des.* Afghan. 95 J5 30.45N 63.00E
Datong China 103 K5 40.12N 113.12E
Daud Khel Pakistan 95 L5 32.53N 71.34E
Daugava *r.* Europe 43 F2 57.03N 24.00E
Daugavpils Latvia 43 F1 55.52N 26.31E
Dauphin Canada 62 H3 51.09N 100.05W
Dauphiné *f.* France 44 F4 45.00N 5.45E
Davangere India 96 F3 14.30N 75.52E
Davao Phil. 105 H5 7.05N 125.38E
Davao G. Phil. 105 H5 6.30N 126.00E
Davenport U.S.A. 65 H5 41.40N 90.36W
Daventry England 10 D3 52.16N 1.10W
David Panama 71 H2 8.26N 82.26W
Davis Str. N. America 63 M4 66.00N 58.00W
Dawa Wenz *r.* Ethiopia 87 C3 4.11N 42.06E
Dawlish England 13 D2 50.34N 3.28W
Dawqah Oman 95 H2 18.38N 54.05E
Dawson Canada 62 E4 64.04N 139.24W
Dawson Creek *town* Canada 62 F3 55.44N 120.15W
Daxian China 103 J4 31.10N 107.28E
Dayr az Zawr Syria 94 F6 35.20N 40.08E
Dayton U.S.A. 65 J4 39.45N 84.10W
Daytona Beach *town* U.S.A. 65 J2 29.11N 81.01W
Dead Sea Jordan 94 E5 31.25N 35.30E
Deal England 11 G2 51.13N 1.25E
Death Valley *f.* U.S.A. 64 C4 36.00N 116.45W
Debak Malaysia 104 E4 1.30N 111.28E
Debar Macedonia 56 E4 41.31N 20.30E
Debenham England 11 G3 52.14N 1.10E
Debrecen Hungary 54 G2 47.30N 21.37E
Decatur U.S.A. 65 I4 39.44N 88.57W
Deccan *f.* India 96 F4 18.00N 76.30E
Děčín Czech Rep. 54 D4 50.48N 14.15E
Dee *r.* Scotland 19 G2 57.07N 2.04W
Dee *r.* Wales 12 D5 53.13N 3.05W
Deele *r.* Rep. of Ire. 16 B2 54.51N 7.29W
Degodia *f.* Ethiopia 87 C3 4.15N 41.30E
De Grey *r.* Australia 110 A3 20.12S 119.11E
Dehra Dun India 97 F7 30.19N 78.00E
Dej Romania 55 H2 47.08N 23.55E
Delano Peak *mtn.* U.S.A. 64 D4 38.23N 112.22W
Delap-Uliga-Djarrit Marshall Is. 108 M7 7.07N 171.22E
Delaram Afghan. 95 J5 32.11N 63.25E
Delaware *d.* U.S.A. 65 K4 39.00N 75.30W
Delft Neth. 42 D4 52.01N 4.23E
Delfzijl Neth. 42 F5 53.20N 6.56E
Delhi India 96 F6 28.40N 77.14E
Deliçe *r.* Turkey 57 L4 40.27N 34.07E
De Longa Str. Russian Fed. 59 T5 70.00N 178.00E
Del Rio U.S.A. 64 F2 29.23N 100.56W
Demirkazik *mtn.* Turkey 57 L2 37.50N 35.10E
Democratic Republic of Congo Africa 86 B4 2.00S 22.00E
Dempo *mtn.* Indonesia 104 C3 4.02S 103.07E
Denakil *f.* Ethiopia/Eritrea 85 I3 13.00N 41.00E
Denau Uzbekistan 95 K6 38.20N 67.54E
Denbigh Wales 12 D5 53.11N 3.25W
Denbighshire *d.* Wales 9 D3 53.07N 3.20W
Den Burg Neth. 42 D5 53.03N 4.47E
Dendermonde Belgium 42 D3 51.01N 4.07E
Den Helder Neth. 42 D4 52.58N 4.46E
Denizli Turkey 57 I2 37.46N 29.05E
Denmark Europe 43 B1 56.00N 9.00E
Denmark Str. Greenland/Iceland 63 P4 66.00N 25.00W
Denny Scotland 17 F4 56.02N 3.55W
Denpasar Indonesia 104 F2 8.40S 115.14E
D'Entrecasteaux Is. P.N.G. 110 E5 9.30S 150.40E
Denver U.S.A. 64 F4 39.45N 104.58W
Dêqên China 102 H3 28.45N 98.58E
Dera Ghazi Khan Pakistan 96 E7 30.05N 70.44E
Dera Ismail Khan Pakistan 96 E7 31.51N 70.56E
Derby Australia 110 B4 17.19S 123.38E
Derby England 10 D3 52.55N 1.28W
Derby *d.* England 9 E3 52.55N 1.28W
Derbyshire *d.* England 9 E3 53.12N 1.28W
Derg *r.* N. Ireland 16 B2 54.44N 7.27W
Derg, Lough Donegal Rep. of Ire. 20 D4 54.37N 7.55W
Derg, Lough Tipperary Rep. of Ire. 20 C2 52.57N 8.18W
Derry *r.* Rep. of Ire. 20 E2 52.35N 6.38W
Derryveagh Mts. Rep. of Ire. 20 C4 55.00N 8.10W
Dersingham England 11 F3 52.51N 0.30E
Derudeb Sudan 94 E2 17.32N 36.06E
Derwent *r.* England 15 G2 53.44N 0.57W
Derwent Resr. Derbys. England 15 F2 53.24N 1.44W
Derwent Resr. Durham England 15 F3 54.51N 2.00W
Derwent Water *l.* England 14 D3 54.35N 3.09W
Desaguadero *r.* Argentina 75 C3 34.00S 66.40W
Desappointement, Iles du *is.* Pacific Oc. 109 R5 14.02S 141.24W
Desaquadero *r.* Bolivia 76 D3 18.24S 67.05W
Dese Ethiopia 85 H3 11.05N 39.40E
Deseado Argentina 75 C2 47.44S 65.56W
Des Moines U.S.A. 65 H5 41.35N 93.35W
Desna *r.* Russian Fed./Ukraine 55 L4 50.32N 30.37E
Dessau Germany 48 F4 51.51N 12.15E
Desvres France 42 A2 50.40N 1.50E
Detroit U.S.A. 65 J5 42.23N 83.05W
Deva Romania 54 H1 45.54N 22.55E
Deventer Neth. 42 F4 52.15N 6.10E
Deveron *r.* Scotland 19 G2 57.40N 2.30W
Devils Lake *town* U.S.A. 64 G6 48.08N 98.50W
Devizes England 10 D2 51.21N 2.00W
Devon *r.* England 15 G2 53.04N 0.50W
Devon *r.* Scotland 17 F4 56.07N 3.52W
Devon *d.* England 9 D2 50.50N 3.40W
Devon I. Canada 63 J5 75.00N 86.00W
Devonport Australia 110 D1 41.09S 146.16E
Devrez *r.* Turkey 57 L4 41.07N 34.25E
Dewsbury England 15 F2 53.42N 1.38W
Dezful Iran 95 G5 32.24N 48.27E
Dezhou China 103 L5 37.29N 116.11E
Dhahran Saudi Arabia 95 H4 26.18N 50.08E
Dhaka Bangla. 97 I5 23.42N 90.22E
Dhamar Yemen 94 F1 14.33N 44.24E
Dhanbad India 97 H5 23.47N 86.32E
Dhaulagiri *mtn.* Nepal 97 G6 28.39N 83.28E
Dhule India 96 E5 20.52N 74.50E
Diamantina *r.* Australia 110 C3 26.45S 139.10E
Dibrugarh India 97 I6 27.29N 94.56E
Dickinson U.S.A. 64 F6 46.54N 102.48W
Dida Galgalu *f.* Kenya 87 B3 3.00N 38.00E
Didcot England 10 D2 51.36N 1.14W
Dieppe France 44 D6 49.55N 1.05E
Diest Belgium 42 E2 50.59N 5.03E
Digby Canada 65 M5 44.30N 65.47W
Digne-les-Bains France 44 G4 44.05N 6.14E
Dijon France 44 F5 47.20N 5.02E
Diksmuide Belgium 42 B3 51.01N 2.52E
Dili Indonesia 105 H2 8.35S 125.35E
Dillon U.S.A. 64 D6 45.14N 112.38W
Dimapur India 97 I6 25.54N 93.45E
Dimitrovgrad Bulgaria 56 G5 42.01N 25.34E
Dinan France 44 B6 48.27N 2.02W
Dinant Belgium 42 D2 50.16N 4.55E
Dinar Turkey 57 J3 38.05N 30.09E
Dinard France 44 B6 48.38N 2.04W
Dinaric Alps *mts.* Bosnia./Croatia 56 C6 44.00N 16.30E
Dindigul India 97 F3 10.23N 78.00E
Dingle Rep. of Ire. 20 A2 52.08N 10.19W
Dingle B. Rep. of Ire. 20 A2 52.05N 10.12W
Dingwall Scotland 19 E2 57.35N 4.26W
Dipolog Phil. 105 G5 8.34N 123.28E
Dire Dawa Ethiopia 85 I2 9.35N 41.50E
Dirranbandi Australia 110 D3 28.35S 148.10E
Disappointment, C. South Georgia 75 F1 54.53S 36.08W
Disappointment, L. Australia 110 B3 23.30S 122.55E
Disko I. Greenland 63 M4 69.45N 53.00W
Diss England 11 G3 52.23N 1.06E
Distington England 14 D3 54.36N 3.32W
District of Columbia *d.* U.S.A. 65 K4 38.55N 77.00W
Distrito Federal *d.* Brazil 77 F3 15.45S 47.50W
Distrito Federal *d.* Mexico 70 E4 19.20N 99.10W
Diu India 96 E5 20.41N 70.59E
Divinópolis Brazil 77 F2 20.08S 44.55W
Divriği Turkey 57 N3 39.23N 38.06E
Dixon Entrance *str.* Canada/U.S.A. 62 E3 54.10N 133.30W
Diyarbakır Turkey 94 F6 37.55N 40.14E
Djado Plateau *f.* Niger 84 F4 22.00N 12.30E
Djelfa Algeria 84 E5 34.43N 3.14E
Djibouti Africa 85 I3 12.00N 42.50E
Djibouti *town* Djibouti 85 I3 11.35N 43.11E
Dnieper *r.* Europe 55 M2 46.30N 32.25E
Dniestr *r.* Europe 55 K2 46.21N 30.20E
Dniprodzerzhyns'k Ukraine 55 N3 48.30N 34.37E
Dnipropetrovs'k Ukraine 55 N3 48.29N 35.00E
Dniprorudne Ukraine 55 N2 47.23N 34.57E
Doberai Pen. Indonesia 105 I3 1.10S 132.30E
Doboj Bosnia. 56 D6 44.44N 18.02E
Dobrich Bulgaria 57 H5 43.34N 27.52E
Dobrovelychkivka Ukraine 55 L3 48.23N 31.11E
Dochart *r.* Scotland 16 E4 56.30N 4.17W
Docking England 11 F3 52.55N 0.39E
Dodecanese *is.* Greece 53 I4 37.00N 27.00E
Dodge City U.S.A. 64 F4 37.45N 100.02W
Dodman Pt. England 13 C2 50.13N 4.48W
Dodoma Tanzania 86 C4 6.10S 35.40E
Doetinchem Neth. 42 F3 51.57N 6.17E
Doha Qatar 95 H4 25.15N 51.34E
Dokkum Neth. 42 F5 53.20N 6.00E
Dolbenmaen Wales 12 C4 52.58N 4.14W
Dole France 44 F5 47.05N 5.30E
Dolgellau Wales 12 D4 52.44N 3.53W
Dolomites *mts.* Italy 50 D7 46.25N 11.50E
Dolo Odo Ethiopia 87 C3 4.13N 42.08E
Dolyna Ukraine 55 H3 49.00N 23.59E
Dolyns'ka Ukraine 55 M3 48.06N 32.46E
Dominica Windward Is. 71 L4 15.30N 61.30W
Dominican Republic C. America 71 J4 18.00N 70.00W
Don *r.* Russian Fed. 35 G2 47.06N 39.16E
Don *r.* Scotland 19 G2 57.10N 2.05W
Donaghadee N. Ireland 16 D2 54.39N 5.34W
Don Benito Spain 46 C3 38.57N 5.52W
Doncaster England 15 F2 53.31N 1.09W
Donegal Rep. of Ire. 20 C4 54.39N 8.06W
Donegal *d.* Rep. of Ire. 20 C4 54.52N 8.00W
Donegal B. Rep. of Ire. 20 C4 54.32N 8.18W
Donegal Pt. Rep. of Ire. 20 B2 52.42N 9.38W
Donets'k Ukraine 55 O2 48.00N 37.50E
Dongfang China 103 J1 19.04N 108.39E
Dongfangbong China 106 B5 46.20N 133.10E
Dong Hoi Vietnam 104 D7 17.32N 106.35E
Dongotona Mts. Sudan 87 A3 4.00N 33.00E
Dongting Hu *l.* China 103 K3 29.40N 113.00E
Donostia-San Sebastián Spain 46 E5 43.19N 1.59W
Doon *r.* Scotland 16 E3 55.26N 4.38W
Doon, Loch Scotland 16 E3 55.15N 4.23W
Dorchester England 10 C1 50.43N 2.28W
Dordogne *r.* France 44 C4 45.03N 0.34W
Dordrecht Neth. 42 D3 51.48N 4.40E
Dore, Mont *mtn.* France 44 E4 45.32N 2.49E
Dorking England 11 E2 51.14N 0.20W
Dornbirn Austria 54 A2 47.25N 9.44E
Dornoch Scotland 19 E2 57.52N 4.02W
Dornoch Firth *est.* Scotland 19 E2 57.50N 4.04W
Döröö Nuur *l.* Mongolia 102 G7 47.40N 93.30E
Dorset *d.* England 9 D2 50.48N 2.25W
Dortmund Germany 48 C4 51.32N 7.27E
Dothan U.S.A. 65 I3 31.12N 85.25W
Douai France 44 E7 50.22N 3.05E
Douala Cameroon 84 E2 4.05N 9.43E
Douglas I.o.M. 14 C3 54.09N 4.29W
Douglas Scotland 17 F3 55.33N 3.51W
Doullens France 42 B2 50.09N 2.21E
Doune Scotland 16 E4 56.11N 4.04W
Dounreay Scotland 19 F3 58.33N 3.45W
Dourados Brazil 77 E2 22.09S 54.52W
Douro *r.* Portugal 46 A4 41.10N 8.40W
Dove *r.* Derbys. England 10 D3 52.50N 1.34W
Dove *r.* Suffolk England 11 G3 52.21N 1.14E
Dover England 11 G2 51.07N 1.19E
Dover U.S.A. 65 K4 39.10N 75.32W
Dover, Str. of U.K./France 11 G1 51.00N 1.30E
Down *d.* N. Ireland 20 F4 54.20N 6.00W
Downham Market England 11 F3 52.36N 0.22E
Downpatrick N. Ireland 16 D2 54.21N 5.43W
Downpatrick Head Rep. of Ire. 20 B4 54.20N 9.21W
Downton England 10 D1 51.00N 1.44W
Dowshī Afghan. 95 K6 35.38N 68.43E
Drachten Neth. 42 F5 53.05N 6.06E
Drăgăşani Romania 56 G6 44.40N 24.16E
Draguignan France 44 G3 43.32N 6.28E
Drakensberg *mts.* R.S.A. 86 B1 30.00S 29.00E
Drama Greece 56 G4 41.09N 24.11E
Drammen Norway 43 B2 59.45N 10.15E
Dranmore Rep. of Ire. 20 C3 53.16N 8.56W
Draperstown N. Ireland 16 C2 54.48N 6.46W
Drau *r. see* Drava *r.* Austria 54
Drava *r.* Yugo. 56 D6 45.34N 18.56E
Drenthe *d.* Neth. 42 F4 52.52N 6.30E
Dresden Germany 48 F4 51.03N 13.45E
Dreux France 44 D6 48.44N 1.23E
Drobeta-Turnu-Severin Romania 56 F6 44.37N 22.39E
Drogheda Rep. of Ire. 20 E3 53.43N 6.23W
Droitwich England 10 C3 52.16N 2.10W
Dromore N. Ireland 16 C2 54.24N 6.10W
Dronfield England 15 F2 53.18N 1.29W
Drosh Pakistan 95 L6 35.33N 71.48E
Drumheller Canada 62 G3 51.28N 112.40W
Drummore Scotland 16 E2 54.41N 4.54W
Druskininkai Lithuania 55 I5 53.58N 23.58E
Druts' *r.* Belarus 55 L5 53.03N 30.42E
Drygarn Fawr *mtn.* Wales 12 D4 52.13N 3.39W
Drymen Scotland 16 E4 56.04N 4.27W
Duarte, Pico Dom. Rep. 71 J4 19.02N 70.59W
Ḍubā Saudi Arabia 94 E4 27.21N 35.40E
Dubai U.A.E. 95 I4 25.13N 55.17E
Dubawnt L. Canada 62 H4 62.50N 102.00W
Dubbo Australia 110 D2 32.16S 148.41E
Dublin Rep. of Ire. 20 E3 53.21N 6.18W
Dublin *d.* Rep. of Ire. 20 E3 53.20N 6.18W
Dublin B. Rep. of Ire. 20 E3 53.20N 6.09W
Dubno Ukraine 55 I4 50.28N 25.40E
Dubrovnik Croatia 56 D5 42.40N 18.07E
Dubrovytsya Ukraine 55 J4 51.38N 26.40E
Ducie I. Pacific Oc. 109 S4 24.40S 124.48W
Dudinka Russian Fed. 59 K4 69.27N 86.13E
Dudley England 10 C3 52.30N 2.05W
Duero *r. see* Douro *r.* Spain 46
Dufftown Scotland 19 F2 57.27N 3.11W
Dugi Otok *i.* Croatia 56 B6 44.04N 15.00E
Duisburg Germany 48 C4 51.26N 6.45E
Dukhan Qatar 95 H4 25.24N 50.47E
Dukou China 103 I3 26.30N 101.40E
Dulce *r.* Argentina 76 D1 30.40S 62.00W
Duluth U.S.A. 65 H6 46.50N 92.10W
Dulverton England 13 D3 51.02N 3.33W
Dumbarton Scotland 16 E3 55.57N 4.35W
Dumfries Scotland 17 F3 55.04N 3.37W
Dumfries and Galloway *d.* Scotland 8 D4 55.05N 3.40W
Dumyât Egypt 94 D5 31.26N 31.48E
Dunaff Head Rep. of Ire. 16 B3 55.17N 7.31W
Dunany Pt. Rep. of Ire. 20 E3 53.51N 6.15W
Dunbar Scotland 17 G4 56.00N 2.31W
Dunblane Scotland 17 F4 56.12N 3.59W
Duncansby Head Scotland 19 F3 58.39N 3.01W
Dunchurch England 10 D3 52.21N 1.19W
Dundalk Rep. of Ire. 20 E3 54.01N 6.24W
Dundalk B. Rep. of Ire. 20 E3 53.55N 6.17W
Dundee Scotland 17 F4 56.28N 3.00W
Dundee City *d.* Scotland 8 D5 56.28N 3.00W
Dundonald N. Ireland 16 D2 54.36N 5.48W
Dundrum B. N. Ireland 16 D2 54.12N 5.46W
Dunedin New Zealand 111 G1 45.53S 170.31E
Dunfermline Scotland 17 F4 56.04N 3.29W
Dungannon N. Ireland 16 C2 54.30N 6.47W
Dungarvan Rep. of Ire. 20 D2 52.06N 7.39W
Dungeness *c.* England 11 F1 50.55N 0.58E
Dungiven N. Ireland 16 C2 54.56N 6.57W
Dungun Malaysia 104 C4 4.44N 103.26E
Dungunab Sudan 94 E3 21.06N 37.05E
Dunholme England 15 G2 53.18N 0.29W
Dunhua China 106 A4 43.25N 128.20E
Dunhuang China 102 G6 40.00N 94.40E
Dunkerque France 44 E7 51.02N 2.23E
Dunkery Beacon *hill* England 13 D3 51.11N 3.35W
Dun Laoghaire Rep. of Ire. 20 E3 53.17N 6.09W
Dunleer Rep. of Ire. 20 E3 53.49N 6.24W
Dunloy N. Ireland 16 C3 55.02N 6.23W
Dunmore East Rep. of Ire. 20 D2 52.09N 7.00W
Dunmurry N. Ireland 16 D2 54.33N 6.00W
Dunnet B. Scotland 19 F3 58.38N 3.25W
Dunnet Head Scotland 19 F3 58.40N 3.23W
Dunoon Scotland 16 E3 55.57N 4.57W
Duns Scotland 17 G3 55.47N 2.20W

Formby England **14 D2** 53.34N 3.04W
Formentera *i.* Spain **46 F3** 38.41N 1.30E
Formosa Argentina **77 E2** 26.06S 58.14W
Formosa, Serra *mts.* Brazil **77 E3** 12.00S 55.20W
Forres Scotland **19 F2** 57.37N 3.38W
Forssa Finland **43 E3** 60.49N 23.40E
Forst Germany **48 G4** 51.46N 14.39E
Fort Albany Canada **63 J3** 52.15N 81.35W
Fortaleza Brazil **77 G4** 3.45S 38.45W
Fort Augustus Scotland **18 E2** 57.09N 4.41W
Fort Chipewyan Canada **62 G3** 58.46N 111.09W
Fort Collins U.S.A. **64 E5** 40.35N 105.05W
Fort-de-France Martinique **71 L3** 14.36N 61.05W
Fortescue *r.* Australia **110 A3** 21.00S 116.06E
Fort Frances Canada **63 I2** 48.37N 93.23W
Fort George Canada **63 K3** 53.50N 79.01W
Fort Good Hope Canada **62 F4** 66.16N 128.37W
Forth *r.* Scotland **17 F4** 56.06N 3.48W
Fort Liard Canada **62 F4** 60.14N 123.28W
Fort McMurray Canada **62 G3** 56.45N 111.27W
Fort McPherson Canada **62 E4** 67.29N 134.50W
Fort Nelson Canada **62 F3** 58.48N 122.44W
Fort Norman *see* **Tulít'a** Canada **62**
Fort Peck Resr. U.S.A. **64 E6** 47.55N 107.00W
Fortrose Scotland **19 E2** 57.34N 4.07W
Fort Rupert Canada **63 K3** 51.30N 79.45W
Fort St. John Canada **62 F3** 56.14N 120.55W
Fort Scott U.S.A. **65 H4** 37.52N 94.43W
Fort Severn Canada **63 J3** 56.00N 87.40W
Fort-Shevchenko Kazakhstan **58 H2** 44.31N 50.15E
Fort Simpson Canada **62 F4** 61.46N 121.15W
Fort Smith Canada **62 G4** 60.00N 111.51W
Fort Smith U.S.A. **65 H4** 35.22N 94.27W
Fortuneswell England **10 C1** 50.33N 2.27W
Fort Wayne U.S.A. **65 I5** 41.05N 85.08W
Fort William Scotland **18 D1** 56.49N 5.07W
Fort Worth U.S.A. **64 G3** 32.45N 97.20W
Fort Yukon U.S.A. **62 D4** 66.35N 145.20W
Foshan China **103 K2** 23.03N 113.08E
Fougères France **44 C6** 48.21N 1.12W
Foula *i.* Scotland **19 X9** 60.08N 2.05W
Foulness Pt. England **11 F2** 51.37N 0.57E
Fouta Djallon *f.* Guinea **84 C3** 11.30N 12.30W
Fowey *r.* England **13 C2** 50.22N 4.40W
Foxe Basin *b.* Canada **63 K4** 67.30N 79.00W
Foxe Channel Canada **63 J4** 65.00N 80.00W
Foxe Pen. Canada **63 K4** 65.00N 76.00W
Foxford Rep. of Ire. **20 B3** 53.59N 9.07W
Foyle *r.* N. Ireland **16 B2** 55.00N 7.20W
Foyle, Lough Rep. of Ire./N. Ireland **16 B3** 55.07N 7.06W
Foz do Iguaçú Brazil **77 E2** 25.33S 54.31W
Framlingham England **11 G3** 52.14N 1.20E
Franca Brazil **77 F2** 20.33S 47.27W
France Europe **44 D5** 47.00N 2.00E
Franceville Gabon **84 F1** 1.40S 13.31E
Francistown Botswana **86 B2** 21.11S 27.32E
Frankfort U.S.A. **65 J4** 38.11N 84.53W
Frankfurt Germany **48 G5** 52.20N 14.32E
Frankfurt am Main Germany **48 D4** 50.06N 8.41E
Franklin D. Roosevelt L. U.S.A. **64 C6** 47.55N 118.20W
Franz Josef Land *is.* Russian Fed. **58 H6** 81.00N 54.00E
Fraser *r.* Canada **62 F2** 49.05N 123.00W
Fraserburgh Scotland **19 H2** 57.42N 2.00W
Fraser I. Australia **110 E3** 25.15S 153.10E
Freckleton England **14 E2** 53.45N 2.50W
Fredericia Denmark **43 B1** 55.34N 9.47E
Fredericksburg U.S.A. **65 K4** 38.18N 77.30W
Fredericton Canada **63 L2** 45.57N 66.40W
Frederikshavn Denmark **43 B2** 57.26N 10.32E
Fredrikstad Norway **43 B2** 59.15N 10.55E
Freeport City The Bahamas **71 I6** 26.40N 78.30W
Freetown Sierra Leone **84 C2** 8.30N 13.17W
Freiberg Germany **48 F4** 50.54N 13.20E
Freiburg in Breisgau Germany **48 C2** 48.00N 7.52E
Fréjus France **44 G3** 43.26N 6.44E
Fremantle Australia **110 A2** 32.07S 115.44E
French Guiana S. America **74 D7** 3.40N 53.00W
French Polynesia Pacific Oc. **109 Q5** 20.00S 140.00W
Freshwater England **10 D1** 50.40N 1.30W
Fresno U.S.A. **64 C4** 36.41N 119.57W
Fria Guinea **84 C3** 10.13N 13.48W
Friedrichshafen Germany **48 D2** 47.39N 9.29E
Friesland *d.* Neth. **42 E5** 53.05N 5.45E
Frinton-on-Sea England **11 G2** 51.50N 1.16E
Frio, Cabo *c.* Brazil **75 E4** 22.50S 42.10W
Frisa, Loch Scotland **16 C4** 56.33N 6.05W
Frisian Is. Europe **34 D3** 54.00N 7.00E
Frizington England **14 D3** 54.30N 3.30W
Frobisher B. Canada **63 L4** 63.00N 66.45W
Frodsham England **14 E2** 53.17N 2.45W
Frogmore England **10 E2** 51.20N 0.49W
Frohavet *est.* Norway **43 B3** 63.55N 9.05E
Frome England **13 E3** 51.16N 2.17W
Frome *r.* England **10 C1** 50.41N 2.05W
Frome, L. Australia **110 C2** 30.45S 139.45E
Frontera Canary Is. **46 W1** 27.46N 18.01W
Frosinone Italy **50 E4** 41.36N 13.21E
Frøya *i.* Norway **43 B3** 63.45N 8.30E
Fuenlabrada Spain **46 D4** 40.16N 3.49W
Fuerteventura *i.* Canary Is. **46 Y2** 28.20N 14.10W
Fujairah U.A.E. **95 I4** 25.10N 56.20E
Fujian *d.* China **103 L3** 26.30N 118.00E
Fuji-san *mtn.* Japan **106 C3** 35.23N 138.42E
Fukui Japan **106 C3** 36.04N 136.12E
Fukuoka Japan **106 B2** 33.39N 130.21E
Fukushima Japan **106 B3** 37.44N 140.28E
Fulda Germany **48 D4** 50.35N 9.45E
Fulford England **15 F2** 53.56N 1.04W
Fulham England **11 E2** 51.30N 0.14W
Fumay France **42 D1** 49.59N 4.42E
Funabashi Japan **106 C3** 35.42N 139.59E
Funchal Madeira Is. **84 C5** 32.38N 16.54W
Fundy, B. of N. America **65 M5** 44.30N 66.30W
Fürth Germany **48 E3** 49.28N 11.00E
Fushun China **103 M6** 41.51N 123.53E
Fuxin China **103 M6** 42.08N 121.39E
Fuzhou Fujian China **103 L3** 26.01N 119.20E
Fuzhou Jiangxi China **103 L3** 28.03N 116.15E
Fyn *i.* Denmark **43 B1** 55.10N 10.30E
Fyne, Loch Scotland **16 D3** 55.55N 5.23W

G

Gabès Tunisia **84 F5** 33.52N 10.06E
Gabès, G. of Tunisia **84 F5** 34.00N 11.00E
Gabon Africa **84 F1** 0.00 12.00E
Gaborone Botswana **86 B2** 24.45S 25.55E
Gadsden U.S.A. **65 I3** 34.00N 86.00W
Gaer Wales **12 D3** 51.54N 3.11W
Gaeta Italy **50 E4** 41.13N 13.35E
Gaeta, G. of Med. Sea **50 E4** 41.05N 13.30E
Gafsa Tunisia **84 E5** 34.28N 8.43E
Gagarin Russian Fed. **55 N6** 55.38N 35.00E
Gagnon Canada **63 L3** 51.56N 68.16W
Gagra Georgia **57 O5** 43.21N 40.16E
Gainesville Fla. U.S.A. **65 J2** 29.37N 82.31W
Gainesville Tex. U.S.A. **64 G3** 33.37N 97.08W
Gainsborough England **15 G2** 53.23N 0.46W
Gairdner, L. Australia **110 C2** 31.30S 136.00E
Gair Loch Scotland **18 D2** 57.43N 5.43W
Gairloch *town* Scotland **18 D2** 57.43N 5.41W
Galana *r.* Kenya **87 B2** 3.10S 40.10E
Galapagos Is. Pacific Oc. **76 A4** 0.30S 90.30W
Galashiels Scotland **17 G3** 55.37N 2.49W
Galati Romania **55 J1** 45.27N 27.59E
Gala Water *r.* Scotland **17 F3** 55.36N 2.48W
Gáldar Canary Is. **46 Y2** 28.09N 15.40W
Galdhøpiggen *mtn.* Norway **43 B3** 61.38N 8.19E
Gallabat Sudan **94 E1** 12.58N 36.09E
Galle Sri Lanka **97 G2** 6.01N 80.13E
Galley Head Rep. of Ire. **20 C1** 51.31N 8.57W
Gallinas Pt. Colombia **71 J3** 12.20N 71.30W
Gallipoli Italy **50 H4** 40.02N 18.01E
Gallipoli Turkey **56 H4** 40.25N 26.31E
Gällivare Sweden **43 E4** 67.10N 20.40E
Gallup U.S.A. **64 E4** 35.32N 108.46W
Galole Kenya **87 B2** 1.34S 40.01E
Galston Scotland **16 E3** 55.36N 4.23W
Galtee Mts. Rep. of Ire. **20 C2** 52.20N 8.10W
Galveston U.S.A. **65 H2** 29.17N 94.48W
Galveston B. U.S.A. **65 H2** 29.40N 94.40W
Galway Rep. of Ire. **20 B3** 53.17N 9.04W
Galway *d.* Rep. of Ire. **20 B3** 53.25N 9.00W
Galway B. Rep. of Ire. **20 B3** 53.12N 9.07W
Gambia *r.* The Gambia **84 C3** 13.28N 15.55W
Gambier Is. Pacific Oc. **109 R4** 23.10S 135.00W
Gamund *mtn.* Ethiopia **87 B3** 4.08N 38.04E
Gäncä Azerbaijan **58 G2** 40.39N 46.20E
Gandadiwata, Bukit *mtn.* Indonesia **104 F3** 2.45S 119.25E
Gander Canada **63 M2** 48.58N 54.34W
Gandhidham India **96 E5** 23.07N 70.10E
Gandhinagar India **96 E5** 23.15N 72.45E
Gandía Spain **46 E3** 38.59N 0.11W
Gand-i-Zureh *des.* Afghan. **95 J4** 30.00N 62.00E
Ganges *r.* India **97 I5** 23.30N 90.25E
Ganges, Mouths of the India/Bangla. **97 H5** 22.00N 89.35E
Gannett Peak *mtn.* U.S.A. **64 E5** 43.10N 109.38W
Gansu *d.* China **103 I5** 36.00N 103.00E
Gantamaa Somalia **87 C3** 2.25N 41.49E
Ganzhou China **103 K3** 25.52N 114.51E
Gao Mali **84 E3** 16.19N 0.09W
Gaoxiong Taiwan **103 M2** 22.36N 120.17E
Gap France **44 G4** 44.33N 6.05E
Gar China **102 E4** 32.10N 80.00E
Gara, Lough Rep. of Ire. **20 C3** 53.56N 8.28W
Garanhuns Brazil **77 G4** 8.53S 36.28W
Garbahaarey Somalia **87 C3** 3.20N 42.11E
Garba Tula Kenya **87 B3** 0.31N 38.30E
Gard *r.* France **44 F3** 43.52N 4.40E
Garda, L. Italy **50 D6** 45.40N 10.40E
Gardēz Afghan. **95 K5** 33.37N 69.07E
Garelochhead Scotland **16 E4** 56.05N 4.49W
Garforth England **15 F2** 53.48N 1.22W
Gargzdai Lithuania **43 E1** 55.42N 21.21E
Garissa Kenya **87 B2** 0.27S 39.39E
Garmisch-Partenkirchen Germany **48 E2** 47.30N 11.05E
Garonne *r.* France **44 C4** 45.00N 0.37W
Garoowe Somalia **85 I2** 8.17N 48.20E
Garoua Cameroon **84 F2** 9.17N 13.22E
Garron Pt. N. Ireland **16 D3** 55.03N 5.58W
Garry *r.* Scotland **18 E2** 57.05N 4.49W
Garry, Loch Scotland **19 E1** 56.47N 4.13W
Garsen Kenya **87 A2** 2.18S 40.08E
Garstang England **14 E2** 53.53N 2.47W
Garvagh N. Ireland **16 C2** 54.59N 6.42W
Gary U.S.A. **65 I5** 41.34N 87.20W
Gascony, G. of France **44 B3** 44.00N 2.40W
Gascoyne *r.* Australia **110 A3** 25.00S 113.40E
Gashua Nigeria **84 F3** 12.53N 11.05E
Gaspé Canada **63 L2** 48.50N 64.30W
Gaspé Pen. Canada **63 L2** 48.30N 65.00W
Gastonia U.S.A. **65 J4** 35.14N 81.12W
Gata, Cabo de *c.* Spain **46 D2** 36.45N 2.11W
Gatehouse of Fleet Scotland **16 E2** 54.53N 4.12W
Gateshead England **15 F3** 54.57N 1.35W
Gävle Sweden **43 D3** 60.41N 17.10E
Gaya India **97 H5** 24.48N 85.00E
Gaya Niger **84 E3** 11.52N 3.28E
Gaza Asia **94 D5** 31.20N 34.20E
Gaza *town* Gaza **94 D5** 31.30N 34.28E
Gaziantep Turkey **57 M2** 37.04N 37.21E
Gdańsk Poland **54 F6** 54.22N 18.38E
Gdańsk, G. of Poland **54 F6** 54.45N 19.15E
Gdynia Poland **54 F6** 54.31N 18.30E
Geal Charn *mtn.* Scotland **19 F2** 57.06N 3.31W
Gebze Turkey **57 I4** 40.48N 29.26E
Gedaref Sudan **85 H3** 14.01N 35.24E
Gediz Turkey **57 I3** 39.04N 29.25E
Gediz *r.* Turkey **56 H3** 38.37N 26.47E
Gedser Odde *c.* Denmark **54 C6** 54.35N 11.57E
Geel Belgium **42 E3** 51.10N 5.00E
Geelong Australia **110 D2** 38.10S 144.26E
Gejiu China **103 I2** 23.25N 103.05E
Gela Italy **50 F2** 37.03N 14.15E
Gelderland *d.* Neth. **42 E4** 52.05N 6.00E
Gelligaer Wales **12 D3** 51.40N 3.18W
Gelsenkirchen Germany **48 C4** 51.30N 7.05E
Gemlik Turkey **57 I4** 40.26N 29.10E
Genale Wenz *r.* Ethiopia **87 C3** 4.15N 42.10E
General Santos Phil. **105 H5** 6.05N 125.15E
Geneva Switz. **44 G5** 46.13N 6.09E
Geneva, L. Switz. **44 G5** 46.30N 6.30E
Genil *r.* Spain **46 C2** 37.42N 5.20W
Genk Belgium **42 E2** 50.58N 5.34E
Genoa Italy **50 C6** 44.24N 8.54E
Genoa, G. of Italy **50 C5** 43.50N 8.55E
Gent Belgium **42 C3** 51.02N 3.42E
George *r.* Canada **63 L3** 58.30N 66.00W
Georgetown Guyana **74 D7** 6.48N 58.08W
George Town Malaysia **104 C5** 5.30N 100.16E
Georgia Asia **58 G2** 42.00N 43.30E
Georgia *d.* U.S.A. **65 J3** 33.00N 83.00W
Georgian B. Canada **63 J2** 45.15N 80.45W
Georgina *r.* Australia **110 C3** 23.12S 139.33E
Georgiyevka Kazakhstan **102 E7** 49.21N 81.35E
Gera Germany **48 F4** 50.51N 12.11E
Geral de Goiás, Serra *mts.* Brazil **77 F3** 13.00S 45.40W
Geraldton Australia **110 A3** 28.49S 114.36E
Gereshk Afghan. **95 J5** 31.48N 64.34E
Germany Europe **48 D4** 51.00N 10.00E
Gevgelija Macedonia **56 F4** 41.09N 22.30E
Gexto Spain **46 D5** 43.21N 3.01W
Geyik Dag *mtn.* Turkey **57 K2** 36.53N 32.12E
Geyve Turkey **57 J4** 40.32N 30.18E
Gezira *f.* Sudan **82 G6** 14.30N 33.00E
Ghadamis Libya **84 E5** 30.10N 9.30E
Ghaem Shahr Iran **95 H6** 36.28N 52.53E
Ghaghara *r.* India **97 G6** 25.45N 84.50E
Ghana Africa **84 D2** 8.00N 1.00W
Ghardaïa Algeria **84 E5** 32.20N 3.40E
Gharyan Libya **52 F3** 32.10N 13.01E
Ghazaouet Algeria **52 C4** 35.08N 1.50W
Ghaziabad India **97 F6** 28.40N 77.26E
Ghaznī Afghan. **95 K5** 33.33N 68.28E
Giant's Causeway *f.* N. Ireland **16 C3** 55.14N 6.31W
Gibraltar Europe **46 C2** 36.07N 5.22W
Gibraltar, Str. of Africa/Europe **46 C1** 36.00N 5.25W
Gibson Desert Australia **110 B3** 23.10S 125.35E
Gīdolē Ethiopia **87 B4** 5.38N 37.28E
Gien France **44 E5** 47.42N 2.38E
Giessen Germany **48 D4** 50.35N 8.42E
Gifu Japan **106 C3** 35.27N 136.50E
Gigha *i.* Scotland **16 D3** 55.41N 5.44W
Gijón Spain **46 C5** 43.32N 5.40W
Gila *r.* U.S.A. **64 D3** 32.45N 114.30W
Gilbert Is. Kiribati **108 M7** 1.20N 173.00E
Gilf Kebir Plateau *f.* Egypt **94 C3** 23.30N 26.00E
Gilgil Kenya **87 B2** 0.30S 36.19E
Gilgit Jammu & Kashmir **96 E8** 35.54N 74.20E
Gillette U.S.A. **64 E5** 44.18N 105.30W
Gillingham Dorset England **10 C2** 51.02N 2.17W
Gillingham Kent England **11 F2** 51.24N 0.33E
Gill, Lough Rep. of Ire. **20 C4** 54.15N 8.25W
Giluwe, Mt. P.N.G. **110 D5** 6.06S 143.54E
Gilwern Wales **12 D3** 51.51N 3.06W
Gimbala, Jebel *mtn.* Sudan **85 G3** 13.00N 24.20E
Giresun Turkey **57 N4** 40.55N 38.25E
Girona Spain **46 G4** 41.59N 2.49E
Gironde *r.* France **44 C4** 45.35N 1.00W
Girvan Scotland **16 E3** 55.15N 4.51W
Gisborne New Zealand **111 G2** 38.41S 178.02E
Gisors France **42 A1** 49.17N 1.47E
Gizhiga Russian Fed. **59 S4** 62.00N 160.34E
Gizhiga G. Russian Fed. **59 R4** 61.00N 158.00E
Gjøvik Norway **43 B3** 60.47N 10.41E
Glace Bay *town* Canada **63 M2** 46.11N 60.00W
Glacier Peak *mtn.* U.S.A. **64 B6** 48.07N 121.06W
Gladstone Australia **110 E3** 23.52S 151.16E
Glanton England **15 F4** 55.25N 1.53W
Glasgow Scotland **16 E3** 55.52N 4.15W
Glasgow U.S.A. **64 E6** 48.12N 106.37W
Glasgow City *d.* Scotland **8 C4** 55.52N 4.15W
Glass, Loch Scotland **19 E2** 57.43N 4.30W
Glastonbury England **13 E3** 51.09N 2.42W
Glenarm N. Ireland **16 D2** 54.58N 5.58W
Glen Coe *f.* Scotland **16 E4** 56.40N 4.55W
Glendale U.S.A. **64 D3** 33.32N 112.11W
Glendive U.S.A. **64 F6** 47.08N 104.42W
Glengad Head Rep. of Ire. **20 D5** 55.20N 7.11W
Glen Garry *f.* Scotland **18 D2** 57.03N 5.05W
Glengormley N. Ireland **16 D2** 54.41N 5.59W
Glenluce Scotland **16 E2** 54.53N 4.48W
Glen More *f.* Scotland **19 E2** 57.15N 4.30W
Glen Moriston *f.* Scotland **18 E2** 57.10N 4.50W
Glennallen U.S.A. **62 D4** 62.08N 145.38W
Glenrothes Scotland **17 F4** 56.12N 3.10W
Glenshee *f.* Scotland **19 F1** 56.50N 3.28W
Glinton England **11 E3** 52.39N 0.17W
Gliwice Poland **54 F4** 50.17N 18.40E
Głogów Poland **54 E4** 51.40N 16.06E
Glomfjord *town* Norway **43 C4** 66.49N 14.00E
Glorieuses, Is. Indian Oc. **86 D3** 11.34S 47.19E
Glossop England **15 F2** 53.27N 1.56W
Gloucester England **10 C2** 51.52N 2.15W
Gloucestershire *d.* England **9 D2** 51.45N 2.00W
Glusburn England **15 F2** 53.54N 2.00W
Glyder Fawr *mtn.* Wales **12 C5** 53.06N 4.01W
Glynneath Wales **12 D3** 51.45N 3.37W
Gmünd Austria **54 D3** 48.47N 14.59E
Gniezno Poland **54 E5** 52.32N 17.32E
Goa *d.* India **96 E4** 15.30N 74.00E
Goat Fell *mtn.* Scotland **16 D3** 55.37N 5.12W
Gobabis Namibia **86 A2** 22.30S 18.58E
Gobi *des.* Asia **103 I6** 43.30N 103.30E
Gobowen England **10 B3** 52.54N 3.02W
Goch Germany **42 F3** 51.41N 6.10E
Godalming England **11 E2** 51.11N 0.37W
Godavari *r.* India **97 G4** 16.40N 82.15E
Godmanchester England **11 E3** 52.19N 0.11W
Godthåb *see* **Nuuk** Greenland **63**
Goes Neth. **42 C3** 51.30N 3.54E
Goiânia Brazil **77 F3** 16.43S 49.18W
Goiás *d.* Brazil **77 E3** 15.00S 48.00W
Gökçeada *i.* Turkey **56 G4** 40.10N 25.51E
Göksun Turkey **57 M3** 38.03N 36.30E
Gölcük Turkey **57 I4** 40.44N 29.50E
Gold Coast *town* Australia **110 E3** 28.00S 153.22E
Golmud China **102 G5** 36.23N 94.49E
Golpayegan Iran **95 H5** 33.23N 50.18E
Golspie Scotland **19 F2** 57.58N 3.58W
Gómez Palacio Mexico **70 D6** 25.39N 103.30W
Gonaïves Haiti **71 J4** 19.29N 72.42W
Gonbad-e Kavus Iran **95 I6** 37.15N 55.11E
Gondar Ethiopia **85 H3** 12.39N 37.29E
Gondia India **97 G5** 21.27N 80.12E
Gongga Shan *mtn.* China **103 I3** 29.57N 101.55E
Good Hope, C. of R.S.A. **86 A1** 34.20S 18.25E
Goodwick Wales **12 C4** 52.00N 5.00W
Goole England **15 G2** 53.42N 0.52W
Goose L. U.S.A. **64 B5** 41.55N 120.25W
Gorakhpur India **97 G6** 26.45N 83.23E
Gorebridge Scotland **17 F3** 55.51N 3.02W
Gorey Rep. of Ire. **20 E2** 52.40N 6.18W
Gorgan Iran **95 H6** 36.50N 54.29E
Goris Armenia **95 G6** 39.31N 46.22E
Gorizia Italy **50 E6** 45.58N 13.37E
Görlitz Germany **48 G4** 51.09N 15.00E
Gorno-Altaysk Russian Fed. **102 F8** 51.57N 85.58E
Gornyak Russian Fed. **102 E8** 50.59N 81.30E
Gorontalo Indonesia **105 G4** 0.33N 123.05E
Gort Rep. of Ire. **20 C3** 53.03N 8.50W
Gorzów Wielkopolski Poland **54 D5** 52.42N 15.12E
Gosberton England **11 E3** 52.52N 0.09W
Gosford Australia **110 E2** 33.25S 151.18E
Gosforth Cumbria England **14 D3** 54.26N 3.27W
Gosforth T. and W. England **15 F4** 55.02N 1.35W
Goshogawara Japan **106 D4** 40.48N 140.27E
Gospić Croatia **56 B6** 44.34N 15.23E
Gosport England **10 D1** 50.48N 1.08W
Göteborg Sweden **43 B2** 57.45N 12.00E
Gotha Germany **48 E4** 50.57N 10.43E
Gotland *i.* Sweden **43 D2** 57.30N 18.30E
Göttingen Germany **48 D4** 51.32N 9.57E
Gouda Neth. **42 D4** 52.01N 4.43E
Gouin, Résr. Canada **63 K2** 48.38N 74.54W
Goulburn Australia **110 D2** 34.47S 149.43E
Gourdon France **44 D4** 44.45N 1.22E
Governador Valadares Brazil **77 F3** 18.51S 42.00W
Gower *pen.* Wales **12 C3** 51.37N 4.10W
Gowna, L. Rep. of Ire. **20 D3** 53.50N 7.34W
Goya Argentina **77 E2** 29.10S 59.20W
Gozo *i.* Malta **50 F2** 36.03N 14.16E
Graciosa *i.* Canary Is. **46 Z2** 29.15N 13.31W
Gradaús, Serra dos *mts.* Brazil **77 E4** 8.00S 50.30W
Grafham Water *l.* England **11 E3** 52.19N 0.16W
Grafton Australia **110 E3** 29.40S 152.56E
Grafton U.S.A. **64 G6** 48.28N 97.25W
Graham Land *f.* Antarctica **112** 67.00S 60.00W
Grahamstown R.S.A. **86 B1** 33.19S 26.32E
Grain England **11 F2** 51.28N 0.43E
Grampian Mts. Scotland **19 E1** 56.55N 4.00W
Granada Spain **46 D2** 37.10N 3.35W
Gran Canaria *i.* Canary Is. **46 Y1** 28.00N 15.30W
Gran Chaco *f.* S. America **75 C4** 23.30S 60.00W
Grand Bahama *i.* The Bahamas **71 I6** 26.35N 78.00W
Grand Canyon *town* U.S.A. **64 D4** 36.04N 112.07W
Grand Canyon *f.* U.S.A. **64 D4** 36.15N 113.00W
Grand Cayman *i.* Cayman Is. **71 H4** 19.20N 81.30W
Grande *r.* Bahia Brazil **77 F3** 11.05S 43.09W
Grande *r.* Minas Gerais Brazil **77 E3** 20.00S 51.00W
Grande, Bahía *b.* Argentina **75 C1** 50.45S 68.00W
Grande Prairie *town* Canada **62 G3** 55.10N 118.52W
Grand Falls *town* Canada **63 M2** 48.57N 55.40W
Grand Forks U.S.A. **64 G6** 47.57N 97.05W
Grand Island *town* U.S.A. **64 G5** 40.56N 98.21W
Grand Junction U.S.A. **64 E4** 39.04N 108.33W
Grand Manan I. Canada **65 M5** 44.40N 66.50W
Grândola Portugal **46 A3** 38.10N 8.34W
Grand Rapids *town* U.S.A. **65 I5** 42.57N 85.40W
Grangemouth Scotland **17 F4** 56.01N 3.44W
Grange-over-Sands England **14 E3** 54.12N 2.55W
Gran Paradiso *mtn.* Italy **50 B6** 45.31N 7.15E
Grantham England **10 E3** 52.55N 0.39W
Grantown-on-Spey Scotland **19 F2** 57.19N 3.38W
Grants Pass *town* U.S.A. **64 B5** 42.26N 123.20W
Grasse France **44 G3** 43.40N 6.56E
Grassington England **15 F3** 54.04N 1.59W
Grave, Pointe de *c.* France **44 C4** 45.35N 1.04W
Gravesend England **11 F2** 51.27N 0.24E
Grays England **11 F2** 51.29N 0.20E
Graz Austria **54 D2** 47.05N 15.22E
Great Abaco *i.* The Bahamas **71 I6** 26.30N 77.00W
Great Australian Bight Australia **110 B2** 33.20S 130.00E
Great Baddow England **11 F2** 51.43N 0.29E
Great Barrier Reef *f.* Australia **110 D4** 16.30S 146.30E
Great Basin *f.* U.S.A. **64 C4** 39.00N 115.30W
Great Bear L. Canada **62 G4** 66.00N 120.00W
Great Bend *town* U.S.A. **64 G4** 38.22N 98.47W
Great Bernera *i.* Scotland **18 C3** 58.13N 6.50W
Great Blasket I. Rep. of Ire. **20 A2** 52.05N 10.32W
Great Clifton England **14 D3** 54.38N 3.30W
Great Cumbrae *i.* Scotland **16 E3** 55.45N 4.57W
Great Dividing Range *mts.* Australia **110 D2** 33.00S 151.00E
Great Driffield England **15 G3** 54.01N 0.26W
Great Dunmow England **11 F2** 51.53N 0.22E
Greater Antilles *is.* C. America **71 J4** 17.00N 70.00W
Greater London *d.* England **9 E2** 51.31N 0.06W
Greater Manchester *d.* England **9 D3** 53.30N 2.18W
Great Exuma *i.* The Bahamas **71 I5** 23.00N 76.00W
Great Falls *town* U.S.A. **64 D6** 47.30N 111.16W
Great Gonerby England **10 E3** 52.56N 0.40W
Greatham England **15 F3** 54.39N 1.14W
Great Harwood England **15 E2** 53.48N 2.24W
Great Inagua *i.* The Bahamas **71 J5** 21.00N 73.20W
Great Karoo *f.* R.S.A. **86 B1** 32.50S 22.30E
Great Linford England **10 E3** 52.03N 0.46W
Great Malvern England **10 C3** 52.07N 2.19W
Great Nicobar *i.* India **104 A5** 7.00N 93.50E
Great Ormes Head Wales **12 D5** 53.20N 3.52W
Great Ouse *r.* England **11 F3** 52.47N 0.23E
Great Plains *f.* N. America **60 I6** 45.00N 100.00W
Great Rhos *mtn.* Wales **12 D4** 52.16N 3.13W
Great Rift Valley *f.* Africa **82 G4** 7.00S 33.00E
Great St. Bernard Pass Italy/Switz. **44 G4** 45.52N 7.11E
Great Salt L. U.S.A. **64 D5** 41.10N 112.40W
Great Sand Sea *f.* Egypt/Libya **94 C4** 28.00N 25.00E
Great Sandy Desert Australia **110 B3** 21.00S 125.00E
Great Shelford England **11 F3** 52.09N 0.08E
Great Slave L. Canada **62 G4** 61.30N 114.20W
Great Stour *r.* England **11 G2** 51.19N 1.15E
Great Torrington England **13 C2** 50.57N 4.09W
Great Victoria Desert Australia **110 B3** 29.00S 127.30E
Great Whernside *mtn.* England **15 F3** 54.09N 1.59W
Great Yarmouth England **11 G3** 52.36N 1.45E
Gréboun, Mt. Niger **82 D6** 19.55N 8.35E
Greco, Monte *mtn.* Italy **50 E4** 41.48N 14.00E
Gredos, Sierra de *mts.* Spain **46 C4** 40.18N 5.20W
Greece Europe **56 E3** 39.00N 22.00E
Greeley U.S.A. **64 F5** 40.26N 104.43W
Green *r.* U.S.A. **64 E4** 38.20N 109.53W
Green Bay *town* U.S.A. **65 I5** 44.32N 88.00W

Greenland N. America **63 N4** 68.00N 45.00W
Greenlaw Scotland **17 G3** 55.43N 2.28W
Greenock Scotland **16 E3** 55.57N 4.45W
Greensboro U.S.A. **65 K4** 36.03N 79.50W
Greenstone Pt. Scotland **18 D2** 57.55N 5.37W
Greenville Miss. U.S.A. **65 H3** 33.23N 91.03W
Greenwich England **11 F2** 51.29N 0.00
Greenville S.C. U.S.A. **65 J3** 34.52N 82.25W
Greifswald Germany **48 F6** 54.06N 13.24E
Grenå Denmark **43 B2** 56.25N 10.53E
Grenada C. America **71 L3** 12.15N 61.45W
Grenade France **44 D3** 43.47N 1.10E
Grenoble France **44 F4** 45.11N 5.43E
Greta *r.* England **15 F3** 54.31N 1.52W
Gretna Scotland **17 F2** 55.00N 3.04W
Grey Range *mts.* Australia **110 D3** 28.30S 142.15E
Grimsby England **15 G2** 53.35N 0.05W
Grímsey *i.* Iceland **43 Y2** 66.33N 18.00W
Grímsvötn *mtn.* Iceland **43 Y2** 64.30N 17.10W
Grodno Belarus **55 H5** 53.40N 23.50E
Grodzisk Wielkopolski Poland **54 E5** 52.14N 16.22E
Groningen Neth. **42 F5** 53.13N 6.35E
Groningen *d.* Neth. **42 F5** 53.15N 6.45E
Groote Eylandt *i.* Australia **110 C4** 14.00S 136.30E
Grosseto Italy **50 D5** 42.46N 11.08E
Gross Glockner *mtn.* Austria **54 C2** 47.05N 12.50E
Groundhog *r.* Canada **63 J3** 49.40N 82.06W
Groznyy Russian Fed. **58 G2** 43.21N 45.42E
Grudziądz Poland **54 F5** 53.29N 18.45E
Gruinard B. Scotland **18 D2** 57.52N 5.26W
Guadalajara Mexico **70 D5** 20.30N 103.20W
Guadalajara Spain **46 D4** 40.37N 3.10W
Guadalcanal *i.* Solomon Is. **111 E5** 9.30S 160.00E
Guadalete *r.* Spain **46 B2** 36.37N 6.15W
Guadalope *r.* Spain **46 E4** 41.15N 0.03W
Guadalquivir *r.* Spain **46 B2** 36.50N 6.20W
Guadalupe *i.* Mexico **64 C2** 29.00N 118.25W
Guadalupe, Sierra de *mts.* Spain **46 C3** 39.30N 5.25W
Guadarrama, Sierra de *mts.* Spain **46 D4** 41.00N 3.50W
Guadeloupe C. America **71 L4** 16.20N 61.40W
Guadiana *r.* Portugal **46 B2** 37.10N 7.36W
Guadix Spain **46 D2** 37.19N 3.08W
Guajira Pen. Colombia **71 J3** 12.00N 72.00W
Guam *i.* Pacific Oc. **105 K6** 13.30N 144.40E
Guanajuato Mexico **70 D5** 21.00N 101.16W
Guanajuato *d.* Mexico **70 D5** 21.00N 101.00W
Guanare Venezuela **71 K2** 9.04N 69.45W
Guangdong *d.* China **103 K2** 23.00N 113.00E
Guangxi Zhuangzu Zizhiqu *d.* China **103 J2** 23.50N 109.00E
Guangyuan China **103 J4** 32.29N 105.55E
Guangzhou China **103 K2** 23.20N 113.30E
Guanipa *r.* Venezuela **71 L2** 10.00N 62.20W
Guantánamo Cuba **71 I5** 20.09N 75.14W
Guaporé *r.* Brazil **76 D3** 12.00S 65.15W
Guarapuava Brazil **77 E2** 25.22S 51.28W
Guara, Sierra de *mts.* Spain **46 E5** 42.20N 0.00
Guarda Portugal **46 B4** 40.32N 7.17W
Guatemala C. America **70 F4** 15.40N 90.00W
Guatemala City Guatemala **70 F3** 14.38N 90.22W
Guaviare *r.* Colombia **74 C7** 4.00N 67.35W
Guayaquil Ecuador **76 C4** 2.13S 79.54W
Guayaquil, Golfo de *g.* Ecuador **76 B4** 2.30S 80.00W
Guaymas Mexico **70 B6** 27.59N 110.54W
Guba Ethiopia **85 H3** 11.17N 35.20E
Gubkin Russian Fed. **55 O4** 51.18N 37.32E
Gudbrandsdalen *f.* Norway **43 B3** 62.00N 9.10E
Guelma Algeria **52 E4** 36.28N 7.26E
Guelmine Morocco **84 D4** 28.56N 10.04W
Guéret France **44 D5** 46.10N 1.52E
Guernsey *i.* Channel Is. **13 Y9** 49.27N 2.35W
Guerrero *d.* Mexico **70 D4** 18.00N 100.00W
Guge *mtn.* Ethiopia **87 B4** 6.16N 37.25E
Guiana Highlands S. America **74 D7** 4.00N 59.00W
Guildford England **11 E2** 51.14N 0.35W
Guilin China **103 K3** 25.21N 110.11E
Guinea Africa **84 C3** 10.30N 10.30W
Guinea, G. of Africa **82 D5** 3.00N 3.00E
Guinea-Bissau Africa **84 C3** 12.00N 15.30W
Guînes France **42 A2** 50.52N 1.52E
Güiria Venezuela **71 L3** 10.37N 62.21W
Guisborough England **15 F3** 54.32N 1.02W
Guise France **42 C1** 49.54N 3.39E
Guiyang China **103 J3** 26.35N 106.40E
Guizhou *d.* China **103 J3** 27.00N 106.30E
Gujarat *d.* India **96 E5** 22.45N 71.30E
Gujranwala Pakistan **96 E7** 32.06N 74.11E
Gulbarga India **96 F4** 17.22N 76.47E
Gullane Scotland **17 G4** 56.02N 2.49W
Gulu Uganda **86 C5** 2.46N 32.21E
Gumdag Turkmenistan **95 H6** 39.14N 54.33E
Gümüshane Turkey **57 N4** 40.26N 39.26E
Guna India **96 F5** 24.39N 77.19E
Gunnbjørn Fjeld *mtn.* Greenland **63 P4** 68.54N 29.48W
Guntur India **97 G4** 16.20N 80.27E
Gurgueia *r.* Brazil **77 F4** 6.45S 43.35W
Gurupi *r.* Brazil **77 F4** 1.13S 46.06W
Gushgy Turkmenistan **95 J6** 35.14N 62.15E
Guwahati India **97 I6** 26.05N 91.55E
Guyana S. America **74 D7** 5.00N 59.00W
Gwadar Pakistan **96 C6** 25.09N 62.21E
Gwalior India **97 F6** 26.12N 78.09E
Gweebarra B. Rep. of Ire. **20 C4** 54.52N 8.30W
Gweru Zimbabwe **86 B3** 19.25S 29.50E
Gwynedd *d.* Wales **9 D3** 53.00N 4.00W
Gydanskiy Pen. Russian Fed. **58 J5** 70.00N 78.30E
Gyöngyös Hungary **54 F2** 47.47N 19.56E
Györ Hungary **54 E2** 47.41N 17.40E
Gypsumville Canada **62 I3** 51.47N 98.38W
Gyzylarbat Turkmenistan **95 I6** 39.00N 56.23E

H

Haapajärvi Finland **43 F3** 63.45N 25.20E
Haapsalu Estonia **43 E2** 58.58N 23.32E
Haarlem Neth. **42 D4** 52.22N 4.38E
Habaswein Kenya **87 B3** 1.06N 39.26E
Habban Yemen **95 G1** 14.21N 47.04E
Hachijo-jima *i.* Japan **106 C2** 33.00N 139.50E
Hachinohe Japan **106 D4** 40.30N 141.30E
Haddington Scotland **17 G3** 55.57N 2.47W
Haderslev Denmark **43 B1** 55.15N 9.30E
Hadhramaut *f.* Yemen **95 G2** 16.30N 49.30E
Hadleigh England **11 F3** 52.03N 0.58E
Haeābja Iraq **95 G6** 35.11N 45.59E
Haeju N. Korea **103 N5** 38.04N 125.40E
Hagadera Kenya **87 C3** 0.01N 40.21E
Hagar Nish Plateau *f.* Eritrea **94 E2** 17.00N 38.00E
Hagåtña *see* **Agana** Guam **105**
Hagen Germany **42 G3** 51.22N 7.27E
Hags Head Rep. of Ire. **20 B2** 52.56N 9.29W
Hai Tanzania **87 B2** 3.19S 37.08E
Haifa Israel **94 D5** 32.49N 34.59E
Haikou China **103 K1** 20.05N 110.25E
Hā'il Saudi Arabia **94 F4** 27.31N 41.45E
Hailar China **103 L7** 49.15N 119.41E
Hailsham England **11 F1** 50.52N 0.17E
Hainan *i.* China **103 J1** 18.30N 109.40E
Hainaut *d.* Belgium **42 C2** 50.30N 3.45E
Haines U.S.A. **62 E3** 59.11N 135.23W
Hai Phong Vietnam **104 D8** 20.58N 106.41E
Haiti C. America **71 J4** 19.00N 73.00W
Haiya Sudan **94 E2** 18.17N 36.21E
Hajmah Oman **95 I2** 19.55N 56.15E
Hakodate Japan **106 D4** 41.46N 140.44E
Halden Norway **43 B2** 59.08N 11.13E
Halesowen England **10 C3** 52.27N 2.02W
Halesworth England **11 G3** 52.21N 1.30E
Halifax Canada **63 L2** 44.38N 63.35W
Halifax England **15 F2** 53.43N 1.51W
Halkirk Scotland **19 F3** 58.30N 3.30W
Halladale *r.* Scotland **19 F3** 58.32N 3.53W
Hall Beach *town* Canada **63 J4** 68.40N 81.30W
Halle Belgium **42 D2** 50.45N 4.14E
Halle Germany **48 E4** 51.28N 11.58E
Hall Is. Fed. States of Micronesia **108 K7** 8.37N 152.00E
Hall's Creek *town* Australia **110 B4** 18.13S 127.39E
Halmahera *i.* Indonesia **105 H4** 0.45N 128.00E
Halmstad Sweden **43 C2** 56.41N 12.55E
Halstead England **11 F2** 51.57N 0.39E
Haltwhistle England **15 E3** 54.58N 2.27W
Ham France **42 C1** 49.45N 3.04E
Hamadan Iran **95 G5** 34.47N 48.33E
Ḩamāh Syria **94 E6** 35.09N 36.44E
Hamamatsu Japan **106 C2** 34.42N 137.42E
Hamar Norway **43 B3** 60.47N 10.55E
Hambleton Hills England **15 F3** 54.15N 1.11W
Hamburg Germany **48 D5** 53.33N 10.00E
Hämeenlinna Finland **43 F3** 61.00N 24.25E
Hamersley Range *mts.* Australia **110 A3** 22.00S 118.00E
Hamhung N. Korea **103 N5** 39.54N 127.35E
Hami China **102 G6** 42.40N 93.30E
Hamilton Bermuda **71 L7** 32.18N 64.48W
Hamilton Canada **65 K5** 43.15N 79.50W
Hamilton New Zealand **111 G2** 37.47S 175.17E
Hamilton Scotland **16 E3** 55.46N 4.02W
Hamim, Wadi al *r.* Libya **53 H3** 32.06N 23.58E
Hamina Finland **43 F3** 60.33N 27.15E
Hamm Germany **48 C4** 51.40N 7.49E
Hammamet, G. of Tunisia **52 F4** 36.05N 10.40E
Hammerdal Sweden **43 C3** 63.35N 15.20E
Hammerfest Norway **43 E5** 70.40N 23.44E
Hampshire *d.* England **9 E2** 51.10N 1.20W
Hampshire Downs *hills* England **10 D2** 51.18N 1.25W
Hamstreet England **11 F2** 51.03N 0.52E
Hamun-e Jaz Murian *l.* Iran **95 I4** 27.00N 59.20E
Hanamaki Japan **106 D3** 39.23N 141.07E
Handa I. Scotland **18 D3** 58.23N 5.12W
Handan China **103 K5** 36.37N 114.26E
Handeni Tanzania **87 B2** 5.26S 38.02E
Hanggin Houqi China **103 J6** 40.52N 107.04E
Hangzhou China **103 M4** 30.10N 120.07E
Hanmni Mashkel *l.* Pakistan **95 J4** 28.15N 63.00E
Hannibal U.S.A. **65 H4** 39.41N 91.25W
Hannover Germany **48 D5** 52.23N 9.44E
Hanoi Vietnam **104 D8** 21.01N 105.52E
Hantsavichy Belarus **55 J5** 52.49N 26.29E
Hanzhong China **103 J4** 33.08N 107.04E
Haparanda Sweden **43 E4** 65.50N 24.05E
Happy Valley-Goose Bay *town* Canada **63 L3** 53.16N 60.14W
Harare Zimbabwe **86 C3** 17.43S 31.05E
Harbin China **103 N7** 45.45N 126.41E
Hardangervidda *f.* Norway **43 A3** 60.20N 8.00E
Harderwijk Neth. **42 E4** 52.21N 5.37E
Haren Germany **42 G4** 52.48N 7.15E
Hargele Ethiopia **87 C4** 5.19N 42.04E
Hargeysa Somalia **85 I2** 9.31N 44.02E
Har Hu *l.* China **102 H5** 38.20N 97.40E
Hari *r.* Afghan. **95 J6** 35.42N 61.12E
Haria Canary Is. **46 Z2** 29.09N 13.30W
Harlech Wales **12 C4** 52.52N 4.08W
Harleston England **11 G3** 52.25N 1.18E
Harlingen Neth. **42 E5** 53.10N 5.25E
Harlow England **11 F2** 51.47N 0.08E
Harney Basin *f.* U.S.A. **64 C5** 43.20N 119.00W
Härnösand Sweden **43 D3** 62.37N 17.55E
Har Nuur *l.* Mongolia **102 G7** 48.10N 93.30E
Harpenden England **11 E2** 51.49N 0.22W
Harray, Loch of Scotland **19 F4** 59.03N 3.15W
Harricana *r.* Canada **63 K3** 51.10N 79.45W
Harris *i.* Scotland **18 C2** 57.50N 6.55W
Harris, Sd. of Scotland **18 B2** 57.43N 7.05W
Harrisburg U.S.A. **65 K5** 40.35N 76.59W
Harrison, C. Canada **63 M3** 55.00N 58.00W
Harrogate England **15 F2** 53.59N 1.32W
Hârsova Romania **57 H6** 44.41N 27.56E
Harstad Norway **43 D5** 68.48N 16.30E
Harteigan *mtn.* Norway **43 A3** 60.11N 7.05E
Harter Fell *mtn.* England **14 E3** 54.27N 2.51W
Hart Fell *mtn.* Scotland **17 F3** 55.25N 3.25W
Hartford U.S.A. **65 L5** 41.40N 72.51W
Hartland England **13 C2** 50.59N 4.29W
Hartland Pt. England **13 C3** 51.01N 4.32W
Hartlepool England **15 F3** 54.42N 1.11W
Hartlepool *d.* England **9 E3** 54.42N 1.11W
Har Us Nuur *l.* Mongolia **102 G7** 48.10N 92.10E
Harwich England **11 G2** 51.56N 1.18E
Haryana *d.* India **96 F6** 29.15N 76.00E
Haslemere England **10 E2** 51.05N 0.41W
Hasselt Belgium **42 E2** 50.56N 5.20E
Hassi Messaoud Algeria **84 E5** 31.43N 6.03E
Hässleholm Sweden **43 C2** 56.09N 13.45E
Hastings England **11 F1** 50.51N 0.36E
Hatfield England **15 F2** 53.36N 0.59W
Ha Tinh Vietnam **104 D7** 18.21N 105.55E
Hatteras, C. U.S.A. **65 K4** 35.14N 75.31W
Hattiesburg U.S.A. **65 I3** 31.25N 89.19W
Haud *f.* Ethiopia **85 I2** 8.00N 46.00E
Haugesund Norway **43 A2** 59.25N 5.13E
Haukivesi *l.* Finland **43 G3** 62.10N 28.30E
Haut Folin *mtn.* France **44 E5** 47.00N 4.00E
Hauts Plateaux Algeria **52 C3** 34.00N 0.10W
Havana Cuba **71 H5** 23.07N 82.25W
Havant England **10 E1** 50.51N 0.59W
Havel *r.* Germany **48 F5** 52.51N 11.57E
Haverfordwest Wales **12 C3** 51.48N 4.59W
Haverhill England **11 F3** 52.06N 0.27E
Havre U.S.A. **64 E6** 48.34N 109.45W
Havre-St.-Pierre Canada **63 L3** 50.15N 63.36W
Hawaii *i.* Hawaiian Is. **108 P8** 19.30N 155.30W
Hawaiian Is. Pacific Oc. **108 O9** 21.00N 160.00W
Hawarden Wales **12 D5** 53.11N 3.02W
Hawes England **15 E3** 54.18N 2.12W
Haweswater Resr. England **14 E3** 54.30N 2.45W
Hawick Scotland **17 G3** 55.25N 2.47W
Hawke B. New Zealand **111 G2** 39.18S 177.15E
Hawkhurst England **11 F2** 51.02N 0.31E
Hawthorne U.S.A. **64 C4** 38.13N 118.37W
Haxby England **15 F3** 54.02N 1.06W
Hay Australia **110 D2** 34.21S 144.31E
Hay *r.* Canada **62 G3** 60.49N 115.52W
Haydarabad Iran **94 G6** 37.09N 45.27E
Haydon Bridge England **15 E3** 54.58N 2.14W
Hayle England **13 B2** 50.12N 5.25W
Hay-on-Wye Wales **12 D4** 52.04N 3.09W
Hay River *town* Canada **62 G4** 60.51N 115.42W
Haywards Heath *town* England **11 E1** 51.00N 0.05W
Hazarajat *f.* Afghan. **95 K5** 33.00N 66.00E
Hazebrouck France **42 B2** 50.43N 2.32E
Heacham England **11 F3** 52.55N 0.30E
Headcorn England **11 F2** 51.11N 0.37E
Heanor England **15 F2** 53.01N 1.20W
Heathfield England **11 F1** 50.58N 0.13E
Hebei *d.* China **103 L5** 39.20N 117.15E
Hebron Jordan **94 E5** 31.32N 35.06E
Hecate Str. Canada **62 E3** 53.00N 131.00W
Hechi China **103 J2** 24.42N 108.02E
Heckington England **15 G1** 52.59N 0.18W
Hede Sweden **43 C3** 62.27N 13.30E
Heerenveen Neth. **42 E4** 52.57N 5.55E
Heerlen Neth. **42 E2** 50.53N 5.59E
Hefei China **103 L4** 31.55N 117.18E
Hegang China **103 O7** 47.36N 130.30E
Heidelberg Germany **48 D3** 49.25N 8.42E
Heighington England **15 G2** 53.12N 0.28W
Heilbronn Germany **48 D3** 49.08N 9.14E
Heilongjiang *d.* China **103 N7** 47.00N 126.00E
Heinola Finland **43 F3** 61.13N 26.05E
Hekla *mtn.* Iceland **43 Y2** 64.00N 19.45W
Helena U.S.A. **64 D6** 46.35N 112.00W
Helensburgh Scotland **16 E4** 56.01N 4.44W
Heligoland B. Germany **48 D6** 54.00N 8.15E
Hellín Spain **46 E3** 38.31N 1.43W
Helmand *r.* Asia **95 J5** 31.10N 61.20E
Helmond Neth. **42 E3** 51.28N 5.40E
Helmsdale Scotland **19 F3** 58.08N 3.40W
Helmsdale *r.* Scotland **19 F3** 58.06N 3.40W
Helmsley England **15 F3** 54.14N 1.04W
Helong China **106 A4** 42.38N 128.58E
Helsingborg Sweden **43 C2** 56.05N 12.45E
Helsingør Denmark **43 C2** 56.03N 12.38E
Helsinki Finland **43 F3** 60.08N 25.00E
Helston England **13 B2** 50.07N 5.17W
Helvellyn *mtn.* England **14 D3** 54.31N 3.00W
Hemel Hempstead England **11 E2** 51.46N 0.28W
Henan *d.* China **103 K4** 33.45N 113.00E
Henares *r.* Spain **46 D4** 40.26N 3.35W
Henderson I. Pacific Oc. **109 S4** 24.20S 128.20W
Hendon England **11 E2** 51.35N 0.14W
Henfield England **11 E1** 50.56N 0.17W
Hengelo Neth. **42 F4** 52.16N 6.46E
Hengoed Wales **12 D3** 51.39N 3.14W
Hengyang China **103 K3** 26.58N 112.31E
Heniches'k Ukraine **55 N2** 46.10N 34.49E
Henley-on-Thames England **10 E2** 51.32N 0.53W
Hennef Germany **42 G2** 50.47N 7.17E
Henrietta Maria, C. Canada **63 J3** 55.00N 82.15W
Henzada Myanmar **97 J4** 17.38N 95.35E
Herat Afghan. **95 J5** 34.21N 62.10E
Hereford England **10 C3** 52.04N 2.43W
Herefordshire *d.* England **9 D3** 52.04N 2.43W
Herm *i.* Channel Is. **13 Y9** 49.28N 2.27W
Herma Ness *c.* Scotland **19 Z9** 60.50N 0.54W
Hermosillo Mexico **70 B6** 29.15N 110.59W
Herne Germany **42 G3** 51.32N 7.12E
Herne Bay *town* England **11 G2** 51.23N 1.10E
Herning Denmark **43 B2** 56.08N 9.00E
Hertford England **11 E2** 51.48N 0.05W
Hertfordshire *d.* England **9 E2** 51.51N 0.05W
Heswall England **14 D2** 53.20N 3.06W
Hetton England **15 E3** 54.01N 2.05W
Hexham England **15 E3** 54.58N 2.06W
Heysham England **14 E3** 54.03N 2.53W
Heywood England **15 E2** 53.36N 2.13W
Hidaka-sammyaku *mts.* Japan **106 D4** 42.50N 143.00E
Hidalgo *d.* Mexico **70 E5** 20.50N 98.30W
Hidalgo del Parral Mexico **70 C6** 26.58N 105.40W
Higashi-suido *str.* Japan **106 A2** 34.00N 129.30E
Higham Ferrers England **11 E3** 52.18N 0.36W
High Atlas *mts.* Morocco **84 D5** 32.00N 5.50W
Highbridge England **13 E3** 51.13N 2.59W
Highclere England **10 D2** 51.22N 1.22W
Highland *d.* Scotland **8 C5** 57.42N 5.00W
High Peak *mtn.* England **15 F2** 53.22N 1.48W
High Seat *hill* England **15 E3** 54.23N 2.18W
Highworth England **10 D2** 51.38N 1.42W
High Wycombe England **10 E2** 51.38N 0.46W
Hiiumaa *i.* Estonia **43 E2** 58.50N 22.30E
Hijaz *f.* Saudi Arabia **94 E4** 26.00N 37.30E
Hildesheim Germany **48 D5** 52.09N 9.58E
Hillerød Denmark **43 C1** 55.56N 12.18E
Hillside Scotland **19 G1** 56.45N 2.29W
Hilpsford Pt. England **14 D3** 54.02N 3.10W
Hilversum Neth. **42 E4** 52.14N 5.12E
Himachal Pradesh *d.* India **96 F7** 31.45N 77.30E
Himalaya *mts.* Asia **97 G6** 29.00N 84.00E
Hinckley England **10 D3** 52.33N 1.21W
Hinderwell England **15 G3** 54.32N 0.46W
Hindhead England **10 E2** 51.06N 0.42W
Hindley England **14 E2** 53.32N 2.35W
Hindu Kush *mts.* Asia **95 K6** 36.40N 70.00E
Hinnøya *i.* Norway **43 C5** 68.30N 16.00E
Hiraman *r.* Kenya **87 B2** 1.05S 39.55E
Hirosaki Japan **106 D4** 40.34N 140.28E
Hiroshima Japan **106 B2** 34.30N 132.27E
Hirson France **42 D1** 49.56N 4.05E
Hirwaun Wales **12 D3** 51.43N 3.30W
Hispaniola *i.* C. America **71 J5** 20.00N 71.00W
Hitachi Japan **106 D3** 36.35N 140.40E
Hitchin England **11 E2** 51.57N 0.16W
Hitra *i.* Norway **43 B3** 63.30N 8.50E
Hiva Oa *i.* Marquesas Is. **109 R5** 9.45S 139.00W
Hjälmaren *l.* Sweden **43 C2** 59.10N 15.45E
Hjørring Denmark **43 B2** 57.28N 9.59E
Hlybokaye Belarus **55 J6** 55.07N 27.42E
Hobart Australia **110 D1** 42.54S 147.18E
Hobro Denmark **43 B2** 56.38N 9.48E
Hô Chi Minh City Vietnam **104 D6** 10.46N 106.43E
Hoddesdon England **11 E2** 51.46N 0.01W
Hodeida Yemen **94 F1** 14.50N 42.58E
Hodnet England **10 C3** 52.51N 2.35W
Hoek van Holland Neth. **42 D3** 51.59N 4.08E
Hof Germany **48 E4** 50.19N 11.56E
Höfn Iceland **43 Z2** 64.16N 15.10W
Hofsjökull *mtn.* Iceland **43 Y2** 64.50N 19.00W
Hofuf Saudi Arabia **95 G4** 25.20N 49.34E
Hoggar *mts.* Algeria **84 E4** 24.00N 5.50E
Hohhot China **103 K6** 40.49N 111.37E
Hokkaido *i.* Japan **106 D4** 43.00N 144.00E
Holbæk Denmark **43 B1** 55.42N 11.41E
Holbeach England **11 F3** 52.48N 0.01E
Holbeach Marsh England **11 F3** 52.50N 0.05E
Holbrook U.S.A. **64 E3** 34.58N 110.00W
Holderness *f.* England **15 G2** 53.45N 0.05W
Holguín Cuba **71 I5** 20.54N 76.15W
Hollabrunn Austria **54 E3** 48.34N 16.05E
Holland Fen *f.* England **15 G2** 53.02N 0.12W
Hollesley B. England **11 G3** 52.02N 1.33E
Hollington England **11 F1** 50.51N 0.32E
Hollingworth England **15 F2** 53.28N 1.59W
Holme-on-Spalding-Moor England **15 G2** 53.50N 0.47W
Holmfirth England **15 F2** 53.34N 1.48W
Holon Israel **94 D5** 32.01N 34.46E
Holstebro Denmark **43 B2** 56.22N 8.38E
Holsworthy England **13 C2** 50.48N 4.21W
Holt England **11 G3** 52.55N 1.04E
Holyhead Wales **12 C5** 53.18N 4.38W
Holyhead B. Wales **12 C5** 53.22N 4.40W
Holy I. England **15 F4** 55.41N 1.47W
Holy I. Wales **12 C5** 53.15N 4.38W
Holywell Wales **12 D5** 53.17N 3.13W
Homa Bay *town* Kenya **87 A2** 0.32S 34.27E
Homayunshahr Iran **95 H5** 32.42N 51.28E
Homburg Germany **42 G1** 49.19N 7.20E
Home B. Canada **63 L4** 69.00N 66.00W
Homs Syria **94 E5** 34.44N 36.43E
Homyel Belarus **55 L5** 52.25N 31.00E
Hondo *r.* Mexico **70 G4** 18.33N 88.22W
Honduras C. America **70 G4** 15.00N 87.00W
Honduras, G. of Carib. Sea **60 K3** 16.20N 87.30W
Hönefoss Norway **43 B3** 60.10N 10.16E
Hong Kong China **103 K2** 22.30N 114.10E
Honiara Solomon Is. **111 E5** 9.27S 159.57E
Honiton England **13 D2** 50.48N 3.13W
Honley England **15 F2** 53.34N 1.46W
Honolulu Hawaiian Is. **108 P9** 21.19N 157.50W
Honshu *i.* Japan **106 C3** 36.00N 138.00E
Hood, Mt. U.S.A. **64 B6** 45.23N 121.41W
Hood Pt. Australia **110 A2** 34.23S 119.34E
Hoogeveen Neth. **42 F4** 52.44N 6.29E
Hook England **10 E2** 51.17N 0.55W
Hook Head Rep. of Ire. **20 E2** 52.07N 6.55W
Hooper Bay *town* U.S.A. **62 B4** 61.29N 166.10W
Hoorn Neth. **42 E4** 52.38N 5.03E
Hopedale Canada **63 L3** 55.30N 60.10W
Hope, Loch Scotland **19 E3** 58.27N 4.38W
Hope, Pt. U.S.A. **59 V4** 68.00N 167.00W
Horley England **11 E2** 51.11N 0.11W
Horlivka Ukraine **55 P3** 48.17N 38.05E
Hormuz, Str. of Asia **95 I4** 26.35N 56.20E
Horn *c.* Iceland **43 X2** 66.28N 22.27W
Horn, C. S. America **75 C1** 55.47S 67.00W
Hornavan *l.* Sweden **43 D4** 66.15N 17.40E
Horncastle England **15 G2** 53.13N 0.08W
Hornepayne Canada **65 J6** 49.14N 84.48W
Hornsea England **15 G2** 53.55N 0.10W
Horodnya Ukraine **55 L4** 51.54N 31.37E
Horodok Ukraine **55 H3** 49.48N 23.39E
Horrabridge England **13 C2** 50.30N 4.05W
Horsens Denmark **43 B1** 55.53N 9.53E
Horsham Australia **110 D2** 36.45S 142.15E
Horsham England **11 E2** 51.04N 0.20W
Horten Norway **43 B2** 59.25N 10.30E
Horwich England **14 E2** 53.37N 2.33W
Hospitalet de Llobregat Spain **46 G4** 41.20N 2.06E
Hotan China **102 E5** 37.07N 79.57E
Houffalize Belgium **42 E2** 50.08N 5.50E
Houghton-le-Spring England **15 F3** 54.51N 1.28W
Houghton Regis England **11 E2** 51.51N 0.30W
Hourn, Loch Scotland **18 D2** 57.05N 5.35W
Houston U.S.A. **65 G2** 29.45N 95.25W
Hovd Mongolia **102 G7** 48.00N 91.45E
Hove England **11 E1** 50.50N 0.10W
Hoveton England **11 G3** 52.45N 1.23E
Howden England **15 G2** 53.45N 0.52W
Howland I. Pacific Oc. **108 N7** 0.48N 176.38W
Hoy *i.* Scotland **19 F3** 58.51N 3.17W
Hoyanger Norway **43 A3** 61.13N 6.05E
Hoyerswerda Germany **48 G4** 51.26N 14.14E
Höysgöl Nuur *l.* Mongolia **103 I8** 51.00N 100.30E
Hradec Králové Czech Rep. **54 D4** 50.13N 15.50E
Huacho Peru **76 C3** 11.05S 77.36W
Huaibei China **103 L4** 33.58N 116.50E
Huainan China **103 L4** 32.41N 117.06E
Huallaga *r.* Peru **76 C4** 5.05S 75.36W
Huambo Angola **86 A3** 12.47S 15.44E
Huancayo Peru **76 C3** 12.15S 75.12W
Huang He *r.* China **103 L5** 37.55N 118.46E
Huangshi China **103 L4** 30.13N 115.05E
Huascaran *mtn.* Peru **74 B6** 9.20S 77.36W
Hubei *d.* China **103 K4** 31.15N 112.15E
Hubli India **96 E4** 15.20N 75.14E
Hucknall England **15 F2** 53.03N 1.12W
Huddersfield England **15 F2** 53.38N 1.49W
Hudiksvall Sweden **43 D3** 61.45N 17.10E
Hudson *r.* U.S.A. **65 L5** 40.45N 74.00W
Hudson B. Canada **63 J3** 58.00N 86.00W

Kotzebue U.S.A. 62 B4 66.51N 162.40W
Kouvola Finland 43 F3 60.54N 26.45E
Kowloon China 103 K2 22.30N 114.10E
Kovel' Ukraine 55 I4 51.12N 24.48E
Kozan Turkey 57 L2 37.27N 35.47E
Kozani Greece 56 E4 40.18N 21.48E
Kozhikode India 96 F3 11.15N 75.45E
Krabi Thailand 104 B5 8.04N 98.52E
Krâcheh Cambodia 104 D6 12.30N 106.03E
Kragujevac Yugo. 56 E6 44.01N 20.55E
Kraków Poland 54 F4 50.03N 19.55E
Kraljevo Yugo. 56 E5 43.44N 20.41E
Kramators'k Ukraine 55 O3 48.43N 37.33E
Kramfors Sweden 43 D3 62.55N 17.50E
Kranj Slovenia 54 D2 46.15N 14.21E
Krasnoarmiys'k Ukraine 55 O3 48.17N 37.14E
Krasnodar Russian Fed. 58 F2 45.02N 39.00E
Krasnodar Resr. Russian Fed. 57 N6 45.00N 39.15E
Krasnohrad Ukraine 55 N3 49.22N 35.28E
Krasnokamensk Russian Fed. 59 N3 50.10N 118.00E
Krasnovodsk Turkmenistan 58 H2 40.01N 53.00E
Krasnoyarsk Russian Fed. 59 L3 56.05N 92.46E
Krefeld Germany 48 C4 51.20N 6.32E
Kremenchuk Ukraine 55 M3 49.03N 33.25E
Kremenchuk Resr. Ukraine 55 M3 49.20N 32.30E
Krishna r. India 97 G4 16.00N 81.00E
Kristiansand Norway 43 A2 58.08N 7.59E
Kristianstad Sweden 43 C2 56.02N 14.10E
Kristiansund Norway 43 A3 63.15N 7.55E
Kristinehamn Sweden 43 C2 59.17N 14.09E
Krk i. Croatia 56 B6 45.04N 14.36E
Kropotkin Russian Fed. 53 L6 45.25N 40.35E
Krosno Poland 54 G3 49.42N 21.46E
Kruševac Yugo. 56 E5 43.34N 21.20E
Krychaw Belarus 55 L5 53.40N 31.44E
Krymsk Russian Fed. 57 M6 44.56N 38.00E
Kryvyy Rih' Ukraine 55 M2 47.55N 33.24E
Ksar El Boukhari Algeria 52 D4 35.53N 2.45E
Ksar el Kebir Morocco 52 B3 35.01N 5.54W
Kuala Lumpur Malaysia 104 C4 3.08N 101.42E
Kuala Terengganu Malaysia 104 C5 5.10N 103.10E
Kuantan Malaysia 104 C4 3.50N 103.19E
Kuban r. Russian Fed. 57 M6 45.20N 37.17E
Kuching Malaysia 104 E4 1.32N 110.20E
Kugluktuk Canada 62 G4 67.49N 115.12W
Kuh-e Baba Afghan. 95 K5 34.40N 67.30E
Kuh-e Dinar mtn. Iran 95 H5 30.45N 51.39E
Kuh-e Sahand mtn. Iran 95 G6 37.37N 46.27E
Kuhmo Finland 43 G4 64.04N 29.30E
Kuito Angola 86 A3 12.25S 16.58E
Kūl r. Iran 95 I4 27.00N 55.45E
Kulal, Mt. Kenya 87 B3 2.44N 36.56E
Kuldīga Latvia 43 E2 56.58N 21.59E
Kŭlob Tajikistan 95 K6 37.55N 69.47E
Kulunda Russian Fed. 102 D8 52.34N 78.58E
Kumamoto Japan 106 B2 32.50N 130.42E
Kumanovo Macedonia 56 E5 42.08N 21.40E
Kumasi Ghana 84 D2 6.45N 1.35W
Kumbakonam India 97 F3 10.59N 79.24E
Kumi Uganda 87 A3 1.26N 33.54E
Kumla Sweden 43 C2 59.08N 15.09E
Kumluca Turkey 57 J2 36.23N 30.17E
Kumo Nigeria 84 F3 10.02N 11.50E
Kunashir i. Russian Fed. 106 E4 44.25N 146.00E
Kungrad Uzbekistan 58 H2 43.05N 58.23E
Kunlun Shan mts. China 102 E5 36.40N 85.00E
Kunming China 103 I3 25.04N 102.41E
Kuohijärvi l. Finland 43 F3 61.20N 24.10E
Kuopio Finland 43 F3 62.51N 27.30E
Kupa r. Croatia 56 C6 45.30N 16.20E
Kupang Indonesia 105 G1 10.13S 123.38E
Kup"yans'k Ukraine 55 O3 49.41N 37.37E
Kuqa China 102 E6 41.43N 82.58E
Kŭrdzhali Bulgaria 56 G4 41.39N 25.22E
Kure Atoll Hawaiian Is. 108 N9 28.25N 178.25W
Kuressaare Estonia 43 E2 58.12N 22.30E
Kurgan Russian Fed. 58 I3 55.20N 65.20E
Kuria Muria Is. Oman 95 I2 17.30N 56.00E
Kurikka Finland 43 E3 62.37N 22.25E
Kuril Is. Russian Fed. 59 R2 46.00N 150.30E
Kuril Trench f. Pacific Oc. 117 Q8
Kurmuk Sudan 85 H3 10.33N 34.17E
Kurnool India 97 F4 15.51N 78.01E
Kursk Russian Fed. 55 O4 51.45N 36.14E
Kuršumlija Yugo. 56 E5 43.09N 21.16E
Kurume Japan 106 B2 33.20N 130.29E
Kurun r. Sudan 87 A4 5.40N 33.50E
Kurunegala Sri Lanka 97 G2 7.28N 80.23E
Kushiro Japan 106 D4 42.58N 144.24E
Kuskokwim r. U.S.A. 62 B4 60.50N 161.20W
Kuskokwim B. U.S.A. 62 B3 59.45N 162.25W
Kuskokwim Mts. U.S.A. 62 C4 62.50N 156.00W
Kustanay Kazakhstan 58 I3 53.15N 63.40E
Kütahya Turkey 57 I3 39.25N 29.56E
Kuujjuaq Canada 63 L3 58.10N 68.15W
Kuusamo Finland 43 G4 65.57N 29.15E
Kuwait Asia 95 G4 29.20N 47.40E
Kuwait town Kuwait 95 G4 29.20N 48.00E
Kuznetsk Russian Fed. 58 G3 53.08N 46.36E
Kvaløya i. Norway 43 D5 69.45N 18.20E
Kwale Kenya 87 B2 4.10S 39.27E
KwaMashu R.S.A. 86 C2 29.45S 30.56E
Kwa Mtoro Tanzania 87 B1 5.14S 35.22E
Kwangju S. Korea 103 N5 35.07N 126.52E
Kwania, L. Uganda 87 A3 1.48N 32.45E
Kwanobuhle R.S.A. 86 B1 33.30S 25.26E
Kwilu r. Dem. Rep. of Congo 86 A4 3.18S 17.22E
Kwoka mtn. Indonesia 105 I3 1.30S 132.30E
Kyakhta Russian Fed. 103 J8 50.22N 106.30E
Kyle of Durness est. Scotland 18 E3 58.32N 4.50W
Kyle of Lochalsh town Scotland 18 D2 57.17N 5.43W
Kyle of Tongue est. Scotland 19 E3 58.27N 4.26W
Kyllini mtn. Greece 56 F2 37.56N 22.22E
Kyoga, L. Uganda 86 C5 1.30N 33.00E
Kyoto Japan 106 C2 35.04N 135.50E
Kyparissia Greece 56 E2 37.15N 21.40E
Kyrgyzstan Asia 102 C6 41.30N 75.00E
Kythira i. Greece 56 F2 36.15N 23.00E
Kythnos i. Greece 56 G2 37.25N 24.25E
Kyushu i. Japan 106 B2 32.00N 131.00E
Kyustendil Bulgaria 56 F5 42.18N 22.39E
Kyzyl Russian Fed. 59 L3 51.42N 94.28E
Kzyl-Orda Kazakhstan 58 J2 44.52N 65.28E

L

Laâyoune W. Sahara 84 C4 27.10N 13.11W
La Banda Argentina 75 C5 27.44S 64.14W
Labé Guinea 84 C3 11.17N 12.11W
Labrador f. Canada 63 L3 54.00N 61.30W
Labrador City Canada 63 L3 52.54N 66.50W
Labrador Sea Canada/Greenland 63 M4 60.00N 55.00W
Laccadive Is. Indian Oc. 96 E3 11.00N 72.00E
Laceby England 15 G2 53.33N 0.10W
La Chaux-de-Fonds Switz. 44 G5 47.07N 6.51E
Lachlan r. Australia 110 D2 34.21S 143.58E
La Crosse U.S.A. 65 H5 43.48N 91.15W
La Demanda, Sierra de mts. Spain 46 D5 42.10N 3.20W
Ladhar Bheinn mtn. Scotland 18 D2 57.04N 5.35W
Ladiz Iran 95 J4 28.57N 61.18E
Ladoga, L. Russian Fed. 58 F4 61.00N 32.00E
Ladybank Scotland 17 F4 56.17N 3.08W
Ladybower Resr. England 15 F2 53.23N 1.42W
Lae P.N.G. 110 D5 6.45S 146.30E
Læso i. Denmark 43 B2 57.16N 11.01E
Lafayette U.S.A. 65 H3 30.12N 92.18W
Lagan r. N. Ireland 16 D2 54.37N 5.54W
Laggan, Loch Scotland 19 E1 56.57N 4.30W
Lagh Bogal r. Kenya 87 B3 1.04N 40.10E
Lagh Bor r. Kenya/Somalia 87 C3 0.30N 42.04E
Lagh Dima r. Kenya/Somalia 87 C3 0.30N 41.09E
Lagh Kutulu r. Kenya 87 C3 2.10N 40.53E
Laghouat Algeria 52 D3 33.49N 2.55E
Lagh Walde Kenya 87 B3 2.48N 38.54E
La Gomera i. Canary Is. 46 X2 28.08N 17.14W
Lagos Nigeria 84 E2 6.27N 3.28E
Lagos Portugal 46 A2 37.05N 8.40W
La Grande 2, Résr de Canada 63 K3 53.35N 77.10W
La Grande 3, Résr de Canada 63 K3 53.35N 74.55W
La Grande 4, Résr de Canada 63 K3 53.50N 73.30W
La Gran Sabana f. Venezuela 71 L2 5.20N 61.30W
Lahad Datu Malaysia 104 F5 5.05N 118.20E
Lahat Indonesia 104 C3 3.46S 103.32E
Laḥij Yemen 94 F1 13.04N 44.53E
Lahore Pakistan 96 E7 31.34N 74.22E
Lahti Finland 43 F3 61.00N 25.40E
Laidon, Loch Scotland 16 E4 56.39N 4.38W
Laihia Finland 43 E3 62.58N 22.01E
Lainio r. Sweden 43 E4 67.26N 22.37E
Lairg Scotland 19 E3 58.01N 4.25W
Laisamis Kenya 87 B3 1.38N 37.47E
Lajes Brazil 77 E2 27.48S 50.20W
La Junta U.S.A. 64 F4 37.59N 103.34W
Lake City U.S.A. 65 J3 30.05N 82.40W
Lake District f. England 14 D3 54.30N 3.10W
Lakeland town U.S.A. 65 J2 28.02N 81.59W
Lakeview U.S.A. 64 B5 42.13N 120.21W
Lakki Pakistan 95 L5 32.35N 70.58E
Lakonia, G. of Greece 56 F2 36.35N 22.42E
Laksefjorden est. Norway 43 F5 70.40N 26.50E
Lakshadweep d. India 96 E3 11.00N 72.00E
La Línea de la Concepción Spain 46 C2 36.10N 5.21W
La Louvière Belgium 42 D2 50.29N 4.11E
La Mancha f. Spain 46 D3 39.00N 2.30W
Lamar U.S.A. 64 F4 38.04N 102.37W
Lamard Iran 95 H4 27.22N 53.20E
Lambay I. Rep. of Ire. 20 E3 53.30N 6.01W
Lambourn England 10 D2 51.31N 1.31W
Lambourn Downs hills England 10 D2 51.32N 1.36W
Lamego Portugal 46 B4 41.05N 7.49W
Lamia Greece 56 F3 38.53N 22.25E
Lamlash Scotland 16 D3 55.32N 5.08W
Lammermuir Hills Scotland 17 G3 55.51N 2.40W
Lampang Thailand 104 B7 18.16N 99.30E
Lampeter Wales 12 C4 52.06N 4.06W
Lamu Kenya 87 A2 2.20S 40.54E
Lamu I. Kenya 87 A2 2.17S 40.52E
La Nao, Cabo de c. Spain 46 F3 38.42N 0.15E
Lanark Scotland 17 F3 55.41N 3.47W
Lancashire d. England 9 D3 53.53N 2.30W
Lancaster England 14 E3 54.03N 2.48W
Lancaster Canal England 14 E2 54.00N 2.48W
Lancaster Sd. Canada 63 J5 74.00N 85.00W
Landes f. France 44 C4 44.40N 0.40W
Landguard Pt. England 11 G2 51.55N 1.18E
Land's End c. England 13 B2 50.03N 5.45W
Landshut Germany 48 F3 48.31N 12.10E
Lanesborough Rep. of Ire. 20 D3 53.40N 8.00W
Langavat, Loch Scotland 18 C2 57.48N 6.58W
Langavat, Loch Scotland 18 C3 58.04N 6.45W
Langeland i. Denmark 43 B1 54.50N 10.50E
Langholm Scotland 17 F3 55.09N 3.00W
Langøya i. Norway 43 C5 68.50N 15.00E
Langport England 13 E3 51.02N 2.51W
Langres France 44 F5 47.53N 5.20E
Langsa Indonesia 104 B4 4.28N 97.59E
Langstrothdale Chase hills England 15 E3 54.13N 2.15W
Languedoc f. France 44 E3 43.30N 3.00E
Lanivet England 13 C2 50.27N 4.45W
Länkäran Azerbaijan 95 G6 38.45N 48.50E
Lannion France 44 B6 48.44N 3.27W
Lansing U.S.A. 65 J5 42.44N 84.34W
Lanzarote i. Canary Is. 46 Z2 29.00N 13.55W
Lanzhou China 103 I5 36.01N 103.45E
Laoag Phil. 104 G7 18.14N 120.36E
Lao Cai Vietnam 104 C8 22.30N 104.00E
Laois d. Rep. of Ire. 20 D2 53.00N 7.20W
Laon France 42 C1 49.34N 3.37E
Laos Asia 104 C7 19.00N 104.00E
La Palma i. Canary Is. 46 X2 28.50N 18.00W
La Palma del Condado Spain 46 B2 37.23N 6.33W
La Paz Bolivia 76 D3 16.30S 68.10W
La Paz Mexico 70 B5 24.10N 110.17W
La Perouse Str. Russian Fed. 106 D5 45.50N 142.30E
La Plata Argentina 75 D3 34.52S 57.55W
La Plata, Río de est. S. America 75 D3 35.15S 56.45W
Lappajärvi l. Finland 43 E3 63.05N 23.30E
Lappeenranta Finland 43 G3 61.04N 28.05E
Lappland f. Sweden/Finland 43 E5 68.10N 24.00E
Laptev Sea Russian Fed. 59 O5 74.30N 125.00E
Lapua Finland 43 E3 62.57N 23.00E
L'Aquila Italy 50 E5 42.22N 13.25E
Larache Morocco 46 B1 35.12N 6.10W
Laramie U.S.A. 64 E5 41.20N 105.38W
Laredo U.S.A. 64 G2 27.32N 99.22W
Largs Scotland 16 E3 55.48N 4.52W
La Rioja Argentina 76 D2 29.26S 66.50W
Larisa Greece 56 F3 39.36N 22.24E
Larkana Pakistan 96 D6 27.32N 68.18E
Larnaca Cyprus 57 K1 34.54N 33.39E
Larne N. Ireland 16 D2 54.51N 5.50W
Larne Lough N. Ireland 16 D2 54.50N 5.47W
La Rochelle France 44 C5 46.10N 1.10W
La Roche-sur-Yon France 44 C5 46.40N 1.25W
La Romana Dom. Rep. 71 K4 18.27N 68.57W
La Ronge Canada 62 H3 55.07N 105.18W
Larvik Norway 43 B2 59.04N 10.02E
La Sagra mtn. Spain 46 D2 37.58N 2.35W
Las Cruces U.S.A. 64 E3 32.18N 106.47W
La Seine, Baie de France 44 C6 49.40N 0.30W
La Selle mtn. Haiti 71 J4 18.23N 71.59W
La Serena Chile 76 C2 29.54S 71.16W
Las Marismas f. Spain 46 B2 37.05N 6.20W
Las Nieves, Pico de mtn. Canary Is. 46 Y1 27.56N 15.34W
Las Palmas de Gran Canaria Canary Is. 46 Y2 28.08N 15.27W
La Spezia Italy 50 C6 44.07N 9.49E
Las Vegas U.S.A. 64 C4 36.10N 115.10W
Latacunga Ecuador 76 C4 0.58S 78.36W
Latakia Syria 94 E6 35.31N 35.47E
Latheron Scotland 19 F3 58.17N 3.22W
Latina Italy 50 E4 41.28N 12.52E
La Tortuga i. Venezuela 71 K3 11.00N 65.20W
Latvia Europe 43 E2 57.00N 25.00E
Launceston Australia 110 D1 41.25S 147.07E
Launceston England 13 C2 50.38N 4.21W
Laurencekirk Scotland 19 G1 56.50N 2.30W
Lausanne Switz. 44 G5 46.32N 6.39E
Laut i. Indonesia 104 F3 3.45S 116.20E
Laval France 44 C6 48.04N 0.45W
Lavenham England 11 F3 52.06N 0.47E
Lawdar Yemen 95 G1 13.53N 45.53E
Laxey I.o.M. 14 C3 54.14N 4.24W
Laxford, Loch Scotland 18 D3 58.25N 5.06W
Laysan I. Hawaiian Is. 108 N9 25.46N 171.44W
Leane, L. Rep. of Ire. 20 B2 52.03N 9.33W
Leatherhead England 11 E2 51.18N 0.20W
Lebanon Asia 94 E5 34.00N 36.00E
Lębork Poland 54 E6 54.33N 17.44E
Lecce Italy 50 H4 40.21N 18.11E
Lech r. Germany 48 E3 48.45N 10.51E
Lechlade England 10 D2 51.42N 1.40W
Ledbury England 10 C3 52.03N 2.25W
Lee r. Rep. of Ire. 20 C1 51.53N 8.25W
Leech L. U.S.A. 65 H6 47.10N 94.30W
Leeds England 15 F2 53.48N 1.34W
Leek England 15 E2 53.07N 2.02W
Leeming England 15 F3 54.18N 1.33W
Lee Moor town England 13 C2 50.25N 4.01W
Leer Germany 48 C5 53.14N 7.27E
Leeuwarden Neth. 42 E5 53.12N 5.48E
Leeuwin, C. Australia 110 A2 34.00S 115.00E
Leeward Is. C. America 71 L4 18.00N 61.00W
Lefkada i. Greece 56 E3 38.44N 20.37E
Legaspi Phil. 105 G6 13.10N 123.45E
Legnica Poland 54 E4 51.12N 16.10E
Leh Jammu & Kashmir 97 F7 34.09N 77.35E
Le Havre France 44 D6 49.30N 0.06E
Leiah Pakistan 95 L5 30.58N 70.56E
Leicester England 10 D3 52.39N 1.09W
Leicestershire d. England 9 E3 52.30N 1.00W
Leichhardt r. Australia 110 C4 17.35S 139.48E
Leiden Neth. 42 D4 52.10N 4.30E
Leigh England 15 E2 53.30N 2.33W
Leighton Buzzard England 10 E2 51.55N 0.39W
Leinster, Mt. Rep. of Ire. 20 E2 52.37N 6.47W
Leipzig Germany 48 F4 51.20N 12.20E
Leiston England 11 G3 52.13N 1.35E
Leith Scotland 17 F3 55.59N 2.09W
Leith Hill England 11 E2 51.11N 0.21W
Leitrim d. Rep. of Ire. 20 D4 54.08N 8.00W
Leixlip Rep. of Ire. 20 E3 53.22N 6.30W
Leizhou Pen. China 103 J2 20.40N 109.30E
Lek r. Neth. 42 D3 51.55N 4.29E
Leksozero, Ozero l. Russian Fed. 43 G3 63.40N 30.52E
Lelystad Neth. 42 E4 52.32N 5.29E
Le Mans France 44 D5 48.01N 0.10E
Lena r. Russian Fed. 59 O5 72.00N 127.10E
Leninsk-Kuznetskiy Russian Fed. 58 K3 54.44N 86.13E
Lens France 44 E7 50.26N 2.50E
Leoben Austria 54 D2 47.23N 15.06E
Leominster England 10 C3 52.15N 2.43W
León Mexico 70 D5 21.10N 101.42W
León Spain 46 C5 42.35N 5.34W
Leova Moldova 55 K2 46.29N 28.12E
Le-Puy-en-Velay France 44 E4 45.03N 3.54E
Lerum Sweden 43 C2 57.46N 12.12E
Lerwick Scotland 19 Y9 60.09N 1.09W
Lesatima mtn. Kenya 87 B2 0.17S 36.37E
Les Cayes Haiti 71 J4 18.15N 73.46W
Leshan China 103 I3 29.34N 103.42E
Leskovac Yugo. 56 E5 43.00N 21.56E
Lesotho Africa 86 B2 29.30S 28.00E
Les Sables-d'Olonne France 44 C5 46.30N 1.47W
Lesser Antilles is. C. America 71 K3 13.00N 67.00W
Lesser Slave L. Canada 62 G3 55.30N 115.00W
Lestijärvi l. Finland 43 F3 63.32N 24.40E
Lesvos i. Greece 56 G3 39.10N 26.16E
Leszno Poland 54 E4 51.51N 16.35E
Letchworth England 11 E2 51.58N 0.13W
Lethbridge Canada 62 G2 49.43N 112.48W
Leti Is. Indonesia 105 H2 8.20S 128.00E
Le Touquet-Paris-Plage France 42 A2 50.31N 1.36E
Letterkenny Rep. of Ire. 20 D4 54.56N 7.45W
Leuchars Scotland 17 G4 56.23N 2.53W
Leuser, Gunung mtn. Indonesia 104 B4 3.50N 97.10E
Leuven Belgium 42 D2 50.53N 4.45E
Leven England 15 G2 53.54N 0.18W
Leven Scotland 17 G4 56.12N 3.00W
Leven, Loch A. and B. Scotland 18 D1 56.43N 5.05W
Leven, Loch P. and K. Scotland 17 F4 56.13N 3.23W
Levens England 14 E3 54.16N 2.47W
Leverkusen Germany 48 C4 51.02N 6.59E
Lévis Canada 65 L6 46.47N 71.12W
Lewes England 11 F1 50.53N 0.02E
Lewis i. Scotland 18 C3 58.10N 6.40W
Lexington U.S.A. 65 J4 38.02N 84.30W
Leyburn England 15 F3 54.19N 1.50W
Leyland England 14 E2 53.41N 2.42W
Leyte i. Phil. 105 G6 10.40N 124.50E
L'gov Russian Fed. 55 N4 51.41N 35.16E
Lhasa China 102 G3 29.41N 91.10E
Lhazê China 102 F3 29.08N 87.43E
Lhokseumawe Indonesia 104 B5 5.09N 97.09E
Lianyungang China 103 L4 34.37N 119.10E
Liaoning d. China 103 M6 41.30N 123.00E
Liaoyuan China 103 M6 42.53N 125.10E
Liard r. Canada 62 F4 61.56N 120.35W
Libenge Dem. Rep. of Congo 86 A5 3.39N 18.39E
Liberal U.S.A. 64 F4 37.03N 100.56W
Liberec Czech Rep. 54 D4 50.48N 15.05E
Liberia Africa 84 D2 6.30N 9.30W
Libin Belgium 42 E1 49.58N 5.15E
Liboi Kenya 87 C3 0.23N 40.50E
Libourne France 44 C4 44.55N 0.14W
Libreville Gabon 84 E2 0.30N 9.25E
Libya Africa 84 F4 26.30N 17.00E
Libyan Desert Africa 85 G4 23.00N 26.10E
Libyan Plateau f. Africa 94 C5 30.45N 26.00E
Lichfield England 10 D3 52.40N 1.50W
Lichinga Mozambique 86 C3 13.19S 35.13E
Lida Belarus 55 I5 53.50N 25.19E
Liddel r. England/Scotland 17 G3 55.04N 2.57W
Lidköping Sweden 43 C2 58.30N 13.10E
Liechtenstein Europe 44 H5 47.08N 9.35E
Liège Belgium 42 E2 50.38N 5.35E
Liège d. Belgium 42 E2 50.32N 5.35E
Lieksa Finland 43 G3 63.13N 30.01E
Lienz Austria 54 C2 46.50N 12.47E
Liepaja Latvia 43 E2 56.30N 21.00E
Liévin France 42 B2 50.27N 2.49E
Liffey r. Rep. of Ire. 20 E3 53.21N 6.14W
Lifford Rep. of Ire. 20 D4 54.50N 7.29W
Ligurian Sea Med. Sea 50 C5 43.10N 9.00E
Likasi Dem. Rep. of Congo 86 B3 10.58S 26.47E
Lilla Edet Sweden 43 C2 58.10N 12.25E
Lille Belgium 42 D3 51.14N 4.50E
Lille France 44 E7 50.39N 3.05E
Lillehammer Norway 43 B3 61.06N 10.27E
Lilleshall England 10 C3 52.44N 2.24W
Lillestrøm Norway 43 B2 59.58N 11.05E
Lilongwe Malawi 86 C3 13.58S 33.49E
Lima Peru 76 C3 12.06S 77.03W
Limassol Cyprus 57 K1 34.40N 33.03E
Limavady N. Ireland 16 C3 55.03N 6.57W
Limburg d. Belgium 42 E3 51.00N 5.30E
Limburg d. Neth. 42 E3 51.15N 5.45E
Limeira Brazil 77 F2 22.34S 47.25W
Limerick Rep. of Ire. 20 C2 52.40N 8.37W
Limerick d. Rep. of Ire. 20 C2 52.30N 8.37W
Limingen l. Norway 43 C4 64.50N 13.40E
Limnos i. Greece 56 G3 39.55N 25.14E
Limoges France 44 D4 45.50N 1.15E
Limousin f. France 44 D4 45.30N 1.30E
Limoux France 44 E3 43.04N 2.14E
Limpopo r. Mozambique 86 C2 25.14S 33.33E
Linares Spain 46 D3 38.05N 3.38W
Lincoln England 15 G2 53.14N 0.32W
Lincoln U.S.A. 64 G5 40.49N 96.41W
Lincolnshire d. England 9 E3 53.10N 0.32W
Lincolnshire Wolds hills England 15 G2 53.22N 0.08W
Lindesnes c. Norway 43 A2 58.00N 7.05E
Lindfield England 11 E2 51.01N 0.05W
Lindi Tanzania 86 C4 10.00S 39.41E
Lindos Greece 57 I2 36.05N 28.05E
Line Is. Pacific Oc. 108 P6 3.00S 155.00W
Linfen China 103 K5 36.07N 111.34E
Lingen Germany 48 C5 52.32N 7.19E
Lingfield England 11 E2 51.11N 0.01W
Linhares Brazil 77 F3 19.22S 40.04W
Linköping Sweden 43 C2 58.25N 15.35E
Linkou China 106 B5 45.18N 130.17E
Linlithgow Scotland 17 F3 55.58N 3.36W
Linney Head Wales 12 B3 51.37N 5.05W
Linnhe, Loch Scotland 16 D4 56.35N 5.25W
Linosa i. Italy 50 E1 35.52N 12.50E
Linxia China 103 I5 35.31N 103.08E
Linz Austria 54 D3 48.19N 14.18E
Lions, G. of France 44 F3 43.00N 4.15E
Lipari Is. Italy 50 F3 38.35N 14.45E
Lipetsk Russian Fed. 55 P5 52.37N 39.36E
Liphook England 10 E2 51.05N 0.49W
Lipova Romania 54 G2 46.05N 21.40E
Lippe r. Germany 48 C4 51.38N 6.37E
Lisala Dem. Rep. of Congo 86 B5 2.08N 21.37E
Lisbon Portugal 46 A3 38.44N 9.08W
Lisburn N. Ireland 16 C2 54.31N 6.03W
Liscannor B. Rep. of Ire. 20 B2 52.55N 9.25W
Liskeard England 13 C2 50.27N 4.29W
Lismore Australia 110 E3 28.48S 153.17E
Lismore Rep. of Ire. 20 D2 52.08N 7.59W
Lisnaskea N. Ireland 16 B2 54.15N 7.28W
Liss England 10 E2 51.03N 0.53W
Listowel Rep. of Ire. 20 B2 52.27N 9.30W
Lithuania Europe 55 H6 55.00N 24.00E
Little Andaman i. India 97 I3 10.50N 92.38E
Littleborough England 15 E2 53.39N 2.05W
Little Cayman i. Cayman Is. 71 H4 19.40N 80.00W
Little Dart r. England 13 D2 50.54N 3.53W
Little Falls town U.S.A. 65 H6 45.59N 94.21W
Littlehampton England 11 E1 50.48N 0.32W
Little Inagua i. The Bahamas 71 J5 21.30N 73.00W
Little Karoo f. R.S.A. 86 B1 33.40S 21.40E
Little Minch str. Scotland 18 C2 57.40N 6.45W
Little Ouse r. England 11 F3 52.34N 0.20E
Littleport England 11 F3 52.27N 0.18E
Little Rock town U.S.A. 65 H3 34.42N 92.17W
Liupanshui China 103 I3 26.50N 104.45E
Liuzhou China 103 J2 24.17N 109.15E
Līvāni Latvia 55 J7 56.20N 26.12E
Liverpool England 14 E2 53.25N 3.00W
Livingston Scotland 17 F3 55.54N 3.31W
Livingstone Zambia 86 B3 17.50S 25.53E
Livny Russian Fed. 55 O5 52.25N 37.35E
Livorno Italy 50 D5 43.33N 10.18E
Lizard England 13 B1 49.58N 5.12W
Lizard Pt. England 13 B1 49.57N 5.15W
Ljubljana Slovenia 54 D2 46.04N 14.28E
Ljungan r. Sweden 43 D3 62.20N 17.19E
Ljungby Sweden 43 C2 56.49N 13.55E
Ljusdal Sweden 43 D3 61.49N 16.09E
Llanarth Wales 12 C4 52.12N 4.18W
Llanbadarn Fawr Wales 12 C4 52.24N 4.05W
Llanberis Wales 12 C5 53.07N 4.07W

Puttalam Sri Lanka **97 F2** 8.02N 79.50E
Putumayo *r.* Brazil **76 D4** 3.00S 67.30W
Puvurnituq Canada **63 K3** 60.10N 77.20W
Puy de Dôme *mtn.* France **44 E4** 45.46N 2.56E
Pwllheli Wales **12 C4** 52.53N 4.25W
Pyaozero, Ozero Russian Fed. **43 G4** 66.00N 31.00E
Pyapon Myanmar **97 J4** 16.15N 95.40E
Pyasina *r.* Russian Fed. **59 K5** 73.10N 84.55E
Pyè Myanmar **97 J4** 18.50N 95.14E
Pyhä *r.* Finland **43 F4** 64.30N 24.20E
Pyhäselkä *l.* Finland **43 G3** 62.25N 29.55E
Pyinmana Myanmar **97 J4** 19.45N 96.12E
Pyle Wales **13 D3** 51.32N 3.42W
Pyongyang N. Korea **103 N5** 39.00N 125.47E
Pyramid L. U.S.A. **64 C5** 40.00N 119.35W
Pyrenees *mts.* France/Spain **46 F5** 42.40N 0.30E
Pyrgos Greece **56 E2** 37.42N 21.27E
Pyryatyn Ukraine **55 M4** 50.14N 32.31E

Q

Qaanaaq Greenland **63 L5** 77.30N 69.29W
Qalat Afghan. **95 K5** 32.07N 66.54E
Qamanittuaq *see* **Baker Lake** Canada **63**
Qamdo China **102 H4** 31.11N 97.18E
Qasigiannguit Greenland **63 M4** 68.50N 51.00W
Qatar Asia **95 H4** 25.20N 51.10E
Qattâra Depression *f.* Egypt **94 C4** 30.00N 27.30E
Qayen Iran **95 I5** 33.44N 59.07E
Qazvīn Iran **95 G6** 36.16N 50.00E
Qena Egypt **94 D4** 26.08N 32.42E
Qeshm Iran **95 J4** 26.58N 56.17E
Qiemo China **102 F5** 38.08N 85.33E
Qilian Shan *mts.* China **102 H5** 38.30N 99.20E
Qingdao China **103 M5** 36.04N 120.22E
Qinghai *d.* China **102 H5** 36.15N 96.00E
Qinghai Hu *l.* China **103 I5** 36.40N 100.00E
Qingjiang China **103 L4** 33.30N 119.15E
Qinhuangdao China **103 L5** 39.55N 119.37E
Qinzhou China **103 J2** 21.58N 108.34E
Qiqihar China **103 M7** 47.23N 124.00E
Qom Iran **95 H5** 34.40N 50.57E
Qomishēh Iran **95 H5** 32.01N 51.55E
Quang Ngai Vietnam **104 D7** 15.09N 108.50E
Quang Tri Vietnam **104 D7** 16.46N 107.11E
Quantock Hills England **13 D3** 51.06N 3.12W
Quanzhou China **103 L2** 24.57N 118.36E
Quchan Iran **95 I6** 37.04N 58.29E
Québec Canada **63 K2** 46.50N 71.15W
Québec *d.* Canada **63 K3** 51.00N 70.00W
Queenborough England **11 F2** 51.24N 0.46E
Queen Charlotte Is. Canada **62 E3** 53.00N 132.30W
Queen Charlotte Sd. Canada **62 F3** 51.00N 129.00W
Queen Elizabeth Is. Canada **63 I5** 78.30N 99.00W
Queen Mary Land Antarctica **112** 72.00S 100.00E
Queen Maud G. Canada **62 H4** 68.30N 100.00W
Queen Maud Land *f.* Antarctica **112** 74.00S 20.00E
Queensland *d.* Australia **110 D3** 23.30S 144.00E
Quelimane Mozambique **86 C3** 17.53S 36.51E
Querétaro Mexico **70 D5** 20.38N 100.23W
Querétaro *d.* Mexico **70 D5** 21.03N 100.00W
Quetta Pakistan **96 D7** 30.15N 67.00E
Quezaltenango Guatemala **70 F3** 14.50N 91.30W
Quezon City Phil. **104 G6** 14.39N 121.01E
Quibdó Colombia **71 I2** 5.40N 76.38W
Quilon India **96 F2** 8.53N 76.38E
Quimper France **44 A5** 48.00N 4.06W
Quincy U.S.A. **65 H4** 39.55N 91.22W
Qui Nhon Vietnam **104 D6** 13.47N 109.11E
Quintana Roo *d.* Mexico **70 G4** 19.00N 88.00W
Quito Ecuador **76 C4** 0.14S 78.30W
Quoich, Loch Scotland **18 D2** 57.04N 5.15W
Quoile *r.* N. Ireland **16 D2** 54.20N 5.42W
Quseir Egypt **94 D4** 26.04N 34.15E
Quzhou China **103 L3** 28.57N 118.52E

R

Raahe Finland **43 F4** 64.42N 24.30E
Raalte Neth. **42 F4** 52.22N 6.17E
Raasay *i.* Scotland **18 C2** 57.25N 6.02W
Raasay, Sd. of Scotland **18 C2** 57.25N 6.05W
Raas Kaambooni *c.* Somalia **87 C2** 1.36S 41.36E
Raba Indonesia **104 F2** 8.27S 118.45E
Rabat Morocco **84 D5** 34.02N 6.51W
Rabigh Saudi Arabia **94 E3** 22.48N 39.01E
Rach Gia Vietnam **104 D6** 10.02N 105.05E
Radom Poland **54 G4** 51.26N 21.10E
Radomsko Poland **54 F4** 51.05N 19.25E
Radstock England **10 C2** 51.17N 2.25W
Rafḥa Saudi Arabia **94 F4** 29.36N 43.32E
Rafsanjan Iran **95 I5** 30.24N 56.00E
Raglan Wales **12 E3** 51.46N 2.51W
Ragusa Italy **50 F2** 36.56N 14.44E
Rahimyar Khan Pakistan **96 E6** 28.25N 70.18E
Raichur India **96 F4** 16.15N 77.20E
Rainier, Mt. U.S.A. **64 B6** 46.52N 121.45W
Raipur India **97 G5** 21.16N 81.42E
Raivavae *i.* Pacific Oc. **109 Q4** 23.52S 147.40W
Rajahmundry India **97 G4** 17.01N 81.52E
Rajanpur Pakistan **96 E6** 29.06N 70.19E
Rajapalaiyam India **96 F2** 9.26N 77.36E
Rajasthan *d.* India **96 E6** 27.00N 74.00E
Rajkot India **96 E5** 22.18N 70.53E
Rakhiv Ukraine **55 I3** 48.02N 24.10E
Rakitnoye Russian Fed. **55 N4** 50.52N 35.51E
Rakvere Estonia **43 F2** 59.22N 26.28E
Raleigh U.S.A. **65 K4** 35.46N 78.39W
Rame Head England **13 C2** 50.18N 4.13W
Ramhormoz Iran **95 G5** 31.14N 49.37E
Ramlat Dahm *f.* Yemen **94 F2** 17.00N 45.00E
Râmnica Vâlcea Romania **56 G6** 45.06N 24.22E
Ramsbottom England **15 E2** 53.38N 2.20W
Ramsey England **11 E3** 52.27N 0.06W
Ramsey I.o.M. **14 C3** 54.19N 4.23W
Ramsey B. I.o.M. **14 C3** 54.20N 4.20W
Ramsey I. Wales **12 B3** 51.53N 5.21W
Ramsgate England **11 G2** 51.20N 1.25E
Ramu Kenya **87 C3** 3.55N 41.09E
Rancagua Chile **75 B3** 34.10S 70.45W
Ranchi India **97 H5** 23.22N 85.20E
Randalstown N. Ireland **16 C2** 54.45N 6.20W
Randers Denmark **43 B2** 56.28N 10.03E
Rangiroa *i.* Pacific Oc. **109 Q5** 15.00S 147.40W
Rangpur Bangla. **97 H6** 25.45N 89.15E
Rankin Inlet *town* Canada **63 I4** 62.52N 92.00W
Rannoch, Loch Scotland **19 E1** 56.41N 4.20W
Rannoch Moor *f.* Scotland **16 E4** 56.38N 4.40W
Ranong Thailand **104 B5** 9.58N 98.35E
Rantauprapat Indonesia **104 B4** 2.05N 99.46E
Raoul *i.* Pacific Oc. **108 N4** 29.15S 177.55W
Rapa *i.* Pacific Oc. **109 Q4** 27.35S 144.20W
Rapallo Italy **50 C6** 44.20N 9.14E
Raphoe Rep. of Ire. **16 B2** 54.52N 7.36W
Rapid City U.S.A. **64 F5** 44.06N 103.14W
Rarotonga *i.* Cook Is. **108 P4** 21.14S 159.46W
Ra's al Hadd *c.* Oman **95 I3** 22.32N 59.49E
Ra's al Hilal *c.* Libya **53 H3** 33.00N 22.10E
Ras Dashan *mtn.* Ethiopia **85 H3** 13.20N 38.10E
Ra's Fartak *c.* Yemen **95 H2** 15.38N 52.15E
Rasht Iran **95 G6** 37.18N 49.38E
Ra's Madrakah *c.* Oman **95 I2** 19.00N 57.50E
Ras Muhammad *c.* Egypt **53 J2** 27.42N 34.13E
Ras Tannurah Saudi Arabia **95 H4** 26.40N 50.05E
Rat Buri Thailand **104 B6** 13.30N 99.50E
Rathdrum Rep. of Ire. **20 E2** 52.55N 6.14W
Rathenow Germany **48 F5** 52.37N 12.21E
Rathfriland N. Ireland **16 C2** 54.14N 6.10W
Rathkeale Rep. of Ire. **20 C2** 52.32N 8.56W
Rathlin I. N. Ireland **16 C3** 55.18N 6.12W
Rath Luirc Rep. of Ire. **20 C2** 52.20N 8.40W
Raton U.S.A. **64 F4** 36.54N 104.27W
Rattray Head Scotland **19 H2** 57.37N 1.50W
Rättvik Sweden **43 C3** 60.56N 15.10E
Rauma Finland **43 E3** 61.09N 21.30E
Raunds England **11 E3** 52.21N 0.33W
Ravenna Italy **50 E6** 44.25N 12.12E
Ravensthorpe Australia **110 B2** 33.35S 120.02E
Rawaki *i.* Kiribati **108 N6** 3.43S 170.43W
Rawalpindi Pakistan **96 E7** 33.40N 73.08E
Rawicz Poland **54 E4** 51.37N 16.52E
Rawlins U.S.A. **64 E5** 41.46N 107.16W
Rawson Argentina **75 C2** 43.15S 65.53W
Rawtenstall England **15 E2** 53.42N 2.18W
Rayleigh England **11 F2** 51.36N 0.36E
Razgrad Bulgaria **56 H5** 43.32N 26.30E
Reading England **10 E2** 51.27N 0.57W
Reading *d.* England **9 E2** 51.27N 0.57W
Rebiana Sand Sea *f.* Libya **94 B3** 24.00N 22.00E
Reboly Russian Fed. **43 G3** 63.50N 30.49E
Rechytsa Belarus **55 L5** 52.21N 30.24E
Recife Brazil **77 G4** 8.06S 34.53W
Reconquista Argentina **77 E2** 29.08S 59.38W
Red *r.* U.S.A. **65 H3** 31.10N 91.35W
Red Bluff U.S.A. **64 B5** 40.11N 122.16W
Redcar England **15 F3** 54.37N 1.04W
Redcar and Cleveland *d.* England **9 E4** 54.35N 1.00W
Red Deer Canada **62 G3** 52.15N 113.48W
Redding U.S.A. **64 B5** 40.35N 122.24W
Redditch England **10 D3** 52.18N 1.57W
Redhill England **11 E2** 51.14N 0.11W
Red Lake *town* Canada **63 I3** 50.59N 93.40W
Red Lakes U.S.A. **65 H6** 48.00N 95.00W
Redruth England **13 B2** 50.14N 5.14W
Red Sea Africa/Asia **85 H4** 20.00N 39.00E
Red Wharf B. Wales **12 C5** 53.20N 4.10W
Ree, Lough Rep. of Ire. **20 D3** 53.31N 7.58W
Regensburg Germany **48 F3** 49.01N 12.07E
Reggane Algeria **84 E4** 26.30N 0.30E
Reggio Italy **50 D6** 44.40N 10.37E
Reggio di Calabria Italy **50 F3** 38.07N 15.38E
Regina Canada **62 H3** 50.30N 104.38W
Reigate England **11 E2** 51.14N 0.13W
Ré, Ile de *i.* France **44 C5** 46.10N 1.26W
Reims France **44 F6** 49.15N 4.02E
Reindeer L. Canada **62 H3** 57.00N 102.20W
Reinosa Spain **46 C5** 43.01N 4.09W
Reliance Canada **62 H4** 62.45N 109.08W
Relizane Algeria **52 D4** 35.45N 0.33E
Rena Norway **43 B3** 61.06N 11.20E
Renfrewshire *d.* Scotland **8 C4** 55.50N 4.30W
Reni Moldova **55 K1** 45.28N 28.17E
Rennell *i.* Solomon Is. **111 F4** 11.45S 160.00E
Rennes France **44 C6** 48.06N 1.40W
Reno U.S.A. **64 C4** 39.32N 119.49W
Reno *r.* Italy **50 E6** 44.36N 12.17E
Republic of Ireland Europe **20 D3** 53.00N 8.00W
Republic of South Africa Africa **86 B1** 30.00S 27.00E
Repulse Bay *town* Canada **63 J4** 66.35N 86.20W
Resistencia Argentina **77 E2** 27.28S 59.00W
Reşiţa Romania **56 E6** 45.17N 21.53E
Resolute Bay *town* Canada **63 I5** 74.40N 95.00W
Resolution I. Canada **63 L4** 61.30N 65.00W
Retford England **15 G2** 53.19N 0.55W
Rethel France **42 D1** 49.31N 4.22E
Rethymno Greece **56 G1** 35.22N 24.29E
Réunion *i.* Indian Oc. **117 L4** 20.00S 55.00E
Reus Spain **46 F4** 41.10N 1.06E
Reutlingen Germany **48 D3** 48.30N 9.13E
Revillagigedo Is. Mexico **70 B4** 19.00N 111.00W
Rewa India **97 G5** 24.32N 81.18E
Reykjavík Iceland **43 X2** 64.09N 21.58W
Reynosa Mexico **70 E6** 26.09N 97.10W
Rezekne Latvia **43 F2** 56.30N 27.22E
Rhayader Wales **12 D4** 52.19N 3.30W
Rheine Germany **42 G4** 52.17N 7.26E
Rhine *r.* Europe **34 D3** 51.53N 6.03E
Rhode Island *d.* U.S.A. **65 L5** 41.30N 71.30W
Rhodes *i.* Greece **57 I2** 36.12N 28.00E
Rhodope Mts. Bulgaria **56 G4** 41.35N 24.35E
Rhondda Wales **12 D3** 51.39N 3.30W
Rhondda Cynon Taff *d.* Wales **9 D2** 51.38N 3.25W
Rhône *r.* France **44 F3** 43.25N 4.45E
Rhosllanerchrugog Wales **12 D5** 53.03N 3.04W
Rhyl Wales **12 D5** 53.19N 3.29W
Riau Is. Indonesia **104 C4** 0.50N 104.00E
Ribble *r.* England **14 E2** 53.45N 2.44W
Ribe Denmark **43 B1** 55.19N 8.47E
Ribeira *r.* Brazil **77 F2** 24.44S 47.31W
Ribeirão Prêto Brazil **77 F2** 21.09S 47.48W
Riberalta Bolivia **76 D3** 10.59S 66.06W
Richmond England **15 F3** 54.24N 1.43W
Richmond U.S.A. **65 K4** 37.34N 77.27W
Rifstangi *c.* Iceland **43 Y2** 66.32N 16.10W
Rift Valley *f.* Kenya **87 B3** 2.00N 35.30E
Rift Valley *d.* Kenya **87 B2** 1.05N 35.45E
Riga Latvia **43 F2** 56.53N 24.08E
Riga, G. of Latvia **43 E2** 57.30N 23.50E
Rigside Scotland **17 F3** 55.35N 3.46W
Riihimäki Finland **43 F3** 60.45N 24.45E
Rijeka Croatia **56 B6** 45.20N 14.25E
Rimini Italy **50 E6** 44.01N 12.34E
Rimouski Canada **63 L2** 48.27N 68.32W
Rimsdale, Loch Scotland **19 E3** 58.18N 4.10W
Ringkøbing Denmark **43 B2** 56.06N 8.15E
Ringsted Denmark **54 B6** 55.27N 11.49E
Ringvassøy *i.* Norway **43 D5** 70.00N 19.00E
Ringwood England **10 D1** 50.50N 1.48W
Riobamba Ecuador **76 C4** 1.44S 78.40W
Rio Branco Brazil **76 D3** 10.00S 67.49W
Río Cuarto *town* Argentina **75 C3** 33.08S 64.20W
Rio de Janeiro Brazil **77 F2** 22.50S 43.17W
Rio de Janeiro *d.* Brazil **77 F2** 22.00S 42.30W
Río Gallegos Argentina **75 C1** 51.35S 69.15W
Rio Grande *town* Brazil **77 E1** 32.03S 52.18W
Rio Grande *r.* N. America **64 G2** 25.55N 97.08W
Río Grande *r.* Nicaragua **71 H3** 12.48N 83.30W
Rio Grande do Norte *d.* Brazil **77 G4** 6.00S 36.30W
Rio Grande do Sul *d.* Brazil **77 E2** 30.00S 53.30W
Ríohacha Colombia **71 J3** 11.34N 72.58W
Rio Verde *town* Brazil **77 E3** 17.50S 50.55W
Ripley England **15 F2** 53.03N 1.24W
Ripon England **15 F3** 54.08N 1.31W
Risca Wales **12 D3** 51.36N 3.06W
Rivera Uruguay **77 E1** 30.54S 55.31W
Rivière-du-Loup *town* Canada **63 L2** 47.50N 69.32W
Rivne Ukraine **55 J4** 50.39N 26.10E
Riyadh Saudi Arabia **95 G3** 24.39N 46.44E
Rize Turkey **57 O4** 41.03N 40.31E
Roadford Resr. England **13 C2** 50.42N 4.14W
Roanne France **44 F5** 46.02N 4.05E
Roanoke U.S.A. **65 K4** 37.15N 79.58W
Roanoke *r.* U.S.A. **65 K4** 36.00N 76.35W
Robertsfors Sweden **43 E4** 64.12N 20.50E
Roberval Canada **63 K2** 48.31N 72.16W
Roca, Cabo da *c.* Portugal **46 A3** 38.40N 9.31W
Rocha Uruguay **75 D3** 34.30S 54.22W
Rochdale England **15 E2** 53.36N 2.10W
Rochefort Belgium **42 E2** 50.10N 5.13E
Rochefort France **44 C4** 45.57N 0.58W
Rochester England **11 F2** 51.22N 0.30E
Rochester U.S.A. **65 K5** 43.12N 77.37W
Rochford England **11 F2** 51.36N 0.43E
Rockford U.S.A. **65 I5** 42.16N 89.06W
Rockhampton Australia **110 E3** 23.22S 150.32E
Rockingham Forest *f.* England **11 E3** 52.30N 0.30W
Rock Springs U.S.A. **64 E5** 41.35N 109.13W
Rocky Mts. N. America **60 I6** 42.30N 109.30W
Rodel Scotland **18 C2** 57.47N 6.58W
Rodez France **44 E4** 44.21N 2.34E
Rodos *town* Greece **57 I2** 36.24N 28.15E
Roe *r.* N. Ireland **16 C3** 55.06N 7.00W
Roermond Neth. **42 E3** 51.12N 6.00E
Roeselare Belgium **42 C2** 50.57N 3.06E
Rogaguado, Lago *l.* Bolivia **76 D3** 13.00S 65.40W
Rokiškis Lithuania **43 F1** 55.59N 25.32E
Rolla U.S.A. **65 H4** 37.56N 91.55W
Roma *i.* Indonesia **105 H2** 7.45S 127.20E
Romain, C. U.S.A. **65 K3** 33.01N 79.23W
Romania Europe **53 H6** 46.30N 24.00E
Rombas France **42 F1** 49.15N 6.10E
Rome Italy **50 E4** 41.54N 12.29E
Romford England **11 F2** 51.35N 0.11E
Romney Marsh *f.* England **11 F2** 51.03N 0.55E
Romny Ukraine **55 M4** 50.45N 33.30E
Romsey England **10 D1** 51.00N 1.29W
Rona *i.* Scotland **18 D2** 57.33N 5.59W
Ronas Hill Scotland **19 Y9** 60.32N 1.26W
Ronda Spain **46 C2** 36.45N 5.10W
Rondônia *d.* Brazil **76 D3** 12.10S 62.30W
Rondonópolis Brazil **77 E3** 16.29S 54.37W
Rønne Denmark **43 C1** 55.07N 14.43E
Ronneby Sweden **54 D6** 56.12N 15.18E
Ronse Belgium **42 C2** 50.45N 3.36E
Roosendaal Neth. **42 D3** 51.32N 4.28E
Roosevelt I. Antarctica **112** 79.00S 161.00W
Roosevelt, Mt. Canada **62 F3** 58.26N 125.20W
Roquefort France **44 C4** 44.02N 0.19W
Roraima *d.* Brazil **77 D5** 2.00N 62.00W
Roraima, Mt. Guyana **74 C7** 5.11N 60.44W
Røros Norway **43 B3** 62.35N 11.23E
Rosa, Monte *mtn.* Italy/Switz. **44 G4** 45.56N 7.51E
Rosario Argentina **75 C3** 33.00S 60.40W
Roscoff France **44 A6** 48.44N 4.00W
Roscommon Rep. of Ire. **20 C3** 53.38N 8.13W
Roscommon *d.* Rep. of Ire. **20 C3** 53.38N 8.11W
Roscrea Rep. of Ire. **20 D2** 52.57N 7.49W
Roseau Dominica **71 L4** 15.18N 61.23W
Roseburg U.S.A. **64 B5** 43.13N 123.21W
Rosenheim Germany **48 F2** 47.51N 12.09E
Roskilde Denmark **54 C6** 55.39N 12.05E
Roslavl' Russian Fed. **55 M5** 53.55N 32.53E
Rossel I. P.N.G. **110 E4** 11.27S 154.05E
Ross Ice Shelf Antarctica **112** 82.00S 170.00W
Rossington England **15 F2** 53.29N 1.01W
Rosslare Harbour Rep. of Ire. **20 E2** 52.17N 6.23W
Rosso Mauritania **84 C3** 16.29N 15.53W
Ross of Mull *pen.* Scotland **16 C4** 56.19N 6.10W
Ross-on-Wye England **10 C2** 51.55N 2.36W
Ross Sea Antarctica **112** 73.00S 170.00W
Røssvatnet *l.* Norway **43 C4** 65.50N 14.00E
Rostock Germany **48 F6** 54.06N 12.09E
Rostov-na-Donu Russian Fed. **58 F2** 47.15N 39.45E
Rota *i.* N. Mariana Is. **105 L6** 14.10N 145.15E
Rothbury England **15 F4** 55.19N 1.54W
Rother *r.* England **11 E1** 50.57N 0.32W
Rotherham England **15 F2** 53.26N 1.21W
Rothes Scotland **19 F2** 57.31N 3.14W
Rothesay Scotland **16 D3** 55.50N 5.03W
Rothwell England **10 E3** 52.25N 0.48W
Roti *i.* Indonesia **105 G1** 10.30S 123.10E
Rotterdam Neth. **42 D3** 51.55N 4.29E
Rotuma *i.* Fiji **111 G4** 11.00S 176.00E
Roubaix France **44 E7** 50.42N 3.10E
Rouen France **44 D6** 49.26N 1.05E
Round Hill England **15 F3** 54.24N 1.03W
Round Mt. Australia **110 E2** 30.26S 152.15E
Rousay *i.* Scotland **19 F4** 59.10N 3.02W
Rovaniemi Finland **43 F4** 66.29N 25.40E
Royale, Isle U.S.A. **65 I6** 48.00N 88.45W
Royal Leamington Spa England **10 D3** 52.18N 1.32W
Royal Tunbridge Wells England **11 F2** 51.07N 0.16E
Royan France **44 C4** 45.37N 1.01W
Roye France **42 B1** 49.42N 2.48E
Royston England **11 E3** 52.03N 0.01W
Royton England **15 E2** 53.34N 2.08W
Rozdil'na Ukraine **55 L2** 46.50N 30.02E
Ruabon Wales **12 D4** 52.59N 3.03W
Rub' al Khali *des.* Saudi Arabia **95 H3** 20.20N 52.30E
Rubha Coigeach *c.* Scotland **18 D3** 58.06N 5.25W
Rubha Hunish *c.* Scotland **18 C2** 57.42N 6.21W
Rubha Reidh *c.* Scotland **18 D2** 57.51N 5.49W
Rubtsovsk Russian Fed. **58 K3** 51.29N 81.10E
Rudnaya Pristan' Russian Fed. **106 C4** 43.46N 135.14E
Rudnya Russian Fed. **55 L6** 54.55N 31.07E
Rudnyy Kazakhstan **58 I3** 53.00N 63.05E
Rufiji *r.* Tanzania **86 C4** 8.02S 39.17E
Rugby England **10 D3** 52.23N 1.16W
Rugby U.S.A. **64 G6** 48.24N 99.59W
Rugeley England **10 D3** 52.47N 1.56W
Rügen *i.* Germany **48 F6** 54.30N 13.30E
Ruhr *r.* Germany **48 C4** 51.27N 6.41E
Rukwa, L. Tanzania **86 C4** 8.00S 32.20E
Rum *i.* Scotland **18 C1** 57.00N 6.20W
Ruma Yugo. **56 D6** 44.59N 19.51E
Rum Cay *i.* The Bahamas **71 J5** 23.41N 74.53W
Runcorn England **14 E2** 53.20N 2.44W
Rundu Namibia **86 A3** 17.52S 19.49E
Ruoqiang China **102 F5** 39.00N 88.00E
Rurutu *i.* Pacific Oc. **108 P4** 22.25S 151.20W
Ruse Bulgaria **56 G5** 43.50N 25.59E
Rushden England **11 E3** 52.17N 0.36W
Russian Federation Europe/Asia **58 J4** 62.00N 80.00E
Ruteng Indonesia **104 G2** 8.35S 120.28E
Ruthin Wales **12 D5** 53.07N 3.18W
Rutland *d.* England **9 E3** 52.40N 0.43W
Rutland Water *l.* England **10 E3** 52.39N 0.40W
Rutog China **102 D4** 33.30N 79.40E
Ruza Russian Fed. **55 O6** 55.40N 36.12E
Rvdsar Iran **95 H6** 37.12N 50.00E
Rwanda Africa **86 B4** 2.00S 30.00E
Ryan, Loch Scotland **16 D2** 54.56N 5.02W
Ryazan' Russian Fed. **55 P6** 54.37N 39.43E
Ryazhsk Russian Fed. **55 Q5** 53.40N 40.07E
Rybinsk Russian Fed. **58 F3** 58.01N 38.52E
Rybinsk Resr. Russian Fed. **58 F3** 58.30N 38.25E
Rybnik Poland **54 F4** 50.06N 18.32E
Ryde England **10 D1** 50.44N 1.09W
Rye England **11 F1** 50.57N 0.46E
Rye *r.* England **15 G3** 54.10N 0.42W
Rye B. England **11 F1** 50.53N 0.48E
Ryotsu Japan **106 C3** 38.06N 138.28E
Ryukyu Is. Japan **103 N3** 26.00N 126.00E
Rzeszów Poland **54 H4** 50.04N 22.00E

S

Saale *r.* Germany **48 E4** 51.58N 11.53E
Saarbrücken Germany **48 C3** 49.15N 6.58E
Saaremaa *i.* Estonia **43 E2** 58.30N 22.30E
Saarlouis Germany **42 F1** 49.21N 6.45E
Šabac Yugo. **56 D6** 44.45N 19.41E
Sabadell Spain **46 G4** 41.33N 2.07E
Sabah *d.* Malaysia **104 F5** 5.00N 117.00E
Sabana, Archipiélago de Cuba **71 H5** 23.30N 80.00W
Sabha Libya **84 F4** 27.04N 14.25E
Sabinas Mexico **70 D6** 27.51N 101.10W
Sabkhat al Hayshah *f.* Libya **53 G3** 31.30N 15.15E
Sable, C. Canada **63 L2** 43.30N 65.50W
Sable, C. U.S.A. **65 J2** 25.00N 81.20W
Sable I. Canada **63 M2** 44.00N 60.00W
Şabya Saudi Arabia **94 F2** 17.09N 42.37E
Sabzevar Iran **95 I6** 36.13N 57.38E
Sachs Harbour Canada **62 F5** 72.00N 124.30W
Sacramento U.S.A. **64 B4** 38.32N 121.30W
Sacramento Mts. U.S.A. **64 E3** 33.10N 105.50W
Sado *r.* Portugal **46 A3** 38.29N 8.55W
Sadoga-shima *i.* Japan **106 C3** 38.00N 138.20E
Säffle Sweden **43 C2** 59.08N 12.55E
Saffron Walden England **11 F3** 52.02N 0.15E
Safi Morocco **84 D5** 32.20N 9.17W
Safonovo Russian Fed. **55 M6** 55.08N 33.16E
Sagar India **97 F5** 23.50N 78.44E
Sagunto Spain **46 E3** 39.40N 0.17W
Sahara *des.* Africa **84 F3** 24.00N 12.00E
Saharan Atlas *mts.* Algeria **84 E5** 34.20N 2.00E
Sa'idabad Iran **95 I4** 29.28N 55.43E
Saidpur Bangla. **97 H6** 25.48N 89.00E
Saimaa *l.* Finland **43 F3** 61.20N 28.00E
St. Abb's Head Scotland **17 G3** 55.54N 2.07W
St. Agnes England **13 B2** 50.18N 5.13W
St. Agnes *i.* England **13 A1** 49.53N 6.20W
St. Albans England **11 E2** 51.46N 0.21W
St. Alban's Head England **10 C1** 50.35N 2.04W
St.-Amand-les-Eaux France **42 C2** 50.27N 3.26E
St.-Amand-Montrond *town* France **44 E5** 46.43N 2.29E
St. Andrews Scotland **17 G4** 56.20N 2.48W
St. Anne Channel Is. **13 Z9** 49.43N 2.12W
St. Ann's Head Wales **12 B3** 51.41N 5.11W
St. Anthony Canada **63 M3** 51.24N 55.37W
St. Asaph Wales **12 D5** 53.16N 3.26W
St. Augustine U.S.A. **65 J2** 29.54N 81.19W
St. Austell England **13 C2** 50.20N 4.48W
St. Austell B. England **13 C2** 50.16N 4.43W
St. Barthélémy *i.* Leeward Is. **71 L4** 17.55N 62.50W
St. Bees England **14 D3** 54.29N 3.36W
St. Bees Head England **14 D3** 54.31N 3.39W
St. Brelade Channel Is. **13 Z8** 49.12N 2.13W
St. Brides B. Wales **12 B3** 51.48N 5.03W
St.-Brieuc France **44 B6** 48.31N 2.45W
St. Catharines Canada **65 K5** 43.10N 79.15W
St. Catherine's Pt. England **10 D1** 50.34N 1.18W
St. Clears Wales **12 C3** 51.48N 4.30W
St. Cloud U.S.A. **65 H6** 45.34N 94.10W
St. Columb Major England **13 C2** 50.26N 4.56W
St. Croix *r.* U.S.A. **65 H5** 44.40N 92.42W
St. Croix *i.* U.S.V. Is. **71 L4** 17.45N 64.35W
St. David's Wales **12 B3** 51.54N 5.16W
St. David's Head Wales **12 B3** 51.55N 5.19W
St.-Dié France **44 G6** 48.17N 6.57E
St.-Dizier France **44 F6** 48.38N 4.58E
Saintes France **44 C4** 45.44N 0.38W
St.-Étienne France **44 F4** 45.26N 4.26E
Saintfield N. Ireland **16 D2** 54.28N 5.50W
St. Gallen Switz. **44 H5** 47.25N 9.23E
St.-Gaudens France **44 D3** 43.07N 0.44E
St. George's Grenada **71 L3** 12.04N 61.44W

St. George's Channel U.K./Rep. of Ire. **20 E1** 52.00N 6.00W
St. Germans England **13 C2** 50.24N 4.18W
St. Govan's Head Wales **12 C3** 51.36N 4.55W
St. Helena *i.* Atlantic Oc. **116 I5** 16.00S 6.00W
St. Helena B. R.S.A. **86 A1** 32.35S 18.00E
St. Helens England **14 E2** 53.28N 2.43W
St. Helens, Mt. U.S.A. **64 B6** 46.12N 122.11W
St. Helier Channel Is. **13 Z8** 49.12N 2.07W
St. Ives Cambs. England **11 E3** 52.20N 0.05W
St. Ives Cornwall England **13 B2** 50.13N 5.29W
St. Ives B. England **13 B2** 50.14N 5.26W
St.-Jean, L. Canada **65 L6** 48.35N 72.00W
St. John Canada **63 L2** 45.16N 66.03W
St. John Channel Is. **13 Z8** 49.15N 2.08W
St. John *r.* Canada **63 L2** 45.30N 66.05W
St. John *i.* U.S.V. Is. **71 K4** 18.21N 64.48W
St. John's Antigua **71 L4** 17.07N 61.51W
St. John's Canada **63 M2** 47.34N 52.41W
St. John's Pt. N. Ireland **16 D2** 54.13N 5.39W
St. Jordi, G. of Spain **46 F4** 40.50N 1.10E
St. Joseph U.S.A. **65 H4** 39.45N 94.51W
St. Joseph, Lac *l.* Canada **63 I3** 51.05N 90.35W
St. Just England **13 B2** 50.07N 5.41W
St. Keverne England **13 B2** 50.03N 5.05W
St. Kilda *i.* Scotland **18 A2** 57.49N 8.34W
St. Kitts-Nevis Leeward Is. **71 L4** 17.20N 62.45W
St. Lawrence *r.* Canada/U.S.A. **63 L2** 48.45N 68.30W
St. Lawrence, G. of Canada **63 L2** 48.00N 62.00W
St. Lawrence I. U.S.A. **62 A4** 63.00N 170.00W
St.-Lô France **44 C6** 49.07N 1.05W
St. Louis Senegal **84 C3** 16.01N 16.30W
St. Louis U.S.A. **65 H4** 38.40N 90.15W
St. Lucia Windward Is. **71 L3** 14.05N 61.00W
St. Magnus B. Scotland **19 Y9** 60.25N 1.35W
St.-Malo France **44 B6** 48.39N 2.00W
St.-Malo, Golfe de *g.* France **44 B6** 49.00N 2.00W
St. Margaret's Hope Scotland **19 G3** 58.50N 2.57W
St. Martin Guernsey Channel Is. **13 Y9** 49.27N 2.34W
St. Martin Jersey Channel Is. **13 Z8** 49.13N 2.03W
St. Martin *i.* Leeward Is. **71 L4** 18.05N 63.05W
St. Martin's *i.* England **13 A1** 49.57N 6.16W
St. Mary's *i.* England **13 A1** 49.55N 6.16W
St. Matthew I. U.S.A. **62 A4** 60.30N 172.45W
St. Maurice *r.* Canada **65 L6** 46.21N 72.31W
St. Mawes England **13 B2** 50.10N 5.01W
St. Moritz Switz. **44 H5** 46.30N 9.51E
St.-Nazaire France **44 B5** 47.17N 2.12W
St. Neots England **11 E3** 52.14N 0.16W
St.-Niklaas Belgium **42 D3** 51.10N 4.09E
St.-Omer France **42 B2** 50.45N 2.15E
St. Ouen Channel Is. **13 Z8** 49.13N 2.14W
St. Peter Port Channel Is. **13 Y9** 49.27N 2.32W
St. Petersburg Russian Fed. **58 F3** 59.55N 30.25E
St. Pierre and Miquelon *is.* N. America **63 M2** 47.00N 56.15W
St. Pölten Austria **54 D3** 48.13N 15.37E
St.-Quentin France **44 E6** 49.51N 3.17E
St. Sampson Channel Is. **13 Y9** 49.29N 2.31W
St. Vincent and the Grenadines C. America **71 L3** 13.10N 61.15W
St. Vincent, C. Portugal **46 A2** 37.01N 8.59W
St.-Vith Belgium **42 F2** 50.15N 6.08E
St. Wendel Germany **42 G1** 49.27N 7.10E
Saipan *i.* N. Mariana Is. **105 L7** 15.12N 145.43E
Sajama *mtn.* Bolivia **76 D3** 18.06S 69.00W
Sakai Japan **106 C3** 34.37N 135.28E
Sakakah Saudi Arabia **94 F5** 29.59N 40.12E
Sakakawea, L. U.S.A. **64 F6** 47.30N 102.20W
Sakarya *r.* Turkey **57 J4** 41.08N 30.36E
Sakata Japan **106 C3** 38.55N 139.51E
Sakhalin *i.* Russian Fed. **59 Q3** 50.00N 143.00E
Sakura Japan **106 D3** 35.43N 140.13E
Sal *i.* Cape Verde **84 B3** 16.45N 23.00W
Sala Sweden **43 D2** 59.55N 16.38E
Salado *r.* Argentina **77 D1** 31.40S 60.41W
Salado *r.* Mexico **70 E6** 26.46N 98.55W
Şalalah Oman **95 I2** 17.00N 54.04E
Salamanca Spain **46 C4** 40.58N 5.40W
Salar de Arizaro *f.* Argentina **76 D2** 24.50S 67.40W
Salar de Atacama *f.* Chile **76 D2** 23.30S 68.46W
Salar de Coipasa *l.* Bolivia **76 D3** 19.20S 68.00W
Salar de Uyuni *l.* Bolivia **76 D2** 20.30S 67.45W
Salavat Russian Fed. **58 H3** 53.22N 55.50E
Salayar *i.* Indonesia **104 G2** 6.07S 120.28E
Sala y Gómez, I. Pacific Oc. **109 U4** 26.28S 105.28W
Salcombe England **13 D2** 50.14N 3.47W
Saldanha R.S.A. **86 A1** 33.00S 17.56E
Sale Australia **110 D2** 38.06S 147.06E
Sale England **15 E2** 53.26N 2.19W
Salehurst England **11 F1** 50.58N 0.29E
Salekhard Russian Fed. **58 I4** 66.33N 66.35E
Salem India **97 F3** 11.38N 78.08E
Salem U.S.A. **64 B5** 44.57N 123.01W
Salerno Italy **50 F4** 40.41N 14.45E
Salerno, G. of Med. Sea **50 F4** 40.30N 14.45E
Salford England **15 E2** 53.30N 2.17W
Salgado *r.* Brazil **77 G4** 4.27S 37.46W
Salihli Turkey **57 I3** 38.29N 28.08E
Salihorsk Belarus **55 J5** 52.41N 27.29E
Salina U.S.A. **64 G4** 38.50N 97.37W
Salinas U.S.A. **64 B4** 36.40N 121.38W
Salinas Grandes *f.* Argentina **76 D2** 29.37S 64.56W
Salinosó Lachay, Punto *c.* Peru **76 C3** 11.20S 77.29W
Salisbury England **10 D2** 51.04N 1.48W
Salisbury U.S.A. **65 K4** 38.22N 75.37W
Salisbury Plain *f.* England **10 D2** 51.15N 1.55W
Salitre *r.* Brazil **77 F4** 9.23S 40.35W
Salluit Canada **63 K4** 62.10N 75.40W
Salmon *r.* U.S.A. **64 C6** 45.50N 116.50W
Salmon Arm Canada **62 G3** 50.41N 119.18W
Salmon River Mts. U.S.A. **64 D5** 44.30N 114.30W
Salo Finland **43 E3** 60.23N 23.10E
Sal'sk Russian Fed. **53 L6** 46.30N 41.33E
Salta Argentina **76 D2** 24.46S 65.28W
Saltash England **13 C2** 50.25N 4.13W
Saltcoats Scotland **16 E3** 55.37N 4.47W
Saltee Is. Rep. of Ire. **20 E2** 52.08N 6.36W
Saltillo Mexico **70 D6** 25.30N 101.00W
Salt Lake City U.S.A. **64 D5** 40.45N 111.55W
Salto Uruguay **77 E1** 31.23S 57.58W
Salton Sea *l.* U.S.A. **64 C3** 33.25N 115.45W
Salvador Brazil **77 G3** 12.58S 38.20W
Salween *r.* Myanmar **97 J4** 16.30N 97.33E
Salyan Azerbaijan **95 G6** 39.36N 48.59E
Salzburg Austria **54 C2** 47.54N 13.03E
Salzgitter Germany **48 E5** 52.02N 10.22E
Samandağı Turkey **57 L2** 36.07N 35.55E
Samani Japan **106 D4** 42.09N 142.50E
Samar *i.* Phil. **105 H6** 11.45N 125.15E
Samara Russian Fed. **58 H3** 53.10N 50.15E
Samara *r.* Ukraine **55 N3** 48.27N 35.07E
Samarinda Indonesia **104 F3** 0.30S 117.09E
Samarra' Iraq **94 F5** 34.13N 43.52E
Sambalpur India **97 G5** 21.28N 84.04E
Sambas Indonesia **104 D4** 1.20N 109.15E
Sambre *r.* Belgium **42 D2** 50.29N 4.52E
Same Tanzania **87 B2** 4.04S 37.44E
Samoa Pacific Oc. **108 N5** 13.55S 172.00W
Samos *i.* Greece **56 H2** 37.44N 26.45E
Samothraki *i.* Greece **56 G4** 40.26N 25.35E
Sampit Indonesia **104 E3** 2.34S 112.59E
Samsø *i.* Denmark **54 B6** 55.52N 10.37E
Samsun Turkey **57 M4** 41.17N 36.22E
San Mali **84 D3** 13.21N 4.57W
Sana Yemen **94 F2** 15.23N 44.14E
San Ambrosio *i.* Chile **109 X4** 26.28S 79.53W
Sanandaj Iran **95 G6** 35.18N 47.01E
San Andrés, I. de Colombia **71 H3** 12.35N 81.42W
San Antonio U.S.A. **64 G2** 29.25N 98.30W
San Antonio, C. Cuba **71 H5** 21.50N 84.57W
San Benedicto, I. Mexico **70 B4** 19.10N 110.50W
San Bernardino U.S.A. **64 C3** 34.07N 117.18W
San Blas, C. U.S.A. **65 I2** 29.40N 85.25W
San Cristóbal Venezuela **71 J2** 7.46N 72.15W
San Cristóbal, I. Galapagos Is. **76 B4** 0.50S 89.30W
San Cristobal *i.* Solomon Is. **111 F4** 10.40S 162.00E
San Cristóbal de la Laguna Canary Is. **46 X2** 28.29N 16.19W
Sanda I. Scotland **16 D3** 55.17N 5.34W
Sandakan Malaysia **104 F5** 5.52N 118.04E
Sandane Norway **43 A3** 61.47N 6.14E
Sanday *i.* Scotland **19 G4** 59.15N 2.33W
Sanday Sd. Scotland **19 G4** 59.11N 2.35W
Sandbach England **15 E2** 53.09N 2.23W
Sandhurst England **10 E2** 51.21N 0.49W
San Diego U.S.A. **64 C3** 32.45N 117.10W
Sandnes Norway **43 A2** 58.51N 5.45E
Sandnessjøen Norway **43 C4** 66.01N 12.40E
Sandoway Myanmar **97 I4** 18.28N 94.20E
Sandown England **10 D1** 50.39N 1.09W
Sandpoint *town* U.S.A. **64 C6** 48.17N 116.34W
Sandviken Sweden **43 D3** 60.38N 16.50E
Sandwich England **11 G2** 51.16N 1.21E
Sandy England **11 E3** 52.08N 0.18W
Sandy C. Australia **110 E3** 24.42S 153.17E
Sandy Lake *town* Canada **63 I3** 53.00N 93.00W
San Felipe Mexico **70 B7** 31.03N 114.52W
San Félix *i.* Chile **109 W4** 26.23S 80.05W
San Fernando Phil. **104 G7** 16.39N 120.19E
San Fernando Spain **46 B2** 36.28N 6.12W
San Fernando de Apure Venezuela **71 K2** 7.53N 67.15W
San Francisco U.S.A. **64 B4** 37.45N 122.27W
San Francisco, C. de Ecuador **76 B5** 0.38N 80.08W
San Francisco de Paula, C. Argentina **75 C2** 49.44S 67.38W
Sangha *r.* Congo **82 E4** 1.10S 16.47E
Sangir Is. Indonesia **105 H4** 2.45N 125.20E
Sangkulirang Indonesia **104 F4** 1.00N 117.58E
Sangli India **96 E4** 16.55N 74.37E
Sangmélima Cameroon **84 F2** 2.57N 11.56E
Sangre de Cristo Range *mts.* U.S.A. **64 E4** 37.30N 106.00W
Sangue *r.* Brazil **77 E3** 11.00S 58.30W
San Jorge, Golfo de *g.* Argentina **75 C2** 46.00S 66.00W
San José Costa Rica **71 H3** 9.59N 84.04W
San Jose U.S.A. **64 B4** 37.20N 121.55W
San José *i.* Mexico **70 B6** 25.00N 110.38W
San Juan Argentina **76 D1** 31.33S 68.31W
San Juan Puerto Rico **71 K4** 18.29N 66.08W
San Juan *r.* Costa Rica **71 H3** 10.50N 83.40W
San Juan *r.* U.S.A. **64 D4** 37.20N 110.05W
San Juan Bautista Paraguay **77 E2** 26.37S 57.06W
San Juan Mts. U.S.A. **64 E4** 37.30N 107.00W
Şanlıurfa Turkey **57 N2** 37.08N 38.45E
Sanlúcar de Barrameda Spain **46 B2** 36.46N 6.21W
San Lucas, C. Mexico **70 B5** 22.50N 110.00W
San Luis, Lago de *l.* Bolivia **76 D3** 13.40S 64.00W
San Luis Obispo U.S.A. **64 B4** 35.16N 120.40W
San Luis Potosí Mexico **70 D5** 22.10N 101.00W
San Luis Potosí *d.* Mexico **70 D5** 23.00N 100.00W
San Marino Europe **50 E5** 43.55N 12.27E
San Marino *town* San Marino **50 E5** 43.55N 12.27E
San Martín *r.* Bolivia **76 D3** 13.05S 63.48W
San Martín, L. Argentina **75 B2** 49.00S 72.30W
San Matías, Golfo *g.* Argentina **75 C2** 41.30S 64.00W
San Miguel El Salvador **70 G3** 13.28N 88.10W
San Miguel *r.* Bolivia **76 D3** 12.25S 64.25W
San Miguel de Tucumán Argentina **76 D2** 26.47S 65.15W
Sanming China **103 L3** 26.25N 117.35E
Sanndray *i.* Scotland **18 B1** 56.53N 7.31W
San Pablo Phil. **104 G6** 13.58N 121.10E
San Pedro Paraguay **77 E2** 24.08S 57.08W
San Pedro, Sierra de *mts.* Spain **46 B3** 39.20N 6.20W
San Pedro Sula Honduras **70 G4** 15.26N 88.01W
San Pietro *i.* Italy **50 C3** 39.09N 8.16E
Sanquhar Scotland **17 F3** 55.22N 3.56W
San Quintín, C. Mexico **64 C3** 30.20N 116.00W
San Remo Italy **50 B5** 43.48N 7.46E
San Salvador El Salvador **70 G3** 13.40N 89.10W
San Salvador *i.* The Bahamas **71 J5** 24.00N 74.32W
San Salvador de Jujuy Argentina **76 D2** 24.10S 65.20W
San Sebastian de la Gomera Canary Is. **46 X2** 28.06N 17.06W
San Severo Italy **50 F4** 41.40N 15.24E
Santa Ana El Salvador **70 G3** 14.00N 89.31W
Santa Ana U.S.A. **64 C3** 33.44N 117.54W
Santa Barbara U.S.A. **64 C3** 34.25N 119.41W
Santa Catarina *d.* Brazil **77 E2** 27.00S 50.00W
Santa Clara Cuba **71 H5** 22.25N 79.58W
Santa Cruz Bolivia **76 D3** 17.58S 63.14W
Santa Cruz, I. Galapagos Is. **76 A4** 0.40S 90.20W
Santa Cruz de la Palma Canary Is. **46 X2** 28.41N 17.46W
Santa Cruz de Tenerife Canary Is. **46 X2** 28.27N 16.14W
Santa Cruz do Sul Brazil **77 E2** 29.42S 52.25W
Santa Cruz Is. Solomon Is. **111 F4** 10.30S 166.00E
Santa Elena, B. de Ecuador **76 B4** 2.10S 80.50W
Santa Elena, C. Costa Rica **70 G3** 10.54N 85.56W
Santa Fé Argentina **77 D1** 31.38S 60.43W
Santa Fe U.S.A. **64 E4** 35.41N 105.57W
Santa Isabel *i.* Solomon Is. **111 E5** 8.00S 159.00E
Santa Maria Brazil **77 E2** 29.40S 53.47W
Santa Maria U.S.A. **64 B3** 34.56N 120.25W
Santa Maria *r.* Mexico **70 C7** 31.10N 107.05W
Santa Maria di Leuca, C. Italy **50 H3** 39.47N 18.24E
Santa Marta Colombia **71 J3** 11.18N 74.10W
Santander Spain **46 D5** 43.28N 3.48W
Santarém Brazil **76 E4** 2.26S 54.41W
Santarém Portugal **46 A3** 39.14N 8.40W
Santa Rosa Argentina **75 C3** 36.00S 64.40W
Santa Rosa U.S.A. **64 B4** 38.26N 122.34W
Santa Rosalía Mexico **70 B6** 27.20N 112.20W
Santiago Chile **75 B3** 33.30S 70.40W
Santiago Dom. Rep. **71 J4** 19.30N 70.42W
Santiago Spain **46 A5** 42.52N 8.33W
Santiago de Cuba Cuba **71 I5** 20.00N 75.49W
Santo André Brazil **77 F2** 23.39S 46.29W
Santo Antão *i.* Cape Verde **84 B3** 17.00N 25.10W
Santo Domingo Dom. Rep. **71 K4** 18.30N 69.57W
Santoña Spain **46 D5** 43.27N 3.26W
Santos Brazil **77 F2** 23.56S 46.22W
San Valentin *mtn.* Chile **75 B2** 46.33S 73.20W
São Carlos Brazil **77 F2** 22.01S 47.54W
São Francisco *r.* Brazil **77 G3** 10.10S 36.40W
São José do Rio Prêto Brazil **77 F2** 20.50S 49.20W
São Luís Brazil **77 F4** 2.34S 44.16W
São Marcos, Baia de *b.* Brazil **77 F4** 2.30S 44.15W
Saône *r.* France **44 F4** 45.46N 4.52E
São Paulo Brazil **77 F2** 23.33S 46.39W
São Roque, C. de Brazil **77 G4** 5.00S 35.00W
São Sebastião, I. de Brazil **77 F2** 23.53S 45.17W
São Tiago *i.* Cape Verde **84 B3** 15.00N 23.40W
São Tomé *i.* São Tomé & Príncipe **84 E2** 0.19N 6.43E
São Tomé, Cabo de *c.* Brazil **75 E4** 21.54S 40.59W
São Tomé & Príncipe Africa **84 E2** 1.00N 7.00E
São Vicente Brazil **77 F2** 23.57S 46.23W
Sã Paulo *d.* Brazil **77 F2** 22.05S 48.00W
Sapporo Japan **106 D4** 43.05N 141.21E
Sapri Italy **50 F4** 40.04N 15.38E
Saqqaq Greenland **63 M5** 70.00N 52.00W
Saqqez Iran **95 G6** 36.14N 46.15E
Sarab Iran **95 G6** 37.56N 47.35E
Sara Buri Thailand **104 C6** 14.32N 100.53E
Sarajevo Bosnia. **56 D5** 43.52N 18.26E
Sarandë Albania **56 E3** 39.52N 20.00E
Saransk Russian Fed. **58 G3** 54.12N 45.10E
Sarasota U.S.A. **65 J2** 27.20N 82.32W
Saratov Russian Fed. **58 G3** 51.30N 45.55E
Saravan Iran **95 J4** 27.25N 62.17E
Sarawak *d.* Malaysia **104 E4** 3.00N 114.00E
Sardindida Plain *f.* Kenya **87 C3** 2.30N 40.00E
Sardinia *i.* Italy **50 C4** 40.00N 9.00E
Sarektjåkkå *mtn.* Sweden **43 D4** 67.25N 17.45E
Sar-e Pol Afghan. **95 K6** 36.13N 65.55E
Sargodha Pakistan **96 E7** 32.01N 72.40E
Sarh Chad **85 F2** 9.08N 18.22E
Sarī Iran **95 H6** 36.33N 53.06E
Sarigan *i.* N. Mariana Is. **105 L7** 16.43N 145.47E
Sarıyer Turkey **57 I4** 41.11N 29.03E
Sark *i.* Channel Is. **13 Y9** 49.26N 2.22W
Şarkişla Turkey **57 M3** 39.21N 36.27E
Särna Sweden **43 C3** 61.40N 13.10E
Sarny Ukraine **55 J4** 51.21N 26.31E
Saros, G. of Turkey **56 H4** 40.32N 26.25E
Sarpsborg Norway **43 B2** 59.17N 11.06E
Sarrebourg France **44 G6** 48.43N 7.03E
Sarria Spain **46 B5** 42.47N 7.25W
Sarthe *r.* France **44 C5** 47.29N 0.30W
Sasebo Japan **106 A2** 33.10N 129.42E
Saskatchewan *r.* Canada **62 H3** 53.25N 100.15W
Saskatchewan *d.* Canada **62 H3** 55.00N 105.00W
Saskatoon Canada **62 H3** 52.10N 106.40W
Sassandra Côte d'Ivoire **84 D2** 4.58N 6.08W
Sassari Italy **50 C4** 40.43N 8.33E
Sassnitz Germany **48 F6** 54.32N 13.40E
Satpura Range *mts.* India **96 F5** 21.50N 76.00E
Satu Mare Romania **54 H2** 47.48N 22.52E
Saudhárkrókur Iceland **43 Y2** 65.45N 19.39W
Saudi Arabia Asia **94 F3** 25.00N 44.00E
Sault Sainte Marie Canada **63 J2** 46.32N 84.20W
Sault Sainte Marie U.S.A. **65 J6** 46.30N 84.21W
Saumlakki Indonesia **105 I2** 7.59S 131.22E
Saundersfoot Wales **12 C3** 51.43N 4.42W
Saurimo Angola **86 B4** 9.38S 20.20E
Sava *r.* Yugo. **56 E6** 44.50N 20.26E
Savaii *i.* Samoa **108 N5** 13.36S 172.27W
Savannah U.S.A. **65 J3** 32.09N 81.01W
Savannah *r.* U.S.A. **65 J3** 32.10N 81.00W
Savannakhét Laos **104 C7** 16.34N 104.55E
Save *r.* Mozambique **86 C2** 21.00S 35.01E
Savona Italy **50 C6** 44.18N 8.28E
Sawel Mt. N. Ireland **16 B2** 54.49N 7.03W
Sawston England **11 F3** 52.07N 0.11E
Sawtry England **11 E3** 52.27N 0.15W
Sawu *i.* Indonesia **105 G1** 10.30S 121.50E
Sawu Sea Pacific Oc. **105 G2** 9.30S 122.30E
Saxilby England **15 G2** 53.17N 0.40W
Saxmundham England **11 G3** 52.13N 1.29E
Sayhut Yemen **95 H2** 15.12N 51.12E
Saylac Somalia **85 I3** 11.21N 43.30E
Saynshand Mongolia **103 K6** 44.58N 110.10E
Scafell Pike *mtn.* England **14 D3** 54.27N 3.12W
Scalasaig Scotland **16 C4** 56.04N 6.12W
Scalby England **15 G3** 54.18N 0.26W
Scalp *mtn.* Donegal Rep. of Ire. **16 B3** 55.05N 7.22W
Scalp *mtn.* Galway Rep. of Ire. **20 C3** 53.00N 8.29W
Scalpay *i.* High. Scotland **18 D2** 57.18N 5.58W
Scalpay *i.* W.Isles Scotland **18 C2** 57.52N 6.40W
Scandinavia *f.* Europe **34 E4** 65.00N 18.00E
Scapa Flow *str.* Scotland **19 F3** 58.53N 3.05W
Scarba *i.* Scotland **16 D4** 56.11N 5.42W
Scarborough England **15 G3** 54.17N 0.24W
Scarp *i.* Scotland **18 B3** 58.02N 7.07W
Schaffhausen Switz. **44 H5** 47.42N 8.38E
Schagen Neth. **42 D4** 52.47N 4.47E
Schefferville Canada **63 L3** 54.50N 67.00W
Schelde *r.* Belgium **42 D3** 51.13N 4.25E
Schiehallion *mtn.* Scotland **19 E1** 56.40N 4.08W
Schiermonnikoog *i.* Neth. **42 F5** 53.28N 6.15E
Schleswig Germany **48 D6** 54.32N 9.34E
Schwaner Mts. Indonesia **104 E3** 0.45S 113.20E
Schwedt Germany **48 G5** 53.04N 14.17E
Schweinfurt Germany **48 E4** 50.03N 10.16E
Schwerin Germany **48 E5** 53.38N 11.25E
Scilly, Isles of England **13 A1** 49.55N 6.20W
Scole England **11 G3** 52.22N 1.10E
Scotland U.K. **8-9**
Scottish Borders *d.* Scotland **8 D4** 55.30N 2.53W
Scottsbluff U.S.A. **64 F5** 41.52N 103.40W
Scourie Scotland **18 D3** 58.20N 5.09W
Scranton U.S.A. **65 K5** 41.25N 75.40W
Scridain, Loch Scotland **16 C4** 56.22N 6.06W
Scunthorpe England **15 G2** 53.35N 0.38W
Scuol Switz. **44 G5** 46.48N 10.18E
Seaford England **11 F1** 50.46N 0.08E
Seamer England **15 G3** 54.14N 0.27W
Seascale England **14 D3** 54.24N 3.29W
Seaton Cumbria England **14 D3** 54.41N 3.31W
Seaton Devon England **13 D2** 50.43N 3.05W
Seaton Delaval England **15 F4** 55.05N 1.31W
Seattle U.S.A. **64 B6** 47.35N 122.20W
Sebastián Vizcaíno B. Mexico **70 B6** 28.20N 114.45W
Sechura, Bahía de *b.* Peru **76 B4** 5.30S 81.00W
Secunderabad India **97 F4** 17.27N 78.27E
Sedan France **44 F6** 49.42N 4.57E
Sedbergh England **14 E3** 54.20N 2.31W
Seefin *mtn.* Rep. of Ire. **20 D2** 52.13N 7.36W
Segovia Spain **46 C4** 40.57N 4.07W
Segura, Sierra de *mts.* Spain **46 D3** 38.00N 2.50W
Seiland *i.* Norway **43 E5** 70.30N 23.00E
Seinäjoki Finland **43 E3** 62.45N 22.55E
Seine *r.* France **44 D6** 49.28N 0.25E
Sekondi-Takoradi Ghana **84 D2** 4.59N 1.43W
Selaru *i.* Indonesia **105 I2** 8.15S 131.00E
Selatan I. Indonesia **104 C3** 3.00S 100.18E
Selatan, Tanjung *c.* Indonesia **104 E3** 4.20S 114.45E
Selattyn England **10 B3** 52.54N 3.05W
Selawik U.S.A. **62 C4** 66.35N 160.10W
Selby England **15 F2** 53.47N 1.05W
Selkirk Canada **62 I3** 50.10N 96.52W
Selkirk Scotland **17 G3** 55.33N 2.51W
Sellindge England **11 G2** 51.07N 1.00E
Selsey England **10 E1** 50.44N 0.47W
Selsey Bill *c.* England **10 E1** 50.44N 0.47W
Selvas *f.* Brazil **77 D4** 8.00S 68.00W
Selwyn Mts. Canada **62 E4** 63.00N 130.00W
Selwyn Range *mts.* Australia **110 C4** 21.35S 140.35E
Seman *r.* Albania **56 D4** 40.53N 19.25E
Semarang Indonesia **104 E2** 6.58S 110.29E
Semenivka Ukraine **55 M5** 52.08N 32.36E
Seminoe Resr. U.S.A. **64 E5** 42.05N 106.50W
Semipalatinsk Kazakhstan **102 E8** 50.26N 80.16E
Semnan Iran **95 H6** 35.31N 53.24E
Semois *r.* France/Belgium **42 D1** 49.53N 4.45E
Sendai Japan **106 A3** 38.20N 140.50E
Senegal Africa **84 C3** 14.15N 14.15W
Sénégal *r.* Senegal/Mauritania **84 C3** 16.00N 16.28W
Senja *i.* Norway **43 D5** 69.20N 17.30E
Senlis France **42 B1** 49.12N 2.35E
Sennar Sudan **85 H3** 13.31N 33.38E
Sens France **44 E6** 48.12N 3.18E
Seoul S. Korea **103 N5** 37.30N 127.00E
Sepik *r.* P.N.G. **105 K3** 3.53S 144.33E
Sept-Îles *town* Canada **63 L3** 50.13N 66.22W
Seram *i.* Indonesia **105 H3** 3.10S 129.30E
Seram Sea Pacific Oc. **105 H3** 2.50S 128.00E
Serang Indonesia **104 D2** 6.07S 106.09E
Serbia *d.* Yugo. **56 E5** 43.52N 21.00E
Seremban Malaysia **104 C4** 2.42N 101.54E
Serengeti Nat. Park Tanzania **87 A2** 2.20S 34.55E
Serengeti Plains *f.* Kenya **87 B2** 3.30S 37.50E
Serere Uganda **87 A3** 1.31N 33.25E
Seret *r.* Ukraine **55 I3** 48.38N 25.52E
Sergipe *d.* Brazil **77 G3** 11.00S 37.00W
Seria Brunei **104 E4** 4.39N 114.23E
Serov Russian Fed. **58 I3** 59.42N 60.32E
Serowe Botswana **86 B2** 22.25S 26.44E
Serpukhov Russian Fed. **55 O6** 54.53N 37.25E
Serranías del Burro *mts.* Mexico **70 D6** 28.30N 102.00W
Serres Greece **56 F4** 41.04N 23.32E
Serui Indonesia **105 J3** 1.53S 136.15E
Sestroretsk Russian Fed. **43 G3** 60.09N 29.58E
Sète France **44 E3** 43.25N 3.43E
Sete Lagoas Brazil **77 F3** 19.29S 44.15W
Setesdal *f.* Norway **43 A2** 59.20N 7.25E
Sétif Algeria **84 E5** 36.09N 5.26E
Seto-naikai *str.* Japan **106 B2** 34.00N 132.30E
Settat Morocco **84 D5** 33.04N 7.37W
Settle England **15 E3** 54.05N 2.18W
Setúbal Portugal **46 A3** 38.31N 8.54W
Setúbal, B. of Portugal **46 A3** 38.20N 9.00W
Seul, Lac *l.* Canada **65 H7** 50.20N 92.30W
Sevastopol' Ukraine **55 M1** 44.36N 33.31E
Seven Heads Rep. of Ire. **20 C1** 51.34N 8.42W
Sevenoaks England **11 F2** 51.16N 0.12E
Severn *r.* Canada **63 J3** 56.00N 87.40W
Severn *r.* England **10 C2** 51.50N 2.21W
Severnaya Zemlya *is.* Russian Fed. **59 L5** 80.00N 96.00E
Severo-Kurilsk Russian Fed. **59 R3** 50.40N 156.01E
Seville Spain **46 C2** 37.24N 5.59W
Seward U.S.A. **62 D4** 60.05N 149.34W
Seward Pen. U.S.A. **62 B4** 65.00N 164.10W
Seychelles Indian Oc. **85 J1** 5.00S 55.00E
Seydhisfjördhur Iceland **43 Z2** 65.16N 14.02W
Seydişehir Turkey **57 J2** 37.25N 31.51E
Seym *r.* Russian Fed. **55 M4** 51.30N 32.30E
Sfântu Gheorghe Romania **56 G6** 45.52N 25.50E
Sfax Tunisia **84 F5** 34.45N 10.43E
Sgurr Dhomhnuill *mtn.* Scotland **18 D1** 56.47N 5.25W
Sgurr Mor *mtn.* Scotland **18 D2** 57.41N 5.01W
Shaanxi *d.* China **103 J4** 34.00N 109.00E
Shabeelle *r.* Somalia **85 I2** 0.30N 43.10E
Shaftesbury England **10 C2** 51.00N 2.12W
Shahr-e Kord Iran **95 H5** 32.40N 50.52E
Shandong *d.* China **103 L5** 35.45N 117.30E
Shandong Pen. China **103 M5** 37.00N 121.30E
Shanghai China **103 M4** 31.13N 121.25E
Shangqiu China **103 L4** 34.21N 115.40E
Shangzhi China **106 A5** 45.13N 127.59E
Shanklin England **10 D1** 50.38N 1.10W
Shannon *r.* Rep. of Ire. **20 C2** 52.39N 8.43W
Shannon, Mouth of the *est.* Rep. of Ire. **20 B2** 52.29N 9.57W
Shantar Is. Russian Fed. **59 P3** 55.00N 138.00E
Shanxi *d.* China **103 K5** 36.45N 112.00E
Shaoguan China **103 K2** 24.54N 113.33E
Shaoxing China **103 M3** 30.02N 120.35E

Shaoyang China **103 K3** 27.43N 111.24E
Shap England **14 E3** 54.32N 2.40W
Shapinsay *i.* Scotland **19 G4** 59.03N 2.51W
Shaqrā' Saudi Arabia **94 G4** 25.17N 45.14E
Sharjah U.A.E. **95 I4** 25.20N 55.26E
Shark B. Australia **108 G4** 25.30S 113.30E
Shashemene Ethiopia **85 H2** 7.13N 38.33E
Shashi China **103 K4** 30.16N 112.20E
Shasta, Mt. U.S.A. **64 B5** 41.35N 122.12W
Shawinigan Canada **65 L6** 46.33N 72.45W
Shchigry Russian Fed. **55 O4** 51.52N 36.54E
Sheberghan Afghan. **95 K6** 36.40N 65.42E
Sheelin, Lough Rep. of Ire. **20 D3** 53.48N 7.20W
Sheep Haven *b.* Rep. of Ire. **16 B3** 55.12N 7.52W
Sheerness England **11 F2** 51.26N 0.47E
Sheffield England **15 F2** 53.23N 1.28W
Shelby U.S.A. **64 D6** 48.30N 111.52W
Shelikof Str. U.S.A. **62 C3** 58.00N 153.45W
Shengena *mtn.* Tanzania **87 B2** 4.17S 37.52E
Shenyang China **103 M6** 41.50N 123.26E
Shenzhen China **103 K2** 22.32N 114.08E
Shepetivka Ukraine **55 J4** 50.12N 27.01E
Sheppey, Isle of England **11 F2** 51.24N 0.50E
Shepshed England **10 D3** 52.46N 1.17W
Shepton Mallet England **13 E3** 51.11N 2.31W
Sherborne England **10 C1** 50.56N 2.31W
Sherbrooke Canada **63 K2** 45.24N 71.54W
Shereiq Sudan **94 D2** 18.44N 33.37E
Sheridan U.S.A. **64 E5** 44.48N 107.05W
Sheringham England **11 G3** 52.56N 1.11E
's-Hertogenbosch Neth. **42 E3** 51.42N 5.19E
Sherwood Forest *f.* England **15 G2** 53.10N 0.55W
Shetland *d.* Scotland **8 E7** 60.20N 1.15W
Shetland Is. Scotland **19 Y9** 60.20N 1.15W
Shiant Is. Scotland **18 C2** 57.54N 6.20W
Shibam Yemen **95 G2** 15.56N 48.38E
Shibîn el Kôm Egypt **53 J3** 30.33N 31.00E
Shieldaig Scotland **18 D2** 57.31N 5.40W
Shiel, Loch Scotland **18 D1** 56.50N 5.35W
Shifnal England **10 C3** 52.40N 2.23W
Shijiazhuang China **103 K5** 38.04N 114.28E
Shikarpur Pakistan **96 D6** 27.58N 68.42E
Shikoku *i.* Japan **106 B2** 33.30N 133.00E
Shikoku-sanchi *mts.* Japan **106 B2** 33.50N 133.40E
Shikotan-to *i.* Russian Fed. **106 E4** 43.47N 148.45E
Shildon England **15 F3** 54.37N 1.39W
Shillong India **97 I6** 25.34N 91.53E
Shimoga India **96 F3** 13.56N 75.31E
Shimoni Kenya **87 B2** 4.38S 39.20E
Shimonoseki Japan **106 B2** 34.02N 130.58E
Shingu Japan **106 C2** 33.44N 135.59E
Shining Tor *hill* England **15 E2** 53.16N 2.01W
Shin, Loch Scotland **19 E3** 58.06N 4.32W
Shipley England **15 F2** 53.50N 1.47W
Shipston on Stour England **10 D3** 52.04N 1.38W
Shīraz Iran **95 H4** 29.36N 52.33E
Shire *r.* Mozambique **86 C3** 17.44S 35.17E
Shizuishan China **103 J5** 39.17N 106.52E
Shizuoka Japan **106 C2** 35.00N 138.28E
Shklow Belarus **55 L6** 54.16N 30.16E
Shkodër Albania **56 D5** 42.03N 19.30E
Shkodër, L. Albania/Yugo. **56 D5** 42.10N 19.18E
Shostka Ukraine **55 M4** 51.53N 33.30E
Shpola Ukraine **55 L3** 49.00N 31.25E
Shreveport U.S.A. **65 H3** 32.30N 93.46W
Shrewsbury England **10 C3** 52.42N 2.45W
Shropshire *d.* England **9 D3** 52.35N 2.40W
Shuangjiang China **103 H2** 23.25N 99.49E
Shuangyashan China **103 O7** 46.37N 131.22E
Shumagin Is. U.S.A. **62 C3** 55.00N 160.00W
Shumen Bulgaria **56 H5** 43.15N 26.55E
Shuqrah Yemen **95 G1** 13.21N 45.42E
Shushtar Iran **95 G5** 32.04N 48.53E
Shwebo Myanmar **97 J5** 22.35N 95.42E
Shwegyin Myanmar **97 J4** 17.56N 96.59E
Shymkent Kazakhstan **102 B6** 42.16N 69.05E
Siahan Range *mts.* Pakistan **95 J4** 27.30N 64.30E
Šiauliai Lithuania **54 H6** 55.51N 23.20E
Siaya Kenya **87 A3** 0.05N 34.18E
Šibenik Croatia **56 B5** 43.45N 15.55E
Siberia *f.* Asia **117 O9** 62.00N 110.00E
Siberut *i.* Indonesia **104 B3** 1.30S 99.00E
Sibi Pakistan **96 D6** 29.31N 67.54E
Sibiloi Nat. Park Kenya **87 B3** 4.00N 36.30E
Sibiu Romania **56 G6** 45.47N 24.09E
Sibolga Indonesia **104 B4** 1.42N 98.48E
Sibsey England **15 H2** 53.02N 0.01E
Sibu Malaysia **104 E4** 2.18N 111.49E
Sibut C.A.R. **85 F2** 5.46N 19.06E
Sichuan *d.* China **103 I4** 30.30N 103.00E
Sicily *i.* Italy **50 E2** 37.30N 14.00E
Sidi bel Abbès Algeria **84 D5** 35.15N 0.39W
Sidi Kacem Morocco **52 B3** 34.15N 5.39W
Sidlaw Hills Scotland **17 F4** 56.31N 3.10W
Sidmouth England **13 D2** 50.40N 3.13W
Sidoan Indonesia **104 G4** 0.19N 120.12E
Sidon Lebanon **94 E5** 33.32N 35.22E
Siedlce Poland **54 H5** 52.10N 22.18E
Siegen Germany **48 D4** 50.52N 8.02E
Siena Italy **50 D5** 43.19N 11.20E
Sierra Leone Africa **84 C2** 8.30N 12.00W
Sierra Nevada del Cocuy *mtn.* Colombia **71 J2** 6.30N 72.21W
Siglufjördhur Iceland **43 Y2** 66.09N 18.55W
Sigüenza Spain **46 D4** 41.04N 2.38W
Sihanoukville Cambodia **104 C6** 10.32N 103.28E
Siilinjärvi Finland **43 F3** 63.05N 27.40E
Siirt Turkey **94 F6** 37.56N 41.56E
Sikar India **96 F6** 27.33N 75.12E
Sikasso Mali **84 D3** 11.18N 5.38W
Sikeston U.S.A. **65 I4** 36.53N 89.35W
Sikhote-Alin Range *mts.* Russian Fed. **59 P2** 45.20N 136.50E
Sikkim *d.* India **97 H6** 27.30N 88.30E
Sil *r.* Spain **46 B5** 42.24N 7.15W
Silesian Plateau *mts.* Poland **54 F4** 50.30N 19.30E
Silifke Turkey **57 K2** 36.22N 33.57E
Siling Co *l.* China **102 F4** 31.40N 88.30E
Silistra Bulgaria **56 H6** 44.07N 27.17E
Siljan *l.* Sweden **43 C3** 60.50N 14.40E
Šilutė Lithuania **54 G6** 55.18N 21.30E
Silver City U.S.A. **64 E3** 32.47N 108.16W
Silverstone England **10 D3** 52.05N 1.03W
Silverton England **13 D2** 50.49N 3.29W
Simanggang Malaysia **104 E4** 1.10N 111.32E
Simbirsk Russian Fed. **58 G3** 54.19N 48.22E
Simēn Mts. Ethiopia **94 E1** 13.30N 37.50E
Simeuluë *i.* Indonesia **104 B4** 2.30N 96.00E
Simferopol' Ukraine **55 N1** 44.57N 34.05E
Simojärvi *l.* Finland **43 F4** 66.06N 27.03E
Simplon Pass Switz. **44 H5** 46.15N 8.03E
Simpson Desert Australia **110 C3** 25.00S 136.50E
Sinai *pen.* Egypt **94 D4** 29.00N 34.00E
Sinaloa *d.* Mexico **70 C5** 25.00N 107.30W
Sincelejo Colombia **71 I2** 9.17N 75.23W
Sinclair's B. Scotland **19 F3** 58.30N 3.07W
Sines Portugal **46 A2** 37.58N 8.52W
Singa Sudan **94 D1** 13.09N 33.56E
Singapore Asia **104 C4** 1.20N 103.45E
Singapore *town* Singapore **104 C4** 1.20N 103.45E
Singaraja Indonesia **104 F2** 8.06S 115.07E
Singida Tanzania **86 C4** 4.45S 34.42E
Singkawang Indonesia **104 D4** 0.57N 108.57E
Sinj Croatia **56 C5** 43.42N 16.38E
Sinkat Sudan **94 E2** 18.50N 36.50E
Sinop Turkey **57 L4** 42.02N 35.09E
Sint Maarten *i.* Neth. Ant. **71 L4** 18.05N 63.05W
Sion Mills N. Ireland **16 B2** 54.47N 7.30W
Sioux City U.S.A. **64 G5** 42.30N 96.28W
Sioux Falls *town* U.S.A. **64 G5** 43.34N 96.42W
Sioux Lookout *town* Canada **63 I3** 50.07N 91.54W
Sipacate Guatemala **70 F3** 13.56N 91.10W
Siping China **103 M6** 43.15N 124.25E
Sipora *i.* Indonesia **104 B3** 2.10S 99.40E
Sira *r.* Norway **43 A2** 58.13N 6.13E
Siracusa Italy **50 F2** 37.05N 15.17E
Siret *r.* Romania **55 J1** 45.28N 27.56E
Sirte Libya **85 F5** 31.10N 16.39E
Sirte, G. of Libya **85 F5** 31.45N 17.50E
Sisak Croatia **56 C6** 45.30N 16.21E
Sisimiut Greenland **63 M4** 66.55N 53.30W
Sisophon Cambodia **104 C6** 13.37N 102.58E
Sisteron France **44 F4** 44.16N 5.56E
Siteia Greece **56 H1** 35.13N 26.06E
Sitka U.S.A. **62 E3** 57.05N 135.20W
Sittard Neth. **42 E2** 51.00N 5.52E
Sittingbourne England **11 F2** 51.20N 0.43E
Sittwe Myanmar **97 I5** 20.09N 92.55E
Sivas Turkey **57 M3** 39.44N 37.01E
Siverek Turkey **57 N2** 37.46N 39.19E
Sivrihisar Turkey **57 J3** 39.29N 31.32E
Siwa Egypt **94 C4** 29.11N 25.31E
Sjælland *i.* Denmark **43 B1** 55.30N 12.00E
Skaftárós *b.* Iceland **43 Y1** 63.40N 17.48W
Skagen Denmark **43 B2** 57.44N 10.36E
Skagerrak *str.* Denmark/Norway **43 B2** 57.45N 8.55E
Skagway U.S.A. **62 E3** 59.23N 135.20W
Skaill Scotland **19 G3** 58.57N 2.43W
Skara Sweden **43 C2** 58.23N 13.25E
Skarzysko-Kamienna Poland **54 G4** 51.08N 20.53E
Skegness England **15 H2** 53.09N 0.20E
Skellefte *r.* Sweden **43 E4** 64.44N 21.07E
Skellefteå Sweden **43 E4** 64.45N 21.00E
Skelmersdale England **14 E2** 53.34N 2.49W
Skerries Rep. of Ire. **20 E3** 53.34N 6.07W
Ski Norway **43 B2** 59.43N 10.52E
Skibbereen Rep. of Ire. **20 B1** 51.33N 9.15W
Skiddaw *mtn.* England **14 D3** 54.40N 3.09W
Skien Norway **43 B2** 59.14N 9.37E
Skikda Algeria **84 E5** 36.50N 6.58E
Skipton England **15 E2** 53.57N 2.01W
Skive Denmark **43 B2** 56.34N 9.03E
Skokholm I. Wales **12 B3** 51.42N 5.17W
Skomer I. Wales **12 B3** 51.45N 5.18W
Skopje Macedonia **56 E4** 41.58N 21.27E
Skövde Sweden **43 C2** 58.24N 13.52E
Skovorodino Russian Fed. **59 O3** 54.00N 123.53E
Skye *i.* Scotland **18 C2** 57.20N 6.15W
Skyros *i.* Greece **56 G3** 38.50N 24.33E
Slamet *mtn.* Indonesia **104 D2** 7.10S 109.10E
Slaney *r.* Rep. of Ire. **20 E2** 52.21N 6.30W
Slatina Romania **56 G6** 44.26N 24.23E
Slave *r.* Canada **62 G4** 61.10N 113.30W
Slave Lake *town* Canada **62 G3** 55.17N 114.43W
Slavyansk-na-Kubani Russian Fed. **57 N6** 45.14N 38.08E
Sleaford England **15 G2** 53.00N 0.22W
Sleat, Sd. of Scotland **18 D2** 57.07N 5.45W
Sleights England **15 G3** 54.26N 0.40W
Slieve Anierin *mtn.* Rep. of Ire. **16 B2** 54.06N 7.58W
Slieve Beagh *mtn.* N. Ireland **16 B2** 54.21N 7.12W
Slievecallan *mtn.* Rep. of Ire. **20 B2** 52.50N 9.20W
Slieve Car *mtn.* Rep. of Ire. **20 B4** 54.04N 9.39W
Slieve Donard *mtn.* N. Ireland **16 D2** 54.11N 5.56W
Slievenamon *mtn.* Rep. of Ire. **20 D2** 52.26N 7.37W
Slieve Snaght *mtn.* Rep. of Ire. **20 D5** 55.12N 7.20W
Sligo Rep. of Ire. **20 C4** 54.17N 8.28W
Sligo *d.* Rep. of Ire. **20 C4** 54.10N 8.35W
Sligo B. Rep. of Ire. **20 C4** 54.18N 8.40W
Sliven Bulgaria **56 H5** 42.41N 26.19E
Slobozia Romania **56 H6** 44.34N 27.23E
Slough England **11 E2** 51.30N 0.35W
Slough *d.* England **9 E2** 51.30N 0.35W
Slovakia Europe **54 F3** 49.00N 19.00E
Slovenia Europe **54 D1** 46.00N 14.30E
Slov''yans'k Ukraine **55 O3** 48.51N 37.36E
Slovyechna *r.* Belarus **55 K4** 51.41N 29.41E
Sluch *r.* Belarus/Ukraine **55 J5** 52.08N 27.31E
Słupsk Poland **54 E6** 54.28N 17.01E
Slutsk Belarus **55 J5** 53.02N 27.31E
Slyne Head Rep. of Ire. **20 A3** 53.25N 10.12W
Slyudyanka Russian Fed. **103 I8** 51.40N 103.40E
Smallwood Resr. Canada **63 L3** 54.00N 64.00W
Smarhon' Belarus **55 J6** 54.28N 26.20E
Smila Ukraine **55 L3** 49.15N 31.54E
Smoky *r.* Canada **62 G3** 56.10N 117.21W
Smøla *i.* Norway **43 A3** 63.20N 8.00E
Smolensk Russian Fed. **55 M6** 54.49N 32.04E
Smolikas *mtn.* Greece **56 E4** 40.06N 20.55E
Smolyan Bulgaria **56 G4** 41.34N 24.45E
Snaefell *mtn.* Iceland **43 Z2** 64.48N 15.34W
Snaefell *mtn.* I.o.M. **14 C3** 54.16N 4.28W
Snaith England **15 F2** 53.42N 1.01W
Snake *r.* U.S.A. **64 C6** 46.15N 119.00W
Sneek Neth. **42 E5** 53.03N 5.40E
Snettisham England **11 F3** 52.53N 0.30E
Snizort, Loch Scotland **18 C2** 57.35N 6.30W
Snøtinden *mtn.* Norway **43 C4** 66.30N 14.00E
Snov *r.* Ukraine **55 L4** 51.45N 31.45E
Snowdon *mtn.* Wales **12 C5** 53.05N 4.05W
Soay *i.* Scotland **18 C2** 57.09N 6.13W
Sobral Brazil **77 F4** 3.45S 40.20W
Sochi Russian Fed. **58 F2** 43.35N 39.46E
Society Is. Pacific Oc. **108 P5** 17.00S 150.00W
Socorro, I. Mexico **70 B4** 18.45N 110.58W
Socotra *i.* Yemen **85 J3** 12.30N 54.00E
Sodankylä Finland **43 F2** 67.21N 26.31E
Söderhamn Sweden **43 D3** 61.19N 17.10E
Södertälje Sweden **43 D2** 59.11N 17.39E
Sodo Ethiopia **85 H2** 6.52N 37.47E
Södra Kvarken *str.* Sweden/Finland **43 D3** 60.20N 19.00E
Sofia Bulgaria **56 F5** 42.41N 23.19E
Sognefjorden *est.* Norway **43 A3** 61.10N 5.50E
Sohâg Egypt **94 D4** 26.33N 31.42E
Soham England **11 F3** 52.20N 0.20E
Soignies Belgium **42 D2** 50.35N 4.04E
Soissons France **44 E6** 49.23N 3.20E
Söke Turkey **56 H2** 37.46N 27.26E
Sokhumi Georgia **57 O5** 43.01N 41.01E
Sokółka Poland **54 H5** 53.25N 23.31E
Sokoto Nigeria **84 E3** 13.02N 5.15E
Sokoto *r.* Nigeria **84 E3** 11.23N 4.05E
Solapur India **96 F4** 17.43N 75.56E
Solihull England **10 D3** 52.26N 1.47W
Solikamsk Russian Fed. **58 H3** 59.40N 56.45E
Sollefteå Sweden **43 D3** 63.09N 17.15E
Solomon Is. Pacific Oc. **111 F5** 8.00S 160.00E
Solomon Sea Pacific Oc. **110 E5** 7.00S 153.00E
Sölvesborg Sweden **54 D6** 56.03N 14.33E
Solway Firth *est.* England/Scotland **17 F2** 54.52N 3.30W
Solwezi Zambia **86 B3** 12.11S 26.23E
Soma Turkey **57 H3** 39.10N 27.36E
Somalia Africa **85 I2** 5.30N 47.00E
Sombor Yugo. **56 D6** 45.48N 19.08E
Somerset *d.* England **9 D2** 51.09N 3.00W
Somerset I. Canada **63 I5** 73.00N 93.30W
Somerton England **13 E3** 51.03N 2.44W
Sommen *l.* Sweden **43 C2** 58.05N 15.15E
Songea Tanzania **86 C3** 10.42S 35.39E
Songkhla Thailand **104 C5** 7.13N 100.37E
Son La Vietnam **104 C8** 21.20N 103.55E
Sono *r.* Brazil **77 F4** 8.59S 48.12W
Sonora *r.* Mexico **70 B6** 28.45N 111.55W
Sonora *d.* Mexico **70 B6** 29.20N 110.40W
Soria Spain **46 D4** 41.46N 2.28W
Soroca Moldova **55 K3** 48.08N 28.12E
Sorocaba Brazil **77 F2** 23.30S 47.32W
Sorol *i.* Fed. States of Micronesia **105 K5** 8.09N 140.25E
Sorong Indonesia **105 I3** 0.50S 131.17E
Soroti Uganda **87 A3** 1.42N 33.37E
Sørøya *i.* Norway **43 E5** 70.30N 22.30E
Sorraia *r.* Portugal **46 A3** 39.00N 8.51W
Sorsele Sweden **43 D4** 65.32N 17.34E
Sortavala Russian Fed. **43 G3** 61.40N 30.40E
Soshanguve R.S.A. **86 B2** 25.38S 28.11E
Sosna *r.* Russian Fed. **55 P5** 52.38N 38.50E
Sosnowiec Poland **54 F4** 50.18N 19.08E
Souk Ahras Algeria **52 E4** 36.17N 7.57E
Souris *r.* Canada **64 G6** 49.38N 99.35W
Sousse Tunisia **84 F5** 35.48N 10.38E
South *d.* Yemen **95 G1** 14.30N 47.30E
Southam England **10 D3** 52.16N 1.24W
South America 74
Southampton England **10 D1** 50.54N 1.23W
Southampton *d.* England **9 E2** 50.54N 1.23W
Southampton I. Canada **63 J4** 64.30N 84.00W
South Anston England **15 F2** 53.22N 1.13W
South Atlantic Ocean 72
South Australia *d.* Australia **110 C3** 29.00S 135.00E
South Ayrshire *d.* Scotland **8 C4** 55.15N 4.40W
South Bank England **15 F3** 54.35N 1.10W
South Bend U.S.A. **65 I5** 41.40N 86.15W
Southborough England **11 F2** 51.10N 0.15E
South Carolina *d.* U.S.A. **65 J3** 34.00N 81.00W
South Cave England **15 G2** 53.46N 0.37W
South China Sea Asia **104 E6** 12.30N 115.00E
South Dakota *d.* U.S.A. **64 F5** 44.30N 100.00W
South Dorset Downs *hills* England **10 C1** 50.40N 2.25W
South Downs *hills* England **11 E1** 50.54N 0.34W
South East C. Australia **110 D1** 43.38S 146.48E
Southeast Pacific Basin *f.* Pacific Oc. **116 D2**
Southend-on-Sea England **11 F2** 51.32N 0.43E
Southend-on-Sea *d.* England **9 F2** 51.32N 0.43E
Southern Alps *mts.* New Zealand **111 G1** 43.20S 170.45E
Southern Ocean **108 F1** 52.00S 110.00E
Southern Uplands *hills* Scotland **17 F3** 55.30N 3.30W
Southery England **11 F3** 52.32N 0.23E
South Esk *r.* Scotland **19 G1** 56.43N 2.32W
South Georgia *i.* Atlantic Oc. **75 F1** 54.00S 37.00W
South Gloucestershire *d.* England **9 D2** 51.35N 2.40W
South Horr Kenya **87 B3** 2.10N 36.55E
South I. New Zealand **111 G1** 43.00S 171.00E
South Kirkby England **15 F2** 53.35N 1.25W
South Kitui Nat. Res. Kenya **87 B2** 1.45S 38.40E
South Korea Asia **103 N5** 36.00N 128.00E
South Lanarkshire *d.* Scotland **8 D4** 55.40N 3.45W
Southminster England **11 F2** 51.40N 0.51E
South Molton England **13 D3** 51.01N 3.50W
South Ockendon England **11 F2** 51.32N 0.18E
South Orkney Is. Atlantic Oc. **112** 60.50S 45.00W
South Pacific Ocean **109 R3** 35.00S 140.00W
South Platte *r.* U.S.A. **64 G5** 41.09N 100.55W
Southport Australia **110 E3** 27.58S 153.20E
Southport England **14 D2** 53.38N 3.01W
South Ronaldsay *i.* Scotland **19 G3** 58.47N 2.56W
South Sandwich Is. Atlantic Oc. **72 H1** 58.00S 27.00W
South Saskatchewan *r.* Canada **62 H3** 53.15N 105.05W
South Shetland Is. Antarctica **112** 62.00S 60.00W
South Shields England **15 F4** 55.00N 1.24W
South Tyne *r.* England **15 E3** 54.59N 2.08W
South Uist *i.* Scotland **18 B2** 57.15N 7.20W
South Walls *i.* Scotland **19 F3** 58.45N 3.07W
Southwell England **15 G2** 53.05N 0.58W
Southwest Pacific Basin *f.* Pacific Oc. **116 A4**
Southwold England **11 G3** 52.19N 1.41E
South Woodham Ferrers England **11 F2** 51.39N 0.36E
South Wootton England **11 F3** 52.47N 0.26E
South Yorkshire *d.* England **9 E3** 53.28N 1.25W
Sovetsk Russian Fed. **54 G6** 55.02N 21.50E
Sovetskaya Gavan' Russian Fed. **103 Q7** 48.57N 140.16E
Soweto R.S.A. **86 B2** 26.16S 27.51E
Spain Europe **46 C4** 40.00N 4.00W
Spalding England **11 E3** 52.47N 0.09W
Span Head *hill* England **13 D3** 51.09N 3.51W
Sparti Greece **56 F2** 37.04N 22.28E
Spartivento, C. Calabria Italy **50 G2** 37.55N 16.04E
Spartivento, C. Sardinia Italy **50 C3** 38.53N 8.51E
Spassk Dal'niy Russian Fed. **106 B4** 44.37N 132.37E
Spátha, C. Greece **56 F1** 35.42N 23.43E
Speke G. Tanzania **87 A2** 2.18S 33.25E
Spencer G. Australia **110 C2** 34.30S 136.10E
Spennymoor *town* England **15 F3** 54.43N 1.35W
Sperrin Mts. N. Ireland **16 B2** 54.48N 7.06W
Spey *r.* Scotland **19 F2** 57.40N 3.06W
Speyer Germany **48 D3** 49.19N 8.26E
Spijkenisse Neth. **42 D3** 51.52N 4.19E
Spilsby England **15 H2** 53.10N 0.06E
Spitsbergen *is.* Arctic Oc. **58 D5** 78.00N 19.00E
Split Croatia **56 C5** 43.32N 16.27E
Spofforth England **15 F2** 53.57N 1.26W
Spokane U.S.A. **64 C6** 47.40N 117.25W
Spratly Is. S. China Sea **104 E5** 9.00N 112.50E
Spree *r.* Germany **48 F5** 52.32N 13.15E
Springfield Ill. U.S.A. **65 I4** 39.49N 89.39W
Springfield Miss. U.S.A. **65 H4** 37.11N 93.19W
Springhill Canada **65 N6** 45.39N 64.03W
Sprowston England **11 G3** 52.38N 1.22E
Spurn Head England **15 H2** 53.35N 0.08E
Srebrenica Bosnia. **56 D6** 44.06N 19.20E
Srednekolymsk Russian Fed. **59 R4** 67.27N 153.35E
Sretensk Russian Fed. **103 L8** 52.15N 117.52E
Sri Lanka Asia **97 G2** 7.30N 80.50E
Srinagar Jammu & Kashmir **96 E7** 34.08N 74.50E
Stadskanaal Neth. **42 F4** 52.58N 6.59E
Staffa *i.* Scotland **16 C4** 56.26N 6.21W
Stafford England **10 C3** 52.49N 2.09W
Staffordshire *d.* England **9 D3** 52.50N 2.00W
Staines England **11 E2** 51.29N 0.31W
Stalbridge England **10 C1** 50.57N 2.22W
Stalham England **11 G3** 52.46N 1.31E
Stalowa Wola Poland **54 H4** 50.40N 22.05E
Stamford England **11 E3** 52.39N 0.29W
Stamford Bridge *town* England **15 G2** 53.59N 0.53W
Standish England **14 E2** 53.36N 2.41W
Stanley England **15 F3** 54.53N 1.42W
Stanley Falkland Is. **75 D1** 51.45S 57.56W
Stanley, Mt. Uganda/Dem. Rep. of Congo **82 G5** 0.20N 30.50E
Stannington England **15 F4** 55.06N 1.40W
Stanovoy Range *mts.* Russian Fed. **59 O3** 56.00N 125.40E
Stansted Mountfitchet England **11 F2** 51.55N 0.12E
Stanton England **11 F3** 52.19N 0.53E
Stara Zagora Bulgaria **56 G5** 42.26N 25.37E
Starbuck I. Kiribati **108 P6** 5.37S 155.55W
Stargard Szczecinski Poland **54 D5** 53.21N 15.01E
Starokostyantyniv Ukraine **55 J3** 49.48N 27.10E
Start B. England **13 D2** 50.17N 3.35W
Start Pt. England **13 D2** 50.13N 3.38W
Staryy Oskol Russian Fed. **55 O4** 51.20N 37.50E
Stavanger Norway **43 A2** 58.58N 5.45E
Staveley England **15 F2** 53.16N 1.20W
Stavropol Highlands Russian Fed. **58 G2** 45.00N 42.30E
Steenwijk Neth. **42 F4** 52.47N 6.07E
Steep Holm *i.* England **13 D3** 51.20N 3.06W
Stefansson I. Canada **62 H5** 73.30N 105.30W
Steinfurt Germany **42 G4** 52.09N 7.21E
Steinkjer Norway **43 B3** 64.00N 11.30E
Stenness, Loch of Scotland **19 F4** 59.00N 3.15W
Sterling U.S.A. **64 F5** 40.37N 103.13W
Sterlitamak Russian Fed. **58 H3** 53.40N 55.59E
Stevenage England **11 E2** 51.54N 0.11W
Stewart Canada **62 F3** 55.56N 130.01W
Stewart *r.* Canada **62 E4** 63.40N 139.25W
Stewart I. New Zealand **111 F1** 47.02S 167.51E
Stewarton Scotland **16 E3** 55.41N 4.31W
Steyning England **11 E1** 50.54N 0.19W
Steyr Austria **54 D3** 48.04N 14.25E
Stikine *r.* Canada **62 E3** 56.45N 132.30W
Stilton England **11 E3** 52.29N 0.17W
Stinchar *r.* Scotland **16 E3** 55.06N 5.00W
Stirling Scotland **17 F4** 56.07N 3.57W
Stirling *d.* Scotland **8 C5** 56.10N 4.20W
Stjørdalshalsen Norway **43 B3** 63.30N 10.59E
Stob Choire Claurigh *mtn.* Scotland **18 E1** 56.50N 4.49W
Stockholm Sweden **43 D2** 59.20N 18.05E
Stockport England **15 E2** 53.25N 2.11W
Stockton U.S.A. **64 B4** 37.59N 121.20W
Stockton-on-Tees England **15 F3** 54.34N 1.20W
Stockton-on-Tees *d.* England **9 E4** 54.34N 1.20W
Stoer, Pt. of Scotland **18 D3** 58.16N 5.23W
Stoke on Trent England **10 C3** 53.01N 2.11W
Stoke-on-Trent *d.* England **9 D3** 53.01N 2.11W
Stokesay England **10 C3** 52.25N 2.49W
Stokesley England **15 F3** 54.27N 1.12W
Stolin Belarus **55 J4** 51.52N 26.51E
Stone England **10 C3** 52.55N 2.10W
Stonehaven Scotland **19 G1** 56.58N 2.13W
Stony Rapids *town* Canada **62 H3** 59.14N 103.48W
Stony Tunguska *r.* Russian Fed. **59 L4** 61.40N 90.00E
Stora Lulevatten *l.* Sweden **43 D4** 67.00N 19.30E
Storavan *l.* Sweden **43 D4** 65.45N 18.10E
Store Bælt *str.* Denmark **43 B1** 55.30N 11.00E
Støren Norway **43 B3** 63.03N 10.16E
Stornoway Scotland **18 C3** 58.12N 6.23W
Storrington England **11 E1** 50.55N 0.28W
Storsjön *l.* Sweden **43 C3** 63.10N 14.20E
Storskrymten *mtn.* Norway **43 B3** 62.20N 9.00E
Storuman Sweden **43 D4** 65.05N 17.10E
Storuman *l.* Sweden **43 D4** 65.14N 16.50E
Stotfold England **11 E3** 52.02N 0.13W
Stour *r.* Dorset England **10 D1** 50.43N 1.47W
Stour *r.* Suffolk England **11 G2** 51.56N 1.03E
Stour *r.* Warwicks. England **10 D3** 52.11N 1.43W
Stourbridge England **10 C3** 52.28N 2.08W
Stourport-on-Severn England **10 C3** 52.21N 2.16W
Stowbtsy Belarus **55 J5** 53.30N 26.44E
Stowmarket England **11 F3** 52.11N 1.00E
Stow-on-the-Wold England **10 D2** 51.55N 1.42W
Strabane N. Ireland **16 B2** 54.50N 7.29W
Stradbroke England **11 G3** 52.19N 1.16E
Stralsund Germany **48 F6** 54.18N 13.06E
Stranda Norway **43 A3** 62.18N 6.56E
Strangford Lough N. Ireland **16 D2** 54.28N 5.35W
Stranorlar Rep. of Ire. **16 B2** 54.48N 7.47W

Stranraer Scotland 16 D2 54.54N 5.02W
Strasbourg France 44 G6 48.35N 7.45E
Stratford-upon-Avon England 10 D3 52.12N 1.42W
Strathaven *town* Scotland 16 E3 55.41N 4.05W
Strathbeg, Loch of Scotland 19 H2 57.37N 1.53W
Strathbogie *f.* Scotland 19 G2 57.24N 2.50W
Strathmore *f.* Angus Scotland 17 F4 56.34N 3.10W
Strathmore *f.* High. Scotland 18 E3 58.25N 4.38W
Strathspey *f.* Scotland 19 F2 57.25N 3.25W
Strathy Pt. Scotland 19 E3 58.35N 4.01W
Stratton England 13 C2 50.49N 4.31W
Stratton St. Margaret England 10 D2 51.35N 1.45W
Straubing Germany 48 F3 48.53N 12.35E
Straumnes *c.* Iceland 43 X2 66.30N 23.05W
Streatley England 10 D2 51.32N 1.10W
Street England 13 E3 51.07N 2.43W
Stretham England 11 F3 52.21N 0.14E
Stroma, I. of Scotland 19 F3 58.41N 3.09W
Stromboli *i.* Italy 50 F3 38.48N 15.14E
Stromness Scotland 19 F3 58.58N 3.19W
Strömsund Sweden 43 C3 63.51N 15.35E
Stronsay *i.* Scotland 19 G4 59.07N 2.36W
Stronsay Firth *est.* Scotland 19 G4 59.05N 2.45W
Stroud England 10 C2 51.44N 2.12W
Struer Denmark 43 B2 56.30N 8.37E
Strule *r.* N. Ireland 16 B2 54.43N 7.25W
Struma *r.* Greece 56 F4 40.45N 23.51E
Strumble Head Wales 12 B4 52.03N 5.05W
Strumica Macedonia 56 F4 41.26N 22.39E
Stryy Ukraine 55 H3 49.16N 23.51E
Stryy *r.* Ukraine 55 I3 49.16N 24.18E
Studley England 10 D3 52.16N 1.52W
Stupino Russian Fed. 55 P6 54.53N 38.07E
Sturry England 11 G2 51.18N 1.07E
Sturt Stony Desert Australia 110 C3 28.30S 139.58E
Stuttgart Germany 48 D3 48.47N 9.12E
Styr *r.* Belarus/Ukraine 55 J5 52.07N 26.35E
Suakin Sudan 85 H3 19.04N 37.22E
Subotica Yugo. 56 D7 46.04N 19.41E
Suceava Romania 55 J2 47.39N 26.19E
Suchan *r.* Russian Fed. 106 B4 42.53N 132.56E
Suck *r.* Rep. of Ire. 20 C3 53.16N 8.03W
Sucre Bolivia 76 D3 19.05S 65.15W
Sudak Ukraine 55 N1 44.52N 34.57E
Sudan Africa 85 G3 14.00N 30.00E
Sudbury Canada 63 J2 46.30N 81.01W
Sudbury England 11 F3 52.03N 0.45E
Sudd *f.* Sudan 85 H2 7.50N 30.00E
Sudeten Mts. Czech Rep./Poland 54 E4 50.30N 16.30E
Suez Egypt 94 D4 29.59N 32.33E
Suez Canal Egypt 94 D5 30.40N 32.20E
Suez, G. of Egypt 94 D4 28.48N 33.00E
Suffolk *d.* England 9 F3 52.16N 1.00E
Suguta *r.* Kenya 87 B3 0.36N 36.04E
Suguti B. Tanzania 87 A2 1.44S 33.36E
Şuḩar Oman 95 I3 24.23N 56.43E
Suhl Germany 48 E4 50.37N 10.43E
Suir *r.* Rep. of Ire. 20 D2 52.17N 7.00W
Suizhou China 103 K4 31.46N 113.22E
Sukabumi Indonesia 104 D2 6.55S 106.50E
Sukadana Indonesia 104 E3 1.15S 110.00E
Sukhinichi Russian Fed. 55 N6 54.07N 35.21E
Sukkur Pakistan 96 D6 27.42N 68.54E
Sula *i.* Norway 43 A3 61.10N 4.50E
Sulaiman Ranges *mts.* Pakistan 90 I5 30.00N 68.00E
Sula Is. Indonesia 105 H3 1.50S 125.10E
Sulawesi *i.* Indonesia 104 G3 2.00S 120.30E
Sulina Romania 55 K1 45.08N 29.40E
Sullana Peru 76 B4 4.52S 80.39W
Sulmona Italy 50 E5 42.04N 13.57E
Sulu Archipelago Phil. 105 G5 5.30N 121.00E
Sulu Sea Pacific Oc. 104 G5 8.00N 120.00E
Sumatra *i.* Indonesia 104 C3 2.00S 102.00E
Sumba *i.* Indonesia 104 F2 9.30S 119.55E
Sumbawa *i.* Indonesia 104 F2 8.45S 117.50E
Sumburgh Scotland 19 Y8 59.53N 1.16W
Sumburgh Head Scotland 19 Y8 59.51N 1.16W
Summer Isles *is.* Scotland 18 D3 58.01N 5.26W
Sumqayıt Azerbaijan 58 G2 40.35N 49.38E
Sumy Ukraine 55 N4 50.55N 34.49E
Sunart, Loch Scotland 18 D1 56.42N 5.45W
Sunda Str. Indonesia 104 C2 6.00S 105.50E
Sunderland England 15 F3 54.55N 1.22W
Sundsvall Sweden 43 D3 62.22N 17.20E
Sunga Tanzania 87 B2 4.25S 38.04E
Sungaipenuh Indonesia 104 C3 2.00S 101.28E
Sungurlu Turkey 57 L4 40.10N 34.23E
Suolijärvet *l.* Finland 43 F4 66.18N 28.00E
Suonenjoki Finland 43 F3 62.40N 27.06E
Superior U.S.A. 65 H6 46.42N 92.05W
Superior, L. N. America 65 I6 48.00N 88.00W
Suq ash Shuyukh Iraq 95 G5 30.53N 46.28E
Sur Oman 95 I3 22.23N 59.32E
Surab Pakistan 95 K4 28.29N 66.16E
Surabaya Indonesia 104 E2 7.14S 112.45E
Surakarta Indonesia 104 E2 7.32S 110.50E
Surat India 96 E5 21.10N 72.54E
Surendranagar India 96 E5 22.42N 71.41E
Surgut Russian Fed. 58 J4 61.13N 73.20E
Surigao Phil. 105 H5 9.47N 125.29E
Surin Thailand 104 C6 14.53N 103.29E
Suriname S. America 74 D7 4.00N 56.00W
Surrey *d.* England 9 E2 51.16N 0.30W
Surtsey *i.* Iceland 43 X1 63.18N 20.37W
Susangerd Iran 95 G5 31.40N 48.06E
Sutak Jammu & Kashmir 97 F7 33.12N 77.28E
Sutherland *f.* Scotland 19 E3 58.20N 4.20W
Sutlej *r.* Pakistan 96 E6 29.26N 71.09E
Sutterton England 11 E3 52.54N 0.06W
Sutton England 11 F3 52.23N 0.07E
Sutton Bridge England 11 F3 52.46N 0.12E
Sutton Coldfield England 10 D3 52.33N 1.50W
Sutton in Ashfield England 15 F2 53.08N 1.16W
Suva Fiji 111 G4 18.08S 178.25E
Suvorov I. Cook Is. 108 O5 13.15S 163.05W
Suwałki Poland 54 H6 54.07N 22.56E
Suzhou Anhui China 103 L4 33.38N 117.02E
Suzhou Jiangsu China 103 M4 31.21N 120.40E
Suzu Japan 106 C3 37.20N 137.15E
Suzuka Japan 106 C2 34.51N 136.35E
Svalbard *is.* Norway 58 D5 76.00N 15.00E
Svapa *r.* Russian Fed. 55 N4 51.44N 34.56E
Sveg Sweden 43 C3 62.02N 14.20E
Svendborg Denmark 43 B1 55.04N 10.38E
Svetogorsk Russian Fed. 43 G3 61.07N 28.50E
Svitavy Czech Rep. 54 E3 49.45N 16.27E
Svitlovods'k Ukraine 55 M3 49.04N 33.15E
Svobodnyy Russian Fed. 59 O3 51.24N 128.05E
Swabian Alps *mts.* Germany 48 D3 48.20N 9.30E
Swadlincote England 10 D3 52.47N 1.34W
Swaffham England 11 F3 52.38N 0.42E
Swains I. Samoa 108 N5 11.03S 171.06W
Swakopmund Namibia 86 A2 22.40S 14.34E
Swale *r.* England 15 F3 54.05N 1.20W
Swanage England 10 D1 50.36N 1.59W
Swan Is. Honduras 71 H4 17.25N 83.55W
Swanley England 11 F2 51.24N 0.12E
Swansea Wales 12 D3 51.37N 3.57W
Swansea *d.* Wales 9 D2 51.35N 4.10W
Swansea B. Wales 12 D3 51.33N 3.50W
Swaziland Africa 86 C2 26.30S 31.30E
Sweden Europe 43 C2 63.00N 16.00E
Sweetwater U.S.A. 64 F3 32.37N 100.25W
Swift Current *town* Canada 62 H3 50.17N 107.49W
Swilly, Lough Rep. of Ire. 20 D5 55.10N 7.32W
Swindon England 10 D2 51.33N 1.47W
Swindon *d.* England 9 E2 51.33N 1.47W
Swineshead England 11 E3 52.57N 0.10W
Świnoujście Poland 54 D5 53.55N 14.18E
Switzerland Europe 44 G5 47.00N 8.00E
Swords Rep. of Ire. 20 E3 53.28N 6.13W
Sybil Pt. Rep. of Ire. 20 A2 52.10N 10.27W
Sydney Australia 110 E2 33.55S 151.10E
Sydney Canada 63 L2 46.10N 60.10W
Syktyvkar Russian Fed. 58 H4 61.42N 50.45E
Sylarna *mtn.* Norway/Sweden 43 C3 63.01N 12.13E
Sylt *i.* Germany 43 B1 54.50N 8.20E
Syracuse U.S.A. 65 K5 43.03N 76.10W
Syr Darya *r.* Asia 58 I2 46.00N 61.12E
Syria Asia 94 E5 35.00N 38.00E
Syrian Desert Asia 94 E5 32.00N 39.00E
Syzran Russian Fed. 58 G3 53.10N 48.29E
Szczecin Poland 54 D5 53.25N 14.32E
Szczecinek Poland 54 E5 53.42N 16.41E
Szczytno Poland 54 G5 53.34N 21.00E
Szeged Hungary 54 G2 46.16N 20.08E
Székesfehérvár Hungary 54 F2 47.12N 18.25E
Szekszárd Hungary 54 F2 46.22N 18.44E
Szombathely Hungary 54 E2 47.12N 16.38E

T

Tabas Iran 95 I5 33.36N 56.55E
Tabasco *d.* Mexico 70 F4 18.30N 93.00W
Tabatinga, Serra da *mts.* Brazil 77 F3 10.00S 44.00W
Tábor Czech Rep. 54 D3 49.25N 14.41E
Tabora Tanzania 86 C4 5.02S 32.50E
Tabrīz Iran 95 G6 38.05N 46.18E
Tabuaeran *i.* Kiribati 108 P7 3.52N 159.20W
Tabuk Saudi Arabia 94 E4 28.25N 36.35E
Täby Sweden 43 D2 59.29N 18.04E
Tacloban Phil. 105 G6 11.15N 124.59E
Tacna Peru 76 C3 18.01S 70.15W
Tacoma U.S.A. 64 B6 47.16N 122.30W
Tacuarembó Uruguay 77 E1 31.42S 56.00W
Tadcaster England 15 F2 53.53N 1.16W
Taegu S. Korea 103 N5 35.52N 128.36E
Taejon S. Korea 103 N5 36.20N 127.26E
Taf *r.* Wales 12 C3 51.45N 4.29W
Taganrog Russian Fed. 53 K6 47.14N 38.55E
Taganrog, G. of Ukraine/Russian Fed. 53 K6 47.00N 38.30E
Tagbilaran Phil. 105 G5 9.38N 123.53E
Tagula I. P.N.G. 110 E4 11.30S 153.30E
Tagus *r.* Portugal 46 A3 39.00N 8.57W
Tahat, Mt. Algeria 84 E4 23.20N 5.40E
Tahiti *i.* Îs. de la Société 109 Q5 17.37S 149.27W
Taibei Taiwan 103 M2 25.05N 121.32E
Taidong Taiwan 103 M2 22.49N 121.10E
Tain Scotland 19 E2 57.49N 4.02W
Tainan Taiwan 103 M2 23.01N 120.14E
Taiping Malaysia 104 C4 4.54N 100.42E
Taita Hills Kenya 87 B2 3.20S 38.17E
Taivalkoski Finland 43 G4 65.35N 28.20E
Taivaskero *mtn.* Finland 43 E5 68.02N 24.00E
Taiwan Asia 103 M2 23.30N 121.00E
Taiwan Str. China/Taiwan 103 M2 25.00N 120.00E
Taiyuan China 103 K5 37.50N 112.30E
Taizhong Taiwan 103 M2 24.09N 120.40E
Ta'izz Yemen 94 F1 13.35N 44.02E
Tajikistan Asia 102 C5 39.00N 70.30E
Tak Thailand 104 B7 16.47N 99.10E
Takabba Kenya 87 C3 3.25N 40.11E
Takamatsu Japan 106 B2 34.28N 134.05E
Takaoka Japan 106 C3 36.47N 137.00E
Take-shima *i.* see Tok-to *i.* Japan 106 B3
Taklimakan Shamo *des.* China 102 E5 38.10N 82.00E
Talagang Pakistan 95 L5 32.55N 72.25E
Talara Peru 76 B4 4.38S 81.18W
Talaud Is. Indonesia 105 H4 4.20N 126.50E
Talavera de la Reina Spain 46 C3 39.58N 4.50W
Talca Chile 75 B3 35.28S 71.40W
Talcahuano Chile 75 B3 36.40S 73.10W
Taldykorgan Kazakhstan 102 D6 45.02N 78.23E
Talgarth Wales 12 D3 51.59N 3.15W
Taliabu *i.* Indonesia 105 G3 1.50S 124.55E
Tallahassee U.S.A. 65 J3 30.28N 84.19W
Tallinn Estonia 43 F2 59.22N 24.48E
Taloyoak Canada 63 I4 69.30N 93.20W
Talsi Latvia 43 E2 57.15N 22.36E
Taltson *r.* Canada 62 G4 61.35N 112.12W
Tamale Ghana 84 D2 9.26N 0.49W
Tamanrasset Algeria 84 E4 22.50N 5.31E
Tamar *r.* England 13 C2 50.28N 4.13W
Tamaulipas *d.* Mexico 70 E5 24.00N 98.20W
Tama Wildlife Res. Ethiopia 87 B4 6.00N 36.00E
Tambach Kenya 87 B3 0.32N 35.32E
Tambacounda Senegal 84 C3 13.45N 13.40W
Tambelan Is. Indonesia 104 D4 0.59N 107.35E
Tambov Russian Fed. 58 G3 52.44N 41.28E
Tambre *r.* Spain 46 A5 42.50N 8.55W
Tâmega *r.* Portugal 46 A4 41.04N 8.17W
Tamiahua Lagoon Mexico 70 E5 21.30N 97.20W
Tamil Nadu *d.* India 97 F3 11.15N 79.00E
Tampa-St. Petersburg U.S.A. 65 J2 27.58N 82.38W
Tampere Finland 43 E3 61.32N 23.45E
Tampico Mexico 70 E5 22.18N 97.52W
Tamworth Australia 110 E2 31.07S 150.57E
Tamworth England 10 D3 52.38N 1.42W
Tana *r.* Kenya 87 C2 2.32S 40.32E
Tana, L. Ethiopia 85 H3 12.00N 37.20E
Tanafjorden *est.* Norway 43 G5 70.40N 28.30E
Tanami Desert Australia 110 C4 19.50S 130.50E
Tanana U.S.A. 62 C4 65.11N 152.10W
Tanaro *r.* Italy 50 C6 45.01N 8.46E
Tando Adam Pakistan 96 D6 25.46N 68.40E
Tandragee N. Ireland 16 C1 54.21N 6.26W
Tanega-shima *i.* Japan 106 B2 30.32N 131.00E
Tanga Tanzania 87 B1 5.07S 39.05E
Tanganyika, L. Africa 86 B4 5.37S 29.30E
Tangier Morocco 84 D5 35.48N 5.45W
Tangshan China 103 L5 39.37N 118.05E
Tanimbar Is. Indonesia 105 I2 7.50S 131.30E
Tanjay Phil. 105 G5 9.31N 123.10E
Tanjona Bobaomby *c.* Madagascar 86 D3 11.58S 49.14E
Tanjona Vohimena *c.* Madagascar 86 D2 25.34S 45.10E
Tanjungkarang Telukbetung Indonesia 104 D2 5.28S 105.16E
Tanjungpandan Indonesia 104 D3 2.44S 107.36E
Tanjungredeb Indonesia 104 F4 2.09N 117.29E
Tank Pakistan 95 L5 32.13N 70.23E
Tanna *i.* Vanuatu 111 F4 19.30S 169.20E
Tanta Egypt 94 D5 30.48N 31.00E
Tanzania Africa 86 C4 5.00S 35.00E
Tao'an China 103 M7 45.25N 122.46E
Taourirt Morocco 52 C3 34.25N 2.53W
Tapachula Mexico 70 F3 14.54N 92.15W
Tapajós *r.* Brazil 77 E4 2.40S 55.30W
Tapauá *r.* Brazil 76 D4 5.40S 64.20W
Tapi *r.* India 96 E5 21.05N 72.45E
Taquari *r.* Brazil 77 E3 19.00S 57.27W
Tar *r.* Rep. of Ire. 20 D2 52.15N 7.48W
Tara *r.* Yugo. 56 D5 43.23N 18.47E
Tarakan Indonesia 104 F4 3.20N 117.38E
Taranaki, Mt. New Zealand 111 G2 39.20S 174.05E
Tarancón Spain 46 D4 40.01N 3.01W
Tarangire Nat. Park Tanzania 87 B2 4.00S 36.00E
Taranto Italy 50 G4 40.28N 17.14E
Taranto, G. of Italy 50 G4 40.00N 17.20E
Tarapoto Peru 76 C4 6.31S 76.23W
Tarbat Ness *c.* Scotland 19 F2 57.52N 3.46W
Tarbert A. and B. Scotland 16 D3 55.57N 5.45W
Tarbert A. and B. Scotland 16 D3 55.51N 5.25W
Tarbert W.Isles Scotland 18 C2 57.55N 6.50W
Tarbes France 44 D3 43.14N 0.05E
Târgu-Jiu Romania 56 F6 45.03N 23.17E
Târgu Mureş Romania 55 I2 46.33N 24.34E
Târgu Secuiesc Romania 55 J2 46.00N 26.08E
Tari P.N.G. 105 K2 5.52S 142.58E
Tarija Bolivia 76 D2 21.33S 64.45W
Tarīm Yemen 95 G2 16.03N 49.00E
Tarim Basin *f.* China 102 E5 40.00N 82.00E
Tarime Tanzania 87 A2 1.20S 34.20E
Tarleton England 14 E2 53.41N 2.50W
Tarn *r.* France 44 D4 44.15N 1.15E
Tarnica *mtn.* Poland 54 H3 49.05N 22.44E
Tarnów Poland 54 G4 50.01N 20.59E
Taroudannt Morocco 52 B3 30.31N 8.55W
Tarragona Spain 46 F4 41.07N 1.15E
Tarsus Turkey 57 L2 36.52N 34.52E
Tartu Estonia 43 F2 58.20N 26.44E
Tarṭūs Syria 57 L1 34.55N 35.52E
Tashkent Uzbekistan 102 B6 41.16N 69.13E
Tasiilaq Greenland 63 O4 65.40N 38.00W
Tasikmalaya Indonesia 104 D2 7.20S 108.16E
Tasmania *d.* Australia 110 D1 42.00S 147.00E
Tasman Sea Pacific Oc. 111 F2 38.00S 160.00E
Tatarbunary Ukraine 55 K1 45.49N 29.34E
Tatarsk Russian Fed. 58 J3 55.14N 76.00E
Tatar Str. Russian Fed. 59 Q2 47.40N 141.00E
Tatvan Turkey 94 F6 38.31N 42.15E
Taubaté Brazil 77 F2 23.00S 45.36W
Taung-gyi Myanmar 97 J5 20.49N 97.01E
Taunton England 13 D3 51.01N 3.07W
Taunus *mts.* Germany 48 D4 50.07N 8.10E
Taupo, L. New Zealand 111 G2 38.45S 175.30E
Taurus Mts. Turkey 57 K2 37.15N 34.00E
Taverham England 11 G3 52.40N 1.13E
Tavira Portugal 46 B2 37.07N 7.39W
Tavistock England 13 C2 50.33N 4.09W
Tavoy Myanmar 97 J3 14.07N 98.18E
Tavy *r.* England 13 C2 50.27N 4.10W
Taw *r.* England 13 C3 51.05N 4.05W
Tawau Malaysia 104 F4 4.16N 117.54E
Tawe *r.* Wales 12 D3 51.38N 3.56W
Tawitawi *i.* Phil. 104 G5 5.05N 120.00E
Tay *r.* Scotland 17 F4 56.21N 3.18W
Tay, Loch Scotland 16 E4 56.32N 4.08W
Tayma' Saudi Arabia 94 E4 27.37N 38.30E
Taymyr, L. Russian Fed. 59 M5 74.20N 101.00E
Taymyr Pen. Russian Fed. 59 L5 75.30N 99.00E
Tây Ninh Vietnam 104 D6 11.17N 106.07E
Tayport Scotland 17 G4 56.27N 2.53W
Taytay Phil. 104 F6 10.47N 119.32E
Taz *r.* Russian Fed. 58 J4 67.30N 78.50E
Taza Morocco 52 C3 34.16N 4.01W
T'bilisi Georgia 58 G2 41.43N 44.48E
Te Anau, L. New Zealand 111 F1 45.25S 167.43E
Tébessa Algeria 52 E4 35.22N 8.08E
Tebingtinggi Indonesia 104 B4 3.20N 99.08E
Tecuci Romania 55 J1 45.49N 27.27E
Tedzhen Turkmenistan 95 J6 37.26N 60.30E
Tees *r.* England 15 F3 54.35N 1.11W
Tees B. England 15 F3 54.40N 1.07W
Tefé *r.* Brazil 76 D4 3.35S 64.47W
Tegucigalpa Honduras 70 G3 14.05N 87.14W
Teguise Canary Is. 46 Z2 29.03N 13.36W
Tehran Iran 95 H6 35.40N 51.26E
Tehuantepec, G. of Mexico 70 F4 16.00N 95.00W
Teide, Pico del *mtn.* Canary Is. 46 X2 28.17N 16.39W
Teifi *r.* Wales 12 C4 52.05N 4.41W
Teign *r.* England 13 D2 50.32N 3.36W
Teignmouth England 13 D2 50.33N 3.30W
Teith *r.* Scotland 17 E4 56.09N 4.00W
Tekirdağ Turkey 56 H4 40.59N 27.30E
Tel Aviv-Yafo Israel 94 D5 32.05N 34.46E
Teles Pires *r.* Brazil 77 E4 7.20S 57.30W
Telford England 10 C3 52.42N 2.30W
Telford and the Wrekin *d.* England 9 D3 52.42N 2.30W
Teme *r.* England 10 C3 52.10N 2.13W
Temirtau Kazakhstan 102 C8 50.05N 72.55E
Temple U.S.A. 64 G3 31.06N 97.22W
Temple Ewell England 11 G2 51.09N 1.16E
Templemore Rep. of Ire. 20 D2 52.48N 7.51W
Temryuk Russian Fed. 57 M6 45.16N 37.24E
Temuco Chile 75 B3 38.45S 72.40W
Tena Ecuador 76 C4 1.00S 77.48W
Tenasserim Myanmar 97 J3 12.05N 99.00E
Tenbury Wells England 10 C3 52.18N 2.35W
Tenby Wales 12 C3 51.40N 4.42W
Ten Degree Channel Indian Oc. 97 I2 10.00N 92.30E
Tendo Japan 106 D3 38.22N 140.22E
Tenerife *i.* Canary Is. 46 X2 28.10N 16.30W
Tengiz, L. Kazakhstan 102 B8 50.30N 69.00E
Tennessee *r.* U.S.A. 65 I4 37.10N 88.25W
Tennessee *d.* U.S.A. 65 I4 36.00N 86.00W
Tenryu *r.* Japan 106 C2 34.42N 137.44E
Tenterden England 11 F2 51.04N 0.42E
Teófilo Otôni Brazil 77 F3 17.52S 41.31W
Tepic Mexico 70 D5 21.30N 104.51W
Teplice Czech Rep. 54 C4 50.40N 13.50E
Teraina *i.* Kiribati 108 O7 4.30N 160.02W
Teramo Italy 50 E5 42.40N 13.43E
Terebovlya Ukraine 55 I3 49.18N 25.44E
Teresina Brazil 77 F4 4.50S 42.50W
Tergnier France 42 C1 49.39N 3.18E
Termez Uzbekistan 95 K6 37.15N 67.15E
Terminillo, Monte *mtn.* Italy 50 E5 42.29N 13.00E
Términos Lagoon Mexico 70 F4 18.30N 91.30W
Termoli Italy 50 F4 41.58N 14.59E
Tern *r.* England 10 C3 52.40N 2.38W
Ternate Indonesia 105 H4 0.48N 127.23E
Terneuzen Neth. 42 C3 51.20N 3.50E
Terni Italy 50 E5 42.34N 12.44E
Ternopil' Ukraine 55 I3 49.35N 25.39E
Terrace Canada 62 F3 54.31N 128.32W
Terrassa Spain 46 F4 41.34N 2.00E
Terre Haute U.S.A. 65 I4 39.27N 87.24W
Terrington Marsh England 11 F3 52.47N 0.15E
Terschelling *i.* Neth. 42 E5 53.25N 5.25E
Teseney Eritrea 94 E2 15.05N 36.41E
Teslin Canada 62 E4 60.10N 132.42W
Test *r.* England 10 D1 50.55N 1.29W
Tetas, Punta *c.* Chile 76 C2 23.32S 70.39W
Tetbury England 10 C2 51.37N 2.09W
Tete Mozambique 86 C3 16.10S 33.30E
Tetney England 15 G2 53.30N 0.01W
Tétouan Morocco 84 D5 35.34N 5.22W
Teviot *r.* Scotland 17 G3 55.36N 2.26W
Teviothead Scotland 17 G3 55.20N 2.56W
Tewkesbury England 10 C2 51.59N 2.09W
Texarkana U.S.A. 65 H3 33.28N 94.02W
Texas *d.* U.S.A. 64 G3 32.00N 100.00W
Texel *i.* Neth. 42 D5 53.05N 4.47E
Texoma, L. U.S.A. 64 G3 34.00N 96.40W
Tezpur India 97 I6 26.38N 92.49E
Thai Binh Vietnam 104 D8 20.27N 106.20E
Thailand Asia 104 C7 16.00N 101.00E
Thailand, G. of Asia 104 C6 11.00N 101.00E
Thai Nguyên Vietnam 104 D8 21.31N 105.55E
Thal Desert Pakistan 95 L5 31.30N 71.40E
Thame England 10 E2 51.44N 0.58W
Thame *r.* England 10 D2 51.38N 1.10W
Thames *r.* England 11 F2 51.30N 0.05E
Thanh Hoa Vietnam 104 D7 19.50N 105.48E
Thar Desert India 96 E6 28.00N 72.00E
Thasos *i.* Greece 56 G4 40.40N 24.39E
Thatcham England 10 D2 51.25N 1.15W
Thaton Myanmar 97 J4 16.56N 97.20E
Thaxted England 11 F2 51.57N 0.21E
The Bahamas C. America 71 I5 23.30N 75.00W
The Calf *mtn.* England 14 E3 54.21N 2.32W
The Cheviot *mtn.* England 15 E4 55.29N 2.10W
The Everglades *f.* U.S.A. 65 J2 26.00N 80.30W
The Gambia Africa 84 C3 13.30N 15.00W
The Great Oasis Egypt 94 D3 24.30N 30.40E
The Grenadines *is.* Windward Is. 71 L3 12.35N 61.20W
The Gulf Asia 95 H4 27.00N 50.00E
The Hague Neth. 42 D4 52.05N 4.16E
Thelon *r.* Canada 62 I4 64.23N 96.15W
The Marsh *f.* England 11 F3 52.50N 0.10E
The Minch *str.* Scotland 18 D3 58.10N 5.50W
The Mullet *pen.* Rep. of Ire. 20 A4 54.10N 10.05W
The Mumbles Wales 12 C3 51.34N 4.00W
The Naze *c.* England 11 G2 51.53N 1.17E
The Needles *c.* England 10 D1 50.39N 1.35W
The North Sd. Scotland 19 G4 59.18N 2.45W
Theodore Roosevelt *r.* Brazil 77 D4 7.33S 60.24W
The Old Man of Coniston *mtn.* England 14 D3 54.22N 3.08W
The Pas Canada 62 H3 53.50N 101.15W
The Pennines *hills* England 15 E3 54.40N 2.20W
The Rhinns of Galloway *f.* Scotland 16 D2 54.50N 5.02W
The Slot *str.* Solomon Is. 111 E5 7.30S 157.00E
The Snares *is.* New Zealand 103 L2 48.00S 166.30E
The Solent *str.* England 10 D1 50.45N 1.20W
The Sound England 13 C2 50.20N 4.10W
Thessaloniki Greece 56 F4 40.38N 22.56E
Thessaloniki, G. of Med. Sea 56 F4 40.10N 23.00E
The Storr *mtn.* Scotland 18 C2 57.30N 6.11W
Thet *r.* England 11 F3 52.25N 0.44E
Thetford England 11 F3 52.25N 0.44E
Thetford Mines Canada 65 L6 46.05N 71.18W
The Trossachs *f.* Scotland 16 E4 56.15N 4.25W
The Wash *b.* England 11 F3 52.55N 0.15E
The Weald *f.* England 11 F2 51.05N 0.20E
Thiers France 44 E4 45.51N 3.33E
Thiès Senegal 84 A3 14.48N 16.56W
Thika Kenya 87 B2 1.04S 37.04E
Thimbu Bhutan 97 H6 27.29N 89.40E
Thionville France 44 G6 49.22N 6.11E
Thira *i.* Greece 56 G2 36.24N 25.27E
Thirlmere *l.* England 14 D3 54.32N 3.04W
Thirsk England 15 F3 54.15N 1.20W
Thiruvananthapuram India 96 F2 8.41N 76.57E
Thisted Denmark 43 B2 56.57N 8.42E
Thomastown Rep. of Ire. 20 D2 52.31N 7.08W
Thompson Canada 62 I3 55.45N 97.54W
Thornaby-on-Tees England 15 F3 54.34N 1.18W
Thornbury England 10 C2 51.36N 2.31W
Thorne England 15 G2 53.36N 0.56W
Thornhill Scotland 17 F3 55.15N 3.46W
Thornton England 14 E2 53.53N 3.00W
Thrapston England 11 E3 52.24N 0.32W
Thuin Belgium 42 D2 50.21N 4.20E
Thule *see* Qaanaaq Greenland 63
Thun Switz. 44 G5 46.46N 7.38E
Thunder Bay *town* Canada 63 J2 48.25N 89.14W
Thüringian Forest *mts.* Germany 48 E4 50.40N 10.50E
Thurles Rep. of Ire. 20 D2 52.41N 7.50W
Thursby England 14 D3 54.51N 3.03W
Thurso Scotland 19 F3 58.35N 3.32W
Thurso *r.* Scotland 19 F3 58.35N 3.32W

Valdai Hills Russian Fed. 35 G3 57.10N 33.00E
Valday Russian Fed. 55 C5 57.59N 33.10E
Valdepeñas Spain 46 D3 38.46N 3.24W
Valdés, Pen. Argentina 75 C2 42.30S 64.00W
Valdez U.S.A. 62 D4 61.07N 146.17W
Valdivia Chile 75 B3 39.46S 73.15W
Val d'Or *town* Canada 63 K2 48.07N 77.47W
Valdosta U.S.A. 65 J3 30.51N 83.51W
Valdres *f.* Norway 43 B3 61.00N 9.10E
Valence France 44 F4 44.56N 4.54E
Valencia Spain 46 E3 39.29N 0.24W
Valencia Venezuela 71 K3 10.14N 67.59W
Valencia, G. of Spain 46 F3 39.38N 0.20E
Valencia de Alcántara Spain 46 B3 39.25N 7.14W
Valenciennes France 44 E7 50.22N 3.32E
Vale of Evesham *f.* England 10 D3 52.05N 1.55W
Vale of Glamorgan *d.* Wales 9 D2 51.27N 3.22W
Vale of Pickering *f.* England 15 G3 54.11N 0.45W
Vale of York *f.* England 15 F3 54.12N 1.25W
Valera Venezuela 71 J2 9.21N 70.38W
Valier, Mont *mtn.* France 44 D3 42.48N 1.04E
Valinco, G. of Med. Sea 44 H2 41.40N 8.50E
Valjevo Yugo. 56 D6 44.16N 19.56E
Valka Latvia 43 F2 57.44N 26.00E
Valkeakoski Finland 43 F3 61.17N 24.05E
Valkenswaard Neth. 42 E3 51.21N 5.27E
Valladolid Spain 46 C4 41.39N 4.45W
Valledupar Colombia 71 J3 10.10N 73.16W
Valletta Malta 50 F1 35.53N 14.31E
Valley *town* Wales 12 C5 53.17N 4.34W
Valley City U.S.A. 64 G6 46.57N 97.58W
Valparaíso Chile 75 B3 33.05S 71.40W
Vals, C. Indonesia 105 J2 8.30S 137.30E
Valverde Canary Is. 46 X1 27.48N 17.55W
Vammala Finland 43 E3 61.20N 22.54E
Van Turkey 94 F6 38.28N 43.20E
Van, L. Turkey 94 F6 38.35N 42.52E
Vancouver Canada 62 F2 49.13N 123.06W
Vancouver I. Canada 62 F2 50.00N 126.00W
Vänern *l.* Sweden 43 C2 59.00N 13.15E
Vänersborg Sweden 43 C2 58.23N 12.19E
Vanimo P.N.G. 105 K3 2.40S 141.17E
Vännäs Sweden 43 D3 63.56N 19.50E
Vannes France 44 B5 47.40N 2.44W
Vantaa Finland 43 F3 60.13N 25.01E
Vanua Levu *i.* Fiji 111 G4 16.33S 179.15E
Vanuatu Pacific Oc. 111 F4 16.00S 167.00E
Varanasi India 97 G6 25.20N 83.00E
Varangerfjorden *est.* Norway 43 G5 70.00N 29.30E
Varaždin Croatia 56 C7 46.18N 16.20E
Varberg Sweden 43 C2 57.06N 12.15E
Vardar *r.* Greece 56 F4 40.31N 22.43E
Varese Italy 50 C6 45.48N 8.48E
Vârful Bihor *mtn.* Romania 54 H2 46.26N 22.43E
Vârful Moldoveanu *mtn.* Romania 56 G6 45.36N 24.32E
Varkaus Finland 43 F3 62.15N 27.45E
Varna Bulgaria 57 H5 43.13N 27.57E
Värnamo Sweden 43 C2 57.11N 14.03E
Várpalota Hungary 54 F2 47.12N 18.09E
Vasa Barris *r.* Brazil 77 G3 11.07S 37.08W
Vaslui Romania 55 J2 46.38N 27.44E
Västerås Sweden 43 D2 59.36N 16.32E
Västerdal *r.* Sweden 43 C3 60.32N 15.02E
Västervik Sweden 43 D2 57.45N 16.40E
Vasyl'kiv Ukraine 55 L4 50.12N 30.15E
Vatersay *i.* Scotland 18 B1 56.56N 7.32W
Vatnajökull *mts.* Iceland 43 Y2 64.20N 17.00W
Vättern *l.* Sweden 43 C2 58.30N 14.30E
Vavau Group *is.* Tonga 108 N5 19.50S 174.30W
Växjö Sweden 43 C2 56.52N 14.50E
Vaygach *i.* Russian Fed. 58 H5 70.00N 59.00E
Vechte *r.* Neth. 42 F4 52.39N 6.01E
Veendam Neth. 42 F5 53.08N 6.52E
Veenendaal Neth. 42 E4 52.03N 5.32E
Vega *i.* Norway 43 B4 65.40N 11.55E
Vejle Denmark 43 B1 55.43N 9.33E
Velen Germany 42 F3 51.53N 6.59E
Veles Macedonia 56 E4 41.43N 21.49E
Vélez-Málaga Spain 46 C2 36.48N 4.05W
Velhas *r.* Brazil 74 E5 17.10S 44.49W
Velikiye Luki Russian Fed. 58 F3 56.19N 30.31E
Velikiy Novgorod Russian Fed. 58 F3 58.30N 31.20E
Velino, Monte *mtn.* Italy 50 E5 42.09N 13.23E
Velizh Russian Fed. 55 L6 55.36N 31.13E
Vellore India 97 F3 12.56N 79.09E
Vel'sk Russian Fed. 58 G4 61.05N 42.06E
Venachar, Loch Scotland 16 E4 56.13N 4.19W
Vendôme France 44 D5 47.48N 1.04E
Venezuela S. America 74 C7 7.00N 65.20W
Venezuela, G. of Venezuela 71 J3 11.30N 71.00W
Venice Italy 50 E6 45.26N 12.20E
Venice, G. of Med. Sea 50 E6 45.20N 13.00E
Venray Neth. 42 E3 51.32N 5.58E
Venta *r.* Latvia 43 E2 57.22N 21.31E
Ventnor England 10 D1 50.36N 1.11W
Ventspils Latvia 43 E2 57.22N 21.31E
Vera Spain 46 E2 37.15N 1.51W
Veracruz Mexico 70 E4 19.11N 96.10W
Veracruz *d.* Mexico 70 E4 18.00N 95.00W
Vercelli Italy 50 C6 45.19N 8.26E
Verdalsøra Norway 43 B3 63.47N 11.23E
Verde *r.* Brazil 77 E2 21.18S 51.50W
Verde *r.* Paraguay 77 E2 23.00S 57.45W
Verde *r.* U.S.A. 64 D3 33.22N 112.20W
Verdun France 44 F6 49.10N 5.24E
Verín Spain 46 B4 41.55N 7.26W
Verkhoyansk Russian Fed. 59 P4 67.25N 133.25E
Verkhoyansk Range *mts.* Russian Fed. 59 O4 66.00N 130.00E
Vermont *d.* U.S.A. 65 L5 44.00N 72.30W
Verona Italy 50 D6 45.27N 10.59E
Versailles France 44 E6 48.48N 2.08E
Verviers Belgium 42 E2 50.36N 5.52E
Vervins France 42 C1 49.50N 3.55E
Verwood England 10 D1 50.53N 1.53W
Vesoul France 44 G5 47.38N 6.09E
Vesterålen *is.* Norway 43 C5 68.55N 15.00E
Vestfjorden *est.* Norway 43 C4 68.10N 15.00E
Vestmannaeyjar *is.* Iceland 43 X1 63.30N 20.20W
Vesturhorn *c.* Iceland 43 Z2 64.17N 14.54W
Vesuvius *mtn.* Italy 50 F4 40.48N 14.25E
Vettore, Monte *mtn.* Italy 50 E5 42.50N 13.18E
Veurne Belgium 42 B3 51.04N 2.40E
Vézère *r.* France 44 D4 44.53N 0.55E
Viana do Castelo Portugal 46 A4 41.41N 8.50W
Viborg Denmark 43 B2 56.28N 9.25E
Vibo Valentia Italy 50 G3 38.40N 16.06E
Vic Spain 46 G4 41.56N 2.15E
Vicenza Italy 50 D6 45.33N 11.32E
Vichy France 44 E5 46.07N 3.25E
Victoria Canada 62 F2 48.26N 123.20W
Victoria U.S.A. 64 G2 28.48N 97.00W
Victoria *r.* Australia 110 B4 15.12S 129.43E
Victoria *d.* Australia 110 D2 37.20S 144.10E
Victoria I. Canada 62 G5 71.00N 110.00W
Victoria, L. Africa 86 C4 1.00S 33.00E
Victoria, Mt. Myanmar 97 I5 21.12N 93.55E
Victoria, Mt. P.N.G. 110 D5 8.55S 147.35E
Victoria de las Tunas Cuba 71 I5 20.58N 76.59W
Victoria Falls *f.* Zimbabwe/Zambia 86 B3 17.58S 25.45E
Vidin Bulgaria 56 F5 43.58N 22.51E
Viedma Argentina 75 C2 40.45S 63.00W
Viedma, L. Argentina 75 B2 49.40S 72.30W
Vienna Austria 54 E3 48.13N 16.22E
Vienne France 44 F4 45.32N 4.54E
Vienne *r.* France 44 D5 47.13N 0.05W
Vientiane Laos 104 C7 18.01N 102.48E
Vierzon France 44 E5 47.14N 2.03E
Vietnam Asia 104 D6 15.00N 108.00E
Vignemale, Pic de *mtn.* France 44 C3 42.46N 0.08W
Vigo Spain 46 A5 42.15N 8.44W
Vijayawada India 97 G4 16.34N 80.40E
Vik Iceland 43 Y1 63.25N 19.00W
Vikna *i.* Norway 43 B4 64.59N 11.00E
Vilagarcía Spain 46 A5 42.35N 8.45W
Vilaine *r.* France 44 B5 47.30N 2.25W
Vila Real Portugal 46 B4 41.17N 7.45W
Vila Velha Brazil 77 F2 20.20S 40.17W
Vilcabamba, Cordillera *mts.* Peru 76 C3 12.40S 73.20W
Vilhelmina Sweden 43 D4 64.38N 16.40E
Viljandi Estonia 43 F2 58.22N 25.30E
Vilkaviškis Lithuania 54 H6 54.39N 23.02E
Villach Austria 54 C2 46.37N 13.51E
Villahermosa Mexico 70 F4 18.00N 92.53W
Villaputzu Italy 50 C3 39.28N 9.35E
Villarrica Paraguay 77 E2 25.45S 56.28W
Villarrobledo Spain 46 D3 39.16N 2.36W
Villavicencio Colombia 74 B7 4.09N 73.38W
Villefranche-sur-Saône France 44 F5 46.00N 4.43E
Villena Spain 46 E3 38.39N 0.52W
Villeneuve France 44 D4 44.25N 0.43E
Villers-Cotterêts France 42 C1 49.15N 3.05E
Villeurbanne France 44 F4 45.46N 4.54E
Vilnius Lithuania 55 I6 54.40N 25.19E
Vilvoorde Belgium 42 D2 50.56N 4.25E
Vilyuy *r.* Russian Fed. 59 O4 63.37N 119.00E
Vilyuysk Russian Fed. 59 O4 63.46N 121.35E
Viña del Mar Chile 75 B3 33.02S 71.35W
Vindel *r.* Sweden 43 D3 63.56N 19.54E
Vinh Vietnam 104 D7 18.42N 105.41E
Vinkovci Croatia 56 D6 45.17N 18.49E
Vinnytsya Ukraine 55 K3 49.11N 28.30E
Viranşehir Turkey 57 N2 37.13N 39.45E
Vire France 44 C6 48.50N 0.53W
Virginia *d.* U.S.A. 65 K4 37.30N 79.00W
Virgin Is. (British) C. America 71 L4 18.30N 64.30W
Virgin Is. (U.S.A.) C. America 74 C8 18.30N 65.00W
Virton Belgium 42 E1 49.35N 5.32E
Vis *i.* Croatia 56 C5 43.03N 16.10E
Visby Sweden 43 D2 57.37N 18.20E
Viscount Melville Sd. Canada 62 H5 74.30N 104.00W
Viseu Portugal 46 B4 40.40N 7.55W
Visginas Lithuania 55 J6 55.34N 26.20E
Vishakhapatnam India 97 G4 17.42N 83.24E
Viso, Monte *mtn.* Italy 50 B6 44.38N 7.05E
Vistula *r.* Poland 54 F6 54.23N 18.52E
Viterbo Italy 50 E5 42.26N 12.07E
Viti Levu *i.* Fiji 111 G4 18.00S 178.00E
Vitim *r.* Russian Fed. 59 N3 59.30N 112.36E
Vitória +Espírito Santo Brazil 77 F2 20.19S 40.21W
Vitória da Conquista Brazil 77 F3 14.53S 40.52W
Vitoria-Gasteiz Spain 46 D5 42.51N 2.40W
Vitsyebsk Belarus 55 L6 55.10N 30.14E
Vittel France 44 F6 48.12N 5.57E
Vizcaíno, Sierra *mts.* Mexico 70 B6 27.20N 114.30W
Vizianagaram India 97 G4 18.07N 83.30E
Vlaams Brabant *d.* Belgium 42 D2 50.54N 4.45E
Vlaardingen Neth. 42 D3 51.55N 4.20E
Vladimir Russian Fed. 58 G3 56.08N 40.25E
Vladivostok Russian Fed. 59 P2 43.09N 131.53E
Vlieland *i.* Neth. 42 D5 53.15N 5.00E
Vlissingen Neth. 42 C3 51.27N 3.35E
Vlorë Albania 56 D4 40.28N 19.27E
Vltava *r.* Czech Rep. 54 D4 50.22N 14.28E
Voe Scotland 19 Y9 60.21N 1.15W
Voi Kenya 87 B2 3.23S 38.34E
Vojvodina *d.* Yugo. 56 D6 43.30N 20.00E
Volda Norway 43 A3 62.09N 6.05E
Volga *r.* Russian Fed. 58 G2 45.45N 47.50E
Volga Uplands *hills* Russian Fed. 35 H3 53.15N 45.45E
Volgograd Russian Fed. 58 G2 48.45N 44.30E
Völklingen Germany 42 F1 49.15N 6.50E
Volnovakha Ukraine 55 O2 47.36N 37.32E
Volodymyr-Volyns'kyy Ukraine 55 I4 50.51N 24.19E
Vologda Russian Fed. 58 F3 59.10N 39.55E
Volokonovka Russian Fed. 55 O4 50.28N 37.52E
Volos Greece 56 F3 39.22N 22.57E
Volta, L. Ghana 84 E2 7.00N 0.00
Volta Redonda Brazil 77 F2 22.31S 44.05W
Volzhskiy Russian Fed. 58 G2 48.48N 44.45E
Vordingborg Denmark 54 B6 55.00N 11.54E
Vorkuta Russian Fed. 58 I4 67.27N 64.00E
Voronezh Russian Fed. 55 P4 51.40N 39.13E
Vosges *mts.* France 44 G5 48.00N 7.00E
Voss Norway 43 A3 60.38N 6.25E
Vostok I. Kiribati 108 P5 10.05S 152.23W
Vouziers France 42 D1 49.24N 4.42E
Voznesens'k Ukraine 55 L2 47.34N 31.21E
Vranje Yugo. 56 E5 42.34N 21.52E
Vratsa Bulgaria 56 F5 43.12N 23.33E
Vrbas *r.* Bosnia./Croatia 56 C6 45.06N 17.29E
Vršac Yugo. 56 E6 45.08N 21.18E
Vung Tau Vietnam 104 D6 10.21N 107.04E
Vuollerim Sweden 43 E4 66.26N 20.40E
Vyatka Russian Fed. 58 G3 58.38N 49.38E
Vyaz'ma Russian Fed. 55 N6 55.12N 34.17E
Vyborg Russian Fed. 43 G3 60.45N 28.41E
Vychegda *r.* Russian Fed. 35 H4 61.15N 46.28E
Vyrnwy, L. Wales 12 D4 52.46N 3.30W

W

Wa Ghana 84 D3 10.07N 2.28W
Wabag P.N.G. 105 K2 5.28S 143.40E
Wabasca *r.* Canada 62 G3 58.22N 115.20W
Wabash *r.* U.S.A. 65 I4 38.25N 87.45W
Wabe Gestro *r.* Ethiopia 87 C3 4.11N 42.09E
Wabush Canada 63 L3 53.00N 66.50W
Waco U.S.A. 64 G3 31.33N 97.10W
Waddan Libya 85 F4 29.06N 16.03E
Waddenzee Neth. 42 E5 53.15N 5.05E
Waddington England 15 G2 53.10N 0.32W
Waddington, Mt. Canada 62 F3 51.30N 125.00W
Wadebridge England 13 C2 50.31N 4.51W
Wadhurst England 11 F2 51.03N 0.21E
Wadi Halfa Sudan 85 H4 21.55N 31.20E
Wad Medani Sudan 85 H3 14.24N 33.30E
Wagga Wagga Australia 110 D2 35.07S 147.24E
Wahpeton U.S.A. 64 G6 46.16N 96.36W
Waigeo *i.* Indonesia 105 I3 0.05S 130.30E
Wainfleet All Saints England 15 H2 53.07N 0.16E
Waingapu Indonesia 104 G2 9.30S 120.10E
Waini Pt. *c.* Guyana 74 D7 8.24N 59.48W
Wainwright U.S.A. 62 C5 70.39N 160.00W
Wajir Kenya 87 C3 1.46N 40.05E
Wakayama Japan 106 C2 34.12N 135.10E
Wakefield England 15 F2 53.41N 1.31W
Wake I. Pacific Oc. 108 L8 19.17N 166.36E
Wakkanai Japan 106 D5 45.26N 141.43E
Wałbrzych Poland 54 E4 50.48N 16.19E
Wales *d.* U.K. 8-9
Wallasey England 14 D2 53.26N 3.02W
Wallingford England 10 D2 51.36N 1.07W
Wallis and Futuna *is.* Pacific Oc. 108 N5 13.16S 176.15W
Walney, Isle of England 14 D3 54.05N 3.12W
Walsall England 10 D3 52.36N 1.59W
Waltham on the Wolds England 10 E3 52.49N 0.49W
Walton on Thames England 11 E2 51.23N 0.23W
Walvis Bay *town* Namibia 86 A2 22.50S 14.31E
Wandsworth England 11 E2 51.27N 0.11W
Wangqing China 106 A4 43.20N 129.48E
Wantage England 10 D2 51.35N 1.25W
Warangal India 97 F4 18.00N 79.35E
Warboys England 11 E3 52.24N 0.06W
Warburton *r.* Australia 110 C3 27.55S 137.15E
Ward Hill Scotland 19 F3 58.54N 3.20W
Ward's Stone *mtn.* England 14 E3 54.03N 2.36W
Wareham England 10 C1 50.41N 2.08W
Waremme Belgium 42 E2 50.42N 5.15E
Warlingham England 11 E2 51.19N 0.04W
Warminster England 10 C2 51.12N 2.11W
Warrego *r.* Australia 110 D3 30.25S 145.18E
Warrenpoint N. Ireland 16 C2 54.06N 6.15W
Warri Nigeria 84 E2 5.36N 5.46E
Warrington England 14 E2 53.25N 2.38W
Warsaw Poland 54 G5 52.15N 21.00E
Warsop England 15 F2 53.13N 1.08W
Warta *r.* Poland 54 D5 52.45N 15.09E
Warwick England 10 D3 52.17N 1.36W
Warwickshire *d.* England 9 E3 52.10N 1.30W
Washington England 15 F3 54.55N 1.30W
Washington U.S.A. 65 K4 38.55N 77.00W
Washington *d.* U.S.A. 64 B6 47.00N 120.00W
Washington, Mt. U.S.A. 65 L5 44.17N 71.19W
Waskaganish *see* Fort Rupert Canada 63
Wast Water *l.* England 14 D3 54.25N 3.18W
Watampone Indonesia 104 G3 4.33S 120.20E
Watchet England 13 D3 51.10N 3.20W
Waterford Rep. of Ire. 20 D2 52.16N 7.08W
Waterford *d.* Rep. of Ire. 20 D2 52.10N 7.40W
Watergate B. England 13 B2 50.28N 5.06W
Waterloo U.S.A. 65 H5 42.30N 92.20W
Waterlooville England 10 D1 50.53N 1.02W
Water of Saughs *r.* Scotland 19 G1 56.47N 2.36W
Watertown U.S.A. 64 G5 44.54N 97.08W
Watford England 11 E2 51.40N 0.25W
Watlington England 10 D2 51.38N 1.00W
Watson Lake *town* Canada 62 F4 60.07N 128.49W
Watten, Loch Scotland 19 F3 58.29N 3.20W
Watton England 11 F3 52.35N 0.50E
Wau Sudan 85 G2 7.40N 28.04E
Waveney *r.* England 11 G3 52.29N 1.46E
Wear *r.* England 15 F3 54.55N 1.22W
Weddell Sea Antarctica 112 73.00S 42.00W
Wedmore England 13 E3 51.14N 2.50W
Weener Germany 42 G5 53.11N 7.21E
Weert Neth. 42 E3 51.14N 5.40E
Weifang China 103 L5 36.44N 119.10E
Weihai China 103 M5 37.30N 122.04E
Weinan China 103 J4 34.25N 109.30E
Weldiya Ethiopia 85 H3 11.50N 39.36E
Welkom R.S.A. 86 B2 27.59S 26.44E
Welland *r.* England 11 E3 52.53N 0.00
Wellesley Is. Australia 110 C4 16.42S 139.30E
Wellingborough England 10 E3 52.18N 0.41W
Wellington Shrops. England 10 C3 52.42N 2.31W
Wellington Somerset England 13 D2 50.58N 3.13W
Wellington New Zealand 111 G1 41.17S 174.46E
Wells England 13 E3 51.12N 2.39W
Wells, L. Australia 110 B3 26.50S 123.20E
Wells-next-the-Sea England 11 F3 52.57N 0.51E
Welmel Shet' *r.* Ethiopia 87 C4 5.37N 41.00E
Welshpool Wales 12 D4 52.40N 3.09W
Welwyn Garden City England 11 E2 51.48N 0.13W
Wem England 10 C3 52.52N 2.45W
Wembley England 11 E2 51.34N 0.18W
Wemyss Bay *town* Scotland 16 E3 55.52N 4.52W
Wendo Ethiopia 85 H2 6.40N 38.27E
Wendover England 10 E2 51.46N 0.46W
Wenlock Edge *hill* England 10 C3 52.33N 2.40W
Wensleydale *f.* England 15 E3 54.19N 2.04W
Wensum *r.* England 11 G3 52.37N 1.20E
Wenzhou China 103 M3 28.02N 120.40E
Wesel Germany 42 F3 51.39N 6.37E
Weser *r.* Germany 48 D5 53.15N 8.30E
Wessel, C. Australia 110 C4 10.59S 136.46E
Wessel Is. Australia 110 C4 11.30S 136.25E
West Australian Basin *f.* Indian Oc. 117 O5
West Bengal *d.* India 97 H5 23.00N 87.40E
West Berkshire *d.* England 9 E2 51.25N 1.19W
West Bridgford England 10 D3 52.56N 1.08W
West Bromwich England 10 D3 52.32N 1.59W
West Burra *i.* Scotland 19 Y9 60.05N 1.21W
Westbury England 10 C2 51.16N 2.11W
West Calder Scotland 17 F3 55.51N 3.34W
West Dunbartonshire *d.* Scotland 8 C4 55.58N 4.30W
Western *d.* Kenya 87 A3 0.30N 34.30E
Western Australia *d.* Australia 110 B3 25.00S 123.00E
Western Desert Egypt 94 C4 27.30N 28.00E
Western Ghats *mts.* India 96 E4 15.30N 74.30E
Western Isles *d.* Scotland 8 B6 57.40N 7.10W
Western Sahara Africa 84 C4 25.00N 13.30W
Western Sayan *mts.* Russian Fed. 59 L3 53.00N 92.00E
Wester Ross *f.* Scotland 18 D2 57.37N 5.20W
Westerschelde *est.* Neth. 42 C3 51.25N 3.40E
West Falkland *i.* Falkland Is. 75 C1 51.40S 60.00W
West Fen *f.* Cambs. England 11 E3 52.32N 0.00
West Fen *f.* Lincs. England 15 G2 53.03N 0.02E
West Frisian Is. Neth. 42 D5 53.20N 5.00E
Westhill Scotland 19 G2 57.09N 2.16W
West Kirby England 14 D2 53.22N 3.11W
West Lavington England 10 D2 51.17N 2.00W
West Linton Scotland 17 F3 55.45N 3.21W
West Loch Roag Scotland 18 C3 58.17N 6.52W
West Lothian *d.* Scotland 8 D4 55.55N 3.30W
West Malling England 11 F2 51.18N 0.25E
Westmeath *d.* Rep. of Ire. 20 D3 53.30N 7.30W
West Mersea England 11 F2 51.46N 0.55E
West Midlands *d.* England 9 E3 52.25N 2.00W
Weston-super-Mare England 10 C2 51.20N 2.59W
West Palm Beach *town* U.S.A. 65 J2 26.42N 80.05W
Westport Rep. of Ire. 20 B3 53.48N 9.32W
Westray *i.* Scotland 19 G4 59.18N 2.58W
Westray Firth Scotland 19 F4 59.13N 3.00W
West Siberian Plain *f.* Russian Fed. 58 J4 60.00N 75.00E
West Sussex *d.* England 9 E2 50.58N 0.30W
West Terschelling Neth. 42 E5 53.22N 5.13E
West Virginia *d.* U.S.A. 65 J4 39.00N 80.30W
West-Vlaanderen *d.* Belgium 42 B2 51.00N 3.00E
Westward Ho! England 13 C3 51.02N 4.15W
West Yorkshire *d.* England 9 E3 53.45N 1.40W
Wetar *i.* Indonesia 105 H2 7.45S 126.00E
Wete Tanzania 87 B1 5.03S 39.44E
Wetherby England 15 F2 53.56N 1.23W
Wetzlar Germany 48 D4 50.33N 8.30E
Wewak P.N.G. 105 K3 3.35S 143.35E
Wexford Rep. of Ire. 20 E2 52.20N 6.28W
Wexford *d.* Rep. of Ire. 20 E2 52.25N 6.30W
Wexford B. Rep. of Ire. 20 E2 52.25N 6.15W
Weybridge England 11 E2 51.23N 0.28W
Weyburn Canada 64 F6 49.41N 103.52W
Weymouth England 10 C1 50.36N 2.28W
Whalsay *i.* Scotland 19 Z9 60.22N 0.59W
Whangarei New Zealand 111 G2 35.43S 174.20E
Wharfe *r.* England 15 F2 53.50N 1.07W
Wheeler Peak *mtn.* Nev. U.S.A. 64 D4 38.59N 114.29W
Wheeler Peak *mtn.* N.Mex. U.S.A. 64 E4 36.34N 105.25W
Whernside *mtn.* England 15 E3 54.14N 2.25W
Whitburn Scotland 17 F3 55.52N 3.41W
Whitby England 15 G3 54.29N 0.37W
Whitchurch England 10 C3 52.58N 2.42W
Whitchurch Wales 13 D3 51.32N 3.14W
White *r.* U.S.A. 65 H3 33.53N 91.10W
Whitecourt Canada 62 G3 54.10N 115.38W
Whitehaven England 14 D3 54.33N 3.35W
Whitehead N. Ireland 16 D2 54.45N 5.43W
Whitehill England 10 E2 51.06N 0.52W
Whitehorse Canada 62 E4 60.41N 135.08W
White L. Australia 110 B3 21.05S 129.00E
White Mt. Peak U.S.A. 64 C4 37.40N 118.15W
White Nile *r.* Sudan 85 H3 15.45N 32.25E
Whitesand B. England 13 C2 50.20N 4.20W
White Sea Russian Fed. 58 F4 65.30N 38.00E
White Volta *r.* Ghana 84 D2 9.13N 1.15W
Whitfield England 11 G2 51.09N 1.15E
Whithorn Scotland 16 E2 54.44N 4.25W
Whitland Wales 12 C3 51.49N 4.38W
Whitley Bay *town* England 15 F4 55.03N 1.25W
Whitney, Mt. U.S.A. 64 C4 36.35N 118.17W
Whitstable England 11 G2 51.21N 1.02E
Whittlesey England 11 E3 52.34N 0.08W
Whyalla Australia 110 C2 33.04S 137.34E
Wichita U.S.A. 64 G4 37.43N 97.20W
Wichita Falls *town* U.S.A. 64 G3 33.55N 98.30W
Wick Scotland 19 F3 58.26N 3.06W
Wick *r.* Scotland 19 F3 58.26N 3.06W
Wickford England 11 F2 51.38N 0.31E
Wickham England 10 D1 50.54N 1.11W
Wickham Market England 11 G3 52.09N 1.21E
Wicklow Rep. of Ire. 20 E2 52.59N 6.03W
Wicklow *d.* Rep. of Ire. 20 E3 53.00N 6.25W
Wicklow Head Rep. of Ire. 20 F2 52.58N 6.00W
Wicklow Mts. Rep. of Ire. 20 E2 53.06N 6.20W
Widecombe in the Moor England 13 D2 50.35N 3.48W
Wide Firth Scotland 19 F4 59.02N 3.00W
Widnes England 14 E2 53.22N 2.44W
Wieluń Poland 54 F4 51.14N 18.34E
Wiener Neustadt Austria 54 E2 47.49N 16.15E
Wiesbaden Germany 48 D4 50.05N 8.15E
Wigan England 14 E2 53.33N 2.38W
Wigston England 10 D3 52.35N 1.08W
Wigton England 14 D3 54.50N 3.09W
Wigtown Scotland 16 E2 54.52N 4.26W
Wigtown B. Scotland 16 E2 54.47N 4.15W
Wijchen Neth. 42 E3 51.48N 5.44E
Wildhorn *mtn.* Switz. 44 G5 46.22N 7.22E
Wilhelmshaven Germany 48 D5 53.32N 8.07E
Wilkes Land *f.* Antarctica 112 69.00S 130.00E
Willebroek Belgium 42 D3 51.04N 4.22E
William, Mt. Australia 110 D2 37.20S 142.41E
Williams Lake *town* Canada 62 F3 52.08N 122.09W
Williamsport U.S.A. 65 K5 41.16N 77.03W
Willingdon England 11 F1 50.47N 0.15E
Williston U.S.A. 64 F6 48.09N 103.39W
Williston L. Canada 62 F3 55.00N 126.00W
Williton England 13 D3 51.09N 3.20W
Willmar U.S.A. 65 G6 45.06N 95.00W
Wills, L. Australia 110 B3 21.15S 128.40E
Wilmington Del. U.S.A. 65 K4 39.46N 75.31W
Wilmington N.C. U.S.A. 65 K3 34.14N 77.55W
Wilmslow England 15 E2 53.19N 2.14W
Wilson's Promontory *c.* Australia 110 D2 39.06S 146.23E
Wilton England 10 D2 51.05N 1.52W
Wiltshire *d.* England 9 D2 51.20N 2.00W
Wiltz Lux. 42 E1 49.59N 5.53E
Wimblington England 11 F3 52.31N 0.06E
Wimborne Minster England 10 C1 50.48N 2.00W
Wimereux France 42 A2 50.46N 1.37E

References
BP Amoco Statistical Review, 1999
Caribbean Tourism Organisation, 1999
Convention on International Trade in Endangered Species
FAO Statistical Databases, 1998
Regional Trends 34 1999 Edition HMSO
UK National Statistics, 1999
UNESCO Statistics, 1998
UN Population Information Network (POPIN)
US Census Bureau, 1999
USGS Minerals Yearbook, 1999
World Bank Organisation, 1998
World Energy Council, Energy Data Centre, 1998
World Health Organisation, 1998
World Tourism Organisation, 2000
World Trade Organisation, Statistics Division, 1999

Photo credits
Satellite images : Science Photo Library
Cover : Images Colour Library

Acknowledgements
General Bathymetric Chart of the Oceans (GEBCO)
International Hydrographic Organisation, Monaco
National Atlas and Thematic Mapping Organisation, Calcutta, India
Ministry of Planning and National Development, Nairobi, Kenya
Instituto Geográfico e Cartográfico, São Paulo, Brazil
Rotterdam Municipal Port Management, Rotterdam, Netherlands